KT-526-673

A HISTORY OF
PRIVATE LIFE

Philippe Ariès and Georges Duby
General Editors

IV · From the Fires
of Revolution
to the Great War

A HISTORY OF PRIVATE LIFE

IV · From the Fires of Revolution to the Great War

Michelle Perrot, Editor

Arthur Goldhammer, Translator

The Belknap Press of
Harvard University Press
CAMBRIDGE, MASSACHUSETTS
LONDON, ENGLAND

Copyright © 1990 by the President and Fellows
of Harvard College
All rights reserved
Printed in the United States of America
10 9 8 7 6 5 4 3
Originally published as Histoire de la vie Privée, vol. 4,
De la Révolution à la Grande Guerre, © Editions du Seuil,
1987.

Library of Congress Cataloging-in-Publication Data
(Revised for vol. 4)

A history of private life.

Translation of: Histoire de la vie privée.
Includes bibliographies and indexes.
Contents: v. 1. From pagan Rome to Byzantium /
Paul Veyne, editor—v. 4. From the fires of revolution to
the Great War / Michelle Perrot, editor; Arthur
Goldhammer, translator.
1. Manners and customs—Collected works. 2. Family
—History—Collected works. 3. Civilization—History
—Collected works. 4. Europe—Social conditions—
Collected works. I. Ariès, Philippe. II. Duby,
Georges.
GT2400.H5713   1987   390'.009   86-18286

ISBN 0-674-39978-1 (alk. paper) (cloth)
ISBN 0-674-40003-8 (pbk.)

Contents

Trouville's casino terrace attracted a large crowd. In the late 19th century the beach was a salon where people could meet family and friends without paying much heed to ocean or sun. (Sirot-Angel Collection.)

A HISTORY OF
PRIVATE LIFE

From the Fires
of Revolution
to the Great War

Introduction

Michelle Perrot

*F*OR a long time historians, like bourgeois Victorians, hesitated on the threshold of private life, held back by modesty, incompetence, and respect for a system of values according to which public figures were the heroes and makers of the only history worth recounting: the grand history of states, economies, and societies.

To cross that threshold required no less than a reversal in values. The private became something other than a realm of curses, taboos, and darkness; it became a place of pleasures and servitudes, conflicts and dreams. And, for a time at least, it was recognized as the center of people's lives, a place worthy of visiting, a legitimate object of study. Privacy is an experience of the present age.

Many factors, including great events and great books, have contributed to the current ascendancy of the private. Among these, politics deserves first mention. The despotism of totalitarian states and the excessive interventionism of democracies even in such neglected areas as risk management—what Michel Foucault has called "the rationality of the abominable and the rationality of the ordinary"—have led to reflection on the mechanisms of power and to a search for the means to resist, whether through small groups or even by isolated individuals, the tentacles of social control. Today's worker looks upon his or her home as an ever more personalized refuge from the boss's surveillance and the discipline of the factory. The practice, widespread in Western societies, of willing personal property to children is not merely a result of bourgeoisification but a form of struggle against the dread of death.

Ideology, rhetoric, and practice in the spheres of economics, politics, and ethics were recast in the early twentieth century to embrace "the masses"; lately, however, there has been increased emphasis on specificities and differences. Societies are now analyzed in terms not of broad classes but of age cohorts, gender categories, ethnic groups, and regional differences. The women's movement has emphasized gender differences as the motor of history. Young people think of themselves as a distinct group and have adopted distinctive styles in clothing and music. The self, whether psychoanalyzed or retold in autobiography (or oral history), has asserted its vitality and volubility. Processes of sectorization, dissociation, and dissemination are at work everywhere.

These complex phenomena have given rise to investigations of the relations between the public and the private, the collective and the individual, the masculine and the feminine, the external and the internal. Out of these investigations has come an abundant literature, of which I can mention only a few major authors and works. While Albert Hirschman (*Shifting Involvements,* 1981) focuses on a regular cycle alternating between periods of intense public involvement and periods in which private objectives predominate, other writers have noted fundamental long-term trends of privatization and individualization. Norbert Elias (*The Civilizing Process,* 1939) holds that privatization is consubstantial with civilization. By examining treatises on "civilities" since the time of Erasmus, he shows how the refinement of that aspect of sensibility known as "modesty" has caused acts such as wiping one's nose, defecating, and lovemaking, once unabashedly performed in public, to be relegated to the discreet shadows. A change in the nature of the individual's self-awareness stemming from new attitudes toward the body led to new ways of eating, washing, and making love—and therefore to new forms of private life.

Louis Dumont sees the development of individualism as the feature that distinguishes the West from the holism of the East, of societies such as the Indian, for example, in which personal interests are subordinated to society's imperious ends. The Renaissance marks the beginning of this fundamental change, of which the Declaration of the Rights of Man and of the Citizen is in a sense the charter. It takes a great deal of time, however, for the abstract legal individual to become a reality—indeed, this process occupies the whole extent of the period with which this book is concerned, the nineteenth and early twentieth centuries.

Jürgen Habermas and Richard Sennett concern themselves with the relatively brief period since the Enlightenment. They attempt to understand how bourgeois liberalism achieved an equilibrium between the public and private spheres, an equilibrium that, both writers argue, has subsequently been disrupted. They do not interpret this equilibrium in the same way, however. For Habermas the state, capitalizing on various forms of exclusion and discontent, assumed a growing role in achieving social harmony. Sennett focuses on the growing tyranny of private life, which eventually drove out the kind of public man who had flourished in eighteenth- and nineteenth-century bourgeois cities— a public man for whom the theater was the central form of expression.

The nineteenth century was the golden age of private life, a time when the vocabulary and reality of private life took shape. Privacy as an idea was elaborated with great sophistication. Civil society, private life, intimate relations, and the life of the individual, though conceptualized as concentric circles, actually overlapped.

This book is concerned with the history of the nineteenth-century model of private life. It begins with the tumult of the French Revolution, during which Rousseau's dream of social transparency came up against the reality of social differences. From the Revolution, that great and contradictory event, flowed the whole nineteenth century. Our story ends with the dawn of a new modernity, tragically cut short by the coming of the First World War. The effects of the war were complex. In some ways the evolution that was under way was impeded, in other ways it was hastened or redirected. But it was never completely halted.

In writing this history we draw on sources that are overabundant yet wanting, garrulous but silent, frank yet reticent. Because the private was at the heart of the political and economic thought and social, moral, and medical concerns of the day, it gave rise to endless theoretical treatises, both normative and descriptive, centered on the family. Public archives, however, are little concerned with private life. The state was as yet reluctant to intervene in the life of the family, which was entrusted with managing a rather amorphous civil society. Only family conflict, a disturbing source of violence, called for intervention. Thus police and court records are of interest. In contrast to the eighteenth century, when the police had served as protectors and confidants, in the nineteenth century they gradually relinquished that role. No longer did victims turn to the police for help; the police increasingly intervened on their own. People turned instead to the courts, accentuating a tendency to substitute the force of law for private vengeance. Unfortunately, until recently court records in France were kept in local record offices, and many have been irretrievably lost through neglect. Only those records kept in Series U of the Departmental Archives are usable, and these are subject to legal time limitations that apply to the use of "personal" documents. Still, criminal records have enabled historians to breach the walls of intimacy.

Private archives, the most direct and fertile of sources concerning private life, are distributed unequally across different social classes, and access to them, as well as the likelihood of their preservation, is a matter of chance. Private records survive only when there is suitable storage, an interest in maintaining the memory of earlier generations, a notoriety that transforms private papers into relics, or a curiosity on the part of descendants fascinated by history or genealogy. At present there is a tendency to value these family treasures highly. Yet private letters and such personal literature as diaries, autobiographies, and memoirs, though precious testimony, do not constitute true documents of private life. Their contents are dictated by rules of propriety and a need for self-dramatization. Nothing is less spontaneous than a letter, nothing less transparent than an autobiography, which is designed to conceal as much as it reveals. Nevertheless, the subtle stratagems of camouflage and display bring us at least to the gateway of the fortress.

The nineteenth-century novel, much concerned with family intrigues and private dramas, is fiction "truer" than many products more immediately derived from experience. Yet we make use of it only with great caution and in certain respects—the study of life styles, for instance—in full awareness of the importance of aesthetic mediations and of the specific requirements of literary production. Nevertheless, the heroes of literature live in each of us, and we are imbued with the music of the novel.

The search for private life raises difficult problems. Because so few studies have been made, it has been necessary to attempt a synthesis without the needed analyses; we have been forced to cobble together a narrative from fragmentary findings. If we succeed in stimulating further work to extend, challenge, and contradict our own, we will have made a valuable contribution.

There are other difficulties. Foremost among them is the disparate nature of the sources, a disparity that has resulted in an undue emphasis on urban issues. Rural private life, its image frozen in folklore, more often than not eludes our grasp. In the city all eyes are on the bourgeoisie. Despite the remarkable efforts of the series' researchers, whom I wish to take this opportunity to thank, the illustrations heighten the impression that we see nothing else, so completely does the bourgeoisie monopolize the scene. Nevertheless, we have tried to be careful not only to examine the interaction between the private and the social but also to appreciate the originality implicit in the variety of forms of private life, a variety that is a product not just of imitation and the desire for distinction but of a combination of diverse elements for specific ends.

Another problem is the impossibility of encompassing the entire Western world in a single volume. The abundance of sources, the complexity of the issues, the scarcity of previous work on the subject, and above all the construction of "national spaces" made our decision all but inevitable. French society is therefore our central concern. Outside it we touch only on the English case, because England offers the most fully developed form of private life in the period and because English society is the society about whose private life most is known and whose influence on France was greatest.

The history of private life calls for specialized methods. The standard approaches of economic and social history are insufficient. Historical demography, though indispensable, offers only a crude framework. Historical anthropology and what is known as the "history of mentalities" are more stimulating because they attempt to relate theory and practice over time. Suggestions from ethnomethodology (Goffman's "presentation of self in everyday life") and microhistory have proved useful, as have others from the sociology of culture. To all these disciplines our debt is great. But perhaps the greatest debt of all is to recent feminist reflection on the public and the private, the formation of distinct spheres of life, and relations between the sexes in family and society.

Still, we are left with the difficulty of understanding anything more than the external and public face of private life, with the impossibility of passing through the looking glass. In this realm the effable creates the ineffable, light produces darkness. The unsaid, the unknown, the unknowable—and our tragic awareness thereof—increase apace with the knowledge that digs vast chasms of unfathomable mystery beneath our feet. Perhaps we need other interpretive tools inspired by semiotics or psychoanalysis. We are also left with the irreducible opacity of the object, an opacity we must somehow penetrate in order to advance beyond the social history of private life, that is, in order to write the history not of groups and families but of individuals, of their representations and emotions—a history of ways of doing, living, feeling, and loving, of the impulses of the heart and the body, of fantasy and dream. Along with a Balzacian history of family intrigues we would like a Nervalian history of desire and a musical, Proustian history of intimacy.

Here, then, is our work, the work of six authors in search of a thousand characters. It is a history concerned with France in the nineteenth century. For a curtain-raiser we have an extraordinary duo: the French Revolution and the English home. Next we bring on stage the actors: the family and others. The setting is one of houses and gardens. In the wings is the solitary individual, with his or her secrets and intimacies. And in the background, still dimly discernible, is the statue of the Commendatore, the shadow of the state. For the history of private life is more than anecdotal; it is the political history of everyday life.

Attributed to François Gérard, *The Fatherland in Danger, or the Enlistment of Volunteers*, circa 1797–1799. The revolution in the forum. Public duty takes precedence over private life, which vanishes in the transparency of community. (Vizille, Museum of the French Revolution.)

✎ 1 ✎

The Curtain Rises

Lynn Hunt
Catherine Hall

Walter Deverell, *A Pet*. A solitary woman talks to a bird while standing in a doorway leading to an English garden. (London, Tate Gallery.)

Introduction

Michelle Perrot

THE eighteenth century refined the distinction between public and private. The public, represented as the state's possession, the *res publica,* had to some extent been deprivatized. The private, once of little or negative significance, had been revalued to the point where it now stood as a synonym for happiness. It was already understood in a familial and spatial sense, but this understanding was far from encompassing all of the many forms of social interaction.

THE FRENCH REVOLUTION AND FOREIGN INFLUENCES

The French Revolution interrupted this evolution dramatically and suddenly, though in a contradictory fashion whose long- and short-term consequences must be distinguished. At the time "private" or special interests were regarded as shadowy influences likely to foster conspiracy and treason. Transparency—an absence of barriers between individuals—was assumed to be the condition of public life. The revolutionaries set out to change hearts and habits, to reshape space and time, and within this new world to create a new man, different from the old in appearance, language, and feeling. Working from the outside in, the Revolution taught citizens new symbols and gestures that would eventually influence their innermost selves.

In the long run, however, the Revolution sharpened the distinction between the public and private spheres, emphasized family values, and led to a differentiation of sexual roles by setting up a contrast between political men and domestic women. Though patriarchal, the Revolution recognized divorce and limited paternal powers in many respects. It also proclaimed individual rights and established, in the form of a right of security, a primitive form of the principle of habeas corpus (which even in today's France is inadequately protected). As early as 1791, article 184 of the Penal Code specified harsh penalties for violation of guarantees against unreasonable search and seizure in private homes (*l'inviolabilité du domicile*).

It would take an entire volume to recount the tumultuous history of the Revolution as it impinged on the sphere of private life in law and custom, rhetoric and daily practice. In the first chapter of this section, Lynn Hunt, a specialist on the period, portrays in broad strokes the nature of an event whose fires still glowed on the horizon of the nineteenth century.

In the next chapter Catherine Hall considers the differentiation of public and private (now identified with the family), along with the increasingly strict differentiation of gender roles in early-nineteenth-century England as a result of the combined effects of Evangelical preaching, Utilitarian writings, and economic changes that resulted in a separation of home and workplace.

The English middle class, which found its true identity in this new domestic ideal, played a crucial role in its development. The ideal spread from the middle class to the working class, which was subjected to sermons on the virtues of the good housewife. The working class adopted the model, but in its own way and for its own ends. Meanwhile, the gentry developed a more intimate style of social life and transformed their castles into country houses. From nursery to garden the gentle pleasures of home flourished under the wings of the "angels of domesticity."

What influence did this model exert on French society, then in search of a new equilibrium between business and pleasure? The English influence was spread in a hundred different ways—by travelers, dandies, exiles, merchants, nurses, and governesses—among the French upper classes, with whom Anglophilia was a mark of distinction. Innumerable traces of this process can be found in such diverse areas as hygienic practices (soap, water closets, bathtubs), fashions in clothing, words such as "home," "baby," and "comfort," and certain vogues in sports, courtship, and lovemaking, all of which penetrated to the deepest levels of French society. Around 1900 trade unionists called for the emulation of British standards in parks, urban beautification, sports, and leisure activities. Posters of the Confédération Général du Travail (CGT), much like Cruikshank's engravings, advocated the eight-hour day and the "English week." And this glorification of England came in spite of a recurrent Anglophobia, encouraged by each new economic and political conflict.

The emphasis on Britain was probably justified, particularly in the first half of the nineteenth century. Subsequently, a culturally powerful Germany and, in the early twentieth century, the United States exerted a growing and sometimes rival attraction. More generally, we may ask to what extent foreign influences affected private life in France even outside such disputed border regions as Alsace, Nice, and Savoy.

Frenchmen in the time of Rousseau and Stendhal had traveled to Italy as adolescents and there they had been initiated in the ways of love and their aesthetic sensibilities had been formed. For a Frenchwoman like Geneviève Bréton, Italy continued to play this role, but was this true for many of her countrymen? At what times in the nineteenth century were the influences of northern or eastern or southern Europe greatest? The question cannot be answered. In any case, cultural influences are one thing, private life is another. Nor is a life style a simple composite of more or less naturalized individual elements, although these influences must be taken into account.

In its openness to outside influences France is a profoundly contradictory country. Its demographic characteristics—early decline in the birth rate, continued high death rate, and consequently low rate of population growth—were unique in Europe and made it a land of immigration. In the second half of the nineteenth century Belgians, Italians, and east-European Jews driven out by pogroms arrived in large numbers. Nearly 100,000 Jews entered France between 1880 and 1925, and 80 percent of them settled in Paris. In all, the immigrant population of France increased from 380,000 in 1851 to more than a million in 1901, or 2.9 percent of the total population (6.3 percent of the Paris population). Immigrants were, by definition, poor and unattractive. So much is clear from the suspicion with which Jews from central Europe were met by assimilated Jews who had lived in France for a long time, or from the xenophobia with which French workers greeted Italian immigrants, particularly in times of crisis. In order to survive, immigrants had to maintain their family structures and traditional ways. Yet legislation, such as the law of 1889 on naturalizations, encouraged them to assimilate. What impact did this immigration have on the practices and concepts of private life?

Jacobin France appears to have been quite self-confident. Its schools, an instrument of unification, fostered a coherent if rather rigid model of citizenship as well as manners. The schools taught people how to carry themselves, stigmatized dialects, corrected accents, and with undoubted efficacy forced domestic as well as foreign immigrants to accommodate to a Procrustean bed. In a related vein, French hostility to Freud's ideas and refusal to acknowledge sexuality as a key dimension of personality can perhaps be interpreted as another indication that the French conception of selfhood and intimacy was fairly hermetic. Clearly private life in the nineteenth century cannot easily be separated from the national cultures within which it flourished.

Louis Léopold Boilly, *Triumph of Marat*. A mixed revolutionary crowd of men and women, young and old, all wearing different costumes, gathers around Marat, "the friend of the people" and denouncer of "private interests." (Lille, Museum of Fine Arts.)

The Unstable Boundaries of the French Revolution

Lynn Hunt

URING the French Revolution the boundaries between public and private life were very unstable. *La chose publique, l'esprit publique,* invaded spheres of life that were normally private. Yet paradoxically an aggrandizing public space and the politicization of everyday life ultimately may have been responsible for the development of a more sharply differentiated private space in the early nineteenth century. An ever-expanding publicity of life, especially between 1789 and 1794, provided an impetus for the romantic withdrawal into the self and a withdrawal of the family into a more clearly defined domestic space. Before this happened, however, private life had to endure the most systematic assault ever seen in Western history.

The revolutionaries took the distinction between public and private very much to heart. Nothing particular (and all interests were by definition particular) was supposed to divide the general will of the new nation. From Condorcet to Thibaudeau to Napoléon, the watchword was the same: "I was the man of no party." Factional or party politics—the politics of private groups or individuals—was considered synonymous with conspiracy; "interests" was a code word for betrayal of the nation.

In the midst of revolution, private meant factional, and privacy was equated with the secrecy that facilitated plotting. Accordingly, the revolutionaries insisted on an all-pervasive publicity. Only unceasing vigilance and constant attendance to *la chose publique* ("public things," now very widely defined) could prevent the emergence of private interests and factions. Political meetings had to be open to the public; meetings of the legislature derived legitimacy from large gallery attendance and repeated interruption. Any salon, coterie, or private circle was subject to immediate denunciation. The expression of private interests in the public realm of politics was defined as counterrevolutionary. "There is only one party, that of the schemers," exclaimed Chabot, "the rest are the party of the people."[1]

This obsessive insistence on excluding private concerns from the public realm soon had the paradoxical effect of effacing the boundaries between public and private. Just as social terms such as aristocrats and sansculottes became infused with political meaning—a sansculotte could be labeled an aristocrat if he did not support the Revolution with sufficient ardor—so too private character took on public, political meaning. In October 1790 Marat denounced the National Assembly as "composed almost entirely of former nobles, prelates, lawyers, king's men, officials, jurists, men without soul, without morals, without honor, and without a sense of decency; enemies of the revolution by principle and by station." The majority of the legislators "is composed only of shrewd rascals, unworthy charlatans." They were "corrupt men, cunning and treacherous."[2] It was not enough to hold the wrong political position; the opposition had to be lacking in basic human qualities. If the public man was not defending the Revolution in the right way, the private man had to be corrupt. Where Marat led, others followed. In 1793 a "moderate, Feuillant [name for an earlier moderate faction], aristocrat" was defined in a semiliterate placard as "He who has not improved the lot of poor and patriotic humanity, though obviously having the capacity to do so. He who, out of wickedness, does not wear a cockade of three-inch circumference; he who has bought clothes other than national, and especially those who do not glory in the title and headdress of the sansculotte." Dress, language, attitudes toward the poor, providing jobs in the city and on the land—all had become gauges of patriotism. What separated the private from the public man?

The conflation of private moral character with public, political behavior was not limited to the local sectional assemblies of Paris and the more radical newspapers. The most notorious single instance may have been Robespierre's speech of 5 February 1794 "Sur les principes de morale politique" (On the Principles of Political Ethics). In making his case that "the mainspring of popular government in revolution is both virtue and terror," the spokesman for the Committee of Public Safety contrasted the virtues of the Republic with the vices of the monarchy: "In our country we want to substitute morals

Louis David, *Costume for Municipal Officials, with Mantle,* 1794. The greatest artists helped to shape the new styles. David designed this proposed new uniform for municipal officials; it drew on ancient, Renaissance, and civic republican models. (Versailles, Museum of History.)

for egoism, probity for honor, principles for customs, duties for properties, the empire of reason for the tyranny of fashion, scorn of vice for the scorn of misfortune, pride for insolence, greatness of soul for vanity, love of glory for love of money, good people for good company, merit for intrigue, genius for wit, truth for glitter, the charm of happiness for the boredom of sensuality, the greatness of man for the pettiness of the great." It followed that "in the system of the French Revolution, what is immoral is impolitic, what is corrupting is counterrevolutionary."

Although the revolutionaries believed that private interests (by which they meant factional or small-group interests) should not be represented in the public arena of politics, they were convinced that private character and public virtue were closely related. As the Temporary Commission of Republican Vigilance Established in "Emancipated City" (Lyons) put it in November 1793: "to be truly Republican, each citizen must experience and bring about in himself a revolution equal to the one which has changed France . . . every man who opens his soul to the cold speculations of interest; every man who calculates the worth of a piece of land, an office, a talent . . . all such men who dare to call themselves Republicans have

Journée of 1 Prairial, Year III: Ferraud, a Representative of the People, Is Assassinated in the National Convention. One of the last of the revolutionary *journées:* the sansculottes invade the Convention. Although women really were part of the crowd, their presence was also a standard part of the mythical representation of bloody violence. (Paris, Bibliothèque Nationale.)

The Directory, or the War of Appearances. The new bourgeoisie makes fun of those who have failed to learn the lesson of the Revolution and still dress in the old aristocratic style. (Paris, Bibliothèque Nationale.)

deceived nature . . . let them flee the land of liberty, for they will soon be recognized for what they are and will soak this land with their impure blood." In short, the revolutionary vision of politics was Rousseauist. A good public life depended upon transparent private hearts. There could be no mediation between the state and the individual by parties or interest groups; but individuals were expected to accomplish interior, private revolutions that mirrored the revolution taking place in the state. As a consequence, private life was intensely politicized; the public threatened to engulf the private. "The Republic," according to the Lyonnais revolutionaries, "takes only free men to its bosom."

Changing Appearance

One of the most telling examples of the public invasion of private space was the recurrent concern with clothing. From the opening of the Estates General in 1789, dress was invested with political significance. Michelet imagined the difference between the sober deputies of the Third Estate at the head of the opening procession—"a mass of men, dressed in black . . . modest clothes"—and "the brilliant little band of deputies of the nobility . . . with their plumed hats, their laces, their gold trim." The result, according to the English John Moore, was

The Bastille Destroyed, or the Little Victory and *The Drum of the Nation,* engravings by Louis-Marin Bonnet after Jean-Baptiste Huet. Children's games provided an opportunity for civic education and the display of new fashions. (Paris, Bibliothèque Nationale.)

Young Frenchwoman on Her Way to the Champ-de-Mars for Drill. (Paris, Bibliothèque Nationale.)

that "a great plainness or rather shabbiness of dress was . . . considered as a presumption of patriotism."[3]

In 1790 fashion journals depicted a "Costume à la Constitution" for women, which in 1792 became the "Equality outfit with a hat very à la mode among Republican women." According to *Le Journal de la mode et du goût,* the "grande dame" of 1790 wore "colors striped in the national fashion," and "the patriotic woman wore royal blue, with a hat of black velvet, hatband, and tricolor cockade. Among men fashion was perhaps less precisely defined at first, but *le costume* soon became a powerfully charged semiotic system. It revealed the public meaning of a man's private character. Moderates and aristocrats could be identified by their disdain for wearing the cockade. After 1792 the red cap of liberty, the short jacket known as the *carmagnole,* and loose-fitting trousers seemed to define the sansculotte, that is, true republican sentiment.

Dress became so politically invested that in October 1793, the Convention had to reaffirm the "liberté de costume." The decree seems innocuous enough: "No person of either sex may constrain any other citizen or citizeness to dress in a particular manner . . . under pain of being considered and treated as a suspect." The National Convention's discussion reveals, however, that the decree was directed particularly against women's clubs whose members were wearing red liberty caps and forcing other women to follow them. In the opinion of the deputies—at this most radical moment of the Revolution, the period of dechristianization—the politicization of dress was threatening to subvert the definition of the sexual order. Fabre d'Eglantine linked the liberty cap to the masculinization of women: "Today they ask for the red liberty cap: they will not be satisfied with that; they will soon demand a belt with pistols." Armed women would be more dangerous in the long breadlines; worse yet, they were forming clubs. Continuing his denunciation, he observed that "these clubs are not composed of mothers of families, daughters of families, sisters occupied with their younger brothers or sisters, but of adventuresses, knights-errant, emancipated women, and amazons."[4] The applause that interrupted Fabre indicated that he had touched a sensitive nerve among the deputies, who voted the next day to suppress all women's clubs because they subverted the "natural" order, that is, they "emancipated" women from their exclusively familial (private) indentities. In response to a women's deputation to city hall two weeks later, Chaumette declared, "since when is it decent to see women abandoning the pious care of their households, the cribs of their children, to come to public places, to harangues in the galleries, at the bar of the senate?" According to even the most radical Jacobin leaders, women were properly associated with private life, and their active participation qua women in the public sphere was rejected by all but a handful of men.

Despite the Convention's apparent defense of the individual's right to dress as he pleased, the state was becoming more and more involved in this area. All men were required by law to wear the tricolor cockade after 5 July 1792, all French citizens, regardless of sex, after 3 April 1793. In May 1794 the Convention asked the artist-deputy David to present his views and suggestions for improving national dress. He produced eight drawings, including two of civilian uniforms. There was very little difference between the proposed civilian costume and those of officials. Both included a short, open tunic held together by a sash at the waist, close-fitting hose, short boots or shoes, a kind of toque, and a three-quarter-length cloak. The costume combined Antique, Renaissance, and theatrical themes. David's civilian costume was worn, if at all, only by the young clients of the master artist. Nevertheless, the very idea of a civilian costume, which originated in the Popular and Republican Society of the Arts, shows that some hoped to erase the line between public and private altogether. All citi-

The "Ladies of Orleans" march in ranks, flowers in their hats and rifles on their shoulders. In the carefully planned festivals of 1793, attributes and functions were assigned in a calculated manner. (Paris, Bibliothèque Nationale.)

Le Sueur, *Patriotic Woman's Club*. Decent and charitable women who remained true to their roles as mothers and wives wear "constitutional" bonnets. Women's clubs were closed by the decree of 9 Brumaire, Year II (November 1793) on the grounds that they were in conflict with woman's purely private role. (Paris, Musée Carnavalet.)

zens, whether or not they were soldiers, would be in uniform. The Society of the Arts artists insisted that the present mode of dressing was unworthy of a free man; if private character was to be revolutionized, then dress too had to be entirely renovated. How could equality be achieved if social distinctions continued to be expressed in dress? Not surprisingly, the dress of women seemed less important to both artists and legislators. According to Wicar, women need change little "except their ridiculously overdone handkerchiefs." Since they were to be confined to private roles, there was no need for women to wear the national uniform of citizens.

Even when the state abandoned the grandiose project for the reform and standardization of men's private dress, dress continued to hold political meaning. The *muscadins* (young dandies) of the Thermidorean reaction wore white linen and attacked supposed Jacobins who did not powder their hair. "Le costume à la victime" of the muscadins included a square-necked coat, elegant shoes, and hair long on the sides; they were armed with short, leaded canes. In general, the Revolution led to a loosening and lightening of dress. For women, this meant a trend toward greater and greater display of bare skin until one journalist commented, "Several goddesses appeared in dresses so light and so transparent that they they denied desire the sole pleasure on which it thrives: the pleasure of guessing."[5]

The most intimate objects of private space were stamped with public signs of revolutionary ardor. "Revolution beds" or "Federation beds" could be found in the homes of prosperous patriots. Porcelain and faience of every sort came painted with republican designs or vignettes. Snuffboxes, shaving mugs, mirrors, chests of all sorts, even chamberpots, were painted with scenes of the revolutionary *journées* or with allegorical settings. *La liberté, l'égalité, la prospérité, la victoire*—all in the varied shapes of lovely, young goddesses graced the private spaces of the republican bourgeoisie. Even poor tailors and shoemakers might have a revolutionary calendar with its new dating system and the ubiquitous republican vignettes on their walls. Portraits of revolutionary and ancient heroes or historical tableaux of the Revolution's founding events certainly did not entirely supplant the woodcuts and engravings of the Virgin Mary and the saints, nor can we assume that popular attitudes changed profoundly during this experiment in political education. Yet the intrusion of new public symbols into private spaces was an essential element in the creation of a revolutionary tradition. And all those portraits of Bonaparte and the varied representations of his victories helped found the Napoleonic myth. The refurnishing of private space had long-term public consequences thanks to the politicizing will of the revolutionary leadership and their followers.

The Changing Decor of Daily Life

Just as political symbols invaded the usually private domains of life, so too the signs of private life invaded public spaces. The familiar *tu* went public. In October 1793 a sansculotte militant petitioned the Convention, "in the name of all my constituents to *tutoyer* without distinction those of either sex to whom they speak individually [the *vous* was plural as well as formal for 'you'] on pain of being declared suspect." His reasoning was that this practice would lead to "less arrogance, less distinction, less enmity, more obvious familiarity, more of a leaning toward fraternity, and consequently more equality." The deputies refused to require the *tu* form in

Changing Language

Wallpaper decorated with cockade and trophy, circa 1793 or 1794. The Revolution even left its mark on the decor of bedrooms and salons. (Vizille, Museum of the French Revolution.)

public, but its use became common in the most radical revolutionary circles. The use of "familiar" language—"tu" was much more widespread among the lower classes—in the public arena had a self-consciously disruptive effect that threatened the normal rules of public discourse.

Even more shocking was the massive intrusion of vulgarity into public, printed, political discourse. Right-wing newspapers such as the *Actes des Apôtres* and *Les Sabats jacobites* and anonymous pamphlets such as *La Vie privée de Blondinet Lafayette, général des bluets* began the trend in the earliest years of the Revolution by parodying Catholic ritual and promoting the elegantly smutty witticisms so appreciated in the highest circles of the ancien régime. Newspapers of the left, especially Hébert's *Père Duchesne*, took up the challenge almost immediately—but in a much more vulgar tone. Soon, the "buggers," the "ass-wipes," and various forms of "fuck," appeared regularly in print, along with an unending variety of fashionable profanity from "by Thunder!" to "twenty-five thousand million firecrackers." In Hébert's case, as in many others, vulgarity reached its nadir in descriptions of Marie Antoinette: "The Austrian tigress was regarded in every court as the most miserable *prostitute* in France. She was accused publicly of wallowing in the mire with her valets, and it was impossible to tell which lout was responsible for the puny, gangrened hunchbacks that came out of her three-tiered belly."[6]

Marie Antoinette was portrayed as the inversion of everything a woman was supposed to be: a wild animal rather than a civilizing force; a prostitute rather than a wife; a monster giving birth to deformed creatures rather than a mother. She was the ultimate, vicious expression of what the revolutionaries feared women would become if they entered the public realm: hideous perversions of female sexuality. This hideous perversion seemed to require an equally repulsive language usually found only in men's locker-room stories. In the public realm it was used to destroy the aura of queenship, of nobility, of deference.

In many other ways language reflected the oscillations of the line between public and private. The revolutionary state tried to regulate the use of private language by requiring French instead of patois and dialect. Barère explained the government's position: "The language of a free people must be one and the same for everyone." The battle between public and private became a linguistic one; the new schools were designed to propagate French, especially in Brittany and Alsace, and all the acts of government were published in that language. In many parts of France, consequently, public speech was nationalized, and patois and dialect were privatized in some measure by the experience.

For some, the creation of a private language compensated for the loss of private lives. Soldiers, who in effect lost their private lives when conscripted, developed their own veterans' slang *(parler des Grognards)* to distinguish themselves from civilians *(pékins)*. They had their own terms for equipment, uniforms, army divisions, battlefield incidents, pay—even for the numbers in the game of lotto (2 was "the little chickie" and 3, "the Jew's ear"). The German enemy was known as "une tête de choucroute," the English more simply as "le goddam."

Symbols of the familiar and the familial developed remarkable political—and therefore public—powers in this period of confusion. The emblem of the Republic, the Roman goddess of liberty, often had an abstract, faraway look on official seals, statues, and vignettes. But in many representations she took on the familiarity of a young girl or a young mother. Soon she became known, first in derision and then in affection, as Marianne, the most common of girls. A female figure, at a time when women lacked most concrete political rights, could nevertheless (or because of this?) become the icon of the new Republic. Engravings portrayed Napoléon himself saving her from the abyss of discord and division in 1799. To be effective, power had to command affection; for this reason it had on occasion to be familiar.

The political discourse and iconography of the revolutionary decade told a family story. At the beginning the king was portrayed as the benevolent father, who would recognize the problems of the kingdom and put them in order with the help of his newly adult sons (in particular, the deputies of the Third Estate). When, in June 1791, he tried to flee the country, this plot line became impossible to sustain. The now more radical sons increasingly demanded fundamental changes and eventually insisted that they replace the father altogether. The need to eliminate the tyrannical father was then complemented by a remarkable fury against the woman who had never successfully been represented as motherly; Marie Antoinette's much-described adultery was an insult to the nation and in some sense was taken to justify her terrible end. Displacing the royal couple in the new family matrix of power was the

Marianne and the Republican Family

LA FRANCE RÉPUBLICAINE.

Ouvrant son Sein à tous les Français.

A nimbus of light surrounds this republican brunette with her ample maternal bosom. Her cap is adorned with the Gallic cock, and from her neck hangs a carpenter's level, a symbol of equality. (Paris, Bibliothèque Nationale.)

Republican calendar for Year III (1794), designed and engraved by P.-L. Debucourt. Conceived by Gilbert Romme and Fabre d'Eglantine, members of the National Convention, it was an extremist attempt to revamp time. The year began with the spring equinox. Each month consisted of three ten-day *décades,* a device for eliminating Sunday with its religious connotations. Each day honored a different plant or agricultural implement. Wearing a Phrygian cap, Philosophy reestablishes the natural order. (Paris, Bibliothèque Nationale.)

fraternity of revolutionaries that protected the fragile sisters of liberté and égalité. There is never a father present in the new representations of the Republic, and mothers, except very young ones, also are largely absent. The parents had disappeared from this family, leaving the brothers to create a new world and protect their now orphaned sisters. On occasion, especially in 1792–1793, the sisters were imagined as active participants in the Revolution, but for the most part, they were represented as in need of protection. The Republic *(La République)* was cherished, but for support it depended on the people *(le peuple),* a formidable, masculine force.

PUBLIC INSTITUTIONS AND PRIVATE BELIEFS

The Catholic Church

The effects of the Revolution on private life were not entirely "symbolic," that is, concerned with such manifestations of political culture as dress, language, and political ritual. In many other areas the revolutionary state directly challenged the power of ancien-régime social institutions—the church, the corporations, the nobility, the village community, and the extended family—and in the process carved out new space for the individual and his private rights.

This process was not without resistance and ambiguities, many of which are evident in the state's struggle with its chief competitor for control of private life: the Catholic Church. Catholicism, at once a privately experienced set of beliefs and a publicly practiced set of rituals, a collection of individuals and a powerful institution, was the locus of the Revolution's most intense public (and perhaps private) struggles. In good liberal fashion, the revolutionaries initially hoped to base their regime on general religious tolerance; questions of religious belief were to be private affairs. But old habits and the ever-increasing need for funds dictated a more ambiguous solution: confiscation of church lands and a "civil constitution" for the clergy. Bishops were to be elected, much like other public officials, and the successive revolutionary assemblies required oaths of loyalty from the clergy and curtailed the wearing of clerical vestments. As support of the *réfractaires* (clergy who refused to swear allegiance to the regime) became associated with counterrevolution, the state increasingly controlled the place, the time, and the manner of worship. With the Concordat of 1801, Napoleon renounced the most extreme manifestations of state control, but only at the price of recognition

This republican teacher has a Roman profile, a virginal veil, and a young girl's breasts. The primer from which she teaches is the Declaration of the Rights of Man and of the Citizen. (Paris, Bibliothèque Nationale.)

of the state's permanent right to interfere in matters of faith.

Although many Catholic parishioners desired reform, they did not easily acquiesce to state control. To defend their church and its rituals, many heretofore private individuals, especially women and children, adopted public roles for the first time. The constitutional church was strangled, according to Abbé Grégoire, by "lewd and seditious women." They hid "nonjurors" (those who refused to take the oath), helped to organize clandestine masses and even "white masses" (masses without a priest), urged their men to petition the government for the reopening of churches after Thermidor, refused to have their children baptized or married by juring priests, and, when all else failed, rioted in the name of religious freedom. Old popular saints were revived and, especially in areas of counter-revolution, new martyrs were created. Recitation of the rosary at *veillées* (evenings spent together socializing) became an act of political resistance. "Suzanne sans peur" was bold enough to publish her resistance in a pamphlet found in the village of Villethiery in the Yonne Department in the Year VII: "There is no governmental despotism anywhere that equals ours. They tell us, you are free and sovereign, while we are regimented to the point that we are forbidden to sing or play in our Sunday best, not even allowed to kneel to give homage to the Supreme Being."[7]

Under assault by the state and by the more determined urban revolutionaries, religion was privatized. By 1794, after

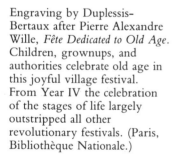

Engraving by Duplessis-Bertaux after Pierre Alexandre Wille, *Fête Dedicated to Old Age*. Children, grownups, and authorities celebrate old age in this joyful village festival. From Year IV the celebration of the stages of life largely outstripped all other revolutionary festivals. (Paris, Bibliothèque Nationale.)

Jean-Jacques Rousseau, *Emile*, book 4. *Sansculotte Paying Homage to the Supreme Being*. The sansculotte in the role of Citizen Emile's "vicar of Savoy": "I believe that the world is governed by a wise and powerful will. I see it, or, rather, I feel it." (Paris, Bibliothèque Nationale.)

The new rituals of secular marriage stressed the importance of mutual consent and the public authorities. The religious aspects of marriage survived, however, in such symbols as the altar, the goddess (Reason?), and the eye of the Supreme Being. Below: *The Marriage Oath.* (Paris, Bibliothèque Nationale.) Page 29, left: *National Guardsman Marries Before the Supreme Being.* (Paris, Bibliothèque Nationale.)

emigration, deportation, execution, imprisonment, abdication, and marriage, there were very few priests left to practice a public religion. Devotion had to take place at home, within the family, or in small, trusted groups. But as soon as restrictions were lifted in any way, private people came forward to proclaim their faith publicly. Parish churches used for grain storage, stables, manufacturing of saltpeter, fishmarkets, or club meetings were restored and reconsecrated. Sacred vessels and vestments were dug up out of hiding, and someone—a schoolteacher or former official if a priest could not be found—was asked to conduct the service. In many places, especially outside the towns, the *décadi* (rest day of the Revolutionary calendar) was ignored, and on Sunday villagers gathered to flaunt their unwillingness to work. The consequence of this dramatic intermixing of private and public concerns was the establishment of an enduring new structure of religious practice: women remained the mainstay of the church they had so tenaciously defended, and men became at best *pratiquants saisonniers* (occasional churchgoers). New forms of public life—the cabaret and the café—now claimed the male population.

In no domain was the invasion of public authority more evident than in family life. Marriage was secularized, and the ceremony, to be considered binding, had to be performed before a municipal official. Under the ancien régime marriage was formalized by the exchange of consent from the two parties; the priest was only a witness to the exchange. By the far-reaching decree of 20 September 1792, the official not only had charge of the civil registers but also declared the couple united in the eyes of the law. Public authority was now taking an active part in the formation of the family. The state determined the obstacles to marriage; reestablished and regulated the process of adoption; accorded rights (severely restricted under the civil code) to illegitimate children; instituted divorce; and limited parental powers. By attempting to establish a new national system of education, the National Convention proceeded on the principle that children, as Danton said, "belong to the Republic before they belong to their parents." Bonaparte himself insisted that "the law takes the child at birth, provides for his education, prepares him for a profession,

The Family and Public-Private Boundaries

Anonymous, miniature on ivory, 1793–1795. Liberty, without a cap but with a sword at her side, places a wreath on Equality, symbolized by the carpenter's level. Revolutionary images in the form of miniatures circulated widely. (Vizille, Museum of the French Revolution.)

regulates how and under what conditions he can marry, travel, and choose a profession."

The legislation on family life demonstrates the competing concerns of the revolutionary governments. The protection of individual liberty, the maintenance of family solidarity, and the consolidation of state control had to be balanced. During the period of the National Convention, in particular, though even earlier, the revolutionary state gave priority to the protection of individuals against the possible tyranny of family and church. Lettres de cachet were especially repugnant because they had been used by families to intern children who were simply rebellious or prodigal. Nevertheless, with the institution of family courts in August 1790, the legislators encouraged family resolution of disputes between family members, including eventually divorce (made possible by another law promulgated on 20 September 1792). The Civil Code was far less preoccupied with the happiness and autonomy of the individual, especially of women, emphasizing the powers of the father. The powers attributed to the family courts were either restored to the father as head of the family or taken over by state courts. In general, the state often limited family or church control only in order to increase its own; it guaranteed individual rights, encouraged family solidarity, and limited parental powers.

The Right to Divorce

The tension between individual rights, family maintenance, and state control is very marked in the case of divorce, which was instituted for the first time in French history during the Revolution. Divorce was the logical consequence of the liberal ideas expressed in the Constitution of 1791. Article 7 had secularized marriage: "The law henceforth regards marriage only as a civil contract." If marriage was a civil contract based on consent, it could be broken. Such reasoning was given further impetus by the force of circumstances. The Civil Constitution of the Clergy had divided the Catholic Church, and in many communes couples were refusing to take marriage vows before a *jureur* (clergyman who had taken the oath of allegiance to the government). By secularizing marriage, the state gained control over the civil registers (births, deaths, marriages) and replaced the church as the ultimate authority in questions of family life. In debates over divorce, which, despite the novelty of the proposed law, were not very extensive, other reasons for instituting divorce were cited: relief for

Anonymous, miniature on ivory, 1796. A woman carries messages back and forth from prison. Her basket too was a weapon. (Vizille, Museum of the French Revolution.)

The law of 1792 made divorce
easy but not advisable. The
highly family-oriented morality
of the Revolution denounced
destructive passions and
appealed to reason and the
interests of the children, a new
notion that actually played a
less central role than the
iconography might suggest.
Le Sueur, *Divorce*. (Paris,
Musée Carnavalet.)
Divorce, 1793. (Paris,
Bibliothèque Nationale.)

the unhappy couple; the liberation of women from marital despotism; and freedom of conscience for Protestants and Jews, because the religion of these groups did not proscribe divorce.

The divorce law of 1792 was remarkably liberal. Seven grounds for divorce were admitted: insanity; conviction for crimes entailing corporal punishment or loss of civil rights; crimes, brutality, or grave injury inflicted by one partner on the other; notorious dissoluteness of morals; abandonment for at least two years; absence without news for at least five years; emigration (when taken as a sign of counterrevolutionary intentions). In such cases, divorce was granted immediately. In addition, a couple could divorce by mutual consent with at most a four-month delay, and divorce was granted also for incompatibility of temperament or character after a six-month period of attempted reconciliation. A one-year wait was required before remarriage. The judicial procedures involved were so inexpensive that divorce was available to most of the population; most strikingly, it was available to both women and men on equal terms. At that time it was the most liberal law anywhere in the world.

Under Title VI of the Napoleonic Civil Code, the number of grounds for divorce was reduced to three: conviction for crimes entailing corporal punishment or loss of civil rights; brutality; or adultery. In line with Napoleon's general reaffirmation of paternal powers, the rights of women were severely curtailed. The husband could seek divorce on the basis of his wife's adultery, but the wife could only request divorce if her husband "kept his concubine in their family home" (article 230). Moreover, if she was convicted of adultery, she was liable to two years imprisonment, while he escaped any punishment. Divorce by mutual consent was maintained, but with many restrictions: the husband had to be at least twenty-five years old; the wife between twenty-one and forty-five years of age; the length of the marriage had to be between two and twenty years duration; and parental permission had to be obtained. There were some 30,000 divorces in France between 1792 and 1803, but many fewer afterward (divorce was abolished in 1816). In Lyons, to take an example that has been closely studied, there were 87 divorces a year between 1792 and 1804, and only 7 a year between 1805 and 1816. In Rouen, 43 percent of the 1,129 divorces between 1792 and 1816 were granted between 1792 and 1795; after 1803 there were only 6 divorces granted a year.

The Experience of Divorce

Did the possibility of divorce have a real impact on the private lives of the new citizens of the Republic? In the cities, certainly, but far less so in the countryside. In Toulouse, for example, there were 347 divorces between 1792 and 1803, but in the rural districts of Revel and Muret there were only 2 each during the same period. In the big cities such as Lyons and Rouen, as many as 3–4 percent of the marriages contracted during the Revolution had been broken by divorce by 1802—within at most ten years of marriage. Around 1900, after the reinstitution of divorce in 1884, the divorce rate was 6.5 percent—probably not much higher than the rate of the 1790s, given that divorce was readily available only during the ten years after 1792. Divorced couples came from all strata of urban society, though artisans, merchants, and professionals may have divorced somewhat more often. Women apparently benefited from the new laws; in two-thirds of the cases in Lyons and Rouen brought by one or the other spouse (not mutual consent), the proceedings were initiated by women. Divorce was not often based on mutual consent: in only one out of four or five cases did the couple seek a divorce jointly.

The primary causes of divorce under the 1792 law were abandonment or prolonged absence. The next most-cited cause was incompatibility. Even the driest statistics tell a sad story on occasion: one-quarter of those citing abandonment in Lyons complained that the absence of a spouse had lasted ten years or more! Fully half of the spouses had been gone five years or more. The Revolution offered some the occasion to bring the legal situation in line with reality. And that reality included some perennial problems. Men and women cited abandonment and incompatibility in nearly equal numbers as their reason for seeking a divorce, but are we surprised to learn that women were much more likely to complain of brutality? The records of the family courts and later the civil courts are filled with stories of husbands assaulting their wives, often on returning home from the cabaret, with fists, brooms, crockery, fire irons, and sometimes even knives.

Divorce legislation was not intended simply to liberate the individual from the constraints of an unhappy domestic situation. The unhappy couple had to work out the divorce arrangements through a family court or a family meeting, depending on the kind of divorce requested. These were composed of relatives (or friends if relatives were lacking), chosen by the husband and wife to decide the merits of the case and property settlements and child custody. Divorce was apparently quite readily accepted, since only one-third to one-half of the petitions for divorce were dropped (presumably in part because of family pressure). The number of cases pursued to completion is surprising, given the novelty of divorce and the church's resistance to it. Even most constitutional bishops only accepted divorce on the condition that it not lead to remarriage during the lifetime of the other spouse. Nevertheless, about one-fourth of the men and women who obtained divorces remarried. (After 1816 the church accepted these remarriages if the original marriages had been secular ones, on the grounds that such marriages had no validity.) Petitions for divorce rarely led to custody battles—partly because many of those seeking divorce had no underage children (three-fifths of the divorcing couples in Lyons and Rouen had no minor children), and partly because neither the courts nor the parents seemed to consider children an integral part of the family unit. Evidence for the latter, though largely negative, is nonetheless convincing: children were rarely cited in the depositions of the couple or in court records; the decisions made for the custody of children were rarely if ever disputed; and frequently the couple mentioned that they had children, without giving their names or even, on occasion, the number of them in the family.

Divorce proceedings provide one of the few windows onto private sensibility during the Revolution. It is not clear how much changed in the affective life of the individual during this troubled time. P. J. B. Nougaret tells the story of a daughter made pregnant by her married lover. Her mother pretends to be pregnant so that they can go off to the country until the daughter gives birth, thus protecting the daughter's honor. This exemplary mother in *Paris ou le rideau levé* (published in Year VIII) seems untouched by the revolutionary experience. The problems experienced in marital relations were probably much the same as they had been before 1789. The Revolution certainly did not invent wife-beating. But the very possibility of divorce must have had some influence on marriage. Now there were women, such as the Lyonnaise Claudine Ramey, who wanted to leave her husband because "she could not be happy with him."[8] For many, love had to be the foundation of marriage. And marriage itself seemed to enjoy an unusual vogue during the Revolution; the average annual number of marriages jumped from 239,000 under Louis XVI to 327,000 in 1793. Not all of these were for love alone; the proportion of marriages in which the husband was less than twenty-five years old and ten years younger than his wife grew from 9–10 to 19 percent in 1796—probably because marriage was the best means of avoiding conscription.

Private Feelings of Important Public Persons

It is very difficult to discover the meaning of private life for the revolutionaries. The memoirs of leading political figures are remarkably impersonal. They are devoted almost entirely to the panorama of public life, not unlike the memoirs of their ancien-régime predecessors; most aspects of private life—love, marital relations, or personal health, for example— are left in the shadows, as if irrelevant to the great experiment in founding a new nation. Even memoirs written much later shared many of the same characteristics. La Revellière-Lépeaux, who composed his in the early 1820s and included many typically romantic passages about his early loves, devoted only one chapter out of three volumes to his "private life before the Revolution." Private life seemed to end with the coming of the Revolution and begin again only with retirement from public life. He described his early meeting with the future deputy Leclerc (of Maine-et-Loire) at the secondary school *(collège)* in Angers as "one of the remarkable circumstances of my private life." The experience of public life in the Revolution had colored almost all of his reminiscences of the past. The only private life that La Revellière-Lépeaux discussed were the major events of his family life: his search for a wife and his feelings about her and his children. When detailing the revolutionary experience, he omits all but his political judgments. The private and the political did not mix.

Even Madame Roland wrote in this conventional style. Faced with the guillotine, she wrote her "Notices historiques sur la Révolution," which were much like the memoirs of politicians involved in day-to-day political affairs. At the same time, however, she also recalled her early years in her memoirs, which she conceived of as an exercise in private history: "I propose to use my spare time in captivity to retrace what is personal to me." In those pages she described life with her parents in great detail, and she devoted much more space to her own private feelings than did La Revellière-Lépeaux. She was torn by grief when her mother died, yet was much more detached when describing her early thoughts about M. Roland: "his gravity, his morals, his habits, all devoted to work, caused me to regard him, in a manner of speaking, without sex, or as a *philosophe* who only existed through reason."

In letters written during the 1780s Madame Roland had managed to combine a consuming interest in political developments with an ongoing fascination for the details of daily life. Nevertheless, the fast pace and all-absorbing public life of the years after 1789 made it impossible for her to become the Madame de Sévigné of the revolutionary era; she was too caught up in affairs of the moment to write leisurely letters. She recognized the impact of the Revolution on private life immediately and on 4 September 1789 wrote: "if an honorable man can follow the torch of love, it is only after having lighted it at the sacred fire of love of country." The year 1789 was the great dividing line in her private life because it was the watershed in national politics. As a result, her more personal "private memoirs" covered only the period up to the beginning of the Revolution. Even near death, however, Madame Roland was able to express her feelings about her daughter: "I hope that one day she will be able to fulfill, in peace and obscurity, the touching duties of wife and mother."[9] Involvement in public life had destroyed the mother's private life, and she hoped her daughter would meet a different fate—a happy private life away from the public eye.

Living and Dying

What little we can discover about the private feelings of people during the 1790s and early 1800s indicates considerable preoccupation, first with the revolutionary process, and then with the building of empire. Everyone was touched in some way: sons were sent to war; priests were deported; churches were converted to secular uses and then reconsecrated; lands sold at auction were repurchased when an émigré family returned; marriages were celebrated in a different way; and divorce was possible. Even private names were affected. In 1793 and 1794, especially, children were named Brutus, Mucius-Scaevola, Périclès, Marat, Jemappes, or even Navette, Betterave, or Messidrice. Boys were more likely than girls to be given revolutionary first names, illegitimate and abandoned children more than legitimate ones. The vogue for revolutionary names subsided quickly after 1794, but there were still occasional echoes, a Prairial, Epicure-Démocrite, or Marie-Liberté, well into the nineteenth century. Private names became carriers of public traditions.

Preoccupation with revolutionary events can be seen in the few extant letters and autobiographical fragments written by ordinary people. Jacques-Louis Ménétra, a Parisian glazier, described his experience with revolutionary politics in his journal. Although his version is original, he often uses the language of the Thermidorean rulers: "The Frenchman breathed nothing but blood . . . The Convention under Robespierre was nothing more than a den of denouncers and vindictive men trying to destroy one party in order to substitute another." In his letters to his brother, the Parisian bookseller Nicholas Ruault described the va-et-vient of Parisian and national politics in great detail, almost to the exclusion of all else. Yet both men wrote of their family lives on occasion (though never in the detail of Madame Roland's *Mémoires*). Ruault interrupted his correspondence when his only son died, and then explained his silence: "The fever or *the doctor has robbed* us of all we hold most dear in the world. What do we have to live for now?" Ménétra told of his daughter's divorce and remarriage and hoped that she would forget "the pain and grief that she suffered with her first monster of a husband." During the widespread miseries of 1795, he proudly announced: "I was living very well. We did not feel the famine at all . . . We had good food."

Those whose lives were more pathetic left little behind to tell the story of their private lives. Death rates were highest in 1794, 1804, and 1814 (though not higher than in 1747). The number of suicides was highest in crisis years; the numbers seemed to be increasing between 1798 and 1801, and under the Empire they reached their apogee in 1812. Under Napoleon, there were about 150 suicides a year in Paris; the method chosen by almost all suicides was jumping into the Seine River. Three times as many men killed themselves as women, no doubt because the proscriptions of Catholic doctrine had a stronger hold on women. The suicides of Paris were not rootless vagrants who just happened to end their unhappy days while in the capital. They were men and women in decline, whose often difficult existence seemed to be worsening. They left little behind other than the clothing they were wearing and the testimony of the relatives, friends, and neighbors who identified the bodies. We know virtually nothing of their innermost feelings except that death in the muddy waters of the Seine seemed preferable to continued struggle.

THE REVOLUTION OF THE MARQUIS DE SADE

In describing private life during the Revolution, we usually must rely on the quantitative measures of social history

Louis Léopold Boilly, *Galerie du Palais-Royal*. Gathering place for libertines at the end of the ancien régime and during the Revolution, the Palais Royal later became filled with private shops and businesses, where some traded goods while others traded on their charms. (Paris, Musée Carnavalet.)

(the rates of divorces and of suicides) and on the direct testimony of those few members of the elite who had occasion to write down their "private" thoughts. We know very little about what most people experienced within themselves. What did the soldier think about in his tent, the prisoner in his cell, the militant's wife while cooking, a prostitute walking the streets or lying in bed at night unable to sleep? We do not even know that these fleeting moments of private consciousness meant much to the people of the revolutionary era. But there is one extreme example of a private consciousness that cannot be overlooked—that of the Marquis de Sade. Sade explored the outer limits of sexuality, surely one of the most important dimensions of the private self; in many ways his explorations still define the boundaries of modern consciousness. Is it coincidental that most of his major writings were composed between 1785 and 1800?

Nothing about the early life of Donatien-Alphonse-François de Sade hints much about the author of *Justine, La Philosophie dans le boudoir,* and *Les 120 Journées de Sodome.* He was educated at Louis-le-Grand before entering the royal army, like many other young noblemen and future heads of titled families. At the age of twenty-three he married, and within months he was confined in Vincennes by lettre de cachet for "débauche outrée," the beginning of a long career of libertinism punctuated by prison. He spent eleven years in Vincennes and the Bastille between 1778 and 1790, and was permanently imprisoned after 1801. Despite his noble lineage, Sade managed to survive the Revolution in Paris, writing plays and even serving as a revolutionary official (secretary of the Section des Picques) before he was imprisoned for several months in 1794 (in the same prison with Laclos).

Sade was a notorious libertine before 1789, but during the Revolution, thanks to his writings, he became even more infamous. *Justine* went through six editions in the decade after its publication in 1791. The 300-page novel was expanded to 810 pages in *La Nouvelle Justine* published in 1797; *Juliette,* published the same year, was over 1,000 pages long. Both *Aline et Valcour* and *La Philosophie dans le boudoir* were published in 1795. It was as the author of *Justine* that Sade was most frequently denounced in the newspapers; *La Nouvelle Justine* and *Juliette,* the other two novels in the *Justine* cycle, landed him in prison for the last time. The number of editions and continuing notoriety of *Justine* indicates that his name was well known during the Revolutionary epoch. *Lolotte et Fanfan*

(1788), the best-known novel of Ducray-Duminil, the extravagant sentimentalist who wrote in the style of the English novelist Anne Radcliffe, went through no less than twelve editions, but Ducray-Duminil was the most popular author of the time. In this era of constant novel production (4,000–5,000 between 1790 and 1814, according to one estimate) and a rapidly growing taste for novel-reading, enhanced by the new reading rooms that multiplied in Paris after 1795, the Sadian oeuvre had a significant public.

Sade's philosophical tales undermined revolutionary ideals, not by rejecting them but by taking them to their most repulsive possible conclusion. According to Blanchot, "he formulates a kind of Declaration of the Rights of Eroticism," in which nature and reason served the desires of an absolute egotism. The conventional triumph of virtue over vice was reversed, again and again. Sade himself claimed, "I am only a machine in her [Nature's] hands that she moves at her will." In the new world of absolute equality only power, often brutal, cruel power, mattered. Birth, privilege, all distinctions disappeared in the face of this revolutionary regime in which there was no law (at least in the conventional sense). Liberty, equality, and even fraternity were glorified and yet perverted in the Sadian novels. Liberty was the right to pursue pleasure without regard for the law, for convention, for the wishes of others (and this limitless liberty for a few special men usually meant bondage for the chosen women). There could be equality in the pursuit of pleasure, and no one had a special birthright to it, but only the most ruthless and self-regarding would win (and they would almost always be male). And what more striking fraternity than the four friends of *Les 120 Journées* or the Society for the Friends of Crime of *Juliette,* whose rules and rituals parodied the Freemason lodges and the thousands of Societies of the Friends of the Constitution (Jacobins) of the Revolutionary decade.

In Sade's novels *le privé* has a very special place. It is necessary to the most extreme, most cruel enjoyment, and it is almost always figured as a prison. As Barthes remarks, "Sadian privacy is only the theatrical form of solitude."[10] Caves, crypts, underground passages, and excavations were among the favorite places of Sade's protagonists. The ultimate in the secret and in solitude were those châteaux specially chosen because they were cut off from the outside (the social)

The Declaration of the Rights of Eros

Jean-Jacques Lequeu, *The Isle of Love*. This depicts an enchanted isle of amorous delights—the architectural embodiment of a literary myth. All sorts of flowers, birds, and animals can be found in this palace, which embodies a variety of other influences and fantasies, all disciplined by a perfect symmetry. (Paris, Bibliothèque Nationale.)

world. The château of Silling in the Black Forest is the locale of *Les 120 Journées de Sodome;* in *Justine* it was the château of Sainte-Marie-des-Bois. There is very little description of the exterior of the châteaux, and the interior is always described in terms of imprisonment: the emphasis is on closure but also on repetitive order. At Silling, "it was necessary, I say, to wall up all the gates by which one could enter and to lock oneself in the place as thoroughly as in a besieged citadel . . . The wish was granted; we had barricaded ourselves in to such a degree that it was no longer possible to recognize where the gates had been, and we took up our place in the inside." Once inside this world cut off from the outside, this absolutely private world, there was a rigid insistence on order. Perversion did not mean anarchy; it meant *systematic* overturning of all taboos, regular, repetitive confrontation of all limits, until pleasure demanded actual murder.

Sade's Private Women

In this hyperprivate space the objects of pleasure and the objects of regulation were usually women: "tremble, guess, obey, anticipate, and perhaps you will not be completely wretched" *(Les 120 Journées).* With few exceptions, the women in Sade's novels are unfree, and they rarely experience pleasure of their own accord. "Pleasure shared is pleasure diminished." Conventional heterosexual love in the novels is exceptional; the vagina is almost always ignored in favor of other orifices. Women are the objects of male aggression and have virtually no physical identity. *Juliette* seems to be the exception, but even she must continually rob and kill just to survive. In a kind of Tocquevillian twist, the equality and fraternity between men only serves their complete despotism over women. Many of the female victims are aristocrats, but the new man of the Sadian world reestablishes a kind of feudal power in the isolation of the château as a cell.

Sade's attitude toward women cannot be considered typical, yet the Sadian oeuvre alerts us to the special role women played in their association with the private. In Sade's novels the private is where women (and sometimes children, including young boys) are imprisoned and tortured for the sexual benefit of men. Is this not a characteristic Sadian reductio ad absurdum of the general view of sansculottes and Jacobins alike that women's place was in the private realm? The revolutionaries limited women's roles to those of mother and sister—dependent for their identity on husbands and brothers; Sade turned them into professional whores or women whose major attribute was their susceptibility to being enslaved by men—their only identity was as sexual objects. In both representations women had no autonomous identity—or at least the male figures wished them to have none, for women were imagined as potential subverters, as if it was all too obvious that they would not willingly accept their assigned roles. Why else did the Jacobins speak so harshly about the chaos created when women claimed rights as public actors? Why else did Sade insist so obsessively on the enclosed château? "To prevent attacks from without, which were little feared, and invasions from within, which were dreaded far more" *(Les 120 Journées)*.

The depiction of women as particularly suited to the private (and unsuited to the public) was common in almost every French intellectual circle at the end of the eighteenth century. The treatise of Pierre Roussel, *Du système physique et moral de la femme* (1775), became the standard point of reference in discourse on women. The woman was figured as the inverse of the man. Women were identified with their sexuality, their bodies; men were identified by their minds, their energy. The uterus defined the woman and determined the consequences for her emotional and moral being. The female reproductive system was thought to be especially sensitive, a sensitivity enhanced by the weaker cerebral matter of women. Women were weaker muscularly and sedentary by inclination. The combination of mental and muscular weakness with emotional sensitivity made women functionally well-suited for child-rearing. Thus, the uterus defined the place of women in society as mother. The discourse of the doctors had the same consequences as the discourse of politicians.

During the Revolution, Roussel occasionally wrote for *La Décade philosophique,* the Ideologue newspaper, and he was an associate of the section morale of the Second Class of the Institute. His younger colleague Georges Cabanis shared his views on women. Biologically, men were strong, defiant, and enterprising; women were weak, timid, and dissimulating. Despite his friendship with Mme de Stael and Mme Condorcet, Cabanis rejected all scholarly and political roles for women; such careers would undermine the family, the basis of civil society, the rock of the natural order. Cabanis's disciple and fellow Ideologue, Jacques-Louis Moreau (de la Sarthe), aimed to further the new science of "moral anthropology" with his two-volume study of the *Histoire naturelle de la femme* (1803). His views are familiar: "if it is correct to state that the male is only male at certain moments, but that the female is female all her life, it is principally to this [uterine] influence that this must be attributed; it is this influence that continually recalls woman to her sex and gives all of her conditions such a pronounced physiognomy." It follows then, that "women are more disposed than men to believe in spirits and ghosts; that they adopt all superstitious practices more readily; that their prejudices are more numerous; that they made in great measure the fortune of mesmerism." It was not surprising that such creatures were susceptible to the influence of counterrevolutionary priests and to the most appalling forms of sexual bondage.

In the nineteenth century women were restricted to the private sphere more than ever before. Although this trend began in the second half of the eighteenth century, the Revolution gave it greater impetus, thus reshaping relations between men and women and conceptions of the family. Women were increasingly associated with the "home," with private spaces, not only because industrialization made it possible for middle-class women to define themselves or be defined in this way, but also because the French Revolution had demonstrated the potential—and danger for men—of overturning the "natural" sexual order.

Woman became the figure of fragility who had to be protected from the outside world (the public); she was the representation of the private. Women were to be confined to private spaces because of their supposed biological defects, but the private itself had proved fragile in the face of the politicization and publicization of the revolutionary process. If the state could regulate family life and recast the measures of the time of day and the months of the year, if politics could determine the names of babies and the choice of clothing, then private life might disappear altogether. And the more private life came under pressure, through the secularization of marriage, limitations on worship, and mass mobilization, the more unstable the previously natural order seemed to become. Women might decide to dress like men and insist on fighting at the front; if "unhappy," they might demand divorces. The loss of deference toward kings, queens, nobles, and rich men seemed to call into question the deference of wife for husband, perhaps even the deference of children for father.

The revolutionaries themselves felt the need to draw the line, to place women on the side of the private and men on the side of the public. From 1794 onward, through 1803, 1816, and continuing through the nineteenth century, this line between public and private, men and women, politics and family, became more rigidly drawn. Even the most radical revolutionaries could not bear the tension created by the public invasion of the private. Well before Thermidor they gradually separated themselves from their own handiwork. But the shock waves they created continued to be felt right through the 1970s, when French law concerning family life at last returned to some of the principles of 1792: the divorce law of 11 July 1975 made divorce as easy as it had been in 1792; the law of 4 June 1970 removed the vestiges of male marital supremacy challenged in the early years of the Revolution; and the law of 3 January 1972 insured the rights of illegitimate children that had first been applied in the year II. What better measure could there be of the "modernity" of revolutionary principles and of the long-lasting effects—for better *and* worse—of the revolutionary heritage?

Sir Edwin Landseer, *Queen Victoria and Prince Albert at Windsor with the Princess Royal* (detail). The royal couple: an ideal marriage. (Collection of H. M. Elizabeth II.)

✒ The Sweet Delights of Home

Catherine Hall

IN ENGLAND 1820 was the year of Queen Caroline. Caroline of Brunswick, the "injured Queen of England," was the wife of George, the Prince Regent, son of George III. The marriage was an arranged one and little love was lost between husband and wife. They separated almost immediately after the wedding; their only issue was a daughter, Princess Charlotte. While George was left free to enjoy his love life, his friendships, and his political intrigues, Caroline was expected to live the restricted life of a royal wife, though without the presence of a husband. Her vulgar German ways—or so George saw them—her indiscretions, and her careless talk infuriated the prince, who longed to be rid of her. Faced with his implacable hostility and control over their daughter, Caroline left England to pursue the life of a wandering aristocrat on the Continent.

In 1820 George III died and the Regent, who had acted for his father during the king's periods of madness, assumed the full regalia of monarchy. But was Caroline to be recognized as his queen? George IV was determined that she should not be and insisted that her name be excluded from the liturgy. Furious at being denied what she considered her rights, Caroline set sail for England. She landed in a storm of controversy and was greeted with glee by the Radicals, enemies of the king who welcomed the opportunity to attack him. The king's ministers counseled negotiations, but they were unable to convince the king, who insisted on divorcing his wife, utilizing a special procedure of the House of Lords for the attempt.

This public trial of the queen captured the nation's imagination in 1820. Such a spectacle had never before been seen.

Caroline, The "Injured Queen"

To Be. or. not To Be!

George IV and Caroline, the "insulted queen": the beginning of the royal soap opera. (Paris, Bibliothèque Nationale.)

For weeks the royal scandal filled columns in the national and provincial press as their lordships listened to evidence of scandal in high places, of illicit sexual relations between mistress and servants, of loveless marriage. The peers of the realm sat in judgment on one woman, who contended with the power of the crown and the majesty of their lordships. But public opinion did not rally in support of the king. Instead, there was a revulsion against him as he massed his troops, gathered his informers, and marshaled his evidence, while never risking an appearance in court. Meanwhile the queen was attended by large crowds as she went to and from the palace of Westminster, the only woman in a chamber of men. Her popularity soared as more and more sordid details about her behavior were revealed, but revealed by foreign servants whose loyalty and truthfulness increasingly came under suspicion. Her petty indiscretions were as nothing compared to the rising tide of indignation on her behalf—indignation at the injustice of her being accused by one whose own indiscretions had been the subject of gossip for decades, indignation at the injustice of one poor woman being the victim of the rotten machinery of crown and state, indignation at the whole corrupt nature of aristocratic expectations of marriage for which Caroline was unfairly paying the price.

At the heart of the widescale popular support for Queen Caroline was a distinctive set of ideas about the proper relations between men and women, about the nature of marriage, and about the place of domesticity in a decent society. Marriages based on money could not hope to succeed. Such arrangements could not hope to provide the basis for a lasting union. The queen's protagonists presented her as a virtuous heroine, her mistreatment by one man making it imperative for other men to come to her rescue. She was a hapless victim whose salvation depended on the chivalry of those knights who would fight on her behalf, who would don their armor and mount their steeds in her defense. Every "manly and courageous arm" must be raised to save her from insult, and thus save the good name of England. Fathers, husbands, brothers, all were called upon to "stand firm in a woman's cause." Caroline's helplessness, her aloneness and dependence, were at the heart of the call to arms. She could not save herself; others must do so. The brightest ornament of English civilization was its "domestic virtue." Unless this were maintained, degeneracy and decay could follow. In a characteristic moment, the London brassfounders and coppersmiths mounted a demonstration in support of the queen. It was led by eight knights on horseback in full armor, wearing white plumes and attended by squires. All those in the procession carried brass rods and many wore brass hats; the whole cavalcade was attended by brass bands. The return to chivalry, so powerful an impulse in early-nineteenth-century England, was fueled by ideals of manliness and femininity that had echoes in many other discourses of the period. But the brave knight who rode to the rescue of his helpless lady wanted to be sure that it was a pure and virtuous heroine whom he would snatch from the jaws of the royal dragon.

Caroline was an unlikely princess to play this role. But her lapses were transformed into the malicious creations of scheming Italian servants, her lines recast as those of the fragile, dependent victim, the mother whose child had been torn from her breast. Her mythic role in the royal melodrama was far more appealing to the popular imagination than the salacious details of her falls from grace. Caroline as wronged queen of an unpopular king was infinitely more sympathetic a figure than Caroline, vulgar and promiscuous. The mismatch between the woman and the myth was revealed by the collapse of her hold on public opinion once the king had in effect lost the case and was forced to abandon the attempt to divorce her. Her hopes that the London crowd would enable her to insist on a joint coronation were dashed, and the king was crowned in triumph alone. But his enjoyment of this moment depended on his defeat at the hands of "the public" and the end of his attempts to persecute his unfortunate queen.

The Queen Caroline affair marked one of the first public moments at which a new view of marriage and of sexual relations was demonstrated as having significant popular support. John Bull, that symbol of English manliness and honor, caroled in his "Ode to George the Fourth and Caroline his wife":

> A *Father* to the *Nation* prove,
>   A *Husband* to thy *Queen,*
> And safely in thy people's Love,
>   Reign tranquil and serene.[1]

The "people" insisted that kingship meant familial responsibilities at home as well as paternal responsibilities toward citizens. Being a proper king meant being a proper husband and father too. Tranquillity in the nation could not be achieved unless there was serenity in the home. Domestic virtue was at the heart of English civilization, and the people could love only when their kingly father exemplified such virtues. The regent, with his contempt for the sanctity of marriage and his rejection of family life, had brought into disrepute values that were dearly held by significant sectors of English opinion. Immoral practices might be commonplace among the aristocracy, but that simply revealed the level of corruption of aristocratic life. People should marry for love and companionship, not money; they should take their duties as parents seriously; men should care for and protect their womenfolk, whose nature it was to be dependent; home should be a place of rest and tranquillity, not of conflict and strife.

The "injured queen" left her mark on the public conduct of monarchy. George's successors, William and Adelaide, were celebrated as the ideal loving couple. Victoria, the "Rosebud of England," became the model wife and mother. A popular preacher proclaimed in 1854: "The throne of our homely and our honoured Queen flourishes amid the happy homes, and upon the loyal hearts of her people. One of her highest titles to our confidence and affection is found in her own domestic virtues. She *is a Queen*—a real Queen—but she is a real *Mother,* and a true *Wife.*"[2] Victoria's claims to the loyalty and love of her subjects depended on her own capacity to love as a true woman should. Just as George IV could not expect the obedience of his people without a firm base at home in his manly character as husband and father, so Victoria in representing true femininity evoked the fealty of her subjects, while reminding them that she was a woman like any other. Every family should be an empire of love, with the father as monarch, the woman as queen. The royal soap opera required kings and queens and their families to represent behavior and practices which we recognize in ourselves but which are lifted to a more glamorous and exalted sphere. After 1820 it was clear that in order to be popular the monarch must be domesticated. Sexual licentiousness was out; marriage and the family were definitely in.

The Message of the Evangelicals: Change Your Way of Life

The criticism of aristocratic sexual relations, of a double standard that accepted male infidelity but castigated adulterous women, and of forms of marriage that belittled care and companionship was articulated mainly by groups within the bourgeoisie. In 1820 the middle-class Radicals led the way because the defense of a particular view of the family and domesticity was tied to an attack on the king. Sir Francis Burdett, the celebrated Westminster M.P., and James Mill, friend of Bentham and leading Utilitarian, were among the queen's most vociferous supporters, and in the House of Lords her cause was championed by Henry Brougham, a founder of the *Edinburgh Review*. But there were no necessary connections between such a view of the family and Radical politics. Indeed, many who were shocked by their bedfellows supported the queen's cause and assisted in the creation of a moral majority linking Anglicans with Unitarians, Tories with Whigs and Radicals. That moral majority was the outcome of decades of intellectual struggle during which new meanings had been developed, new definitions offered, as to what constituted proper relations between men and women.

Central to the development of such new discourses was the emergence in the late eighteenth century of Evangelicalism, a reform movement within the Anglican Church. In part a reaction to Methodism, with its low social connections and popular appeal, Evangelicalism aimed to reform the church from within, primarily through its appeal to those with wealth and rank. In its early years the movement relied particularly on declassé gentry for support. Its best-known protagonists, William Wilberforce and Hannah More, appealed to the upper class to bring about a needed revitalization of English life. The Evangelical message focused on sin, guilt, and the possibilities of redemption. Conversion, seeing the light, and understanding one's nature as a sinner were essential. Without individual awareness of the depths of human sin and the possibility of redemption and salvation through Christ, there could be no hope. Individual spiritual life was at the heart of the Evangelicals' worldview, and they saw the collapse of the quality of that life as the cause of spiritual and moral decadence in eighteenth-century society. Society was rotten to the core, but its rottenness was the result of religious emptiness. Nominal Christianity, as they labeled the shallow practices of those who attended church and read the Bible without ever listening in their hearts to the Word, was no route to salvation. *Real* Christianity must be based on a total commitment to starting anew, beginning life afresh. From the moment of conversion and recognition of all that was un-Christian, men and women who saw themselves as sinners and sought salvation could hope that their spirits would be washed clean. They could struggle for a truly religious way of life that would involve breaking all old habits, examining critically every individual and social act, and reflecting on the Christian meaning of every thought and practice.

Arthur Hughes, *Bed Time* (detail), 1862. Evening prayer: a maternal duty. (Preston, Harris Museum.)

Such a faith demanded much of its adherents. It aimed at the transformation of the individual self, the becoming of a new person in Christ. This required powerful supports—an internal system of checks, already used by the Puritans and represented by the diaries and journals of the seriously religious, and also external supports from clergy and others among the faithful who could assist in the ceaseless struggle to live as a new soul. Such a struggle involved the endless minutiae of daily life: relations with family and friends, relations with servants and employees, the giving and taking of orders, the eating of meals, and the enjoyment of leisure pursuits, whether at work or at home, in the church or the stable. God was watching and listening, and those all-seeing and all-hearing eyes and ears had to become the internal conscience. It was necessary to scrutinize every aspect of human behavior. A real Christian had to live a spiritual life every minute, every hour, every day, and every year; every action and every thought had to be judged within the eternal scheme. Self-knowledge was of the essence of salvation. As that favorite poet of the Evangelicals, the Puritan John Milton wrote:

> For not to know at large of things remote
> From use, obscure and subtle, but to know
> That which before us lies in daily life
> Is the prime wisdom.[3]

To know one's self and the state of one's soul was the "prime wisdom." The second major duty was to carry God's Word to others, to evangelize. The Evangelical creation of a new life started with themselves, but their next aim was to reform the whole society. This improving zeal was greatly strengthened by the fear which affected the British upper class in the wake of the French Revolution. Terrified by events in France, some segments of English society responded by arguing that the top priority was to put one's own house in order. Whereas for Radicals that reordering had to do with the demand for representative government and the critique of Old Corruption, for Evangelicals the problem was one of sin and immorality. The only way to reinvigorate society was by carrying the Word to as many as possible, building a new religious base from the bottom up. Events in France were a warning of what was to come if a revolution in the "manners and morals" of the nation did not take place.

Such a revolution had to begin with individual salvation. The union of each soul with Christ, the experience of rebirth,

were essential prerequisites for the challenge to moral degeneracy and decay. The renunciation of self was vital: "self must be denounced and laid in the dust that Christ may be all in all," one woman wrote.[4] The heart must be surrendered to holy obedience, the will trained to submission. The act of private prayer was highly regarded. Evangelicals placed personal faith at the heart of the religious experience and stressed the importance of Bible-reading, study, and prayer. Such private introspection, aided by the keeping of diaries and journals, should be supported by family prayer. As the religious household gathered each day to pray, they could act as checks and guides to each other, discussing the details of individual falls from grace, taking comfort together in Christ's capacity to understand and forgive.

The religious household provided the best supports for a Christian life. Because the world was filled with pride and sin, real religionists sought to escape into the tranquillity and seclusion of the Christian life. Here the false gaiety of the theater or assembly room could be replaced by the inner peace gained through knowledge of the Savior. Rejection of "the world"

John Philipp, *Presbyterian Catechizing*. Reading a holy book in a family setting. (Edinburgh, National Gallery of Scotland.)

In 19th-century England, the
family listened while the father
read from the Bible. Two
pictures show attitudes ranging
from comfort to rigidity: a
difference of period as well as
representation.

Right: Anonymous, *Family
Worship*. Below: Samuel Butler,
Family Prayers, 1864.
(Cambridge, St. John's
College.)

presented more difficulties for the men associated with Evangelicalism than for the women, since their business activities were not considered conducive to a religious life, whereas the domestic activities of middle- and upper-class women were recognized as more prone to the development of Christian practices. The household was vital to Evangelicals, as it had been to the Puritans before them, providing as it did a secure haven from the pressures of the outside world and a place of peace in which master and mistress could exercise control over their children and servants. Evangelicals saw the family as central to their struggle to reform manners and morals. Families could be the "little church" which the Puritans had dreamt of, the "little state" subject to its master and able to pursue truly Christian practices, whatever was occurring in the world around it.

Hannah More's Family Ethic

Emphasis on the importance of daily life meant that Evangelicals sought to develop rules of conduct that could be adhered to. The celebrated Evangelical writer Hannah More was preeminent in the attempt to provide models for Christian men and women, models that offered guidance in the practicalities of daily life. Her father was a landed gentleman whose income failed and whose daughters were obliged to start a school in order to support themselves. More became a well-known woman writer and intellectual before her conversion in the late 1770s. A friend of the famous actor and manager David Garrick and of the celebrated Dr. Johnson, she was also a member of the Bluestockings, a group of literary ladies who met in London to talk and discuss the issues of the day. Her conversion to serious Christianity, like that of her friend William Wilberforce, was not sudden. Gradually religion began to alter her attitudes and values significantly. She started to commit her life to serious Christian endeavor, and in the 1780s she wrote a series of books designed to shake the complacency of the English upper class and encourage them to seek moral reformation.

As for so many of her generation, the French Revolution proved a watershed for Hannah More. Her skills were applied increasingly, in part at the request of the government, to convincing all classes of society of the vital importance of the Christian message. Her celebrated series of cheap repository tracts was one of the main weapons in the intellectual armory of the establishment. The Evangelically inspired attempt to win the hearts and minds of the people through propagandizing traditional paternalism combined with Christian revivalism marked the soft underside of the iron glove of repression so effectively wielded by Pitt in the 1790s. In tracts for the poor More preached obedience to those in authority and emphasized the joys to come in the heavenly home. A modest, humble, and hardworking life would find pleasure in God's eyes. But More's political conservatism, which she shared with most Evangelicals since they scorned the things of this world and focused on the inner spiritual life, was at odds with her religious radicalism and her insistence on making life anew. The spiritual passion and moral certainty of her writing made More one of the most widely read authors of her period.

More's fundamental quest was for religious salvation. She saw the family as crucial for that salvation, and familial duties were preeminent in the attempt to lead a Christian life. All men and women possessed individual souls and, therefore, the possibility of life eternal, but the duties of men and women were markedly different. More's early writing delineated proper conduct for men and women in a prescriptive manner and essay form. Some of these books were very popular. But her later writing, imbued with a new urgency and seeking to win support for her ideas, to persuade as well as instruct, was more imaginative. Her most popular work was her only novel, *Coelebs in Search of a Wife,* published in 1807. It immediately became the talk of the metropolis and of provincial towns and found its way into far-flung corners of the empire. *Coelebs* was written for the middle class, for More had abandoned her exclusive appeal to the upper class and now saw the middle class as crucial to the struggle for moral regeneration. Although Evangelicalism had developed among the fringes of the gentry, it soon became clear that its most powerful support came from groups that constituted the middle class. Merchants, manufacturers, bankers, traders, farmers, doctors, and lawyers, together with their wives and children, made up the congregations of most parishes where Evangelicalism acquired a strong hold, together with some artisans and men in new clerical occupations. It never acquired powerful support from the poor, where Methodism was to be preeminent among those with religious inclinations.

Coelebs represents the gathering together of More's ideas about the proper relations between men and women, how each in different ways should pursue spiritual life. The hero is a young Christian with a comfortable income drawn from landed property, who, after the death of his parents, goes in search of a wife. The novel, intended to instruct as well as entertain, is packed with prescriptions on the conduct of daily life—from the care of children to responsibilities toward servants, from the place of business in a man's life to the place of domestic duties for women, from the cultivation of gardens and the creation of proper homes to instructing the poor. In the course of his travels Coelebs goes first to London where he is shocked by the superficiality and shallowness of metropolitan life with its endless and unsatisfying search for pleasure. He finds the young ladies he meets in the city empty and frivolous, without a serious thought in their heads and with no capacity for selfless endeavor. He retreats to the country, always thought of by Evangelicals as a setting more conducive to the religious life, separate as it is from the worst ravages of the urban world. Here he meets and stays with the best friends of his deceased parents, the Stanley family.

The Stanleys are the perfect religious family, a household that not only encourages a proper spiritual life among its inmates but also provides a beacon of light for those who visit. Mr. Stanley, the patriarch, is a model of Christian manliness, exemplifying all those virtues which the Evangelicals were defining as necessary to a new form of masculinity that would challenge the older patterns of rude vigor and sportsmanship and celebrate instead gentleness and tenderness combined with manly authority. His real religion informs all of his daily life and underpins all of his actions. Mr. Stanley's concerns are not those of the traditional eighteenth-century gentleman preoccupied with hunting, shooting, and fishing, drink, and food. Rather he is a landlord with a serious moral purpose, determined to fulfill his responsibilities to his tenants and seeing those responsibilities as moral and religious as well as economic. He is immensely serious about familial duties, whether as a husband or a father. In Mr. Stanley we see a loving and considerate husband and father. It is manly, Hannah More tells us, to be family-based, to enjoy domestic life and willingly to take responsibility for children. The form of masculinity linked to sexual dissipation, drink, and indulgence is to be abhorred. The new Christian man must allow his religious calling to be the center of his being, whether that calling is to be a gentleman farmer, a merchant, a clergyman, or a lawyer. Whatever his employment, he must perform it in a religious spirit. He must exercise his authority as master of his business and of his household with proper Christian care.

*The Two Spheres: Public
Man and Private Woman*

The Evangelical man was seen as a person with responsibilities and cares in the public world. The woman, however, was seen as centered in her home and family. Hannah More believed that men and women were born to occupy different spheres. This was the rule of Nature as well as of custom and propriety. Nature had defined men and women differently, each sex with its own qualities; attempts to step out of one's sphere were doomed to disaster. More's detestation of Mary Wollstonecraft was based not only on her rejection of the Paineite radicalism of the 1790s but also on her conviction that Wollstonecraft's plea for equality between the sexes was unnatural and immoral. The biological construction of the male and female expressed their different human destinies, she believed; for a woman to seek success in the same sphere as the man was a denial of the special tasks and duties God had assigned to her. "The fin was not more clearly bestowed on the fish," she wrote, "nor the wing given to the bird that he should fly, than superior strength of body, and a firmer texture of mind was given to man, that he might preside in the deep and daring scenes of action and of council: in the complicated arts of government, in the contention of arms, in the intricacies and depths of science, in the bustle of commerce, and in those professions which demand a higher reach, and a wider range of powers."[5] More elaborated the observable biological distinctions between men and women into a series of characteristics that she labeled "naturally" masculine and feminine.

Evangelical ideas about femininity began with the assumption that woman's godliness was linked to her maternal and wifely duties. Eve had fallen because of her unabashed sensuality. But Mary, the mother of Christ, had given new hope to womanhood by bearing Jesus. Saint Paul, a mentor for numerous Evangelicals including Hannah More, had instructed women that their duty was to manage the house. Woman's profession was to be a wife and mother. The home was the proper sphere of her influence and her action. The wider theaters of public life were not for her. She could shine at home, the gentle moon to her husband's sun, the modest violet showing its beauties only to those with time and patience.

Evangelicals firmly believed in the right of all, male or female, to salvation, but this commitment to spiritual equality did not mean a belief in social equality. The different spheres of male and female action, the "smaller circle" which the woman encompassed, meant that in social terms she was subordinate to her husband. "Wives, submit yourselves unto your own husbands, as it is fit in the Lord," Saint Paul had written,[6] and who had the authority to challenge it? This did not mean that women lacked influence. Men had power in the world, but women could influence men, and in this lay their special skill. It was their particular responsibility to care for men in such a way that men would listen to them, would heed their advice, would value their words. In an Evangelically inspired household, where spiritual life was understood as the key, women occupied a position of dignity and status that depended on their relation to men but that carried with it a recognition of their special and exclusive skills.

Evangelicalism offered middle-class men and women new identities, new ways of giving meaning to their lives and making sense of some of their experience. Faced with a rapidly changing world in which the old preeminence of title and land no longer seemed adequate, real religion offered a new scale of values in which respect for landed wealth and paternalism certainly played a part, but in which the capacity to lead a spiritual life was judged as more important than the trappings of nobility. As William Cowper, that favorite Christian poet of the middle classes, wrote:

> My boast is not that I deduce my birth
> From loins enthroned or rulers of the earth
> But higher far my proud pretensions rise
> The son of Parents passed into the skies.[7]

The proudest claim any man or woman could make was to walk with Christ. The moral certainty that tended to accompany such views gave serious Christians the energy and zeal to work hard in the Lord's vineyards.

The favorite maxim of a prominent Victorian Evangelical was said to be: "It is better to wear out than to rust out."[8] This motto would be a fitting epitaph for many of his brethren. Their energy was indefatigable, for they were convinced that they were doing the work of the Lord. Evangelicalism, which began as a reform movement within the Anglican church, was unable to establish its predominance for many decades. By the middle of the nineteenth century, however, Evangelical influence was pervasive within the Anglican church, and its hold on institutions of both church and state was extensive. Hard work had achieved this: training clergymen, endowing parishes; establishing schools and Sunday schools where Evangelical doctrines could be taught; ensuring that Evangelical protagonists were well represented on public bodies; publishing tracts, pamphlets, journals; raising money to spread the Word; propagandizing whenever and wherever there was an opportunity. Such an aggressive enterprise was bound to make enemies. From the vituperations of Cobbett to the caricatures of Dickens or Thackeray, Evangelicals offered a rich target for hostile pens. But the hostility was in part a measure of their success. From the heartlands of the new urban areas where they had worked hard to build new churches and establish new ministries, to the rural parishes of England where they replaced sleepy pluralists with energetic young clergymen backed by wealthy laymen, gradually built up support until by the 1850s they were well placed, even in the church hierarchy.

By the early nineteenth century the campaign of the Anglican Evangelicals to save England from moral decay was strengthened by the rise of nonconformist evangelicalism. The group that had been central to eighteenth-century dissent—Quakers, Unitarians, and Presbyterians—survived, often with dwindling membership but with a high proportion of the influential upper middle classes in their congregations. Meanwhile the membership and support for New Dissent—as the Methodists, Independents, and Baptists are sometimes called—rose rapidly. The New Dissenters shared with Angli-

In mid-19th-century England men and women lived in separate spheres. At home we see women, children, and servants. It is teatime, and the fire is being poked for Aunt Emily. Left: *Aunt Emily's Visit,* circa 1845. Right: Meanwhile, at the Royal Exchange, men do business. (1847.)

can Evangelicals a belief in the conversion experience and the power of salvation and grace, as well as a belief that the struggle facing them was a spiritual struggle, to win the hearts and minds of the people of England to a religious life, and that the army of Christ must battle with the enemies of the light, whether Owenites, socialists, or other dangerous radicals and atheists. From the 1790s to the 1840s the efforts of evangelical Christians to fight the good fight were unceasing. Despite deep and continuing hostilities between Anglicans and Dissenters over the relation between church and state, in the struggle to counteract the danger of irreligion, serious Christians were prepared to work together in the name of the Lord.

These same Christians also shared assumptions as to the proper roles of men and women. Evangelical discourses on manliness and femininity, articulated particularly by Hannah More and requiring significant reworkings of late-eighteenth-century alternative discourses, became their new orthodoxy. More, together with the Evangelical poet William Cowper, who wrote about the pleasures of a quiet home life and domesticity, provided the framework for the emergence of new male and female subjects. The Christian man was one who would look after dependents, whether of his own family or his employees; whose power and authority derived from his moral stature rather than physical prowess; who, though his theater of life encompassed business and politics, loved his

home. The Christian woman was defined by her relation to others as a wife and a mother, finding her fulfillment in her duties to home and family, occupying her "relative sphere" with full knowledge of the influence she could wield. By the mid-nineteenth century the visions of Cowper and More, who were challenging notions of masculinity associated with the gentry and aristocracy which had no place for religious sensibility, and also the dangerous arguments of Wollstonecraft and her comrades who believed that men and women could be equal, had become the commonsense assumptions not only of serious Christians but of the English middle classes.

Popularizing Domesticity

How did this transformation come about? Why, by 1820, could public opinion decree that English kings should not despise the bonds of matrimony and of family life? How had Hannah More, a dangerous and radical subversive in the eyes of some in the established church in the 1780s and 1790s, become a household name, quoted from pulpits, lauded in a myriad of texts? Why had earlier ideas about woman's voracious sexuality been abandoned and a new stress on her modesty, her natural passivity adopted? When had established assumptions as to male and female partnership in the family economy been replaced by new beliefs about the man's duty to provide financially for his wife and children? Why was the labor of married women, so long counted on, now confined for the respectable to domestic duties? When had women come to see their profession as that of wife and mother, while men discovered an enormously wide variety of new skills and occupations, from land agent to civil engineer, from manager to insurance agent? Why did the middle classes come to believe in separate spheres and organize their lives around such beliefs?

Clergymen preached on the different duties of men and women and followed those beliefs in church organization. Men took the active and the public roles, women the supportive and private. Men could enter the ministry, which increasingly required specialized training, women could not. In dissenting chapels, where the church membership was also its governing body, men began to take on more responsibilities. Small informal chapels of the eighteenth century could become large and powerful bodies by the nineteenth. Population growth, the expansion of towns, and the increased wealth of the middle class meant that new opportunities were available, new facilities required, new needs recognized.

Take the example of a small Independent chapel in the center of Birmingham, a rapidly growing industrial town whose wealth was based on the metal industries. By mid-century Carr's Lane had become a well-established and relatively wealthy foundation, with a large church building, which had been specially constructed and continuously improved, two full-time ministers, and a Sunday congregation composed mainly of the middle- and lower-middle-class which often exceeded one thousand. The major figure there from 1805 to 1857 was the Reverend John Angell James, known throughout Britain for his preaching and writing. In his popular works such as *The Young Man's Friend and Guide through Life to Immortality, Female Piety,* and *The Family Monitor, or a Help to Domestic Happiness* James taught that men should be kings and masters of their households, that married women should devote their time and attention exclusively to the household (unless there were very strong reasons for this not to be the case), and that a religious household was the only possible basis for a stable society. The minister was appointed by the membership who paid for his services. Only the male members, however, could vote when a new minister was chosen; only the male members could serve as trustees and be responsible for the finances of the chapel; only the male members could occupy the new offices established in the chapel. The office of deacon, for example, was filled by men elected from the membership to support and assist the minister. Women were allowed to be chapel members for, as Saint Paul said, "There is neither Jew nor Greek, there is neither bond nor free, there is neither male nor female: for ye are all one in Christ Jesus."[9] That spiritual oneness was not reflected in the social relations of the chapel. Men and women occupied different spheres there, just as elsewhere. Women were allowed to speak at the Carr's Lane chapel meetings, by no means a privilege that could be assumed in all dissenting chapels. They were welcomed as auxiliaries in the work of the chapel—delivering tracts, teaching in girls' Sunday schools, visiting the poor at home, acting as volunteers, and carrying out the marching orders of the clergy—this was the extent of their role.

The attempt to build separate sexual spheres into middle-class institutions was not confined to religious institutions. Evangelical Christians were exceedingly active in the establishment of new cultural ventures, and here as well, a distinction between male and female activities was often written into the constitutions and enshrined in the custom and practice of such societies. Take literary and philosophical institutions, for example, or the art societies set up in so many towns. Membership was open to both men and women, but the part they played differed greatly according to sex. Men were active on committees, served as officers, were elected fellows in recognition of their contributions in particular fields; they could give as well as attend lectures and enjoy all the facilities provided. On the other hand, women, though they paid the same membership fees, could take no part in the formal organization, usually could vote only by proxy, and frequently were barred from events such as the all-male annual dinner, which was an occasion for the gentlemen to enjoy a "convivial" evening with plenty of food and drink. The Birmingham Philosophical Institution, like many others, did not permit women to use the reading room, which was treated as an all-male sanctum, a place where the men could read their newspapers in peace, undisturbed by female chatter. Not surprisingly, such societies were regarded primarily as masculine preserves. Few women joined, though many enjoyed the use of certain facilities by dint of their relationship to a male member—daughter, wife, or sister. In the later nineteenth century, as women gained confidence and increasingly felt the restrictions of their definition as private persons, marginal to the public world of men, they began to demand and gain access to many such clubs and societies. In the early nineteenth century, however, when middle-class men, proud of their success in business and commerce and confident about their religious inspiration, increasingly sought to reshape the world in their own image, that image sharply differentiated between the spheres of men and women.

THE CADBURY FAMILY

Meanwhile the material circumstances of life for middle-class men and women were changing in ways that also contributed to a sharper division of labor between the sexes. Farmers, manufacturers, merchants, and professionals were able to make sense of the material changes in their own lives through an ideology which emphasized the different duties and responsibilities of different members of the family according to gender. Take a family such as the Cadburys, shopkeepers in Birmingham since the late eighteenth century. Richard Tapper Cadbury, born in the West Country, was apprenticed

The second generation of Cadburys, a Quaker family: John, Candia, and their six children pose in front of their house in Edgbaston in 1847. (Birmingham Reference Library.)

to a draper. He came from an established Quaker family, and Quakers had a tight network of religious, economic, and social connections throughout the country. His apprenticeship was served in Gloucester, his years as a journeyman in London; then, seeing an opening for a silk mercer and draper in Birmingham, he settled there in 1794. His father, in addition to paying his apprenticeship fees and furnishing introductions to the Quaker community in each town he went to, had given him enough capital to start a modest business. In 1800 Richard, together with his wife, Elizabeth, and his rapidly growing family moved in above the shop he had acquired on Bull Street, one of Birmingham's main thoroughfares. It was common practice at that time for middle-class families to live above or next to their business premises. Ironmasters lived next door to their foundries, lawyers had offices in their houses, shopkeepers lived above the shop. Only the very wealthy upper middle classes could aspire to have a house separate from their family enterprise.

As a girl Elizabeth Cadbury did not have access to the sort of training her husband had. Few apprenticeships were open to women, the assumption being that they would pick up any necessary knowledge on the job, learn to help in whatever ways they could. Only the rich did not expect their wives to work in the family enterprise. A farmer's wife might be responsible for the dairy, a merchant's wife help in the warehouse or counting house, a manufacturer's widow carry on the business when her husband died. Elizabeth Cadbury helped in the shop when extra hands were needed and looked after the business when her husband was away; she organized the large household, which included apprentices and female shop assistants as well as her own immediate family. In the first fifteen years of married life she bore ten children, eight of whom survived; her own mother, in old age, lived with them.

In such a household there were always mouths to feed, clothes to wash, shirts to make and mend, water to carry up- and downstairs. Yet, with the help of two women servants who did some of the domestic work, Elizabeth Cadbury managed to take an active part in the business. When Richard went to London in search of new fabrics for the shop he wrote to her: "Bombazines I have been after but I find it difficult to get all my colours. Such as I have met with are very nice and tomorrow I am to look out my black ones."[10] He inquired anxiously whether there was any news from Ireland about the linens they were expecting and told her that he had already acquired "some coloured and scarlet whittles and scarves" and had ordered a bonnet for their daughter Sarah. His letters brim with a mixture of business and family details, all part and parcel of the shared business and social life of man and wife.

In 1812 the shop was doing well and Richard Tapper Cadbury rented a modest second house in Islington Row on the outskirts of the town, almost in the country. The younger children went there to live with their nurse and their pets, which included pigeons, rabbits, a dog, and a cat. An extra piece of land was rented on which fruit and vegetables could be grown. Mrs. Cadbury was now supervising two households, and with her elder daughters she moved constantly between them. In 1827 she was unwell, but soon afterward Richard was happy to report to one of their daughters that she was recovered enough to have had a busy day in town, bustling about at the shop without any ill effects. The sons, meanwhile, followed in their father's footsteps, each being apprenticed in different towns and in different branches of the retail trade. The eldest son, Benjamin, was apprenticed to a draper, in preparation for taking over the family business.

John, the second son, was trained as a dealer in tea and coffee.

Their sisters had no such formal training. They were their mother's apprentices, learning from her not only the secrets of baking and household management but also the art of combining such skills with a readiness to help in the shop whenever assistance was required. They could tend fruit and vegetables in the garden, or help their mother put down old carpets in the winter to give the house some extra warmth, or pop into the shop to give their father a hand. The business was part of the life of every family member. As Elizabeth Cadbury wrote when the Bull Street premises were being altered and they were worried as to the effects this would have on the light in the parlor, "I suppose we must not complain as it is for the business."[11]

But business practices were gradually changing in such a way as to make this kind of familial involvement increasingly difficult. Married women had no right to make contracts, to sue or be sued, or to enter into partnerships. Their marital status meant that in law their husbands were responsible for them; they had no independent legal existence. Only single women and widows could enter into business on their own account, and their opportunities often arose at the death of husbands and fathers. In the eighteenth century, in family enterprises such as that of the Cadburys, husband and wife operated as an informal partnership, sharing the cares and anxieties of business along with other aspects of domestic life. The man carried legal responsibility for the concern, but in day-to-day life there were few sharp demarcations of function. There were, however, a variety of tasks connected with the business which only the man could do. It was always Richard Tapper Cadbury who traveled in search of stock, for example, and although married women had the right to pledge credit in their husbands' names, Elizabeth Cadbury seems to have left the payment of bills to her husband. The informal partnership was one which assumed ultimate male authority.

The growth of manufacture and commerce and the transformation of agriculture resulted in the development of new business practices that threatened such customary and informal relations. In a period when partnerships provided the major basis for expansion, the legal restrictions barring married women and the customary expectations concerning daughters meant that the overwhelming majority of partnerships were

Division of Labor and Separation of Home and Workplace

In the shop: men and women on either side of the counter. The specialty grocery business remained a male bastion. (1846.)

between men, usually related by kin or associated through religious belief. Apprenticeships gradually died out, but the new forms of education and training, devised especially to deal with the needs of the commercial classes, were not open to women. The need for boys from middle-class families to learn bookkeeping, for example, was widely recognized, and the early nineteenth century saw many new educational ventures aiming to provide men with the basic skills necessary to become captains of industry. Meanwhile, girls were still being educated at home. Once young men had moved into business, it was easy for them to develop the contacts and associations with other men so necessary to maintain credit, negotiate loans, and acquire new customers. It was hard for women to enter the new world of commercial transactions. Loans which had once been negotiated informally increasingly had to be done through banks. Corn which had been sold in the marketplace was now sold in the corn exchange—a facility used exclusively by men. Similarly, the stock exchange, built especially for the ever expanding financial market, was no place for a woman.

Drapery was the first business that systematically exhibited the characteristics of modern retailing. Unlike many other traders who had to combine production and distribution—such as the butcher killing and preparing his meat or the baker baking and selling his bread—the draper was relatively free from production functions. Only thread had to be prepared for sale. Developments in textile production, particularly cotton, resulted in an expanding mass market for cloth, and by the 1820s the drapery shops in towns and cities were flourishing. Drapers, able to concentrate their capital on shop improvements, were frequently the first to introduce plate-glass windows, window displays, and gas lighting. They also led the field in price ticketing and cash trading, two of the next developments.

The Cadbury drapery business expanded and prospered. Meanwhile John had established his tea and coffee store next door. He not only introduced the latest retailing improvements—he was particularly proud of his plate-glass windows—but also decided to branch out into the manufacture of cocoa as soon as he had enough capital. To do this he established a completely separate factory and ran the two sides of the business simultaneously. He and his first wife, Priscilla, who died in 1828, after they had been married only two years, lived, like his parents before him, over the shop. In 1832 he married for the second time, a merchant's daughter Candia, and until the birth of their first child they lived in Bull Street. Shortly thereafter they moved from the center of town to nearby Edgbaston.

Edgbaston was the suburban development, approximately a mile from Birmingham, which the Evangelical Lord Calthorpe, a substantial landowner, had been planning from the early 1800s. Calthorpe designed the area as a select site, to provide genteel homes and gardens for the middle classes, away from the dirt, bustle, and uncongenial neighbors who were an inevitable part of living in the center of town. The leases were carefully controlled, so shopkeepers could not turn their homes into business premises, manufacturers could not set up workshops in their gardens. Wide roads were laid out, many trees planted, and in time churches and parks established. Edgbaston prided itself on its combination of charming villas and rural landscape; it offered the best of the city in the country. To live in such an area necessitated a division between work and home, since family enterprises could not be run from Edgbaston homes. Calthorpe's creation, one of the first of its kind, was based on the premise that middle-class people

The size of the Cadbury warehouse suggests the extent of their commercial organization. (Based on a sketch by Richard Cadbury; Birmingham Reference Library.)

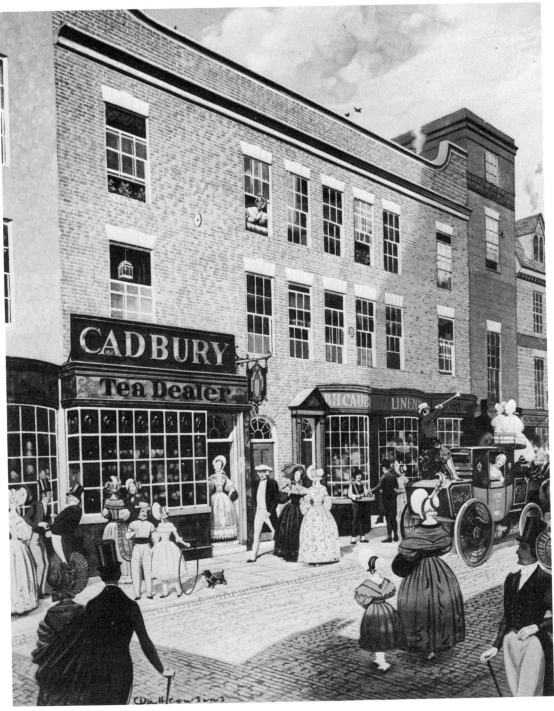

Drawing by E. Wall Cousins. Bull Street, Birmingham, around 1824: the Cadbury kingdom. To the right is father Richard's linen shop; to the left, son John's tea and coffee shop. (Birmingham Reference Library.)

increasingly would want homes separate from their workplaces and a family life separate from the life of the business. "The sweet caresses and endearments of wife and children" were to be set apart from "the cares and anxieties of business."

Economic and commercial changes encouraged such a separation. As the scale of the Cadbury enterprise grew there were more and more aspects of the work with which a woman could not be involved. The factory was a short distance from the house, and Candia could not oversee it in the way her mother-in-law had cared for the shop at the same time she was looking after small children. Branching out meant a greater division of labor, the employment of more male workers, the elaboration of financial records—all easier for men to deal with. Both John and his father were involved in the planning and building of an impressive new market hall, which facilitated better distribution and was part of the formalization of more advanced commercial practices so characteristic of this period. Business and commerce were becoming a male sphere, with the women retailers who survived concentrating in shops associated with food and with female clothing. In deciding to create a new domestic setting for themselves and their children, free from the interference of work associations, the young Cadburys implicitly accepted the ideas associated with separate spheres.

Cottage and Nursery

John and Candia's new house was to be their family home for nearly forty years. They gradually altered and extended its modest size as their family grew and money became available. Candia spent her time at home, caring for the children, cooking, washing, looking after the garden. As their daughter Maria later described it, the house was "almost cottage like in appearance and too small without many alterations, but its countrylike surroundings decided our parents to take it, make more rooms, and lay out the gardens to their own taste . . . our Mother was exceedingly fond of gardening, but our Father was greatly occupied with business and town affairs and other interests and he had very little time during the week for his garden."[12] The house soon had a playroom, later turned into a schoolroom, and a nursery upstairs for the little ones. The lives of Candia and her children were focused on home and school, while her husband used the Edgbaston home as a happy base from which he could be active in the town world of business and politics.

Large, middle-class house in neoclassical style. Berwickshire in the late 1850s.

A home such as this, with dining room and drawing room, with schoolroom and nursery, was a new concept. Such differentiation of space had not been possible in the town crescents of the eighteenth century, nor had it been considered desirable. The novel idea of separate rooms for children and of a demarcation between eating and cooking was associated with the idea of a different space for men to work in. Such homes had major implications for furnishing, as warmth and comfort were increasingly stressed. J. C. Loudon, during this period the arbiter of taste in matters of architectural design, internal furnishings, and garden layout for the middle classes, instructed his readers in his immensely popular manuals as to what a nursery was, how a drawing room should be equipped, what delights the garden could offer in terms of shared enjoyments for husband and wife.

For if homes designed exclusively for domestic living were new, so were the gardens that surrounded them. During the eighteenth century a square with a shared walkway and an iron fence was considered sufficient. By the mid-nineteenth century a garden had become an important feature of middle-class life. Tamed nature, enclosed by trees and hedges to ensure privacy, provided a perfect setting for family life. Men could tend trees and vines, for Loudon was at pains to assure them that there was nothing menial in this kind of manual labor, delighting in an hour's relaxation over it after returning from the pressing exigencies of a day in town. Women's special responsibility was the flowers—a natural association between the sweet and gentle feminine nature and the delicacy and fragrance of blossoms. (It was in this period that linguistic relationships were often made between women and flowers.) Meanwhile a mother could teach her young children to tend plants and grow seeds in their own small gardens.

John and Candia Cadbury's home and garden in Edgbaston provide a concrete manifestation of a particular view of family life, of the special duties of men and women and their different relations to the social world. The vision of Hannah More, set in an idealized and gentrified world, had turned into the bricks and mortar of middle-class homes. The religious commitment to establish a new way of life that would make possible a constant attention to spiritual experience and which demanded a religious household had found material form in

Home, Work, and Virtue

Gardening, a pastime of women and children, could also be a family passion and teacher of virtue. (1864.)

the gradual separation and demarcation of men's and women's work. While men faced ever-widening opportunities in the expanding business and professional sectors and were increasingly defined in terms of their occupational and public activities, women moved away from that world and made motherhood and domestic management their profession. That division between male and female worlds had a religious connotation, for the marketplace was considered dangerously amoral. The men who operated in that sphere could save themselves only through constant contact with the moral world of the home, where women acted as carriers of the pure values that could counteract the destructive tendencies of the market. Home was the place of sweet delights, the haven for the harassed and anxious man who had to produce the material wealth on which that home depended. His manliness was based on his ability to provide for his dependents; the femininity of his wife and daughters rested on their capacity to be dependent. A man's dignity lay in his occupation; a woman's gentility was destroyed if she had one. By mid-century the middle-class ideal of breadwinning husband and domesticated wife and children had become so widespread that the registrar general was able not only to introduce the new category of "housewife" to the census but also to state in his introduction to the report on 1851: "The possession of an entire house is strongly desired by every Englishman; for it throws a sharp well-defined circle round his family and hearth—the shrine of his sorrows, joys and meditations."[13]

The Dominance of Middle-Class Values

Many Englishmen would have been astonished at the registrar general's assumption that they desired "entire" houses, but his claim to speak for all on this issue draws attention to the extent to which middle-class discourses had become common parlance. This had resulted in part because of the evangelizing zeal of serious Christians and other groups of the middle class, such as the Utilitarians, who aimed to reconstruct the world in their own image. They hoped to convert both the upper classes and the laboring poor to their beliefs and tried to encourage them to behave in specified ways. The aristocracy and gentry should abandon their licentious and indolent ways, the poor should become industrious. All should recognize the importance of a stable family life and a proper domestic setting. On this last issue evangelicals of every description and Utilitarians agreed. The great Jeremy Bentham himself was a firm believer in the different spheres and abilities of men and women, and assumptions as to the proper relations between the sexes underpinned Utilitarian policies quite as much as those of the evangelicals. For the Benthamites, however, separate spheres were a taken-for-granted commonplace rather than an article of moral principle. The extent to which they accepted it as natural reflects the influence of the protagonists of dual spheres by the early nineteenth century.

How successful were the middle-class improvers and to what extent did the stockingers, handloom weavers, cotton spinners, small masters, publicans, and traders who made up the "industrious classes" of the early nineteenth century adopt the new domestic values associated with evangelicalism? Across the country innumerable schools, Sunday schools, and philanthropic ventures of every kind were established, all with middle-class notions of what was properly male and female. In recommending domestic values to Sunday-school pupils,

Moral Instruction of the Poor

The Mechanics Institute of Manchester, 1825, offered education to the working man. (University of Manchester.)

Sunday schools run by
Christian charities taught the
poor to read and inculcated
morality. They were
caricatured as much as they
were praised. These
illustrations accentuate the
positive.

charity schoolgirls, or aged and infirm women, middle-class women at the same time defined their own "relative sphere" and their sense of the proper place of working-class women. That place was either as servants in the homes of their betters or as respectable and modest wives and mothers in their own homes. A Society for Aged and Infirm Women, for example, sought money on behalf "of those who have discharged the relative duties of a wife and mother" and were left, perhaps deserted, in their old age.[14] The organizers paid the strictest attention to establishing whether the women really deserved such assistance, whether their lives had been humble and respectable. Boys and girls were taught separately in schools, often in different buildings and with emphasis on different achievements. Self-improvement societies and debating societies were for men only. The new Mechanics Institutes, which often had strong Benthamite backing, were initially exclusively male and hoped to train men not only to be more industrious, rational, and scientific but also to be better husbands, fathers, and brothers. As the first report of one such institute stressed, a man's entire family would benefit from his involvement with such an establishment. He himself would become more sober, intelligent, and tranquil; his presence at home would create more pleasure; he would learn to organize his finances better, so he would have more money for his children's education; his wife would learn by his example to be cleaner, neater, and more caring of the home. In sum, the family would become a living example of domestic bliss.

These were grandiose claims. Not surprisingly, working-class men and women were not miraculously transformed into respectable and sober men, domestic and home-loving women, by the action of institutions formulated by the middle class. But, as many historians have demonstrated, nor did they simply reject the values of this dominant culture. As Robert Gray has shown in his study of the aristocracy of labor in late-nineteenth-century Edinburgh, a process of negotiation took place between dominant and subordinate, negotiation that resulted in the emergence of distinctive concepts of dignity and respectability, influenced by middle-class values yet holding to a belief in trade-union action and a strong sense of class pride. Similarly, David Vincent in his study of the meaning of "useful knowledge" to working-class autobiographers has demonstrated the independence from middle-class meanings of the term and the creation of a separate and class-specific concept.[15]

George Cruikshank. *The Bottle,* 1847. Three of a series of eight celebrated Cruikshank engravings demonstrating the ravages of alcohol. Before: a happy home, but the husband holds out a tempting cup to his wife. After: the husband, unemployed, drinks with money obtained by pawning the family's clothing. Finally: "Disputes and violence are the natural consequences of frequent use of the bottle." This manner of educating the masses was widely imitated, even by the trade unions.

The same story could be told with regard to male and female spheres. Working-class men and women did not adopt the middle-class view of a proper way of life in its entirety. But aspects of religious and secular discourses on masculinity, femininity, and domestic life did have resonance in some sections of the working class, did make sense of some experiences and did appeal to some needs.

Consider the temperance movement. Temperance, it has been argued, is a prime example of the successful assertion of middle-class hegemony. Workingmen became volunteers in the cause of middle-class respectability. They aimed to improve themselves, to educate themselves, to raise themselves socially. The total abstinence movement had originated with class-conscious workingmen and there were many connections between them and the Chartist movement, but the radical belief in individual improvement was vulnerable to assimilation to the cultural patterns of the middle class. Arguments against drink used a strong appeal to home and family, for one of the major evils associated with alcohol was its propensity to ruin working-class families. In the famous series of engravings by the extremely popular Cruikshank entitled *The*

Bottle the first image is of a respectable and modest working-class family enjoying a meal in their simple but clean and comfortable home. They represent the model happy family, with clothes carefully mended, a family portrait, the younger children playing, a fire burning cozily in the grate, and a lock on the door ensuring that the home would remain a place of refuge and security. Then the man offers his wife a drink, and in scene after scene Cruikshank documents the horrifying destruction of the home and family, ending up with the husband insane, having murdered his wife with a bottle, the youngest child dead, and the other two having become a pimp and a prostitute. It was a cliché of temperance lecturers to rely on the comparison between the unhappy home of the drunkard and the contented domestic idyll of the temperate worker. A reformed drunkard poetically declares:

Richard Redgrave, *The Poor Teacher,* 1843. The pretty young tutor is a lonely figure, condemned by poverty to dress in austere black. She symbolizes the loneliness of women in the 19th century. (London, Victoria and Albert Museum.)

I protest that no more I'll get drunk—
For I find it the bane of my life!
Henceforth I'll be watchful that nought shall destroy
That comfort and peace that I ought to enjoy
In my children, my home and my wife.[16]

Such protestations did not simply imply the acceptance of middle-class ideals of domesticity. Workingmen and women developed their own notions of manliness and femininity, which, though affected by dominant conceptions, nevertheless had inflections of their own. John Smith, a Birmingham temperance enthusiast, argued: "The happiness of the fireside is involved in the question of temperance, and we know that the chief ornament of that abode of happiness is woman. Most of the comforts of life depend upon our female relatives and friends, whether in infancy, in mature years, or old age."[17] Here he touched on a vital nerve, for the workingman's comforts of life did indeed depend on female relatives. But those female relatives needed different skills from their middle-class sisters. Middle-class idealogues stressed the moral and managerial aspects of womanhood, for wives were to provide moral inspiration and manage the running of their households; working-class blueprints for the good wife and mother emphasized the practical skills associated with cooking, cleaning, and bringing up children. Dignity and self-worth for women lay in doing those tasks well.

The acceptance by some segments of the working class of a version of domesticity is illustrated by the writing of two key thinkers and political activists—Francis Place and William Cobbett. Place, born in 1771, was apprenticed in the leather breeches trade and later became a very successful tailor. He spent his entire life in London where he was deeply involved in the radicalism of the 1790s, particularly as secretary of the London Corresponding Society, and he played an important part in the trade-union reform of the 1820s. In later years he was a committed Benthamite and, since financial success enabled him to retire from business, he was able to lead the life of a full-time reformer. In his youth, however, Place had experienced great poverty, and he had been fully engaged in the life of a late-eighteenth-century artisan. He drew on familiar assumptions as to the role of women, assuming, for example, that his wife would help with his work whenever it was necessary. But he was also deeply committed to improving working-class manners and morals, and his autobiography delights in detailing the ways in which improvements in the cultural patterns and habits of the laboring poor had taken place. He loved to recount the disappearance of the street games of his youth, which had exhibited open enjoyment of

Praise for the Good Homemaker: Francis Place

Illustration from *Cottage Economy*. Rural life, self-sufficiency, and thrifty housewives made for happy families and stable societies.

sexuality, and he strongly disapproved of the drinking habits of workingmen and consequent neglect of their families—of which his own father was a prime example.

Place was a firm believer in the desirability of an "entire" house long before the registrar general penned his comments. "Nothing conduces so much to the degradation of a man and a woman," he believed, "in the opinion of each other, and of themselves in all respects; but most especially of the woman; than her having to eat and drink and cook and wash and iron and transact all her domestic concerns in the room in which her husband works, and in which they sleep." He was delighted when he was able to get new lodgings with a small closet at the end in which he could work. "It enabled my wife to keep the room in better order. it was advantageous too in its moral effects. Attendance on the child was not as it had been always, in my presence. I was shut out from seeing the fire lighted the room washed and cleaned, and the cloathes washed and ironed, as well as the cooking."[18]

As a boy Place had been apprenticed; his wife, who had worked as a servant, had no formal skills. When he was able to find work, Place could earn far more than his wife could command, but she was able to help him with some of the work involved in making trousers, at the same time caring for the children and the household. His lifelong interest in self-education inspired him to read, to think, and to write. As his income grew, he was able to buy books and to mix with well-known intellectuals, though the social distance between them was never bridged. Jeremy Bentham and James Mill encouraged Place to write his autobiography in order to demonstrate how a workingman could rise to wisdom and prosperity from the most unpropitious of backgrounds.

His wife's self-improvement was of a different kind. She learned to be an excellent dressmaker and milliner, able to "catch a fashion at a glance and instantly adapt it to any purpose she wished." She remained a simple woman, in her husband's account, happy to be known as a good manager, wife, and mother, rather than aspiring to step beyond her sphere. While the improvements so lauded by Place included making new opportunities for men, the hope of acquiring an education, abandoning dissolute habits, and becoming a rational man, for women the approved aspiration was to be a good wife and mother.

William Cobbett and "Cottage Economy"

William Cobbett, the writer and journalist E. P. Thompson claims was the most important intellectual influence on postwar Radicalism, exhibits the same structures of feeling on the question of male and female spheres. It was Cobbett who created the Radical culture of the 1820s, Thompson suggests, "not because he offered its most original ideas, but in the sense that he found the tone, the style, and the arguments which could bring the weaver, the schoolmaster, and the shipwright into a common discourse. Out of the diversity of grievances and interests he brought a Radical consensus."[19]

But Cobbett's Radical consensus placed women firmly in the domestic sphere. He was categorically in favor of home life and what he saw as established and well-tried household patterns. Happy families, he argued, were the basis for a good society. In writing *Cottage Economy* Cobbett hoped to contribute to the revival of homely and domestic skills which he considered seriously threatened by the development of a wage economy. His vision of an idealized past required a reworking of old ideas, which were presented as though long established; a new version of old patriarchal relations was offered as if it had always existed. *Cottage Economy* gave detailed instructions on the brewing of beer, not only because it could be made more cheaply at home but also because a good home brew would encourage men to spend their evenings with their families rather than at the tavern. A woman who could not bake, Cobbett thought, was "unworthy of trust and confidence . . . a mere burthen upon the community." He assured fathers that the way to construct a happy marriage for their daughters was to "make them skilful, able and active in the most necessary concerns of a family." "Dimples and cherry cheeks" were not enough; it was knowing how to brew and bake, to milk cows and churn butter, that made a woman a "person worthy of respect." What could please God more than the picture of "the labourer, after his return from the toils of a cold winter day, sitting with his wife and children round a cheerful fire, while the wind whistles in the chimney and the rain pelts the roof?"[20]

Cobbett had no use for what he considered the newfangled ideas about femininity associated with sections of the middle class. He hated the false gentility, as he saw it, of farmers' wives who turned their front rooms into parlors, bought pianos, and taught their daughters to have airs and graces. He wanted the farmer's wife to go back to the dairy, keep farm laborers living in, and feed them as she should. But he was not simply asking for a return to the past, since he claimed all manner of new rights for workingmen. They should have the right to a manly wage which would allow them to support their wives and children, not in luxury but in decency and honesty. They should have the right to independence of thought, freedom to read what they chose and to say what they believed. Most important of all, they should have the right to vote; representation should be based not on the owning of property but on honorable labor and the concept that a workingman's property lay in his skill. As head of the household, men should be obeyed by their wives and children, and men should speak for their dependents both politically and legally. Wives could not act independently and could not vote, "because the very nature of their sex makes the exercise of this right incompatible with the harmony and happiness of society."[21]

The acceptance of feminine passivity and docility, the belief that domesticity was "natural" to women and that the division between the sexes was the only possible basis for social harmony, and the acceptance of the theory of separate gender roles, which came from the heart of radical working-class culture, indicate the extent to which such assumptions had come to underlie thinking about sexual differences in sections of the working class.

The convergence of Evangelical ideas with those of some of the male working class can be seen in the development of a state policy on female labor in the 1840s. The period of the 1830s and 1840s saw the confirmation of men as responsible political citizens, while women for the most part were condemned to public silence. An important aspect of this was the idea, present in both Place and Cobbett, that a man should earn a "family wage" sufficient to support himself, his wife, and his children. Such an ideal of male sufficiency and female dependence, already firmly established within middle-class culture, was to become embedded in working-class practice as well. The bargaining procedures that developed within the skilled male trade unions were premised on the notion of the "family wage." Again, this was not the straightforward acceptance of middle-class standards, but rather an adaptation and reshaping of specific class ideals.

In the early 1840s middle-class fears and anxieties about the employment of women in unsuitable work came to a head over the issue of female labor in the mines. It was already firmly established that for a middle-class woman to work for money labeled her as unfeminine. In the case of the laboring poor, standards differed somewhat. It was acceptable for women to be employed in jobs that were an extension of their "natural" female role. There was no offence to propriety in seeing women servants cleaning, cooking, caring for children. Work as dressmakers or milliners was also appropriate, as were jobs concerned with the preparation and presentation of food. But some jobs were deemed to be deeply inappropriate for women, especially when they took place in mixed settings. For women to work underground was perhaps the most blatant rejection of Evangelical notions of femininity. A commission was appointed to inquire into conditions of child labor in the mines, and the officials were shocked and horrified at the evidence of female conditions of work that emerged. Their assumptions as to the nature of femininity were outraged by the spectacle of women in various stages of undress working alongside men. The affront to public morality and the fears generated as to the imminent collapse of the working-class family and consequently of working-class morality led to the campaign, spearheaded by Evangelicals, for the exclusion of women from underground work.

Working-class miners supported the ban that was imposed, but not for the same reasons as the middle-class campaigners. As Angela John has shown, they did not accept the

Illustrations from "First Report on the Mines," 1842. The parliamentary reports known as "blue papers" because of their blue covers owed their impact to crude but suggestive engravings such as these, which revealed to many people the nature of the conditions under which women and children toiled in the mines. Top: hauling coal, a job normally done by young girls. Bottom: a young woman drags a hopper of coal to which she is hitched by a harness. (Paris, Bibliothèque Nationale.)

judgment of commissioners such as Tremenheere that female exclusion was, "the first step towards raising the standard of domestic habits and the securing of a respectable home."[22] They resented middle-class interlopers who tried to tell them how to live their lives and how to organize their families. They demanded control of their own families and better lives for their wives and daughters, insisting that if the wives of the owners of the coal mines could stay at home, then so should theirs. The miners stressed that their wives were entitled to a decent life above ground and attacked those owners who continued to employ women illegally. They had another powerful motive for supporting exclusion. The Miners Association of Great Britain and Ireland was formed in 1842, three days before the date designated for women under eighteen to leave the pits. As clearly stated in the *Miner's Advocate,* the union was firmly opposed to female employment. It sought to control miners' hours of labor and obtain the highest possible wages. For women to work was seen as a direct threat to this enterprise, for women's work kept wages down. For their own reasons the men who worked in the mines wanted to be able to support their women at home. The women, unable to speak publicly, had no say in the matter. They hated the working conditions but needed the money. But their voices were not heard, and in one of the major public issues of the 1840s, blazoned across newspaper headlines, men were legitimated as workers, women as wives and mothers, by the state, by middle-class philanthropists, and by workingmen.

In 1820 George IV learned the hard way that the great English middle class valued familial loyalty and domestic values. But were the aristocracy and gentry touched by the apparent hegemony of middle-class views of gender difference? Both Lawrence Stone and Rudolph Trumbach have argued that there was a marked shift toward a new view of domesticity among the landed classes in the eighteenth century. Stone believes the new views were inspired by the elite of the mercantile and financial bourgeoisie.[23] A new version of gentility was lauded in magazines such as *The Spectator*. That gentility became associated with novel demarcations of function for men and women. Such discourses were then taken up, reworked, and elaborated by the Evangelicals. The increase in the economic, political, and social power of the middle classes in the early nineteenth century was further reflected in the

The Aristocracy and the "New Privacy"

VOLUME V.

Price, 4s. Plain; 4s. 6d. Gilt.

London: W. S. Johnson, 60, St. Martin's Lane; Simpkin, Marshall, and Co.
Edinburgh: Messrs. Oliver and Boyd; J. Menzies.—Dublin: Mc'Glashan;
Curry and Co.—Liverpool; Philip and Son; and of all Booksellers.

Frontispiece of one of the leading magazines devoted to home life and the family circle. People of different ages share the comforts of the "nest."

adoption of practices that had their origins in the social ranks of farmers, manufacturers, and merchants by their "betters," the aristocracy and gentry. As Leonore Davidoff argues, "essentially middle class patterns of behaviour were grafted on to the honorific code of the aristocracy or gentry to produce the widened concept of 'gentility.'"[24]

Or, as Mark Girouard puts its, by mid-century the upper classes had moved closer to the upper middle classes, the social gap between them had narrowed. "The upper classes adjusted their image to make it acceptable to middle class morality. They became—some quite genuinely, others at least superficially—more serious, more religious, more domestic and more responsible."[25]

Middle-class criticism of the upper classes, of their indolence, their corruption, their immorality, was at its height in the 1820s and 1830s; it subsided as the aristocracy and gentry became more attached to domestic values. They created what Girouard calls the "moral home," centered on a happy and sheltered family life with family prayers, Sabbath observance, and a regularized routine of domestic life. Women, excluded from participation in the market or in the public world, ruled the private one through the system of etiquette, the rules of "Society" and of the "Season." They were the leaders of society and acted as gatekeepers; they made the decisions as to social acceptance and rejection. The principle of this regulation was personal knowledge: no one could be accepted who was not personally known. Social life became more exclusive and more private, taking place in the homes of the rich, with access only to the known. Family and kin played a vital part in this controlled social interaction; having connections was of the essence of acceptance. The privatized havens of the middle classes, sheltering women and children, restoring men to allow them to reconfront the exigencies of the business world, had a somewhat different inflection in the operation of the exclusive world of society.

The interest of aristocracy and gentry in more privacy, more segregation, was reflected in the building and remodeling of their homes. Servants were housed upstairs in middle-class villas; in a country home it was possible to make them entirely invisible through the use of separate staircases. Servants' quarters were made more elaborate with no mingling of the sexes and only one or two occupants to each room. Children were given special accommodations close to their parents; Loudon's "nurseries" became ubiquitous. Many

J. C. Loudon, *Encyclopedia of Cottage, Farm and Villa Architecture and Furniture* (London, 1839). The comforts of home called for functional furniture, in which the English pioneered. This 1839 encyclopedia offers a veritable catalogue of different models, including "lady's pieces" such as work tables, sofas, and stools for the sewing room. There is also a high chair for the baby. (Paris, Bibliothèque Nationale.)

1066   COTTAGE, FARM, AND VILLA ARCHITECTURE.

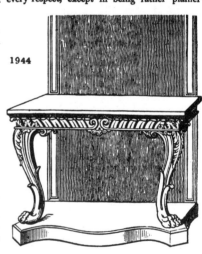

which resembles the preceding one in every respect, except in being rather plainer These are very useful articles for industrious young ladies. We have seen some of them, and also of the articles in the two preceding and two following paragraphs, in Mr. Dalziel's show-room, of much more elaborate beauty, executed in the rarest exotic woods, and finished with French polish; but we have preferred giving these simple Designs, as likely to be more generally useful.

2115. *Lady's Work Tables.* Figs. 1947 and 1949 are fitted up with drawers for holding cottons; and they have bag frames, which are of wood, covered with fluted silk, and fringed at bottom for containing work.

2116. *Sofa Tables.* Figs. 1948, 1950, 1951, and 1952 are four different varieties of sofa or occasional tables for drawingrooms. Drawers may be introduced under the tops; but the effect is not then so good, as it requires the upper part of the frame to be made

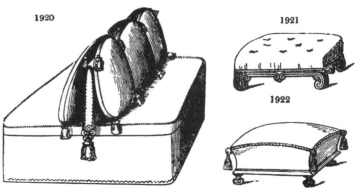

houses had self-contained family wings with the parent's bed-room, a nursery, and sitting room. Bedrooms for bachelors were usually located on different corridors from those for the ladies—and sometimes even in a different wing. Smoking rooms were introduced, for men only; morning rooms were primarily for the ladies' use. The entire house became stratified into different areas for ladies and gentlemen, with the hall acting as the meeting place inside. Once again the garden offered the perfect setting for the two sexes to meet in perfect complementarity. The modest aspirations of the villa dwellers of Edgbaston in the 1830s had been turned into the grandiose Gothic dreams of the landed classes.

"Sweet Home": The Jeweler's House

In 1820, the year of Queen Caroline's vindication, James Luckcock, a Birmingham jeweler who had managed to secure a "modest competency" and retire from business at the age of fifty-nine, settled with his wife, a son, and a daughter into a small house in Edgbaston which he had built on land acquired from Lord Calthorpe. He had constructed the home of his dreams, one "snug and comfortable," and "keeping within moderate bounds as to size and expense." He had divided the land into two lots and rented the other house as an investment. In his own premises he had "all my heart could wish. The house and garden planned by myself, the situation picturesque, secluded and charming; the aspect, a southern slope; the soil deep and highly productive; and the whole plantation rapidly rising to beauty and perfection." In his garden he planted horse chestnut and mountain ash, "as I have always considered a few full grown venerable and majestic trees essential to the character of a respectable country mansion." In addition to growing his own vegetables, he chose for flowers "the humble cowslip and unpretending fox glove, the meek snowdrop as well as the chaste and elegant lily or the magnificent Piony." This was in keeping with his lifelong political radicalism, for in this period certain flowers such as pinks and carnations were associated with artisans, others, like dahlias, were more gen-teel and expensive. Luckcock's garden was embellished with urns replete with inscriptions to domestic harmony, and the canal at the end of the garden was tastefully hidden by a hedge to make it appear like a river. Here, at Lime Grove, he realized the "climax of happiness," "satisfied with retirement from the world and all its specious and unsatisfactory delusions . . . blest with the possession of a little Paradise."[26]

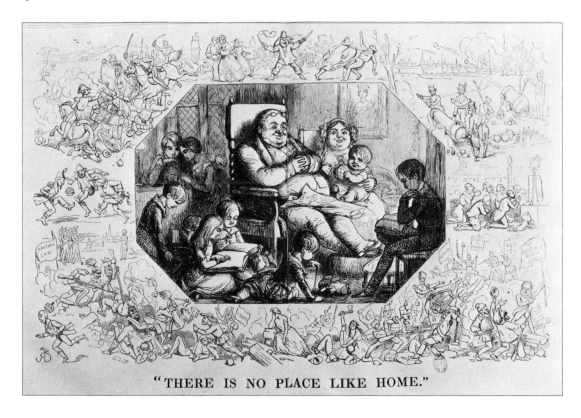

"THERE IS NO PLACE LIKE HOME."

Drawing by Richard Doyle for *Punch, the London Charivari,* the famous satirical weekly founded in 1841 (vol. 17, 1849). The Victorian family—beneath the picture of Victoria an islet of tranquillity in the midst of a world in revolution—was often the butt of *Punch*'s satire. (Paris, Bibliothèque Nationale.)

There Luckcock passed his time, gardening, writing books, meeting with his friends, organizing the construction of a new Sunday-school building for the Birmingham Unitarians, attending reform meetings, and continuing to play the part of an active public man. Once he became seriously ill and feared death. An enthusiastic amateur poet, he was so bold as to write a poem about himself *for* his wife. Adopting his wife's persona, it cataloged some of the virtues of the husband she would miss, as in these lines:

> Who first inspir'd my virgin breast,
> With tumults not to be express'd,
> And gave to life unwonted zest?
>   My husband.
>
> Who told me that his gains were small,
> But that whatever might befal,
> To me he'd gladly yield them all?
>   My husband.

Who shunn'd the giddy town's turmoil,
To share with me the garden's toil,
And joy with labour reconcile?
                    My husband.

Whose arduous struggles long maintain'd
Adversity's cold hand restrain'd
And competence at length attain'd?
                    My husband's.[27]

Few husbands may have gone so far as to sing praises of themselves in the names of their wives. Nevertheless, Luckcock's life and dreams were echoed in countless hearts. In the English national imagination by the mid-nineteenth century home was indeed a place of sweet delights. But those delights were experienced differently by men and women. Men could mix the cares, anxieties, and deep satisfactions of public life with the secluded charms of home. For women there was rarely such duality; home was their "all in all," the "natural" site of their femininity.

A summer Sunday in a small provincial town. The family has gathered around the elderly grandparents, perhaps to celebrate a birthday. These are people of modest station, who pose crowded together on the sidewalk in a space that is partly private, partly public. The room visible in the background however, has layers of drapes—a mark of respectability. (Sirot-Angel Collection.)

2

The Actors

Michelle Perrot
Anne Martin-Fugier

Châteauroux, around 1900. He is a cabinetmaker, she the daughter of vintners. Her dreams of grandeur and beauty are evident in this studio photograph of the parents with their three daughters, Andrée, Madeleine, and Thérèse. (Private collection.)

Introduction

by Michelle Perrot

THE primary theater of private life in the nineteenth century was the family, which established the characters and roles, the practices and rites, the intrigues and conflicts, typical of the private sphere. Civil society's invisible hand, the family was both nest and nexus.

The family reigned triumphant in the doctrine and rhetoric of all parties from conservative to liberal and even libertarian, which celebrated it as the basic cell of the organic social order. Actually, it was far more chaotic and varied than this triumphal portrait suggests. The nuclear family had only just emerged from broader and still persistent systems of kinship, whose nature varied with locale and setting, social level and cultural tradition.

As a totalitarian unit the family sought to regulate its members' activities. Increasingly, however, individuals rebelled against its discipline. Hidden tensions developed between generations, between the sexes, and between individuals determined to control their own destinies. The tensions at times became explosive. By comparison with the past, families now turned more readily to the courts to settle disputes, and this practice insidiously made them vulnerable to outside control.

Increased state intervention also threatened the autonomy of the family, especially the poor family. Unable to rely on the family to do its bidding in all cases, the state acted in its stead, particularly with regard to management of that most precious form of social capital, children.

To be sure, private life encompassed a much broader range of behaviors than is included under the heading of the family. Partly for political reasons, however, the nineteenth-century family tended to subsume all the functions of private life and to define its rules and norms. Prisons and boarding schools, barracks and convents, vagabonds and dandies, nuns and lesbians, bohemians and toughs, celibate individuals and institutions, often were obliged to define themselves in relation to the family or on its margins. It was the center; they were the periphery.

Dominique Ingres, *The Stamaty Family*, 1818. Family portraits were much in demand in the first half of the 19th century, and some of the greatest painters of the age turned their talents to the task. This portrait of the Stamaty family is a classic of the genre. Each person strikes a pose: the father with his Napoleonic gesture, the mother in her finery, the slender young woman at the piano, the adolescent with his unruly hair, and the young child, whose sex is revealed by his toys. (Paris, Louvre.)

✃ The Family Triumphant

Michelle Perrot

THE French Revolution had attempted to subvert the boundary between public and private, to construct a new man, and to reshape the daily routine by restructuring space, time, and memory. This grandiose project had been thwarted, however, by individual resistance. Mores had proved stronger than laws.

The revolutionary experience had made a strong impression on contemporary thinkers. For Benjamin Constant, George Sand, and Edgar Quinet it was a subject for continued reflection. In what respects had the Revolution altered their lives and the lives of their fellow citizens, and in what respects had it failed to do so? Sand described how the peasants of Berry resisted the use of the familiar *tu*—against the wishes of the *petits messieurs* of the city, new members of the bourgeoisie who prided themselves on addressing Sand's grandmother, the once-noble Mme. Dupin, as *tu*. Constant stressed the importance of reserve: "In those days I listened to the most animated harangues. I saw the most energetic demonstrations. I was witness to the most solemn oaths. Nothing happened. The nation engaged in these activities as though they were ceremonies, in order to avoid argument, and then everyone returned home with no more idea or sense of commitment than before."[1]

This observation explains why the relation between public and private is a central concern of all postrevolutionary political theory. Defining the relation between state and civil society, between the collective and the individual, became the major problem of the day. While laissez-faire and the "invisible hand" remained the prevalent ideas in economic thought, which rested on the laurels of the eighteenth century, political thinkers felt a need to trace the contours of "private interests" and specify how such interests ought to be organized. The newest political idea of the day probably was that the family is the basic cell of society. Domesticity had a fundamental regulatory function; it played the role of the hidden god.

This idea was shared throughout Europe. Catherine Hall has shown how notions of domesticity were developed simultaneously by Evangelicals and Utilitarians in early nineteenth-century Britain. In civil society Bentham's "panopticon" took the form of the sovereign gaze of the father as head of the family, master of the household under God or in accordance with reason.

Hegel: The Family,
Foundation of Civil Society

The idea of a close correspondence between public and private was perhaps most fully developed by the philosopher Hegel. In *Principles of the Philosophy of Right* (1821) he analyzed relations among the individual, civil society, and the state. The foundation of law, Hegel argued, is the individual, for all rights are vested in the person. The body defines the self, which requires personal property in order to objectify itself. Suicide is the ultimate symbol of the sovereignty of the self, just as crime is the symbol of the self's responsibility. But the individual is subordinate to the family, which along with corporate bodies constitutes one of the essential "circles" of civil society. Without the family the state would be forced to deal with "inorganic collectivities," that is, mobs, with the attendant risk of despotism.

For Hegel the family is the safeguard of natural morality. It is based on monogamous marriage by mutual consent. Within the family passions are unnecessary, even dangerous. The best marriage is the arranged marriage, in which inclination follows rather than precedes the contract. The family is a construct of reason and will, held together by material as well as spiritual bonds (such as memory). Its patrimony is both an economic necessity and a symbolic affirmation. The family, an "object of piety for its members," is a moral being, "a single person whose members are contingent." It is headed by the father, whose death alone liberates his heirs and marks the end of the family unit—a whole greater than the sum of its parts, which must submit to its discipline. Thus the nineteenth-century family was a "holistic group" in Louis Dumont's sense. Roles were distributed by gender in accordance with the "natural characteristics" of the sexes and in keeping with passive-active, interior-exterior dichotomies typical of

Pierre-Alexandre Jeanmiot, *The Introduction.* Mother or procuress? What has the young lady with the vacant stare done wrong, that she should be offered to this boor, a chain smoker who doesn't even bother to remove his hat? The deliberate ambiguity of the painting suggests the ambiguity of the situation itself. (Paris, Petit Palais.)

nineteenth-century thought. "Man's real, substantial life is in the state, in science, and so on, as well as in combat and labor in contact with the external world and with himself." "Woman's substantial destiny lies in the objective morality of the family, whose piety is the expression of moral tendencies." Children are at once members of the family and individuals in their own right. As free individuals, they must be educated, but without indulging the playfulness that sets the child apart from the adult. When they come of age they should be ready to have families of their own, "with the sons as heads and the daughters as spouses." In truth, however, the son does not fully accede to his new status until his father is dead. The freedom to make a will is limited by family law. On this point Hegel was severely critical of the arbitrariness of Roman law. He rejected primogeniture and the exclusion of daughters from inheritance. To him what was important was not the lineage, with its heavy feudal overtones, but the family, the cornerstone of modern society. Civil society consists of circles of "concrete, independent persons," of myriads, "multitudes of families." It is nothing other than "the unity of scattered family groups."[2]

Kant's Household

While Hegel concerned himself with the macrosocial interaction of public and private, Kant was interested primarily in the household. For him domestic rectitude was the triumph of reason. The home extinguished the individual's desire to escape, giving him roots and subjecting him to a discipline. The household was ruled by "a law of this world, a conservative law, which silences the call of the wild, of the barbarian forest in man's breast." The home is the foundation of morality and the social order. It is the heart of private life, subject to the discipline of the father, who alone is capable of domesticating instincts and taming his wife. The threat of domestic warfare is always present. "A woman may turn into a vandal; a child, contaminated by its mother, may turn weak or vengeful; a servant may reclaim his liberty." The woman, focus of the home, also poses a threat to its well-being. "If she escapes, she may immediately become a rebel and a revolutionary."[3] Hence, as Kant knew full well, the legal status of women was contradictory: as an individual she enjoyed individual rights, but as a member of a family she was subject to the law of the family, in essence monarchical. A persistent opposition runs through nineteenth-century thought between the woman with desires and the domesticated woman.

The Liberal Family

Because of the need to resolve acute problems of political, legal, and social reconstruction in the aftermath of the Revolution, France was a particularly fertile source of ideas about the family in the early nineteenth century. French thinking may be classed under three main headings: the boundary between public and private (or the notion of public and private spheres); the nature of civil society; and male and female roles.

Liberals from Germaine de Staël to Alexis de Tocqueville were keen to establish a clear boundary between public and private, in order to safeguard the private interests that they saw as constituting the strength of the nation. "The Republic will gain the love of its citizens," Mme. de Staël wrote, "only if it respects the particularity of private wealth." She called upon the state "not to demand, not to pressure."[4] Benjamin Constant observed that "liberty will be all the more precious to us as the exercise of our political rights leaves us more time to devote to our private interests."[5] Both contrasted the ancient world, whose citizens lived to take part in politics and war, with the modern world, in which individuals, properly encouraged by an attitude of laissez-faire, engaged in commerce and industry. In order to concentrate on their private activities, citizens entrusted public affairs to representatives. The separation of complementary public and private spheres required representative government, and the specialization of political activity required skilled and ultimately professional practitioners.

Guizot fully grasped this need. In terms reminiscent of Hegel, he analyzed the several functions of government. In order to preserve order and liberty social power, arbiter of civil society, had to be properly aligned with the political power that determined the overall direction of society's activities. This latter power was to be entrusted to men of talent, to an elite of organizers: it was a business for men, not for salons in which the company was mixed and the atmosphere frivolous. Though largely domestic, social power was not feminine. The father, head of the family, was its central element, although his power, being "the expression of a higher reason, more apt than others to distinguish the just from the unjust," was not arbitrary. The family, Guizot held, was a place where negotiations went on constantly; it was a model of democracy. "Nowhere else is the right of suffrage more real or extensive. Suffrage comes closest to being universal within the family."[6]

Royer-Collard and Tocqueville were equally concerned

Francisque Grenier de Saint-Martin, *Introduction of a Paris Bridegroom-to-be,* 1830s. This ridiculously fashionable suitor is greeted warmly by the father of a well-to-do provincial family and with friendliness by the mother. The would-be innocent lowers her eyes demurely and stares at her sewing. The introduction, a courtly ritual that became a matrimonial one, was a frequent subject of satirical painting. (Paris, Bibliothèque des Arts Décoratifs.)

about the content of civil society. In Royer's view, "the Revolution left nothing in place but individuals . . . From a society reduced to dust emerged centralization."[7] He saw "natural associations" such as the commune and the family as the antidote to Jacobinism. Tocqueville, though sensitive in many ways to the attractions of private life, was keenly aware of the perils of excessive individualism, the individualism of "*chacun chez soi, chacun pour soi*" (every man in his own home, every man for himself) favored by Baron Dupin. "Despotism, which by its nature is fearful, sees man's isolation as its best guarantee of survival, and normally it does all it can to keep men apart . . . It bestows the name of good citizens on those who keep strictly to themselves." All Tocqueville's work revolves around the problem of reconciling private happiness with public action. He advocated associations and celebrated the virtues of the American family, virtues from which he believed a social bond might be forged. "Democracy stretches social bonds but tightens natural ones. It brings relatives together even as it pushes citizens apart." For liberals the family, in a sense the "natural" community, was the key to individual happiness and the public good.[8]

The Traditionalists

The family was also the major concern of traditionalists, typified by Louis de Bonald under the Restoration and, later and in a very different way, by Frédéric Le Play and his school. Traditionalists were critical of the decline of morals, the perversion of sex roles, and effeminization. Dissolute families and women who shirked their duties were made scapegoats for military defeats and social unrest. The Restoration and Ordre Moral were in this respect typical, as was the twentieth century's Vichy Regime.[9]

Under the Restoration the traditionalist offensive was three-pronged. In the religious sphere, respect for the family was one of the favorite themes of missionaries. "Where are you better off than in the bosom of your family?" ran one hymn in 1825. In the political sphere, traditionalists attacked divorce, which had been legalized in 1792 but was banned again in 1816. In the ideological sphere, Bonald was the apostle of the family. Widely read by the provincial nobility (and often cited by Renée de Lestrade, the maternal heroine of Balzac's *Mémoires de deux jeunes mariées*), he helped raise the moral standards of an aristocracy eager to polish its image. Nevertheless, visions of ostentatious luxury and aristocratic

Paul Gavarni, *Un Mariage de raison*, 1839. A middle-class marriage of convenience (perhaps a shotgun wedding?) during the July Monarchy. The smug satisfaction of the relatives and the sarcastic looks of the jolly "bachelors" who escort their "trapped" comrade are in sharp contrast to the crestfallen appearance of the young couple. Gavarni was a shrewd observer of contemporary ways, especially of male-female relations. (Paris, Bibliothèque Nationale.)

debauch remained deeply rooted in the popular psyche, so deeply that traces of it survive today in the comments of the guides who show tourists through abandoned châteaux. In fact, however, those visions fed on an earlier period: the golden age of aristocracy.

An indication of Bonald's thinking about the family can be found in his speech to the Chamber of Deputies in favor of abolishing divorce (December 26, 1815). Divorce, he argued, is intrinsically perverse, not only for the unjustified suffering it brings to women and children but also for moral reasons. Implicitly recognizing the rights of passion, he devotes an extraordinary amount of attention to the question of love in marriage. Love, usually demanded by women, weakens paternal authority: "A veritable domestic democracy, it allows the wife, the weaker sex, to rise up against marital authority." A woman's grandeur, however, consists in submission to her husband or, if she is a widow, to her eldest son, heir to the family home. The foundation of the monarchical state, the family is itself a paternal monarchy, an aristocratic society guaranteeing stability, longevity, and continuity. The father is its natural head, just as the father-king is the natural leader of France, which is also a household. To restore the monarchy was to restore paternal authority. "In order to wrest the state from the hands of the people, the family must be wrested from the hands of women and children." Marriage is not only a civil contract but at the same time a religious and political act. "The family requires mores, and the state requires laws. Strengthen domestic power, a natural element of public power, and consecrate the total dependence of women and children, a guarantee of steadfast obedience in the people."

Le Play, or "The Family, Principle of the State"

Simon Durand, *A City-Hall Wedding*. This satirical painting attacked both the city-hall wedding, which was considered a thing of no consequence, and marriage itself. Would the bridegroom show up to marry this forlorn lady, who is obviously past her prime? (Paris, Bibliothèque Nationale.)

The thought of Frédéric Le Play was neither counterrevolutionary nor liberal.[10] His originality lay in an attempt to use sociological observation to further the family cause. Hostile to state expansion, Le Play hoped to reinvigorate civil society by making families happier, defining happiness as "moral law plus bread." In *Ouvriers européens* (1877) he wrote: "Private life stamps public life with its character. The family is the foundation of the state." Le Play was the antithesis of a liberal, however. For him the selfishness of private interests in the jungle of laissez-faire, unchecked urbanization and industrialization, and neglect of the Ten Commandments and of fundamental moral precepts were the causes of that awful scourge, proletarianization. As a remedy he proposed resto-

E. Beaudoin, *At the Photographer's*. The column and drapery were the photographer's customary props, as in this portrait of a widowed father posing with his two children. The portraits on the wall are probably of the deceased mother and child. (Paris, Bibliothèque Nationale.)

ration of the so-called stem family, the family whose property was transmitted to a single heir chosen by the parents. (In the Pyrenees this undivided patrimony was called the *melouga;* in Gévaudan it was the *oustal*.) Le Play contrasted the stem family with the unstable family created by the Civil Code, which provided for equal division of the parents' estate among all children, as well as with the patriarchal family, in which all power was concentrated in the hands of a hereditary patriarch. He believed that hierarchy was not only "natural" but also depended on talent and merit.

Respect for hierarchies was one condition of equilibrium. But leaders must also respect and protect their subordinates. The "social question" and increasing state intervention were consequences of patrons' failure to live up to their obligations. Paternalism and patronage offered the best kind of social re-lations, and the father was naturally the head of the family. Yet Le Play and his disciple Emile Cheysson also attached great importance to the virtues of the housewife. Le Play's monographs are a rich source of information about the roles, responsibilities, and powers of the mother in lower-class fam-ilies, as well as about household chores.

The ideas of Le Play and of *Réforme sociale* were probably the most advanced of those nineteenth-century thinkers and

The Fourierist phalanstery was often favorably portrayed. Note the religious syncretism in this picture. (*L'Illustration,* 1846.)

movements that made the family the focus of their theory and practice. Such ideas fell into disrepute for political and ideological reasons associated with the triumph of the Republic and of the Durkheimian school of sociology that supported it. The family was an innocent victim of this episode in that for a long time it ceased to be an object of research interest in the social sciences.

The Socialists and the Family

Before Marxism dismissed private life as a bourgeois, not to say petty-bourgeois, product, socialists attached great importance to the family.[11] Although all nineteenth-century socialists were critical of the family, few went so far as to envision its complete elimination. Equally rare were those who envisioned a subversion of traditional sex roles, for belief in a natural inequality of the sexes was deeply rooted. Nevertheless, a wide variety of solutions to the problems of the family were proposed. Among the extreme libertarians were Fourier, Enfantin, the feminist Claire Démar, and 1840s communists such as Théodore Dézamy, whose *Code de la communauté* objected to the puritanical "familyism" of Cabet's *Icarie.* "No more broken homes! No more home child-rearing! No more familyism! No more marital domination! Freedom of marriage! Perfect equality of the sexes! Free divorce!" proclaimed Dézamy, while Cabet lashed out at voluntary celibacy and viewed "concubinage and adultery" as "inexcusable crimes." Clearly *Icarie* was a work of relentless moral didacticism and outright machismo. At Nauvoo, the American city where he attempted to found a utopian community, Cabet found himself at odds with women who refused to trade their finery for uniforms.

Fourier's radicalism was the exception, the "absolute extreme," in regard to both sex roles and relations between the sexes. Though he denounced women as "the proletarians' proletarians," he also saw their emancipation as the key to progress: "The extension of women's privileges is the general principle of all social progress." Within the Fourierist phalanstery he advocated complete equality, interchangeable roles, total freedom of choice in regard to sex partners, late marriage, and easy divorce. Malthusian in his wariness of population growth, he was not Malthusian at all in his advocacy of contraception and abortion. Fourier's radicalism in sexual matters frightened his disciples, including Considérant and such female followers as Zoé Gatti de Gamond, who expurgated his works and refused to publish the most revolutionary of them, *Le Nouveau Monde amoureux*.[12] The Fourierist community established at Guise (in Aisne) by Godin repudiated what was called "pivotal" morality and in this respect was closer to *Icarie* than to Fourier's idea of the phalanstery. Moreover, Godin's own companion, like the wives of other "great men," was relegated to the shadows.

The Saint-Simonians after Enfant, the majority of communists, and socialists of Christian bent such as Pierre Leroux, Constantin Pecqueur, Louis Blanc, and even Flora Tristan favored modernizing the family institution, equality of the sexes including equality in education, and the right of divorce. But in their eyes monogamous marriage remained the foundation of the nuclear family—a family held together by powerful emotional bonds and in which children were the center of attention. After 1840 most feminists (including those of 1848, who saw the state as a "great household") accepted these moderate positions, which could be readily accommodated to their demands for civil equality and which offered concrete opportunities for action. George Sand, staunchly profamily though quite free in her personal life, belongs to this group.

Finally, there was a traditionalist wing of socialism, which

Gustave Courbet, *Pierre Joseph Proudhon and His Children* (detail), 1865. Proudhon without his daughters is not the whole Proudhon. "Fatherhood filled an immense void in me," said the anarchist theorist, a good family man. (Paris, Petit Palais.)

included Buchez, the Christian socialists of *L'Atelier,* and disciples of Lamennais and Proudhon. This group held that the inequality of the sexes was natural and ineradicable; that women must obey, indeed that their liberty lies in obedience; and that marriage, the safeguard of order and morality, ought to be indissoluble and patriarchal. Proudhon in particular consistently proclaimed the creative superiority of the virile principle, of chastity over sensuality, of work over pleasure. For the theorist of anarchy, the conjugal family was the living cell of a private organism that he hoped would devour the public sphere and annihilate the state.

From Fourier to Proudhon there was clearly no trend toward greater freedom. Socialists of course had to meet two sets of demands: those of the ambient bourgeois morality, which criticized the "bestiality" of the proletariat and forced socialist moralists to adopt a stiff posture of respectability, and those of their working-class and popular clients, for whom the family economy and family ethics were the basic components of class consciousness.

The socialists' own vision of social transformation also changed with time. In the first half of the century socialists believed in a practical, grass-roots revolution. Virtuous communities—communes, family-based working groups—would set an example of altruistic small enterprise for others to follow. The resulting desire for what Rousseau called transparency gave rise to a dispute over "publicity of morals" between Enfantin and certain female Saint-Simonians who insisted on rights of privacy to ensure the dignity of women. In *Ma loi d'avenir* (My Law of the Future) Claire Démar lashed out at certain marriage rites and at "the publicity of the scandalous legal battles that fill our courts and tribunals with such words as adultery, impotence, and rape and lead to disgusting investigations and arrests."

With Blanquism and even more with Marxism the problem of the seizure of power was posed in different terms. Political revolution was indispensable as a prelude to economic revolution; power was to be seized at the top, from the state. In social analysis the mode of production supplanted the family, and mores were relegated to the superstructural framework. Engels subscribed to the conclusions of Bachofen, and especially Morgan, concerning the existence of a matriarchy in primitive, happy, egalitarian, but barbarian times and held that the abolition of this monarchy was "the great historical defeat of the female sex." Yet he viewed the socialist revolution and seizure of control over the means of production as the necessary if not sufficient condition for restoring equality between the sexes. Women were urged to subordinate feminist issues to the class struggle, of which the battle between the sexes was seen as a derivative. Feminism was henceforth condemned as bourgeois almost by essence, and long years of misunderstanding between feminists and socialists began.

Marxism (and the socialist movement over which it now exerted considerable influence) also dismissed anthropology as "idealist." This dismissal was but a consequence of Marx's explicit critique, in *The German Ideology,* of Hegel's *Philosophy of Right* and of Marx's denial of the dualism of state and civil society, individual and citizen.[13] An impoverished Marxian analysis consequently underestimated the importance of possessions, bequests, and death.

It was not only Marx's social theory that neglected the family, however, but also Durkheim's.[14] Interested exclusively in universal social facts, Durkheim "pulverized anthropology" by neglecting the spatial dimension. At the same time, positivist historiography focused exclusively on politics and nation-building and excluded the private sphere from its field of view.

Yet even as the family disappeared as an explanatory concept in the social sciences, it occupied a more important place than ever in the political thought of such founders of the Third Republic as Grévy, Simon, and Ferry. Thinking about the family vanished; the politics of the family began. The reason for this was that the functions of the family—functions assumed as well as assigned—now outweighed its heuristic value.

The atom of civil society, the family administered private interests whose development was essential to the power of states and the progress of humanity. As the linchpin of production, it kept the economy running and managed the transmission of wealth from generation to generation. As a reproductive cell, it produced children and assumed responsibility for their early socialization. As the guardian of the race, it was responsible for racial purity and health. As the crucible of national consciousness, it inculcated symbolic values and memories of the nation's founding. It fostered citizenship as well as civility.

The "good family" was the underpinning of the state, especially for republicans.[15] Love of the family and love of the

Disdéri, *Family Group,* circa 1870. A family skillfully posed at the foot of a staircase leading to a handsome bourgeois home. Nothing is left to chance in the composition. The only man in the group, seated slightly apart, holds the youngest child on his knees, but his elbow rests on an open book.

fatherland (with its many mothers) belonged to the same spectrum of feeling, and both were linked to respect for humanity. Accordingly, the state took a growing interest in the family— at first only in the poorest families, the weak link in the chain of generations, but later in all families. Throughout most of the nineteenth century, however, the family acted independently. Beneath the veneer of centralization there was much variety owing to religious and political traditions, social class, and local differences.

FAMILY AND PATRIMONY

A network of individuals and collection of properties, the family was also a name, a blood line, a material and symbolic patrimony to be inherited and passed on. It was a flow of ownership regulated in the first instance by law.

In principle the Civil Code had abolished ancient customary laws, prohibited wills, eliminated primogeniture, and established equal partition of estates among male and female heirs. In many respects these changes constituted a revolution, and they were perceived as such. When Pierre Rivière, the "red-eyed parricide" of the Norman bocage, killed his mother (and for good measure his sister and brother as well), was it not in part because his mother enjoyed full power over the family property, a state of affairs completely at odds with Norman custom? This woman, who repeatedly made contracts only to break them, was in his eyes a devil and a menace.

Did the Civil Code really set "the rules of the bourgeois peace," as André Arnaud maintained? On the contrary, it is striking to find how strongly traditional values of inheritance persisted and how much the father retained the preeminent position in this patrilinear system of inheritance.[16] The husband "alone administers community property" (Article 1421). His powers were limited only by stipulations in the marriage contract. But marriage contracts, a characteristic feature of areas ruled by written law, declined steadily over the course of the century, even in Occitania where the *régime dotal* (dowry held in escrow as opposed to becoming community property) was usually maintained. The decline is particularly noticeable in Provence and Languedoc as well as in the Occitanian hinterland. The same trend has been noted in Normandy: in Rouen, J.-P. Chaline found that 43 percent of marriages were covered by contracts in 1819–20, compared with 24 percent at midcentury and only 17 percent on the eve of World War

I.[17] The *régime dotal,* which protected the wife's property and preserved at least part of the family patrimony in case of bankruptcy, survived only among the bourgeoisie, where it was employed as a precautionary tactic by capitalists whose fortunes were family-based.

In France estate divisions upon inheritance generally resulted in small holdings and helped to retard or at any rate modulate industrialization by slowing the rural exodus, in contrast to what took place in Britain. In many regions, however, particularly those in which the stem family predominated, resistance to the Civil Code was quite strong. In Gévaudan, for example, families anxious to preserve their *oustal* circumvented the Code in a variety of ways.[18] The parents—or at any rate the all-powerful father—entered during their lifetime into various arrangements designed to keep the family holdings intact and in the hands of the most capable (and/or preferred) son. In some cases dispossessed "cadets" were compensated. (Children sometimes left home temporarily just to lay their hands on the cash compensation to which they were entitled by relinquishing their share of the family property.) More often, however, they remained unmarried and worked the land or even entered service as domestics. As

Albert Auguste Fourié, *Wedding Dinner at Yport.* The rural wedding feast, this one in the Caux region, was a classic subject of genre painting. The late 19th century abandoned the truculence of Flemish painting in favor of a more tender style. The apple blossoms are out: the painter has seen to it that nature is in harmony with the heart. (Rouen, Musée des Beaux-Arts.)

individualism gained ground, however, it became increasingly difficult to secure the consent on which this system depended.

In fact, much of the population received no inheritance of any kind. From the beginning to the end of the nineteenth century, two-thirds of men and women died intestate.[19] The concentration of wealth actually increased. In Paris, 1 percent of the population possessed 30 percent of the wealth in 1820–1825; by 1911 the comparable figure had decreased to only 0.4 percent. The situation was much the same in Bordeaux and Toulouse. It was worse in Lille, a proletarian city: there, 8 percent of the population held 90 percent of the wealth in 1850 and 92 percent in 1911. The middle class had made a genuine advance, but its rise still had little effect on the distribution of wealth. This finding tends to corroborate the notion of a stalled society with limited social mobility and much family tension over the issue of property.

Forms of Possession

In the aggregate, accumulation of wealth was relatively insignificant. Nevertheless, the acquisitive desire remained strong, and real estate was its primary object. For the bourgeoisie owning land was an indispensable sign of social prominence; the poor wanted a place of their own. The father of Henri Beyle (Stendhal) thought of nothing but his "estate," and among the petty-bourgeois of Grenoble in the early nineteenth century, money, "a necessity of life, unfortunately as indispensable as toilets but which must never be mentioned," remained a taboo subject, but "the word 'real estate' was uttered with respect."

In the middle of the Second Empire 18 percent of income came from investments in urban real estate and 41 percent from agricultural production, compared with only 5.9 percent from investments in stocks and bonds. Over the second half of the century the appeal of securities increased steadily thanks to the development of corporations, new banking strategies, and a speculative rise in prices as new heirs began to diversify their wealth. Bonds supplanted ground rent. It became common for people even among the provincial petty bourgeoisie to follow prices on the stock exchange. One respectable lady in a small town in Berry, the daughter of vintners and the widow of a carpenter, subscribed to a financial journal and amassed a portfolio of bonds, including bonds issued by the Russian government and the city of Budapest; she also bought a piano for her daughters.

Office of a small family business? The boss is not far away—his boater is on the hatrack. A typewriter has replaced the sewing machine that used to sit on this young secretary's stand. (Sirot-Angel Collection.)

Jacques Capdevielle has shown how this acquisitive spirit spread through all strata of society to become the foundation of the radical-opportunist Third Republic, the linchpin of whose policy was the equation "citizens equal property owners."[20] Stocks and bonds—which packaged ownership in discrete, divisible units—accorded well with democracy. Capdevielle notes a surprising consensus on the question of property in the late nineteenth century, a consensus embraced by socialists and even anarchists. The "good father," that hero of the revolutionary sansculottes and pillar of the Republic, was a small property owner wealthy enough to leave something to his heirs. Gambetta, in a speech delivered in Auxerre in 1874, praised "small fortunes, small capital, the whole world of the small that is democracy."

Slowly a capitalist spirit began to take shape. As it worked its way into conversation and family correspondence, the family's image of itself changed.

WORK AND THE FAMILY ECONOMY

With or without a patrimony the family was an economic system. The Industrial Revolution, which proceeded in different places at very different rates, did not destroy the family economic system but used and strengthened it.[21] Some scholars have gone so far as to speak of a "family mode of production." That may be too strong a term, but families did constitute networks of accumulation, know-how, and solidarity.

In the countryside the household was the basic economic unit. The family and the land were one, and the needs of both took precedence in the lives of individual family members. The *oustal* system in Gévaudan was an extreme case, but even where the patrimonial system was less rigid the family was a business, its home a workplace. The roles of parents and children, young and old, men and women were strictly defined. Although those roles were complementary, they were not necessarily without conflict. At times, moreover, migration could lead to changes in this economic structure and organization.

Protoindustrial development relied heavily on the family cell, on the coincidence of workplace and residence. Weavers offer the best example of a domestic industrial economy characterized by endogamy and sexual division of labor. The putting-out system proved quite resistant to factory-based

industrialization, and though weavers were extremely poor, many who moved on remained nostalgic for the old ways.[22] The development of electricity revived dreams of the home factory, which Peter Kropotkin saw as a libertarian road to independence.

The small family business—store or workshop—is another French dream that has persisted stubbornly despite the vulnerability of small businesses to bankruptcy and the attendant risk of family dishonor. Subcontractors thrive in certain branches of heavy industry. To be one's own boss remains a deep-seated ambition, and to work at home remains an ideal in a country where workers long refused to carry lunchboxes or eat in cafeterias—they preferred to have their wives bring hot lunches to the plant at noontime—and where barricades went up when a proposed reduction in the lunch break would have made it impossible to eat at home (the Houlme Affair of 1827 in Rouen). Here, the family economy bolstered a whole way of life. Industrialization in France had to reckon with these social facts. Factories were located in villages, close to the sources of manpower. Whole families were employed and paid as units; in textile mills the male worker was assisted by his wife and supervised his children. Disciplinary problems were resolved instantly.

The grocer was a personage in the neighborhood, available to serve as witness or confidant. This one, with a watchchain on his waistcoat and assisted by his wife and a clerk, kept a wine and "gourmet specialty" shop that sold to cooks from well-to-do households. (Sirot-Angel Collection.)

Along a street leading to the mine entrance, a row of identical houses, each containing two apartments. Note the attached sheds and tiny gardens, the curtains in all the windows. This is a typical company town, a system conceived in the late 19th century to attract workers to the mines. *The Mines of Bruay,* 1889. (Paris, Bibliothèque Nationale.)

The mill owner himself set the example. He lived near the plant, sometimes on the factory grounds. His wife kept the books, and he invited employees to share in family occasions. Paternalism was the first system of industrial relations. Its benefits flowed to a core group of key workers whose reliability was essential. The system was feasible only where willing workers resided near the workplace. Paternalistic industrialism spoke the language of the family: the owner was the "father"; the workers were one big "family"; bankruptcy was equivalent to "death."

If consensus broke down, the system collapsed. Such a collapse occurred in the second half of the nineteenth century in certain cooperatives, which were actually "truck systems" in disguise. Workers increasingly demanded cash wages instead of payment in kind, which created intolerable bonds of dependency and came to be seen as a modern form of serfdom. One could easily draw a parallel between the crisis in the "natural" family and the crisis in the industrial family, both overwhelmed by the rising tide of individualism.

Strength of the Family Economy

Even outside the factory a strict family economy governed proletarian living conditions. The father's wages paid for all essentials, and his income was supplemented as soon as possible by whatever the children could earn. This fact explains why the birthrate among workers remained quite high for a long period of time. Proposals to limit child labor met with hostility because the long-range views of social planners clashed with the short-term interests of families whose poverty limited their vision. The planners envisioned a different economic equilibrium, a different occupational pattern. But for workers, limiting births, like other measures to aid children, was costly, hence rare.

Women's work, interrupted by periods of motherhood, was also subject to the demands of family life. In any case a woman's income was merely a supplement to her husband's wages. But the old idea of supplementary income took on new meaning in the nineteenth century. Sometimes the woman's earnings were earmarked for special purposes, primarily child care and housekeeping. This income was important to the housewife because it enhanced her status. Workers repeatedly praised the indispensable homemaker and offered ideological justification for what was fundamentally an economic necessity. Woman's quasi-professional work in the home was portrayed as a consequence of her "natural" qualities, unwittingly lending support to economists who characterized domestic work as unproductive labor. In hard times a woman's supplementary earnings could become crucial. Workers who

In the mining industry housing was crucial for establishing and maintaining the social hierarchy. This engineer's house was large, with a monumental doorway, balcony, and ornate dormers. Other signs of distinction include the landscaped lawn and the horse and carriage. But the surroundings were a reminder of the industrial environment. *The Mines of Bruay,* 1889. (Paris, Bibliothèque Nationale.)

suffered long months of unemployment in 1884 survived, they said, because their wives did hours of house-cleaning and laundering. It should come as no surprise that women generally remember times of crisis as periods of additional work for themselves.

Family gardens—small vegetable gardens found in many urban settings, and even abutting the Paris fortifications—offered another hedge against poverty and misery, as did the exchange of services and commodities in what was essentially a barter economy. This kind of exchange required the existence of horizontal communities, whose disappearance explains why contemporary societies are more vulnerable to unemployment and more dependent on the state than societies in the past. Where such communities still exist, as in Italy and Greece, the underground economy, based largely on family and neighborhood ties, continues to be important.

The family of course was more than the soup pot and the family budget. It regulated marriage strategies in a setting where occupational groups traditionally formed essentially endogamous communities. It also played an important role in the geographic mobility that was such an important part of a worker's apprenticeship and a significant vehicle of social change.[23] For workers, migrations and changes of residence were never accidental; considerations of kinship and occupation determined where people went. Knowing relatives and coworkers made it easier for the newly arrived worker to find a niche in his adopted city. And if necessary he could retreat to the country, because he retained ties to the place he had left. When Simon Parvery, a porcelain worker in Limoges, was injured in an accident, he was able to return to a family farm. Families also provided needed services, acting as employment agencies and banks. In certain highly structured ethnic groups, such as the colony of Auvergnats in Paris,[24] families helped to conceive strategies of social advancement. With the family's help, the "savages" tamed the city.

Before the era of compulsory schooling, families educated their members, especially in reading. (The so-called Jacotot method was intended for use by fathers and mothers, who were far more literate than is generally believed.) Raspail relied on families to spread medical information and clinical techniques. The working-class family was not a carbon copy of the bourgeois order but, as Jacques Rancière has said, "a natural place for appropriation of knowledge and emancipation of the poor."[25]

The family served capitalism in the nineteenth century by managing capital accumulation; it was the primary focus of what is sometimes called primitive accumulation. Business history is primarily family history—a history whose great events are marriages and funerals, windfalls and accidents. The nuclear family had the qualities needed to thrive in the "takeoff phase" of industrial development: "The domestic spirit, the notion of private life, proved ideally suited to the secret, unconvivial, antlike labors required by early industrialization."[26]

Employers relied on family systems both to support and to discipline workers. Family secrets were business secrets. Marriage contracts effected mergers and diversifications. Businesses that passed into the hands of capable heirs could be well managed and even boldly progressive. But when firms fell into the hands of stupid or profligate offspring, they failed, and once-great houses declined. Even financial practices were shaped by the family. Limited partnerships, supremely useful in a period of self-financed enterprise, reflected family structure. After 1867 families adapted to the new corporate form of organization, which enabled them to increase the firm's capital yet retain a majority of shares and thus effective control of the business while protecting their personal property.

Business genealogy in this period reflects the genealogies of the families that controlled the firms. The textile industry in the Nord offers striking examples of growth through family connections. In Roubaix, for instance, the Mottes formed connections with numerous industrial families: the Bossuts, the Lagaches, the Brédarts, the Wattines, the Dewawrins, and others. The Pollet family controlled Redoute. In Lille the Thieriez and the Wallaerts dominated industry, as the Willots have done in more recent times. Business was also influenced by individual ideologies and personal traits. In Normandy, where aristocratic nostalgia was a powerful influence, restrictions on marriages were stringent, and the resulting clannishness and tendency to invest in land proved inimical to industrial growth. Among iron- and steelmakers the Schneiders and Wendels were no less aggressive than the textile entrepreneurs. But their deep local roots led them to develop a style of aristocratic paternalism. The company town of Le Creusot was another form of quasi-feudal domination of a region and its people.

The founders of the large department stores raised the "happy household" to the pinnacle of honor. Today one can

Primitive Accumulation and Family Capitalism

This monument in Verjux (Saône-et-Loire) features the very Victorian portrait of the woman who was queen-mother of the Bon Marché department stores, the widow Boucicaut, née Marguerite Guérin (1816–1887). (Paris, Bibliothèque Marguerite-Durand.)

The Bon Marché, at the corner of the rue du Bac and the rue de Sèvres, replaced the Petit Thomas, forerunner of the department store. What made "the ladies happy" was also their perpetual temptation, lord of their imaginations, and governor of their appearances. (Sirot-Angel Collection.)

still view the edifying saga of Cognacq, founder of Le Samaritaine, and his wife, Louise Jay, in a diorama on the top floor of the main branch in Paris. One panel exalts the hardworking marriage of this ideal couple, shown at home at night doing the books by lamplight. When the owner of Bon Marché died, his widow, Mme. Boucicaut, having no heir capable of taking over the business but determined to keep it in the family, took charge herself, and her successors have honored this exemplary loyalty to the firm by encouraging marriages between the store's managers and major stockholders. Another device for legitimating capital by associating it with labor is the practice of choosing executives from the company's own work force, promoting from within in order to constitute a "moral if not a biological family." This practice leads to strict supervision of executives' private lives and to a "merciless domestication" of the firm.

This family domination should not be viewed as charac-

teristic of a primitive stage of industrial development. Louis Bergeron notes: "Large private and, more recently, public industry is much less free of family domination than is generally believed . . . Among business leaders family connections still determine career trajectories."[27] Analyzing the influence of private relations in contemporary public life by studying the case of the Cossé-Brissac family, Pierre Bourdieu and Monique de Saint-Martin show how family connections influence political decisions.[28] In other words, the state has been colonized by certain families, even if they are not the "two hundred families" of notorious legend. Hence family affairs are sometimes state secrets and vice versa.

A family legacy is more than just material goods. A heritage comprises a portfolio of connections, a symbolic capital in the form of reputation, situation, and status, "a heredity of responsibilities and virtues"[29]—in short, the greatest of protections and the worst of inequalities. At the time of the *Madame Bovary* trial Flaubert wrote his brother Achille: "They ought to know at the Ministry of the Interior that in Rouen we are what is called *a family,* that is, that we have deep roots in the region, and that in attacking me, especially for immorality, they will injure many people" (January 3, 1857).

FAMILY: SEX AND BLOOD

The family was assigned other missions: the reproduction of numerous healthy and fertile offspring and the satisfaction of sexual needs without deceit, scandal, or risk of debilitation. The urgency of these missions increased with time, for in the latter part of the nineteenth century people became obsessed with the declining birthrate and fears of degeneracy.

The idea that marriage is the surest way of achieving a prudent and therefore healthy sexuality can probably be traced back to Antiquity. Michel Foucault has shown how an ideal of moderate conjugal life took shape in the Rome of the Antonines under the auspices of the Stoics.[30] In the nineteenth century, which invented nothing, republicans readily invoked this ancient morality. As for the Puritan influence, one of the most popular and often reprinted works of the day was Benjamin Franklin's *Poor Richard's Almanac,* which preached the doctrine of waste not, want not, and counseled moderation in all things. Doctors, the modern priests, sanctified marriage as a regulator of energy and a way of avoiding dangerous commerce with prostitutes, injurious to the race.

In the second half of the century, what Jean Borie has called "mythologies of heredity" were developed by physicians and novelists (such as the Zola of *Fécondité* and *Docteur Pascal*), by fear of the great "social scourges"—tuberculosis, alcoholism, and syphilis—and by terror of flaws transmitted by tainted blood. Because of these hereditary weaknesses the family came to be seen as a weak link to be protected from danger through constant vigilance. Chastity was recommended, even to young men, whose escapades had once been tolerated as a mark of virility, while young women were required to remain virgins.

The nuclear family, that temple of normal sexuality, established norms and discredited outside sexual activity. The marriage bed was the approved altar for the celebration of sexual rites. No longer was it surrounded by curtains. Instead it was protected by thick bedroom walls and by a locked door through which the children were only rarely allowed to pass, whereas parents could enter the children's bedrooms at any time. Formerly punctilious, the Church advised confessors to cease vexing married people—married women in particular—with importunate questions. The sanctified marital bed was to be left in peace. The family—in Foucault's words "the crystal of sexuality"—was also the guardian of the blood line, the protector of the health of the race. Beware the weak links in the chain. Even neo-Malthusian anarchists, eager to liberate women and the poor from the burdens of uncontrolled reproduction, succumbed to the appeal of eugenics, to the dream of racial purification that grew out of the ambiguous doctrines of Social Darwinism.

Thus the family was buffeted by contradictory forces. On the one hand the roles it was found or assigned to fill accentuated its ubiquity, its strength, and its powers and compelled it to close ranks around its terrible secrets. It became more and more jealous of its privacy, while at the same time its anxiety deepened. To one woman worried about her child's upbringing Freud is supposed to have remarked, "Never mind. Whatever you do will be wrong."

On the other hand, increasing awareness of the family's demographic and social role compelled those in power—philanthropists, physicians, the state—to envelop the family in solicitude, to penetrate its mysteries, and to invade its fortress. At first intervention was directed at poor families, at the least

well off, at those deemed unsuited to their role, particularly their role in caring for children. By the turn of the twentieth century judges, doctors, and policemen were invoking the "child's interest" to justify ever-expanding incursions into the private sphere.

In many cases, however, the family itself, gnawed by doubts or faced with difficulties and internal conflicts, was complicit in seeking outside intervention. Social control was not just an outside gaze, a matter of heightened surveillance, but a far more complex interaction of desires and grievances. In Gévaudan at the end of the nineteenth century requests for judicial intervention increasingly came from families or from individuals persecuted by their families.

The family—society's "invisible hand" and the economy's "hidden God"—was at times a conspirator within the very heart of democracy; it straddled the ambiguous boundary between public and private. That boundary snaked its way through the heart of the family, its location varying with time, place, and milieu; at the same time it twisted its way through the home. All this background is essential if we are to understand the intensity of the energies that drove the family, of the conflicts that tore it apart, and of the passions that welled up within it.

This 1882 bedroom, designed and carried out by the studio of Auguste Godin (1816–1883) and Jeanselme (rue des Grands-Augustins), was done in a transitional style. It retains something of the formality of the salon yet serves as a private office. The bed still has a canopy, but as the altar of family life it occupies the center of the room. The mirror on the armoire was an aid in grooming. (*L'Illustration,* 1882.)

FAMILY TYPES AND PRIVATE LIFE

"It is a question of the family," said Michelet, like a good Jacobin. In reality of course there is not the family, but families. But although the singular is wrong, we will sometimes use it. Literature, which is focused on the rise of the urban bourgeoisie and fascinated by Paris, is partly to blame for the misconception. The way in which the French national identity has been constructed is another cause.

The plural ought to be used because of the tremendous diversity of family types. In the history of privacy the urban-rural divide is a major fault line; other differences arise from the social environment, religious influences, and even political affiliations. How does being a Catholic, Protestant, or Jew affect private practices? Is there anything special about a Calvinist father or a Jewish mother? Did freethinking modify relations between the sexes or ways of seeing the body? Is there an effective socialist morality? Does being anarchist affect amorous behavior? Between the two world wars Armand made free love the touchstone of individual liberation, and his newspaper *En dehors* reported on comrades' experiences in this regard. The history of Victor Coissac and his "Harmony colony" show how powerful resistance in this area was, however. It was a long way from theory to practice.

Stendhal, evoking his mother's death in *La Vie de Henry Brulard,* describes her feelings and manner of expressing them and contrasts the "hearts of Dauphiné" with the "hearts of Paris": "Dauphiné has its own way of feeling, a lively, stubborn, argumentative way that I have never encountered anywhere else. To perceptive eyes music, scenery, and novels must look different with every three-degree change in latitude."

What Stendhal with his great sensitivity to regional differences explained in terms of climate, Hervé Le Bras and Emmanuel Todd attribute to the extreme variety of family structures found in France, so extreme that "from an anthropological point of view France ought not to exist." Critical of the overly general character of a history of *mentalités* more concerned with temporal change than with geographical variety, they emphasize the diversity of kinship systems found in different regions of France. In this respect, "there is as much difference between Normandy and Limousin as there is between England and Russia." Refining Le Play's system of classification, they identify three major types: first, regions of nuclear structure where the age at marriage and rate of celibacy are less stable than in other regions—Normandy, the interior parts of western France, Champagne, Lorraine, Orléanais, Burgundy, and Franche-Comté; second, regions of complex family structure where marriage is subject only to loose controls, including the southwestern quarter of France, Provence, and the Nord; and third, regions of complex family structure where marriage is subject to strict controls, including Brittany, the Basque country, the southern Massif Central, Savoy, and Alsace.[31]

In each area one finds systems of authority based on different family behaviors. These systems affect not only relations between parents and children but also the age of marriage and relations between husband and wife. "Each of these major family types corresponds to a particular type of family feeling . . . Each family structure gives rise to specific tensions and pathologies." Rates of illegitimacy and suicide, forms of

At the turn of the century photography recorded the rural scene. For this picture everyone posed in his or her finest attire and was placed according to rank or function. The masters are seated and well dressed, while the servants are dressed for work. The obligatory smile is forthright in the masters, restrained in the servants. In the center is a charming little girl who is treated affectionately. (Sirot-Angel Collection.)

Marcel Baschet, *Francisque Sarcey*. Teatime in a fin-de-siècle bourgeois family. Note the servant with cap, the men dressed in black, and the mistress of the house who, dressed in white, smiles at the arriving guests. (Paris, Private collection.)

violence, and even political opinions are strongly correlated with this fundamental variable. The argument of Le Bras and Todd is highly schematic and necessarily simplistic, and we do not agree with them in every detail. We do concede, however, that our analysis is insufficiently attentive to social and still more to regional differences.

In part the problem is one of lack of primary data, despite the work of the French ethnological school, especially that of Elisabeth Claverie and Pierre Lamaison, whose importance for the subject of this book is considerable. Their results are based on extensive research into judicial archives, which may lead them to overemphasize conflict. Nevertheless, their work is a welcome antidote to the view that family life in traditional societies was harmonious and serene. Much work in cultural and structural anthropology is directed at what is stable and invariant in social life, and the effect is to give an impression of static societies. There was nothing static about nineteenth-century society, however, not even in the most isolated rural areas. Society was constantly on the move, affecting the boundary between the public and the private as well as ways of living, feeling, loving, and dying.

To be sure, powerful unifying factors were at work: the

law; institutions; language; that steamroller of differences, the school; the media; and consumer items that conveyed "Paris fashions" throughout the country. Adored as much as it was feared, the capital exerted a powerful attraction on the rest of the country, and men and things circulated between Paris and the provinces in a way that tended to standardize the forms of private life.

Yet resistance to standardization was also surprisingly strong. According to Eugen Weber, it was only World War II that spelled "the end of the *terroir*."[32] And the only unity in the working class was in the rhetoric of bourgeois fear and later of militant consciousness. Family secrets and individual mysteries persisted and changed, and it is these secrets and mysteries, thus far barely glimpsed, that we must now try to understand.

The family was serious business, and so was being photographed for these children, forced to remain still far too long. In the late 19th century men began to dress in light-colored English tweeds, while women turned to darker colors.

Family Life

The family describes itself, thinks of itself, and represents itself as a unified entity maintained by a constant flow of blood, money, sentiments, secrets, and memories.

Scattered families kept in touch through letters. Correspondence was facilitated by improvements in postal service. Already underway in the first half of the nineteenth century, these were accelerated in the second half by the construction of railroads and other technological advances that helped make this the great century of paper. Receiving frequent, regular, and above all "fresh" news of family members became a necessity. On April 3, 1830, that indefatigable letter-writer George Sand asked to be sent from Paris some of "that yellow and blue letter paper that is so ugly and so fashionable." She compared the postmarks of letters received with the dates they were posted. The mailman, who not only distributed the mail but also kept people informed of the correct time—the time according to the railway station clock—was an expected and honored visitor.

Children away at school were expected to write weekly letters home. When husband and wife were briefly separated, they wrote every two or three days. Beyond the nucleus of the family, more distant relatives wrote according to a schedule determined by degree of kinship. For some, New Year's Day was the one annual occasion for sending bulletins of family health and summaries of births, deaths, marriages, illness, and examinations passed during the course of the previous year. Such subjects were the meat and potatoes of regular correspondence. Caroline Chotard-Lioret, who has studied some 11,000 letters written between 1860 and 1920 by mem-

Correspondence

bers of a bourgeois family in Saumur, has been able to show what people could and could not say in letters.[33] Among the things people in this particular family did not talk about were money, death, and sex. They did write about illness, routine details, and of course children. Other families were concerned with different subjects. The Goblots were obsessed with educational achievements. A mother and daughter whose published letters reveal only their first names—Emilie and Marthe—had much more to say about money and physical matters; they talked of illnesses and colics but also about things that strike us as almost indecent, for the boundary between propriety and impropriety is constantly shifting.

Letters were not spontaneous effusions but what M. Bossis has called "symbols of compromise" between the public and the private, the individual and the social.[34] The audience for family correspondence was not an individual but a group; letters passed from person to person, staking out their territory as they went. Confidences were muted, and intimacy was impossible. The letters at issue here were written by literate, articulate people. Some of the letter-writers were frustrated authors who found in correspondence an acceptable outlet for their energies. Many women experienced the same "rage to write" as George Sand and her friends at the Couvent des Anglaises; excluded from writing for the general public, they threw themselves with vengeful pleasure into writing letters. Some devoted hours a day to the task. Men too continued to hone their epistolary skills, though in the twentieth century their thoughts turned to technology and crafts and away from writing.

The gap between the sexes was not as great as that between town and country. In the cities some of the poor relied on public letter-writers, whose conventions insinuated themselves into private correspondence. In the country news arrived by word of mouth more often than by letter. When migrant masons returned to Creuse, a festival marked the occasion; during long winter vigils they recounted their adventures in the city. After 1900 postcards became an extremely popular means of communication. A family of five from Melun—the father a gardner, the mother a housewife, and three daughters who worked in offices—exchanged more than a thousand postcards between 1904 and 1914. The more frequent exchange of news was accompanied by a tendency toward more concise, informative messages.

Regular, formal family gatherings were both an important form of communication and a demonstration of family unity.[35] For religious and ethnic minorities family gatherings were a means of survival and even resistance, hence particularly important events. Until quite recently some two hundred members of the Monod clan met for an annual tea at which each person present was identified by a name tag. Another Protestant family, the Reclus, convened to celebrate the father's birthday.[36]

During this time the family photograph developed into a full-fledged genre, a way of commemorating family events. By the turn of the twentieth century many families kept photographs neatly arranged in albums. Until World War I families of modest means photographed only weddings, but after 1914 photography became increasingly popular as a means of recording all sorts of occasions. Soldiers about to leave for the front often posed with their wives and children, and family photos of the departure were often found on the dead in the trenches.

Before the era of photography wealthier families had commissioned portraits.[37] Family galleries, rows of ancestral portraits in oil or photographs, were a way of visually displaying the family line. Such galleries embodied family memories in material form, a matter of great concern in a century preoccupied with evolution and with the transmission of property and values from generation to generation. In the Nord and Rouen in the late nineteenth century bourgeois families researched their genealogies, possibly in the secret hope of discovering illustrious ancestors. (They were more likely to prove how far they had come up in the world.) Sumptuous burial vaults in cemeteries sheltered the remains of family members and affirmed the unity of the clan for all to see.

In the nineteenth century autobiographies, particularly those of "ordinary folk,"[38] were more commonly stories of a family than of an individual. Addressed to later generations, these autobiographical writings dwelt on the writer's childhood and roots, as if the writers wished to measure the distance they had traveled. If they had succeeded, they prided themselves on that distance; if they had failed, they might offer it as an excuse. Condorcet advocated a history of "the masses of families." George Sand, whose *Histoire de ma vie* is actually more a history of her family than of her life, exhorted the poorer classes to follow her example: "Artisans, you who are beginning to understand all, who are beginning to know how to write, do not forget your dead. Perpetuate the lives of your fathers for the benefit of your sons; fashion your own titles and coats of arms, if you like, but do it, all of you," for "the people have their ancestors, just as much as kings."

Memory depends on commemoration. In perpetuating oral tradition women no doubt played a key role.[39] Such memory was of course foreshortened and reconstituted, and events were less important than the way in which they were represented. Italian immigrants in Lorraine elaborated a mythic memory of their origins that made its way into their conversation. Accounts of their journey from Italy magnified the role of the founder of their community and his odyssey.

Rituals and Styles

Family life, both public and private, was staged according to definite rules. Among the bourgeoisie, fascinated by the court life of old, the rules were erected into an elaborate code. Manuals of etiquette replaced the "books of civilities," which, as Norbert Elias has shown, had contributed since the time of Erasmus to the sophistication of private behavior.[40] People also were instructed by novels, which may be consulted as legitimate historical sources because they reveal more fully than other sources the ideals of private life that fascinated their perspicacious authors. Private archives yield valuable information.

The rituals of bourgeois life reveal a threefold temporal structure, attuned to the day, the year, and the life. This model, as detailed as a book of etiquette and as binding as an aristocratic ritual, was of such normative importance that considerable space can be devoted to it, for from it we learn how people wished to live. With minor differences this same model was adopted in all major European cities. It even influenced the court. Louis-Philippe, so proud of his big double bed, wished above all else to be a good father, in Tocqueville's words, "sober in his behavior, simple in his habits, measured in his tastes." At Versailles we learn from *Emilie* that "the queen's salon is remarkable only for a large work table with drawers to which the princesses hold the keys and in which they place their work. Here the royal family gathers." Later we learn from Octave Aubry that Empress Eugénie, who had a particular interest in rearing children, "takes care of her own child as would an ordinary mother. She dresses him, rocks him, and sings him Spanish tunes." The court succumbed to

Summer Evening in the Country,
1898. She reads, he smokes,
drinks coffee, and dreams.
Alone together at the beginning
of a dubious night. (Paris,
Bibliothèque Nationale.)

the "family craze" that had begun in the city. This striking reversal of the usual pattern was a triumph of the bourgeoisie. Family life became a fashion and a model of government.

To be sure, these rituals were subject to many variations in response to both tradition and inner necessity. One example is that of the Lutheran families in Alsace who considered it prudent to take certain precautions against the possibility of renewed religious conflict. Although the integration of Protestants and Jews into the nation had made decisive progress in the nineteenth century, there was always a danger that something might go wrong. Lutheran parents therefore customarily chose two sets of godparents for their children, one Catholic, the other Lutheran. In case of trouble the child could seek protection from one or the other. In the Jewish community friction developed in the 1880s with the arrival of immigrants from central and eastern Europe. In the Pletzl, the Jewish quarter of Paris in the Marais, it was common in the Belle Epoque to find small chapels set up in the shops of haberdashers and tailors; recent immigrants worshiped in these chapels rather than attend official services in the major synagogues. Or, to take another example, Auvergnats found it easy to adapt to Paris precisely because they maintained family and regional traditions: their own cooking, dances, and holidays such as Saint-Michel and Saint-Ferréol. They returned regularly to their native villages on specially chartered "Bonnet trains." Similarly, Italian immigrants clung to their customs, and even their priests, although this reluctance to give up old ways involved them in occasional fracases with French workers.

Although the family took the place of God, religious trappings clung tenaciously to certain rituals. Although free-thinking was generally on the wane, 38.7 percent of all burials in Paris in the period 1884–1903 were civil burials, as were 21.5 percent of burials of men in Carmaux in 1902–1903. Contrast these figures with the 50 percent civil burials recorded in Saint-Denis, a working-class suburb of Paris, in 1911. Secularization had made its greatest inroads among the working population. Civil marriages accounted for 40 percent of the total in Hénin-Liétard. New phraseology for wills and new rituals were developed by so-called solidarity societies. In Roubaix the Freethinkers' church performed fifty burials annually. At these men and women carried the coffin themselves. At the cemetery speakers eulogized the deceased while bells were rung.

Emancipation had its limits. Some workers requested religious burials only to be refused by the priest. In the Nord refusals of this kind triggered riots. Of all religious ceremonies, First Communion resisted change more successfully than any other, perhaps because no substitute rite of passage had been found to mark the beginning of adolescence. In de-Christianized regions a child's First Communion was often a subject of dispute in working-class households (where the man of the house was likely to harbor anticlerical sentiments).

Rituals tell us about beliefs, but they tell even more about ways of life. Social differences marked all these rituals profoundly, in ways that rural anthropologists have studied in great detail. Less work has been done on urban workers, where attention has focused more on class than on family issues and everyday life. In the nineteenth century workers' private rituals had little in common with the private rituals of the bourgeoisie. Workers' rituals were situated differently with respect to both space and time. Their theater of choice was the street, the café, or the outdoors. This public character of private ritual accounts for the increasing expenditure on clothes. Even the poorest Italians in the Lorraine Basin were preoccupied with cutting a fine figure on Sundays. Work filled their lives. The absence of vacations and genuine leisure time

(as opposed to unemployment) was a major difference between the worker and the bourgeois. The worker's "Holy
Monday" (that is, Monday taken off from work) with the
comrades had little in common with the bourgeois's Sunday.
Family meals and outings were ways in which workers celebrated, however. Working-class neighborhood life was more
noticeably coeducational than bourgeois life. In the clamor
around the turn of the century for the English work week,
the need to spend time with the family was an important
argument; yet it would be wrong to infer that workers were
necessarily imitating the petty bourgeoisie.

Rituals were subtle combinations of diverse ingredients,
part public and part private, part rural and part urban.
Through ritual, social groups took possession of the spaces in
which they lived and sought to give style to their existence.

What misfortune or dishonor led this young man to blow his brains out in a garret apartment? In romantic Paris suicide was on the rise, but having a family generally promoted stability. The use of firearms remained a privilege of the educated class. (Paris, Bibliothèque des Arts Décoratifs.)

Problems and Conflicts

The nineteenth-century family found itself in a contradictory situation. Its power and dignity reinforced by society, which saw it as an essential agent of social control, the family attempted to impose its own ends on individual members; the group interest was declared to be more important than individual interests. Yet egalitarianism was also honored, and individualism made quiet but steady progress. As a result, the family was subjected to centrifugal forces, which led to conflict and at times to disintegration. The family was a microsociety, and not only its integrity but its most intimate recesses were under attack.

Defense of the family honor remained the most basic rule. Honor required keeping the family's deepest secrets, secrecy being the mortar that held the family together and created a fortress against the outside world. But that very mortar had been known to create cracks and crevices in its structure. Cries and whispers, creaking doors, locked drawers, purloined letters, glimpsed gestures, confidences and mysteries, sidelong and intercepted glances, words spoken and unspoken—all these created a universe of internal communications, and the more varied the interests, loves, hatreds, and shameful feelings of individual family members, the more subtle those communications were. The family was an endless source of drama. Novelists drew on it constantly, and fragments of the rich saga of private life occasionally could be read in the newspapers. "Not every family is a tragic affair, but every tragedy is a family affair."[41]

As the century progressed, rebellion against the family—primarily the father but in some cases the mother or an envied brother—assumed more violent forms. In order to survive, the family was forced to evolve. Individuals showed less willingness to suffer its constraints. The bourgeois family in particular was the target of criticism by artists and intellectuals, by unmarried dandies who denounced marriage laws and by bohemians who mocked hypocritical conventions. The family also came under attack by rambunctious adolescents and by women determined to live lives of their own choosing. Though buffeted on the eve of World War I by heavy seas, the family ship did not go down. Yet many who abandoned ship did so with relief, with a sense of deliverance, and with the hope of embarking on a personal adventure, only to end in horror.

Money

Money was a primary source of conflict, for the family was the repository of a patrimony. Hegel deemed that patrimony essential to the family's very existence, but Marx denounced it as the germ of corruption. Money was crucial to many arranged marriages, and among the wealthy arranged marriages were the norm. Unkept promises led to recriminations. When dowry payments fell into arrears, husbands turned accountants and scrutinized their in-law's books. In southern France many jurists recommended the *régime dotal* as a way of preserving a woman's rights, but husbands who found their hands tied by this legal separation of property tried to circumvent the system's restrictions in any way they could. Consider the case of Clémence de Cerilley, who rather imprudently married a retired military officer. The gentleman in question forced her to draw up will after will, each more favorable to himself than the last, until one day, with his own family's backing, he had her declared insane and locked up, leaving himself free to administer her properties. So great were the legal prerogatives of the husband that Clémence's family had great difficulty extricating her from this predicament. In particular, it proved impossible to obtain a legal separation, since Clémence did not allege "injuries or violence or threats or mistresses under the conjugal roof," as required by article 217.

The Cerilley family correspondence offers further examples of conflicts over money, especially inherited money. One cousin claimed to have been done out of a 60,000-franc bequest from his maternal grandfather; he used this claim as grounds for challenging the family's financial arrangements. In another case, brothers and sisters, all of whom had been on affectionate terms with their father, fell to bickering over the provisions of his will, split hairs about a certain set of wooden bowls, and ultimately went to court to settle the dispute.

The most serious conflicts involved inheritances, and problems frequently arose, even though parents took precautions by giving children gifts during their lifetime and by working out settlements prior to death. Unfortunately the valuation of family property cannot be carried out with mathematical precision. Desire, fantasies, a sense of entitlement— all these perturbing influences came into play. Rich as they were, the Brame brothers went at one another tooth and nail over the château de Fontaine near Lille; they plotted endlessly and on occasion even resorted to violence. The affair became such a sore subject that Jules, the eldest brother, felt compelled to leave an account of this fratricidal battle for his descendants.

At a more humble level we find family members counting sheets and handkerchiefs in the linen closet, a fact that tells us just how important these items were both to the family economy and to what Norbert Elias has called the "civilizing process." Pettiness could go to such extremes as counting teaspoons or—the height of unreason—breaking up libraries to satisfy egalitarian sensibilities. The death of a father or ancestor could become an occasion for settling scores, a time for each family member to calculate the advantages of the others or to claim that some special devotion to the deceased established title to an extra share of the inheritance; inevitably some people felt wronged. When a family squabbled in public, no one escaped unscathed, not even the most affectionate of sisters or the closest of cousins. Bad feeling often lingered and sometimes hardened into permanent estrangement. Disputes became subjects of family conversation and correspondence, at least where there was no tacit ban on discussing monetary matters.

Usually these family disputes remained confidential, the only outside witness being the notary, who in the most serious cases might be called in to serve as arbiter. At times the pressures were extreme, especially in rural areas where property was a matter of survival. In Gévaudan it became increasingly common for children who deemed themselves deprived by their father's designation of a principal heir to protest the choice. Toward the end of the nineteenth century children might go to court rather than seek private vengeance. This willingness to air family secrets in public was a sign that the traditional sense of family was on the wane.

Families considered business failure a tragedy, and among

Jules Breton, *Monday,* 1858. During the Second Empire many urban workers, particularly in northern France, were in the habit of taking off "Holy Monday" and celebrating with joyous libations among friends—an old custom among artisans. Housewives worried about their budgets sometimes invaded the male preserve of the tavern and angrily urged their husbands to return home. Breton, a native of Courrières (Pas-de-Calais), painted many scenes of popular life, for the most part in rural settings. This painting was considered one of the best works in the Salon of 1859. (Saint Louis [Missouri] University Gallery of Art.)

industrialists and businessmen a bankruptcy could destroy a family's name and sap its patrimony. As the law evolved, however, private wealth was increasingly distinguished from corporate wealth. Corporations supplanted partnerships, so that the property of collateral branches of the family ceased to be jeopardized by bankruptcy. Nevertheless, some old-fashioned families clung to older forms of organization. Such families had a rough time between the First and Second World Wars, when it was easy for an incompetent heir to squander in a few years family wealth that had been amassed over a long period.

The question of money frequently poisoned daily life. Husband and wife clashed over the household budget. The wife was the steward of household funds, the *ministre des finances* she was called among the poor. Totally dependent on her husband, she was sometimes obliged to deceive him about household accounts. Tempers often flared over monetary matters. Henri Leyret described payday: "On that day the neighborhood took on a very special air, a mixture of gaiety and anxiety, of animation and expectation, as if the dreary pressures of the week were about to blossom forth in new life. Housewives waited in the windows or on the doorsteps of their homes. Some, impatient or anxious, even set out to meet their husbands on the way home from work . . . In the streets scolding voices could be heard; inside angry, filthy words were flung about, hands were raised, tears flowed, and children wailed; while at the tavern the atmosphere was one of joy and intoxication—intoxication with song more than with wine."[42]

Leyret also described the bullying to which children, particularly older children, were subjected when parents suspected them of not handing over all their earnings. Girls, especially flirtatious ones, were suspected of streetwalking. Money became a bone of contention between adolescents searching for freedom and their working parents.

Honor

A family's patrimony did not consist solely of money and property. The family also possessed a symbolic capital in the form of honor. Anything that injured the family's reputation or besmirched its name threatened that honor. When attacked by an outsider, the family united. Compromising behavior by one of its members placed the family in a difficult situation. It might respond in many ways: by jointly assuming responsibility and making amends, by punishing the guilty individual in a family tribunal, perhaps even expelling the black sheep, or by joining in a conspiracy of silence. But woe unto the person who brought scandal upon the family!

Scandal—the notion was a central one, yet its meaning varied. Tricaud remarks that "the noble sensitive to the slightest danger of humiliation yet little troubled by a mountain of debt was a commonplace figure of history and literature."[43] Nineteenth-century France knew many different codes of honor, and it would be interesting to explore in detail just what, under various circumstances, constituted a scandal. Broadly speaking, honor was more a question of morality and biology than of economics. A sexual offense or an illegitimate birth was much more severely condemned than a bankruptcy, although bankruptcy was less tolerated than it is today. In short, dishonor arrived through women, over whom the mark of shame always hovered.

Because illegitimacy was harshly condemned, unwed (or adulterous) mothers sometimes resorted to abortion or infanticide; others chose to give birth in the maternity wards of out-of-town hospitals and then put their children up for adoption. To stem the slaughter of newborn bastards, the Empire in 1811 instituted "orphans' towers," which later became a subject of heated controversy. In 1838 Lamartine, speaking in the Chamber of Deputies, defended the towers as the best way of protecting family honor. He argued for "social paternity" against Malthusian deputies fearful of the proliferation of the poor. "The illegitimate child should be received as a guest. The human family ought to envelop that child with love"— the human family, not the child's actual family, which wanted nothing to do with the shameful offspring. The number of abandoned children had increased from 67,000 in 1809 to 121,000 in 1835, however, and the towers, blamed for this scourge, were phased out. In 1860 only twenty-five were still in existence, and these were closed by ministerial order.

From that date on a woman who wished to give up her child did so by making public declaration of her desire at a government office. An unwed mother who wished to raise her offspring received an allowance equivalent to the cost of a hospital nurse. Abandoned children became the responsibility of the Office of Public Assistance, at least in Paris, where

Until their institution was abolished in 1860, the nuns of the rue d'Enfer in Paris took in abandoned children day and night. Children were given up not only by forsaken women but also, as this picture suggests, by poor couples, who might someday reclaim their baby. (Paris, Bibliothèque Nationale.)

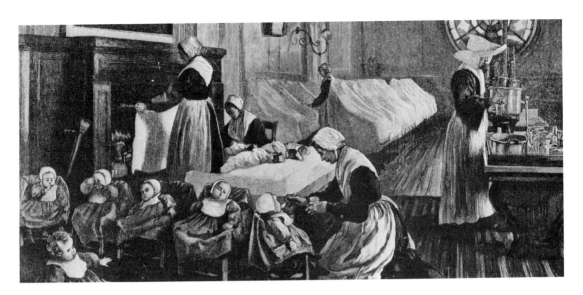

the problem was most serious. This office generally placed its charges in rural homes. Orphanages such as the Prince-Imperial and training schools such as the Apprentices' School of Auteuil were not established until the second half of the century.

Illegitimacy was scandalous, for it was the visible sign of an offense against virginity or marital fidelity, hence a threat to the social order. The guilty woman and those closest to her thought of nothing but hiding the offense, of getting rid of its spoiled fruit. Mothers often abetted their daughters in infanticide. Frequently a neighbor or even a household member would denounce the crime. Sometimes a persistent rumor was enough to attract the attention of mayor and gendarmes.

Some women, whether acting on principle or out of emotion, chose to keep their illegitimate offspring. Often the grandparents would raise the child for a time, long enough for the mishap to be forgotten or perhaps for the unfortunate woman to find herself a husband willing to claim paternity. For people of modest station, among whom illegitimacy was not such an explosive issue, such a course was fairly common, but among the upper classes it required much careful negotiation. It was not easy to find a mate for an unwed mother, and sometimes financial compensation had to be offered to attract a husband. Take the case of Marthe, a young aristocrat made pregnant by a servant; when she insisted that she needed a man sexually, her whole family set out to find her an ac-

By 1882 orphans were kept in public institutions, still run by nuns with the assistance of wet nurses who lived on the premises in order to avoid the risks of transporting the children to the countryside. ("Children on Welfare: The Nursery," *L'Illustration*, 1882.)

ceptable husband. The man they came up with turned out to be a brute: taking advantage of her "guilt," he swindled and beat her. Ultimately she asked for a divorce, once again incurring the disapproval of her Catholic relations. The child, who had been sent to live with a nurse, died at age four or five, not really mourned by anyone. In fact death was the usual fate of the bastard, a child no one wanted, cared for, or loved. It has been estimated that 50 percent of all children born out of wedlock died in the year they were born. Not until people became aware of the so-called crisis of natality (a declining birthrate) during the Second Empire did the state act to stem this loss of potential citizens. State aid for unwed mothers marked the beginning of French family policy, though it was of little use in rehabilitating the mothers who received it. Many had been banished by their families only to be greeted with scorn by the institutions that were supposed to help them.

The birth of a bastard, the *mauvaise naissance,* was an inexpiable shame for the mother and an indelible taint on her child. The illegitimate child was subject to exploitation and humiliation of all kinds. In the villages of Gévaudan bastards were called all sorts of names. *Champi* (dialect for waif) was one, and people who saw *champis* as potential delinquents treated them accordingly. The path from orphanage to reform school was well trodden. Ahead lay the army. The Commune and the Great War treated these outcast children as cruelly as any wicked stepmother.

So heavy was the burden of illegitimate birth that some autobiographies seem to have been written deliberately to protect the author's guilty secret. Xavier-Edouard Lejeune—*Calicot*—created a picaresque adventure to hide what a pitiless birth certificate revealed to his descendants. Many born out of wedlock but later legitimized learned the secret of their birth only late in life and to their great chagrin. Knowledge of illegitimate birth sometimes led to wild speculation about a person's possible ancestors.

At the beginning of the nineteenth century Aurore de Saxe—Mme Dupin—had raised her son Maurice's illegitimate son, Hippolyte Chatiron, without problems. Throughout his life Hippolyte was treated as George Sand's half brother (except in the matter of inheritance). As the century progressed, however, the condemnation of illegitimacy became more severe. No doubt this heightened severity accounts in part for the decline in the number of illegitimate births and the increase in the number of premarital conceptions and postmarital legitimations.

Tainted Blood

As it became increasingly widespread to portray the family as "genetic capital," anxieties over marriage and birth increased accordingly. People became obsessed with the fear of giving birth to an abnormal child, for abnormalities were considered signs of hidden sin. The pages of popular science magazines were filled with monsters. *La Nature,* for instance, abounded in descriptions of strange births, of creatures whose malformations were all the more worrisome because the cause was unknown. Did not such births reflect some hidden taint? Sideshows and museums of anatomy such as Dr. Spitzner's attracted nervous but fascinated crowds. People shunned the handicapped and at times reproached them as though they sensed in the victim's affliction a mark of invisible transgression. A deformed child was an embarrassment and sometimes an object of hatred. One of Flaubert's correspondents, Mlle. de Chantepie, told him (in a letter dated July 17, 1858) the story of a child named Agathe who was mistreated by her parents because she was deformed. "Her face was all right, but her enormous head sat atop a horribly misshapen child's body." She was beaten, humiliated, kept shoeless, and ultimately declared insane.

Syphilis was believed to be the primary cause of birth defects. The health of prospective brides and grooms was therefore a matter of concern, and if investigation turned up a hidden vice, shame and perhaps anger ensued. Families whispered about such mishaps, which hovered in the background and fascinated subsequent generations as time deepened the mystery. Caroline Chotard-Lioret has turned up an interesting example in the Boileau family correspondence. Eugène Boileau's mother, Aimée Braud, was a woman whose inadequate dowry led to a bad marriage and who rose in rebellion against her ill-matched husband. After accusing this spouse of having contracted a "shameful disease," she refused to share his bed. One day, while he was briefly at home between two trips, she displayed the bed linen in front of the house—a highly symbolic exposure of the household's most intimate secrets. Later, in desperation, Aimée left her husband's home and sued to obtain custody of their three children, who had

The Medicine of Venus without the Doctor. Syphilis was a "shameful disease" that people hid even from their doctors; this accounts for the success of a variety of dubious forms of self-treatment. (Paris, Bibliothèque Nationale.)

been spirited off to Belgium by their father. She then shut herself up in her house at Rochefort, where she died half-mad. The family spoke of this ancestor only in veiled terms. Her tragedy may explain why her son Eugène was so keen to raise a stable family in a harmonious household.

Madness

Biological defects, that new source of dishonor and family conflict, were the focus of Zola's epic saga of the Rougon-Macquart family, spread over many novels. One great fear, which grew more substantial in the century that witnessed the birth of the clinic, was mental illness. A "deranged" daughter could easily discourage her sisters' suitors. Because she cast doubt on the mental equilibrium of those who shared her blood, she caused them shame. The oddest thing about the case of Adèle Hugo was that the whole family, except for the mother, closed ranks to protect the great Victor's reputation against any harm that might be caused by his extravagant offspring; to the curious they uniformly recounted an expurgated version of Adèle's story. The family drew together and expelled the anomaly from its midst.

Delinquency was not always a matter of scandal. The boundaries of respectability changed with time and social milieu. Community codes of honor do not always coincide with the law. Poaching and trespassing were so widespread in the nineteenth century that the law was forced to retreat. The child who filched from the woods, the woman who gathered fuel from the forest floor, and even the poacher were winked at by nearly everyone. In the cities in the early nineteenth century poor mothers frequently set their children to begging or even pilfering. In the lower orders survival was the paramount rule, and morals were quite tolerant.

Once a family rose to the level of the petty bourgeoisie, however, respect for the law and good manners became central concerns. The debauchee, the alcoholic, the spendthrift, the deadbeat, the gambler, and the swindler were undesirables and, as such, severely reproached. In business a man was expected to honor his debts. The undisciplined heir was subject to harsh sanctions by his family. Baudelaire, judged hopelessly inept by his relatives, was placed under the supervision of a guardian. His correspondence with his mother, Mme. Aupick, was filled with complaints about his financial difficulties and his conflicts with the attorney charged with remitting his regular allowance. The rule of bourgeois propriety was never to give cause to be talked about—an ideal of discreet mediocrity. Eccentricity was a kind of scandal.

Swindling and fraud were widely tolerated, particularly if directed against a highly alien state. By contrast, bankruptcy was perceived not just as an individual failure but as a moral fault. Balzac's César Birotteau offered himself up as expiatory victim. Reimbursing his creditors became an act of "reparation," and his rehabilitation took on religious value. It was not uncommon in the nineteenth century for bankrupts to commit suicide. Philippe Lejeune has shown how some bankrupts, feeling a need to justify themselves to their offspring, turned to autobiography.[44] Highly anticapitalist bourgeois women in the Nord closed their doors to bankrupts suspected of illegal trafficking or of leading dissolute lives. Only with the rise of the corporation was business separated from the family and capitalism liberated from the idea of honor.

The nineteenth century made sexuality—the sexuality of the family—a subject of science. In all the norms and rules governing sexual behavior, the family was the center, the administrator, even if it often relinquished its role to others: the priest and, even more, the doctor, who was the great expert on sexual identity, the confidant in case of difficulty, and the source of new hygienic precepts. Yet even the physician's role was limited by the fact that people were reluctant to turn to him for help.

Normally the role of the family in sexual matters was

Sexual Shame

Pious image published by Bouasse-Lebel (1860–1870) to commemorate a reception for Children of Mary. The Immaculate Conception became dogma in 1854, and the cult of the Virgin reached a peak at around this time. (Private collection.)

shrouded in silence. We know very little about it. Incest, which Fourier in *Le Nouveau monde amoureux* claimed was a common practice, is particularly elusive. Sexual tolerance varied depending on the milieu, the act, the age, and the gender of the person involved. Inequality between men and women was probably greatest here. Virility was a question of phallic prowess, which could be demonstrated fairly freely on women and especially young girls. In Gévaudan girls were raped with near impunity. Even offenses against young children were tolerated so long as they did not become public. In the second half of the nineteenth century the courts punished these offenses more severely than in the past, presumably a sign of heightened sensitivity. At the end of the century some prosecutors began to raise the issue of inadequate punishment of rapists.

Greater attention began to be paid to the sexuality of adolescents and women. The pubescent adolescent was seen as a person in the throes of an identity crisis potentially dangerous both to himself and to society; every adolescent was seen as a potential criminal. And the sexuality of women was a concern because, as always, misfortune arrives through the distaff side. A perennial source of anxiety, female sexuality was controlled by the Church, which played a major role in this area. Adoration of the Virgin, repeated recitation of the rosary under the supervision of older girls, and worship in congregations of Children of Mary all helped girls protect their virginity. Piety combatted the evils of the world and the dance hall. Caroline Brame's confessor's paramount admonition was, "Above all, no waltzing." Even among the lower strata of society a daughter's virginity was valuable capital: fathers and brothers accompanied girls to dances, where encounters between men and women frequently were brutal.

Although female infidelity was an offense of the utmost gravity, male adultery was all but universally tolerated except where the man openly kept a concubine, a practice that was strongly condemned and, if it involved the family home, subject to legal sanction. Among the bourgeoisie, women rarely knew of their husbands' affairs, so there was little they could do. Women of more modest station, however, alerted by rumors or chance encounters in the street, could speak their minds and on occasion rebel against their husbands, especially when they felt that an affair injured them financially and threatened their ability to provide for their children. *La Gazette des tribunaux* resounded with the insults they hurled at unfaith-

Achille Devéria, *A Young Woman Receives the Counsel of Her Guardian Angel,* 1830. This guardian angel will have to work hard to protect the young lady from the young suitor's somber attractions. Romanticism exalted virginity, an obstacle that served to inflame the passions. (Paris, Bibliothèque des Arts Décoratifs.)

ful husbands or the "tramps" they courted. Around the turn of the century a few even resorted to the most feared weapon of all: vitriol.

TYPES OF CONFLICT

Most family conflicts were settled in the privacy of the home. Propriety, a sense of privacy, fear of what people would say, and an obsession with respectability—all were reasons to stifle conflicts. The fundamental precepts of peasant and bourgeois alike were to keep troubles private, to keep outsiders out, and to wash one's dirty laundry at home. These principles strengthened the boundary between "us" and "them"—the always threatening outside world. Discretion was more difficult for workers than for the wealthy; they were not protected by forests or walls. "From my bed I could hear everything that went on in X's house," said the witness in one criminal case. More exposed than any other group, workers, perhaps for that reason, were more reluctant to talk about themselves.

In case of conflict some families set up what amounted to their own private tribunals to ask for amends or to expel those guilty of some offense. Warring parties or hostile clans some-

Vicente Palmaroli, *The Confession*. A lascivious parody of confession: the young woman in white, seated in an odd sort of beach chair, listens to the confessions of a lover dressed like a priest. (Madrid, Prado.)

times formed, and people refused to speak to or to see one another. Diplomatic efforts might be made within the family to deal with such disputes by careful seating arrangements at family gatherings, judicious organization of family ceremonies, or shrewd negotiation. Burials were frequently occasions of reconciliation; death divided, but it also drew families together. Unmarried uncles or aunts often devoted themselves to mending rents in the family fabric, rifts often compounded by stubborn myths. At times unpleasantness remained long after its origins had been forgotten. Pious souls prayed for harmony to be restored, for many people dreamed of being able to present their families as happy and united, as harmonious tribes, proud and serene, for the benefit of others and for future generations—and so they were often depicted in family photographs.

Violence

Bourgeois families rarely resorted to physical attack. The fisticuffs of country folk were rejected in favor of more subtle though no less devastating forms of aggression. Adopting the strategy of the mole or the spider, hostile family members worked in darkness and silence to undermine seemingly impregnable reputations, even to destroy their enemies.

Poisoning, the most extreme of solutions, was greatly facilitated by the development of arsenic and later phosphorus. In 1840 Dr. Cornevin wrote: "There is a crime which lurks in the shadows, which creeps into the family home, which frightens society, which seems, owing to the artifices of its employment and the subtlety of its effects, to defy the apparatus and the analysis of science, which intimidates, through doubt, the consciences of juries, and which is proliferating at a frightening rate year after year: that crime is poisoning." An old tradition associated the crime of poisoning with women, whose weakness and nature inclined them to act by stealth and whose domestic occupations offered ample opportunity. Marie Lafarge, who despite persistent denials was convicted in 1838 of having poisoned a husband who did not live up to her dreams, served as a prototype for the suspicions of many a mother-in-law after the death of a beloved son. Between 1825 and 1885 crime records reveal 2,169 cases of poisoning which claimed 831 victims; 1,969 suspects were charged in these crimes, 916 of them men and 1,053 (or 53 percent) women. (Compare this with the fact that women were accused in only 20 percent of crimes overall.) Poisoning reached a peak in the years between 1840 and 1860 and declined sharply thereafter. Even at its height, however, it never lived up to the fantasies of the age.

Among rural people and workers, fighting was more common, and brawls between groups of brothers or cousins were a quick, convenient way of settling scores. Wife-beating was a male prerogative. Battery and abuse were alleged by 80 percent of women asking for separation from their husbands. Husbands, often drunk or in need of a physical outlet after a long day at work, beat their wives not so much for infidelity as for being spendthrifts and bad housekeepers. "Dinner wasn't ready and the fire had gone out," was one man's excuse for beating his wife to death.

Indeed death sometimes was the denouement of that popular classic, the marital squabble. Joëlle Guillais-Maury has studied a hundred "crimes of passion" committed in late-nineteenth-century Paris. Nearly all of them were acts committed by men, usually young men, against women, in revenge for an offense against the man's honor. Murder was a way for a man to say, "You are my woman, you belong to me." Guillais-Maury's cases involved both married and unmarried women who refused to sleep with men they did not like or who took a lover or who walked out on a man with whom they had been living. With surprising vitality and extremely blunt language these women insisted on their freedom of choice and movement. They also openly avowed their desires and complained of the men's infidelity, brutality, and either impotence or sexual tyranny. "It was hell," one of them said. Their bodies, they asserted, were subject to no law but their own. But they paid dearly for these claims, often with their lives.[45]

Women were the principal victims of family violence of every variety. Flaubert's mistress, Louise Pradier, was thrown out by her husband: "They took her children from her. They took everything. She lives on an income of 6,000 francs in a furnished room without a maid, in misery" (letter from Flaubert dated May 2, 1845). Flaubert also mentions a working-class woman who had an affair with a prominent citizen of Rouen. As a result, her husband killed her, sealed her body in a bag, and threw it into the water; for this crime he was sentenced to just four years in prison. One staple of the crime reports of the period was the woman whose body was hacked to pieces, a paroxysmal illustration of the violent opposition of some men to woman's desire for emancipation.

Deuxième Année. — N° 83.   Huit pages : CINQ centimes   Dimanche 7 Septembre 1890.

Le Petit Parisien

TOUS LES SAMEDIS
SUPPLÉMENT LITTÉRAIRE
5 CENTIMES

SUPPLÉMENT LITTÉRAIRE ILLUSTRÉ

TOUS LES JOURS
Le Petit Parisien
5 CENTIMES

"The Ville-d'Avray Affair," *Le Petit Parisien,* September 17, 1890. It was rare for a bourgeois wife to kill her husband, and in any case she would have been more likely to use poison than a knife, a man's weapon. These paradoxical details amused the readers of illustrated supplements to the major newspapers. Crime stories dramatized the problems of private life. (Paris, Musée des Arts et Traditions Populaires.)

Private Vengeance

Violence as a form of private vengeance, both inside and outside the family, remained quite common among the poorer classes of society. Anne-Marie Sohn, who has scoured a half-century of judicial archives in search of female roles, has found almost no cases of private vengeance outside those classes.[46] Louis Chevalier has described the violence of working-class brawls in the first half of the nineteenth century.[47] Men clashed outside taverns and dance halls, often over women. (Italians, alleged to be adept at seduction, were often victims.) Young toughs slashed each other to pieces in vacant lots or in the deserted environs of Paris's outer walls. If the police attempted to intervene, they could easily find both sides in a brawl arrayed against the forces of order. Such brawling suggests a direct, unmediated relation to the body.

In the countryside the vendetta in its pure form was scarcely to be found anywhere outside of Corsica. From homicide statistics and administrative reports, however, it is possible to identify a "region of vengeance" covering almost the whole southern part of the Massif Central, including Velay, the Vivarais, and Gévaudan, an area that some demographers have identified as one of patriarchal family structure. Through investigation of lengthy series of criminal records, Claverie and Lamaison have unearthed a variety of kinds of revenge. They also note a connection between rising family tensions and the difficulties faced by disinherited younger sons proletarianized by the stagnation of the economy. Intense frustration sometimes caused rocks to fall unexpectedly, fires to break out, or murderous brawls to take place; there were also strange cases of bewitchment.[48]

Yet at the same time Claverie and Lamaison note that people were increasingly willing to turn to the police, to use legal violence as the means of, or substitute for, private violence. Filing complaints gradually supplanted setting fires or starting riots. But people hesitated to go to court, for they were intuitively aware of the fact that a lawsuit brought into play a whole new set of rules, under which everyone, plaintiffs and defendants alike, risked exposure. Attempts were often made to settle out of court, to reach an amicable understanding. If these efforts failed, however, the suit or criminal trial might be allowed to proceed. At one time people had not minded being forced to appear in court or even being sent to prison; these were affronts to be endured with panache and bravado. Now they became matters of dishonor, and dishonor alone was sometimes enough to satisfy the thirst for vengeance. This use of the courts signifies an increasingly individualized conception of justice, a conception that helped put the courts, once shunned by the poor, at the very center of working-class behavior.

The right to private vengeance, which was fairly widely acknowledged by juries, at least in regard to crimes of passion and particularly where female adultery was the motive, became less acceptable to criminologists after the turn of the twentieth century. These experts looked upon private vengeance as a mark of primitivism or even madness; writing in *La Revue des deux mondes* in 1910, Brunetière, a spokesman for enlightened opinion, called such behavior a "negation of the law, a return to barbarism, a regression to animality."

Legal Vengeance

There was nothing novel about filing a complaint with the authorities. Yves and Nicole Castan have studied the way in which people in Languedoc used the courts in the early modern era.[49] Arlette Farge and Michel Foucault have shown how families used lettres de cachet and the police when domestic peace was threatened.[50] In the nineteenth century these kinds of behavior took on new forms: the recourse to reform schools (to which youths were sent on request by their families) and confinement for psychiatric reasons under the law of 1838.

Although the number of youths sent to reform school was small (a record 1,527 confinement orders were issued in 1869), some 74,090 youths served time between 1846 and 1913. These institutions were particularly important in the Seine département (including Paris), which accounts for 75 percent of all confinement orders issued between 1840 and 1868 and for 62 percent of those issued between 1896 and 1913. At first the reform schools were primarily an instrument of the wealthier classes, but their use expanded to the poorer strata of society, particularly after an 1885 law exempted poor families from paying the cost of the inmate's room and board. In 1894–95, 78 percent of all applications to send a child to reform school came from the families of manual laborers. The high proportion of young women in the reform schools is striking. Between 1846 and 1913, 40.8 percent of inmates were female, a figure far in excess of the proportion of females among juvenile delinquents (16 to 20 percent from 1840 to 1862, 10 to 14 percent from 1863 to 1910). Fathers confined

Child Martyr, 1877. Physical punishment of children varied with the country, the educational system, and attitudes toward the body. (Paris, Bibliothèque Nationale.)

girls whom they feared would become pregnant or who were guilty of "misbehavior," which was the main reason cited for sending young women away. Virginity remained the most precious form of capital.

Reform schools became an object of bitter controversy between those who favored unconditional parental authority and those who championed the "interests of the child" and tended to blame the family environment for youthful misdeeds—men such as the Catholic jurist Bonjean, head of the Société Générale des Prisons, editor of *La Revue pénitentiaire,* and author of *Enfants révoltés et parents coupables* (Rebellious Children and Guilty Parents, 1895). At the end of the century it was far more common to denounce not youthful offenders but ill treatment by beastly parents, whom it was proposed to relieve of their responsibilities. Despite the law of 1889 (concerning the removal of parents from responsibility for their children) and that of 1898 (concerning parental mistreatment), reform schools continued to operate in deteriorating conditions until 1935. That year a new law made the confinement of children in reform schools illegal but allowed parents to place their children in correctional institutions, where conditions were so deplorable that there was hardly any difference. This hesitance to interfere with institutions for dealing with youthful offenders has been explained as the result of a powerful consensus, encompassing both the broad public and legal experts, concerning the principle of authority.[51] The changes do, however, indicate a diminution of the privacy of the poor vis-à-vis the state. In the name of the child's interest— the interest of the child considered as a social being—the state exerted growing power over families, for better or worse.

The law of 1838 enabled families to confine in institutions people classed not as dangerous, undesirable, or undisciplined but as insane. Hence the asylum was not the successor of the Bastille but a radically different kind of institution. It symbolizes the medicalization of confinement, in which medical authority outweighed governmental authority. No prefect was allowed to sign a confinement order unless a doctor had issued a certificate of insanity.[52] This medical authority may well have been put to illegitimate uses, and some deviant behavior may have been unreasonably categorized as "madness," but the fact remains that governmental authority in this regard was now limited by the need for medical certification.

Confinement in Mental Institutions

One example of the abuse of medical authority was the case, mentioned earlier, of Clémence de Cerilley, whose husband, with the aid of his greedy family and the backing of a physician, had her committed on grounds that included "exaggerated mystical beliefs." Another was the case of Hersilie Rouy, subjected to "voluntary commitment" through the machinations of a half brother who, in the hope of winning her inheritance, enlisted the support of one Dr. Pelletan. The compliant doctor certified that Hersilie, an unmarried artist (who, being an independent woman, had sought to live in solitude), was suffering from "acute monomania"; as a result of this she spent fourteen years in an asylum. Still another case of abuse was that of Mme Dubourg, whose husband had her locked up because she refused to go to bed with him; ultimately he killed her. In recent years we have rediscovered such women as Adèle Hugo and Camille Claudel, who apparently were confined as a result of arbitrary decisions on the part of families intent on safeguarding the reputations of two famous men.

A more subtle issue concerns the notion of normality implicit in the nosology of female mental illness.[53] Female mental illness often involved allegations of exaggeration or excess, particularly in regard to amorous passion and above all when that passion assumed forbidden forms: love of the father, lesbianism, love for a younger man, clitorism, or the mere exercise of free choice. Trélat, the author of *La Folie lucide* (1861), wrote: "All women are made for feeling, and feeling is almost hysteria."[54] Sexual and familial disequilibrium, he maintained, was the principal source of dementia. Conversely, family harmony was a guarantee of sanity.

Madness could be a consequence of a genuine family misfortune. Among insane women there were many abandoned lovers, women who had made bad marriages or who had been deceived by their husbands, and mothers mourning lost children. Male insanity seems to have had more to do with the vicissitudes of public and professional life. Bankruptcy, peculation, gambling—these were the things that women denounced as the causes of madness among men—and men constituted a majority of asylum inmates.

Although the police continued to use their authority to have troublesome individuals committed, more and more inmates entered mental institutions as the result of a private tragedy or family conflict of which the physician was the sole judge and arbiter.

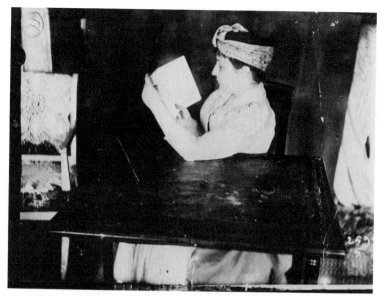

Camille Claudel, Adèle Hugo: two famous victims whose stories, recently brought to light, surely bear witness to a good many others. (Paris, Bibliothèque Marguerite-Durand; Paris, Musée Victor Hugo.)

Separation and Divorce

There were less dramatic ways of ending a troubled marriage. Although divorce was abolished in 1816 and not reinstated until 1884, separation was allowed. Bernard Schnapper has studied the nature and evolution of legal separation from 1837 (when statistical records first become available) until 1914.[55] Separations were rare: at their peak, around 1880, there were only around 4,000 per year, or about thirteen for every ten thousand marriages. The number of separations grew very noticeably after 1851, when a law was passed making legal assistance available to anyone who applied for separation. Previously the procedure had been used mainly by the bourgeoisie, but now it was embraced by the poorer classes. In the period 1837–1847, only 24 percent of applicants had been "workers, servants, or housekeepers," but this figure rose sharply to 48.8 percent in the period 1869–1883. Furthermore, separation was a female institution. The percentage of female applicants ranged from 86 to a high of 93. Most were older women, often mothers, with many years of marriage behind them. Usually they were women pushed to the breaking point not so much by their husbands' infidelity as by abuse: "It was the battered woman and not the deceived woman who filed for separation." Separation was most common in northern France, in the more highly urbanized and better educated parts of the country. In short, it was a sign of modernity, as was divorce, whose geographical distribution in 1896 was virtually the same as that of separation. Dalloz's legal dictionary finally noted an expansion of the acceptable grounds for separation: case law is a good indicator of changing mores.

Divorce exhibited similar characteristics: the same distribution, the same preponderance of female applicants (80 percent), and the same grounds (either battery or mental cruelty was cited in 77 percent of the applications in 1900). Divorce was a slightly more bourgeois institution than separation, however. Compared with applications for separation, applications for divorce show a higher proportion of office workers and professional people. A consequence of the Revolution, divorce (first legalized in 1792) was particularly popular among urban women. Bonald and the ultramonarchists campaigned for and obtained its abolition in 1816. Later, radicals such as Alfred Naquet made divorce a central issue once again, and in alliance with the Opportunists they succeeded in having it reinstated in 1884. To be sure, the positions of husband and wife remained highly unequal. Husbands were allowed to

Numéro 249.

PRIX DU NUMÉRO : 40 CENTIMES

4 Octobre 1884.

A. ROBIDA
RÉDACTEUR EN CHEF

La Caricature

JOURNAL
HEBDOMADAIRE

Abonnements d'un an, Paris et départements : 20 francs. — Union postale : 24 francs. — Trois mois : 7 francs. — Bureaux : 7, rue du Croissant

FESTIN DE DIVORCE. — Texte et Dessins par A. ROBIDA

FESTIN DE DIVORCE

« Le Tribunal civil de la Seine vient de pronon-
» cer le divorce entre Monsieur Eugène Pont-
» douilly et Madame Pontdouilly, née Berjou.
» Monsieur Pontdouilly et Mademoiselle Berjou,
» ex-dame Pontdouilly, ont le plaisir de vous en
» faire part.
» Et vous prient d'assister à la signature à la
» mairie et au repas de divorce qui aura lieu au
» restaurant ***, le ..... »

Not always a tragedy, divorce was sometimes by mutual consent. Robida's optimistic humor reflects a striking change in attitudes and the decline of the old belief in the indissolubility of marriage. *La Caricature* was one of the best satirical papers of the early Third Republic. *La Caricature*, October 4, 1884. (Paris, Bibliothèque des Arts Décoratifs.)

introduce as evidence compromising letters received by their wives, but wives could not use letters received by their husbands. For a woman to call her husband "scum and skunk" was grounds for divorce; for a man to call his wife "cow and sow" was not. In 1904, however, a law was passed making it legal for a divorced person to marry his or her companion in adultery, and in 1908 another law provided that after three years of legal separation either party could file for and be granted a divorce. Thus the divorce laws were liberalized, to the great scandal of outraged conservatives led by the writer Paul Bourget. Despite the misgivings of Catholics and the disapproval of the devout, divorce became an accepted part of life, although it still remained quite rare—only 15,000 divorces were granted in 1913. Still, divorce challenged the notion that marriage was indissoluble and asserted the right of a husband or wife to look for love or simply for happiness and understanding, thereby strengthening the idea, accepted today, that marriage is a free contract.

Before that point could be reached, people's thinking about marriage had had to evolve considerably, and France had had to move a considerable distance toward separation of church and state under the Third Republic. Even more important, it had taken a long struggle by feminists and their allies to change people's minds. From Claire Démar and George Sand (whose first novels, *Indiana* and *Lélia* were briefs in favor of divorce) to Maria Deraisme and Hubertine Auclert, the feminist clamor for divorce had been unrelenting. That clamor became especially insistent when institutions were weak, as in the early days of the Third Republic. In 1873 Léon Richer published *Le Divorce* and, while the Ordre Moral was still at the height of its power, launched an energetic campaign to revise the Civil Code. In 1880 Olympe Audouard and Maria Martin founded the Society of Friends of Divorce, whose organ was *Le Libérateur*. From 1880 to 1884 the campaign was particularly intense.

At the turn of the century, however, feminists apparently became wary lest inequality between the sexes make divorce a powerful weapon in the hands of unfaithful husbands. "Man tires of amorous relations more quickly than woman," Marguerite Durand wrote in *La Fronde*. She warned against granting divorce on the request of one party only and pointed out the danger that it might become a legal means of getting rid of an aging and unwanted spouse. Women, because of their weak social position, required guarantees against abandon-

On July 14, 1881, at the Bastille, a group known as "The Rights of Women," in conjunction with the newspaper *La Citoyenne* (founded by Hubertine Auclert and first published on February 13, 1881) organized a demonstration in favor of political and civil equality for women. (Paris, Bibliothèque Marguerite-Durand.)

In 1887 Hubertine Auclert (1848–1914), the most active of French "suffragettes," wrote: "Political rights are the key to all other rights for women." A police report indicated that "Hubertine Auclert is believed to be suffering from madness and hysteria, a disease that causes her to look upon men as her equals and to seek contact with them." (Paris, Bibliothèque Marguerite-Durand.)

ment; to provide those guarantees would take complete revision of the Civil Code. On April 6, 1880, Hubertine Auclert burst in on a wedding ceremony in the *mairie* of Paris's fifteenth arrondissement and addressed the young bride and groom thus: "*Citoyen et citoyenne,* you have just sworn an oath before a man who represents the Law, but what you have sworn makes no sense. Woman, being man's equal, owes him no obedience." Another century would have to pass before she would be heard.

Paul Mathey, Untitled. Household chores are done and children play while the father is away. (Paris, Musée d'Orsay.)

✑ Roles and Characters

Michelle Perrot

THE FATHER FIGURE

Figurehead of the family as well as of civil society, the father dominates the history of private life in the nineteenth century. Law, philosophy, and politics all conspired to establish and legitimate his authority. From Hegel to Proudhon, from the theorist of the state to the father of anarchy, the power of the father enjoyed majority support. The father bestowed his name upon the child, and, in Kant's words, "legal birth is the only true birth." Deprived of the king, traditionalists sought to restore the father. Revolutionaries and republicans were no less eager to bolster his authority. Republicans placed the keys to the city in the father's hands.[1] Deploring the decline of paternal punishment, Jules Simon wrote: "It is an axiom of political science that authority must be made omnipotent in the family so that it becomes less necessary in the state. Our great republican assemblies erred when they reduced the power of the husband and father."[2]

Republicans deliberated beneath the gaze of Marianne; meanwhile, with statuary all the rage, figures of women became ubiquitous: at the feet of great men or arranged in decorative wreaths around their brows. This extreme investment in symbolism, this frantic celebration of "the Muse and the Madonna," was a way of heightening the differentiation of public from private space.

Portalis wrote: "Differences in the nature of husband and wife imply differences in their respective rights and duties." In the name of nature, the Civil Code granted the husband absolute superiority in the household and the father absolute superiority in the family; the wife and mother were legally

The Rights of Man

Albert Auguste Fourié, *En Famille.* Monsieur, madame, baby, and big sister: in the corner of the salon between the piano and the drapes, the typical nuclear family enjoys a moment of intimacy. (*L'Illustration,* 1892.)

incapacitated. The married woman ceased to be a responsible individual; unmarried and widowed women shouldered far greater responsibilities. Article 213 of the Civil Code all but stripped married women of legal capacities: "The husband is obliged to protect his wife, the wife to obey her husband." A married woman could not serve as guardian of a minor child or be included in family councils; distant male relatives were preferred to fill these roles. A married woman could not witness deeds. If she left her husband's home, she could be returned by the public authorities and compelled to "perform her duties and enjoy her rights in complete liberty." The adulterous woman could be punished by death because her crime struck at what was most sacred in the family: legitimacy of descent. In Gévaudan brief affairs were tolerated, but pregnancies were closely scrutinized. The woman who gave birth to an illegitimate child could expect no mercy. The adulterous man risked nothing, protected as he was by masculine complicity. Custom had required men to marry women they made pregnant; the new Civil Code prohibited paternity suits.

The system of community property, which placed the wife's property under the authority of her husband, gained ever wider acceptance. Neither wife nor minor child (whose legal status was in many ways similar) had the right to determine how their earnings would be spent until a 1907 law finally loosened restrictions in this regard. In late-nineteenth-century Aude wages of couples who worked in the vineyards were paid to the husband. A woman's property was protected only under the *régime dotal,* or else under the terms of a marriage contract providing for complete separation of the wife's property from that of the husband. But in general only the wealthy employed marriage contracts, and even they were less and less likely to do so. Although the Civil Code may have protected the well-to-do, it left poor women at a striking disadvantage. Some men ascribed to the husband even greater powers than the law provided. Alexandre Dumas the younger believed that a deceived husband had every right to avenge himself. Proudhon listed six cases (including immodesty, drunkenness, theft, and wanton spending) in which "the husband may kill his wife in strict paternal justice" (*La Pornocratie ou les Temps modernes,* 1875).

The father's omnipotence extended to the children. Greater sensitivity to childhood had by no means reduced the family's authority or the father's power. In this respect the French Revolution had limited itself to minor reforms: abrogation of paternal authority over grown children, elimination of the right to disinherit an heir, and limitation of the father's right to punish his children. Robespierre proposed taking children from their parents at the age of seven or eight and raising them in common so as to inculcate respect for new ideas, but the matter was never brought up for debate.

Despite Le Play's claim that the Revolution, by abolishing the right to make wills, had "killed the father," the Civil Code actually perpetuated many old ideas. Even the grown child was required to "show sacred respect at the sight of his progenitors," and, if "nature and law loosen the bonds of paternal authority on the child, reason tightens the knots." Until 1896 no one under the age of twenty-five could marry without parental consent.

A father could request that his child be arrested and held in state prisons just as he had been able to do under the old system of lettres de cachet. Thus, the state lent its support to the system of paternal punishment and, by acting as the father's proxy, helped maintain order in families. The conditions under which the public authorities acted were established by Articles 375 to 382 of the Civil Code (Book I, Title IX): "The father who has very serious grounds for discontent with a child's behavior" was permitted to appeal to a local court known as the *tribunal d'arrondissement*. Until the age of sixteen the child could be held for no more than one month; from age sixteen until majority he could be held for up to six months. Formalities were minimal, as were the guarantees

It took quite a long time for photography to invade the domestic interior, where people had to pose among the props of everyday life. The relatively bare setting reflects early-20th-century ideas of domestic comfort. (Sirot-Angel Collection.)

against abuse. No written statement was required and no judicial formalities except perhaps the arrest warrant itself, which did not have to specify the reasons for the arrest. If the child, once released from jail, "committed new offenses," a fresh detention could be ordered. In order to allow poor families to avail themselves of this service, the state, in 1841 and again in 1855, agreed to meet the cost of feeding and housing the prisoner if the family could not pay. The child held as a result of paternal punishment was treated in much the same way as the juvenile delinquent found to have acted "without cognizance": if the family, that is, the father, was unwilling to take the child back, he (or she) could be held in prison until he reached his majority.

The insane and feeble-minded had no rights as citizens. Under the law of 1838 they could be held on request of their families. The husband's power over his wife was confirmed in this area too, as is shown by the story of Clémence de Cerilley, the sister of Emilie, whose family had to go to extraordinary lengths to secure her release from a confinement obtained with little difficulty by her husband. Confinement of "madwomen" increased dramatically over the course of the nineteenth century: from 9,930 in 1845–1849 the number of female lunatics rose to 20,000 in 1871, according to Yanick Ripa. In 80 percent of the cases these women were committed at the behest of men (a third of them husbands, the rest fathers and employers).[3] It is true that women filed even more petitions for commitment than men, such petitions being used largely as a means of maintaining order in the family.

Powers

The father's powers were twofold. He totally dominated public space. He alone enjoyed political rights. Politics was exclusively a male bastion in the nineteenth century, so much so that Guizot recommended that political matters not be discussed in that female preserve, the high-society salon. The comtesse Arconati-Visconti, in whose salon republicans gathered at the end of the century, was asked by Gambetta to exclude women for a day in order to facilitate serious discussion; she complied.

The father's powers were also domestic. They were exercised over the private sphere, which was not, as is sometimes thought, the exclusive domain of women, even if the role of women in it did increase. Man was master first and foremost through the power of money. In bourgeois households he controlled expenditures by limiting his wife's allowance to a sum often barely adequate to cover basic needs. The affectionate Caroline Orville could not understand why her husband, in a time of war and separation (1871), made such a fuss over a dressmaker's bill, the only expenditure she allowed herself, because she "wished to be presentable"—as it was her duty to be. Even the most generous of men wielded power through their control of the purse, as is evident in the case of Victor Hugo, who, concerned about the unity of the "tribe," sought to keep his family with him in Guernsey by denying those who wished to escape the money they needed for travel. His scrutiny weighed particularly heavily on his wife and on his daughter Adèle, who were totally dependent on him. Hugo complained that he was nothing but the family "treasurer."[4] But how could it have been otherwise? The financial power of the father was tempered only in the cities, where wives of workers and shopkeepers won the much-coveted position of "family minister of finance."

Fundamental decisions were left to the father. In the economic sphere his powers even seemed to increase. In northern France in the first half of the nineteenth century bourgeois women played an important role in managing family businesses, serving as bookkeepers, secretaries, or even, as in the case of Mélanie Pollet, plant managers.[5] In the second half of the century, however, they retreated to their homes, now located away from the plant with which they had nothing more to do.

Decisions concerning education, particularly of sons, and marriages were made by the father. Martin Nadaud's mother saw little reason for her son to attend school, because she wanted to put him to work in the fields as soon as possible. His father decided otherwise, however, in this instance showing enlightened thinking. Many matches were made by fathers; mothers, moved by sentiment as in the comedies of Molière, took the side of their tearful daughters. Mme Hugo, for instance, took Adèle's side in her bitter battle with Victor.

In many cases the father's decision was based on scientific argument and reason. In opposition to women—devout and mysterious, overly moved by sentiment, tempted by passion, prey to madness—the male, the father, was supposed to protect the rights of intelligence. On such grounds Kant, Comte, and Proudhon laid claim to primacy in the household on behalf of the father; the home was too important to be left to feeble women.

On the same grounds a husband had the right to monitor

Trousers were for men only. Woe unto the couple in which the woman wore the pants! This possibly deceived husband reminds his wife, on her knees, who is boss. A fin-de-siècle variation on a very old subject. (Paris, Bibliothèque des Arts Décoratifs.)

his wife's acquaintances, visits, travels, and correspondence. At the end of the nineteenth century there was a major controversy over this issue, one that reveals both the extent of an individualistic feminism (shared by some men) and its limitations. No measure was actually taken to protect the privacy of a woman's correspondence, and most magistrates held against women who attempted to invoke this right. In March 1887 *Le Temps* asked its readers to express their opinions on the question and published some of the many responses it received. A strong proponent of a husband's authority over his wife, Alexandre Dumas the younger stated that "a husband who has doubts about his wife and who hesitates to inform himself by opening the letters she receives is an imbecile." A priest cited Church doctrine: "The husband is master in the home." Pressensé, striking a balance between the law and mores, offered a far subtler opinion, whereas Juliette Adam and Mme de Peyrebrune came down clearly on the side of freedom, although with important reservations. Adam believed that everyday reality was in contradiction with the Civil Code. A woman could "achieve freedom in spite of the law." She could correspond "with her mother, her sisters, her daughters, and her friends." Mme de Peyrebrune stressed the logic of the jurists' position, a "consequence of laws restricting a woman's moral freedom in marriage." Hence the law needed changing. In 1897 the *substitut* for the *procureur général* of the court of appeals of Toulouse reviewed arguments on both sides in a lecture delivered at the court's annual opening session, only to conclude that the husbands' rights were legitimate and that most women were happy to be protected from themselves by being forced to submit to their spouse's will. In case law the question was no less controversial. One thorny question concerned the secrecy of confidential letters, which were not supposed to be communicated to third parties. This right of secrecy was so powerful that when the recipient of confidential letters died, it was accepted that the sender could ask that the letters be returned. The problem for judges was to determine whether or not a husband should be regarded as a third party.[6]

The Father's House

Although the man of the house was often away, he still dominated the home. He had rooms of his own: the smoking room and billiard parlor to which the men retired to talk after a formal dinner; the library, because books—and bibliophilia—remained a masculine affair; and the office, which the children never entered without trembling. According to the Goncourt brothers, Sainte-Beuve was never truly himself except in his second-floor den, far from the nagging women on the floor below. Even working women had no office in the home, the office being an extension of public space into the private space of the household. Pauline Reclus-Kergomard, who became a kindergarten inspector in 1879, sorted her papers on the dining room table, while her husband Jules daydreamed in his empty office, much to the dismay of her son.[7]

In the salon roles were divided and positions marked out. Kant defined male and female roles quite strictly. Victor Hugo's salon, in which the men stood in a group in the center of the room while the seated women formed a wreath around the periphery, may be taken as a model of its kind. Men chose interior decor to a much greater extent than is generally believed. According to manuals of etiquette, when a well-bred man prepared to marry, he and his future mother-in-law jointly selected furnishings for what would become the couple's home. But Jules Ferry "inundated his brother with letters concerning the apartment [he] desired" for his future home with Eugénie Risler and with directives "concerning the moving and the color of the curtains and rugs."[8] A veritable Pygmalion, Ferry also taught his wife how to dress, how to choose her hats, and how to exploit her natural beauty. Men displayed women to advantage not only on the stage and through fash-

In the 19th century men met
and relaxed in clubs, cafés, and
billiard halls, places where no
respectable woman would set
foot.

Right: *The Café La Manille,*
1899. (Paris, Bibliothèque
Nationale.)
Below: Amédée Julien Marcel-
Clément, *Le Billard,* 1900.

ion but also in the home. Wealthy men—great collectors—filled their homes with acquisitions and fantasies. For them interior decoration was not feathering a nest but creating an image.

Victor Hugo dreamed of a home that would be the center of his world—and therefore of *the* world. Exile in Guernsey provided him with an opportunity in the form of Hauteville House, which he personally purchased, renovated, and decorated. His wife objected, confiding to her sister, "I do not like to see us owning property." Adèle, who loved travel and cities, was only too well aware of the bondage implicit in striking roots as well as of the loneliness that her children would be enforced to endure for want of young companions. "I concede that with your fame, your mission, your personality, you have chosen a rock in which you are admirable in your proper setting, and I understand that your family, which amounts to something only through you, is sacrificing itself not only to your honor but also to your image," she wrote Victor in 1857. "I love you, I belong to you, and I will obey you. But I cannot be an abject slave. There are circumstances in which a person needs to be free." A patriarch, the father sat enthroned like a god in the tabernacle of his home.

Hugo, called by his son a "gentle tyrant," was probably one of the most grandiose father figures of the century. To a sublime degree he bore all the physical and moral marks of fatherhood: generosity and despotism, devotion and power. He also exhibited all the foolishness and pettiness of the bourgeois male with his mistresses and his fear of what people might say. And he displayed the selfishness and cruelty of one who preferred to see his demented daughter locked up in a *maison de santé* rather than endure the opprobrium her presence at home might bring to "our name." Of his daughter he wrote, "A misfortune can occur at any time," and Henri Guillemin remarks that he seemed to hope for one. The power of a father whose glory was impugned might extend to murder, in which case "killing the father" was no mere symbol but a necessary means of survival.

The nineteenth century offers many examples of triumphant and dominating father figures. Many creative men turned their homes into studios and their wives and daughters and sisters into secretaries. Examples include Proudhon, Elisée Reclus, Renan, and Marx. We know a great deal about Marx's home life from his correspondence with his daughters and their correspondence among themselves. They adored him, and he was an attentive father, but he could also be tyrannical and meddlesome when it came to their choice of husbands or careers. Eleanor was virtually forced to give up the stage and renounce her love for Lissagaray in favor of Aveling, whose socialism her father preferred but who eventually betrayed her. Secluded with the ailing Marx, who did not understand her, Eleanor joined the army of young women sacrificed to their father's reputations and desires. Yet it was often the same father who opened the gates of the world to a young woman, for his power was the supreme form of male power, exercised over everyone but most of all over the weak, the dominated and protected.

The father figure was a part of Protestant, Jewish, and atheist as well as Catholic culture. Not an exclusively bourgeois phenomenon, the powerful father belonged to society as a whole. Proudhon, for whom paternity was a powerful urge, construed fatherhood as a kind of honor. As a young man he thought of procuring himself a child by "paying a monetary compensation to a young woman whom I would have seduced for the purpose." At forty-one he married a young working-class woman of twenty-seven, "simple, gracious, and naive," devoted to work and to her duties, "the gentlest and most docile of creatures," a woman he had glimpsed in the street and to whom he had proposed in a letter that might have been a textbook specimen of the genre. He chose his wife to take the place of his mother: "Had she lived, I would not have married." But "instead of love I had the fantasy of a home and fatherhood . . . My wife's gratitude gained me three daughters, blond and pink, whose mother nursed them herself and whose existence fills all my soul." He went on to write that "paternity has filled an immense void in me." It was "like a magnification of my existence, a kind of immortality."

Paternity was the most basic way for a proletarian male to perpetuate his memory, property, and reputation. The traditional rural definition of male honor in terms of paternity and virility was taken up by the working class, whose identity it helped to shape.

The Death of the Father

Of all the scenes of private life, the death of the father was the most significant, the most charged with meaning and emotion. This was the scene recounted in stories and painted in pictures. The deathbed was no longer the place where a man expressed his last wishes; these were now regulated by

Jules Boquet, *Mourning*. An increasingly acute awareness of the individual in the 19th century made death a more important, wrenching, and private affair than ever before. Many men died young, leaving women alone to guard their memories. (Rouen, Musée des Beaux-Arts.)

Medal inscribed "To Our Father." (Paris, Bibliothèque Nationale.)

law. Still, it was the scene of final farewells, transfers of power, great gatherings, pardons, and reconciliations, and of course it was also the source of new rancor born of terminal injustice.

A mother died discreetly. Widowed, alone, advanced in age, she had already watched her children leave home. Rarely was she allowed to retain possession of the key to business premises or domestic pantry. In Gévaudan she was more likely than not regarded as one more mouth to feed by the child designated to be her husband's heir, who might grudgingly offer her and her other children lodging in the family home.

When a father was about to die, he "summoned his children," as in the fable. In Lille, Caroline Brame witnessed the death of old Louis Brame, known as Bon-Papa, the founder of a dynasty. The feuding brothers gathered around the death-bed. Caroline's diary describes the scene: "Bon-Papa kissed us all. Then he called my father and my Uncle Jules to his side, handed them his books, explained the state of his affairs, and commended his servants. On his face there was an expression of ineffable heavenliness." Proudhon's father, a poor cask maker, chose to die in princely fashion, at the end of a meal to which he had invited relatives and friends to say his fare-wells: "I wanted to die among you. Now serve the coffee."

In any family the father's death was a major economic and emotional blow. It was the event that dissolved the family and allowed other families to come into being and individuals to go their separate ways. In some families, therefore, indi-vidual members longed for the father's death, so there were stringent laws against parricide. A sacrilegious act for which acquittal was rare, parricide led almost certainly to the scaffold and left a blot on the family name.

There were many ways of killing a father short of murder, however, including the child's own neurosis. Sartre saw Flau-bert's illness as "murder of his father," Achille-Cléophas, who wanted young Gustave to enter a career in the law. "Gustave would become a notary. He would become a notary because he was one already, by virtue of a predestination that was nothing other than the will of Achille-Cléophas."[9] Sartre con-tinues: "Flaubert's neurosis was the father himself, that abso-lute other, that superego within, which had constituted him as impotent negativity." His father's death lifted an unbearable burden from Flaubert's shoulders. The day after the burial he declared himself cured. "Its effect on me was like the effect of cauterization on a wart . . . At last! At last! I was going to work."

The death of the father was an important element in the

serialized novels of the early nineteenth century, novels in which family structure played a powerful role. The father's death was the only way for a son to achieve maturity and take a wife of his own.

Abolition of the right to make wills, which Le Play called a murder of the father, allowed and encouraged estates to be broken up and dissolved the power of patriarchy. In regions where the extended family was dominant, this abolition was seen as a destructive move and therefore resisted; in other areas, such as central France, it was welcomed as progressive. In 1907 Emile Guillaumin denounced the old customs of the extended family as "an exploitation of children by their father" and hoped that such abuse would be banned forever. Even in regions where Occitanian culture survived, tensions over this issue grew over the course of the century.

As the nineteenth century progressed, the father's legal prerogatives were slowly—very slowly—eroded. This erosion was due partly to growing demands by women and children and partly to increasing intervention by the state, particularly in the lives of poor families, on the grounds that the father was incapable of providing for certain vital needs. The law of 1889 on paternal incompetence and of 1898 on the mistreatment of children afforded the state a greater role, ostensibly in order to protect the interests of the child. The law of 1912, the culmination of repeated efforts since 1878, finally granted women the right to go to court to prove paternity in cases not only of abduction or rape but also of "fraudulent seduction" (where documentary evidence could be produced). Proponents of the law—philanthropists, legislators, and clergy—championed the unwed mother and the abandoned child.

Increased legal capacity for wives attests to a reduction in the powers of the husband; so does the right of divorce (granted in 1884) and separation, most divorces coming at the behest of the woman. Study of case law confirms this impression. Consider, for example, the question of visiting rights for the maternal grandparents of separated couples' children who are in the custody of their father. Until the Second Empire fathers had no obligation to allow visits by grandparents. In 1867, however, a precedent-setting decision granted the request of the maternal grandparents, "in the interest of the child."

But the law did no more than grant its timid and belated sanction to steady, silent pressures emanating from within the family itself, pressures that ultimately resulted in the family's transformation. The democratic family, based on free contract, which Tocqueville observed in early nineteenth-century America was not a natural, evolutionary consequence of modern society; rather it was the result of a compromise—a compromise which itself stimulated new desires.

MARRIAGE AND HOUSEHOLD

Marriage, the crucible of the family, has been the focus of numerous anthropological and demographic studies, whose results need be described here only briefly. In the next chapter Anne Martin-Fugier will describe marriage ceremonies, and later Alain Corbin will discuss the growing importance of sentiment, of demands for emotional and sexual fulfillment.

For now let us confine our attention to a few important features of nineteenth-century marriage. The heterosexual couple established a powerful norm, which led to the rejection of homosexuality and celibacy. The nineteenth century characteristically was focused on marriage, which fulfilled innumerable functions. Marriage was both a strategic alliance and a device for meeting sexual needs. In the words of Michel Foucault, "the family was the agent of exchange between sexuality and marriage. It transported law and the legal di-

The inevitable marriage photo preserved the memory of a "great day." Studio backdrop. (Sirot-Angel Collection.)

mension into the apparatus of sexuality, and it transported the economy of pleasure and intensity of sensation into the rules of marriage."[10] The exchange rate varied, but the bourgeoisie was the power behind this particular economy: consciousness of the body was a form of consciousness of self. Marriage and desire were not always compatible—far from it. Conflict between the two was often the source of family drama and marital tragedy. The more rigorous a family's marital strategy, the more it sought to channel or stifle desire. As individualism became a more powerful force, people began to rebel against arranged marriages—the source of many a romantic drama and of countless crimes of passion.

These characteristic features of nineteenth-century marriage are reflected in demographic statistics. The marriage rate was generally high and stable (around sixteen per thousand), with the exception of two depressed periods, one during the Second Empire, the other, more marked, in the years 1875–1900. This second decline in the marriage rate worried demographers, who had previously been concerned by a drop in the birthrate. The result was a moralistic campaign against celibacy. The celibacy rate was in fact quite low: only slightly more than 10 percent of men and 12 percent of women above the age of fifty remained unmarried.

A second remarkable demographic feature of the period was a lowering of the age of marriage. In traditional societies late marriage (related to the need to provide for a family) was the principal means of contraception. Proudhon said that his ancestors married "as late as possible." Wary of sexual influence, he continued to favor late marriage. In the nineteenth century, however, earlier marriage became possible for two reasons. First, attitudes toward contraception changed (even if the methods remained quite rudimentary). Second, acceptance of smaller amounts of property as sufficient to support a family made it easier to consider marriage at an earlier age.

Peasants on small plots, workers, and even bourgeois wanted to set up their own households as soon as possible. "In the civilized world," Taine wrote, man's principal needs are "an occupation and a home." A home of one's own was also the best way of escaping parental authority and living independently. Women especially began to seek younger, more desirable partners and refused to marry graybeards. When George Sand expressed astonishment at the nearly forty years' difference in age between her grandmother and her grandfather, Dupin de Francueil, she elicited her grandmother's splendid response: "It was the Revolution that brought

The League of Fathers and Mothers of Large Families was founded by Captain Maire in 1908 to encourage reproduction in a country whose birthrate had allegedly fallen too low. Parents with at least four children were eligible for membership. The league pressed the authorities for "laws offering protection and assistance to those who represent the country's future." Captain Maire, shown in this picture, obviously practiced what he preached. (Paris, Bibliothèque Marguerite-Durand.)

old age into the world." The gentle Caroline Brame rebelled against these customs. Attending the marriage of a young woman to "a friend of her father's, a man twice her age," she commented: "That [kind of marriage] would not please me at all" (*Journal,* 25 November 1864). Her tastes led her to a young man of her own age, nineteen, of whom her family did not approve.

In truth, average rates and tendencies do not mean much in areas that depended heavily on family structures. The maps drawn up by Hervé Le Bras and Emmanuel Todd are eloquent in this regard. "The rate of early marriage is a good indicator of the type of control exerted by the social system over young adults . . . A high marriage age indicates an authoritarian family structure. This type of structure yields large numbers of bachelors, who live all their lives as grown-up children or eternal uncles in the families of their married brothers or sisters."[11] The age of marriage for women was particularly high in Brittany, the southern Massif Central, the Pays Basque, Savoy, and Alsace in 1830; by 1901 it had declined somewhat. Malthusian practices persisted in Catholic areas, since the Church preferred the "restraint" of late marriage to other forms of birth control.

The proper social choice of a mate was an important element of family strategy. Homogamy and even endogamy were prominent tendencies in all regions and at all levels of society. This is explained in part by patterns of sociability: people married their peers because they saw them in the ordinary course of life. Social reproduction (in Pierre Bourdieu's sense) was a natural result of these processes, which, though deterministic in their operation, should not be allowed to obscure the freedom of individuals to conform or rebel in a variety of ways.

Marriage with Peers

Endogamy, widespread in rural areas under the ancien régime, declined in the nineteenth century owing to migration. And even those who migrated continued to be subject to family rules. Auvergnats and Limousins who, in the first half of the century, commuted back and forth between Paris and the countryside in a regular seasonal flow, had sexual contacts in the city but married in their native villages. One such person was Martin Nadaud, whose village marriage was the result in part of personal attractiveness (a glance was enough to seduce his intended), in part of scrupulous obedience to his father's wishes.

Men, more mobile than women, were probably the primary beneficiaries of this loosening of contraints. This hypothesis is confirmed by Martine Segalen's study of Vraiville in the Eure département[12] (see the table that follows).

Local marriages of native
residents of Vraiville
(percentage).

Period	Men	Women
1753–1802	63.0	86.0
1853–1902	41.9	89.2

As early as the final third of the eighteenth century an increase in social mixing is evident in the cities. Numerous demographic studies (in Caen, Bordeaux, Lyons, Meulan, Paris, and elsewhere) have shown that the proportion of marriages with persons born outside the city walls increased steadily. Urban neighborhoods soon came to look like rural villages. In nineteenth-century Belleville, "men and women met and married within a very limited space."[13] Familiarity took the place of communal life. Glances, conversation, and flirtation exploded the old proprieties.

Everywhere the rate of homogamy was high. Among bourgeois families, where marriages were dictated by family and company interests, homogamy was the rule; its level was highest where several distinguishing characteristics came into play, as among Protestant industrialists in the cotton trade in Rouen, whose names combined to form a veritable ballet of consanguine cousins. In Gévaudan marriages were governed by strict principles designed to maintain equilibrium among the *oustals;* the circulation of property, dowries, and women was governed by regular cycles. Sons who would inherit married younger daughters; a dowried sister married a younger son.

Workers were also subject to this exchange economy. Glass workers, ribbonmakers, and metalworkers in the Lyons region married within their own groups and before witnesses from the same trade.[14] Work interacted with private life in what scholars call "technical endogamies" based on occupational group, family, and locale. Such endogamic systems have been identified among ribbonmakers in Saint-Chamond, among glass workers in Givors, and among cabinetmakers in the faubourg Saint-Antoine of Paris, where professional as well as radical political traditions were passed from father to son.

In groups where social mobility was minimal there was acute sensitivity to minute hierarchical differences. Marie, a nineteen-year-old glovemaker from Saint-Junien in Haute-Vienne, lived opposite a cousin who happened to be a skiver, a relatively skilled specialty in the glove trade. "There was no thought of romance" between these two young people, according to a scholar who studied Marie's family. "In the workers' hierarchy Marie was too far inferior to her cousin even to consider marriage."

Individuals were keen to discover what amounted to dowries in disguise. Diligent servants and workers were highly prized as wives. Young workers like Norbert Truquin in Lyons saved money to pay off their debts or to start a business. Women acted as the savings institutions of the lower classes.

Impossible Marriages

In 1828 the *Journal des débats* reported on a crime of passion. A working girl of nineteen, the daughter of a tailor, was courted by a coworker of twenty, who escorted her home, "holding her by the arm," and asked her parents for her hand. The family held a council and decided that the young man was neither earnest enough nor talented enough to marry their daughter. The young woman's father did not like the young man's looks: "He doesn't look right to be a tailor." The daughter later testified that "by all appearances I thought I loved him, but since my parents were against it I gave him up." Dismissed, the young man was seized by a murderous rage, his desire thwarted by the iron will of the group. Many nineteenth-century crime stories tell of impossible loves.

For petty-bourgeois families the right marriage could lead to social advancement. Marriage was therefore a matter for strategic calculation and prohibitions. Homogamy was less marked than among workers; individuals sought to marry above their station. Postal clerks, for example, were reluctant to marry coworkers because they dreamed of having wives who did not have to work. Many female postal workers therefore remained unmarried, because they in turn were unwilling to marry manual laborers. For women the price of independence was often solitude. For men climbing the ranks of society, money was less important than a woman's class, distinction, qualities as a homemaker, and even beauty. Charles Bovary was dazzled by Emma, who had a parasol, white skin, and the "fine education" of a "city miss." Well-to-do, he could afford the luxury of a pretty wife with a maid to relieve her of domestic chores.

Marriage was a negotiation conducted by relatives (such as matchmaking aunts), friends, clergymen, and others. Many factors had to be carefully weighed. About 1809 one penniless noble from Lozère who had set his aunt the mission of finding him a wife wrote to inform her of his requirements. At the top of the list was an inheritance sufficient to enable him to keep his house at Mende and his château. One hundred thousand francs would suffice for a person of the same station as himself, but "for a station inferior to mine, her property must more or less compensate for the difference in our positions."[15]

Matrimonial strategies became increasingly diverse and complex as the century progressed. Wealth took many forms: cash, property, businesses, and "expectations." Other elements came into play. Among the terms of exchange were name, reputation, situation (the liberal professions were highly regarded), class, and beauty. Like a king, a rich, elderly man sought to marry a young and beautiful woman. Women distinguished themselves through their appearance in order to attract men. Men in need of cash might accept an unwed mother with property, someone like the heroine of *Marthe*.

Love and Marriage

Personal predilection, of which Hegel was so wary, and even passion, of which families disapproved, also entered the scene. In the second half of the nineteenth century more and more people hoped to reconcile strategic marriage with love and happiness. Such was the dream of Emma Bovary: "Had she been able to establish her life on some great, solid heart, then virtue, affection, sensuality, and duty would have merged into one." Women, for whom marriage was life's only prospect, were especially subject to these influences. Claire Démar (*Ma Loi d'avenir,* 1833) called for a radical change in the education of young girls, who were "left in ignorance even of what men look like." She criticized marriage as "legal prostitution," advocated free choice of a partner, the "need for a fully physical trial of flesh by flesh," and the right of infidelity. Too far ahead of her time, Démar committed suicide; her Saint-Simonian comrades watered down her text and turned it into a tract favoring motherhood.

Less radical, Aurore Dupin, at this time still Mme. Dudevant and not yet George Sand, in a long letter to Casimir dated 15 November 1825, explained her view of their misunderstanding, the disparity in tastes and pleasures that separated them: "I saw that you did not like music, and I stopped spending time on it because the sound of the piano drove you away. You read to be obliging, but after a few lines the book fell from your hands because you were bored and sleepy . . . I began to feel a genuine sorrow at the thought that our tastes might never coincide in the slightest."

Baudelaire too dreamed of shared tastes, but outside marriage. On the day after his breakup with Jeanne after fourteen years of cohabitation, he sighed: "I catch myself thinking, as I look at some handsome object or beautiful scenery or anything at all agreeable, 'Why isn't she with me, why isn't she here to admire that with me or to buy that with me?'" (Letter to Mme. Aupick, 11 September 1856).

Men wanted something more from marriage: not passive submission but consent, and if not an active wife, then at least a loving one. Certain men even wanted a relationship between equals. Michelet counseled men to "create their own wives," and Jules Ferry, a strong supporter of different roles and different spheres for men and women, nevertheless was proud of his marriage to Eugénie Risler: "She is republican and philosophical. She feels as I do on all subjects, and I am proud to feel as she does" (letter to Jules Simon, 7 September 1875).

Eugène Boileau, whose correspondence with his fiancée

has been studied, expressed to perfection the new ideal of the republican couple, which was freethinking, thoroughly imbued with Roman stoicism, and religiously devoted to marital harmony: "When I hear people say 'Marriage . . . is slavery!' I shout, 'No, marriage is tranquillity, it is happiness, it is freedom. Through it, and through it alone, man (by which I mean both sexes)—man having developed to the full can achieve true independence. For he then becomes a complete being, constituting in his very duality the unique human personality" (letter to Marie, 24 March 1873). The ambition was to achieve total unity and therefore self-sufficiency in marriage: "Do not admit anyone else into our private life, into our thoughts." The husband became the confidant of his wife: "I cannot counsel you too strongly to take no other confidant but your friend, to open your heart (but fully) to none other than your husband, to him who is to be, who soon will be, and who I dare say already is at one with you."[16]

HOME LIFE: WOMAN'S REVENGE?

Women, though in general dominated, enjoyed compensations designed to reconcile them to their situation. They were relatively protected. The law concerned itself less with them than with men. For bourgeois women whose mission in life was to keep up appearances, ostentatious luxury had its charms. And women lived longer than men. Certain avenues of action were open to them, particularly as private values changed over the course of a century concerned with utility, anxious for its children, and troubled by its own contradictions. Already Kant had asked how to resolve the contradiction between personal rights—a woman being a person—and the essentially monarchical marital rights of the master. His answer was "personal rights with real modalities." Feminism attacked this chink in the armor of law, as did the "social maternity" rhetoric of church and state. But what were the implications for daily life?

Martine Segalen, Yvonne Verdier, Agnès Fine, and others have done much to clarify the role and place of women in French rural society. Segalen, for one, has registered her strong disagreement with the pessimistic but sketchy accounts of nineteenth-century travelers such as Abel Hugo. Instead, she emphasizes the complementarity of chores in an environment where public and private merged imperceptibly. What

In Rural Society

emerges from her work is a general impression of harmonious equilibrium between the sexes.[17]

Yvonne Verdier has described the leading personalities of Minot in Burgundy as well as their cultural roles, which she sees as rooted in their "biological destinies": "From a woman's biological destiny it was but a short step to her social destiny."[18] Female help (usually employed in the laundry), dressmakers, and cooks wielded knowledge and power in village life. By no means were they shut up in the home.

Agnès Fine has analyzed how mother-daughter and male-female relations affected the contents of a bride's trousseau.[19] From there she has gone on to study how biological facts were accommodated to social realities through symbolism.

These descriptions have a timeless character. The peacefulness of the culture tends to mask the tensions and conflicts that Elisabeth Claverie and Pierre Lamaison focus on their work. In the *oustal* system, in which exchange of women was rigorously determined by exchange of property, wives were often beaten and were not allowed to keep the keys to the pantry. Some were forced to steal in order to survive. Female loyalties were generally destroyed by marriage and fear of

Left: Claude Monet, *Lunch,* 1868. (Frankfurt, Städelsches Kunstinstitut.) Below: Mary Louise McMonnies, *Visit to a Park.* (Rouen, Musée des Beaux-Arts.) Bourgeois women with children and servants at table and in the garden. Note the tranquil serenity of the Monet and the dreamy atmosphere of the McMonnies.

men. Illegitimate pregnancies were severely punished. The lot of unmarried women was particularly difficult. Widows, regarded as dangerous owing to their supposed sexual appetites, were sometimes thrown out of their homes and forced to live in huts with a few belongings and handouts. Young women were preyed upon by shepherds and employers and often raped by men who felt they were making a legitimate display of virility. "Rape was experienced as a variant on the usual behavior of men toward women . . . The idea of bringing charges seems to have been impossible to conceive or formulate. Sexual normality included a range of consequences: violence, frustration, death."[20] Did this particularly harsh oppression of women result from a complex kinship system in which women had a greater likelihood of inheriting property than in other places? In addition, the southeast Massif Central was an area where vendettas were still carried on and blood crimes were common. The contrast between the peaceful and violent images of rural life may also be an artifact of the sources used: proverbs and customs on the one hand, court documents related to conflict on the other.

Mistresses of Bourgeois Households

Urban households seem to have been simpler than rural ones. Here again, however, there was much variety depending on social level and type of housing. The distance from home to workplace was an important factor in determining the autonomy of domestic life, as is abundantly clear from Bonnie Smith's portrait of bourgeois women in northern France. In the first half of the nineteenth century these women participated in the family business, kept the books, and, rather than buy a silk dress, invested in the firm. By the second half this tradition had died out; it was carried on only by elderly widows. In the 1850s and 1860s most women withdrew from the business world and retreated into their homes. Those homes themselves changed as industrial relations took a less paternalistic turn. Plant owners ceased to live within the factory walls or close to the plant gate. As they became wealthy, they fled the smoke, odors, and sight of poverty, congregating in new sections of old cities: on the boulevard de Paris in Roubaix, for example, where sumptuous villas—veritable "châteaux"—were built and where workers came to jeer during strikes. Women now administered the household, their large staffs of servants, and their equally large families, the product of Catholic beliefs and even more of the marital strategies of northern France's textile families.

Out of this environment emerged a domestic morality whose main tenets Smith describes as faith against reason, charity against capitalism, and reproduction as self-justification. Reproduction gave meaning to even the most insignificant activity of the child-burdened *bourgeoise:* between 1840 and 1900 the average number of children per family increased from five to seven. Everything mattered: from cleanliness and interior decoration to quasi-religious adherence to a tyrannical schedule (see the *heures du jour* drawn by Devéria); from the most trivial of woman's work—for one always had to be busy—to obsession with household accounts, which tormented the mistress who had to make do with what her husband granted her and who often had to account to him for every expenditure. Each detail took on moral significance, more symbolic than economic in nature. A woman's life was a language, a ritual, governed by a strict code. Highly self-conscious, these *bourgeoises* of the Nord were neither passive nor resigned. On the contrary, they attempted to turn their vision of the world into a judgment, often peremptory, of the way things were. That vision has sometimes been called "Christian feminism." (Can it be considered feminism? Not if feminism is defined as a quest for equality, for what was claimed here was difference.) It was expressed by novelists such as Mathilde Bourdon, author of *La Vie réelle,* and by Julia Bécour and Joséphine de Gaulle, who wrote a sort of domestic epic in which good and evil, women and men, confront each other. The men's destructive lust for power and money brings chaos and death. Angels of the hearth, the book's virtuous blonde heroines restore sweet harmony to the household.

To varying degrees this same model of consummate domesticity—with a tinge of saintliness that is not altogether Victorian because it bears earmarks of an older Marianism—was found at all levels of the bourgeoisie. Obviously the size of a family's fortune affected the number of servants and the splendor of the household as well as family beliefs and values. The aristocratic nostalgia that remained such a powerful force in the faubourg Saint-Germain was elsewhere tempered by a growing emphasis on utility, which affected the French bourgeoisie more than is generally believed. Some scholars stress the fact that women of the leisure class served a symbolic function; the luxury in which they lived expressed the possession that was the very essence of their husbands' being and also perpetuated the etiquette of the court. Others emphasize the importance of the domestic economy and of the mistress of the household in that economy. Still other scholars note that women's power was based on the child and its needs in regard to health and education. Feminists invoked motherhood in pressing their demands. The French insistence on the difference between men and women no doubt set French feminism apart from its British and American counterparts, which were more exclusively concerned with equal rights for women.

The Homemaker

Among the urban populace the homemaker was an important figure. Most women, whether married or not, were homemakers. Most homemakers were in fact housewives—that is, legitimately married women—especially in families with children. A relatively poor family required a woman "at home." Being at home did not necessarily mean being inside; housing was often of such poor quality that the dwelling was more gathering place than residence. The homemaker performed many different functions. She bore and raised the children—and in working-class families, among the last to limit births, children were still numerous. Wives of artisans and shopkeepers sent their progeny off to wet nurses, but the poorest women suckled their own, baring their breasts like the female traveler in Daumier's drawing of a third-class railway coach. A woman took her children with her wherever she went. As soon as they could walk they became her escort, and children out with their mothers were familiar figures in popular drawings and in early photographs of the city. Very young children also went out alone; intrepid "urchins" played together in streets and yards. Little by little, however, mothers became obsessed with the dangers of the street, which included accidents and bad company. Increasingly the homemaker's day and movements were governed by the child's schedule, especially by school hours.

The homemaker's second function was to care for the family, to perform all sorts of household chores. She shopped for the best price on food, which she obtained by purchase, barter, and indeed gathering, for even in big cities there were many places where food could be had for the picking. She prepared meals, including a separate lunch for her husband if he worked away from home. She fetched water and fuel, kept the home in good repair, and took care of linen and clothing, which included washing, tailoring, mending, and patching. All this took time—lots of it. Le Play's family budgets tried to measure the time spent in doing the laundry, this being the

first domestic chore that the state attempted to rationalize by constructing mechanized washhouses based on the English model during the Second Empire.

Finally, the homemaker sought to provide a supplementary income for the family by cleaning other houses, taking in laundry, running errands, making deliveries (of items such as bread, the *porteuse de pain* being a familiar figure of the time), and selling items from streetcorner stalls to other women constantly in search of bargains.

Gradually, especially over the last thirty years of the nineteenth century, the highly organized and rationalized garment industry began to exploit this vast labor force of women at home. The first sewing machines were highly coveted, and many housewives dreamed of owning their own Singer. But the machines kept women confined to the home, unable to frequent the streets as in the past. Because of the abuses of the sweating system, factories, in which work was less lonely, better supervised, and more amenable to public scrutiny than in isolated sweatshops, ultimately won out.

As the family minister of finance, the homemaker enjoyed certain ambiguous powers. Around the middle of the nine-

Edgar Degas, *Laundresses.* Advances in cleanliness made laundering linen, whether at home or for wages, a major activity of women and made the washhouse an important gathering place. The laundress was a familiar figure in 19th-century Paris, as was the washerwoman in the countryside. (Stanford, California, Private collection.)

"In the home . . . in the factory." Was the sewing machine the "great glory of women," as Gaston Bonheur imagined? Widely used in the textile industry and coveted by working women as well as by the bourgeoisie, it was also their cross to bear.

teenth century large numbers of French workers began turning their wages over to their wives to handle. Occasionally arguments associated with this weekly ritual resounded through the neighborhood, but in general it should probably be considered a victory for women, tired of waiting for handouts from their husbands. By gaining control of the family finances, however, women became responsible for what they spent. Although they had the power to decide what was bought—and already their patronage was eagerly sought by the large department stores and the first rather decorous advertisements—their chief responsibility was to cope with poverty, if need be sacrificing their own needs to make ends meet. Leaving such male comestibles as meat and wine to the head of the household and sugar to the children, the housewife all too often subsisted on café au lait; the *côtelette de la couturière* (seamstress' cutlet) was a piece of Brie.

Nevertheless, this modest control over the family budget gave women power that even today is greatly prized by housewives in relatively modest families. Women had other areas of responsibility as well, including care of—as contemporaries might have put it—body and soul. Doctors were too expensive for a worker's family to consult except in rare circumstances, so women relied on age-old remedies and on the advice of the new hygienic science. The use of camphor was recommended by Raspail, the "physician of the poor," who, aware of the traditional role of women in hygienic matters, addressed his advice especially to them.[21]

Female literacy improved rapidly in the nineteenth century, and many mothers taught their children to read. Women were avid readers of serialized fiction. Even as the big newspapers sought to tame the imagination of the people, women kept it alive. The Church catered to women, and many who enjoyed the religious festivals and the warm social life of the parish led an active religious life—not without conflict with husbands who had a more materialistic outlook.

The housewife was plain-spoken, often a rebel in private as well as in public. Many paid dearly for their free spirits, becoming targets of violence or crimes of passion. As time passed, opportunities for women to participate in public life became less frequent though more routine. It is not at all clear that modernization enhanced the power of working-class women, since outside forces now encroached on the private sphere from all directions and the models for workers to emulate were mostly masculine. Women thus found themselves torn between conflicting roles and had difficulty finding

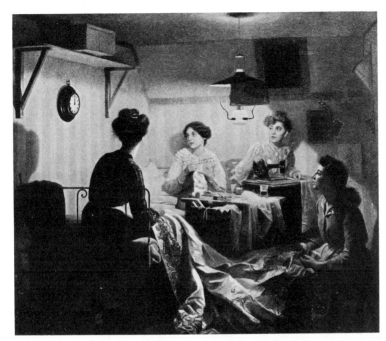

Left: *The Stroke of Midnight.*
(Paris, Bibliothèque Nationale.)
Seamstresses hard at work in a
loft look anxiously at the clock.
Note the contrast between the
bare surroundings and the
sumptuous fabric. Below:
Marie Petiet, *The Ironers.*
(Paris, Bibliothèque Nationale.)
Surrounded by fine linen,
young women ironing amuse
themselves with gossip.

their place. On all sides they were exhorted to retreat into the home—witness the CGT's posters advocating the English-style workweek. Some women lost interest in a world of trade unions and politics that paid them no heed.

PARENTS AND CHILDREN

The child in the nineteenth century was more than ever the center of the family, which invested in it not only emotionally but also economically, educationally, and existentially. As heir, the child represented the family's future, its projected image of itself, its dream, and its way of doing battle with time and death.

This investment, one indication of which was the increasingly abundant literature on childhood, was not necessarily focused on the individual child. Stendhal said that his father "did not love me as an individual but rather as a son obliged to carry on his family name" *(Henry Brulard)*. The group took precedence over the individual, and in France the notion of the "child's interest" developed quite late. Even then it usually applied only to higher collective interests, to the child as social being.

Actually the child was not an exclusive possession of the family but the future of the nation and the race, tomorrow's producer and progenitor, citizen and soldier. Between the child and the family—especially the poor family, presumed incapable of caring for its own—a host of third parties intervened: philanthropists, physicians, and statesmen determined to protect, educate, and discipline the young. The first social legislation passed in France was intended to protect children: the law of 1841 limiting the duration of factory work. Although this legislation proved relatively ineffective, its symbolic and legal significance was considerable because it marked the first step away from liberal justice and toward social justice.[22]

Childhood was an area in which public and private met and sometimes clashed. As much as childhood was an issue of power, it was also an object of knowledge. The effects of this knowledge, developed in the latter third of the nineteenth century by physicians, psychologists, and jurists, were contradictory. It strengthened social control, but it also contributed to an image of childhood as unfathomable mystery.

The Secrets of Procreation   In France, which Moheau in the late eighteenth century described as a country quick to discover the "baneful secrets"

James Jacques Tissot, *Hide and Seek,* ca. 1877. In this comfortable English home, crammed with bibelots and tinged with the exotic, the children are not confined to the nursery. (Washington, D.C., National Gallery of Art.)

of birth control, the birthrate declined quite early. Available techniques did not permit "planning" births, but they did allow restricting them: the birthrate declined from 32.9 per thousand in 1800 to 19 per thousand in 1910. Demographers, troubled by the trend, turned the private act of birth into the public issue of "natality." Having children was in part an act of discretion, although the degree to which this freedom existed varied with region and milieu. According to Hervé Le Bras and Emmanuel Todd, these disparities were the result of parental will as formed by family structures. The ideological factors that are usually emphasized were shaped by preexisting molds. Three areas in which the birthrate was unusually low in 1861 stand out clearly: Normandy, Aquitaine, and Champagne. In each region, however, the low average birthrate was achieved in a different way. In Aquitaine it was common for families to have only one or two children. In Normandy there were widely divergent extremes of behavior, with abnormally high numbers of couples who chose to have no children (in Orne, for example) as well as abnormally high numbers who won the Cognacq Prize for producing nine or more children after twenty-five years of marriage. Le Bras and Todd go so far as to speak of "neurotic behavior."[23]

The rising rate of illegitimacy, which Edward Shorter has described as a sign of sexual liberation, confuses the picture somewhat.[24] It seems to admit many different interpretations. Le Bras and Todd contrast the situation in the north and east, where many illegitimate offspring were recognized by marriage, with the Mediterranean south, where men recognized their children but did not marry the mother. The first situation was one of greater equality between the sexes and greater freedom for women; in the second situation, the coercive power of the extended family was paramount.

Here we can penetrate no further into the thicket of historical demography other than to point out just how complex the subject is, even when it comes to ascertaining facts, let alone proposing interpretations. What Le Bras calls "the secret history of fertility" is in fact a bewildering host of incompatible theories. Social, biological, and ideological determinisms are all toyed with, even if childbirth ultimately is analyzed as the result of a "parental decision." Among ideological factors, incidentally, the "ravages" of individualism are frequently cited, and feminism is often treated as nothing more than a peculiarly harsh form of individualism.

The parental decision that is made in bed brings us face

to face with the most intimate matters of sex and love. It should come as no surprise that the truth is elusive, especially when the mysteries of the marriage bed are compounded by the opacity of time and the silence of parents and progeny alike. Rare is the child who knows whether its birth was a matter of chance or desire.

In any case, the birthrate declined even though the average age at marriage decreased. No doubt the decision not to have children resulted from growing awareness of what raising a child meant. People took better care of children, coddled and loved them more than in the past, but produced fewer of them. Little is known about how births were prevented. Some couples used no birth control other than abstinence; to avoid having babies women "slipped away." Coitus interruptus left the decision to the male, who labored under an obligation to "be careful." In wealthier homes people relied more on techniques imported from England or learned in brothels; one such technique was douching, which required a ready supply of water and accounted for the success of the bidet—delayed, we are told, by concerns about its decency.[25] In 1906 libertarian neo-Malthusians, eager to teach birth-control techniques to

The newborn is king in this suburban family, which seems to be suffering a bit from the chill of spring. (Sirot-Angel Collection.)

proletarian women, adopted the slogan "Women, learn to be mothers only when you choose" and distributed condoms and absorbent sponges. Their propaganda often offended women, who were faced with impossible demands and perhaps shocked at such intrusion into their private affairs. In case of "mishap" many women preferred, all things considered, to seek an abortion. Abortion became increasingly common, particularly among urban married women with several children; by the turn of the twentieth century it seems to have been used as a form of contraception. Is Angus MacLaren right to view this use of abortion as an expression of feminism in the lower strata of society, or at any rate as an expression of the will of women unwilling to accept either an unwanted birth or the horrors of infanticide?[26] The latter, though still common in the first half of the nineteenth century, was severely repressed under the Second Empire (with as many as a thousand prosecutions annually), and its prevalence diminished. Isolated cases of infanticide continued to occur, however, among serving girls in the country and lonely maids in sixth-story Paris bedrooms who faced the shame of raising an illegitimate child.

Despite progress in birth control in the nineteenth century, the inadequacy of means of contraception made "accidents" common. People spoke, not always in the most joyful tones, of "falling pregnant" and "being in a sad pass." Unwanted children who were not killed faced a risky future, whether they were abandoned or simply accepted into the family as a judgment of fate.

Yet people also ardently desired children, not just for family reasons or because their role required it but because they wished to be parents. For women parenthood was a reason for existing, but men too felt the desire for children. "A woman without children is a monstrosity," according to Louise, the protagonist of Balzac's *Mémoires de deux jeunes mariées* (Memoirs of Two Young Brides). "We are made solely to be mothers." Ten months after her marriage Caroline Brame-Orville confided to her diary: "my great sorrow is not to have a baby, whom I would love so and who would make me accept the serious life I am leading" (January 1, 1868). In order to have a child she spares no effort, including medical treatment, a cure at Spa, and a visit to the pope, whose benediction she thanks for the birth, fourteen years later, of a daughter she names Marie-Pie (Mary Pius) in homage. Gustave de Beaumont discussed his wife's pregnancy with Tocqueville. Beaumont was so concerned about her that he deferred writing his book, torn between his desire to be a father and his sorrow at his wife's suffering: "There are moments when, out of consideration for the poor mother, I would send the child if I could to all the devils . . . I nevertheless look upon the expected event as a blessing, and our ardent desire to see you experience a similar fate is the substance of all our conversations and hopes" (June 10, 1838). In parallel or perhaps in conjunction with the development of maternal sentiment, a paternal sentiment for "baby" also developed, even though the infant was still regarded almost as a fetus and took so long to develop a truly human visage.

The desire for children did not extend to adoption. Filiation by blood remained a firmly rooted idea. Although the first steps toward institutionalizing adoption were taken under the Second Empire, changes in this realm, particularly in regard to transmission of the family name, were slow in coming.

Birth is a strictly private—and feminine—act, even in the way it is told and remembered (and among women it is an inexhaustible topic of conversation). Its theater was the family bedroom, or in the best of cases the parents' bedroom, and men were excluded, except for the doctor who, thanks to the medicalization of childbirth, assisted more and more frequently at the bedsides of relatively wealthy clients. Lower fees, as well as tradition and modesty, ensured that midwives retained a dominant though declining position. Giving birth in a hospital was a sign of poverty or, even worse, of shame and solitude; unwed country girls came to the city to give birth in the hospital before abandoning their babies. In western, southwestern, and central France, Le Bras and Todd tell us that the "rejection of bastard children brought mothers to hospitals."[27] The shift to hospital births did not come until after the First World War. Even then it was slow, affecting mainly the most progressive circles in Paris, where women hoped to improve their child's chances in a country whose infant mortality rate remained among the highest in Europe. For both mother and child birth was often a traumatic experience.

Home Birth

The declaration of a child's birth at the town hall—that bestowal of a name which for Kant was the only real birth— was made by the father. The child who entered the world thus also entered the family and society.

Bébé, Baby

Victor Lecomte, *Birth*. Note the presence of men—the husband and the doctor—in the temple of birth. Hospital births did not become commonplace until after World War II. In 1880 only poor and illegitimate children were born in hospitals. (Nantes, Musée des Beaux-Arts.)

Childhood, once seen as a largely undifferentiated stretch of time, much the same for boys and girls, was now divided into three strategic phases: early childhood (up to the age of eight), childhood proper, and adolescence. Adolescence, the crucial age of puberty and sexual identification, was a worrisome time when heightened surveillance was essential. At eight, children were regarded as having attained the age of reason; accordingly they drew the attention of legislators, physicians, and moralists.[28] The baby (French used the English word *baby* until the 1880s, after which it became *bébé*) did not come into its own until much later, although a vogue for breast-feeding did develop in the upper classes in the eighteenth century. Paradoxically, more children were handed over to wet nurses in the nineteenth century than ever before, and abandonment of infants set new records. Yet by the end of the century a new science of child-rearing *(puériculture)* had emerged.

Mary Louise McMonnies, *Roses and Lilies.* "Maternity is the passion of the day," wrote Delphine de Girardin in 1840. Here, a mother, her small daughter, and a doll: a feminine trinity set amid the saccharine sweetness of roses and lilies. The subject, a common one for French and even more for English painters, was a favorite of female painters. (Rouen, Musée des Beaux-Arts.)

Though awareness of infancy was slow to form, signs of its advent are unmistakable. The attentive mother refused to swaddle her baby and employed an English nurse. Renée de L'Estoril (in Balzac's *Mémoires de deux jeunes mariées*) was seen as a pioneer. By the end of the nineteenth century every good mother took an active part in caring for her own infant, now regarded as a full-fledged individual and affectionately referred to by pet names. Jenny and Laura Marx were fertile mothers who for all their diligence were nevertheless obliged to mourn some of their offspring; they kept their father, Karl, informed of their youngsters' feats. Bourgeois correspondence often has the flavor of nursery rhyme. Caroline Brame-Orville kept daily records of the awakenings of her much-coveted daughter Marie. Berthe Morisot portrayed this maternal contemplation of the cradle on canvas. Yet the cradle continued to connote the physical functions. Its place was in the privacy of the home, and Flaubert burst out laughing when he saw one on stage. Even the most attentive fathers rarely gave their children more than a casual glance. Gustave de Beaumont began to take an interest in his son when he began to walk: "Now he can come hunting with me with a wooden rifle"—an initiation into the manly arts.

The Sexless World of Early Childhood

At all levels of society tending to very young children was woman's work. Early childhood was feminized: boys and girls wore dresses and long hair until age three or four and often longer, and they played freely underneath their mother's or a servant's skirts. In France the child's bedroom was a late invention. In 1873 Viollet-le-Duc designed one for a house he was building, because "one must plan for everything." Children's toys were everywhere, especially in the kitchen (as can be seen in many paintings from the period). In cities toys became a consumer item, manufactured on a large scale and sold in department stores. In rural homes factory-made toys were unknown; in poorer families fathers made the toys. Vingtras-Vallès long remembered a wagon his father had carved for him out of a piece of fir. While making the toy the father had injured himself, and young Vingtras-Vallès had been spanked by his mother, who felt the need to punish both the "spoiled" child and the indulgent father. Dolls had a large place in the child's world. In the early nineteenth century they were not sex-typed, but puppets on which children lavished affection before they themselves became objects of their par-

Blanche Demanche, *The Favorites.* For a lonely little girl, a doll was a substitute for another person—a child to care for, a friend to confide in. (Salon of 1914.)

ents' affection. George Sand wrote some marvelous pages about memories of her dolls.

Because there were still few schools for very young children, early education was the task of mothers, who taught reading by means of the Jacotot method. As children came to be more highly valued, women devoted themselves all the more diligently to this task, which fostered in them a desire to better their own education. Aurore Dudevant came to feminism through maternal love: "I have long told myself that profound knowledge is of no use to our sex, that we ought to seek virtue and not knowledge in letters, that our goal was achieved when study of the good made us good and sensible, and that, on the contrary, when we did not refrain from science, we became pedantic, ridiculous, and lost all the qualities for which we were loved. I still think that my principle was correct, but I am afraid that I took it too literally. Today I realize that I have a son whom I must prepare for the more thorough lessons that he will receive when his childhood is over. I need to be prepared to give him that early education, and I want to make myself ready" '(letter to Zoé Leroy, 21 December 1825).

As the child grew, the nature of its education depended on its sex and social background. Fathers began to play a part, at least in the education of sons. In bourgeois families the father sometimes served as tutor, and working-class fathers

Paul Thomas, *Good Upbringing*, 1896. In the midst of sewing, a good mother pauses to hear her child recite her lessons. (Paris, Bibliothèque Nationale.)

trained apprentices or led groups of workers. A father rarely took an interest in the education of his daughters, except in certain intellectual and mostly Protestant milieus. In the Reclus family daughters as well as sons went to Germany to complete their studies, after which they obtained positions as tutors or nannies with English and German families. Girls who wished to travel met little opposition. Guizot, who oversaw his daughter's education, wrote affectionate letters in which he pointed out her spelling mistakes. Paternal feelings may have developed more freely with daughters than with sons, for a father felt none of the competitiveness with a daughter that he might experience with a male rival. We also find quite modern instances of affectionate friendship between father and daughter, particularly where the father was liberated and the daughter intelligent, and especially when the mother was more traditional-minded than her child. Geneviève Bréton clashed with the woman she called her "Queen Mother," who detested artists "who are not of Society," but she enjoyed a bantering relationship with her father: "We love each other greatly. We always understand each other, even when we say nothing, for we are both quiet people" (*Journal*, p. 28). Her father was a very proper man, however, who forced Geneviève to throw away all her perfume because he "could not admit that a young lady might be pleasing to smell." In particular he would not allow her to wear iris powder, "a decent, suitable perfume for a well-bred young lady" (*Journal,* p. 43). Certain young women keen for emancipation rejected their mothers and all they stood for, choosing masculine models instead. Germaine de Staël had this to say about her father: "When I see him, I ask myself if I could have been born of his union with my mother. My answer is no: my father alone sufficed to bring me into the world." (This statement is open to any number of Freudian interpretations.)

Relations between mothers and sons also took many forms. Affectionate friendship made an exemplary pair of Aurore de Saxe (later George Sand) and her son Maurice Dupin, whose relationship remained virtually unruffled even through adolescence. Vingtras-Vallès resented his mother's determination to make a gentleman of him. Rimbaud hated his mother, and in the case of Pierre Rivière, frustrated by the newfound power of women, hatred festered to the point of murder. Pity was what Gustave Flaubert felt for his widowed mother, from whom he was never able to free himself. In principle, however, a mother's power over her son was limited by law. Mothers could not become guardians, for example. Widows were an exception in that their rights were relatively well protected, even in marriages made under the rules of community property. As a result, sons often had a hard time with widowed mothers. The image of the mother and of her domestic powers figured powerfully as an antifeminist theme in early twentieth-century literature. Georges Darien, François Mauriac (Génitrix), and later André Breton portrayed men's age-old terror of maternal power. "Mothers!" Breton wrote, "We relive Faust's fright. We are gripped by an electric sensation at the mere sound of these syllables, in which lurk powerful goddesses from other times and places."

Mothers bore much greater responsibility for rearing their daughters, whom the state, by delaying public education for women, abandoned and whom the Church entrusted to their care, a decision which had the effect of instituting, from adolescence onward, a subtle division between body and soul.[29] Mothers initiated their daughters into the world; the confessor introduced them to morality and to God. No doubt the intention was to perpetuate the conservative and commemorative role of women. Mothers had a most important mission: to marry off their daughters. *Pot-Bouille* paints a neurotic but, to judge by contemporary letters, not exaggerated portrait of their frenzied efforts toward that goal: balls, receptions, piano lessons, and embroidery were all part of it. In rural families the trousseau was the physical embodiment and symbol of the marriage bond. Agnès Fine's study of southwestern France gives prominence to the cultural and emotional content of "this long history of mother–daughter relations."[30]

Because daughters were closer to their mothers and more dependent on them than were sons, they suffered more from the mother's absence or death. This suffering was particularly severe in the case of the eldest daughter, who was often called on to take the mother's place. Private diaries sometimes served as a compensation for the absent mother, as can be seen in the case of Caroline Brame.

Familiarity

Everyday relations between parents and children varied enormously from town to country. In rural areas displays of affection were discouraged. Social, religious, and political differences had an important impact. Different conceptions of authority and self-presentation influenced the individual's choice of words and gestures. Within the family we find contradictory tendencies. Physical gestures and the expression of emotions were controlled more tightly than ever before. Only women and the poor were permitted to shed tears in moments of pain or solitude. Children were corrected for mistakes in language or for bad posture; they were told to sit straight, eat properly, and so on. On the other hand, exchanges of affection between parents and children were tolerated and even desired, at least in bourgeois families. Caresses were considered appropriate in many circumstances, an encouragement to the development of young bodies. Though very modest, Caroline Brame sighed after her father died that she would no longer feel the warmth of his caress. Traveling in Greece around 1860, Edmond About remarked how cool Athenians were in private compared with the warmth of the French.

Another sign of closeness was the familiar *tu,* which came into common use among parents and children. "In the past people used *tu* with their servants and not with their children. Today they use *tu* with their children and not with their servants," Legouvé noted approvingly. In *Les Pères et les enfants au XIXe siècle* (Fathers and Children in the Nineteenth Century) we read that "*tu* should be used regularly with one's children, so that *vous* can be used with them from time to time as a sign of discontent." This explains why George Sand was so sensitive to the fact that her grandmother called her *vous*.

Not only George Sand but also liberal educators like Legouvé were firmly opposed to corporal punishment. "The old method horrifies me," Sand wrote, "and I think I would cry louder than [the children] if I beat them." But what was the reality? Social differences are perhaps more evident here than anywhere else. Remember that, in a society that had known feudalism and abolished it, corporal punishment had particular significance: it was the ultimate mark of infamy.

In bourgeois homes children were even less likely to be beaten than in aristocratic ones. Here and there one still found martinets with their rods, but disapproval became more pronounced. The rod was not spared in *collèges* or in certain *lycées* that claimed to enforce military discipline. George Sand shuddered with horror at the proctor of the Lycée Henri IV, "a ferocious champion of absolute authority . . . who authorized an intelligent father to order his Negro to beat his son in front of the entire class, which lined up in ranks to witness this spectacle, suited to the Creole or Muscovite taste, and which was threatened with severe punishment at the least sign of

Physical Punishment

Surprised in His Slumbers, 1866. A pleasant disorder reigns in this small coeducational elementary school. The teacher uses a cat-o'-nine-tails on the sleeping student, to the amusement of some of his classmates. The rationalist reform of education had yet to transform this classroom.

(Paris, Bibliothèque Nationale.)

disapproval."[31] Increasingly, however, adolescents, such as Baudelaire and his comrades at Lyons in 1832, rebelled against such methods, and their families protested. The protest grew so loud that boarding schools advertised in their brochures that they did not use corporal punishment. The state itself intervened, and repeated bulletins reminded teachers and others that "children must never be struck." One such bulletin went to mental asylums in 1838, and two others concerning the primary schools were issued in 1834 and 1851. Under Jules Ferry the rules became even more stringent. A regulation dated 6 January 1881 stated: "It is strictly forbidden to inflict corporal punishment of any kind." A study of the evolution of *pédagogies du corps,* methods of training and disciplining the body, shows how other forms of discipline, aimed at achieving internalization of rules, took the place of these more physical methods.[32] The goal became one of "touching the soul more than the body," as Beccaria had hoped the penal system would do. The gulf between public schools and religious schools widened, the latter clinging to older concepts of education in such matters as hygiene and punishment. Countless autobiographies attest to the fact that when it came to using the iron rule, religious brothers and nuns were in the rearguard, at least in schools that taught lower-class children.

I am interested here not in the history of educational methods as such but in the way family demands influenced the educational system to restrain its authoritarian tendencies. In this first intrusion by parents into the sacred world of the schools, the private guided the public; private mores became state law.

In the countryside and among the poor and petty-bourgeois segments of the urban population, however, blows abounded. "Hide-tannings" (to use a Gévaudan expression that occurs in Albert Simonin's description of his childhood in La Chapelle at the beginning of the century) or spankings were perfectly acceptable so long as they did not exceed certain limits. Spankings were usually administered with the bare hand; sticks and whips were reserved for masters of apprentices and guards in institutions as a mark of external physical force. Being beaten was a part of every nineteenth-century worker's childhood memories, as Perdiguier, Gilland, Truquin, Dumay, and Toinou attest. In workshops even more than in factories the impudent or clumsy apprentice was apt to receive a thrashing from the older workers assigned to teach him his trade.

Underlying these punishment practices was a series of images. People believed that the rebellious will in children had to be tamed, and that children had to learn about the harshness of life. "Son, this will make a man of you." Physical violence was an inherent part of the idea of virility. Some people, having internalized the model, actually prided themselves on the beatings they had received and perhaps embellished the reality. But growing numbers of children and, above all, adolescents rebelled. Militant workers, especially anarchists, claimed to have derived their hatred of authority from the crushing experience of beatings. Self-consciousness is first of all consciousness of one's body.

Investment in the Child

Parent-child relations developed in two ways in the nineteenth century. Parents increasingly invested in the child as the future of the family, often in ways that limited the child's freedom. The family of Henri Beyle (Stendhal) pursued its dream of aristocratic distinction through him; he lived a cloistered childhood. Little Jacques Vingtras-Vallès had to bear the burden of his family's wish to rise in society. His father was an assistant teacher *(répétiteur)* in a *collège;* his mother wanted him to be a *professeur.* Combining peasant gruffness with a thirst for respectability, she imposed an iron discipline on the youth. To begin with she carefully monitored his appearance; he was expected to be clean, stand straight, and wear proper clothing ("I am often in black"); these good habits would encourage him to internalize the value of order. He never received an embrace or heard an affectionate word from his mother. "My mother says that children must not be spoiled, and she whips me every morning. When she has no time in the morning, the whipping is put off till noon, rarely later than four o'clock." And further: "My mother sees to it that I receive an education. She doesn't want me to be a countrywoman like her. My mother wants her Jacques to be a gentleman."

To be an heir was no simple matter. If the child fell short of what was expected or refused to go along with his family's wishes, the results could be tragic. Ambitions were shattered. The child felt guilty. The parent brooded over his betrayal. Think of Baudelaire, who never overcame the remorse he felt toward his mother, Mme Aupick. Or Van Gogh, whose letters to his brother Theo are filled with the hopeless rebellion of the "bad son." A source of existential anxiety, nineteenth-century family totalitarianism was in many ways profoundly neurotic.

But the child was also an object of love. After 1850 if a child died his relatives went into mourning, just as they would for an adult. In private they might cry over a lock of his hair. Was this only bourgeois sentimentalism? Not at all. In Lorraine, the heart of the iron and steel industry, mothers, wives of workers, "all lived in sorrow for their lost children. [They] wiped away their tears with checkered handkerchiefs whenever they met."[33] In education Legouvé proclaimed "the superiority of the principle of affection" and advocated respect for the child's autonomy. Children should be raised for themselves, not for their elders; their interests might not coincide with the group interests. They alone were responsible for their destinies, hence the important thing, according to liberal ed-

Outdoor Storytelling. Children socialize in the country. What is this young storyteller saying that so fascinates his listeners? (Paris, Bibliothèque Nationale.)

ucators, was to develop initiative even at the price of a certain ambiguity in their training; in this way the students would be free to make individual choices later on.

We gain some sense of how children looked and talked from the many observations that were made of them, including the intrusive observations of school records. The stereotypes vanish in a bewildering variety of concrete notations of the child's language, gestures, sexual behavior, and play. By this time childhood was seen as a special moment in life. Every autobiography began with and dwelt on childhood, while the bildungsroman traced the childhood and youth of the hero. Opposed to the rest of life, childhood became the foundation of adulthood, and the child became a person.

The adolescent, unknown in traditional societies, came into clear focus. Buffon and, even more, Rousseau had called attention to the rewards and dangers of that period of life that stretched from the time of First Communion to the baccalaureate or conscription for boys and to marriage for girls. The whole of book IV of Rousseau's *Emile* is devoted to "this critical moment," the moment of sexual identity. "We are in a sense born twice, once to exist, the other time to live; once for the species, the other time for sex . . . Just as the roaring of the sea begins long before the tempest, so is this stormy development heralded by newborn passions. An obscure fermentation warns of the impending danger."

Adolescence, the "Critical Age"

The notion of adolescence as a critical moment was revived repeatedly in the nineteenth century, most notably by physicians, who between 1780 and 1840 wrote dozens of theses on puberty in boys and girls and on remedies to deal with it. Adolescence, it was argued, is a danger not only to the individual but also to society. The adolescent in search of his identity is a narcissist seeking his own moral and physical image. Mirrors fascinate him. To Max Stirner he was the "One" and therefore apt to dissolve the bonds of society. Durkheim was of the same opinion. If young people committed suicide more readily than their elders, it was because they were not fully integrated into society. In addition, the adolescent's sexual appetite made him prone to violence, brutality, and sadism (toward animals, for example). He had a liking for rape and blood.

From this characterization of the adolescent it was but a short step to the notion of the adolescent criminal, whom Duprat analyzed in a work typical of the concerns of the day

Marie Bashkirtseff, *The Meeting*, 1883. Children socialize in the city. Younger children gather around a bigger youth, almost an adolescent. There is a mixture of curiosity and envy in this little "fraternity of terror." Note the school uniforms and the familiar black school bag. (Paris, Musée d'Orsay.)

entitled *La Criminalité dans l'adolescence. Causes et remèdes d'un mal social actuel* (Criminality in Adolescence. Causes and Remedies of a Contemporary Social Ill). According to Duprat, the adolescent is a "born vagabond." Enamored of travel and movement and profoundly unstable, he engages in "flights analogous to those of hysterics and epileptics, who are unable to resist the impulse to travel." The adolescent has a pathology of his own, including such afflictions as "hebephrenia," defined as "a need to act in defiance of every obstacle and danger." Such disorders could drive the adolescent victim to murder.

The most troubling thing about the adolescent was the sexual mutation he was undergoing and his thoughts about that transformation. Michel Foucault has shown how the "schoolboy's sex" became the primary object of that "will to know" about sex that for Foucault is typical of modern society.[34] Physicians, the primary observers of the body, stirred up concern about such issues as masturbation, homosexuality in boarding schools, and perverse behavior among childhood friends. To be sure, male and even female homosexuality ceased to be a crime so long as public decency was not offended, but "inversion" became an anomaly that was scrutinized as though it were a disease. Central to this concern was the adolescent with his "bad habits." How to deal with adolescent sexuality was a primary concern of educators and a major social anxiety. Specialized knowledge was needed. How could the family do enough on its own?

Many families, enamored of aristocracy or Rousseauism and afraid of contact with the vulgar and perverse, dreamed of educating their children at home under the watchful eye of the parents; English tutors and nannies were preferred. The young Stendhal remembered the stifling isolation in which his parents kept him in order to prevent any contact "with the children of the common people": "They never allowed me to speak to a child of my own age . . . I had to endure endless homilies on paternal love and the duties of children." He survived by lying and dreamed of nothing but escape. The Directory's Ecole Centrale would be his deliverance.

Adolescents share a moment of silent contemplation.

It was considered necessary for children of a certain age to be sent away to boarding school. Girls of fifteen to eighteen attended boarding school to complete their moral education and preparation for social life and to acquire the "art of pleasing" needed in the matrimonial salons. Boys lived in the barracklike atmosphere of the *collèges* and *lycées,* where they prepared to pass the baccalaureate, that distinguishing mark of the bourgeoisie. These schools did not have a good reputation. Baudelaire was bored to death in one: "I am so bored that I cry for no reason," he wrote his mother on August 3, 1838. George Sand was distressed at having to send her son to one. Comparing the "angelic soul of this true adolescent," a delicate, androgynous youth who resembled her own father and who had been raised by an attentive mother, to the "ill-groomed, poorly educated *collégien* infatuated by some crude vice that has already made him insensitive to the primary ideal," she was saddened that she could no longer educate her son at home. "In decent, quiet families it ought to be a duty to keep the children at home and not force them to learn about life at a *collège* in which the only equality is won with the fist."[35] Boarding schools were blamed for masturbation and homosexuality. Roger Martin du Gard, in his posthumous and

A typical class in a republican lycée studies beneath the watchful eye of the teacher. (Rouen, Musée National de l'Education.)

largely autobiographical novel *Le Lieutenant-Colonel de Mau-mort,* described the sexual life of a *collège* around 1880: "Solitary onanism was the rule, shared pleasure the exception." Public opinion, especially conservative opinion, nevertheless blamed the boarding schools for the "effeminization" of youth, the defeat of 1870, and the depopulation of France. Poor and peasant families who wished to prolong their sons' education were obliged to send them to boarding schools, but bourgeois families kept their boys at home and sent them to study as day students whenever possible. For Ernest Legouvé as well as George Sand, this arrangement was the best possible solution to the educational problem. More than ever before, bourgeois families wished to set the tone of their offspring's life, to serve as cocoon and private tutor to their children. In opposition to the secular state and its public schools, they treated education as a private affair, thereby contributing to the success of so-called *écoles libres,* or private schools.

Nevertheless, the affection that enveloped the child was tainted by wariness of the adolescent, still suspected of seditious tendencies. The very surveillance to which adolescents were subjected was an invitation to secrecy. Adolescents invented a hundred stratagems to win a modicum of privacy.

Recess at a secondary school in Meaux: adolescents under surveillance.

Girls study in the rather informal classroom of a girls' private school, of which there were many before (and after) the Ferry laws. (Rouen, Musée National de l'Education.)

They read novels during study time or after curfew; they wrote poetry; they kept diaries; and they dreamed. All these activities constituted an inner life. Friendships were important. The friendships that girls made at boarding school were often cut short by marriage. Boys formed groups consolidated by various rites of initiation and represented by symbolic figureheads, like the "Bachelor" whom Flaubert and his friends from the *collège* of Rouen invented to be the hero of their imaginary adventures. Sometimes these groups persisted in later life as cliques in the worlds of business and government. Life in large nineteenth-century boarding schools was frequently disrupted by individual or collective rebellion. After 1880, however, such disruptions became less common, as if the establishment of the Third Republic had made them unnecessary. Yet the Republic was no more willing than the monarchies of the nineteenth century had been to permit youth to play the role in festival celebration and sexual regulation that it had played in traditional societies. Youths were no longer treated as a group but as individuals, whose only duties were to follow orders and keep silent. When young people rebelled, therefore, their rebellion was usually individual rather than political, and it pitted them against the family, not the state.

This characterization applies to poor as well as to bourgeois youth. From the time of his First Communion (or receipt of a graduation certificate) to his conscription in the army, the

Croquet at a lay convent, or how not to educate young ladies. (Sirot-Angel Collection.)

young worker lived with his family and brought home his pay. (The *livret,* or pay booklet, abolished for adult workers, was still issued to youths.) In occupational groups where the family structure remained intact, as among miners, to marry before going into the service was considered a betrayal of the family. Nevertheless, according to various investigations, such as one conducted in 1872 into "working conditions in France," young people were showing signs of impatience. In the factories of La Voulte in Ardèche, "many [young workers] left home the minute they started earning money and went to live in boardinghouses, just as unmarried foreign workers would do." In the textile industry of Picardy, young men and even young women of sixteen or seventeen were taking lodgings and no longer giving their pay to their families. Accordingly, in certain households it was agreed that after the age of eighteen the children would share only part of their pay with their families or that they would pay a "negotiated" price for room and board.

Auguste Flandrin, *Paul and Hippolyte as Children*. A family of painters from Lyons. Auguste (1804-1843), the eldest, drew his two younger brothers, Jean-Paul (1811–1902) and Hippolyte (1809–1864), who had the most successful career of the three. (Private collection.)

BROTHERS AND SISTERS

In addition to the vertical relations between parents and children, there were horizontal relations between siblings.[36] Even among peers, however, inequalities and sometimes com-

Two sisters photographed during the Second Empire. Such photographs were common among the upper classes, less so among the working class. When Xavier-Edouard Lejeune, a draper's assistant, tried to persuade his provincial grandmother to allow her picture to be taken during a brief visit to Paris during this same period, the elderly woman became frightened on the way and fled home. (Sirot-Angel Collection.)

petition resulted from differences of sex, rank, age, talent, and possibly parental favoritism. Competition was most intense in regions where the eldest son received special treatment. In Gévaudan, for example, tensions between older and younger siblings increased in the nineteenth century, at times to murderous heights; neither lawsuits nor emigration provided an adequate safety valve. Younger siblings often found themselves in a subordinate position, reduced almost to the role of servants and in many cases required to remain celibate.

There was a difference between the playful bickering of youth and the rivalries that erupted when adolescents were confronted with major life decisions or the hatreds that emerged when the time came to divide an inheritance. Family battles broke out when a will was contested or when ownership of a coveted property was disputed. For symbolic as well as material reasons people invariably overvalued those goods of which they were deprived. It is difficult when one is not the favorite.

Before these crucial moments arrived, however, sibling relations exhibited many other qualities. Children took pleasure in jointly challenging the authority of their parents. Younger brothers and sisters were instructed by their elders. An older brother might prove a crucial influence in the choice of a career or in shaping the ideological outlook of a younger sibling. Older sisters often served as teachers of the young. Victor Hugo was warmed by the memory of Léopoldine, a Bible open on her knees, giving Adèle spelling lessons. Big sisters also taught younger girls how to do household chores, groom themselves, and make themselves attractive to boys. The responsibilities of the eldest sister were particularly heavy. In homes where the mother was deceased, she served both the father and the younger children as mother and homemaker, often at the sacrifice of her own aspirations. In poorer families, particularly in rural areas, the eldest sister was often sent out to work in order to help her parents raise her younger brothers and sisters. Or the youngest sister might be expected to care for her elderly parents. Households consisting of two women, an elderly mother and one of her daughters, occur quite often in census figures reported at five-year intervals. A child's responsibilities and duties were thus partly determined by his or her place in the order of birth.

Feelings between siblings were certainly less intense than moral literature made them out, but they did exist, and Alain Corbin sees them as one of the major forms of emotional

These young people, possibly wearing mourning, may have gathered to honor the visit of their brother the seminarian. They look like characters out of Mauriac.

interaction. Gender difference complicated brother-sister relations, which in some ways served as an initiation into relations with the opposite sex. Incest was repressed by stringent religious and social taboos, so these relations rarely took a sexual form, but they may well have been amorous. Bakunin admitted to having felt incestuous love for his sister, and that confession fueled a campaign against him. The fact is that censorship of these matters was so powerful that the veil is only occasionally lifted. Pierre Moignon, a worker and sometime criminal, wrote his sister of his love for her and kept a diary of his hopeless passion that has survived in the record of his trial.

Little Sisters

In relations between an elder brother and younger sister or an elder sister and younger brother, age reinforced the usual paternal or maternal feelings. The little sister in Zola's *Travail* (1901) felt unreserved adulation for her older brother. Though sacrificed to Martial Jordan's ventures without being consulted, she was apparently pleased to play second fiddle and cried tears of joy at the news of her brother's success—the very picture of contentment. The figure of the little sister occurs repeatedly in antifeminist literature of the early twentieth century. The older brother, surrogate for the father and husband, acts as his sister's guide and initiator. To males suffering a crisis of identity it was reassuring to think of themselves as models.

The protective elder sister devoted herself body and soul to the education and advancement of her younger brother. Ernest Renan owed a great deal to his sister Henriette, of whom he left an idealized portrait in *Ma soeur Henriette*. Born in Tréguier in 1811, Henriette was twelve years older than Ernest and tyrannized him from early childhood. She worked as a teacher in Brittany, Paris, and even Poland, refusing several proposals of marriage in order to devote herself to her family. Her savings enabled Ernest to pursue his studies and research. In 1850 brother and sister set up housekeeping together in Paris. "Her respect for my work was extreme. At night she sat by my side for hours, scarcely breathing so as not to interrupt me. Yet she wanted to see me, and the door that separated our two bedrooms was always open." Henriette influenced her brother, particularly in the area of religion, where she preceded him down the road to unbelief. "She was an incomparable secretary for me. She copied all my works and entered into them so deeply that I could rely on her as a living index of my own thought." Trouble came when Ernest fell in love, even though she herself had suggested marriage. "All the storms that love can hold we experienced . . . When she told me that the moment of my union with another woman would be the moment of her departure, my blood ran cold."

After Ernest's marriage to Mlle. Scheffer, Henriette transferred her need for affection to little Ary, her nephew. "The maternal instinct that overflowed in her found its natural outlet here," wrote Renan, who with the heedless nonchalance of a great man wrote of his sister's marvelous relations with his wife: "Each one had her separate place by my side, and there was neither sharing nor exclusion." Henriette, however, never regained the perfect happiness of solitary communion with her brother until she accompanied him, enthusiastically, on a mission to Syria, where she met her death. "That year was in fact the only one of her life which she passed without tears, and virtually her only reward," Ernest wrote.

EXTENDED FAMILIES

Radiating out from the central nucleus of parent and children were networks of kinship whose extent varied according to family type, nature of housing, migration, and social environment. Yet the extended family continued to be a vital entity in the nineteenth century, even among the lower classes. Sunday dinners with the extended family were an institution particularly prevalent among workers.

In rural areas grandparents had long shared homes with their children and grandchildren, although this arrangement could become problematic when the grandparents could no longer work. This situation was much less common in cities because apartments were too small to allow it, although children sometimes offered lodging to elderly parents on a temporary basis. The workers described in Le Play's *Ouvriers des deux mondes* generally kept up relations with their forebears, particularly on the mother's side. Young children were often entrusted to the care of the elderly, and children cared for aging parents. This solidarity between generations tended to weaken over time, however, and elderly people cast off by their children faced the specter of death in a hospice. Hence the question of old age became increasingly acute at all levels

Grandparents

Family gatherings brought couples and generations together. Right: An urban working-class family, as evidenced by the sidewalk, the waxed-paper tablecloth, and the wine glasses. Below: A provincial bourgeois family displays a "modern" preference for a more "natural" look, in which everyone attempts to appear busy rather than engaged in posing for the photographer. (Sirot-Angel Collection.)

of society. In Gévaudan elderly people unhappy with receiving irregular handouts of food preferred a system of maintaining a life interest in their property.

Demands for retirement with pensions grew among wage earners, particularly in the public sector where those demands were addressed to the state. In 1907 asylum attendants wrote the minister of the interior: "Do we not have, as all citizens do, a right to life, and do we not enjoy the same privileges as other occupational groups that are protected by the state and whose future is guaranteed by the state retirement fund?" The refusal of the CGT (Confédération Générale du Travail) to approve the 1910 retirement law was the result of defects in the legislation rather than opposition to a principle that was supported by most workers, as is evident from the letters received by Ferdinand Dreyfus, who dealt with the issue for the newspaper *L'Humanité*. The fact that old age now became a "risk" against which people wished to insure themselves just as they insured themselves against sickness or accident shows both the weakening of family solidarities and the changing perception of the human life span. This consciousness of old age, which according to George Sand's grandmother had been ushered in by the Revolution, is a major change that deserves further study.

The degree to which grandparents took part in the lives of their children depended on distance. Traditionally relieved of educational responsibilities, grandparents could afford the luxury of indulging their grandchildren, of playing grandpa and grandma. But sometimes they took the place of deceased or disabled parents or parents who had for some reason been forced to go abroad. Henri Beyle, whose mother had died, was raised by his grandfather Gagnon. The bastard Xavier-Edouard Lejeune was cared for by his maternal grandparents. Aurore Dupin was educated by her paternal grandmother, who also took in Maurice's natural son Hippolyte Chatiron. Elisée Reclus was taken care of until he was eight years old by his maternal grandparents, who had a decisive influence on him.

Autobiographies almost invariably begin with a portrait of the writer's grandparents; family memory rarely extends back in time earlier than this generation. To the grandchild the grandparents were almost mythical figures. Their lives were the symbolic equivalents of quarters of nobility, and through them the grandchild not only constructed a rudimentary genealogy but also became acquainted with death for the first time. The death of the narrator's grandmother in Proust's

Remembrance of Things Past is a case in point. Grandparents also played a real role in the transmission of knowhow and traditions. In this troubled century accounts by elders of historical events and how they were experienced amounted to a private form of memory. These memories often were filtered through the eyes of women, not only because women lived longer than men but also because they married earlier, so that grandmothers were more likely than grandfathers to play a part in the lives of their grandchildren.

Aunts and Cousins

Also included within the circle of the extended family were uncles, aunts, and cousins. The line was usually drawn at the offspring of first cousins. Among the lower classes this extended family served as backdrop to the migrations of young workers. Among the bourgeoisie extended family members were invited to receptions and vacationed together; during such special times they experienced initiations of various kinds, including sexual. According to Fourier, "aunts invariably claim their nephews' first offerings," and uncles had to muster all their virtue to resist "tender incest with their nieces." Adolescents lusted after the pretty female cousin who, from one summer to the next, had grown into a woman; girls'

Two sisters with their dignified parents and aunts. The youngest girl's virginal white dress is an emblem of her solitude: "No one is lonelier than a young girl," Roger Martin du Gard wrote in *Devenir,* 1908. (Sirot-Angel Collection.)

hearts beat for the handsome male cousin who had begun to affect the manners of the liberated student. When it came to sentimental education, the family met all needs.[37] But if things went too far, if the family name or inheritance were threatened, the family could also clamp down hard.

Uncles and aunts were permitted to serve as guardians. Since widowed mothers were disqualified, the role of aunts and uncles in family councils could be considerable, especially when it came to counseling a widow regarding possible remarriage, to administering the property of orphans, or to requesting the institutionalization of a family member under the law of 1838.

Unmarried aunts hovered about the household and populated the child's world; they often filled the memories of their nephews. Henri Beyle was subjected to the iron rule of his strict Aunt Séraphie, "that female devil . . . the evil genius of my entire childhood," whose influence was compensated by the tenderness of Aunt Elisabeth. Jacques Vingtras describes the bustling activities of his maternal aunts Rosalie and Mariou and his paternal aunts Mélie and Agnès, two elderly spinsters who lived on nothing and eventually joined a small community of béates, devout women, near Puy-en-Velay. With orphaned girls aunts necessarily played a more maternal role. Caroline Brame was chaperoned by her aunt Céline Ternaux, who was no doubt responsible not only for Caroline's marriage but for the marriage of many other girls in her family. Marie Cappelle, the future Mme Lafarge, was initiated into the secrets of marriage by her aunts: "After a rather long and lively breakfast, my aunts took me into the small salon, closed the doors, and began initiating me into the frightening mysteries of my new duties."[38]

Uncles introduced a breath of fresh air into the home. An uncle shared a father's prestige without his faults. He offered nephews an accomplice with whom they could identify. Xavier-Edouard Lejeune delighted in his escapades with his tailor uncle, who used to put on his frock coat and take his nephew to the Barrière du Trône. Albert Simonin admired his uncles: Pierre, the inventor, who owned an automobile well before 1914, and Frédéric, a watchmaker who also lit streetlamps and built his own suburban house. Paul Reclus truly worshiped his uncle, the geographer Elisée Reclus; after his death Paul published his uncle's works. As a surrogate for the father, the uncle might wield considerable power. People were especially fond of making up stories about the fabulous success of far-off uncles: the uncle in America was a standard family myth.

Neighbors and Servants

Beyond the nuclear family and the extended family lay a third circle composed of servants among the well-to-do and chiefly of neighbors among the common folk. In both cases there was consciousness of a boundary line, even a danger. Servants and neighbors helped the family, to be sure, but their presence posed a threat to privacy and their scrutiny could be embarrassing. People had to rely on these helpers, but they also had to be wary of them.

Neighbors could be helpful and hostile at the same time. In villages it was not easy to escape their scrutiny. In Gévaudan "the whole village was aware of everything that was going on, and everyone participated in the game of spying on their neighbors' private lives while protecting their own." A whole semiology of behavior and appearance sprang into being. Some places lent themselves to the mania for spying better than others. One such place was the church, "the village panopticon." People noted who attended mass, how frequently they received communion (and for those who abstained there were questions about absolution), and how long young girls remained in the confessional. Women, being sources of shame, were watched especially closely—particularly that most sensitive region, their bellies. When faces swelled and waists thickened only to thin down suddenly, tongues began to wag. Widows were subjected to special scrutiny. "In the provinces people keep their eyes on widows," according to Mauriac. "They keep track of how long a widow wears the veil. They measure the depths of her sorrow by the length of her crepe. Woe unto the widow who, one torrid summer day, lifts her veil in order to breathe. Those who see her will say: 'There's another one who quickly got over her grief'" (*La Province,* 1926). People watched one another through half-closed shutters. Wisecracks and insinuations were whispered at those centers of gossip and censure, the fountain and washhouse, and from there developed into persistent rumors. Since villages were communities that liked to take care of their own affairs without outside intervention, internal censure was particularly constraining. The neighborhood was the tribunal in which reputations were judged.

Neighborhoods

Was there greater freedom among the lower classes in the cities? Yes, insofar as urban communities were provisional, bonds of interest were looser, circulation was greater, and

there was a relatively strong sense of solidarity against outsiders, especially the police. No, because walls were thin (and squeaking beds told what was going on on the other side), windows left open on summer evenings turned courtyards into resonance chambers that magnified marital quarrels and disputes between neighbors, and people encountered one another in stairways, at public fountains, and in pestilent "jakes," which were a perennial source of conflict. A key figure in every apartment house was the concierge, who was almost invariably a women, the Swiss and porters of an earlier era having gradually disappeared. She was feared because of her intermediate position, straddling public and private, between tenants and landlords and at times in cahoots with the police, who turned to her whenever there was an incident and who sought to recruit her as a spy. Her behind-the-scenes power was considerable: she selected tenants, and no visitor or street

An apartment building in which the presence of a horse perpetuated some rural odors. Nevertheless, this building is equipped with modern conveniences such as sewers and bathrooms. The concierge is in the courtyard, and housekeepers can be seen in the windows.

The Shoe Palace, erected during the Haussmann era. Shoes were still expensive and much coveted by the working-class population. The photographer is standing in the street, and people stand still to look at him, glad to have their picture taken. Marville liked the city empty, but turn-of-the-century postcards liked to portray the bustle of crowded streets. (Sirot-Angel Collection.)

singer could enter the courtyard without her permission. Those who lived in buildings with direct access to the street had greater control over their privacy.

"Most residents confined their existence to a modest, even a tiny expanse of space," Pierre Sansot observed.[39] It was not so much the neighborhood as the street that defined the boundaries of privacy and the zone of familiarity. Shops were key meeting places and had their own code of etiquette and ritual exchanges. Certain familiar figures served as lookouts, confidants, and witnesses; the baker's wife and above all the grocer often became the "ear of the neighborhood or street, or even the confessional."[40] The neighborhood, open to the wider city and to many forms of private behavior, formed a more complex society than the household.

Space was less important than people, neighbors whom a person rarely chose freely and whose affection he needed to win even as he defended himself against them. Neighbors established a code of proper behavior at home as well as in the street, a norm that one had to respect in order to win acceptance, since people tended naturally to exclude those who were different from themselves in nationality, race, and place of origin (down to the province and even canton) and thus to reproduce the status quo. In the first half of the nineteenth century Paris, as Louis Chevalier has shown, was a congeries of villages.[41] On the rue de Lappe, in a *quartier* populated by Auvergnats, certain buildings were inhabited exclusively by people who hailed from the same village. Similarly, at the end of the century, the Pletzl (in the Marais) was filled with Jewish immigrants from central Europe.[42]

What will the neighbors say? was a common refrain. The disapproval, tolerance, or indulgence of one's neighbors determined the law by which one lived. But there were limits beyond which neighbors did not go. The threshold was sacrosanct, and no one crossed it without invitation unless unusual noises were heard or suspicious effluvia or noxious odors were detected. Parents could beat their children, and husbands could beat their wives; that was their affair, and no one would call the police for such a thing. It took a drama of some sort to loosen people's tongues and lead to calls for intervention. Recourse to the police and the courts by private individuals is an interesting indicator of tolerance and of forms of public intervention. In any event, neighborhood problems remained civil matters under the law, and there was a substantial consensus concerning the inviolability of a family's privacy, defined as that which took place within the home.

Little will be said here about house pets, part of the intimate world that Alain Corbin will describe later in this volume. Affection for dogs, birds, and, somewhat later, cats increased over the course of the century, as did public concern about their welfare. Animals were members of the family, and people spoke of them as they might speak about old friends. News about pets was shared, and George Sand's letters include numerous admirable examples of the genre. *Domestic Animals*

Animals sometimes served as tokens of an absent individual. Caroline Brame and Geneviève Bréton were given dogs by the men who loved them. Caroline called her dog Guerrière (Female Warrior) and frequently reminded the animal of its absent master by repeating his name. Geneviève treated her dog as a symbol of the baby she hoped to bear. Dogs were given identities: Mme Dupin's wore a collar that read: "My name is Nérina. I belong to Mme Dupin of Nohant near Châtre." She spent her last days on her mistress's lap and "was buried in our garden underneath a rose bush. The old gardener said that she had been *encavé* rather than *enterré*, for as a Berrichon purist he never would have applied the verb *enterrer* to any but a baptized Christian."

The house pet thus began its long ascent to "personhood,"

not without obstacles, with the result that today the whole issue has became a matter of some embarrassment for the law. Can a person bequeath his or her fortune to a dog, for example? A court in 1983 answered this question in the negative. In the last third of the nineteenth century animal rights were nearly as pressing an issue as children's rights. Feminists were highly sensitive to issues affecting animals, and most were active members of the Society for the Protection of Animals.

Servants

The size and composition of a staff of servants depended on a family's social status and standard of living. Servants were the most visible symbol of status. Hiring a maid marked a family's rise to a higher caste—that of the served, of people able to afford leisure for their women, whose function was to exhibit luxury. Domestic service followed the aristocratic model; servants were hired hands but not independent workers, for they were tied to their employers by bonds of personal dependency. The servant devoted his or her time, body, and even person to the masters. Because of its archaic nature,

Servants found work through patrons, contacts, and placement bureaus. Demand exceeded supply in the late 19th century, attracting many peasants and provincials to the city. (*L'Illustration,* 1891.)

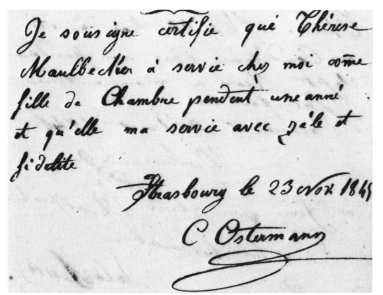

Certificate attesting to the fact that servants were subject to control by both their employers and the municipal authorities. It reads: "I, the undersigned, certify that Thérèse Maulbection(?) served as a maid in my home for one year and that she served me with zeal and loyalty. Strasbourg, 23 Nov. 1849. [signed] C. Ostermann." Surveillance by employers would continue long after municipal supervision had been abolished. (Colmar, Archives of Haut-Rhin.)

servant status was increasingly troubling to people who lived in a democratic society, and by the turn of the twentieth century there were signs that domestic service was on the wane—among them the difficulty of "finding help," of which bourgeois women, including feminists, complained.

The world of servants was hierarchical. At the top of the ladder were tutors and nannies, which only well-to-do families who wished to educate their children at home could afford. These servants were seen as quasi-intellectuals, as often they were. The rise of compulsory education diminished the number of tutors more than the number of nannies, of whom Flaubert wrote in the *Dictionnaire des idées reçues:* they "are always from an excellent family that has suffered misfortunes. Dangerous in the home, corrupt husbands." In 1847 the duc de Choiseul-Praslin, having fallen in love with a young governess, murdered his wife and then committed suicide. This notorious case, which exhibited a member of the aristocracy reduced to a vulgar crime of passion, shook the monarchy. Early-nineteenth-century nannies were usually French; later fashion favored English and German girls. They almost invariably were targets of the master's desire. "Mademoiselle" was obliged to counter her seductive allure by affecting an austere appearance, wearing glasses and a proper bun.

The lot of lower-ranking servants was even more difficult. They wore uniforms and lacked social position. Their

Bécassine was created in 1906 for the *Semaine de Suzette*. She typified the Breton maid, naive but devoted, whose gaffes and bad grammar delighted bourgeois readers. Garrulous though she was, Bécassine had neither mouth nor ears, to show that, as far as what went on in her masters' home was concerned, she was both deaf and dumb. (Paris, Bibliothèque Nationale.)

situation was ambiguous because they were at once inside and outside—a part of the master's family, yet excluded from it, intimate with the household and its secrets, yet obliged to see nothing and above all to say nothing. Bécassine, a comic-strip servant, was portrayed as having no mouth. Increasingly servants were women whose chief relation was with the mistress of the house. As the great aristocratic households were whittled down, domestic staffs were reduced to the *bonne à tout faire,* the all-purpose maid, and petty bourgeois families marked their ambition by hiring a servant. The profession became proletarianized and feminized, a familiar combination that indicated its loss of social prestige.

The most difficult position of all was that of the valet or chambermaid, a nearly extinct species. As long as their personhood was denied there was no problem. Their intimate contact with their masters made no difference, since servants were not sexual beings. In the eighteenth century the marquise du Châtelet could still tranquilly ask her valet Longchamp to attend her in her bath, even though Longchamp himself was sufficiently aware of his virility to be troubled by the request, as he confessed in his memoirs. But within a century and a half the bathroom had become a sanctuary, and masters, unwilling to expose themselves to their servants, hid their nudity behind closed doors. In the *Journal d'une femme de chambre* (Diary of a Chambermaid) Célestine de Mirbeau observed that "Madame dresses alone and does her own hair. She locks herself with two turns of the key in her dressing room, where I am seldom allowed to enter." It was almost as if she regretted this infringement on her prerogatives. Georges Vigarello has shown how this expulsion was preceeded by "more stringent standards of personal appearance."[43]

The need for greater privacy affected not only the bathroom but other parts of the house as well, including the bedroom. A decent woman made her own bed, with servants standing by but not actually present in the room. The woman could see them or at least call them if needed without being seen herself. Jeremy Bentham's brother Samuel designed a system for English households that allowed servants to be called from a distance. Under the Directory in France bells for calling servants became common; "cityoenne Ziguette" (Count Roederer) complained that this change had resulted in a loss of familiarity with the staff. Viollet-le-Duc, whose *Histoire d'une maison* (History of a House, 1873) was intended to be a model, lavished a great deal of attention on vestibules, corridors, and stairways, which were supposed to serve as avenues of circulation and communication as well as escape. Michelet could not bear the scrutiny of servants: "The rich . . . live before their domestics [read: before their enemies]. They eat, sleep, and make love under hateful, mocking eyes. They have no privacy, no secrecy, no home." Hence "the crucial axiom for maintaining peace at home is to live *à deux* rather than *à trois*." This rejection of servants as intruders probably indicates the advent of a new sensibility, yet it is also a sign that servants were coming to be seen as individuals, a development that ultimately spelled the end of domestic service.

The more common way of overcoming the dilemma in the nineteenth century was to deny the servant's individuality, to ignore his or her body. Anne Martin-Fugier has shown how servants were denied personhood to such a degree that their true first and last names were dropped and they were assigned new names when they entered service: "From now on you shall be known as Marie."[44] A servant in principle had

Octave Uzanne, *Woman in Paris.* The bathtub, which like most advances in hygiene originated in England, became common in France in the 1880s. Soon modesty would not allow even a chambermaid as respectful as this one to attend the mistress' bath. (Paris, Bibliothèque Historique.)

Domestic espionage. Servants, whom Michelet referred to as "our enemies," were always eager to discover their masters' secrets. Right: two servants spy on madame through the keyhole. Opposite page: a chambermaid avidly reads her mistress' mail and is in turn caught in the act by the lady herself. Turn-of-the-century salons featured countless paintings on similar subjects, evidence of a growing malaise. The Flemish painter Remy Gogghe, whose work is shown here, specialized in powerful social satire.

Right: Remy Gogghe, *Madame Is Receiving*. (Salon of 1908.) Opposite page: *Mistress of the House and Her Indiscreet Chambermaid*. (Salon of 1904.)

no private life, family life, or sex life, for she had no space or time of her own, nor even any right to space or time. The seventh floor, where servants slept, was often a shabby, promiscuous space that established a distance, a separation ensuring that only furtive pleasures could exist. Mistresses often harbored social and sexual fantasies about what went on upstairs.

Maids were normally unmarried, supposedly without lovers, husbands, or children. If misfortune befell a serving woman, she took care of things on her own. Servants accounted for a high proportion of women prosecuted for infanticide. They filled the hospital maternity wards, refuge of the unmarried mother, and were often obliged to abandon their children after giving birth. When people became concerned about the low birth rate, tolerance of unwed mothers increased. Many servants then kept their children, but the need to raise the children often kept them tied to their jobs.

If it happened that the master of the house was the father

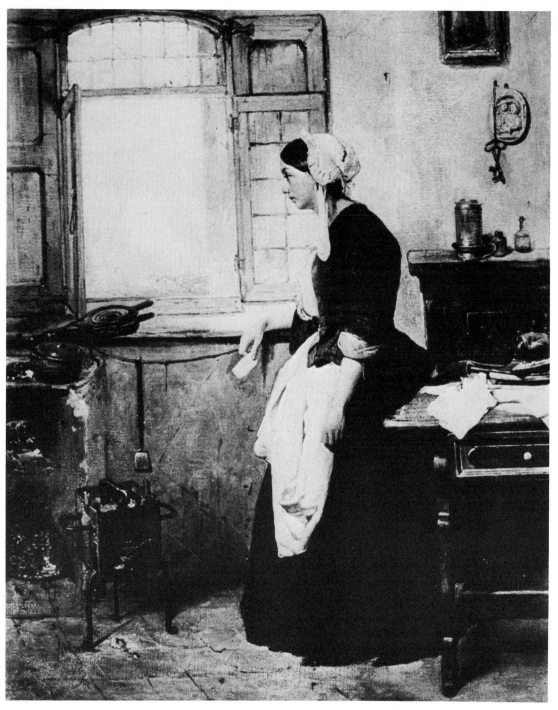

Domenico Induno, *The Letter*. Where is he? Will the man who seduced or promised to marry this young servant with the bulging belly return to claim his child? The old device of using a letter to suggest an absence is here invested with the melancholy of abandonment. (Naples, Capodimonte Museum.)

of a maid's child, the woman was obliged either to disappear or to keep her mouth shut. Helen Demuth, who bore a child by Karl Marx, kept silent about the boy's existence throughout her life. When, much later, after both Helen and Karl were dead, their daughter Eleanor discovered the truth, she fell ill, not because of the affair but because of the lie that had covered it up. Helen Demuth's position in the Marx family, with which she identified to the point of denying herself, is a paradoxical example of the abnegation to which good-hearted serving women were reduced, women like those visible in the corner of the photograph of one family whose name has been forgotten. Some of these women were so devoted to their employers' families that they had no other roof, no family of their own, and watched over their master's children like eternal nannies. Berthe Sarrazin cared for the ailing Toulouse-Lautrec and sent news of his health to his relatives. Sharing in the family spirit was an unconscious means of avoiding suffering and giving life meaning. Thus Céleste Albaret—the model of Proust's Françoise—and Berthe, Nathalie Clifford-Barney's chambermaid, were vigilant, affectionate observers of the greatness of their masters.

This survival of feudal times was incompatible with the development of self-consciousness. If masters were no longer willing to be seen by their servants, servants were no longer willing to endure the negation of their bodies and their very being. Although there were few open rebellions, many made their protests felt. They changed employers, refused orders, spurned advice, and pursued goals of their own. Young maids saved themselves for marriage and were reputed to be good matches. Fewer provincials came to the cities in search of positions in service, in part because by the end of the nineteenth century they were deterred by fears of the "Parisian malady," syphilis. The "servant crisis," reflected by a marked increase in the number of employment offers in the newspapers, a slight rise in wages, the first steps toward the organization of servants, and protective legislation, actually stemmed from private and personal considerations. It was a sign of the democratization of private life.

Jean-Léon Gérome, *The Doorway of the House, with the Artist's Father and Son*. Loneliness at the beginning and at the end of life. (Rouen, Musée des Beaux-Arts.)

On the Fringe

The family model had such normative power in the nineteenth century that it imposed itself on institutions as well as individuals. Vast areas of life were defined as lying outside the family, hence as being suspect. In these areas the rules of private life were blurred, and even the right to privacy was in doubt. The celibate and the solitary—those who chose or were obliged to live outside the family on a temporary or permanent basis—played an important social role.

Imitation of the family governed the lives of some. Ballerinas who danced at the Opera, for instance, had an "opera mother" who tried to find a "father" to protect them in their musical "home." In the penal colony at Mettray, near Tours, prisoners formed "families" composed of "brothers," two of whom were designated "elders." In protest against cloying family life, some bachelors attempted to develop their own unique style: "A curse upon the family, which softens the heart of the brave, which encourages every kind of cowardice, which extracts every conceivable concession, and which marinates you in an ocean of milk and tears." So wrote Flaubert, cousin to the dandies of the nineteenth century, to his friend Louis Bouilhet on October 5, 1855. Flaubert's letter anticipates the words of André Gide: "*Familles, je vous hais*" (Families, I hate you).

Eliminating the family and its domestic theater from private life left two polar opposites: the individual and society. The individual, as Stendhal observed, thrived on selfish curiosity, curiosity necessary if he was to explore the complexities of the emerging public society. Some people yearned for medieval and aristocratic ways, ways that belonged to an outdated, prefamilial society; still others were alive with the attitudes of the avant-garde.

Institutions of the Celibate

Sexual segregation was a fundamental principle of institutions such as schools, prisons, and public welfare agencies whose purpose was to take charge of unmarried and solitary individuals. Convents, seminaries, and to a certain extent the military drew upon volunteers. Other celibate institutions did not, but all employed disciplinary methods honed long ago by the army and the Church. Inmates were physically segregated from the outside world and kept under "panoptic" surveillance so as to prevent communication between peers. Such communication was feared as a source of antihierarchical sentiment and possible perversion, a fear that stemmed from a deep distrust of the inmates' ability to speak to one another and from suspicion of their physical and sexual needs. Nighttime, when the desire for intimacy was greatest, was particularly dreaded.

If possible the authorities would have preferred to confine each inmate in an individual cell, or "box," as the private room was called in English boarding schools, but resources were limited. The prisons, though an extreme case, illustrate the general rule. By the 1840s voices calling for individual cells had gained the ascendancy, and in 1875 a law was passed requiring imprisonment in private cells, but it was never enforced. Guards, pressing inquisitorial eyes to peepholes in cell doors, attempted to control promiscuity. In the nineteenth century, moreover, isolation was widely used as a therapy, from insane asylums to sanatoria.[45] "The genius of suspicion came into the world," Stendhal wrote.

We must take care to avoid dubious parallels. The similarities among these different types of institutions were purely formal. It made a tremendous difference whether a person joined the institutional population voluntarily or involuntarily, as the result of a vocation or for some other reason. In principle, those who responded to a call freely accepted the discipline imposed on them and internalized the rules of the institution. A dualist spirituality prevailed in nineteenth-century convents.[46] The soul was strictly divorced from the body, which was viewed as a source of evil to be silenced, banished from memory, or punished. Ascetic practices, both physical and moral, were designed to help individuals achieve the goal of pure spirituality. In the contemplative orders asceticism was at times carried to extreme lengths, including the symbolic murder of the "Other" who stood in the way of union with God. Many pious adolescent girls dreamed, sometimes with encouragement from their oppressed mothers, of dying

The judas hole or spy window on the cell door enabled the guard to see without being seen. The law of 1875 set forth the principle of the individual cell, which went along with individual surveillance. Solitude was both penance and remedy. (Salon of 1905.)

young. For Thérèse of Lisieux early death was a sublime grace. Devotion did not preclude temptation, however. The passions of heart and flesh lay shrouded in secrecy, hidden in dark, cavernous fortresses of the soul. Within the cloister itself new boundaries between public and private arose. Every detail, every word and sound, stood out with terrifying clarity. "In the seminary," a critical Stendhal wrote, "there is a way of eating a boiled egg that reveals the progress made in the devout life." After Julien Sorel, the hero of Stendhal's novel *The Red and the Black,* decides to forge a new character for himself, "the movement of his eyes gave him a great deal of trouble."

For those who were involuntarily confined, defending privacy was a constant struggle. Sometimes that struggle took the form of insisting on a time or space of one's own, free of surveillance by the authorities and exempt from the tyranny of the group. Vallès in *L'Insurgé* had warm words for "the little room at the end of the dormitory where teachers could go in free moments to work or to dream." At other times privacy might be defended through the formation of private relationships, which alleviated loneliness and established a protective carapace against intrusion by the authorities. Various tactics were developed to circumvent the rules. Free time was closely managed. Movement created confusion that was conducive to exchange. Friends repaired to neutral territory, to dark corners or bathrooms, which in all closed institutions are a haven of liberty and therefore a focus of suspicion.

Designed by architects Gilbert and Lecointe, the Mazas Prison was opened in 1850 on boulevard Diderot in Paris. In class exercises and religious activities cell doors were used to separate the prisoners. This was a tough prison with a high suicide rate, yet it was noted for the ease with which prisoners were able to communicate with one another. (*L'Illustration,* 1881.)

Paul Gavarni, *The Young Man's Life*. Were students carefree, cynical, and much given to traveling? A cliché that came close to the truth. (Paris, Bibliothèque Nationale.)

Investigation has been made of the means by which institutional subcultures develop: the passing of notes, graffiti (the lingua franca of boarding school and prison), jokes, and signs.[47] Complicity and friendship, including "special" friendships, are invested with peculiar intensity in these closed environments, which act as a spur to latent or manifest homosexual feelings and where the other sex—the forbidden sex—is eagerly eroticized or of necessity sublimated. Extreme constraint and extreme desire coexist. The pleasures of reading, eating, and making love are savored all the more because they are hidden. Feelings are so intense that they may become overwhelming. Sometimes, however, enforced self-restraint over a prolonged period induces repression so extreme that it amounts to anesthesia. Simone Buffard is one of many writers who have described how "prison chill" kills all desire and capacity in the prisoner. Erving Goffmann has analyzed the "loss of autonomy" that occurs in mental hospitals and other total institutions, whose inmates become so self-absorbed that it becomes difficult for them to readapt to the outside world.[48]

To date little attention has been devoted to the lives of

the confined, precisely because those lives are out of sight, deliberately hidden from the view of the public and therefore of the historian. What we know about them we know only because the walls have been breached, and it is unlikely that we can make the subtle distinctions required. Although Baudelaire, Vallès, and others who attended religious boarding schools often compared their institutions to prisons, the comparison is accurate only in certain respects. Surveillance techniques and forms of private intercourse in different total institutions may appear similar without really being so. The diversity of these institutions needs to be studied in historical perspective. Which were most susceptible to external influences? In the schools, for example, students' families had a decisive impact on the use of corporal punishment. How did outside attitudes affect such internal matters as mail censorship in barracks and prisons, furlough and parole policies, sleeping arrangements, and personal hygiene? Resistance to discipline and desire for change had a profound impact on even the most rigid and static institutions.

In 1860 France counted some 50,000 prisoners, 100,000 monks and nuns, 163,000 boarding students, 320,000 hospitalized mental patients, and nearly 500,000 soldiers. Each of these tribes had its own forms of private life; they should not be forgotten.

The Unwed

In the nineteenth century few people chose to remain unmarried for life, but many, particularly women, found themselves deprived of a spouse at an early age and left alone for long periods. The age at which people married declined for both sexes, but unequally. In the 1851 census, more than 51 percent of men were unmarried, compared with only 35 percent of women. By the age of thirty-five, however, only 18 percent of men remained unmarried, compared with 20 percent of women. At sixty-five only 7 percent of men were unmarried, whereas the rate of celibacy remained above 10 percent for women in all age groups. In short, the rate of marriage was higher for men than for women, even though men married later; married life offered men convenience and respectability. The dandy Baudelaire remarked in a letter to his mother (December 4, 1854) that he needed "a family at all cost. It's the only way to work and spend less." Gustave de Beaumont, struck, as was his friend Tocqueville, by the spectacle of married life in America, anticipated in a letter to his brother Achille (September 25, 1831) that the American family

Francisco Oller, *The Student*. He reads in desultory fashion, while she sews in silence. They drink coffee in their cozy little apartment. Their relationship is not destined to last long. (Paris, Louvre.)

would soon become the norm: "I fear that we shall arrive at a state of affairs in which bachelors will find themselves in an untenable situation and only fathers with families will enjoy any security at all." Sixty years later Péguy would hail those same "fathers with families" as the "heroes of the modern world."

Great suspicion was attached to celibacy.[49] Although the Church and the sociologist Frédéric Le Play approved of celibacy because it permitted abnegation, society viewed the person who did not marry as "dry fruit." Flaubert in his *Dictionnaire des idées reçues* skewered certain contemporary aphorisms: "Bachelors: all selfish and debauched. They ought to be taxed. A sad old age lies in store for them." The noun *célibataire* (bachelor) applied only to men; in describing women it became an adjective (*femme célibataire,* or spinster). The *Larousse du XIXe siècle* remarked on "the confusion of one Englishman, unfamiliar with the synonyms of our language, who referred to the *garçons* in a restaurant as *célibataires*" (*garçon,* "waiter," can also mean "bachelor"). The *célibataire* was always a male; an unmarried woman *reste fille,* "remained a girl," that is, nothing—or, worse yet, she became, a *vieille fille,* an *anormale,* or a *déclassée* like comtesse Dash.

A Bachelor Party. Young men celebrate with paid companions in a hired room. (Paris, Bibliothèque Nationale.)

Jean-Paul Laurens, *The Student.*
A medieval student as imagined
by a historical painter. (Salon
of 1909.)

Celibacy, whether temporary or permanent, was a very
different experience for men and women. Women lived in
anticipation of marriage; the life of the unmarried young lady
was one of seclusion. By contrast, the young bachelor led a
full, free, and merry life, an apprenticeship, to which marriage, a settling down, spelled an end. Bachelorhood was a
happy time, at least as embellished in memory, a time of
fleeting love affairs, of travel, of camaraderie, and of free-
wheeling relations with other men (see Flaubert's correspondence). It was also the age of "sentimental education" and
sexual experience, when everything was permitted. Young
men "sowed their wild oats" and "got it out of their system."
Nothing changed until the end of the century, when fear of
syphilis slowed some men down. Even among the poorer
classes a period of wanderlust was institutionalized in the form
of the journeyman's *tour de France.* Young workers traveled
from town to town learning their trade and a little something
about life before settling down.

In Paris, students, who often lingered for years over the
arcana of law and medicine, formed a tribe about which such
tenacious myths have grown up that it is hard to judge the

reality. One myth is that of the Latin Quarter, perpetually agitated by political turmoil and under constant surveillance until at least 1851.[50] Another is that of Bohemia, immortalized by Murger; an attempt has been made to pinpoint its boundaries, identify its citizens, trace the changes of its political beliefs and literary tastes, and to follow its denizens in their travels from the boul' Mich to Montmartre and from Montmartre to Montparnasse.[51]

Le Vie de Bohème

Bohemia encompassed several types of citizen. One was the "amateur," the young man who "deserted home and family" to live "the life of adventure," but only for a time before finally settling down. Another was the "artist." Most Bohemians—the "unknown Bohemia"—lived in anonymous poverty, stoic, passive, and never attaining notoriety. "They died for the most part of a disease that science does not dare call by its true name, misery," victims of tuberculosis and the hospitals. "They spit, they cough, and the neighbors become annoyed, so they go to the Charité" (Vallès). A small minority achieved success and recognition: "Their names are on the posters." Many of these were painters, sculptors, and writers, but there were also journalists associated with the *petite presse,* the lesser publishers who bought caricatures, poems, and *blagues* (humorous stories).

Scenes from the Bohemian Life (1851): Café Momus, where Murger's four heroes met their girlfriends. (*L'Illustration,* 1852.)

Bohemia established a model of private life that opposed the bourgeois model point by point. In the first place the bohemian's relation to time and space was the opposite of the bourgeois's. The bohemian lived at night and owned no watch, and he lived in the salons and cafés and on the boulevards of the city. No bohemian could "take ten steps on a boulevard without running into a friend." His greatest pleasure and principal occupation was conversation. He lived and wrote in pubs, libraries, and reading rooms. Bohemians resembled urban workers in their private use of public space. Perpetually hounded by creditors and sheriff's deputies, the bohemian had no fixed domicile, no furniture, and very few possessions of any kind. One of Murger's heroes, Schaunard, carried his belongings with him in cavernous pockets. Often several bohemians shared temporary lodgings, which they excelled at transforming for an evening's celebration with a few sophisticated art objects or hangings or other decorations, set up for the occasion as one might pitch a tent.

Meager bohemians disdained thrift as the virtue of fat

The *grisette,* Musset insisted, was "virtuous, decent, proper, careful, sincere, and gay." This one spurns the advances of a gentleman in too much of a hurry. (Paris, Bibliothèque Nationale.)

cats, and in one night of gala celebration or gambling they could easily squander sums earned, borrowed, or snatched from the communal pot. Bohemians scorned private property and shared everything, including women, who passed from one to another at will. Multiple affairs were the rule, and infidelity was a principle. Schaunard collected locks of hair; he had sixty. *Grisettes* and *lorettes,* young ladies of easy virtue, often paid the price in these affairs, for while relations between the sexes were less hierarchical among bohemians than in other segments of society, they were still unequal. In Bohemia too, man was king, even if some especially shrewd women managed to make their way or at least to take pleasure in living without toil. Some women, enjoying what Sébastien Mercier called a "kind of masculine liberty," made conquests. For female Rastignacs, whose youth and beauty vanquished Paris, Bohemia was but a stepping stone. "I am all alone, and that's nobody's business but my own," said Eugène Sue's improbable subversive Rigolette.

In this communal and public life, love was the one act that required a minimum of privacy. When a couple succumbed to the pangs of desire, it cut itself off from the crowd. For sex, a private room, a closed door, and drawn curtains were indispensable. Sexual intimacy could not be shared, and in that sense, at least, it resembled marriage.

Murger's portrait of Bohemia was as much if not more dream than reality, but it exerted a powerful attraction on young people, particularly those from the provinces. To go to Paris and become a writer, poet, or journalist, to escape the dull bourgeois life—this was an ambition widely shared by those "victims of the book" of whom Jules Vallès later gave a more pessimistic portrait. One symptom, perhaps, is that the subproletariat of *réfractaires* (Bohemians unwilling to become bourgeois) that orbited around the private schools and lesser newspapers never found loneliness more unbearable than on Sunday, the "condemned man's seventh day," when families filled all public space and made them feel left out wherever they went.

Dandies

Dandyism was a more conscious and elaborate rejection of bourgeois life than bohemianism.[52] British in origin and aristocratic in essence, dandyism took distinction for its very principle. Codified by Brummell, Barbey d'Aurevilly, Baudelaire, and Fromentin *(Dominique),* dandyism accentuated difference in a society that was moving toward uniformiza-

Henri Gervex, illustration for Balzac's *La Fille aux yeux d'or,* 1898. "A man becomes rich; he is born elegant," said Balzac, an aristocrat at heart. (Paris, Bibliothèque Nationale.)

Henri Gervex, for *La Fille aux yeux d'or.* Dandyism was fashion and elegance; it was relaxing on the sofa after a brisk horseback ride; and it was the pleasure of friendship between men. (Paris, Bibliothèque Nationale.)

tion. The bohemian leaned to the left politically, the dandy to the right. Antiegalitarian, the dandy hoped to restore an aristocracy based not on money or ancestry but on temperament and style. A dandy was born, not made.

A public man, the dandy, an actor on the urban stage, hid his individuality behind the protective mask of appearance, which he strove to make undecipherable. He was fond of illusion and disguise and exquisitely sensitive to detail, to such accessories as gloves, ties, canes, scarves, and hats. The Goncourt brothers mocked Barbey d'Aurevilley's appearance, the "carnival that parades through the streets of his personality all year long." A dandy, Carlyle said, is "a man who wears clothes . . . He lives to dress." Grooming was one of his primary occupations, and Baudelaire claimed that he never took less than two hours a day with his toilette. Unlike courtiers of old, however, the dandy attached extreme importance to cleanliness of both body and linen—a sign of a new attitude toward the body. Barbey bathed every day, and when the ailing Maurice de Guérin had to return to Le Cayla, his sister Eugénie's greatest concerns were the lack of water and the absence of a dressing room.

Such habits required leisure time and an income sufficient to live without working. Although dandies were better off than bohemians, they were not wealthy men. Contempt for

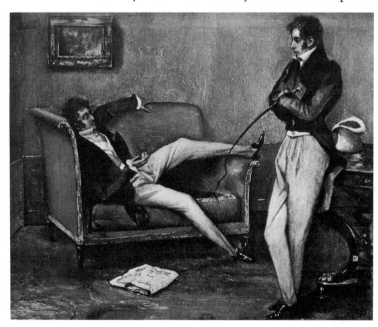

the pursuit of wealth, fondness for ostentatious luxury and gambling, and acceptance of the risks of the gaming table and the possibility of being obliged to live more austerely—all these were part of the dandy's anticapitalist, antibourgeois morality. The dandy hated parvenus (and Jews insofar as they symbolized the manipulator of money), business, and family life. Marriage, he believed, was the worst form of captivity, and women were the chains that enslaved. For dandies carnal pleasure could only be a matter of commerce. Love of boys was best. The word "homosexuality" did not become current until 1891, but the dandy's homosexuality became increasingly pronounced as the values of women and family gained prominence, or so the dandy professed to believe.

The advent of the "new woman" triggered a crisis of male identity throughout Europe. This crisis, interpreted by Otto Weininger in *Sexe et caractère* (1903), probably played a part in the resurgence of pederasty at the end of the nineteenth century, a resurgence described from one man's point of view in Edmond de Goncourt's *Journal*. Contempt for women, or at any rate for the feminine, pointedly evident in Marinetti's 1909 *Futurist Manifesto,* was another of the constants of dandyism, which should be regarded, in Kempf's view, not as misogynist but as "spernogynist" (from the Latin *spernere,* to scorn). "A woman," Flaubert noted, "is the opposite of a dandy; she is natural, that is, abominable." Dandies, pessimistic and therefore hostile to procreation, also spurned children.

Dandyism was an ethic, a conception of life that raised celibacy and vagabondage to the level of conscious resistance. "I hate the herd, the rule, and the level. Bedouin, if you will; citizen, never" (Flaubert to Louise Colet, January 23, 1854). The flâneur, the dandy, and later the apache were the antidotes to that epitome of the bourgeois, M. Prudhomme. Society tolerated the flâneur and dandy but suppressed the apache, who had emerged from the poorer suburbs to threaten the security of the rich.

The Solitude of Women

Solitude, whether voluntary, endured, or simply borne with resignation, created a difficult situation for women because there was, in a radical sense, no place for female solitude in the conceptual framework of the time. Full of pity, Michelet remarked: "The woman who has neither home nor protection dies." A chorus of voices echoed the same sentiment: "If there is one thing that nature teaches us beyond any doubt, it is that

Henri-Georges Bréard, *The Newspaper*. Old women. A relatively educated woman reads aloud from a newspaper to alleviate the loneliness of friends. (Salon of 1914.)

woman is made to be protected, to live with her mother while still a girl and as a wife under the protection and authority of her husband . . . Women are made to hide their lives" (Jules Simon, *L'Ouvrière*, 1861). There was no salvation for a woman outside the home and marriage .

Considered wanton if she lived by her charms and hopeless if she had none, the single woman incurred suspicion, disapproval, and ridicule. An elderly bachelor might have his eccentricities, but he was regarded as silly rather than pitiful. A spinster, however, was someone who had gone to seed, whose bloom had faded. Balzac saw her as a shamefully "unproductive creature." Cantankerous, sharp-tongued, conspiratorial, even hysterical and wicked, the spinster inspired fear, as evidenced by Balzac's Cousine Bette (1847), who like a spider constantly spun her webs of intrigue in the city, that showcase of stereotypes. Not until the twentieth century do we witness the emergence, under the influence of feminists and of writers such as Léon Frappié, of a different portrait of the single woman. Only then were women accorded the right to remain unmarried.

Yet many women did find themselves alone. The 1851 census revealed that 12 percent of women over the age of fifty had never married and that 34 percent were single; the proportions were identical in 1896. At midcentury the percentages of single women were particularly high in western France, in the Pyrenees, and in the southeastern quarter of the Massif Central. Later, regional differences receded, but the number of women living alone in large cities increased dramatically.

This high level of female solitude had been a constant feature of the demography of western Europe since the Middle Ages. Several factors contributed to the phenomenon. First, strategic calculations by families determined which daughters would marry and which would not; younger sisters were often expected to care for aging parents. Most important of all was widowhood; women lived longer than men and remarriage was rare. The Civil Code protected bourgeois widows better than earlier laws had, but the lot of poorer widows was hard. Few had pensions, for they received no credit for housework and jobs done at home, and in any case their wage-earning activities were too intermittent to constitute a "career." (Women employed by the state tobacco industry were an exception to this rule.) The earliest laws, passed only in 1910, concerning pensions for female workers and peasants show just how marginal their position was. Rural cottages and urban garrets, hospitals and asylums, were filled with poor, elderly women, forgotten by all unless a girl's boarding school decided to offer charitable assistance. The history of old age is an important subject that must be studied with careful attention to gender.

Solitude sometimes was the result of a deliberate choice in response to a religious or altruistic vocation (nurse, social worker, schoolteacher) or a decision to favor career over family.[53] Many female postal workers chose to remain unmarried. In 1880, 73 percent of women employed by the post office after the age of fifty lived alone; 55 percent of them had never married (compared with 10 percent in 1975–1980). Their career histories show that they chose to remain single out of a desire for financial and professional independence; their male colleagues were looking for wives who would stay home, not fellow postal workers.[54] Nineteenth-century women who wished to improve their position in society through work were obliged to sacrifice their private lives. Celibacy was the price they paid.

The daily lot of these lonely women was difficult. Women's wages, still seen as a mere supplement to the family

Richard Miller, *Spinsters*. Two elderly spinsters take tea in a cozy salon. (Salon of 1904.)

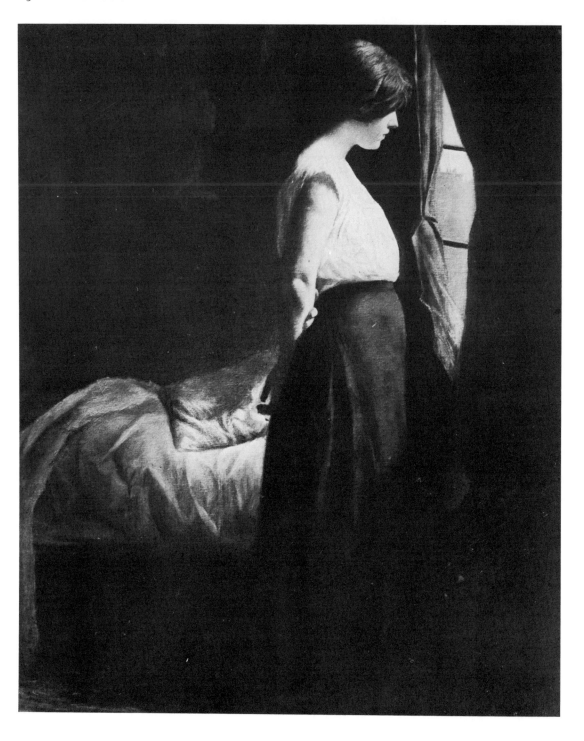

budget, were almost always lower than men's wages. The "female occupations," particularly in the garment trade on which so many women depended, were by nature unskilled. At the turn of the twentieth century, the Office du Travail (Labor Office) investigated conditions among home workers in the highly rationalized garment industry. The reports reveal a world populated by single women, in some cases a mother with her daughters, whose poverty was hidden from view in a sixth-floor walkup. There the working woman kept her treadle-operated Singer going ten to fifteen hours a day. For her daily meal she consumed a "seamstress's cutlet," or sliver of Brie, with a cup of coffee, the Parisian female worker's drug of choice. All things considered, many women preferred to put on a shawl or blouse in the hope of finding a man.

For the youngest workers seduction was a possible resource. A relationship with a man not only made life easier but also resolved the problem of sexuality outside marriage. If a young woman applied for a job at one of the large department stores, the manager often asked if she had a "protector"; without one it seemed impossible that she could make ends meet. Supplanting the *grisette* of an earlier era, many a humble female worker and decent secretary had her "friend," generally a "respectable" man from a somewhat higher social stratum. But for every woman who would have married her lover of many years had he been free, how many women lived on dreams that turned sour when it became clear they had been deceived? Far from being a subversive genre, the romantic novels they so avidly consumed always made it clear that the prince never marries the shepherdess.

It is not known how many single women pooled their resources in order to survive, but the number was certainly large. The census, conducted every five years, counted "households" composed solely of women: mothers, daughters, friends. Researchers such as Villermé and Le Play briefly described these all-female households. Villermé in 1840 noted that women "who have no family and do not live as concubines usually live together in groups of two or three in small studios or rooms, which they furnish jointly."[55] Women did the best they could to cope with a solitude they might not have chosen but in some cases preferred to the unappealing prospect of marriage.

Was there a female equivalent of dandyism? Did some women deliberately resolve to remain unmarried and to live in an unfettered manner of their own choosing? No doubt

Images of feminine solitude. Left: Edmond de Grimberghe, *Melancholy*. A young woman's melancholy at the end of a lonely night. (Salon of 1895.) Above: Charles Vasnier, *Expectation*. A woman awaits the arrival—perhaps—of a man. Women shut up in the home gaze through windows at the world outside. (Salon of 1910.)

there were such women among actresses, about whose private lives little is known. Yet while it was possible for a woman to avoid the shackles of marriage, it was not as easy for her to shun men entirely. Some illustrious courtesans attempted to turn loose morals to their own advantage. Literature has portrayed their lives and fates in contrasting ways. Nana, having put a circle of admiring men at her feet, succumbs to smallpox, a "decomposed Venus." Odette, whom the war enables to become mistress of the duc de Guermantes (in Proust's *Remembrance of Things Past*), is nothing more than a "doddering dowager" by the time she reigns over the faubourg Saint-Germain.

Perhaps female dandyism existed among lesbians after the turn of the century, among women such as Nathalie Clifford-Barney, Renée Vivien, Gertrude Stein, and their friends. Creative aesthetes, champions of Art Nouveau or of the avant-garde, these women, accepted by Paris high society in part because of their foreign origins, claimed the right to live as men. Close to these circles one finds other "new women": journalists, writers, artists, lawyers, physicians, even professors. No longer content with secondary roles, such women accepted no restrictions on their lives or loves. Admired by some, vilified by others, they found nothing easy. To confront the obstacles they needed the friendship—or love—of women and of a few men. The sexual revolution may have been more difficult than the social revolution.

The Homeless

Of all solitary men and women the homeless aroused the greatest suspicion in a society where residence was a condition of citizenship and the hobo was seen as one who rejected the prevailing morality. The peasant who jealously clung to his treasure saw the tramp and the gypsy, in contrast to the familiar hawker, as potential thieves and treated them accordingly. In Gévaudan, villagers cast into a ditch an ironmonger who failed to pay for a glass of wine. A Republic dominated by good family men adopted draconian measures against ne'er-do-wells. Repeat offenders, generally petty thieves and tramps who were declared "unsuited for any kind of work," were sent to Guiana under an 1885 law. Hoboes were subject to confinement and were issued identity cards and health certificates. Tramps were accused of posing a threat to health because allegedly they spread microbes and tuberculosis, among other diseases.[56]

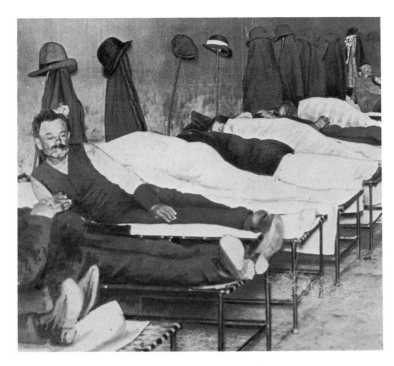

An early-20th-century flophouse. Although certainly more comfortable than the street, these houses were really measures by the authority to control a worrisome population. (Sirot-Angel Collection.)

The celibate, solitary, and homeless were marginals living on the periphery of a society whose center was the family. Their physical and moral lives were complicated. Suspect or accused, they dwelt on the defensive, caught in a net which, though still relatively loose, steadily tightened.

One sign of their archaic status was that their lives were not only solitary but also short, in a world where longevity was a sign of modernity. The celibate died of fatigue or committed suicide. Durkheim saw the group's high suicide rate as proof of nonintegration into society. Migrant workers who moved from the country to the deadly city succumbed to tuberculosis in large numbers. In this group we find silk workers in Lyons, maids in Parisian garrets, and masons from Creuse who rented rooms in the poorer northern and eastern quarters of the city. In fact, tuberculosis, often denounced as the scourge of the celibate, only served to prolong their celibacy, so great was the fear of contagion through marriage.

Solitude, not yet a right of the individual, was a type of relation to oneself and others. It was the very image of what society was not, for this society at any rate valued the orderly warmth of the home above all else.

Jules Alexis Muenier, *Emigrants*. Too romantic for 19th-century France, where internal migrations were more organized and seldom the product of chance, this painting of an emigrant couple is symbolically rich. (Paris, Bibliothèque Nationale.)

Frédéric Bazille, *Family Reunion,* 1867. A family poses in a natural setting, beneath a tree that symbolizes life and duration. (Paris, Musée d'Orsay/Jeu de Paume.)

❧Bourgeois Rituals

Anne Martin-Fugier

A THIRST FOR MEMORY

"Many things were in the air at the château de Fleurville." Camille, Madeleine, Marguerite, and Sophie bustled in anticipation of their cousins' visit. "They came and went, climbed up and down the stairs, ran through the halls, jumped, laughed, cried, and shoved one another." All was ready for the boys' arrival—the château's bedrooms where they would sleep as well as the girls' hearts, aflutter with impatience. Once the bouquets of flowers had been arranged and set out, the preparations were complete, and the comtesse de Ségur's 1859 novel, *Les Vacances* (The Vacation), could begin.

The occasion for the visit was a summer vacation. The extended family gathered; the girls awaited the boys. As proper mistresses they made sure, by attending to such details as the placement of bouquets, that their cousins would be properly welcomed. By generating the emotion that marked the event as an important one, they discharged their role as women, for in general it was a woman's duty to supervise the arrangements for private occasions and to signal those occasions with effusions of sentiment.

Vacation pleasures were characterized not only by spatial location but also by temporal structure. When children gathered, they greeted one another by remembering things past— previous summers:

"'We'll do a lot of silly things, just like two years ago.'
'Do you remember the butterflies we caught?'
'And the ones we didn't catch?'
'And that poor toad—'
'And that little bird—'
'Oh! What a good time we're going to have!' they all shouted, hugging one another for the twentieth time." The

memory, narrated in the past (imperfect) tense, immediately sets the stage for the future. It is a promise and an assurance.

The imperfect, when coupled with a lament for the past, for what will never be again, becomes the romantic imperfect, as in Lamartine's *La Vigne et la maison* (1857):

Efface ce séjour, ô Dieu! de ma paupière,
Ou rends-le-moi semblable à celui d'autrefois,
Quand la maison vibrait comme un grand coeur de pierre
De tous ces coeurs joyeux qui battaient sous les toits!
. . . . .
On eût dit que ces murs respiraient comme un être
Des pampres réjouis la jeune exhalaison;
La vie apparaissait rose, à chaque fenêtre,
Sous les beaux traits d'enfants nichés dans la maison.
. . . . .
Puis la maison glissa sur la pente rapide
Où le temps entasse les jours;
Puis la porte à jamais se ferma sur le vide,
Et l'ortie envahit les cours!

Erase this stay, O God! from my eyelids,
Or make it like that of another day,
When the house used to flutter like a great stone heart,
From all the joyful hearts that beat beneath its roof.
. . . . .
These walls seemed to breathe, as a creature of the vine stock
Takes delight in the exhalation of the young grape;
Through every window life looked rosy
To the beautiful eyes of the children nested within.
. . . . .
Then the house slid down the slippery slope
Where time piles up the days;
Then the door closed forever on the empty house,
And nettles invaded the yards!

For Lamartine, time kills the happiness that made even the stones palpitate.

But happiness can be kept alive in memory, and then the imperfect serves to amass joyous souvenirs that illuminate the present. Not only is the present possible to bear, but, nurtured by memory, it can be exploited to the full; fleeting happy moments, strung together on a thread of time, are converted into fruitful duration.

Ferdinand Heilbuth, *The Snack*. (Paris, Bibliothèque Nationale.)

In this perspective children are doubly important. Their happiness must be assured so that they may amass a capital of joyous souvenirs. At the same time adults accumulate a wealth of irreplaceable memories of a time when their children were young.

The quotidian, banal by essence, assumes a positive value if the trivial moments of which it is composed are transformed into rituals to which a sentimental significance is attached. The mistress of the household who at regular intervals convenes the family around the dining room table is designated as the administrator of happiness. She sets the rhythm of private life, establishes its regularity, and directs the performance.

Repetition is not routine in bourgeois space. It ritualizes, and ritual extends the duration of the moment. Beforehand, one waits, one makes ready; afterward, one comments, one relives the experience. Pleasure lies in anticipating the moments that punctuate the day. Ritualization attaches the value happiness to the event destined to become a souvenir.

Memories, hoarded like capital, were recorded as in a passbook. Mme Alphonse Daudet used the phrase "feminine chronologies" to describe collections, assembled by women, of everyday objects that were treated as relics. One woman

Recording the Passage of Time

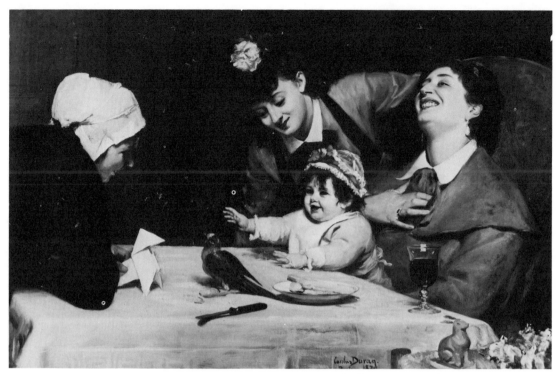

Carolus-Duran, *Laughing Women,* 1838. A child among women. The servant was part of the bourgeois family's universe. (Detroit, Michigan Institute of Arts.)

might collect gloves she had worn, another dresses. Ladies and young misses decorated their "albums" with inscriptions in prose or verse as well as drawings—other forms of relic.

The invention of photography in 1836 set the stage for a new kind of album. Photography became increasingly popular after 1850; the short form "photo" did not appear until 1876. Portraits in oil depicted their subject outside of time, in the eternity of art; photos preserved the moment. Not only did photographs serve as relics useful for spurring the memory; assembled in albums, photographic images revealed the passage of time, the growth of children, and the perpetuation of the family through marriages, births, and baptisms.

In her work on the Boileau family Caroline Chotard-Lioret has discovered three albums containing some forty slides taken between 1860 and 1890. These slides were sent to the Boileaus by various correspondents. Marie Boileau received several letters from her cousins promising to send recent photos of themselves and their families. Through the pictures we can follow the course of individual lives from baptism at age seven to adolescence and on through marriage to adulthood and parenthood and finally old age. This social practice provides "concrete evidence of the size of a family network."[1] When Marie's daughters married in 1901, she sent their portraits to other family members. After 1910 photographs became commonplace. Between 1912 and 1914 Marie's husband, Eugène filled sixteen albums with pictures he had taken.

Private diaries also served as repositories of memory. Gabrielle Laguin, a young bourgeois woman from Grenoble, began her diary in July 1890, when she was sixteen and a half: "Many years from now, perhaps I shall feel pleasure on re-reading these scribblings, begun in a time of youth and joy" (July 12). On October 30 she struck the same chord: "Later, when I am quite old, it will amuse me to reread this diary, to see myself in the mirror of the past as I was then."

Before long her diary became a reference book. In writing it she was creating a history for herself. By inscribing the present between the past and the future, she structured her life. The present is what is least in evidence in these pages; it was immediately transformed into the past, into an object of reference.

The future for Gabrielle consisted of dreams of marriage to her cousin Louis Berruel, aged twenty-eight. On October 3, 1891, those dreams came true. Yet she continued to situate herself with respect to both the past ("Oh! How happy I am! My life's dream came true one month and three days ago.") and the future ("Yes, of course, I do still desire something, and that something is a nice little baby. Will 1892 be the year when I shall experience the pleasure of becoming a mother?"). There her diary ends, at a crucial moment in this young woman's life. Her diary served in part as a place to record confidential observations about her own emotions. Even more important, it enabled her to record the passage of time, to write the history of her life by linking her present to the flow of time.

Twenty years later, Gabrielle's eldest daughter, Renée Berruel, began a diary in a student notebook. The earliest surviving entry dates from 1905, when Renée was thirteen. But she had begun her record much earlier, judging from what she wrote on March 9, 1910, on the five hundredth page of her diary: "Five hundred! They're beginning to mount up! True, it will soon be eight years since I began." It all started with a book. "We were all at Buissière for All Hallows, gathered in the dining room near the fire . . . I didn't know what to do with myself and went browsing through the shelves, where I found Lamartine's *Manuscript of My Mother*. At that moment it occurred to me to keep a diary of my own."[2]

Private diaries can provide invaluable details about the lives of the people who kept them. But they are just as interesting for what they tell us about the desire to mark the passage of time. Regular family correspondences arose out of the same desire. Marie and Eugène Boileau received 11,000 letters between 1873 and 1920, the majority of them from their children and other family members. The letters contain information about children, family business, visits, and above all the health of relatives, but almost nothing about deeply private feelings. Correspondence served a ritual function: it was concrete evidence of an emotional bond between family members. The value of letters lay not so much in what they said as in the regularity of their exchange.

The desire to mark the passage of time in its purest form is seen in the so-called birthday books, which appeared first in England and later in France. In 1892 the publisher Paul Ollendorff published what he called the *Recueil Victor Hugo* (Victor Hugo Anthology). In its preface he remarked that English birthday books were usually filled with selections from Byron or Shakespeare but that he had chosen Hugo in homage to France's national poet. Inside, each recto page was blank except for the indication of a month and day, while the verso page oppposite contained a quote from Hugo.

The birthday book could be used in three different ways. First, a birthday might be observed by noting which of the poet's thoughts corresponded to it. Second, one might comment (or ask a friend to comment) on the poet's lines. Third, the book could be used as a diary; among women this was its primary use.

I have here a birthday book, a *Recueil Victor Hugo,* that once belonged to Claire P. of Châteaufort. At different stages in her life Claire used her book in different ways. Sometimes she marked down important dates and birthdays. Sometimes, usually when life was particularly eventful, as at the time of her engagement or during her trip to Russia, she recorded the events of certain days in detail, as in a diary. Her little book, filled with writing in a hand so small as to be at times illegible, wound up in the hands of an antique dealer; with it we can investigate a life that this woman wished to preserve from oblivion.

Claire was born on September 1, around 1870. Her First Communion was in 1880. She lived sometimes on avenue

Wagram in Paris, sometimes on the shores of Lake Geneva in Montreux, where her family owned a château that was sold on May 30, 1896, after which Claire and her parents moved to a rented villa. As a young lady Claire led a life filled with parties and promenades, but what mattered to her more than anything else was music. The high points of her life were her trip to Russia in 1899; her father's illness, followed on August 17, 1900, by his death; her engagement in February 1902 and marriage in April of that same year to Edmond; and the birth of her son Albert on January 11, 1903.

The birthday book contains a few remarks on Claire's warm and affectionate relations with her husband. On April 6, the day following their wedding, she wrote: "Fair. Edmond and I take a wagon ride out to the mills and back by way of Dampierre and the quays of the Loire. It was lovely . . . I'm delighted. Hawthorn in bloom." On May 15 she had this to say: "The doctor tells me I can look forward to a baby. Surely I have all the symptoms! I'm very pleased, and so is Edmond! He says he loves me even more! And I feel his affection growing every day!" On August 6: "The dear baby I'm expecting is drawing us closer and closer together." She then left for Le Pouliguen with her sister-in-law; Edmond joined the two women there from August 10 to August 17. November 20 was Edmond's name day: "I wished him many happy returns the night before with green plants and ferns."

Albert was born on Sunday, January 11, 1903, and baptized on February 15. After that the entries in the book become less frequent. On September 23 we read: "I leave Luvigny with Bébert and Nounou for Paris and Saumur, where we expect to meet Edmond." On November 26 Albert's first tooth appeared, followed by his second on December 11. On February 22, 1904, the child, aged thirteen and a half months, was photographed in Saumur. On June 19: "Bébert is walking better and better. To the Bellay Pond with him, Edmond. Delightful day." On May 6, 1905: "Return to Saumur—Bébert, Lucie, and I. Edmond *excellent,* happy to see me again after a week apart. Grandma and the sisters and brothers were delighted with Bébert, who was so good and is talking so well for his two years and three months. Amusing! His father is crazy about him!" At this point the diary skips to 1910. Claire takes her son to Montreux on December 8. On December 25: "Very beautiful Christmas tree." On December 31: "All go tobogganing. Ideal day. Took photos. Albert took a toboggan run with Ferdi."

The final entries bear postwar dates. On December 27, 1918, we find: "Nice—Cimiez, villa Rosa. Above the Arenas. Spending the winter with mother, Marie, Albert." And on August 29 of the following year: "1919: Paris, 38, rue de Bellechasse. Spending the winter in Paris."

Claire P.'s birthday book is an ideal source for exploring the question of time in private life. Bedside reading throughout her life, the book clearly marks the major milestones in the life of a person born into good society: First Communion; an adolescence taken up with balls, excursions, and amusements; engagement; marriage; and the birth and baptism of a child. The pace of life is subsequently determined by the child's growth and upbringing. We also learn about the importance of different periods in the year as marked by religious holidays, especially Christmas and Easter.

MORNING, NOON, AND NIGHT

The course of the day is clearly mapped out in the manuals of proper behavior in which the nineteenth century abounded. These manuals were repeatedly reprinted in new variations and adapatations. To give just two examples, Mme Pariset's 1821 *Manuel de la maîtresse de maison* (Manual for the Mistress of the House) was revised by Mme Celnart and reissued in 1913 under the title *Nouveau manuel complet de la maîtresse de maison,* and Mme Gacon-Dufour's *Manuel complet de la maîtresse de maison ou la parfaite ménagère* (Complete Manual of the Mistress of the House, or The Perfect Homemaker), which first appeared in 1826, went through many subsequent editions.

The evolution of these guides followed the progress of urbanization. In the first half of the nineteenth century Alida de Savignac offered two different guides for housewives, one for Paris (*La Jeune maîtresse de maison,* 1836), the other for the country (*La Jeune propriétaire,* 1838). Little by little these books came to be aimed exclusively at urban women, with only an appendix for those who lived in the country. That appendix shrank in size until eventually it disappeared altogether, leaving urban life as the only model and the countryside as no more than a place to vacation in.

These housewives' manuals continued the tradition of the previous century's *ménagers,* or household books. They emphasized the economic rationality of the woman's role as manager of the household. Their popularity is symptomatic of the need to invent a new and exclusively private way of life and a new form of happiness, centered in the family circle. In order to enjoy that happiness the housewife had to learn how to manage time and money in the correct manner, and the new manuals set out to teach her what she needed to know in order to organize her life properly. They also described the various rituals that marked the passage of time and the role to be played in each by the different members of the family.

The leading role was that of the mistress of the household, who was responsible for orchestrating not only everyday ceremonies such as family meals and evenings by the fire but also the visits, receptions, and other social occasions that constituted the family's relations with the outside world. She was obliged to supervise the performance of household chores in such a way as to maximize the well-being of the entire family, her husband above all.

Edgar Degas, *The Bellelli Family,* circa 1860. The females appear before the master of the house. Mme Bellelli's demeanor is dignified and chilly. Her power is all the more impressive in that her daughters reproduce it and share it between them. The painting accurately portrays the role of the bourgeois mother: she was queen of the roost, but a queen who reigned *for him.* (Paris, Louvre.)

For men, time was the time of public life. A man's schedule was dictated by his business. Few men in good society were idle and therefore free to arrange their days as they pleased. Although one manual published in 1828 instructed fashionable men-about-town how to use their idle time, as the century progressed publications for men were increasingly designed as career guides. Fewer and fewer people lived on private incomes.

Home was the haven in which men rested from their outside labors, and everything possible was to be done to make that haven a place of harmony. The house was a nest, a place where time stood still. Not only was this nest idealized, so too was the women who was its mistress. Like a fairy, she was expected to achieve perfection without making a show of the effort required. "Like the mechanic at the opera, she controls everything that happens yet no one sees her doing it."

Schedules

As director of the household a woman worked with one essential tool, her schedule, which she required her servants to observe and which she herself respected scrupulously. Regularity was the fundamental law of managing time. It began with the ritual of arising. The mistress of the house was in theory the first to get up in the morning and the last to go to bed at night. It was recommended that she rise at six-thirty or seven in the summer, at seven-thirty or eight in the winter. From the moment of awakening a women kept a sharp eye out for problems. Even if a maid washed and dressed the children and prepared their breakfast, it was essential that they be seen by their mother before they left for school.

Servants called for discreet but constant surveillance. Middle-class families generally employed three: a valet-coachman, a cook, and a chambermaid. The mistress of the house went over the household books daily with the servants. She then gave orders for the day (including the chores to be done and the day's menus). She inquired about supplies of food, wood, and coal. She checked the dirty linen before the laundress took it away and the clean linen when it was returned the following week.

If there was only one maid in the house, the mistress would be expected to get her hands dirty and help with the chores. But if there were enough servants to handle the work, the lady of the house was free to devote her morning to private pursuits such as reading the mail, playing the piano, sewing, or knitting. Well-bred women did not go out in the morning. If a person chanced to meet a reputable woman in the street at an inappropriate hour, etiquette required that she not be greeted; it was assumed that she was engaged in charitable or religious activities about which she wished to say nothing.

One of the missions assigned the mistress of the house was to make sure that meals, for which the family gathered around the dining room table, were a special time. The article on "Dinner" in the nineteenth-century *Larousse* encyclopedia depicts a typical family meal: "Everybody is there: grand-father, the children, and Baby, the littlest of all, fastened in his high chair. The wine is resting in clear carafes on a spar-kling white tablecloth. The maid fastens napkins around the little ones' necks, then brings out the sorrel soup and the gigot, the shank of which is decorated with a paper cutting. Mother scolds René for eating with his fingers, while Ernest teases his little sister. Baby fidgets in his chair. Father cuts him a tiny piece of meat and places it in his plate, or shakes a bunch of grapes in front of his face before giving it to him." The scene

Meals

A crowded table and relaxed diners, safe from the servants' scrutiny at the end of a meal, when the children made their brief appearance and the jolly uncle told his jokes. The unceremonious round table contributed to the intimacy of the occasion. (Sirot-Angel Collection.)

Jean Béraud, *La Pâtisserie Gloppe at the Rond-Point des Champs-Elysées,* 1889. Pastries and women in this sugary, sensual French pastry shop, a place for a quick snack. (Musée Carnavalet.)

is a noontime dinner in the provinces. In Paris at that hour of the day one would have been eating lunch.

The nomenclature of meals was different in Paris and the provinces. In the provinces one "dined" at midday and "supped" in the evening. In Paris a supper was a cold meal eaten after a ball or lavish party at one or two in the morning. The Parisian terms eventually became standard, but even today in the provinces people sometimes use *dîner* for *déjeuner* and *souper* for *dîner.*

Mealtimes changed over the course of the nineteenth century. Breakfast (*premier déjeuner,* also called *déjeuner à la tasse,* or breakfast in a cup) was taken immediately after waking. It consisted of a cup of milk, coffee, tea, or chocolate together with a *flûte* (thin loaf) or round of toast. "Second breakfast" (*deuxième déjeuner,* also called *déjeuner à la fourchette, déjeuner dînatoire*) was served between ten and noon. It consisted of hors-d'oeuvres, cold meats, and other snacks. Roast meats and salad were served only if the hour was somewhat advanced. Taine's hero Frédéric-Thomas Graindorge breakfasted in Paris in the 1860s at the hour of eleven and consumed cold chicken or partridge and a bottle of Bordeaux.

The dinner hour varied more widely than the time of any other meal. It was constantly being put off until later in the day. Stendhal's *Journal* informs us that in 1805 dinner guests were invited for five o'clock. He himself occasionally dined earlier, as for example on May 3, 1808: "At quarter to four I dined on grilled mutton, fried potatoes, and salad." Mme Pariset wrote in 1821 that eighteenth-century Parisians dined no later than four in the afternoon, whereas now they were eating no earlier than five or often six. In her opinion the reason for the later dinner hour was that earlier in the day men were occupied with business.

By the end of the century dinner guests were invited for around seven-thirty. Etiquette was the opposite of what it is today: people were expected to arrive five to fifteen minutes *early*. Late guests were allowed fifteen minutes' grace, after which the company moved to the dinner table. Some people could not get used to the new dinner hours. The elderly Ragons in Balzac's *César Birotteau* (1837) exhorted their guests to arrive for dinner at five o'clock, "because our sixty- and seventy-year-old stomachs cannot accommodate to the new hours required by fashion." As the dinner hour advanced, people began to adopt the English custom of "five o'clock tea," often served with a light snack.

A meal was not just consumption of food but a family occasion. The homemaker's manuals stressed the importance of the mistress of the house in creating an agreeable atmosphere around the dinner table. Mme Celnart had this to say in her *Manuel des dames* (1833): "Care should be taken with the honors of the dinner table not only when you have guests but also for your husband's sake, in order to make life at home more civilized. I use the word 'civilized' advisedly, for the mark of civilization is the ability to bestow pleasure and dignity on the satisfaction of all our needs. This must be done because the occupations of social life, especially for men, leave almost no time for family life except mealtimes, and because experience and what we know about prolonging life suggest that this time be devoted to gaiety so as to make digestion easy and unobtrusive. Here, then, is ample reason to enliven your meals with gentle conversation."

Outsiders were rarely invited to family lunches, which were consequently served without a tablecloth. The tradition of the family gathering at lunchtime gradually disappeared, however. Men were too busy or worked too far from home to return home for lunch, and there was a steady shift toward a working day interrupted only for lunch, if not at the work place itself, then at least away from home. In 1908 a book entitled *Les Usages du monde* (The Ways of the World) recommended avoiding lunch altogether, because stopping to eat interrupted the day.

Sunday lunch or dinner was usually an elaborate family ritual. Like holidays, these Sunday meals offered regular occasions for family gatherings. Forty years after the fact, George Sand warmly recalled the Sunday dinners of her childhood in the 1810s at the home of her great-uncle Beaumont: "This weekly dinner was an old and most agreeable family custom, and invariably the same guests attended . . . At precisely five o'clock my mother and I would arrive to find my grandmother already seated by the fire in an enormous armchair that was placed opposite the enormous armchair of my great-uncle." Writing in 1895, Maurice Genevoix was similarly nostalgic for the Sunday ritual of a distant past: "We used to dine together—ten of us—at a table in my grandparents' dining room . . . Why, when I think back on those Sunday dinners, do I always think of winter? Perhaps because when I was a child they filled me with a deep sense of harmony and intimacy."[3] Outside lay the cold of night, but inside there was warmth in every sense—the ideal of happiness for thinkers from Rousseau to Michelet.

Day

The afternoon was devoted to social duties, some of which were discharged at home, others outside the home. From 1830 until 1914 women of good society set aside a certain day for receiving guests. At the beginning of the social season they sent out cards engraved with the words, "At home on such and such a day at such and such a time." In the second half of the nineteenth century, after the dinner hour had been advanced, women normally received between two and six o'clock in the provinces and between three and seven o'clock in Paris.

Traditionally the mistress of the house sat to the right of the fireplace. Around 1880 the fashion changed, and the hostess now occupied a chair placed in the center of the salon. She rose to welcome women, elderly men, and priests but remained seated to greet a man. And men did come, even if women were more numerous—men with private incomes and men of letters (the presence of Paul Bourget or Marcel Prévost could enhance the reputation of a salon), to be sure, but also

Mary Cassatt, *Five O'Clock Tea*. Women enjoy an interlude by the fireside. (Boston, Museum of Fine Arts.)

men with more pressing concerns in politics or business who nevertheless managed to squeeze in a moment to be with a wife or friend who was receiving. By the end of the century it had become more difficult for such men to take time off in the afternoon, and many women therefore chose to receive in the evening, from eight-thirty on.

A table was set up in the salon with cakes, petits fours, and sandwiches, and tea was brought to the guests by the daughters of the house. Female guests stayed only a short while, for they often had several receptions to attend in a single afternoon. It was deemed appropriate to stay for fifteen minutes to half an hour.

On arriving and especially on leaving a salon, people generally said nothing so as not to interrupt the conversation. It was better simply to shake hands. In departing it was best to wait for a brief pause in the conversation, then to get up without haste. When the crowd was large, it was permissible to leave "in the English manner," that is, without taking leave of one's hostess. In some salons there was a steady parade of guests entering and leaving on reception day. Georges Vanier reports that his mother received as many as two hundred guests every Friday in her Rouen hôtel.[4]

In the first half of the century a woman receiving guests was expected to occupy her hands in some way. Young Alida

The salon, where social gatherings were held, with and without the participants. Right: A folding table is set up for teatime, an occasion dominated by women and light-colored attire in this well-staffed household. Above: A late-19th-century bourgeois salon at Moulins, filled with bric-a-brac to alleviate the fear of emptiness, as severe here in the provinces as it was in Paris. (Sirot-Angel Collection.)

de Savignac heeded her mother's advice: "In the salon you should embroider or hook rugs while carrying on conversation."[5] According to Mme Celnar (1833), doing needlework helped a woman to be a gracious hostess and offered an opportunity to show her elegance and taste.

Over the next fifty years fashions changed. It came to be considered vulgar for a woman to work while receiving guests. No needlework, rugs, embroidery, or writing materials were permitted to remain in evidence. Private pursuits and social entertaining had become incompatible.

During the Belle Epoque people began to tire of the ritual of the "day." Women who did not wish to be stuck at home one afternoon a week kept their days but received only between the hours of five and six or only on the second and fourth Tuesdays of the month. With the outbreak of war the "day" fell out of fashion.

On afternoons when a woman did not receive at home, she felt obliged to appear in other salons. She was also responsible for keeping up contacts with the family, whose numbers could be legion. Vanier's mother had forty-eight names on her visiting list.

Visits

There were many occasions for visits: "bread-and-butter" visits after dinners or balls to which one was invited, whether or not one actually attended; courtesy calls three or four times a year to persons with whom one wished to maintain good relations but nothing more; congratulatory visits after a wedding, an important appointment, or an award; condolence calls; annual ceremonial visits to a man's superiors, during which the wife's presence was expected; and, before and after a journey, visits to people who might otherwise call while one was away.

If the person on whom one paid a call was not home, the custom was to leave with a servant or concierge a calling card with its corner turned down or folded along its length, depending on the fashion of the moment. A folded or dog-eared card was a sign that the individual had called in person; an unbent card indicated that it had been left by a servant or agent. It was possible to hire the services of a *poseur de cartes,* a card-leaver, through an advertisement in *High-Life,* an early *Who's Who?* of high society. Although such "visits by card" were considered quite vulgar in the 1830s, they subsequently became very popular.

Obligatory visits claimed much of the time of a woman of good society. Shunning the ritual could easily earn a person a reputation for oddity. André Germain, grandson of the founder of the Crédit Lyonnais, in 1906 married Edmée Daudet, daughter of the writer Léon Daudet. André wanted his wife to pay social calls in the afternoon, but she refused and instead went riding, alone, in a carriage in the Bois de Boulogne, after which she took tea in a restaurant and listened to gypsy music. Such rejection of society was of course suspect.

Orchestrating and maintaining social relations was a key aspect of bourgeois life and a responsibility of the mistress of the house, who kept lines of communication open to other households. Women of the petty bourgeoisie were well aware of this responsibility and proclaimed their social standing by holding salons on specified days and by paying and receiving calls. Emulation of the rituals of their betters knit the social fabric together.

Evening Activities

The theater or opera box was an extension of the salon, a fact that may seem paradoxical because the box, though a public place, was treated as though it were private. According to nineteenth-century rules of propriety, a woman could attend the theater alone as long as she sat in a box. If she sat in the orchestra or balcony, however, she had to be accompanied by a man—husband, brother, or relative. Orchestra and balcony were open, exposed spaces in which a woman—unless she wished to be considered a *fille publique,* as promiscuous as the place itself—needed a protector.

A box, however, was an isolated, protected world unto itself, a home transplanted to the theater. In good society it was customary to take an annual subscription to a box, or loge. In Rouen in 1850 a seat in a box at the Théâtre des Arts cost 250 francs for a man and 187 francs for a woman. The most comfortable option was to hire a box equipped with a salon. During the Second Empire such a box, with six seats, went for 1,800 francs.

A woman behaved in her box as though she were in her salon. She could not leave it to wander about the theater, but she could receive friends with the same etiquette as at home, and she might allow them to introduce their relatives.

The nature of evening activities depended on whether only family members were present or there were guests from outside; whether one lived in town or in the country; and

Paul Gavarni, *The Loge.* Midway between public and private, the box was a salon where intrigue at times rivaled that of the performance on stage. (Paris, Dorville Collection.)

whether one was truly well off or lived in relatively modest circumstances. Remember that until the invention of electricity, evenings were engulfed by darkness. Witnesses to the coming of electricity attest to the dramatic changes it brought. Bernard Cazeaux, who was born in Paris in 1909, spent his childhood in a gaslit apartment. Today he can remember the amazement he felt when for the first time he visited a friend whose apartment was lit with electricity. Electricity put an end to dark corners and vanquished the shadows.

This minor revolution did not begin in Paris apartments until 1890. At the beginning of the nineteenth century well-to-do people lit their homes with wax rather than cheaper tallow candles. Some made use of the self-regulating oil lamp invented by Carcel in 1800. Gas lighting became common in private homes after 1825. In 1828 Paris counted 1,500 gas subscribers; by 1872 the number had increased to almost 95,000 and by the end of the century to 220,000. In 1855 a merger of several companies into the Compagnie Parisienne d'Eclairage et de Chauffage par le Gaz resulted in a decline in the price of gas from 0.49 francs to the more affordable 0.30 francs per cubic meter.

A familiar object before the advent of electricity. From "Lighting," in *The Educational Museum.* (Paris, Galerie de l'Imagerie.)

Among Catholics family evenings sometimes began with common prayer, which Mme de Lamartine on September 5, 1802, called "a most touching and useful custom"—useful for the servants, who enjoyed a moment of daily communion with their masters, and useful for the masters, whom prayer reminded of the Christian idea of equality. Some bourgeois families emulated this aristocratic tradition of family prayer.

Family gatherings were often taken up with card and dice games. At Milly in September 1806 Mme de Lamartine played chess with her husband, while their children played and studied the fables of La Fontaine. Reading aloud was an activity that parents and children enjoyed together.

Above all, family evenings were occasions for intimate fireside conversation. In 1828 Horace Raisson ended his book of etiquette entitled *Code civil* with an "Apology for the Fireside": "I should feel remiss if, along with the harsh rules of etiquette and the ceremonious pleasures of the salon, I did not also mention the happiness of domestic life and the common pleasures of the fireside." In order to illustrate those common pleasures, so typical of the nineteenth century, he nevertheless alluded to those earlier generations of Frenchmen who had lived in Gothic castles and who had placed such a high value on the fireplace, thus demonstrating their mastery of the domestic art.

Jean Béraud, *The Ball,* 1878. The grande bourgeoisie socialized in the grand manner, inviting a large but select public for concerts, plays, and dances given in the home. (Paris, Musée Carnavalet.)

Emphasis on the fireside can be compared with the idea of the home as a nest, an idea that gathered force throughout the century and became an obsession toward the end. The fireside image gained prominence even as the fireside proper was disappearing from the home. The handsome buildings that went up in the second half of the century were equipped with hot-air furnaces, which replaced wood and coal stoves in the fireplaces. Public school readers meanwhile popularized the image of the petty-bourgeois family gathered under a lamp and around a stove.

Inviting guests from outside the family transformed the significance of the evening. The number of guests and their familiarity with the members of the household were crucial variables. Throughout the nineteenth century people expressed nostalgia for eighteenth-century forms of sociability. Bourgeois like the Goncourt brothers idealized the *soirées* of that age, which in their eyes had combined the most refined luxury with the most polished conversation.

The noble ladies who frequented the courts of the Bourbons and of Napoleon I helped to create and perpetuate the myth of an ideal ancien-régime type of sociability. In 1836 the duchesse d'Abrantès described, in the *Gazette des salons,* what those soirées of yesteryear had been like. Society in those days consisted of some eighty people who saw one another constantly, and two hundred others who migrated from salon to salon over the course of the week. The men played billiards; the women embroidered or sketched. At two in the morning supper was served—the high point of the evening, during which the conversation turned confidential and "even a little naughty."

The fall of Napoleon I marked the end of this constricted society and the beginning of *raouts,* or "parties" in the English sense, attended indiscriminately by all sorts of people. Mrs. Trollope, who visited Paris in 1835, was sorry that the suppers of old, at which one met the refined people who in her view gave the French way of life its charm, had been replaced by these *raouts*.

Evenings were an ideal time for amateur musicales and theatricals. Friends, especially in the provinces, where cultural diversions were limited and people were obliged to amuse themselves, formed groups of musicians and singers that met regularly at a member's home.

George Sand recounts that in 1810 a troupe of itinerant actors came to La Châtre in her native Berri. Amateur musi-

Octave Uzanne, *The French Woman of the Century. High Society in 1850.* In the 19th century the *raout,* or English-style party, supplanted the private *soirée.* (Paris, Bibliothèque Historique.)

cians in the town formed an orchestra to accompany the play: "In the provinces in those days people were still artists. No locality was too poor or too small to mount a good quartet, and every week people gathered at the home of one music lover or another to make what the Italians call *musica di camera* (chamber music), a reputable and noble form of relaxation that has vanished along with the old virtuosos, the last guardians of the sacred fire in our provinces."[6] George Sand seems to be saying that by 1850, when she wrote her memoirs, people had lost the habit of making music. Actually amateur music-making flourished throughout the century.

Mme B., who was born in 1894, spent her childhood in Caen. A good pianist, she and her brothers and their friends organized an orchestra. They rehearsed during the week and performed every other Sunday for relatives and friends. On the odd Sundays they played bridge (which became quite popular in the Belle Epoque). In Rouen, Félix Bourgeois under the July Monarchy and Georges Vanier under the Third Republic won renown for their singing voices and often graced social gatherings with their performances.

Amateur theater was another widely practiced activity. Charades were the nineteenth century's favorite form of amusement. The *Dictionnaire universel de la vie pratique à la ville et à la campagne* (Universal Dictionary of Practical Life in Town and Country, 1859) explained the workings of this "agreeable pastime, in which everyone takes turns playing the parts of author and spectator." Half the group performed the charade, while the other half looked on and tried to guess the word. If they succeeded, the two teams changed sides.

Other games vied with charades for popularity. In the 1830s *tableaux vivants* became fashionable: "A heavy frame covered with canvas was brought into the salon, and behind it people in costume positioned themselves carefully to represent certain heroes." Georgette Ducrest described in a novel an evening at the home of Mme de Duras during which Baron Gérard agreed to "reproduce his admirable composition, *Corinne.*" But tableaux vivants had one major drawback: to make the images accurate required lengthy preparation, which interrupted the flow of the evening and put a damper on the company.

The charms of conversation were not enough for receptions orchestrated as though they were theatrical spectacles, complete with intermissions. Comedians, singers, magicians, and hypnotists amused the guests. The 1880s showed a marked preference for comedy. Note the men in black, strictly segregated from the women in white. (Paris, Musée Carnavalet.)

In addition to charades, people amused themselves by staging society comedies. These ranged in length from the brief sketch suitable for performance before a small audience of family and friends to the full-blown comedy from the stage of the Français or Gymnase, which idle socialites learned and performed for audiences of as many as four hundred people. Scribe, in particular, enjoyed great success with this audience.

Children imitated their parents by staging amateur plays. At the beginning of each year, for example, Renée Berruel and her sister invited friends over to eat snacks and put on short plays such as *Le Désespoir de Louison, Colombine héritière,* and *Ma Tante Flora.*

People also gave dancing parties at which they took turns playing the piano while others danced contredanses and polkas (*Journal des jeunes filles,* February 1849). The contredanse was in fashion between the First and Second Empires, after which it evolved into the quadrille. The polka came to France by way of Prague in 1844. The waltz, however, had a bad rep-

The ballad was a form of seduction. Here a classical sentimental intrigue for André Theuriet's novel and for the respectable readers of *L'Illustration.* (1890.)

utation. Introduced into France at the end of the eighteenth century, in 1820 it was still banned at court. In 1857 Flaubert was prosecuted for describing a waltz without hiding its sexual component. At the end of the nineteenth century the tango met with similar disapproval.

Amateur entertainment had its limits. For a real *grande soirée* one hired an orchestra to provide dance music. It was also fashionable to hire divas to give private recitals. Thus, evening entertainment might have an intimate character, as it did when the daughters of the house played the piano, or it might become a form of ostentation, as when fashionable professional entertainers were brought in. In either case enjoyment was a private affair.

James Tissot, *Shh!* Artist or daughter? Daughters usually contented themselves with the piano, the "hashish of women." A private concert of chamber music lends an air of distinction to this sumptuous salon, in which the presence of Hindu princes serves as a token of the Empire. (Manchester, City Art Gallery.)

ANNUAL HOLIDAYS

Summer vacation and religious holidays marked out the year's progress. The aristocrat's summer holiday grew into the bourgeois's summer vacation. This period saw the birth of the ideology of relaxation and leisure. The school vacation was eventually lengthened. Believers and nonbelievers, churchgoers and nonchurchgoers—all depended on the Christian calendar. The year proceeded from Christmas to All Hallows, from the birth of Christ to the festival of the dead. Religious holidays in a sense became family holidays. The form remained the same, but the content changed. Christmas, for example, gradually lost its connection with the birth of Jesus in Bethlehem and became a children's holiday. The family honored Christian holidays as a way of celebrating itself.

The Christmas Tree

Christmas trees probably originated in Scandinavia. The Swedes brought them to Germany in the first half of the seventeenth century, during the Thirty Years' War, though the custom did not catch on until the beginning of the nineteenth century. As late as 1765 Goethe, visiting a friend in Leipzig, was astonished to find a Christmas tree in the house. (The customs of Strasbourg, however, confirm that Christmas trees were found in homes there in 1605.)

In 1840 the German custom was introduced simultaneously in England (by Prince Albert) and in France (by Princess Helen of Mecklemburg, the duchesse d'Orléans, and by Protestant families from Alsace and Germany). Encouraged by Empress Eugénie during the Second Empire, the tradition of the Christmas tree took hold. Refugees who left Alsace and Lorraine after the defeat of 1870 helped to spread it. Yet for the lexicographers Littré and Larousse, the Christmas "tree" was nothing more than a "large branch" of fir or sprig of holly decorated with candy and toys for the children.

Late in the century the custom seems to have been "nationalized" by the French. Fully decorated Christmas trees were sent out every year to missionaries in Greenland and colonists in Africa. In French homes Christmas trees were almost identical to those found in homes today.

The Crèche

Littré in 1863 does not allude to crèches in churches or homes. Larousse, a few years later, mentions them, but only in the churches, where they were tended by real, talking people. He delivers a long diatribe against the mangers of Provence, which he finds sacrilegious because they mix the sacred with the profane and provoke laughter among Christians. Yet he notes one sign of progress: the angel is trying to speak French rather than the local dialect. The time has come, he says, to do away with old traditions.

The Christmas tree, introduced in France around 1840, was firmly established by 1900. (Paris, Bibliothèque des Arts Décoratifs.)

Of Scandinavian origin, the Christmas tree came to France by way of Germany. (Paris, Bibliothèque Nationale.)

There must have been many such Nativity scenes in Catholic churches. In 1906, according to Monsignor Chabot, more than 30,000 were sold annually at prices ranging from 20 francs to 3,000 francs. Most consisted of seven or eight basic figures.

Crèches from Marseilles featuring clay figures from Italy became especially popular, because they included not only the traditional sacred figures but also such profane participants as a knife-and-scissors grinder, a tambourine drummer, a man in a trance, a miller, a baker's boy, and so on. Modernity made its presence felt in the form of four- and five-story buildings illuminated at night by candlelight, and of steam locomotives.

The German Example

Before the Christmas tree was imported into France, various French observers expressed their views on this German custom. Oddly enough, they spoke nostalgically, as though the Christmas tree were an old French tradition that had somehow gone out of fashion. *La Gazette des ménages* on December 23, 1830, deplored the fact that in France, and especially in Paris, "the present generation shows little concern for these old customs," in contrast to Germany, a paragon of respect for domestic traditions.

Le Journal des jeunes filles in December 1849 alluded to German customs with similar emotion, expressing regret that

the French did not know how to exploit the magical atmosphere of the holiday. In Germany gifts "dropped from heaven," brought by the Christ child. France would do well to follow the German example and make the year-end holidays an occasion for gathering the generations, and especially the grandparents, around the family hearth.

The opinions voiced in 1830 and 1849 were identical. Both glorified the private aspects of the year-end holidays. In the aftermath of two revolutions (one in 1830, the other in 1848) writers drew a contrast between the instability of public life and the stability of family life: "The joys of the family," the journalist concluded in 1849, "are the one thing, the only happiness, that revolutions can never take from us."

In 1866 Gustave Droz devoted a chapter of his *Monsieur, Madame et Bébé* to a family New Year's celebration. At seven in the morning on New Year's Day, Baby scratched at his parents' door to wish them a happy new year. His father took him into the big bed, the servant came to light the fire, and the cozy stage was set for the exchange of gifts. For Droz, this moment of family happiness was the most precious thing in the world. The whole day was punctuated by charming family tableaux.

Familial pleasures were concentrated in particularly in-

Happy Holidays

tense form on New Year's Day, a day on which the family steeled itself for the coming year. By 1866 it was no longer necessary to invoke the example of Germany. Droz describes the day's activities as though they followed long-established custom. As the century progressed, people apparently became more and more certain that home was a precious and irreplaceable source of happiness. Children became the leading figures in the holiday ritual.

Réveillon and Holiday Gifts

Littré in 1869 defined *réveillon* as "a special meal eaten in the middle of the night, particularly on Christmas night." He does not mention the verb *réveillonner,* nor does he say anything about New Year's Eve. I have been unable to find any indication of family celebrations or dinners on the night of December 31. Flaubert in his letters recalls waiting for midnight to arrive, once while smoking, another time thinking of China.

Catholic families attended midnight mass and afterward ate supper. Since it was customary to give the servants the night off on Christmas Eve, the meal was quite simple. It included two traditional dishes: a sort of vanilla porridge eaten with waffles, and grilled sausage. There were also cold dishes such as truffled turkey, and for dessert there were frozen pastries and sherbets.

All sorts of pastries were cooked for Christmas—*gaufrettes, galettes, chaussons.* Local customs varied, but there is no trace of the Christmas pastry most popular in France today, the *bûche de Noël* (yule log). In the nineteenth century the only yule log was the one placed on the fire on Christmas Eve and intended to burn all night—an old rural tradition that involved staying up all night on Christmas Eve and then attending dawn mass on Christmas morning.

Originally a Catholic custom, the réveillon evolved into a nonreligious celebration in the second half of the nineteenth century. By 1908 the *Usages du siècle* could assert that "everyone celebrates the réveillon." Catholics took their réveillon after midnight mass, while others formed the habit of going to the theater and then enjoying the réveillon. A religious pretext was no longer necessary to celebrate Christmas. The holiday provided a reason for family and friends to gather, and that was enough. Turkey and grilled sausage remained on the réveillon menu, but hot consommé replaced the vanilla porridge, and France adopted the English pudding as the symbol of Christmas. All the magazines published recipes for English pudding (see, for example, *Fémina* for January 1, 1903). Another English custom that spread to France was kissing beneath the mistletoe, which *Fémina* illustrated with a photograph on December 15, 1903.

Etrennes, or New Year's gifts, were gifts given in keeping with an ancient tradition on January 1. This custom developed into an obligation to give New Year's bonuses to the servants, the concierge, the mailman, and others, an obligation that transformed the first of the year into an expensive ordeal. The newspapers lampooned this custom. In January 1830 *La Mode* published a one-act play entitled, "New Year's Day, or Small Gifts Sustain Friendship," which featured a man hounded by a host of people from his valet to his wife, all of whom expected their *étrennes*.

More broadly, the word étrennes was applied to gifts of all sorts exchanged during the year-end holiday season. Some authors, such as Mme de Grandmaison in 1892, attempted to prescribe the proper time for each type of gift: Christmas Day was for gifts *(cadeaux)* to children, New Year's Day for étrennes to adults. In reality, however, adults also exchanged

Eugène Devéria, *New Year's Gifts,* 1846. Books for father, jewelry boxes for the ladies, a hobbyhorse for the little boy, and an album for the little girl, with affection for all. Gift-giving was an honored ritual. (Paris, Musée Carnavalet.)

gifts on Christmas Day, as did children on New Year's Day. In the end all these gifts came to be known indiscriminately as étrennes.

The Christmas Slipper

On Christmas Eve French children put their slippers in front of the fireplace in the hope of finding them filled with gifts in the morning. By whom? The Infant Jesus or Père Noël? Both beliefs coexisted, but little by little Santa Claus gained the upper hand.

Robert's dictionary of proper names tells us that Father Christmas first appeared in Europe in the second half of the nineteenth century, allegedly as an American import and a commercial creation. There can be no doubt that commercial considerations contributed to his success, but retailers did not invent him. The prototype was probably Saint Nicholas or Santa Claus, whose day was December 6 and who, in Nordic countries, was supposed to bring gifts to children who behaved themselves, while his partner the bogeyman left rods for those who disobeyed. It seems likely that Santa Claus was brought by Scandinavian and German immigrants to the United States, where he became commercialized.

Father Christmas was firmly established in Paris at the beginning of the nineteenth century, and he gained in stature as the century progressed. George Sand, born in 1804, recounts her childhood Christmases in *Histoire de ma vie:* "What I have not forgotten is my firm conviction that little Father Christmas, a kindly old man with a white beard, came down the chimney at midnight and left a gift for me in my slipper, which I was supposed to find in the morning. Midnight! That fantastic hour of which children know nothing, which they are told is so late that they cannot possibly stay awake that long. What incredible efforts I made not to fall asleep before the little old man appeared. I was very eager to see him but also afraid. Yet I never could stay awake that long, and the next day my eyes went straight to my slipper on the edge of the hearth. What emotion I felt at the sight of the white paper, for Father Christmas was extremely neat and never failed to wrap his present with great care. I ran barefoot to take possession of my treasure. It was never a magnificent gift, for we were not wealthy, but a cookie or an orange or simply a nice red apple. Yet it seemed so precious to me that I scarcely dared eat it."[7]

Father Christmas has nothing to do with the birth of

Christ, and for a long time the Catholic Church opposed his Christmas role. Catholics pretended that the Infant Jesus brought children gifts on Christmas Eve. According to Francisque Sarcey (*Annales,* December 22, 1889), children saw the Infant Jesus "traveling through the air, clutching an armful of cakes and toys to his breast. They felt his presence, very good and very just, in the air above them. They said to themselves that with him you had to keep to the straight and narrow or your slippers would remain empty." This image never really caught on, however, and the Church, powerless to halt the rising popularity of Father Christmas with his red suit, white beard, and huge basket of gifts, coopted him by making him a faithful messenger of Jesus and the teacher of a simple morality of reward for good behavior.

In the month of December newspapers traditionally published columns proposing gift ideas to their readers. Many of these ideas specifically concerned gifts for women: love seats, sewing tables, "trinkets for the boudoir," colored, perfumed, and glossy writing paper, and fancy visiting cards. An item might be described as "making a nice gift for a woman," but no one would think of saying the same about a man's gift; the category of male gifts simply did not exist in the nineteenth century. At most one finds an occasional reference to necessary items "for men and ladies." This lack of a specific category does not mean that men did not receive gifts, simply that people did not talk about them.

In 1836 the most sophisticated gift one could give a child was a small theater in which "an Asiatic tightrope dance" was "simulated by small paper figures that move without obvious attachments." Other toys mimicked reality: working water mills, singing birds, and female dolls equipped with full trousseaus and "ready for marriage." Dolls were always a sure thing. Stuffed bears came in at the beginning of the twentieth century: Teddy, the American bear, dates from 1903, Martin, the French bear, from 1906.

The *Larousse du XIXe siècle* notes that although children's gifts naturally followed fashion, people had recently begun to give gifts of cultural value: "Good, handsome books are slowly replacing costly frivolities in this January 1 ceremony." Allowance must be made, as usual, for the dictionary's enthusiatic promotion of education and progress. Still, newspapers and magazines did publish lists of books suitable for presents (see, for example, *La Mère de famille,* December 1834, and *La Femme et la famille, journal des jeunes personnes,* 1880).

Punch and Judy for good little girls and boys, whose imaginations were formed by such fare. (Paris, Bibliothèque des Arts Décoratifs.)

Little girls recorded in their diaries the gifts they and their friends received. Holiday gifts were not only a source of immediate pleasure but also an investment for the future, memories that children treasured all their lives. Adults nostalgic for childhood passed that nostalgia on to their children.

New Year's Greetings and Visits

Children, as though in exchange for the gifts they received, offered New Year's greetings to their parents. On December 29, 1877, Elisabeth Arrighi wrote: "We are also preparing our étrennes for papa. Pierre, Amélie, and I are learning *Le Petit Savoyard* and writing it down on a beautiful parchment. And I have learned a piece for two hands and another for four hands that I shall play with mama. Amélie has learned a piece for four hands that she will play with me."[8]

On the first of the year people called on close relatives to offer New Year's greetings: father and mother, uncles and aunts, brothers and sisters exchanged visits. The evening was reserved for grandparents and superiors. The following week was for cousins and other relations, the fortnight for close friends, and the entire month of January for acquaintances. All told, there were many visits to make and many greeting cards to write.

To keep disruption to a minimum, many people were content to send a servant or hire an agent to leave a visiting card at the home of people to whom they wished to present greetings. There was something paradoxical in this Parisian custom, as noted in *Le Figaro,* December 24, 1854: recipients of such delivered cards poured scorn on "compliments at three francs per hundred." But if an acquaintance failed to send a card, the same people complained that "so-and-so is ill-bred. He didn't even send a card on New Year's Day."

Of course vast numbers of cards also were sent by mail. At the end of the century the Paris post office counted more than a million on January 1 alone. The comtesse de Pange reports that she sent and received roughly 1,500 greeting cards.

The Changing of the Seasons: Easter and All Saints' Day

Easter was an important holiday in several respects. Every Catholic was expected to confess and receive communion during the fortnight preceding Easter Sunday. One communion a year, at Eastertime, was the Church's minimum requirement. The Easter fortnight began on Palm Sunday. Germaine de Maulny remembers that on that day toddlers went to mass with a *rampaum* or *rampant,* that is, a small bouquet of leaves, candy, ribbons, garlands, and trinkets, which the priest then blessed. On Holy Thursday, in the afternoon, Germaine's mother took her on a tour of the churches of Limoges. On Good Friday she and her sister were ordered by their mother to throw veils of purple fabric over all the statues of saints in the house. The Maulnys followed the path of the cross to the cathedral as a family.

Easter was the egg holiday. People hid colored Easter eggs and egg-shaped candies in their houses and yards for the children to find, and Easter gifts of all kinds, from lead soldiers to jewelry, were given in egg-shaped packages. (The custom of giving Easter gifts flourished until World War I.) In April 1911 the magazine *Mon chez-moi* published an article on the latest fashion: the floral egg, which might be as simple as a fragrant bouquet or as lavish as a floral case containing a precious gem. These floral eggs were expensive if made by a florist, so the magazine published do-it-yourself instructions.

Easter Sunday, which commemorated the resurrection of Christ, also marked the arrival of spring. Families attended mass together and, no matter what the weather, donned their new clothing, symbolically marking the arrival of spring even if the temperature remained low. Young women, Germaine de Maulny tells us, wore light dresses and Italian straw bonnets festooned with daisies and mouse ears.

All dressed up, noses wiped, these children have come to mumble their respects to grandma and grandpa. In the meantime they steal a glance at the toys that await them. (Paris, INRP, Historical Collection.)

At home the change of season was the time for spring cleaning. Fireplace shovels and tongs were cleaned and greased before being put away until fall. Curtains and wall hangings were taken down and beaten to remove dust, as were rugs. Paintings were cleaned and wool mattress covers combed.

In the nineteenth century there was no long school vacation at Christmas; only December 25 and January 1 were school holidays. Easter vacations became common, however. In the first half of the century classes were suspended for the Thursday, Friday, and Saturday before Easter. In November 1859 this vacation was secularized: lycée students were given a week's vacation following Easter Sunday for family and educational reasons.

Under the Third Republic primary school pupils were given the same Easter vacation as secondary school students. On a motion by the government the Assembly agreed, on March 9, 1886, after extended debate, to make the Mondays following Easter and Whitsunday legal holidays. On August 1, 1892, Easter vacation was extended to begin at noon on the Wednesday before Easter, a step toward the two weeks of Easter vacation that French schools have allowed since February 18, 1925.

Over the nineteenth century the Easter vacation evolved into something like a trimester break. Christmas vacation quickly followed suit. The act of August 1892 also provided for eight special vacation days to be scheduled at the beginning of the school year by decision of the school principal with the advice of the academic council. If these special vacation days were scheduled to fall between December 25 and January 1, students could enjoy a brief vacation. The act of February 1925 made this informal practice official: the number of special vacation days was reduced to two, but Christmas vacation was extended from the end of class on December 23 to the morning of January 3. Thus, the division of the French academic year into three trimesters dates from 1925.

If Easter marked the beginning of spring, All Saints' Day marked the beginning of winter. In the second half of the nineteenth century it became customary for families to visit the graves of family members on that day. Philippe Ariès has shown how a cult of the dead developed in this period, reversing attitudes that had developed in the previous century. At the end of the eighteenth century Paris cemeteries were being closed; the Cemetery of the Innocents was destroyed in 1785 amid general indifference. Around 1850 public opinion changed.

Three factors contributed to the newfound interest in the dead and made it possible for urban cemeteries to survive,

Alfonse Leduc, drawing. During the Second Empire people of relatively modest means began to consume sugar and candy, once a sign of wealth. (Paris, Bibliothèque des Arts Décoratifs.)

Emile Friant, *All Saints' Day*, 1888. Family visits to cemeteries on All Saints' Day became a common custom in the second half of the 19th century. The women wear mourning and contribute to charity in honor of the dead. (Nancy, Musée des Beaux-Arts.)

even in Paris. First, the positivists approved of honoring the dead on the grounds that to do so helped promote the public spirit: "Tombs foster a sense of family continuity, and cemeteries foster a sense of continuity in the city and in mankind," Pierre Laffitte wrote in 1874.[9] Second, Catholics subscribed to the cult of the dead and championed it as though it had always been a part of their practice. This contention may seem puzzling, for a century earlier the Church had been partly responsible for the decline of interest in cemeteries. Its position at that time was that a person's earthly remains were of no importance; all that mattered was eternal life. Third, science bestowed its approval. Scientists proved that proximity to cemeteries posed no danger to the living and that the mephitic influences denounced in the previous century were mere superstitions.

After 1850 the cemetery became "a place to visit, a place

of meditation." In Rouen between 1860 and 1880 the number of family burial vaults with lavish memorials increased markedly. France's defeat in the Franco-Prussian War (1870) encouraged veneration of the dead and respect for their memory. In 1902, 350,000 people, nearly 10 percent of the population, visited the cemeteries of Paris on All Saints' Day.

On Easter women and girls wore light colors, but for All Saints' Day they returned to dark colors, felt hats, muffs, and ankle boots—in short, they "dressed for winter."

SUMMER: FROM COUNTRY HOUSE TO SUMMER VACATION

In Goldoni's celebrated trilogy *La Villegiatura,* staged in Venice in 1761, the author rails against the transformation of the "innocent rural diversion into what it has become nowadays, a passion, a mania, a disturbance." In France at the beginning of the nineteenth century only a small elite spent the summer in country homes. In the 1870s the *Larousse du XIXe siècle* still considered the word *villégiature,* defined as "a recreational sojourn in the country," to be a neologism. Aristocrats and other people of private means, whose business did not require them to be in Paris or other major cities, spent summers in their châteaux, on their country estates, and did not return to town until October or even November, after hunting season. For the elite the year thus fell into two parts: the social season—winter and spring—and the sojourn in the country—summer and part of fall.

Gradually the bourgeoisie began to imitate this aristocratic model. Auguste Villemot made fun of this in his column in *Le Figaro,* May 15, 1856. A woman, he said, might enjoy herself mimicking "rustic simplicity" by setting up house in May in the country just outside Paris, but for a man whose business was in Paris this caricature of château living was simply hell. The journalist might laugh; nevertheless, bourgeois families abandoned the city for its rural environs when the season arrived. "A bourgeois of Grenoble is respected in proportion to the size of his estate," Stendhal wrote. His father owned a house in Chaix, two leagues from the city, and there the family spent the months of August and September. Most bourgeois families in Rouen owned a country house not far from the city; they invited relatives and friends to spend several months of the year with them in the country, and they took advantage of the opportunity to inspect farms they

Fritz Paulsen, 1868. The young men are dressed almost casually, while the young women wear light hats and boldly shortened dresses; their chaperon, however, sticks to a dark bonnet and dress. This summertime stroll conforms to certain rules even as it contributes to loosening them. Note the parasols: the sun was still seen as the enemy of a proper pink complexion. (Paris, Bibliothèque Nationale.)

owned in the surrounding area. Mme G., born in 1888, daughter of a wealthy Bordeaux merchant, recalls that from Easter to All Saints' Day she, along with her parents, brothers, sisters, and a half-dozen servants, went to live in a beautiful house at Pontac, about five miles outside of Bordeaux. Antoine Arrighi was an *avocat* at the court of Napoleon III. Every spring his family abandoned its Paris apartment on the rue de Rennes and went to Auteuil, where Mme Arrighi and her sister, Mme Villetard de Prunières, rented a house with a garden. In 1878 they left Paris on May 11 and returned on October 26. This sojourn just outside Paris is not to be confused with the Arrighis' midsummer excursions to the Channel coast (to Langrune in 1876 and 1877, Saint-Aubin from 1878 to 1884, Mers in 1885, Beuzeval in 1888) or to towns with hot springs (Challes in 1882, La Bourboule in 1886, and Geneva in 1887).

The Paris bourgeoisie and the provincial bourgeoisie followed different patterns, as the foregoing examples illustrate. In the provinces people lived on properties they owned. Parisians did not generally own rural estates, and in any case they would not have been equipped to oversee farm operations. Therefore they rented country homes or vacationed in hotels. Renting made it possible to vacation in different places. Mme D., born in 1876, reports that her father, an official of the Ecole Normale Supérieure, liked change and never took his family to the same place twice for summer vacation. He rented large estates at a rate of 500 francs for the season. During one summer in the 1880s the family occupied a seventeen-room château in Morbihan.

Even those city dwellers who lacked the leisure to spend six months of the year out of town formed the habit of spending Sundays in the country. In a February 10, 1831, review of Aglaé Adanson's popular book *La Maison de campagne* (The Country House) *La Gazette des ménages* had this to say: "Leave Saturday night, go for a stroll on Sunday (if it doesn't rain), and return to the city on Monday morning—that is what many Parisians call going to the country. With a coachman, a gardener, and a cook, these city folk have everything they need for their brief excursions."

Summer Migration

In *Le Figaro*, August 6, 1854, Auguste Villemot described the intense heat of the empty capital: "Every living thing has apparently sought refuge on the railway platforms," where husbands could be seen accompanying wives about to leave for the country or seaside. Only "porters and men of letters" remained in Paris. Villemot was jesting; nevertheless, the reality was astonishing. The journalist put the number of Parisians who had left the city for the summer at 30,000. City people who could afford to travel became "tourists." The word, synonymous with traveler, was first used in 1816, but it was Stendhal who really fixed it in the public mind with his 1838 *Mémoires d'un touriste*. The *Larousse du XIXe siècle* described the tourist as one who "travels out of curiosity and idleness." Tourists were not necessarily walkers or itinerants. Some settled in seaside villas and did not budge (the word *estivant*, "summer resident," was first used in 1920). *La Gazette des touristes et des étrangers*, founded in 1877, reported primarily on coastal resorts. A glance at the summer issues of the fashionable papers shows the importance of the summer migration. All had columns on the society scene in the *villes d'eaux*, an expression that could be applied to seaside resorts as well as to towns with hot springs: "The waters are to the summer what the salons are to the winter," according to the June 5, 1846, *Journal des dames*.

The earliest exploitation of mineral water baths dates

Mineral waters were fashionable in the early 19th century. Vittel experienced a surge of popularity at the end of the Second Empire. (Sirot-Angel Collection.)

from the First Empire: 1,200 people took the cure at Aix-les-Bains in 1809. During the Restoration the French discovered the seacoast. In 1822 the comte de Brancas, subprefect at Dieppe, opened the first ocean bathing establishment and persuaded the duchesse de Berry to visit. From then until 1830 the court transferred itself to Dieppe every July. After 1830 aristocrats from the faubourg Saint-Germain clung to the habit. At that time Dieppe was the only developed coastal resort, although in 1835 people had begun to talk about the tiny beach at Biarritz, which under the Second Empire became the favorite resort of Empress Eugénie. By the end of the July Monarchy, Trouville on the Norman coast had become a fashionable resort, but it was more bourgeois and less chic than Dieppe.

Trains cut the travel time from Paris to the beaches by two-thirds. In 1840 it took twelve hours to go from Paris to Dieppe by carriage; by railway during the Second Empire it took only four hours. In August 1848 the first "pleasure train" was run from Paris to Dieppe. These special weekend trains, which facilitated travel to the Norman coast, became increasingly popular during the second half of the century, so much so that in 1850 the railway company began offering discount tickets (5 francs in third class, 8 francs in second class). Wealthier travelers took the "yellow train" or the "husbands' train." In 1871 it left Paris late Saturday afternoon and returned before noon on Monday, allowing just enough time for harried businessmen to spend Sunday by the sea with their wives and children. The wealthiest travelers could also avail themselves of daily deluxe trains such as the one that ran from Paris to Trouville between July 15 and September 30, 1904. These trains, composed exclusively of parlor cars, offered only first-class tickets, with a supplementary charge for the deluxe service. A round-trip ticket cost more than 50 francs—twenty days' pay for an ordinary worker.

Parisians, who benefited from direct rail connections, were probably more inclined than provincials to leave their homes. To take one example, Parisians vacationing on the coast of Normandy outnumbered Rouennais, who, despite the proximity of the ocean, showed little interest in seaside vacations before 1914. (But the same Rouennais traveled frequently to Paris via a railway that had existed since 1843.)

In addition to summer tourism in the mountains and spas winter tourism developed, especially along the Mediterranean

Alban de Lesgallery, *The Old Harbor in Biarritz,* 1858. Ocean bathing first became fashionable during the Restoration. Biarritz, which began receiving visitors in 1835, became Empress Eugénie's favorite resort. (Private collection.)

coast. (The name "Côte d'Azur" was first used in 1877.) After Nice was annexed to France in 1860, the city became a fashionable winter resort. In the winter of 1861–62, 1,850 families vacationed there; by 1874–75 the number had risen to 5,000, and by 1887 to 22,000. People were naturally attracted by the pleasant climate, but some were perhaps urged to go by their doctors. In the 1890s a change of climate was a fashionable prescription as a preventive for tuberculosis; doctors recommended sojourns in the mountains and winters under mild skies. On the Atlantic coast the "winter city," Arcachon, was an extreme example of the conjunction of medical concerns with tourism. Built from nothing during the Second Empire as a center for the treatment of tuberculosis, the town nevertheless boasted a casino.

Necessary Leisure

During the second half of the century people came to believe that vacations constituted a necessary change in activity and way of life. Restful and beneficial, nature compensated for the ravages of urban and industrial life. The taste for nature was not new. What was new, as Henri Boraud remarks in his study of vacations, "was the inclusion of these concerns into the temporal organization of human activities."[10]

Work time came to be seen as alternating with vacation time, that is, with time spent in nature, travel, or recreation. In rural, artisanal society leisure time had had its place in the course of normal activities. In urban, industrial society leisure was granted to everyone at specified times, especially in the summer. Whereas Rousseau had turned to nature as a way of throwing off constraints on his time, the modern taste for nature, as it spread to new strata of society, structured time more rigidly than ever before. As more and more people succumbed to the appeal of vacations, the year had to be organized in a new way. An article in *La Revue hébdomadaire*, July 6, 1912, entitled "The Vacation Question," stated: "Fifty years ago the person who took a vacation stood out. Today a person stands out if he does not take a vacation." People felt a need to vacation and insisted that they had a right to do so. The first organized leisure activities appeared at the end of the nineteenth century under the auspices of the Touring Club of France (1890), the *Guide Michelin* (1900), and local tourist offices.

We can learn a great deal about the broader evolution of society, which resulted in the shift from the aristocratic notion

Rossi, *Beach,* 1904. Despite the hat with its abundance of ribbons, the beach imperceptibly loosened people up, encouraged them to wear lighter clothing, and favored more spontaneous forms of play. Sport liberated the human body before subjecting it to a new discipline. (Paris, Bibliothèque Nationale.)

of a rural sojourn to the concept of a right to leisure and ultimately to a paid vacation (a right won by French workers in 1936), by examining the history of school vacations. Before the nineteenth century, classes were interrupted for two reasons: religious holidays, which were scattered throughout the year, and agricultural labors, which resulted in such large numbers of absences that primary schools simply closed down. During the nineteenth century, school vacations gradually became divorced from religious and agricultural considerations, and as the justification for vacations became one of affording leisure time to students and teachers, the duration of school holidays increased, particularly under the Third Republic.

Departing for a new life, these young women are seen off by their parents and curé. On the train family discipline melted away, opening up the road to adventure. (Châteauroux, Archives of Indre.)

In the nineteenth century summer vacation lasted at most six weeks, with classes ending around Assumption (August 15) and resuming at the beginning of October. On January 4, 1894, an order was issued allowing two additional weeks of vacation in schools "that arranged for vacation classes." This extension was offered initially as a reward to personnel "who contributed to regular adult and adolescent courses" and later as a prize to teachers who contributed to the success of after-school programs. This order, reissued annually until 1900, ultimately resulted in extension of the normal duration of summer vacation to eight weeks, from August 1 to October 1. On July 20, 1912, a new order increased the summer vacation for secondary schools to ten weeks, from July 14 to October 1, but it was 1935 before this extension was applied to primary schools as well.

Once, boarding students at lycées and private academies had spent the six weeks of vacation at their schools, but that time was past. As late as the Restoration it was not uncommon for children to spend the whole year at boarding school without ever leaving; instances of this practice could still be found under the Second Empire. The minister of public instruction, Victor Duruy, took pity on these youngsters and in August 1866 expressed his wish that they be taken in by lycées on the seacoast. He deserves recognition for the modernity of his outlook, as well as for his dream of organizing educational trips and exchanges.

People increasingly blamed the schools for not embracing real life, and at the same time they discovered the educational as well as health benefits of vacations and leisure time. This new awareness resulted in the rapid spread of summer camps for children. In addition, scouting was first introduced in France in 1911.

Vacations and the Family

"But you can pick up your prizes when you return to school," Mme R.'s mother told her three children when she took them away on vacation on July 1. The children, lycée students, wanted to postpone their departure until after the annual awards ceremony. Mme R. was born in Paris in 1897, and throughout her childhood she spent summer vacations at Langrune on the coast of Normandy. At Easter her parents wrote the villa's owners to reserve their rental, which cost 400 francs. They also hired a piano and a cabana (at 50 francs each) and a young maid who "did the season" for 15 francs a month.

Mme R.'s father, an engineer employed by the state administration of public works, joined the family for a few days
around July 15 and again around September 15 and spent the
month of August with them. The family went bicycling
together.

As adolescents Mme R. and her brothers frequented the
casinos of the "family beaches." Everyone knew everyone else,
and parents were comfortable leaving their children alone to
teach one another how to dance. Different families mingled
to form circles in which young people could safely move with
greater freedom than in Paris.

The casinos, though places of amusement, were also secular temples for the young bourgeois who met on the family
beaches. Although the youngsters who went to them did not
know it, the casinos were similar to the family room that the
Boileau family had built for its own private use. Freethinkers,
the Boileaus, Caroline Chotard-Lioret tells us, had torn down
the chapel on their estate in Vigné in 1894 and replaced it with
this recreational parlor.

The Boileaus' family room was more than seventy-five
feet long and decorated with red velour and wainscotting.
There were two sculpted stone fireplaces with medallions
bearing the initials of Eugène and Isabelle, who had financed
the renovations. The room was inaugurated in 1901 on the
occasion of a double wedding, that of the two Boileau daughters, Jeanne and Madeleine. Later it served as a dining room,
in which Eugène and Marie played host to thirty to fifty
summertime guests. The house at Vigné has been a powerful
bond for the descendants of the Boileaus, helping to keep the
family together. As late as the 1950s all the cousins vacationed
there.

THE GREAT EVENTS OF A LIFETIME

Marriage, a central event, divided a life into two parts. *Marriage*
The continuity of both family and society depended on marriage. In private life time was therefore divided into "before"
and "after," and important events fell into one or the other of
the two periods.

Before marriage an individual's life passed through several
distinct stages: the beginning of adolescence, marked in most
families by First Communion; the end of secondary schooling,
marked in a boy's life by receipt of the baccalaureate (girls

generally did not receive classical instruction in Latin and therefore could not take the examination for the "*bac*"; if they insisted on a diploma, it was usually the *brevet élémentaire*); and the commencement of adult life, the search for a spouse, and engagement. Ultimately came marriage followed by the birth of children. After that, private time flowed more or less uniformly until death, the hours filled with the responsibilities of rearing children and marked by innumerable family occasions.

A young bourgeois passed his baccalaureate after seven years of secondary education, either in the lycées instituted by Napoleon I (later rebaptized royal *collèges,* only to have the name "lycée" restored in 1848) or in private institutions. Until 1930 secondary studies required the payment of tuition, and, although the state gave out scholarships, secondary school was effectively a privilege limited to the upper classes. In 1842 tuition at a royal *collège* like Louis-le-Grand was 100 francs per year for a day student and 700 francs for a boarder. In 1873 a student of rhetoric at a Paris lycée paid 300 francs per year; by the end of the century the cost had risen to 450 francs. A good private institution would cost him 720 francs. Tuition for a boarder at a Jesuit school in Paris amounted to 1,400 francs, or nearly half the salary of a graduate of the Ecole Polytechnique employed as an engineer by the post office. For the sake of comparison, a maid in Paris in 1880 earned wages of 500 francs annually. In 1854, of 107,000 secondary school students, 4,600 received baccalaureates; after 1873 the number increased to 6,000 or 7,000 annually.

The young bourgeois was in theory subject to compulsory military service under the law of 1873. Lots were drawn to determine who would be required to serve five years and who only one year (which in fact amounted to only six months). But a young man who had received the baccalaureate and who volunteered for service before he was called was required to serve only one year, provided he paid a sum of 1,500 francs for equipment. In addition, students who went on to the so-called *grandes écoles* (the most prestigious institutions of higher learning, including the Ecole Polytechnique, the Ecole des Ponts et Chaussées, the Ecole des Mines, and the Ecole Centrale) or who became state functionaries had no difficulty gaining exemption from service.

After the baccalaureate a young man might continue his education by attending law school or medical school or one of the grandes écoles. (University entry fees were high: to register and take examinations cost 1,000 francs for a law student and 3,000 francs for a medical student). Some chose to skip higher education and go directly into a family business. In any event, a man was no longer young by the time he was ready for marriage.

For the young bourgeoise, on the other hand, higher education was not an issue if her goal was marriage—in other words, if she possessed a dowry sufficient to find a husband. Secondary education for women, whether in a boarding school or, after 1880, in one of the lycées established by Camille Sée, was never intended to prepare young women for the baccalaureate, without which there was no hope of entering the university. Upon completing her studies a young woman was eligible to take examinations for the *brevet élémentaire* or the *certificat de fin d'études secondaires,* but she really did not need diplomas. "Leave that worry to those who need to earn their living," was the recommendation Louise Weiss received from her literature teacher at the lycée Molière in 1910.[11] For the needy, private courses to prepare for the baccalaureate were first offered in 1905. The lycées did not offer officially sanctioned preparatory courses until after the war.

The purpose of education for an adolescent girl of bourgeois background was to prepare for her future role as housewife. She learned how to keep house, supervise the servants, converse with her husband, and raise her children. These duties required neither Latin nor science but a veneer of general culture, skill in music and drawing, and theoretical and practical training in cooking, hygiene, and child-rearing. Until marriage the young lady not only acquired the skills and manners she would need for everyday life as well as high society but also completed her education by taking courses at schools for homemakers, such as the Ecole des Mères or the Foyer, and by attending lectures for young ladies of good family at, say, the Université des Annales.

Finding a Mate

Family and friends were of course useful for finding a mate. A best friend's brother or sister was a natural candidate, as were the distant cousins who appeared at family gatherings for weddings, baptisms, and First Communions.

Young people had plenty of opportunities to meet at such events as charity sales, sporting events (such as tennis or skating), and dances. So-called *bals blancs* were debutante balls to which only eligible young men and women were invited. They were called *blancs* because the girls, making their society debut, dressed in white, a symbol of innocence and virginity. Their mothers attended to maintain decorum, evaluate dowries, and compare the eligible young men.

In France it was customary for a young woman to marry the same year in which she made her debut. If she were very young, she might come out two winters in a row. If, by the time a third season arrived, she had found no takers, her prospects plummeted, for people began to have doubts about her virtue, or worse, about the adequacy of her dowry.

One strategy practiced in bourgeois circles was marriage by introduction, arranged by matchmakers who specialized in finding the right mate. For the most part these matchmakers were elderly spinsters, cousins or friends of good families, whose spotless reputations inspired confidence. They arranged meetings between young people who seemed likely to get along with each other. Simone de Beauvoir's parents met in this way, as did the parents of Jacques Chastenet and Edmée Renaudin's aunt and uncle.

Just because a marriage was arranged did not mean that feelings were unimportant. Couples brought together by family or friends sometimes got on together very well. And if two young people fell in love, their parents did not dismiss the possibility of marriage out of hand. They gathered information about the intended spouse's reputation, income, and opinions. Political and religious affiliations were matters of concern: the freethinkers Eugène and Marie Boileau, who had five daughters to marry off, never considered marriage with a Catholic family. One daughter, Madeleine, noticed, on the boulevard in Tours, a pleasantly handsome young man. He turned out to be the son of an industrialist and a Protestant, hence a possible mate. Madeleine's eldest sister, already married, arranged the first interview and subsequently waged an all-out campaign to secure the marriage. Two months later Madeleine was officially engaged, and a month after that, having been baptized the night before, she was married.

The Engagement

A young man who wished to marry might ask a friend to present his proposal to the parents of the young woman. If the proposal was accepted, his parents would then present a formal proposal to the woman's parents. As of that moment the suitor offically became a fiancé and was received as such in the home of his intended. On his first visit a date would be set for the engagement dinner.

Nicolas-Eustache Maurin, *Fraternal Love,* circa 1835. An angelic blonde blesses her sister's engagement. In the Romantic era, gentlemen preferred brunettes. (Paris, Bibliothèque Nationale.)

Both families were invited to the dinner, which was held at the home of the future bride. On that night the young man gave an engagement ring to his fiancée. She too was permitted to make a gift—a man's ring or a locket containing her portrait or a lock of her hair—which she actually presented to her young man a week later, just prior to another dinner, given by his parents.

Before his first visit the engaged suitor sent his fiancée a white bouquet. If he was wealthy, he would send flowers every day from the presentation to the wedding. He might even send flowers to his future mother-in-law. Toward the end of the century etiquette permitted sending flowers of a color other than the traditional white. Following an oriental custom, some men chose flowers that gradually turned redder and redder until on the eve of the wedding they became purple, as a symbol of ardent love. Manuals of etiquette declared this new fashion to be in the worst possible taste.

Every day the young suitor went to pay court to his fiancée, who was always chaperoned by her mother or another family member. A young lady was expected to show reserve in the presence of her intended. She could neither write nor

Wedding contracts were common in bourgeois marriages, particularly in Paris. The father and notary were the principal actors in this male business. Still, for a woman to sign her own name was a step toward individualization. (Paris, Bibliothèque Nationale.)

receive letters without her mother's knowledge. She must not display affection too warmly, lest she give him reason to doubt her modesty and take the bloom off their future together. In theory the future bride and groom were expected to use the engagement period to get to know one another. The fiancée, however, was expected to remain somewhat ethereal, so that it would be that much easier for her partner to idealize her: "Make sure that later, whatever circumstances and perhaps disillusionments may arise, the husband will always retain the memory of a slender, white form and a pure gaze, the sign of a truly innocent soul."[12]

The engagement lasted between three weeks and a few months. Two months was apparently the norm. The newspaper *La Corbeille,* on December 1, 1844, suggested that a meeting often led in the blink of an eye to a wedding: "Before the veritable season of balls comes a season of weddings, which people call 'summer weddings' because they are the result of summer acquaintances and meetings at the spas, in the châteaux, or while traveling." Other marriages were called "winter weddings" because "they are usually the consequence of a contredanse or of a few polite words exchanged at a concert."

During the engagement period the two families worked out the conditions and amounts of the dowry and set a date for the signing of the marriage contract. On that day the couple, together with certain close relatives and friends, appeared before the notary, or in some cases the notary came to the home of the fiancée. In either event the ceremony was the same. While the notary read the marriage contract, the couple feigned indifference, for it would have been unseemly to show concern for money rather than total absorption in love. When the reading was complete, the young man rose to sign the contract, then handed the pen to his future wife. After that the contract was signed by the parents of the couple as well as by the invited guests. If the family wished to honor an important personage among its acquaintances, he would be invited to sign the contract too.

In Paris and other large cities it became customary for a reception with dancing to be held on the night the contract was signed rather than on the wedding night; by 1900 there was no longer any dancing on the wedding day itself. The fiancée danced first with her intended, then with the notary, then with the best man and others in the wedding party.

Marriage contracts were a custom of the bourgeoisie.[13] Only persons of modest means married without a contract and therefore under the laws of community property; the husband became sole administrator of the couple's joint property. The bourgeois marriage contract provided either for contractual separation of property (so that the laws of community

The Contract

Marriage sometimes meant love, but it always meant an alliance between two families, whose respective titles and occupations figure prominently in this wedding announcement. (Paris, Bibliothèque Nationale.)

property applied only to property acquired jointly, and the couple's debts were kept separate) or for legally separate property (the *régime dotal*), which permitted the wife to administer half of her property herself, while the other half, constituting her dowry, was transferred to her husband.

In Paris, broadly speaking, men married women of wealth comparable to their own. Two departures from this norm can be discerned, however. Shopkeepers and merchants sometimes married women of smaller fortune than themselves, whereas civil servants and professional men sometimes married wealthier women. Admittedly civil servants were paid quite poorly: an *auditeur* at the Conseil d'Etat started at 2,000 francs per year, while a judge at the end of his career earned 6,000 francs. In Rouen an engineer with 75,000 francs worth of patents married the daughter of a merchant, who brought him 741,000 francs. The fiancée's dowry allowed the young couple to live in a style appropriate to its rank rather than its income; the husband's position brought the couple prestige and a comforting stability.

If a young man of modest means but graced with diplomas and good career prospects could marry into the bourgeoisie, a dowryless young woman of the bourgeoisie had a good chance of remaining unwed. It was unlikely that she could make up for the absence of a dowry by obtaining an education and pursuing a career. In France in 1914 there were only twelve female lawyers, a few hundred doctors, and slightly more secondary school teachers. A woman who earned her own living stepped down in class.

The Trousseau

During the engagement the bride-to-be completed her trousseau, which included both personal and household linen. The husband contributed only his personal linen. The fiancée saw to it that the household linen was marked with the initials of both families. Normally the trousseau accounted for about 5 percent of the dowry. According to Mme Alq, the value of a modest trousseau (three dozen each of sheets, pillowcases, tablecloths, napkins, serving aprons, and so on) was approximately 2,000 francs in 1881; a lavish trousseau, with items counted by the gross rather than the dozen, might be worth 25,000 francs.

The major difference between a sumptuous and a modest trousseau was in the areas of lace, furs, dressing gowns, and fine lingerie. The comtesse de Pange, who married in 1910, had a trousseau containing dozens of petticoats, culottes, camisoles, linen and silk stockings, long gloves for the evening and short gloves for the daytime. She also had three dresses, dinner gowns, dressing gowns, three tailored walking suits, an otter coat, a silver fox, a sable stole, and four big hats decorated with feathers and flowers.

Owning large amounts of linen was a necessity in rural areas, where linen was washed in great tubs only two or three times a year. In town, where laundries offered regular cleaning service, less linen was required. Georges Vigarello has shown how the history of linen is related to the history of cleanliness and thus to the perception of the body, hence that it has a symbolic as well as a material dimension.[14] Owning linen was a sign of wealth. During the Second Empire people still displayed their linen along with the basket of gifts offered to the bride right up to the eve of the wedding. This custom fell out of fashion on the grounds that it was immodest to exhibit such intimate items as a woman's lingerie.

Linen played an important part in fashion. Between boarding school and marriage young women spent much of their time embroidering bonnets, collars, and cuffs for their trousseaus. Fashion magazines offered models and guidance. *Journal des jeunes personnes,* 1858. (Private collection.)

The Gift Basket

On the day the contract was signed the bridegroom-to-be sent his fiancée a collection of traditional gifts. These were referred to as *la corbeille,* "the basket," because at one time the gifts were given in a basket of wicker lined with white satin. Later it became customary to send the gifts in a small piece of furniture, a sort of escritoire, but by 1900 people were making do with boxes and cases supplied by the stores from which they purchased the items.

Like the trousseau, the basket was worth about 5 percent of the value of the dowry, or approximately one year's income. It contained items of white and black lace that were passed on from generation to generation; people took great care with these items, having them repaired and cleaned when necessary. The basket also contained jewels, family heirlooms perhaps or else more modern settings; precious odds and ends such as fans, bottles, and candy boxes; fabrics; and furs. Cashmere shawls were particularly prized during the July Monarchy and Second Empire. Finally, there was a missal for the wedding mass and a purse filled with new gold coins, fresh from the mint, along with a note inscribed "For your poor."

The trousseau was exhibited in the fiancée's bedroom, the basket in the sitting room. In the most splendid marriages the bridal gifts could be of grandiose proportions. In 1904 the comte and comtesse Greffulhe gave their only daughter in marriage to the duc de Guiche. After the ceremony the guests went to the home of the bride's grandmother, where the 1,250 gifts she had received were exhibited around the "basket."

Fashion magazines such as the *Gazette des salons* (1835–36) described typical "baskets" from various Paris furniture-makers and enumerated their contents, which ranged from gloves to peignoirs and shawls. In 1874 the poet Stéphane Mallarmé, writing in *La Dernière mode* under the pseudonym Marguerite de Ponty, gave a lavish description of the various jewels that might be included in a gift basket.

The Wedding Ceremony

Both civil and religious weddings could be celebrated on the same day, but usually the civil ceremony preceded the religious by a day or two, particularly in Paris, where delays were likely. Only the four witnesses and the couple's closest relatives were invited to the civil ceremony at the city hall. The groom sent a carriage to fetch his two witnesses and another to fetch those of his bride; he then went with his parents to pick up the bride at her home and take her to the city hall. The mayor or his assistant then read the marriage certificate along with Chapter 6 of the Civil Code, which detailed the rights and duties of husband and wife. He asked the bride and groom if they consented to take each other for husband and wife. Next the bride signed the marriage certificate on the civil register, after which she handed the pen to her husband, who thanked her with the words, "Merci, madame."

There was no charge for a civil wedding, but traditionally one gave the mayor an offering for the poor of his district or town. The wedding party then dined and passed the evening at the bride's parents' home. Toward the end of the century it became fashionable to make a very elegant ceremony of the civil wedding; the hall was decorated with flowers and green plants and an orchestra and popular singers were hired. This fashion developed first in connection with purely civil marriages, particularly remarriages after divorce or marriages between Catholics and Jews, where a sumptuous church ceremony was out of the question.

Religious wedding services came in various types, at prices ranging from 10 to 2,000 francs for Catholics and from 15 to 2,000 francs for Jews, with an "extra special" service at 4,000 francs. For Protestants, the wedding service was always free. Depending on the type of service, one obtained the right to use either the main altar or one of the side chapels, a canopy at the church door, and various degrees of lavishness in regard to flowers, lighting, and music. For the right price it was possible to hire singers and musicians from the Opera and Conservatory. Important society marriages were such powerful draws that invitations included tickets to the church lest too large a crowd overwhelm the facilities. In theory, all costs of the church wedding were borne by the groom, whereas the lunch, dinner, and reception were paid for by the parents of the bride. In practice, however, the costs were often divided between the two families, as is shown by the private archives of the Stacklers, a family of Rouen cotton manufacturers. Those costs could be enormous: one Stackler marriage in 1899 came to 5,641 francs—3,200 people were invited.

The priest read the banns in church three Sundays in a row, unless a dispensation had been obtained by payment of a fee. A dispensation was also necessary in order to marry during Advent, Lent, and other special periods; normally there were no weddings on Friday. The money paid for dispensations went to the poor of the parish.

The wedding ceremony was probably the most public of private rites. Everything in it was codified: the composition and order of the procession, the number and selection of bridal attendants, the costumes of bride and groom (white and triumphal black, respectively), and the gestures of consent. The bride was accompanied to the altar by her father, who gave her to her husband. But before pronouncing the sacramental "I do," the bride turned her head toward her mother, as if to ask her consent. Until the end of the nineteenth century only the bride wore a wedding ring. The groom's ring, a fashion that came to France from abroad, did not become customary until the turn of the century, and it was not considered essential.

In the provinces weddings traditionally were occasions for lengthy celebration. On August 29, 1832, George Sand wrote Emile Regnault about the wedding of their friend Duvernet: "I left the church in order to escape the wedding, which has gone on for three days and three nights without letup." Another custom survived in the provinces even after losing favor in Paris: the bachelors in the wedding party attempted to make off with the bride's garters.

When a poet married an orientalist, an unusual informal ceremony was possible. On June 5, 1900, Lucie Delarue-Madrus married the translator of the *Thousand and One Nights* at the church of Saint-Roch, just ten days after the two had met. The bride wore bicycling togs: checkered dress and boater hat. To transport witnesses and family members to the ceremony the couple hired the only four automobile taxis in Paris. People gathered in the street. Bride, groom, and guests retired to a neighborhood restaurant for lunch; the couple did not take a honeymoon.

Such unconventionality was rare. For Jules and Gustave Simon *(La Femme au XXe siècle),* nothing was as sublime as a church wedding. The fact that, from 1879 to 1885, a period during which anticlericalism led to an increase in the number of civil marriages, many women were denied a church wedding outraged the Simons: "We men cannot understand what a church is for a woman. To enter her church, veiled in white, on the arm of her beloved, to the music of the organ, amid clouds of incense and among all her friends, wreathed in smiles or overcome with emotion, is the fulfillment of her childhood dream and a memory to cherish for the rest of her life. Nothing is lost on her—not the flowers or the candles or the sweet songs of the choir boys or the cadences of the priest or the ring placed on her trembling finger or the stole placed on her head or the sacred benediction or her mother's warm embrace behind the sacristy door. When a little girl puts aside her dolls, her greatest joy is to help her older sister put together a trousseau while waiting for her own turn to come. One cannot remove all this from a woman's life." Was this a description of a woman's dream or a man's fantasy?

The Honeymoon

Honeymoons became fashionable in the 1830s. In 1829 the *Code conjugal* depicted the newlywed couple at home the day after the wedding. The bride's mother was the first to visit, followed by close relatives and friends. The couple dined with their parents. Clearly they did not go off on a honeymoon, although the book notes that "the English have an excellent custom, which is to spend this month of happiness in the remote countryside. This practice, which has come to France in recent years, is not the least of the good things we have borrowed from our neighbors."

A honeymoon in the country was a way for a newly wed couple to ensure their privacy, which was always threatened at home by family and social obligations. The *Livre du mariage* (Book of Marriage, 1886) indicated that the purpose of the honeymoon was to ensure a couple's privacy; newlyweds should travel with trunks containing everything necessary to "create a charming environment for themselves wherever they might go." An hour after arriving at the hotel, everything was unpacked and the couple was snug in its nest.

When was the best time to leave on the honeymoon voyage? There were two contending schools of thought. One school held that the English had the right idea, namely, that the couple should leave directly after the ceremony, having been sent off in a shower of rice and white satin slippers. The other held that they ought to wait a while. At the end of the Second Empire the comtesse de Bassanville observed that it was unfashionable to leave immediately. In June 1894 *La Grande dame* noted that "one no longer leaves immediately after the ceremony. Such behavior has become bourgeois. Nowadays the groom takes his wife to his estate or to the nest that he has prepared for her by studying her tastes. Or else the parents go away for a few days, leaving the young newlyweds to themselves." Six to eight weeks later the couple set out on their honeymoon.

At the beginning of the twentieth century the ultimate in chic was to forget the honeymoon voyage altogether and take a room under an assumed name in a luxurious Paris hotel. The trip to Italy had become so traditional that those who wished to set themselves apart from the common herd went elsewhere—to Sweden or Norway, for example. These were the lands of Nordic idealism, and Ibsen and and his tortured heroines were in fashion at the time.

Although an Italian honeymoon may have been thought routine by some, it was a time-honored ritual. Travel agencies offered a choice of two itineraries: via Strasbourg and Switzerland or via Lyons and the Mediterranean coast. Italy and the Mediterranean were the destinations of choice for most newlyweds. Italy was considered the land of love. Its mild climate, beautiful scenery, artistic legacy, and Catholic presence combined to create a climate of diffuse sensuality. The aesthetic and the religious stimulated both the senses and the emotions, and memories of Romeo and Juliet still haunted Verona.

The Mediterranean, "where the orange blossoms," facilitated the discovery of sensuality. The high temperatures and violent beauty of the countryside vanquished flesh and soul, setting the stage for bliss. The warm sensuality of the honeymoon did not necessarily have anything in common with the conjugal sexuality to come.

A wedding night in the family home, under the watchful eye of a very proper mother. Bridegrooms in the late 19th century were advised to exhibit prudence and tact. (Private collection.)

Camille Marbo, who married at Saint-Germain in October 1901, went to Italy with her husband on a six-week honeymoon. She called the custom of the honeymoon trip "barbarous": "A mixture of physical surprises, fatigue, and bewilderment caused by all the excursions and visits to monuments and museums." Her husband wanted to see everything. She found it difficult to keep up. Soon she was pregnant, and she returned from the trip exhausted. A miscarriage left her infertile. Because of such experiences, physicians warned that it was better not to mix too many different activities at once. Newlyweds did best to spend the first weeks of married life in the country, where they could make their acquaintance in an atmosphere of calm. Only afterward should they depart on a honeymoon, which they would then be in a far better position to enjoy.

The logic of this reasoning was sound, but it failed to reckon with the honeymoon's symbolic role. Marcel Prévost, in his *Lettres à Françoise,* defended the traditional honeymoon, which he said deserved credit for "heightening the hope and enthusiasm so necessary to two people who plan to make a life together."[15] Whether the wedding night was a success or a disappointment, the important thing was that the honeymoon leave pleasant memories to mark this crucial moment in marriage. The purpose of the journey was to shape memories by establishing certain images.

In general, the marriage ceremonies focused more on the bride than on the groom or the couple. The wedding day was above all to be the most important day in a woman's life. Excluded from public life, women had a role to play in the private sphere, one which the wedding ceremony reinforced.

Weddings were for good. Divorce remained quite rare. According to the 1901 census, for every 10,000 French men between the ages of eighteen and fifty who married, 53 divorced; and for every 10,000 French women between the ages of fifteen and forty-five who married, 70 divorced.

From Marriage to Family

A high value was placed on intimacy between husband and wife. It became increasingly common for couples to sleep together in double beds. The wisdom of separate bedrooms ceased to be discussed. Mme Pariset had warmly commended the practice in 1821, but this advice disappeared from the 1913 reprinting of her book. An example was set on high: when Louis Philippe showed visitors around the royal apartments, he proudly pointed to the bed he shared with Queen Marie-Amélie. Bourgeois husbands and wives used the familiar *tu* and called each other by silly but touching pet names. César Birotteau called his wife "Mimi," "my beautiful white doe," and "my beloved pussycat."

After marriage much of private time was consumed by children. Newlyweds immediately began to anticipate the birth of a child. Once born, the child was baptized and trained at home until the time came for schooling and for encouraging the youngster's leisure pursuits. The family schedule changed as the child grew. People had fewer children than in the past; more than half of the women born in 1881 produced no more than two children. But they lavished greater attention and invested more of their hopes than ever before in the children they did have.

Greater intimacy between husband and wife accompanied closer family relations generally. Paternity and maternity were rising commodities. The Goncourt brothers noted in their diary for March 26, 1860: "The child and its mother are no longer relegated to the woman's apartments as in the past. The child is shown while still an infant. Parents proudly present the child's nurse. It's as if they were on stage, making a great show of their production. In short, a man is a father today as he would have been a citizen a little less than a century ago—with a great deal of show."

Daumier caricatured fathers proudly showing off their offspring. Many men were also willing, in private, to play with their children and show them affection. The children of Eugène and Marie Boileau came into their room in nightshirts every morning, and the parents took them into their bed. Marie's letters to Eugène when he was away from home in 1883 give the flavor of these morning welcomes: "If only you could see the litter in my bed every morning. They make me lazy, the little darlings. It's anyone's guess who looks the happiest. Jane [age two and a half] throws her pretty little arms around my neck and tries to keep the others from kissing me. She slaps and scratches them and says, 'I want mommy for myself' in her winning little voice and then hugs me as hard as she can. If you were there, dear big Fanfan, how happy I would be, or rather, how happy we would be." Maternity was constantly praised to the skies and declared to be the only really gratifying role for a woman.

As the children grew, their entry into the community of Christians was marked by baptism and communion, religious

Alfred Stevens, *Family Scene*. Monsieur, madame, and bébé: the classic three-member family in a France already tending to limit its population. The husband works at his desk, while the wife holds her child in a Madonnalike manner. (Paris, Musée d'Orsay/Jeu de Paume, Kaganovitch Collection.)

ceremonies that were transformed during the nineteenth century into family occasions, ceremonies that helped strengthen and revitalize family ties.

The Revolution had stripped the Church of responsibility for recording births, marriages, and deaths, turning that function over to the state. When a child was born, its father was required to declare the birth within three days at the town hall of the town in which the child was born. He took with him two witnesses who also lived in the town. Within twenty-four hours after the declaration was made, an official physician paid a call to verify that the birth had indeed taken place and to confirm the child's sex.

Baptism

In principle, baptism also took place within three days after birth. According to the 1859 *Dictionnaire universel de la vie pratique à la ville et à la campagne,* it could be postponed only for grave reasons. But family pressure ultimately resulted in an easing of the religious obligation. The ceremony was often put off for anywhere from six weeks to two or even three months in order to allow the child's mother to attend. If there was fear for the infant's life, however, an emergency baptism could take place sooner. Claire P. of Chateaufort gave birth to a son, Albert, on January 11, 1903, and noted that the infant was privately baptized by abbé Demange on January 17 and formally baptized a month later, on February 15, after which Claire invited the witnesses to lunch.

A child was customarily given three names: one by the parents, one by the godfather, and one by the godmother. During the church ceremony the godfather stood to the right of the woman holding the child, the godmother to the left. Each placed one hand on the baby and the other on the folds of its gown in a symbolic gesture. When the priest asked, "What do you want?" they responded, "We request that this child be baptized." The priest then asked additional questions, to which the godparents responded. Finally they signed the baptismal certificate, after which they shared a meal to which the child's father invited all witnesses to the ceremony.

Traditionally both the godfather and godmother gave presents, but the gift expected from the former was far more substantial than that expected from the latter. The official duty of the godparents was to oversee the child's Christian education if the parents died, but their most important role was to offer the child certain ritual gifts. Like good fairies, they

Eugène Devéria, *Baptism.*
(Paris, Bibliothèque Nationale.)

brought offerings of welcome to the newborn's cradle and continued to ply the youngster with gifts throughout childhood and adolescence.

Godparents also participated in family celebrations. Traditionally the godfather of the first child was the paternal grandfather and the godmother was the maternal grandmother. For the second child the maternal grandfather and the paternal grandmother usually were chosen. If the grandparents were dead, the family turned to the closest relative in each of the two lines, preferably a relative of an earlier generation. The fact that grandparents doubled as godparents is a good example of family autarchy.

The ringing of bells and the distribution of coins to the poor signal the joyful arrival of a new Christian, escorted by his godfather and godmother. Gastl, *Baptism.* (Paris, Bibliothèque Nationale.)

First Communion rivaled marriage as the "greatest day of a person's life," to borrow Flaubert's definition of communion from his *Dictionnaire des idées reçues.* In many respects it was a prefiguration of marriage; the commitment required by the sacrament was enacted before the entire community. The spectacle was orchestrated in such a way as to arouse emotion in the participants as well as the spectators. In the

First Communion

The Happy Grandmother: Return from Communion. The girl kissing her grandmother was also kissing her childhood goodbye. A girl's First Communion was a rite of passage to adolescence, the first of the "best days" of her life, and a prelude to marriage. (Paris, Bibliothèque Nationale.)

Dictionnaire de conversation à l'usage des dames et des jeunes personnes (1841) we read: "The parents [of the communicants], especially the mothers, look on with emotion at this first act of their religious lives, and feel within their hearts the reawakening of inexhaustible love."

The emotion came in part from anticipation of the great day, for which the preparations were lengthy, and in part from the solemnity of the occasion. Elisabeth Arrighi made her First Communion at age twelve, on Thursday, May 15, 1879, at the church of Saint-Germain-des-Prés. In her diary a few days before the year 1879 had even begun she wrote: "Year of my First Communion." She repeatedly alludes to catechism class, in which she made good grades, good enough to win the *grand cachet* and the congratulations of the priests. On Thursday, May 8, she received as gifts a white missal, an ivory box, an ivory crucifix, and various religious books. On Saturday, May 10, she confided to her diary that she hoped her father would receive communion with her on the day of her First Communion. May 11, 12, and 13 were taken up with a retreat. The preacher spoke of death, hell, and heaven. On May 14 she participated in a general confession. Elisabeth was most scrupulous: she accused herself of teasing her little sister and asked God to forgive her. On Sunday, May 18, she recounted the Thursday ceremony in detail. The hymns, the organ music, the crowd, and the procession of little girls in white combined with the intensity of the prayer to create a feeling of exaltation: "Oh! I shall remember the emotion I felt at that moment for the rest of my life." She advanced, "trembling," toward the holy table, knelt, made the sign of the cross, received the host, then returned to her place where she forgot herself in the fervor of prayer and thanksgiving. She was in a state of bliss: "I heard God speaking to my soul, saying to me over and over, 'I am yours, you possess me.'" Inner turmoil manifested itself through the language of love—yet another point in common between First Communion and marriage.

In the nineteenth century First Communion traditionally took place when a child was about twelve. In the thirteenth century the Lateran Council had decided that the child should communicate for the first time at the age of reason or "discretion," that is, when he or she was old enough to distinguish good from evil and the bread of the Eucharist from ordinary bread. The Council of Trent in the sixteenth century again invoked the notion of an "age of discretion," which the learned theologians determined to lie in the range from age nine to

thirteen or fourteen. Custom shifted gradually toward the end of this span of years and away from the beginning.

During the nineteenth century there was discussion in the Church about the wisdom of this choice. In 1853 the provincial councils of Albi, Toulouse, and Auch warned that children should communicate early, "at an age when they are able to discern the body of the Lord yet still retain their original innocence, exempt from the taint of vice." Pius IX condemned the practice of postponing First Communion until a standard and relatively late age, and Cardinal Antonelli explained the pope's views in a letter sent to the bishops of France on March 12, 1866.

Jules Octave Triquet, *Solemn Communion*. Girls on the verge of adolescence receive the benediction of the springtime sun beneath diaphanous white veils. With fervor in their souls and hearts a-flutter, they celebrated virginity with a mixture of affectation and eroticism. (Rouen, Musée des Beaux-Arts.)

The debates over the proper age for First Communion culminated on August 8, 1910, in the issuance of a papal decree, *Quam Singulari Christus Amore*. Pius X ordered that children should receive First Communion as soon as they

Solemn Communion or Private Communion?

In front of the church and in the studio, First Communicants appear in the finery of the day, impeccably groomed and wearing an air of seriousness and clothes designed expressly for the occasion. Girls dressed as brides; boys in their first suits, which in relatively modest families they would continue to wear until they joined the service. (Sirot-Angel Collection.)

acquired a basic knowledge of religion, typically at around age seven.

The pope's order had two purposes, one spiritual, the other material. The spiritual purpose was to eliminate what the pope saw as elements of Jansenism in the delaying of First Communion. The Jansenists portrayed the Eucharist as a reward, whereas the pope held that it should be considered "a remedy to human frailty." If a child seemed to have acquired enough of the rudiments of religion after two years of catechism class, there was something to be gained by urging him to communicate for the first time and thereafter to confess and receive communion frequently. In fact there was no better way to fortify the child's soul. The sacrament was a necessary bulwark against temptation and sin. Ideally early communion was supposed to lead to daily communion and a pure heart.

The second purpose of the pope's order was to diminish the ostentatious display associated with First Communion. Opponents of the papal decree feared that it would "do away with the solemnity that makes First Communion the happiest day of our lives." Mass communion, with all its attendant formality, was introduced in France in the middle of the eighteenth century, at first in certain religious establishments, particularly those run by the Jesuits, and shortly thereafter in the parishes. The practice was still not widespread in 1789 and was not universally adopted until after the Concordat.

The solemn nature of First Communion turned it into a social occasion. Like the marriage ceremony, it was staged in such a way as to leave "an indelible memory." The boys dressed somberly in black suits with white silk armbands, while the girls in their white chiffon dresses and veils resembled little brides. "A girl's whole life unfolds between two veils—the communicant's and the bride's," wrote the comtesse de Gencé in 1910. At communion girls received presents worthy of a wedding basket. Only those not among the family's intimate friends gave religious gifts, such as a missal or rosary. Close friends gave such profane items as jewels, watches, or elegant objets d'art. At the end of the nineteenth century the custom was to lay out the gifts along with the donors' cards, exactly as was done with wedding presents. To complete the parallel, the family lunch that followed high mass concluded with the serving of an elaborate cake.

Lowering the age for First Communion meant making the occasion less of a prefiguration of marriage. No one would give the same gifts to a girl of seven as to an adolescent of twelve—to do so would have been ridiculous. Thus, it was reasoned, the younger child would be less preoccupied with gifts and appearances. But the religious authorities had not reckoned with the volume of commerce that had grown up around the rite of First Communion: "Everything the family wears on that day must be new. The father and mother wear new clothes. For the mother especially, communion was an excellent occasion to obtain from her husband a new dress combining the profane with the sacred. The dressmakers had lines for every budget. For poor girls there were dresses at 3.75 francs with bodice and veil for an additional 0.85 francs. For the wealthiest there were bonnets at 15 francs to go with outfits costing 130 francs and composed of two chiffon skirts with a silk lining. Belts started at 1.45 francs and went all the way up to 40 francs."[16]

No doubt the pope hoped that by reducing the age of First Communion he would also reduce the ostentatious display of profane wealth that went along with it. But he had no intention of diminishing the religious solemnity of the occasion. The grandeur of the ceremony was intended to stir emotion in the parish and arouse sympathy for the communicants on the part of parents, friends, relatives, and parishioners in general. The First Communion service was thus a way of ensuring that at least once a year every Christian would return to the sacrament of the Eucharist.

For a long time First Communion was celebrated at Easter. It gave "praiseworthy impetus to the performance of Easter duties by all." The "Parish Bulletin of Saint-Sulpice" clearly delineated the role to be played by the communicants, that of mediators between God and the other parishioners: "Large numbers of relatives and friends followed them to the altar to receive their God. The others, less fortunate and courageous perhaps, envied their happiness, and surely more than one returned to the privacy of his home and, in giving his child a long embrace, discovered the Jesus he had not received" (May 25, 1909). Through the child the sacrament passed from the Church to the family.

After 1910 a new system was established. This new system respected what the pope had said in *Quam singulari,* yet preserved the splendor of the old First Communion ceremony, which was now divided into two parts. The first part of the new ceremony, which was called the "small" or "private" communion, took place at the age of discretion, age seven. The second part, called the "formal communion," even though essentially it supplanted what had been called "First Communion," was held when the child turned thirteen.

It was impossible simply to shift the traditional First Communion ceremony from age twelve or thirteen to age seven, because that ceremony was not only a religious event but also a rite of passage from childhood to adolescence. Chateaubriand observed as much in his *Mémoires d'outre-tombe*. Young Romans, he wrote, donned the toga when they reached the age of manhood; young Christians received communion. Chateaubriand made his First Communion in April 1791, when he was thirteen. The ceremony marked the "moment when the family decided on the child's future status."[17]

The religious ceremony marking the beginning of adolescence had become an important family celebration, and many were unwilling to give it up. People not only remembered this rite of passage in later years but also commemorated it with souvenirs. To relatives and friends the communicants distributed religious images with their names and the date of the communion ceremony inscribed on the back. They also posed, often kneeling on a prie-dieu, for the traditional communion photograph.

Other Family Occasions

In addition to the annual holidays celebrated by all, each family established its own private rituals. Renée Berruel wrote in her diary on March 23, 1908: "Tonight we celebrated mama's name day. I made a pocketbook, and we sang *Simple Bouquet*. Each of us gave a small vase, and papa gave a chest with four drawers and a mirror."

In *Savoir-vivre* (1879) Clarisse Juranville extolled the virtues of these family celebrations, "stages on life's way when the heart seems to expand." She describes how each member of the family responds to the kindness of the others. Of the little daughter, for example, she writes: "Your father has placed in your room something you've wanted for a long time. Your sister has embroidered a collar for you. Your mother has served a splendid cake in your honor, and your little brother has given you a bouquet and recited a brief compliment." According to Juranville, these occasions were especially important for the grandparents, who longed to be remembered by children and grandchildren. On name days and birthdays grandparents invited the family to dine with them. These regular occasions were excellent opportunities to demonstrate and strengthen family ties.

Wedding anniversaries garnered special attention. They marked a couple's progress across the sea of matrimony, from the cotton anniversary (after one year of marriage) to the porcelain (twenty years), silver (twenty-five years), gold (fifty years), and diamond (after sixty years). Celebration of these occasions by children, grandchildren, and great-grandchildren amounted to commemoration of the family's own founding.

The average life expectancy increased markedly during the nineteenth century. In 1801 it was thirty years; by 1850 it had increased to thirty-eight years for men and forty-one years for women, and by 1913 to forty-eight years for men and fifty-two years for women. But the wealthy were far more likely to live to old age than were the poor. In France between 1870 and 1914, "for forty-year-old males, death claimed 130 white-collar employees and 160 workers for every 90 business owners (death rates per 10,000 in each category)." At Bordeaux in 1823 the average age at death was forty-nine for a wealthy bourgeois compared with thirty-three for a person of

Old Age, Death, and Mourning

Lucien-Hector Jonas, *Golden Anniversary*. A triumph of fidelity, and even more of an equal—and rare—longevity, which truly deserved a speech by the mayor and a gathering of children and grandchildren. Old age enjoyed no other kind of honor in the late 19th century. (Paris, Salon of 1912.)

the lower strata. In Paris in 1911–1913 the mortality rate in the wealthier arrondissements was 11 per 10,000 population compared with 16.5 in the poorer arrondissements. Death rates from tuberculosis were twice as high among the poor.

Consequently the well-to-do were often in a position to enjoy a period of retirement at the end of their lives. Those who worked in independent professions had to bear the cost of retirement on their own; only civil servants received pensions in the nineteenth century. The law of 9 June 1853 provided a pension at age sixty to former soldiers, government employees, and academics with more than thirty years' service. It also set maximum pension amounts: for magistrates, for example, the pension could not exceed either 6,000 francs or two-thirds of the average compensation over the last six years of service, whichever was less.

Few workers received pensions. The only exceptions were those employed in state factories or by the railways or certain large industrial firms. Many workers subscribed to mutual funds. Peasants, who had no form of social security, were obliged to rely on their families for support. The law of 1910 "on pensions for farmers and workers," though controversial and limited in scope, nevertheless shows that people had become aware of the problem.[19]

In the nineteenth century a physician or engineer who retired lived on what he had managed to put aside during his working years. The value of money was stable enough that a professional could retire in his fifties without suffering a decline in his standard of living. Many of the rentiers living in France in those days were of modest middle-class background and enjoyed relatively small incomes. Retirement reflected the ideal of *otium,* or leisure. Once a person was no longer obliged to earn his living, all his time was at his disposal, and he was free to enjoy the pleasures of private life every day.

The well-to-do died at home. To them the hospital was a place of horror, and only those without money or family went there to die. Even the clinics, which served a clientele less impoverished than that of the hospitals, were considered a form of banishment. Death was incorporated into the very design of housing. In 1875 the abbé Chaumont wrote that the master bedroom was a "sanctuary" which someday would be the scene of the final agony. For that reason it should be equipped with a "soothing but instructive image of the death of Saint Joseph."

It was surely more complicated to tend to the dying at

home in Paris and other large cities, where ever since the time of Haussmann apartments had been shrinking. Lack of space made proximity to the dying difficult, particularly since, owing to the discoveries of Pasteur, people had become obsessed with hygiene. Where death had once been a part of life, now it came to be seen as a form of decay. This rejection of death led to what Philippe Ariès has called "hidden death," the relegation of death to the hospitals, a change that took place in the 1930s.

When a person died, those in attendance closed the eyelids of the deceased, straightened the limbs, and covered the body with a white sheet. The face was left uncovered and illuminated, so that the least sign of life would be noted at once. For the same reason the body was watched night and day and never left alone. If the deceased was Catholic, a crucifix and sanctified sprig of holly were placed on the chest. The shutters in the death room were half closed.

A declaration of death was filed at the town hall, and the family then awaited a visit from the coroner, who issued a burial permit. Once the permit was in hand, the town would issue the death certificate. For funeral arrangements the family turned to the town's funeral bureau or to the vicar responsible for religious burials. In Paris there were funeral homes that promised to organize the ceremony "with tact and propriety."

Like marriages, funerals came in several categories. In 1859 a first-class funeral cost 4,125 francs, and a funeral of the ninth and lowest class only 15 francs, counting both the cost of the religious ceremony and services provided by the funeral home. The various classes of funeral differed as to the quality of casket, flowers, and so on as well as the solemnity of the service.

If the deceased was wealthy, a mortuary chapel lit with tapers would be set up in his or her home. Visitors came to pay their respects and sprinkle holy water on the coffin. In families of more modest means, the coffin would be displayed in the entryway, which was draped with crepe to look like a mortuary chapel. As long as the body remained in the house, the family did not gather at the table for meals; each person ate in his or her own bedroom.

When the time came for the funeral procession, male mourners either walked to church bare-headed or rode in carriages. The closest relatives marched at the head of the procession. Female mourners usually went directly to the church without stopping at the home of the deceased. After

Nos parents sont maintenant avec Dieu, et leur partage est avec les saints.

A mortuary image from the mid-19th century and from Turgis, one of the best-known purveyors of religious objects in the Saint-Sulpice quarter, celebrated for its distinguished black and white engravings. After 1880 mortuary images confined themselves to evoking the memory of the dead and avoided mention of the hereafter. (Paris, Bibliothèque Nationale.)

Pierre Marcel-Béronneau, *Painful Duty,* 1900. For a father's death, a major event in the history of a family, tears were permitted and even required. A cortege of women in black with mourning veils and handkerchiefs at the ready. The men will shed their tears at the cemetery, where women were too sensitive to set foot.

the service only relatives and close friends followed the coffin to the cemetery. Early in the nineteenth century the aristocracy still observed an old custom that gradually disappeared as the century progressed: the women of the family did not participate in either the procession or the funeral service. It eventually became customary among the well-to-do for the widow, who at one time had not even been mentioned in death announcements, to lead the mourning for her husband.

The only written evidence of death is to be found in elements of the funeral ritual itself: death announcements, black-bordered writing paper, and notes of expenditures for mourning garb and cemetery upkeep. In November 1900, after the death of her sister, Marie Boileau noted in her account book: "Paid for mourning for the servants and day help: 274 francs; mourning hats and veils from Mme Richard's: 180

francs; for cleanup at the cemetery, 30 francs; to the curé de B. for the offertory: 50 francs."

When people in the nineteenth century spoke of the length of the mourning period, it was to deplore the fact that it was getting shorter. Mme de Genlis in 1812 was just as nostalgic as Blanche de Géry in 1883 for a mythical past in which people supposedly had mourned twice as long, for a lengthy period of mourning was taken as a sign of a righteous society. The reality was otherwise, however. Mourning at court had been shortened by half by an eighteenth-century royal order: husbands were to be mourned for one year, wives, parents, and grandparents for six months, and other family members for one month.

Nineteenth-century mourning periods actually appear to have been longer, and the length of mourning changed little over the course of the century: widows mourned for a year and six weeks in Paris and for two years in the provinces. In 1908 the *Usages du siècle* stressed the difference between the two years of mourning nominally required by etiquette and the reality, which was closer to a year and a half or a year and six weeks. This last figure agrees with that derived from other sources.

Men mourned only half as long for their wives: six months in Paris, a year in the provinces. The *Nouveau manuel complet de la maîtresse de maison* (1913) is the only source that prescribes an equal mourning period, two years, for both widow and widower. It is also the only source to recommend two years of mourning for a father or mother; all the others limit their recommendation to one year or even, in the case of the *Code civil* of 1828, six months. A comparison of this last-named work with subsequent manuals of etiquette suggests that the period of mourning actually increased rather than decreased as the nineteenth century progressed. Mourning for a grandparent increased from four and a half to six weeks, for a brother or sister from two to six months, for an uncle or aunt from three weeks to three months. For first cousins the period remained more or less the same: fifteen days in 1828, fifteen days to a month later on. Under the Second Empire parents began to wear mourning for children who died in early infancy.

Mourning involved three stages. Consider the case of a widow. Her period of high mourning lasted four and a half months in Paris, six months in the provinces. During this time she wore black wool dresses, a hood and veil of black crepe, black linen gloves, and no jewelry except for a bronzed steel belt buckle. She was not supposed to curl her hair or wear perfume. During the next six months, the second stage of mourning, she could wear black silk dresses, a hat with veil, gloves of leather, silk, or kid, and costume jewelry. This period was followed by three more months of partial mourning, during which she might mix white, gray, or lavender with her black clothing and wear jade jewelry. The etiquette of mourning was so complex that a special newspaper, the *Annonces des deuils* (Mourning Announcements), was published in the eighteenth century to furnish specific details about how things were done, such as what day diamonds could be substituted for black stones or silver buckles for bronze ones.

During the period of high mourning the entire household, including children and servants, wore black. Uncles, aunts, and cousins were excepted, however. Carriages were draped in black. Mourners could not appear in public in places devoted to pleasure such as theaters or balls, nor could they participate in public assemblies. For the first six weeks they were not supposed to go out at all, and only close friends were invited in. Women were not allowed to do needlework, even among relatives and friends.

Mourning was also signified by personal items other than clothing. Black-bordered handkerchiefs were used, and writing paper for mourners had a black band about half an inch wide at the top and an eighth of an inch wide at the bottom. Once the mourning period ended, people returned to ordinary white paper, except for widows, who, unless they remarried, continued to write on black-bordered paper for the rest of their lives.

The nineteenth century's attachment to the code of mourning is interesting. Although it was not really respected except by aristocrats and in the wealthiest households, the rules of that code established an image of the ideal ritual, which, like the etiquette of high society, was linked to the monarchical society of the eighteenth century.

Conclusion

On February 22, 1871, Victor Hugo wrote: "I take little Georges and little Jeanne walking whenever I have a free moment. You might describe me as 'Victor Hugo, representative of the people and children's maid.'"[20] The parallel between public and private life is striking. Hugo, far from placing public life on a higher plane, sees his roles as politician and grandfather as being of equal importance.

In 1877, eight years before his death, Hugo published *L'Art d'être grand-père*. Throughout this collection of poems he depicts himself, to borrow the title of one of them, as "Victor, *sed victus*": the great hero, whom no tyrant had been able to make bow down, was "vanquished by a small child"—not just by his own grandchildren but by all the children he saw in the Tuileries and the Jardin des Plantes. He was vanquished by their innocence and by what he saw in them of the divine. Children, he said, are the best defense against the world's nastiness. Let the papers insult him and pour scorn him; if Jeanne went to sleep clutching his finger, he felt enveloped and protected by the little girl's sweetness. God speaks through children, so that when we contemplate a child we find "a profound peace made entirely of stars."

Victor Hugo with Georges and Jeanne at Hauteville House. (Paris, Musée Victor Hugo.)

Children ensure the continuity of time. If "the sons of our sons enchant us," it is because time's thread is knit together through them as the cycle of life repeats itself again and again: "To see my Jeanne's Jeanne—oh, how that would be my dream!" Hugo conjures up an image of Jeanne's wedding day and motherhood: "Jeanne's adventure will still lie ahead of her, in the creature in whom our destiny expands or comes to an end. She will be a mother of young and grave mien." Victor Hugo here gives poetic expression to a religion of the family, a religion that the bourgeoisie normally celebrated in occasions great and small. Sometimes these celebrations were closely associated with religion, sometimes not. They were occasions for sentimentality, tenderness, and joy. The family shared common emotions and rejoiced in its own existence. At the same time it established its own private time scheme, independent of the vicissitudes of history and of public competition. This family time embodied two contradictory qualities. It was regular, owing to the repetition of periodic family rituals. Yet this regular and cyclical time, smooth and uninterrupted—a time that was not oppressive to individuals but that flowed through them, as it were, in a biological continuum—was meant to establish a kind of eternity.

In the final analysis it was this eternal quality of private time that family ceremonies asserted. Marriage was therefore the most important of those ceremonies, and for the same reason children and vacations took on more and more importance. The family, in its ceremonies, blissfully contemplated its eternal incarnation.

A bourgeois street in the neighborhood of the Opera in the early morning hours, prior to the opening of its luxury shops. Marville has left a photographic inventory of Second Empire Paris. (Paris, Bibliothèque Nationale.)

❧ 3 ❧

Scenes and Places

Michelle Perrot
Roger-Henri Guerrand

From the the quarters of the concierge, a tailor, to the cramped garret where a woman alone, sewing, watches a child, this cross-sectional drawing of a house at night shows the gradation of statuses and life styles that fascinated the authors and illustrators of *Tableaux de Paris. Le Magasin pittoresque,* 1847. (Paris, Bibliothèque Nationale.)

✒ At Home

Michelle Perrot

"PRIVATE life should be lived behind walls. No one is allowed to peer into a private home or to reveal what goes on inside," Littré wrote in his *Dictionnaire* (1863-1872). The expression "wall of private life," he says, was coined by Talleyrand, Royer-Collard, or Stendhal some time in the third decade of the nineteenth century.

Private life was walled off in several ways. Within public space small groups—microsocieties—staked out semiprivate areas for their exclusive use. Cities were filled with clubs, aristocratic and bourgeois circles, lodges, gaming parlors, private rooms rented by the night for amorous gatherings, and cafés, cabarets, and bistros—"houses of the people."

These semiprivate gathering places were almost exclusively the province of men. Women, whose reputations suffered from any association with "public" activity, had no place in them. They gathered instead in sewing rooms, churches, and washhouses, places which they sought to preserve from ever more strenuous efforts by men to control them. Civil society was not, despite the wishes of wary legislators, a void; it was honeycombed with cells of conviviality, each with its own secrets.[1]

The dominant classes, fearful of the ignorance and filth of the masses, made sure that safe havens would exist in public places: theater loges were extensions of the private salon; ships and bathhouses had private cabins; first-class compartments avoided indiscriminate mingling of people from different classes and preserved distinctions. "Since the invention of the omnibus," Flaubert wrote, "the bourgeoisie is dead"—this from the writer who made the hackney carriage wandering the city with drawn blinds the very symbol of adultery.[2]

The Household Order

The quintessence of privacy, however, was the home, seat of the family and pillar of the social order. Kant celebrated its metaphysical grandeur: "The house, the residence, is the only rampart against the dread of nothingness, darkness, and the obscurity of the past. Its walls contain all that mankind has patiently amassed over hundreds of centuries. It opposes escape, loss, and absence by erecting an internal order, a civility, a passion of its own. Its liberty flourishes where there is stability and finitude, not openness and infinity. To be at home is to recognize life's slow pace and the pleasures of sedentary meditation . . . Man's identity is thus residential, and that is why the revolutionary, who has neither hearth nor home, hence neither faith nor law, epitomizes the anguish of errancy . . . The man without a home is a potential criminal."[3]

Homes established roots. Housing for workers therefore occupied a prominent place in the strategies of employers intent on creating a stable work force, as well as in the ideologies of family and law and order. Le Play and his disciples, who investigated lower-class housing, have left detailed descriptions that are an invaluable source for the historian, a veritable dissection of popular behavior. Once, the science of physiognomy had sought to describe individual faces on the theory that the face is the mirror of the soul; now the science of sociology described the arrangements of individual rooms on the theory that a room mirrored the life of its occupant. Under the Third Republic the village schoolmaster's home was intended to be a glass house. The teacher's room was a "small sanctuary of order, industriousness, and good taste," in contrast to the "shabby hovel of the messy bachelor, who leaves home as often as he can and who has no taste for anything beautiful," according to Inspector Richard, who in 1881 drew up plans for model housing. The ideal republican missionary was to sleep on an austere bed modeled after the beds at Saint-Cyr, the military academy. His bathroom was to be equipped with white linen and tools for good grooming "that will prove that the tenant respects his person but eschews excessive sophistication." His floor should be kept waxed, and his chairs were to be stuffed with straw and kept "clean of all stains." He should have a "nice library," filled chiefly with classics obtained while a pupil at the *école normale,* or teacher's school. There should be a glass case for scientific collections and a cage "containing songbirds," along with a few green plants discreetly marking the presence of a well-domesticated nature. The schoolmaster's one concession to luxury was to be a "magnificent table covering, made from an old shawl taken from his mother's wardrobe," a token of the teacher's dignified background and careful upbringing by an attentive mother. Later on, it became permissible to add a piano, a few "casts of fine sculpture," and reproductions of masterpieces "brought within reach of every pocketbook by the technique of photogravure." Such a "gentle home" could be visited by all—authorities, parents, and pupils—without fear of blushing at an intrusion upon the teacher's private space.[4]

The home was a political as well as a moral entity. Every voter had to have a residence, and every prominent citizen required a prominent home in town and perhaps a château in the country. The home stood for discipline and reconstruction, a shield against the dangers of revolution. Viollet-le-Duc published his *Histoire d'une maison* in 1873, when memories of the Commune still lighted up the countryside. In 1889, the hundredth anniversary of the French Revolution, the theme of the "social economy section" of the Exposition Universelle was "the home through the ages." Ultimately the domain of government would expand to incorporate the domestic.

In the nineteenth century, however, home was a family affair. The house was where the family gathered, the center of its existence. It was the incarnation of a couple's ambition and the symbol of its success. Starting a family meant moving into a home. Young couples were less and less willing to share the home of parents. Viollet-le-Duc remarked: "I have seen the warmest family feelings consumed and extinguished when married children live together with their forebears."

The English word "home" came into use among the French bourgeoisie in the 1830s; poorer families referred to their "*carrée*," or "digs." In either case, a home of one's own was the sign and sine qua non of independence. Politically at odds with his parents, Gustave de Beaumont and his young wife looked for "a hole to burrow in." In 1839 Beaumont wrote: "Clémentine and I are extremely eager to own a little 'home.' To us, the smallest cottage would seem like heaven on earth, if only we could be our own masters."[5] In 1888 the proletarian Norbert Truquin, who had seen something of the world and of revolution, wrote: "There is no fate more enviable than that of living in your own home *(intérieur)* in the midst of your family." The word "*intérieur*" now referred not so much to the heart of man as to the heart of the household, and it was there that one experienced happiness; similarly, well-being was now conditioned on "comfort." "Put this word in your dictionary," Jean-Baptiste Say advised readers of "the middling class" who glanced at his *Décade philosophique* (1794–1807), "and may you possess all that it implies." He contrasted the "luxury of convenience" with ostentatious expenditure.[6] Home economics, the science of the domestic, insisted on a quiet life.

A house was also property, an investment, in a country where a large proportion of capital was still invested in real estate and where such investment still offered a decent return. Many inheritances consisted chiefly of real property, which, as Jacques Capdevielle has pointed out, was not only a form of ownership but also a hedge against death.[7] How vital was such property? Heirs sometimes fought bitterly over a house and the carefully inventoried objects it contained; their quarrels transformed the cozy nest into a nest of vipers.

A house was like a private kingdom, whose owners sought to appropriate nature by growing gardens and building greenhouses to abolish the seasons; to appropriate art by amassing collections and staging private concerts; to appropriate time by collecting family souvenirs and memorabilia of journeys; and to appropriate space by accumulating books that described the earth and picture magazines such as *Illustrations, Lectures pour tous,* and *Je sais tout* that showed it.[8] Reading, a form of armchair exploration, civilized the world by making it legible; photographs made it visible. The home library was a window on the world; it encompassed the world within the confines of the home.

At the turn of the century people experienced a keen desire to know and dominate the world without leaving home. Technological advances such as electricity and the telephone established communication with the outside world and made it possible to envision a day when everyone might work at home. Many people aspired to own a small family business in which all family members could work under the watchful eye of the father. From Zola (*Travail,* 1901) to Kropotkin, many saw the family business as a kind of utopia with great liberating potential. At home the male uncertain of his social identity might recover his dignity as head of the family.[9]

Artists too imagined a center of elite social life and creation, a "total home" utterly new in form down to its smallest detail. Edmond de Goncourt, in two volumes devoted to *La Maison d'un artiste,* warned that "life threatens to become public"; to ward off that danger he proposed the home as ultimate

Claude Monet, *The Artist's Garden at Vétheuil,* 1880. The calm of the lush, enclosed gardens of the Ile-de-France. The painting of the Impressionists was an equivalent of happiness. (Washington, D.C., National Gallery of Art.)

refuge. Life also threatened to become femininized, and it was up to man to reconquer the house from those priestesses of the quotidian, women. As the twentieth century approached, Joris Karl Huysmans and other men who worried about the new "emancipated" woman shared Goncourt's fears.

"Families, I hate you!" André Gide proclaimed a little later on. "Closed shutters, sealed doors, happiness jealously guarded." Fortress of privacy, the home was protected by walls, servants, and darkness. But it was also a place seething with internal conflict, a microcosm through which ran the tortuous boundary between public and private, male and female, master and servant, parent and child, family and individual. The assignment of rooms for various uses, the location of stairways and corridors, the availability of space for private meditation, for grooming, for physical and spiritual pleasures—all these were governed by strategies of encounter and avoidance shaped in part by desire and concern for the self. Household sounds were an amalgam of cries and whispers, muffled laughter and sobbing, murmurs, surreptitious footsteps, squeaking doors, and the implacable tick of the clock. At the center of all this secrecy was sex.

Bourgeois Interiors

This housing model—this model house—was of course a bourgeois model. From Victorian London to fin-de-siècle Vienna and as far east as Berlin and Saint Petersburg, the bourgeois home came in countless variations. Yet there may have existed a uniform, pan-European, nineteenth-century bourgeois style. This style would have been fostered by the free circulation of architectural ideas and characterized by a subtle mixture of functional rationality, still modest comfort, and nostalgia for the age of aristocracy—a nostalgia that was particularly powerful in countries where court life lingered on. Even in democratic countries the bourgeoisie was slow to assert its own taste, clinging to ideals of elegance borrowed from eighteenth-century salons and châteaux. Whatever validity this hypothesis of a uniform bourgeois style may have, many disparities in social structure, family relations, and sex roles persisted. These disparities stemmed from differences in national, religious, and political cultures and led in turn to differences in domestic architecture and use.

In *The Tongue Set Free: Remembrance of a European Childhood* Elias Canetti compares his various childhood homes.[10] At Ruschuk on the lower Danube, three identical houses—

one for Canetti's parents, one for his grandparents, and one for his uncle and aunt—were built around a courtyard garden, which Gypsies visited on Fridays. Five or six young Bulgarian servants, mountain natives who ran through the house barefoot, were constantly on call. At night they crowded together on the Turkish sofas in the salon and told wolf and vampire stories. In Manchester a nanny was in charge of the upper-story nursery, and young Elias spent long hours alone studying the figures in the wallpaper. On Saturday nights the children went down to the salon and recited poems to amused guests. Sunday mornings were holidays; the children had free access to their parents' room and could climb into their beds—twin beds of course, as was only proper in Protestant England.

The organization of space and time was determined by rituals. In Vienna, where the Canettis occupied an upper-story apartment with balcony, a well-schooled maid sorted out visitors in the waiting room. The family took ceremonial walks to the Prater. "Everything revolved around the imperial family. It set the tone, and that tone governed not only the nobility but also the great bourgeois families." In Zurich, on the other hand, "there was neither a kaiser nor an imperial nobility . . . I was certain, in any case, that in Switzerland every man had his place, everyone counted." It was impossible to banish the maids to the kitchen, as in Vienna; they ate at the table with the family. Canetti's mother was content, and the family was drawn together: "My mother was always there for us. There was no one between us. We never lost sight of her," in an apartment that was remarkably small. Topography follows custom.

The Rural Home: Workspace

The difference between town and country was just as important as the difference between countries. At the turn of the twentieth century a majority of Europeans still lived in the country. In France 69 percent of the population was rural in 1872, 55.8 percent in 1911. Privacy was not unknown in rural homes, but in open farmhouses it could not be taken for granted. The only walls were walls of silence, breached exclusively by confession.

The peasant identity had deep roots. In Picardy or Gévaudan home was more a matter of locality than of structure. To be "from here" someone had to recognize the elements of the landscape, read the signs of the sky and the weather, and identify property lines and recount the history that had deter-

Designed primarily as instruments of work and production, rural houses offered limited space for family life and intimate needs. Styles varied widely, however, according to the region and the wealth of the occupants. Above is a sumptuous country house with bedrooms on a second floor, while the simple farmhouse (right) appears to have accommodated a large number of people in a small space. Achille Quinet, 1877. (Paris, Bibliothèque Nationale.) C. Famin, 1874. (Paris, Bibliothèque Nationale.)

mined them. The *terroir,* the rural locality in the strongest sense of the term, was where people felt they had roots shared with others and perpetuated. Family stories, constantly repeated and scrutinized, created sites of commemoration. The sense of boundaries was very powerful. Outsiders beware—especially tramps and, worse yet, strangers.

The same word that was used for "house"—*casa* or *oustal*—also designated the associated farmland. Overcrowded and of crude construction, the farmhouse was not so much a home as a workplace. The visiting ethnographer and the urban schoolteacher saw nothing but animal-like promiscuity, especially when animals and people slept under one roof. The barn, the woodshed, the ditch bordering pastureland in bocage country, the stand of trees in which shepherd girls shaded themselves in open-field regions—all these were better places for making love and grooming the body than was the common bedroom, shared by the entire family. Each person was constantly under the scrutiny of everyone else. Transgression was difficult and generally required the more or less tacit consent of the group. To hide a pregnancy, much less a birth, must have been torture for any woman who did not enjoy the cooperation of other village women.

"They all kept their eyes on me. My father hovered around me and judged everything I did. He would have pre-

ferred that I never change the straw in my mattress." These words, reported by Elisabeth Claverie and Pierre Lamaison, were spoken by a man of forty-two.[11] Court records such as the one from which this testimony was taken reveal growing impatience with such close supervision, which no doubt became even closer when tensions mounted in the *oustal*. Parental interference became even more unbearable as individualistic attitudes developed, encouraged in part by the greater mobility and wider horizons that came with improvements in transportation ranging from the railroad to the bicycle. (Young people rode bicycles to dances in nearby villages.) After the First World War, many rural women refused to live under the same roof as their mothers-in-law. Some wanted private space; others required certain amenities in order to tend to their appearance, even at the risk of being called "flirtatious." For all these reasons women left the country and flocked to the cities; their exodus led to an increase in the proportion of rural men who did not marry.

Crowded together in filthy hovels, the urban poor developed a different style of private life. They seemed to tolerate indiscriminate mingling even in their recreational activities. Zola regarded the workers' dance as a kind of mating ritual.

The Homes of the Poor

Marville's working-class Paris. Shops and apartment crowd in on one another and break the lines of the facades. Signs everywhere made the city a book. As usual, not a person in sight. (Paris, Bibliothèque Nationale.)

To the upper classes that indiscriminacy was a sign that workers were sexually primitive and uncivilized. Working-class activists, keen to acquire a more dignified image, became increasingly intolerant of rowdy ways. "People live helter-skelter lives, like animals. We are mired in savagery," Jean Allemane observed of workers' lodgings; fifty years earlier Dr. Villermé had said much the same thing in a report on the living conditions of textile workers. Industrialists and public health physicians proposed new housing policies designed to alleviate overcrowding and thus reduce tuberculosis and alcoholism among workers. Toward the end of the nineteenth century people began to speak of "minimal acceptable norms" in housing; standards defined the number of cubic feet of space required per inhabitant and specified basic amenities. Although for a long time the workers' movement showed little interest in the "housing question," after the turn of the century it began to call for "pure air" and "healthy housing."[12]

Although philanthropic efforts yielded undeniable if limited improvements in housing in the period before 1914, these laudable initiatives were hampered by persistent failure to comprehend working-class habits.[13] Forced to "live in the streets," workers made use of public buildings and of open, quasi-private space in the neighborhood. People helped one another and taught newcomers to cope with urban culture. Nineteenth-century workers spent what money they had not on better housing, which was out of reach, but on clothes, which not only could be had but which, as Maurice Halbwachs observed some time ago, were necessary in order to appear in public without embarrassment, to cut a good figure (*bella figura,* as Italian workers, experts on the subject, used to say).

Workers' desires were focused first and foremost on the city. Workers moved frequently, and not just to escape the landlord and his rent-collector; moving was also a sign of social mobility. Workers in Turin, Maurizio Gribaudi has found, moved first to the center of the city, then to the outskirts, then back to the center.[14] This constant movement has all the earmarks of a deliberate social strategy.

For workers, the city was a vast theater in which some rose and others fell, some found fortune and others misfortune. Working people wanted an open city, whose resources they could freely avail themselves of, just as their peasant ancestors had once freely availed themselves of the village's communal lands. They disliked fenced playgrounds and public parks, which excluded the poor and were designed as decent places for the well-to-do to stroll in; working men and women preferred undeveloped fields. Instead of the green spaces proposed by public health advocates, they favored Paris's "black belt," destination of many a Sunday excursion as well as a meeting place for unruly youths. The passageways of the bourgeois downtown, which Walter Benjamin found so fascinating, had their equivalent in a working-class suburb like Levallois-Perret, whose passages the police hesitated to enter, or again in Lille, whose alleyways reproduced rural allegiances right in the heart of town.[15]

Thus people compensated for mediocre housing by relating to the city in a new way. At the same time they also related in new ways to their bodies (many supposedly private acts were performed outdoors) and to things. Leftovers were used, and worn-out items were recycled. A kind of barter economy flourished. Partly independent of the cash economy, the world of barter was one in which working-class women, not confined to the home like their bourgeois counterparts, played a fundamental role.[16] To the poor the city was what the forest was to the poacher. Seen in this way, urban life and rural life had much in common. They differed as to social mobility, but that was primarily a consequence of size.

The urban poor differed from other segments of the society in one important respect: their family networks were not defined by the limits of a locality or the walls of a home. In the second half of the nineteenth century, however, the poor also experienced an ever more powerful desire for space and privacy.

Freedom meant above all freedom to choose one's place of residence. Workers resisted being herded into workmen's housing, whether company towns or just vast housing projects such as the famous Cité Napoléon, which ended in fiasco. "Housing projects have never been popular in France," Audiganne noted in 1860, because they connoted an extension of factory discipline into the home.[17] "Upon returning to our apartments we might find posted on the doors new regulations affecting nearly all our private activities. We would not be masters in our own homes." Rather than accept regulation in exchange for the relative comfort of the projects, workers chose to live in flimsy dwellings such as the "brick and plaster" buildings built in cities that experienced major expansion in the nineteenth century.

The desire for independence had deep roots. It stemmed in part from the peasant's firm attachment to the soil, which proved to be such a powerful brake on industrialization. That attachment to the soil was actually strengthened by the requirements of the protoindustrial family economy, in which the home was first of all a workplace. In the Nord, for example, weavers who worked at home bitterly opposed attempts by some city governments to evict them from their houses for health reasons. But moving weavers from damp cellars to dry and inconvenient lofts showed complete contempt for the requirements of the textile trade. Reybaud observed in 1863 that "efforts were made to entice [weavers] into healthier, better ventilated areas where buildings were more soundly constructed, but to no avail. They resisted being moved."[18] In Lille weavers forcibly evicted from their cellars regrouped in alleyways near the center of town and set up shop at street level.

Once again it was space, location, and use that mattered, not the quality of the "interior," a notion that is scarcely perceptible in the reports of overcrowded dwellings compiled by Le Play and his collaborators in *La Réforme sociale*. These workplace-homes contained little in the way of furniture and other objects: mattresses, kitchen utensils, a table, a few chairs, and occasionally a family chest, which the sympathetic soci-

Space was limited in this modest accountant's apartment. The common room served also as an office and a child's bedroom. But heavy hangings, potted plants, framed pictures and mirror, and flowered wallpaper attest to a concern for domestic comfort. (Jean Migrenne Collection.)

ologist saw as a sign of persistent respect for family roots. Sometimes a meager symbol of pleasure or privacy turned up in one of these bare apartments: a birdcage perhaps (birds were the poor man's pet of choice), or a lace curtain manufactured in Calais, so widely used that they even turn up in the wretched shanties of the Cité Jeanne-d'Arc photographed by Atget at the turn of the century. The walls might boast a color print cut out of a weekly picture magazine or a family photo. The walls were the first surface to be appropriated. Moving meant changing wallpaper; low-priced wallpaper had as dramatic an impact as did low-priced cotton fabrics for women's clothing. In the 1830s Agricol Perdiguier (whose *nom de compagnonnage,* or journeyman's name, was Avignonnais-la-Vertu) lived in a wretched hovel in Paris's faubourg Saint-Antoine. The floor was poorly tiled and the ceiling was supported by "rough-hewn black beams as in country houses." But the room was decorated with "light wallpaper, which lent an air of gaiety." The windows were covered with "muslin curtains through which the leaves of climbing vines can be seen." Although "nearly everything in Agricol Perdiguier's world was repulsive and hateful, when he returned home it was as if he were entering another world."[19]

A Growing Desire for Intimacy

As the working class became less mobile and housing conditions grew worse, grievances and desires emerged more distinctly. In an 1884 parliamentary inquiry into housing, workers, called as witnesses for the first time, bitterly attacked the filthy apartments, "roach hotels," and makeshift buildings in which they were forced to live. Sounding a more positive note, they expressed their wish for a little more space—at least two rooms and, where there were children and "a self-respecting father, three or four rooms would not be too much." Decent sleeping arrangements outweighed the demand for privies. Workers, as soon as they could afford to do so, arranged for children to sleep in a different room from their parents. A wooden bed as opposed to a straw mattress signified settling in. In 1880 a female worker attempted to kill her companion because he spent the money they had been saving for a bed, which would have confirmed their life together as a couple. When the builder Maréchal was planning workers' apartments, however, he dared not make room for private baths: "The [common] people do not ask for bathrooms in their apartments." What workers did want was buildings of modest size with a wide variety of facades, "so that no one can say that they live in a workers' housing project." The sources reveal a dread of regimentation and a yearning for individualized housing.[20]

People needed warmth, cleanliness, and pure air. They also wanted privacy for the family and longed desperately for independence. They liked space in which to build and tinker. For all these reasons they dreamed of owning single-family homes, an idea that was not simply foisted on workers by the bourgeoisie but that was actually the anarchists' fondest wish. Pataud and Pouget envisioned a sort of housing tract containing homes with yards for workers. At about this same time British investigative committees discovered a heightened need for privacy among English workers, "so great is the fear of unwarranted intrusion by one's neighbor."[21] Michel Verret, writing of today's worker, remarks that "workers place greater value on housing than on the city."[22]

People at all levels of society desired greater intimacy within the family, between husband and wife, and among friends. These desires were particularly powerful at the turn of the twentieth century. One form in which they were expressed was a growing reluctance to mingle indiscriminately with neighbors and to accept their restrictions on individual behavior. They increasingly resisted the surveillance practiced in prisons, hospitals, barracks, and boarding schools.

The evangelist David Gétaz was imprisoned at Chalon during the Second Empire. His most unpleasant memory was of the common dormitory and "the breathing of all those men, whose snoring assailed my ears." It was impossible to have a private meeting with his wife: "No outpouring of emotion, no tender affection, none of those sweet words that no stranger should hear, none of those little secrets that people in such situations always want to tell each other." The turnkey prowled about, "as though he had never before seen people who loved each other."[23] Where tokens of love were less inhibited, they were necessarily more private. Modest Caroline Brame was disturbed by the caresses of young newlyweds.[24] Amorous etiquette grew more refined as the mystery surrounding love deepened. Beds in bourgeois apartments no longer sported curtains, because the whole bedroom was now reserved for the bedtime ritual.

Hospital employees in Paris rebelled against being forced to live a barrackslike existence: "Communal living, which once was one of the basic rules of hospital life, has become a heavy burden for most of our employees . . . They suffer from having to eat in dining halls and from having to sleep in dormitories. They do not feel 'at home' in the hospital, and they dream of the privacy and relative comfort of a home of their own. Finally, they want to make sure that outside of working hours their private lives are free of administrative discipline."[25] This was written in 1910 by a municipal councillor named Mesureur, who despite his sympathies judged that the hospital's unmarried female employees were better off being forced to live in the hospital dormitory, where they were safe and the moral climate was healthy. Yet being housed on the premises where one worked was considered a mark of servitude, and workers were reluctant to accept such conditions.

People demanded space not only to make love and to be with their families but simply to live. Norbert Truquin, a laborer from Lyons who was forced to live in a kind of barracks, recalled, "what bothered me most was feeling the presence of another man beside me. It was the first time I'd shared a bed."[26]

Elderly people confined in hospices attempted to carve out a private niche. "It is a constant struggle to keep them from storing rags, old utensils, and cracked pots behind their beds or in some corner of the room. The only value these things have for them is that they are not part of the house-issued clothing and furnishings. These things belong to them, and taken together they symbolize a kind of home."[27] To be sure, this was written by a liberal who favored home care. But resistance to hospitalization on the part of the poor was widely attested. And dying at home ensured that one would not be subjected to autopsy, the ultimate fate of many proletarians.

The desire for a private space of one's own reflected a heightened sense of physical individuality, an awareness of individual personality that some writers carried to extremes. "You have to close your door and windows," Flaubert wrote, "curl up like a hedgehog, light a roaring fire in your fireplace because it's cold, and pluck some great idea from your heart." And further: "Since we can't reach for the sun, we must seal our windows and light the chandeliers in our room."[28]

Great things were at stake in private space. Here the ambitions of power were realized in material form, personal relations took shape, and people discovered themselves. Hence it is not surprising to discover that the house played an important role in art and literature. From Monet's sunny gardens to Matisse's partly open windows to the twilight shadows cast by Vuillard's lamp, painting penetrated the home and hinted at its secrets. Literature, long silent about decor, suddenly began to describe interiors in minute detail, reflecting a change in the way people looked at places and things. What a change

The young lady reading is part of the decor of this 1880s English salon with its bouquets and bibelots. The geometric wallpaper and light curtains heightened the importance of light and created a new style. (London, Victoria and Albert Museum.)

from Stendhal's sketches in *La Vie de Henry Brulard* to the meticulous inventories in Roger Martin du Gard's *Le Lieutenant-Colonel de Maumort*[29] and ultimately to Georges Perec's *La Vie, mode d'emploi*.

Lytton Strachey remembered his childhood home as a place of odd agglomerations of stone and brick, each with its excrescences, ornaments, and characteristic furnishings, its specific and immutable forms, its intense, heavy atmosphere, with which his life was intertwined as intimately as his soul with his body. Such places exert tremendous power; their effects on our lives are subtle and pervasive.[30]

Proust too had powerful memories of rooms in which he had lived: "I envisioned now one, now another of the bedrooms I had occupied in my life, and eventually I remembered all of them in long daydreams that filled the time after I woke up." Theater of private life, scene of the most personal of learning experiences, and focus of childhood memories, the home is a fundamental place of commemoration in which our imaginations dwell forever.

Home: A Place of Commemoration

This apartment building in the Buttes-Chaumont quarter of Paris was designed for the petite bourgeoisie and graced with Art Nouveau inventions. Note the fashionably ornate ivy-leaf wrought iron and the various sculptural motifs. The absence of a monumental entryway and "noble story," along with the determination not to treat the top floor as a place for servants, reflects a change in attitude on the part of architects influenced by the social movement of the early 20th century. (Sirot-Angel Collection.)

Private Spaces

Roger-Henri Guerrand

THROUGHOUT the nineteenth century the dominant class displayed contempt for proletarians. These "barbarians," as the common people were often called by their betters, were too loathsome for words. Dr. Taxil, a physician who lived during the reign of Louis-Philippe, despaired of description: "The third and final class, the vast proletariat, shares, but for a few worthy exceptions, all the hopeless ignorance, superstition, base habits, and depraved morals of the children of the forest. Its vulgarity, rudeness, improvidence, and prodigality, coupled with the burlesque pleasures and orgies that are so harmful to its well-being, cannot—and I say this without prejudice—be described; the portrait would be too hideous."[1]

It would not be difficult to fill an anthology with similar texts. To the conquering bourgeois the proletarian was a savage of the most dangerous variety, a member of an inferior race. "Although some well-to-do Parisians took an interest in the lower classes," Adeline Daumard tells us, "they more or less consciously erected a barrier between the bourgeoisie and the people, and even if they believed in the need for social mobility, their consciences were untroubled, for they considered the lower orders to be their moral as well as social inferiors."[2]

In the new society, where property was the supreme value, an unbridgeable gulf separated owners from workers. In Lille, for example, in 1891 the average net worth of an industrialist was 1,396,823 francs, compared with 68 francs for a worker, or a ratio of 20,541 to 1. By 1908 the average net worth of both worker and industrialist had increased, but the ratio was still 9,075 to 1.[3] How could two social species as dramatically different as these live together?

Accordingly, buildings that housed both rich and poor in apartments on different floors—a type of dwelling that had been common in prerevolutionary France—gradually disappeared. We can trace this change in cross-sectional drawings of apartment buildings. Such drawings were a device used by many nineteenth-century artists, who followed the example set by the demon Asmodée in Le Sage's *Le Diable boiteux*.[4] Older engravings show that apartments on higher floors were less sumptuous and comfortable than those on lower floors, with the garret the least comfortable of all. Even early in the century tenants occupying different floors of older buildings did not know one another, as Balzac and others observed.[5] The occupants of the second, or noble, floor soon moved to newer quarters in more exclusive areas of the city. In Paris this shift began during the Restoration, as new streets were built to the west and north of the city. It ended under Haussmann, who deliberately removed the dangerous classes from the center of town to the outskirts. A cross-section of an apartment building from the Haussmann era would reveal that its tenants were socially homogeneous. In every city of any size posh sections gradually emerged for the wealthy, while proletarians were relegated to ghettos where no member of the upper classes was ever obliged to set foot.

Housing in the Elegant Quarters

During the Second Republic (1848–1851) the government extended building codes that dated back to the ancien régime and set new limits on building height as a function of street width.[6] (Buildings could rise no higher than 11.7 meters on streets of less than 7.8 meters in width; no higher than 14.62 meters on streets from 7.8 to 9.75 meters in width; and no higher than 17.55 meters on streets wider than 9.75 meters.) Napoleon III later added an additional category to accommodate Haussmann's plans: on boulevards more than 20 meters in width, the height of the cornice might be raised to 20 meters, provided that the building stood no more than five stories high (counting the mezzanine). No one floor could exceed 2.6 meters in height in any building.[7]

Haussmann prohibited overhangs that would have protruded into the street, but builders waged an endless battle to restore their precious decorative bulges. Their appetites were finally assuaged by a new ordinance, which stipulated that on streets between 7.8 and 9.75 meters in width, balconies could extend up to 50 centimeters beyond the facade at heights of

5.75 meters or more above the sidewalk.[8] On streets wider than 9.75 meters, balconies higher than 4 meters could protrude out to 50 centimeters; if higher than 5.75 meters, they could extend to 80 centimeters. At the beginning of the twentieth century, buildings still could not exceed 20 meters in height for seven stories including mezzanine, but protrusions of up to 1.2 meters were authorized on streets that were at least 10 meters wide.[9] This concession was enough to allow the development of bay windows, which had begun to appear around 1890, with the purpose of augmenting the lighting in the dining room.

Within the wide latitude afforded by these relatively generous building regulations, architects were free to decorate facades using all the recipes they had learned at the Ecole des Beaux-Arts, which for more than a century stressed the extreme importance of archaeological gingerbread.[10] The late nineteenth century was a time of bitter struggle between the neoclassical and the neo-Gothic styles. Reverence for the classical orders encouraged the use of embedded columns and pilasters of every variety, invariably coupled with pediments, ornamental friezes, and Italianate embossing. In this noble task architects who as students had been awarded the Grand Prix de Rome proved unrivaled, for during their stay at the Villa Medici they had spent much time, pencils in hand, gazing at ancient monuments. Their enemies, abetted by a redoubtable champion in the person of Viollet-le-Duc, worked in Gothic, just as Balzac had written his *Contes drolatiques* in pseudo-Old French. When Jérôme Paturot decided to build himself a house, he turned to a young builder with a full head of hair who offered him his choice of Romanesque or Gothic in any of several varieties: with lancets, radiant, flamboyant, or Lombard.[11]

Any number of mercenaries set out to make names for themselves by plundering the Renaissance. Certain facades from this period offer marvelous textbook illustrations of the whole gamut of sixteenth-century styles. Around the turn of the century the leafy excrescences of Art Nouveau introduced a new note into this simultaneously ancient and medieval landscape, but in most French cities, other than Nancy, Art Nouveau buildings were one of a kind.

What were the more expensive buildings—those with rents high enough to discourage tenants of less than substantial social status—like inside? Under Haussmann the grand bourgeois apartment house achieved its classic form. César Daly's

Théo Petit was one of the architects who did most to popularize Art Nouveau in the early 20th century. He built several handsomely proportioned buildings in Paris and called frequently on the services of the sculptor H. Bouchard, an artist with symbolist as well as populist inclinations. (Paris, Bibliothèque Nationale.)

E. Renaud was one of a group of architects who, during the July Monarchy and afterward, revived the Renaissance style, as in this celebrated building on place Saint-Georges (9th arrondissement). Its ornamentation challenged bourgeois utilitarianism. The symmetry of the facade is impeccable. (Paris, Bibliothèque Nationale.)

L'Architecture privée au XIXe siècle (1864) explored fine distinctions within a genre that had attained a uniform perfection.

According to Daly, the widely respected founder of the *Revue générale d'architecture,* the bourgeoisie of his day had its choice of three types of rental housing. The top-notch apartments were reserved for families of established wealth. Such apartments presented two faces, one to the courtyard, the other to the street. Erected upon stone foundations and basements, buildings rose no higher than five stories—three of impressive proportions. Apartments on the second through fourth floors were connected by a stone staircase. Wooden stairs, marking a diminished social status, led from the top of that staircase to the fifth floor, which was inhabited by less well-to-do families or by friends or children of the families housed below. There was also a service staircase, located either alongside the main staircase or at the rear of the building. Depending on the configuration of the plot on which the building stood, the service staircase was accessible either from the courtyard or through a concealed doorway independent of the main vestibule. The service staircase, always of wooden construction, provided access to the kitchens on every floor as well as to the garrets where the servants slept.

Buildings of this type were heated by a furnace installed in the basement and connected to heating ducts in the floors. Above the third floor, however, this type of heating was ineffective. Warmth was not yet considered an essential amenity in every home, and physicians recommended that bedrooms be kept cold and well-ventilated.

Families of somewhat smaller fortune occupied apartment buildings of the second class. These too were built on stone foundations and basements, but they incorporated an additional floor, making six stories in all. The first and second floors were customarily occupied by commercial businesses. The main staircase was of wooden construction from top to bottom, and there were two apartments on every floor. Yet even this relatively more modest type of building had a service stairway.

The lower fringe of the dominant class occupied apartments of the third class, in six-story buildings with only a single wooden staircase. These buildings had no courtyard, only a small light or air shaft.

What distinguished all three types of apartment building was the presence of a concierge, once found only in aristocratic

Throughout the 19th century the schools of fine arts gave priority to antique and Renaissance models. Every facade was a bravura piece, an anthology, the one above being a deluxe example of the genre which required the services of a sculptor. Everything in this mishmash evokes myths and naturally could be appreciated only by those who had studied the classics. César Daly, *L'Architecture privée au XIXe siècle,* 1872. (Paris, Bibliothèque Nationale.)

An incisive observer of social types, Daumier included the concierge in his abundant gallery of portraits. A number of his lithographs involve tenant-landlord relations. (Paris, Bibliothèque Nationale.)

hôtels. "The concierge in the faubourg Saint-Germain, a man who has seen everything life has to offer and who has nothing to do, gambles with the earnings from his investments. The porter in the Chaussée-d'Antin likes his comfort. In the Stock Exchange quarter the porter reads his newspaper; in the red-light district she is a former prostitute, and in the Marais she is principled, cantankerous, and a creature of whims."[12]

Eugène Sue gave a name to this new character in the human comedy: Monsieur Pipelet, Mr. Janitor.[13] He proved to be a figure of no small social importance in the larger cities and became a favorite target of the satirical papers from *Le Charivari,* which published Daumier's caricatures, to *L'Assiette au beurre,* which in 1900 devoted a special issue to the concierge. Since landlords did not live in their buildings, the concierge was the owner's representative. He collected rents, rented vacant apartments, cleaned hallways and other public areas, and maintained order. Standing on the boundary between the public and the private, he regulated the flow of traffic between street and apartments. Some also accused him of serving the police as an informant; *L'Assiette au beurre* reckoned that he did as much damage as the "stooges" employed by the Church and the army.[14] A few observers remarked that the concierge's quarters were generally uncomfortable, but

In these two "Haussmannian" buildings—left: 95, rue de Vaugirard; right: 39, avenue Mozart—countless examples of which can be found in the residential neighborhoods of Paris and the provinces, the only originality is in the metal bay windows, the winter gardens of the middle bourgeoisie.

there must have been exceptions to this rule. In a novel written by Paul de Kock during the Second Empire, a janitor by the name of Droguin lives the life of Riley in an apartment as stylish as that of any young middle-class family.[15]

Beyond Cerberus, the ample stairwell of one bourgeois apartment building faced the statue of a Neapolitan woman, according to Emile Zola's description; on the head of the statue rested an amphora from which protruded three gaslights with frosted globes.[16] In place of the Neapolitan lady Zola might equally well have chosen a lansquenet or a Moorish woman, who often filled the same office of lampholder—a device occasionally seen even today. The walls were done in mock marble, a specialty item available from any number of firms. The bannister was of cast metal; stairs were covered with red or Oriental runners held in place by copper rods. The elevator, invented in 1867 by the engineer Léon Edoux (who coined the word *ascenseur*), did not come into common use until after 1900.

A Rational Space

Apartment interiors were laid out in accordance with a rational scheme that for many years enjoyed almost universal acceptance. Every apartment had public areas for show, private areas for intimate family gatherings, and purely functional

Félix Lenoir, plan for a dining room, 1874. During the reign of Louis-Philippe numerous catalogs were published with designs to inspire furnituremakers, and the worst extravagances were proposed to wealthy clients. The astonishing buffet in this dining room includes a display plate in the style of Bernard Palissy, two Chinese vases, and a pair of funerary urns. (Paris, Musée des Arts Décoratifs.)

spaces. Just inside the door was a foyer beyond which no visitor could go unless invited. In the foyer callers were sorted out and directed to their proper destination. In some early-nineteenth-century buildings this space was large enough to double as a dining room, as Balzac attests: "The baroness put her daughter up in the dining room, which was promptly converted into a bedroom . . . and the foyer became, as in many households, the dining room."[17]

The dining room, when utilized as intended, was a place of tremendous importance. Here the family put itself on display for its guests. It displayed its silver and exhibited the centerpiece it had commissioned from a fashionable goldsmith. Mealtimes were a highpoint of social intercourse: "It was at table that deals were done, ambitions avowed, and marriages concluded. Gastronomic horizons expanded accordingly. A mark of prestige and a sign of excellence, gourmet dining symbolized conquest; it came to betoken success and prosperity."[18] Countless paintings commemorate meticulously prepared formal dinners, whose menus and settings were planned down to the last detail. Some hosts went so far as to rehearse formal dinners in private before submitting what they had wrought to the scrutiny of guests.

A place for social occasions, the dining room was also the place where family members gathered daily. Over the course of the nineteenth century, however, the dining room apparently lost some of its intimate character, a character that had caught the eye of at least one author: "When dinner was over and the tablecloth had been removed and the oil lamp had been set up, the wife took up her embroidery, the husband took up his book or newspaper, the children gathered their toys, and everyone talked freely."[19] The lady of the house, Cardon tells us, spent most of her time in the dining room because the lighting there was better than anywhere else in the house. He was probably thinking of the old *hôtels* of the faubourg Saint-Germain and the Marais that had been converted into apartments. In most buildings constructed between 1860 and 1880, especially in Paris, the dining room received light only from cramped and dark inner courtyards. It therefore ceased to be used except for meals, because the *petit salon* generally proved to be a much cozier place for reading and needlework.

Of course not all bourgeois enjoyed a *petit salon,* but most were willing to sacrifice a great deal for a *grand salon.* A posh

In upper-class apartment buildings the staircase was intended to create an immediate impression. It was not simply a functional space but a focus of display. That accounts for the elaborate banister, the lamps, and the statues of various materials. Daly, *L'Architecture privée au XIXe siècle.* (Paris, Bibliothèque Nationale.)

apartment was simply inconceivable without this theatrical space, scene of the ritual that linked the new society to the old: the regularly scheduled reception, the "day" on which the lady of the house was "at home" to visitors. Nineteenth-century society painters such as Béraud and Tissot tirelessly magnified these occasions.

Among the pettiest of petty bourgeois, those whose circle was limited essentially to members of the family, the salon, its furniture shrouded with protective covers, went virtually unused. Eventually some interior decorators went so far as to declare the room useless. But they seriously underestimated its symbolic importance: it signified membership in a class. The salon symbolized urbanity and sociability, two characteristics of the bourgeoisie.

In the nineteenth century a heavy veil was thrown over the least manifestation of sexuality. As a result, the master bedroom became a sacred place, a temple consecrated not to voluptuousness but to procreation. Once it had been permissible to receive guests in a room with a bed in it, but that time was past. A taboo was placed on the bedroom, as if it were a sacred place and to enter it without reason entailed some terrible risk.

Léger, proposed bedroom decor, 1844. The canopied bed continued its long career, while the new armoire with mirror, a combination of the cheval glass and the old two-door armoire, caught on quickly. (Paris, Musée des Arts Décoratifs.)

In architectural treatises of the nineteenth century and earlier, no mention is ever made of an area of the home reserved specifically for children. Examination of dollhouses from the period points to the same conclusion. In bourgeois families infants were sent out to wet nurses, and children were placed in boarding schools as early as the first grade.[20]

As the century progressed, bourgeois apartments became more and more like antique shops. Accumulation seems to have been the only guiding principle of interior design. The most diverse eras and civilizations coexisted side by side; a Renaissance dining room might stand next to a Louis XVI bedroom, while a Moorish billiard parlor might open onto a veranda decorated in Japanese style. Fabrics, hangings, silk, and carpets covered every bit of free surface. It was the age of the *tapissier,* and even the legs of the piano were concealed by fabric. It was also the heyday of trimming. The day of the tassel had arrived, and it would take French decorators many years to escape its spell.

Adeline Daumard has proposed an explanation for these remarkable changes in taste.[21] Throughout the nineteenth century the bourgeoisie (especially in Paris, which set the tone for the entire country) lived in terror of riot. Home sweet home was designed to assuage these fears: "Space was symbolically divided; inside meant family and security, outside meant strangers and danger." People became obsessed with the desire that no wall or floor be left bare; bare floors became a mark of poverty. The leading bourgeois magazine, *L'Illustration,* described the new conception of space in its February 15, 1851, issue: "We gathered in the small salon, which was tightly sealed by excellent door curtains, silk pads, and double drapes . . . A good carpet lies underfoot . . . A profusion of fabrics graces the windows, covers the mantelpiece, and hides the woodwork. Dry wood and cold marble are concealed beneath velvet and plush."

In 1885 Maupassant in *Bel-Ami* described the journalist Forestier's apartment in exactly the same terms: "The walls were covered with an old fabric of faded violet studded with small flowers no bigger than a fly. The doors were curtained by a bluish gray fabric, a sort of military twill dotted with bits of red silk. And haphazardly scattered throughout the apartment were chairs of every size and variety, from chaise longues to enormous armchairs to poufs and ottomans, all

Crowded and Cozy

The first half of the 19th century was the golden age of wallpaper, and in this domain, too, pastiche triumphed. To set off neo-Gothic furniture, wallpaper reflected the architectural motifs of Gothic cathedrals dressed up with fanciful curlicues that are striking to behold. (Paris, Musée des Arts Décoratifs.)

covered with Louis XVI silk or with fine Utrecht velvet sporting a garnet design on a cream background."

Foul Odors

The apartment was more than just a place for entertaining guests and enjoying family life. Food had to be cooked, and people had to answer the call of nature. Both of these necessary functions were areas where one might expect a high degree of rationalization, but that expectation is contradicted by the facts. The vital functions involved a direct relation to the body, and when it came to contact with what was considered, "dirty," the new ruling class had raised its standards considerably.[22] Nineteenth-century architects, at once representative of and shaped by the class from which they sprang, turned their backs on the kitchen.[23] That indispensable room was relegated to the depths of the apartment, to that rear portion filled with acrid fumes and odors, where the heat of the oven was bad for the complexion and where decent people most assuredly did not set foot. Not until the end of the nineteenth century did hygienists influenced by Pasteur assail the kitchen as a breeding ground for flies, a dustbin where it was all too easy for Koch's bacillus to thrive.

People similarly took little interest in the *cabinet de toilette* with its complement of porcelain pitchers and bowls. In Paris running water was not available to upper stories until 1865 on the Right Bank and ten years later on the Left Bank. As for the bathroom, if there was one, it hardly mattered if it was relegated to a place far from the bedrooms, since people did not bathe every day. The value of water was not appreciated until after the discoveries of Pasteur, which transformed the washing of hands into a social obligation.

Bourgeois disdain for physical necessities was nowhere more apparent than in the toilet. Hygienic toilets with water flush existed in the eighteenth century, as Mariette's celebrated catalogue attests.[24] These devices failed to catch on throughout the first half of the following century, however. People continued to believe in the value of human waste as fertilizer, and nightsoil men continued to haul their daily loads from Paris to Montfaucon. Gaseous emanations from these cargoes infected the air of the capital. Although people in France were aware of British legislation, in effect since 1855, requiring all waste to be evacuated through sewers, they regarded this practice as a terrible waste; it not only consumed vast quantities of water but also deprived farmers of a valuable resource.

Atget, *Kitchen in a Merchant's House.* If ever a room deserved the appellation catch-all, it was this kitchen. It took time for bourgeois rationality to reorganize the kitchen, which the masters of the premises never set foot in. (Paris, Bibliothèque Nationale.)

This château or hôtel kitchen was fully equipped, including even a water tank, in the days before cast-iron coal stoves were available. (Paris, Bibliothèque des Arts Décoratifs.)

The stenciled floral decoration reflects the influence of Art Nouveau, but no such assemblage of bathroom fixtures could be found in any early-20th-century bathroom. This was an advertisement for the line of products manufactured by Jacob Delafon. Note the bidet, an accessory still a long way from being considered essential. (Paris, Bibliothèque des Arts Décoratifs.)

In Lille waste removal was
long monopolized by a group
of men who crisscrossed the
city in wagons with barrels that
they filled with waste
purchased from housewives
and servants and then resold to
farmers for fertilizer. This
medieval practice endured until
1889. (*Le Lillois*, July 7, 1889;
Lille, Archives départementales
du Nord.)

In Paris the imperial decree of 1809 requiring the use of
cesspits was widely respected, but medieval practices persisted
in the provinces. In Lyons sewage discharge into the Rhone
surprised no one. In Marseilles, 14,000 of 32,653 buildings
noted in the 1886 census had no system for human waste
disposal. Waste was simply accumulated in a potty on each
floor and then disposed of in the gutter. In Bordeaux 12,000
poorly constructed cesspits poisoned the ground water.

Meanwhile, Britain experienced a tremendous vogue for
flush toilets. The golden age of indoor plumbing had begun,
and all Europe studied English methods. Stevens Hellyer's
important book was translated by Poupard, a Parisian con-
tractor who sent his son to study with the master.[25] The
question was definitively resolved for French architectural
theorists, as is clear from the declaration made in 1882 to the
Society of Public Medicine by Emile Trélat, founder of the
Ecole Spéciale d'Architecture: "City dwellers must be carefully
protected from their excretions from the moment they are
produced. The waste outlet, normally kept sealed, should be
opened briefly, and waste should be forcefully expelled from
the residence by a powerful stream of water."

This sudden change of attitude—the abandonment of human waste as fertilizer—was one result of progress in agron-
omy. Peruvian guano (widely used from 1850 to 1880),
nitrates from Chile, and last but not least the whole panoply
of chemical fertilizers developed in the late nineteenth century
ultimately won farmers over. Meanwhile, Pasteur's discoveries had raised fears of microbes: "His experiments have led
people to reject the cesspit as a vast, airless reservoir of the
most dreadful viruses known to man." Adolphe Wazon, the
engineer who wrote these words, flatly condemned the cesspit
and praised the use of sewers for the evacuation of waste, a
new technology made possible in Paris by the extraordinary
system of sewer mains constructed by Eugéne Belgrand during the Second Empire.[26] From just 87 miles of sewer in 1852,
the system expanded to 350 miles in 1869.

The transition to the new system was not made without
recriminations. The law of 1894 concerning hygienic improvements in Paris and the Seine département met with strong
hostility from landlords, for once united in opposition to this
collectivist and tyrannical infringement of their rights.[27] Architects for a long time continued to locate toilets wherever
they pleased, even next to the kitchen, because to concern
oneself with "such things" was considered indecent.

The bourgeois apartment building contained one additional level: the attic, where the servants slept. Such segregation had not existed under the ancien régime; before the Revolution the servants of the house had been part of the family. With the establishment of a new, hierarchically structured society in the early nineteenth century, it was no longer considered appropriate for servants to sleep in the same part of the house as their masters, lest there be an opportunity for "promiscuity." At the bottom of the social ladder, servants were entitled to no more amenities than were needed to reconstitute their strength for long days of Sisyphean labor.

Domestics were therefore obliged to live in tiny cubbyholes on the sixth and seventh floors of elegant apartment buildings. Arranged along a corridor on the top floor of one such building, on the boulevard Saint-Denis in Paris in 1828, were a number of maid's rooms illuminated by skylights. Each room, or rather, cell, contained roughly 40 square feet of space; there was no heat, the furniture was all hand-me-down; and the only facilities were a single spigot and a Turkish toilet on the landing.

There was no shortage of eminent authorities prepared to denounce these scandalous conditions. In *L'Ouvrière* Jules Simon compared Parisian servants' quarters with the Piombi in Venice. Professor Brouardel of the Académie de Médecine raised the specter of tuberculosis descending from the seventh floor and infiltrating even the best-guarded nurseries. Paul Juillerat, the man responsible for establishing records of health conditions in Paris housing, published a brochure detailing the conditions that a maid's room had to meet in order to be considered healthy. At the Tuberculosis Exposition of 1906 two images were displayed side by side: one was a faithful reproduction of a servant's room in a building in the Champs-Elysées quarter of the 8th arrondissement, which ever since the time of Louis-Philippe had been the wealthiest, most fashionable part of the city, the other of a prison cell at Fresnes. The cell was habitable and healthy; the servant's room was not.[28] The situation did not change much until after the Second World War. Servants' masters climbed every mountain in the world, but they never climbed the stairs to the top floor of their own building.

Thus, the bourgeois apartment, hemmed in between ever more congested streets and foul courtyards redolent with kitchen and bathroom odors, was—despite its more than 3,000

Garret-Dwellers

This fine example of a pedestal toilet, installed in a good-sized tiled bathroom, was a rare sight even in luxury apartment buildings until after 1900. It was not until the mid–1880s that the health authorities and the pontiffs of architecture became convinced of the virtues of the flush toilet, an invention brought to a peak of perfection by the English. Hellyer, *Traité de la salubrité des maisons,* 1889. (Paris, Bibliothèque Nationale.)

square feet of living space (newer apartments were smaller)—
nothing more than a deceptively rational facade, a trompe-
l'oeil designed to fool society. It would be the task of the
international movement in modern architecture in the 1920s
and 1930s (a movement anticipated by Francis Jourdain's courageous manifestos of 1910) to destroy this image of a class
that never managed to find a valid architectural form in which
to express itself.

THE CHÂTEAU CALENDAR

Under the ancien régime social ascension culminated in
the acquisition of an *hôtel particulier*. Many nobles lived in
apartments, but France's leading families commissioned the
most renowned architects to design their private residences,
and commoners who came into money hastened to follow
their lead. From the Middle Ages onward an architectural
patrimony was thus constituted, with construction in each
century representative of a style that reflected the contemporary needs and aspirations of the dominant class.

Things changed in the nineteenth century. Because many
property-owners had only recently come into money, they
often were not steeped in an artistic tradition. They did, however, feel a keen desire to display their wealth. Hence they
succumbed to extravagance of every variety yet were unable
to impose conceptions of their own on architects who were
themselves victims of the fashions that the Ecole des Beaux-
Arts of Paris imposed on its students, the vast majority of
whom stemmed from the class in power.[29]

Certain nobles who had emigrated during the Revolution
returned to reclaim their hôtels, while the bourgeoisie hastened
to commission hôtels of its own. A new type of hôtel began
to appear as early as the Restoration. The residential portion
of the building was situated at the rear of the courtyard, while
another section, bordering the street, housed offices and shops.
Allowing for commercial space proved to be a wise investment. In the Nouvelle-Athènes quarter in the northern part
of Paris the architect Constantin—who did a great deal of
work with Dosne, the exchange agent and future father-in-
law of Adolphe Thiers—built neoantique cubes surrounded
by stately gardens. For the comte de Pourtalès, Félix Duban
built a pastiche of an Italian Renaissance villa, which one
entered from the street that runs behind the Church of the
Madeleine.

André-Henri Dargelas, *The Happy Family.* (Wolverhampton Art Library.)

Anonymous, *Country House in Parkland,* England, early 19th century. This sumptuous country house permitted the landlord to oversee his farm while enjoying the pleasures of domesticated nature.

William Powell Frith, *Many Happy Returns of the Day*. The family celebrates Alice's birthday. Note the rich interior, the attentive mothers, the well-behaved children, and the withdrawn gentlemen. The newspaper offered a window on the world. The dividing line between public and private passed through the house. (Harrogate Art Gallery.)

Anonymous, *Woman Seated before a Bust of Her Husband, Year IV.* Alone in her house, this young woman hesitantly begins a letter to her husband, whose statue draws attention to the difference in their ages. The absent husband is at once powerful and vulnerable. His power is reinforced by the public requirement of fidelity, but it is also weakened by the heart's need for sustenance through daily contact and conversation. (Vizille, Museum of the French Revolution.)

Dominique Doncre, *Portrait of Pierre-Louis-Joseph Lecoq and His Family*, 1791. The Revolution had a friendly face for a provincial lawyer in 1791. This compatriot of Robespierre, a judge in the district court of Arras, managed to combine a comfortable and elegant family life with his prestigious new post. (Vizille, Museum of the French Revolution.)

Mihaly Munkacsy, *Paris Interior,* 1877. Countless minor masters spread the taste for interior painting throughout Europe. (Budapest, Magyar Nemzeti Gallery.)

Lorenzo Valles, *Artist's Studio*. The artist's studio, or the painting within a painting, was a favorite subject of an age eager to lay hold of images of itself. Here, another way of representing women. (Rennes, Musée des Beaux-Arts.)

Jules Voirin, *An Auction Sale,* 1880. The passion for objects and collecting endured throughout the history of the Third Republic. The work of art became a commodity. (Nancy, Musée Historique Lorrain.)

Voloskov A. Jacovlevic, *The Tea,* 1851. The family tea was a ritual that brought bourgeois families together from London to Saint Petersburg. (Leningrad, State Russian Museum.)

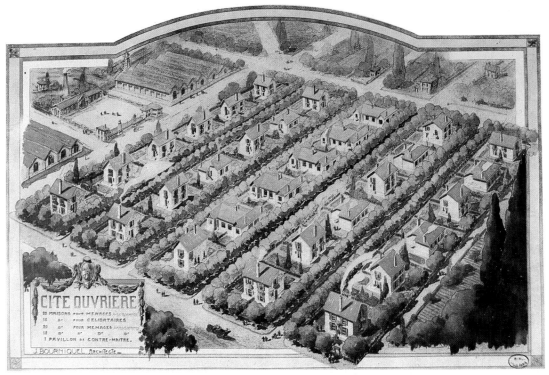

J. Bourniquel, *Pour construire sa maison*, 1919. There is no hierarchical distinction of space in this development, in which the architect has aligned houses along rectilinear streets. By 1920 the ideal of the detached single-family home was no longer challenged except by representatives of the modern movement such as Le Corbusier. (Paris, Bibliothèque Historique de la Ville de Paris.)

Opposite: L. Isabey, *Villas, maisons de ville et de campagne composées sur les motifs des habitations de Paris moderne*, 1864. The pseudo-Gothic style infested 19th-century French architecture. It gave rise to bastard creations with pent roofs and huge gables supported by braces, ridge spikes, and, here, an indescribable belvedere. (Paris, Bibliothèque Historique de la Ville de Paris.)

Pl 40

PLAN DU REZ DE CHAUSSÉE

PLAN DU 1er ÉTAGE

Henri Gervex, *Marriage of Mathurin Moreau,* 1881. Monsieur Moreau officiates at his son's wedding. In the audience, the future Nicholas II is seated, the prince of Wales is standing, and behind him is Emile Zola. The scene is the *mairie* of Paris's 19th arrondissement.

Opposite: Raffaelo Sorbi, *Promenade on the Road to Fiesole,* 1878. Walking was not simply a pleasure recommended by doctors who believed in natural medicine; it was also a codified ritual, with strict social boundaries that everyone was expected to observe. Encounters were possible and introductions were sometimes made, but ostentatious expressions of disdain were just as likely. Anyone could go to the mall to verify his or her position in society. (Paris, Private collection.)

Félix Vallotton, *Woman Arranging Her Hair,* 1900. (Dijon, Musée des Beaux-Arts.)

Opposite: *Lovers' Secrets,* circa 1820. The code of romantic love was developed during the Restoration. An insistence on authenticity, the vogue of the natural, the prudish simplicity of female attire, virile energy tempered by the defeat of the Empire, and the success of poets all laid the groundwork for the accord of souls and encouraged the chaste effusions of lovers. (Paris, Bibliothèque des Arts Décoratifs.)

Ignaz Schockl, *Plan for a Library*. In a century that exploited knowledge, having a room that was used exclusively as a library had important social meaning. Architects who designed such libraries rarely showed concern for functional requirements. Kitsch ran riot as libraries were constructed in a whole range of "neo" styles. (West Berlin, University Library.)

All sorts of follies were committed. During the reign of Louis XVIII a house, located in Moret, which dated from the time of François I, was dismantled and rebuilt brick by brick alongside the Cours-la-Reine. Not far from there, on avenue Montaigne, Prince Napoleon, the emperor's cousin, became infatuated with the idea of reconstructing a Pompeiian villa, a task undertaken by Alfred Normand. A connoisseur of antiquity, Normand was obliged to strike a compromise between the archaeological facts, which he knew perfectly well, and the requirements of modern comfort and the Parisian climate.

Luxurious new residences sprang up in Paris's *beaux quartiers,* residences in which the new gentlefolk—with whom, when necessary to restore luster to a tarnished escutcheon, the old gentlefolk did not disdain to marry—could entertain in lavish style. One such sumptuous new hôtel was built for Emile Gaillard, the comte de Chambord's banker, in the place Malesherbes; it was a masterpiece of brick and stone in the Louis XII style. Another was the neobaroque hôtel built for Menier, the *chocolatier,* opposite the parc Monceau. The Pereire brothers had gained control of 10 of the 19 hectares confiscated in 1848 from what had been called the parc des Orléans and had turned it into a deluxe property. Still another was the Rose Palace built by Boni de Castellane, scion of one of France's oldest families, who had married a billionaire American heiress. The architect, acceding to his client's wishes, had based his plans on the Grand Trianon and imitated the *escalier d'honneur* of the Palace of Versailles.

The provinces did not lag behind the capital. Hôtels in Lille were larger than in Paris.[30] Some had facades as long as 80 feet and as high as 50 feet and offered as much as 3,200 square feet of space distributed over four floors: a basement with kitchens and conveniences; an entresol with two salons, a dining room, and a study; a floor above with bedrooms; and an attic. Outbuildings contained a billiard parlor, a library, stables, and servants' quarters. Lille manufacturers saw themselves as lords of Flanders and made no secret of their ambitions. Just before the war the Dévallée brothers of Lille, sons of an industrialist from Roubaix, decided to act as their own architects when the professionals refused to honor their demands. Although their creation, complete with marble columns, affected a Renaissance air, it was distinguished by the presence of enormous gargoyles. Each room was done in a different style, including the inevitable Moorish. Like a prince

Prince Jérôme Napoléon was not concerned with appearing "modern." He wanted to provide his mistress, the actress Rachel, with a setting worthy of ancient tragedy and came up with this Pompeii-style house on the avenue Montaigne, designed by Normand. Note the tetrastyle Ionic peristyle in front of the house, whose atrium served as backdrop for rooms inspired by antiquity. (Godefroy, Paris, Bibliothèque Historique.)

Vandenbergh, *Watercolor,* 1890–1891. Detached winter gardens were often found in Paris and the provinces. (Lille, Archives départementales du Nord.)

under the influence of a court astrologer, one of the brothers insisted that his sleeping position be determined by the phases of the moon. He therefore had his bed mounted on a shaft turned by Swiss clockwork.

The prize for the most exotic incongruity—in Roubaix of all places—goes to the industrialist Vaissier, the inventor of "Congo soap." In 1890 he asked Paul Achille Dupire to design a château that was to have rested on the backs of four elephants. The architect refused and instead designed an oriental palace capped by a glass dome: "It is the dream of the rajah of India. It is caprice, fantasy, a riot of color and a luminosity of decor achieved right here in our own foggy Flanders."

It was hard to go farther than this in "architectural Wagnerism." Other industrialists from the same province, concerned to keep faith with the historical tradition, preferred neo-Gothic hôtels in the Flemish style, distinguished by a variety of facades equipped with the cusped gables characteristic of northern architecture. The same phenomenon occurred in Brittany, in Rennes, for example, where buildings of eclectic style included regional allusions.[31]

A new type of *grande bourgeoise* residence made its appearance at the end of the century. Because of its deliberately picturesque style, borrowed from an architecture that was

The neo-Gothic fashion lasted until the end of the 19th century. This urban castle with gables and pinnacles is a typical example of the manner pioneered by Viollet-le-Duc. (Paris, Bibliothèque Nationale.)

gaining popularity in coastal resorts, one might call this type of building a hôtel-villa. Far from downtown centers, in areas where it was still possible to purchase large vacant lots, this new type of structure was generally erected in the midst of an English-style garden. It is a much more difficult type of building to describe accurately than was the classical hôtel, for here the most important element was ornamental excess, made possible by the use of polychrome brick and turned wood. Examples can be found in Rouen as well as Lille.[32] These houses are all protuberances, set-backs, bulging bay windows, fancy roofs, protruding beams, and wooden balconies. Such wild departures from the rules of neoclassicism sometimes reveal traces of Art Nouveau in the treatment of a curve or the mixing of different kinds of materials, including metal. This type of construction, with its asymmetrical masses in which doors and windows were placed seemingly at random, can also be found in more modest individual homes, which were later built in large numbers on the outskirts of major cities.

From Billiard Parlor to Greenhouse

As hôtels in the nineteenth century were subjected to the same rationalizing improvements as apartment houses, public and private areas were clearly differentiated. Other amenities, designed to facilitate regular entertaining, attest to a level of

No 19th-century château or bourgeois residence was without a billiard parlor. Architects, having no tradition to refer to, indulged in audacities of every variety. In the "Renaissance" space depicted here, pointless protuberances hang down from the ceiling, while the Dutch-style window, modified to provide as much light as possible, overlooks a pretentious billiard table decorated in the style of the room. Daly, *L'Architecture privée au XIXe siècle*. (Paris, Bibliothèque Nationale.)

C. Giraud, *Veranda of Princess Mathilde, rue de Courcelles.* Princess Mathilde received writers and artists in the hôtel given to her in 1857 by her cousin Napoleon III. Illuminated from above through a glass roof, the winter garden was filled with plants and bushes. (Paris, Musée des Arts Décoratifs.)

luxury made possible by substantial wealth. One of the first of these additions was the billiard parlor. Billiards had been played in Europe since the late Middle Ages, but the number of devotees of the ivory ball increased greatly in the nineteenth century. Daumier produced several lithographs on the theme, including one entitled "A Rainy Day," with the caption: "The guest is sentenced to six hours of compulsory billiards." There was not a single hôtel or château of any size that did not boast this indispensable accoutrement, at which, just as in the time of Louis XIV, famous men excelled.[33]

The real mark of a home of distinction was the greenhouse or winter garden. Zola made sure that the hôtel of the speculator Saccard was equipped with one, attached to the side of the house off the salon—the classic arrangement.[34] Greenhouses began to appear in the first half of the nineteenth century and proliferated rapidly during the Second Empire.[35] The most widely imitated model was the winter garden of Princess Mathilde, granddaughter of Napoleon I, which was the subject of numerous paintings. The garden was located in a vast greenhouse designed to admit light from overhead; under the roof, which rested on Ionic columns, grew ivy, palms, and decorative plants that brought nature right into the heart of Paris.

Louise Abbéma's *Déjeuner dans la serre* (Lunch in the Greenhouse) depicts a less spectacular example. The decor is rather kitsch, with its Louis XIII table with turned legs, African weapons, Moorish platter, and ottomans, all draped with various hangings and exotic plants—an ideal backdrop for the actress Sarah Bernhardt, who was a friend of the artist. In the era of Proust's salons the winter garden added a note of distinction to a home. Only the wealthy could afford to sit beneath palms chatting while snow fell outside. Unlike the verandas of cafés and restaurants, which faced the street, these indoor gardens faced inward, opening onto a private courtyard or garden. Some bourgeois apartments offered pale imitations in the form of a sort of loggia with stained-glass windows attached to the salon and sometimes extending out over the sidewalk.

Neo-Gothic Châteaux

While the grand bourgeois preferred to live in the city, where all serious business was transacted, nobles attempted to reconquer the countryside, which they had abandoned well before the Revolution. They had begun returning to the land prior to the accession of Louis-Philippe, who definitively excluded them from political power. In the country these nobles set themselves the impossible goal of restoring the symbols of feudalism. Gothic architecture therefore became fashionable in legitimist circles, while the bourgeoisie preferred the art of the Renaissance, which, being an era shaped in large part by remarkable individuals, accorded well with the bourgeois's individualist philosophy.

For a long time Viollet-le-Duc was given sole credit for the Gothic revival, which resulted in the construction of hundreds of châteaux throughout France, especially during and after the Second Empire. But a show organized by the Caisse Nationale des Monuments Historiques turned up at least one provincial builder who owed nothing to the man responsible for the restoration of Pierrefonds; further research will certainly lead to the discovery of others.[36] René Hodé, an architect from Anjou, built fourteen châteaux in that region and enlarged and decorated ten *gentilhommières,* aristocratic country homes. He did a great deal of work for legitimist clients, including the comte de Falloux, the comte de La Rochefoucauld, and the comte de Quatrebarbes, clients who spurned the frivolous art of the philosophical eighteenth century. As landowners these men did much to improve their estates, often with scientific knowledge, in the hope of winning the people of the countryside over to the royalist cause—a hope that was crowned with some success.[37]

For these noble clients Hodé designed dream castles, châteaux with symmetrical facades that incorporated all the distinguishing marks of seigneurial residences from the age of chivalry: towers, crenellations, steep slate roofs, windows with mullions, and dormers with peaked canopies. The interiors had to be renovated to suit contemporary taste of course, and different functions were assigned to different places. The kitchens were located in the basement. The ground floor became the principal focus of the house. Around a vestibule connected to the staircase stood the main hall, the dining room, the salon, and the billiard room. A long corridor on

René Hodé, drawing of château de la Baronnière. Viollet-le-Duc's ideal château found a faithful interpreter in the Angevin architect Hodé, who devoted his talent to serving the local aristocracy, which during the Restoration easily regained its pre–1789 social and political preeminence. (Angers, Musée des Beaux-Arts.)

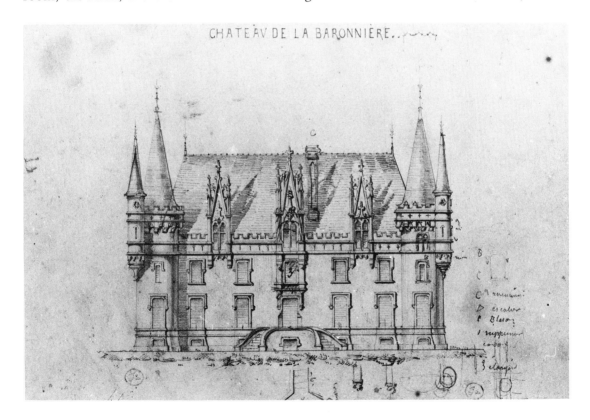

CHATEAU DE LA BARONNIÈRE.

the second floor led to the master bedrooms. On the third
floor another corridor led to guest rooms and to the quarters
of the ranking servants—the children's governess and the master's secretary. A concealed service staircase connected this
level to the second-floor landing. Nineteenth-century châteaux
differed from those of the ancien régime in that they were
isolated: outbuildings and sharecroppers' cottages were hidden
away at a respectful distance. Hodé renovated country houses
in the same spirit. Pulling down the adjoining farmhouse
enabled him to add towers, and eliminating inner walls allowed him to expand the salon and dining room.

Somewhat later, a visitor to the nearby province of the
Vendée, which was even more devoted to the royalist cause
than Anjou, would have found it easy to believe that the comte
de Chambord, the would-be Henri V, had actually been restored to the throne. Two hundred châteaux have been identified as having been built in the Vendée in the nineteenth
century.[38] The Gothic predominated, but here and there the
Renaissance style also left its mark. In the last decade of the
century châteaux were also built in the "Norman" genre,
misleadingly so called because of the abundant use of half-
timbered construction, both genuine and fake. Like provincials
elsewhere, Vendeans felt no need to rely on Paris architects.
For nearly fifty years, Joseph Libaudière, originally from
Nantes and once a student of Pascal, Charles Garnier's assistant
in the construction of the Paris Opera, served in the post of
official architect of the Vendée. Between 1880 and 1906 he
built fourteen neo-Gothic churches and numerous châteaux.
At Bondues, near Lille in northern France, Louis Cordonnier
succumbed to the influence of Neuschwanstein in building a
châteaux for the comte d'Hespel: the edifice he created sported
a dozen pediments with sparrow's-foot decoration, fantastic
chimneys sprouting from steep sloping roofs, a crenellated
tower, and brick walls with white stone coping.

Viollet-le-Duc's conception of the Gothic, diametrically
opposed to this sentimental, Christian, monarchist tendency,
was put forward as the solution to a functional problem. A
staunch foe of the craze for the antique, he envisioned the
Middle Ages not as the age of chivalry but as the age of the
communes that created the first democratic institutions. In
addition to the restoration of Pierrefonds, which was begun
in 1858 and had still not been completed at the end of the
Second Empire, Viollet-le-Duc built five châteaux, all neo-
Gothic, in various parts of France.[39] The most polished of the

lot is certainly the one at Roquetaillade in the Gironde, which was restored and renovated in accordance with the wishes of owners who spared no expense in order to live out their medieval dream.[40] For their money they received an ample share of trefoil and quadrifoil bays, monumental fireplaces, and high-medieval furnishings, all set in a most stylish decor.

The Rothschilds' Glass Palace

The taste for the neo-Gothic produced some dreadful sights, as eighteenth-century structures sprouted towers and dormers. But a few billionaires, whose cultural background included none of these feudal trappings, remained immune to the Gothic disease. In 1829 James de Rothschild bought the château de Ferrières from Fouché's heirs. After the small château, situated next to a lake, had been demolished, the banker asked Joseph Paxton, architect of the Crystal Palace (built for the 1851 London World's Fair), to draw up plans. The cornerstone of the new structure was laid in 1855, and work was completed three years later. The building was square, with four identical towers at the corners and a vast central room with a glass roof, yielding a structure similar to that with which Paxton had first distinguished himself. The glass-roofed central room was surrounded, on the first floor, by ballrooms, salons, a dining room, a billiard parlor, and game rooms; the bedrooms were on the second floor.[41]

Although the architecture of Ferrières owed nothing to the models taught by the Ecole des Beaux-Arts, its interior decor succumbed to the prevailing eclecticism. The central room resembled an antique shop. One salon was done in white in a Louis XVI style; another in leather in a vague Renaissance manner. Comfort was an important concern in the construction of the guest rooms, which were in fact suites complete with foyer, bathroom, and toilet. The kitchens, located underground more than a hundred yards from the château, were connected to the dining room by an underground passage equipped with a small train.

The Rothschilds went to Ferrières in early October and returned to Paris in January. In the country their principal occupation was hunting in the grand French tradition. Hunting also occupied the Harcourts, who every July left their hôtel in the place des Invalides in July for the château de Sainte-Eustoge in the Gâtinais.[42] For them the journey to the country was a major expedition, which involved the transport of, among other things, silver, porcelain, glassware, children's toys, textbooks, and a grand piano. The château, to which rooms had been added, was similar in structure to many others, with a salon, dining room, billiard parlor, and library on the first floor, ten bedrooms for the owners and their guests on the second floor, children's rooms on the third floor, and servants in the attic. The rooms were occupied until Christmas, and the colors of many well-known hunters could be seen on the premises.

The Epiphany of the "Norman Chalet"

In the middle of the nineteenth century both old families and "parvenus" began to congregate in resort towns that were then springing up all along France's coasts.[43] Some of these resorts were the work of experienced promoters; Arcachon, for instance, was built by the Pereire brothers.[44] They were not responsible for the architecture, however, and the initial vogue for colonial villas with verandas did not last long. Contractors were obliged to add a personal touch to every house, resulting in a hodgepodge of neo-Gothic, Moorish, and Swiss styles concealed beneath a garnish of ornamental woodwork.

The Swiss chalet, which had spread beyond the borders of the Helvetic cantons in the eighteenth century and had become fashionable in mountain resorts everywhere, suddenly began to be seen in English-style parks all over the continent, at first in the form of the small country retreat but later as a full-blown country home. The chalet proved particularly attractive to architects designing seaside homes. It became popular with lovers at Deauville, where, just as at Arcachon, every style under the sun could be found.[45] The villa of the princesse de Sagan resembled a Persian palace, while that of the marquise de Montebello mimicked a Louis XIII château. Toward the end of the century a vogue for the picturesque encouraged the use of half-timbered construction, which yielded the so-called Norman chalet. Cornelius Vanderbilt, the American billionaire, had a "cottage" built for himself in this style, and derivatives of this style continue to ravage the French landscape to this day.

WITH THE COTTAGERS

Agricultural questions were much in vogue during the Restoration and July Monarchy, as evidenced by countless articles in the press[46] as well as by the success of novels by

This large villa on the Basque coast shows no trace of the revival of the local style that would soon be all the rage in the area. With its bulging volumes and asymmetrical facade, dominated by an unexpected window, this home reflects some of the audacity of Art Nouveau. (Paris, Bibliothèque Nationale.)

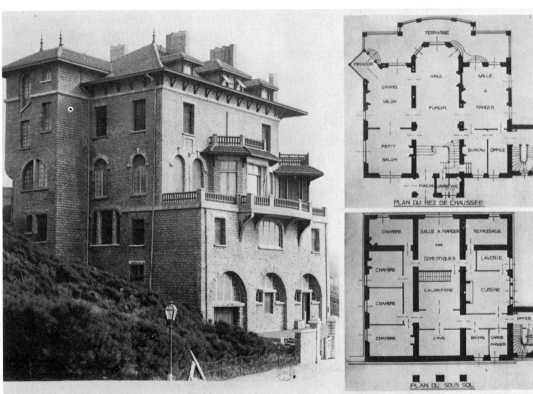

VILLA de M. Orossen, à Biarritz, (Basses-Pyrénées)
M. CAZALIS, architecte, à Biarritz.
Façade de l'entrée et façade de la terrasse.

Balzac and George Sand.[47] Those novels, rife with bias, were surely misleading to their readers. To Balzac the peasant was an indefatigable "rodent" who had been nibbling away at the great estates since the Revolution, an inferior, amoral being who would nevertheless outlive the bourgeoisie. Caught up in the myth of the savage, the author of *Médecin de campagne* saw French peasants much as James Fenimore Cooper had seen the Indians or as Madame Hanska had received the hypocritical homage of her muzhiks, that is, from a great distance. George Sand, for her part, cast her heroes in fine porcelain. Her "refined tillers" and "young shepherds," invariably polite and well-dressed, lived in "cottages that epitomized the poetry of the hamlet." Their tables never lacked for excellent bread or chicken stew, always accompanied by a mouth-watering local wine.

It is therefore pointless to look to either of these authors for precise descriptions of actual living conditions in the countryside, for such descriptions would have seriously undermined the myth or the poetry. As early as the Revolution several architects wrote theoretical treatises on peasant housing that could have done much to improve rural dwellings. Among them was the mysterious François Cointeraux, who in 1790 opened a school of rural architecture, first located in Paris but later moved to Lyons. In numerous books and brochures he set forth his ideas about cobwork construction and noncombustible roofs.[48] In 1802 Lasteyrie du Saillant translated a book with a full appendix of plans that had been published by the agricultural office in London.[49] Several other volumes on rural architecture appeared subsequently,[50] and then during the Second Empire came Louis Bouchard-Huzard's monumental compendium.[51] The authors of these works were concerned primarily with large farms, on which residential quarters were now customarily located at some distance from outbuildings. The choice was made for reasons not of status and prestige but of convenience and hygiene.

Miserable Shanties

What about the small farms that predominated throughout much of France? Victor Considérant, an engineer and disciple of Charles Fourier, painted, in his usual vigorous style, a dark portrait of his rural travels: "Champagne and Picardy, Bresse and the Nivernais, Sologne, the Limousin, Brittany, and the like must be seen, and seen up close. You find rooms that serve as kitchen, dining room, and bedroom for the whole

The sloping roof attests to the age of this rural home with outside staircase, a simple solution to the problem of upper-story access that was found in many parts of France. (Sirot-Angel Collection.)

family: father, mother, and children. They also serve as cellar and attic, and sometimes as stable and barnyard as well. Light is admitted through low, narrow openings. Drafts enter by way of ill-fitting doors and windows. The wind whistles through blackened, broken panes—if there are panes, for there exist whole provinces in which glass is virtually unknown. Occasionally a smoky oil lamp is used for light, but usually the only light comes from the fire. The floor is of rough, damp earth, with puddles here and there. One steps in them, and young children wade in the mud. I myself have seen ducks scour these puddles for food."[52]

Considérant's outcry is confirmed by objective observations. The earliest to come to light dates from the beginning of the July Monarchy. It is contained in a départemental health council report and concerns a village near Troyes.[53] Its author states that every conceivable rule of hygiene is violated in this community of 402 inhabitants. The houses, thatched cottages with earthen walls and no floors or windows, contain single rooms inhabited by as many as ten people: "In this room people prepare their food, discard wet and sweaty clothing, dry and age cheeses, and store or hang salted meats."

A medical thesis from the same period describes dwellings in a village in the Tarn in almost identical terms: "The same hovel is used for preparing food, storing leftovers used for feeding the animals, and storing small farm implements. The sink is in one corner and the beds are in another. Clothes are hung on one side, salted meats on the other. Milk is made into cheese and dough into bread. Even pets share the same room, in which they eat their meals and satisfy their physical needs. The chimney, which is too short and too large in diameter, allows a cold wind to enter, forcing the smoke back into this wretched dwelling, which is home to the farmer and his family."[54]

Only once did Dr. Villermé leave the cities, his customary object of study, to examine the lives of peasants. He said nothing to contradict those who had preceded him: "It is essential to visit the poor Breton peasant in his dilapidated cottage, whose roof extends down almost to the ground and whose interior is blackened by constant smoke from dried heather and gorse. In this miserable hut, where the only light must enter through the door and is extinguished when the door is closed, the peasant and his family live, half-naked, with no furniture other than a crude table, a bench, a cauldron, and a few wooden or earthenware utensils. The bed is a box

of sorts, and the peasant sleeps without sheets on a bale of oats rather than a mattress stuffed with wool, while, if the family is lucky, in another corner of this depressing shanty a meager, sickly cow gives milk to nourish the farmer and his children."[55] Based on information gathered from the prefects, Villermé estimates that some 400,000 peasant dwellings in Brittany have three or fewer openings, counting both windows and doors. Cambry, the author of the celebrated *Voyage dans le Finistère,* had given a similar account of conditions in Brittany fifty years earlier. He described smoky hovels whose floors, never covered with tile or wood, were full of holes into which the children were always stumbling.[56]

At the end of the July Monarchy, Adolphe de Bourgoing, a country gentleman from the Nivernais, published a small book in which he expressed sentiments similar to Considérant's: "The peasant home is small, damp, and ill lighted. More often than not it has no windows. Light and air enter through a single door, which fits so badly that it allows the biting cold to enter in wintertime and in all seasons admits pestilential odors from the dung heap and from the filth rotting in the fetid water that stands in a pool in front of the house."[57]

These thatched cottages, set very close together, represent the rock bottom of peasant habitation. Such "picturesque" dwellings could still be found in many parts of France after the Second World War. (Famin. Paris, Bibliothèque Nationale.)

In the nearby region of Haute-Vienne the situation, as described by one observer to a meeting of the *conseil général*, was identical: "Not one-tenth of the dwellings in our villages meet satisfactory standards of hygiene, health, and above all morality . . . Most farmer's houses consist of a single story, with at most two rooms offering a total of less than 270 square feet of living space. The floor is of damp earth or, at best, ill-matched stones. Ceilings are no higher than 7 feet 9 inches. The hut has one door and one casement about a foot and a half high, but no glass. The kitchen contains a few crude items of furniture along with household and farm implements. The bedroom is used by all without distinction as to age or sex. In the attic it is common to find four, five, or six beds."[58]

Many similar descriptions exist, and there is no need to reproduce their desperate monotony here.[59] The proletarian of the fields, confined along with his animals in a single room, lived in unhealthy conditions for which "clean country air," of whose virtues the peasant was ignorant, did nothing to compensate. The conservative Adolphe Blanqui concurred with the views of the utopian Considérant in these lines, published in the *Journal des économistes:* "Unless you have seen it, as we have done, with your own eyes, you cannot believe the wretched state of the clothing, furnishing, and food of the inhabitants of our countrysides. There are entire cantons in which some items of clothing are still passed on from father to son, where the only kitchen utensils are a few miserable wooden spoons, and where the only furniture is a bench and a rickety table. Hundreds of thousands of men still have no notion of bed sheets. Hundreds of thousands have never worn shoes, and millions have never drunk anything but water and seldom or never eat meat or even white bread."[60]

For some, the cause of the peasant's misery was his individualism. On November 16, 1836, Emile de Girardin wrote in *La Presse* about one commune on the outskirts of Paris, where a total of 1,540 hectares had been "cut up into 38,826 shreds." How could anyone care about the fate of such savages?

Sources of Infection

Under the Second Empire the countryside remained much as it had been under the ancien régime. Four medical theses, concerned with four different regions, all mention cohabitation with animals, lack of ventilation, fireplaces that do not draw, and family members crowded together in a single

This one-room rural house combined kitchen, common room, and bedroom in one area. Note the curtained bed. The cast-iron stove is a sign of modernity. (Borgé Collection.)

room.[61] Such conditions, Dr. Louis Caradec noted, were ideal for the development of certain kinds of disease: "These low, damp, poorly lit, improperly oriented houses, in which humans and animals live crowded together, contribute greatly to the development of scrofula and tuberculosis and tend to ensure that all maladies end in virulent infection. Such conditions engender . . . abcesses, caries, and diseases of the joints. Flaws in the construction of housing and lack of cleanliness are more to blame than diet or heredity for the persistence of scrofula in the countryside."[62]

By the inception of the Third Republic worker and peasant were already being reduced to mythical figures, which were bandied about by the political parties for purposes of their own. Speaking for the left, the former communard Arthur Rank forbade writers to discuss the worker. Meanwhile, the peasant with his hoe became the property of the parties of the right, who jealously guarded the rural myth. When Zola published *La Terre* (The Land) in 1887, he was accused of slandering the French peasant. Without passing judgment, one may note that even with all the resources of the novelist's imagination, a week in the Beauce was hardly long enough for a city dweller to arrive at an accurate description of rural habitation. Such a description was not Zola's goal, and he was content with just two passages, whose wording is almost identical, to describe the farm on which the novel is set: "The square farmyard of La Borderie, closed in on three sides by stables, sheepfolds, and barns, was deserted." A few pages later he writes: "Three long buildings bordered the large square farmyard, the sheepfold at the far end, the barn on the right, and the cowpen, stable, and farmhouse on the left."

Research of a more scientific nature was almost totally nonexistent. Henri Baudrillart's enormous tome contains a few scattered notes.[63] Beyond that, there is only one comprehensive survey of rural habitation in late-nineteenth-century France: *Les Maisons types,* published in 1894 under the editorship of Alfred de Foville. It contains fifty-one monographs covering houses selected from different regions of France; nothing new is added to what was already known from studies published under Napoleon III. The book's general outlook, as well as the conclusions that its authors draw from certain facts which nearly everyone at the time deplored, situate it outside the "progressive" social movement. The book tended to exalt the past in much the same way as the novels of René Bazin did in the 1920s and 1930s. Consider monograph number 23, concerning the region of Valgaudemar: "Although the crowding of family members in cramped quarters may have been regrettable, it did not impair morality. I lived [in this type of house], and I never heard the slightest whisper of scandal. An active life, pious habits, and an austere father and mother were scarcely conducive to any relaxation of morals." And monograph number 46, concerning the Avranches region: "Morality did not suffer from the fact that all, or nearly all, the inhabitants slept in the same room. On the contrary, these conditions resulted in a kind of mutual surveillance. The dormitory is preferable to the cell. Only modesty suffered, but this embarrassment was not as severe as might be imagined by people who have always been accustomed to living in private rooms."

Twelve years earlier Dr. Layet had published an important book, gathering examples from all over France in support of a judgment condemning deficiencies in peasant housing that had been attacked ever since the beginning of the century: "We consider it a duty to show how little concern the peasant has for the salubriousness of his home, within which he is apparently pleased to accumulate any number of factors deleterious to his health. Constant dampness, inadequate replenishment of breathable air, crowding, foul emanations—all these are harmful influences that will have an effect on him, that will

counter if not negate the positive effects of a day spent outdoors in the sun and fresh air."[64]

In this environment dysentery, typhoid, typhus, and cholera were all endemic. In 1888 smallpox claimed 782 lives in
the Lorient district. In 1890 measles killed 232 children in the
same area. In papers submitted to the Académie de Médecine,
Dr. Le Chevallier even claimed that cases of leprosy could still
be found in Brittany.[65]

Medical topography was an active area in nineteenth-
century medicine, and countless essays in the subject repeated
the same findings concerning the unhealthy character of peasant housing. To be sure, there were also exemplary farmhouses, and the same ones—always the houses of masters,
never more than a small minority—were mentioned in work
after work. Not until after the Second World War did rural
Frenchmen decide to change their living conditions and to
subscribe to standards of public hygiene that had long since
been accepted in the cities. The change, when it did come,
came all the more rapidly because it was accomplished by the
people themselves, with guidance from their own farm
organizations.

URBAN DECAY

The conditions under which the suffering classes were
housed have been neglected for far too long by social historians
content to limit their judgments to the aesthetic realm. It is
astonishing to find Henri Sée, a man of the left, attacking
Arthur Young, an Englishman who visited France on the eve
of the Revolution, on the grounds that Young criticized public
hygiene in France's older cities but failed to appreciate such
"picturesque" qualities as winding, narrow streets.[66] More recently a Marville photograph taken during the Second Empire
was published, with a caption alluding to the "picturesque
intimacy of the old city."[67] In light of the historical work of
the last two decades this description seems rather odd.[68]

Throughout the nineteenth century social reformers from
all quarters, from the conservative parties to "antilandlord"
anarchists, denounced the deplorable condition of housing for
the poor. Paris has been studied most thoroughly, and it is
clear that protests began there early in the century. The critics
found workers' housing cramped and conditions generally
unhealthy. Following the cholera epidemic of 1832, which
claimed 18,602 victims in the capital, these charges were con-

This central Paris street, in the Halles district, is a survival of the Middle Ages that endured intact until 1936, even though it had been classified an "unhealthy neighborhood" before 1914. (Sirot-Angel Collection.)

firmed by an official investigation. The report concluded that, "wherever a miserable population lived crowded in filthy, cramped buildings, the epidemic claimed numerous victims."[69] In the narrowest, dirtiest streets, the mortality rate from cholera ran as high as 33.87 percent, compared with 19.25 percent in other areas.

Under the Second Empire, Haussmann concentrated his efforts on the chic sections of Paris, forcing proletarians to move to the outskirts.[70] His excavations created bold new boulevards, but elsewhere hovels proliferated. Louis Lazare reported the following observations in the *Revue municipale* for 1859: "Traveling through Paris as far as the fortifications, we noted 269 alleys, shantytowns, courtyards, passageways, and villas that had been constructed without municipal action or control of any kind. Most of these private properties, subject to the arbitrary government of their owners, are hideous to behold and turn the stomach." Zola, reflecting upon this "arbitrary government" in *L'Argent*, portrayed one landlord surveying his shantytown of "wretched huts made of earth,

The Zone, the black belt of fortifications rendered useless after the Franco-Prussian war, obsessed the imagination of "respectable" Parisians until it was demolished in the mid–1920s.

Atget, *Cité Trébert, Porte d'Asnières,* 1913. Shantytowns, common in Paris long after World War I, were frequently described by social commentators and well known to experts in environmental health. For too long the City of Light was, for many people, anything but. (Paris, Bibliothèque Nationale.)

Drawing by Steinlen for Aristide Bruant's *Dans la rue, chansons et monologues.* Cholera was the major epidemic of the 19th century, and few towns of any size were spared. (Paris, Bibliothèque Historique.)

old boards, and used zinc, like so many heaps of debris arrayed around an inner courtyard." The landlord surveys the scene from his own house, solidly built of stone and located next to the street.

In the last quarter of the century social analysis turned quantitative. Abundant statistics were produced in support of still indispensable qualitative judgments. The official report on the Jeanne-d'Arc, Doré, and Kroumirs housing developments has become a classic example of the kind of social reportage produced by countless physicians and philanthropists.[71]

In working-class areas such as the 11th, 13th, 19th, and 20th arrondissements, investigators discovered housing complexes linked by narrow passages and ruled by powerful landlords. Real-estate promoters rented land for a number of years, then built one-story structures of clapboard and plaster, which they divided into apartments and rented by the week. People also built without authorization on the strip of land next to the fortifications of Paris, which Thiers had designated as a buffer zone where no building was to be allowed; the pointlessness of this precaution was demonstrated by the siege of Paris in 1870. Undeterred by meaningless formalities, new colonizers added buildings to those already present. With a few stakes and some wire bold pioneers carved out plots in what came to be called "apache country." Landlords surreptitiously expanded their holdings and rented to the unsuspecting.[72]

It is not surprising that repeated epidemics claimed many victims in these unhealthy surroundings. Typhoid killed 869 people in Paris in 1873 and 3,352 in 1882. Cholera caused 986 deaths in 1884. Dr. Bucquoy, author of a report on cholera, found that the disease never struck well-built and properly maintained houses whose landlords provided tenants with a supply of fresh water: "We reviewed all the places where the epidemic proved severe, and we did not find a single one in which the elementary rules of hygiene were respected."[73] The last cholera epidemic of the century, in 1892, claimed 1,797 people in the Seine département, 906 of them in Paris alone. Most affected were the 11th arrondissement, with 104 deaths; the 18th, with 116 deaths; and the 19th, with 106 deaths.[74]

A Significant Investigation

The first comprehensive study of overcrowded housing in Paris was the work of Dr. Jacques Bertillon, brother of the inventor of anthropometry and head of the municipal bureau of statistics. In order to compile his figures Bertillon made use of a special questionnaire distributed during the 1891 census. The results from the suburbs proved unusable, however. Too few people returned the questionnaires, and many who did return them filled them out inaccurately, because they feared that the purpose of the investigation was to establish a new tax.

In Paris, however, only 2 percent of the questionnaires went unanswered, and those mainly concerned people who lived alone in relatively small buildings. Ultimately the survey covered 884,345 families. After deploring the fact that it was still impossible to describe living conditions in France with statistical precision, Dr. Bertillon defined what he meant by overcrowding: "We say that there is overcrowding or overpopulation when the number of individuals per household is more than double the number of rooms, for example, when a three-room apartment is occupied by seven people or a four-room apartment is occupied by nine people."[75]

In the capital, the larger the family, the poorer the housing. Only 35 percent of two-person families had more than one room per person; 27 percent of three-person families had at least that much space; 20 percent of four-person families;

18 percent of five-person families; and 13 percent of six-person families. Approximately 331,976 Parisians, 14 percent of the total population, lived in overcrowded conditions, according to Bertillon's definition. The lowest number of inhabitants per room was found in the 8th and 9th arrondissements, where the death rate was also lowest. In crowded areas such as the 13th, 19th, and 20th arrondissements, the death rate was higher.

Rents of the smallest apartments (those costing less than 500 francs per year) increased steadily throughout the nineteenth century. So did wages, which rose 48 percent between 1853 and 1891. But the suffering classes lived in constant insecurity. Wages decreased during periods of depression. When orders fell off, working hours were cut back and some workers were laid off, in what contemporary economists referred to as "normal unemployment." Under such conditions how could a family establish a budget? On several occasions Dr. Octave Du Mesnil pointed out that a worker with steady employment could at best give a rough estimate of his income and expenditures, because allowances had to be made for unemployment and illness. "As for day laborers, who are hired on a day-to-day basis and who can never be sure that there

Preliminary plan for a worker's housing project with glassed-in central court at 58, rue de Rochechouart. Godin's Familistère was influenced by this design. (Paris, Bibliothèque Nationale.)

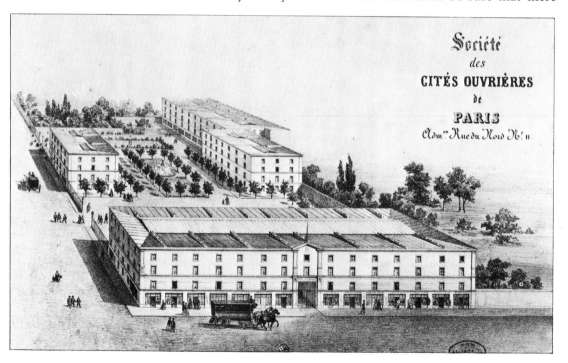

will be work not next week or next month but tomorrow, establishing a budget is simply impossible."[76]

The situation in the provinces was never better than that in Paris, as Louis-René Villermé's celebrated study showed for the July Monarchy. Yet the good doctor was far from regarding himself as a philanthropist, as was Adolphe Blanqui, who nevertheless called for special legislation regarding housing, "whose horrible insalubrity is the primary cause of that constant mortality and anonymous immorality that are decimating and brutalizing the population of some of our largest cities."[77] Medical topographers and boards of health diligently gathered information throughout France concerning housing that not a single responsible official dared call suitable. Their results were read by few people, but other reports reached a far wider audience. *L'Ouvrière,* a book by Jules Simon, the intellectual leader of the opposition to the Second Empire, was one of the most widely read books in the second half of the nineteenth century. It contained full descriptions of urban slums, to which the author appended this conclusion: "All industrial cities offer the same spectacle."[78]

Early in the century enlightened minds grasped the fact that good housing was one of the keys to social peace and one of the best ways of combating utopianism (and, after 1848, socialism). A corporation was set up in Paris in 1849 for the purpose of building apartment complexes *(cités)* in all twelve of the capital's arrondissements. These were to offer healthy, well-ventilated apartments with a kitchen and one or two bedrooms at rents below those being asked for unhealthy apartments. The prince-president invested heavily in the scheme, as did several friends of L'Ordre. The first was built at 58, rue Rochechouart (in the 9th arrondissement); France's first low-rent housing project still stands today.

Inaugurated on November 18, 1851, it was given the imperial title of Cité Napoléon. When the last apartment was rented in 1853, the complex sheltered some six hundred individuals in two hundred apartments, the largest of which contained only one bedroom with fireplace, one large, well-lit sitting room, and one small kitchen, which doubled as an entry foyer. Each floor shared a single toilet and sink. Water was supplied by a fountain in the courtyard. Certain conveniences were much appreciated by the residents: the stairs were cleaned by a janitor; there was a washhouse and a bathhouse;

The Cité Napoléon

child care was provided; and a doctor on the premises offered free consultations every morning and when necessary made house calls.[79]

Armand de Melun and the Law of 1850

While the Cité Napoléon was being built, housing for the poor figured prominently in a series of debates in the Chamber of Deputies. Credit for raising the issue goes to Armand de Melun, the first social Catholic militant to succeed in translating his charitable intentions into concrete legislation.

Melun, who founded the charitable organization Société d'Economie in 1847 and was elected to the Legislative Assembly in 1849, immediately filed a bill concerning health improvements in housing that outlawed unhealthy buildings. He claimed that the proposed legislation was in no way a concession to the socialists and that it posed no threat to the rights of property: "What it attacks is not a principle but a merciless, heartless fact that wants to deny both divine and human laws and that claims the right to use and abuse everything, limited solely by frightful greed."[80] Hence the measures proposed were prudent and Christian, at once progressive and conservative. It was left up to each municipal council to appoint a commission of specialists to inspect buildings and prohibit the rental of any that it deemed unhealthy. Because municipal councils were under no compulsion to avail themselves of this power, and because many were dominated by landlords and notables, the law of April 13, 1850, was largely ineffective and was almost never enforced, except in Paris, where Haussmann used it for his own ends. Still, it was a first step.

During the Second Empire landlords showed little interest in following the example set by the building on rue Rochechouart. In 1854, however, the Cité des Gobelins (on the site that is today 59–61, avenue des Gobelins) was built by Sieur Levesque. This project consisted of a "group of residential units appropriate to the needs of the working class . . . which avoids the drawbacks associated with housing projects in the strict sense"—or so said the promoter, who no doubt wished to absolve himself of any suspicion of Fourierism.

Scholars who have studied charitable projects in Paris have often noted that landlords' profits were highest in the poorest arrondissements, a paradox that Adeline Daumard has been able to explain: "The ratio of income to market value was highest in the poor neighborhoods—not only gross income but also net income, because maintenance costs were

reduced to a minimum, whereas in wealthier neighborhoods and business districts landlords had to please demanding tenants and were often forced to undertake costly repairs and renovations."[81]

With the socialist peril revived by the return of exiled communards from New Caledonia, the founding of the Worker's Party by Guesde and Lafargue, and anarchist agitation against the payment of rent, conservatives rediscovered the value of "individual initiative."

Early Philanthropic Solutions

In 1888 the Philanthropic Society, which for more than a century had played a role on the charitable front and which claimed the support of many illustrious names, became executor of the estate that established the Heine Foundation, a new kind of philanthropic venture. In 1889 the Foundation completed its first project, a building with thirty-five apartments designed by the architect Comte Gilbert de Chabrol and located at 45, rue Jeanne-d'Arc (in the 13th arrondissement). Rents averaged 227 francs per year for a two-room apartment with a total living space of under 310 square feet. Yet some philanthropists involved in the venture were astonished that the birthrate did not shoot up. At almost the same time another building designed by Chabrol went up at 65, boulevard de Grenelle (in the 15th arrondissement). The apartments here were slightly larger than those in the first building and rented for an average of 316 francs.[82]

In 1890 the Paris-Orleans Railway Company (later with the cooperation of the Paris-Lyons-Mediterranean Company) founded the Société des Habitations Economiques, which built four apartment buildings: two at 10–12, rue Dunois (13th arrondissement); a third at 123, rue du Chevaleret (13th arrondissement); and a fourth at 54, rue Coriolis (12th arrondissement). These contained a total of 133 apartments (each with approximately 345 square feet of living space, roughly the same size as the apartments on the rue Jeanne-d'Arc), which rented for 282 francs. Amenities included water, a toilet, and a rubbish chute in each apartment. Apart from these "model apartments," there is nothing else to report in all of Paris. In a city where there were hundreds of charitable foundations the poor had remarkably few friends.

In the provinces too one has to look carefully for buildings constructed at the behest of forward-looking individuals. In Rouen, whose slums earned the distinction of being described in several nineteenth-century works, the engineer and architect Edouard Lecoeur in 1885–86 designed an apartment complex known as the Groupe Alsace-Lorraine, which was built in the poorest section of the city at the behest of an organization of prominent citizens known as the Société Anonyme Immobilière des Petits Logements (Small Apartment Realty Corporation). The complex consisted of six five-story apartment buildings with three apartments per floor, two with three rooms and one with two rooms, as well as fifteen shops on the ground floor. Tenants enjoyed amenities never before seen in working-class housing: gas, flush toilets, rubbish chutes, sewage connections, laundry rooms, an infirmary, and even a cider press—a rare instance of the integration of rural activities into urban life.[83]

Lyons was always a center of philanthropic initiative. In 1886 Edouard Aynard, a banker and politician, along with the railway magnates Félix Mangini and J. Gillet, founded the Société Anonyme des Logements Economiques (Low-Rent Housing Corporation) with a capital of 300,000 francs. On July 1, 1887, five five-story buildings were completed on the rue d'Essling and the rue de la Rèze (3rd arrondissement). Apartments had three rooms, each of which occupied between 118 and 172 square feet. Construction costs were kept low through the use of a "composite material made from slag which hardens with time and turns the building into a veritable monolith."[84] Subsequently other complexes were erected on the rue Jaboulay and the rue d'Anvers; several of these have recently been rehabilitated.

By 1902, when Mangini died, the Société that he had so enthusiastically supported had become, after the Hospices, the largest landowner in Lyons. Its 130 buildings contained some 1,500 apartments and housed nearly 8,000 people. The biased belief that workers were not reliable tenants is refuted by the figures: out of a total rental income of 389,818 francs, only 536.80 francs remained uncollected.

All these efforts were pilot projects, however, undertaken in many cases by intelligent, energetic promoters. Except in Lyons, the results achieved were insignificant compared with the magnitude of the need. Liberals of the day, caught within the limits of their system, did not want to acknowledge that the problem could not begin to be solved until the standard of living had been raised on a vast scale. They remained wary of working people.

The law of November 30, 1894, was the first measure designed to make credit available for the construction of low-rent housing. However, the results proved disappointing to the bill's sponsors, Jules Siegfried and Georges Picot, who had hoped to galvanize the ruling class. Neither the Caisse des Dépôts nor the Caisses d'Epargne, both institutions that held workers' savings, were willing to invest in projects whose goal was to raise the standard of living of those same workers.

Speaking to the Société Française des Habitations à Bon Marché (French Society for Affordable Housing) in February 1905, Picot observed: "In sum, the laws of 1894 and 1895 made only five and a half million francs available to French contractors, whereas the Belgian Savings and Retirement Fund lent more than fifty million francs to Belgian contractors. A small country with only one-sixth of our population accomplished ten times as much!"[85]

France thus limited itself to charitable undertakings. In 1905 the situation was much the same as it had been before 1894; millions of families experienced no improvement in their standard of living. "The worker lives as he can, not as he would like. He cannot choose between spacious and cramped quarters. The only apartments available have one or two bedrooms, rarely three. No matter how many children he has, he must take what is available and pay whatever price is asked. The landlord's demand wins out over the tenant's offer." Such was the conclusion of one investigator, based on his study of working-class housing in Lunéville in 1896. It could have been applied equally well to all of France.

The effects of this situation on families were as bad as the effects on the general level of morality. The author of a study of workers' housing in the Marennes district in 1898 put it this way: "The worker who spends 12 to 15 percent of his wages on rent and who still must house his children in cramped, dirty, unhealthy quarters seeks every opportunity to stay away from home. Because he is unhappy with himself, those around him must endure his bad moods. He goes into debt and will quit his job over a trifle. He then becomes a nomadic worker, dragging his misery from city to city, and his children are just waiting for the time when, liberated at last, they will be able to escape from this environment."

Private initiative in housing was an undeniable failure. The problem made society increasingly uneasy. But how could it have been otherwise, at a time when the social climate was set by opportunism in power? Industrialists and bankers had accepted the republic only on condition that it erect no obstacles to the expansion of capital. Since speculation in stocks was clearly more profitable than the construction of low-rent housing, the ruling class and its propertied supporters enthusiastically invested in stocks.[86] As Léon Say, one of the true leaders of the Third Republic, put it, "Charity has its limits, but good investment has none."

FROM PHALANSTERY TO COMPANY TOWN

Charles Fourier's concept of the harmonious residence has been the secret or declared inspiration of any number of schemes and experiments in working-class housing right down to the present time. The influence of the "prophet of harmony" has yet to be fully measured. As a shrewd observer of the realities of his day, he could hardly ignore what was plain to behold: "Civilized custom makes it possible for thirty workers, men and women alike, to live quite morally and decently in a cramped attic. Our moralists, who oppose union in industry, establish it in the only places where it is inappropriate, in the lodgings of the poor and the sick, whom one sees crowded like sardines in workers' lofts and hospitals."[87] Fourier had seen and lived in "dirty and hideous cities" as well as in villages composed of "clusters of disgusting cottages."[88]

In Fourier's ideal society families would live not in a "chaos of small homes, each dirtier and messier than the next" but in "phalansteries" or "societal palaces" large enough to hold 3,500 people. He provided sketchy plans of such a palace together with a brief description. The idea was taken up by Victor Considérant, one of the first popularizers of Fourier's thought.

Considérant proposed a building not unlike the prototype suggested by the master but specified in full detail and described in well-turned phrases, such as this one describing the structure of a phalanstery: "In the societal construction everything is foreseen and provided for, organized and arranged; man is master over water, air, heat, and light." Each apartment was to be supplied with hot and cold running water and central heating: "A single central furnace will distribute heat to all parts of the building, including galleries, shops, halls, and apartments. This uniform heat will be conducted to the various rooms by a system of pipes equipped with valves, by means of which one may vary and regulate at will the temperature in any part of the societal palace."[89]

The phalanstery was to be divided into apartments of various types designed for every budget, some furnished, others not. A communal restaurant would supply meals at cost. All apartments were to have access to a glassed-in gallery, ventilated in summer and heated in winter. This gallery would link together all the parts of the palace: "The gallery cleaves to the sides of the societal edifice like a long belt that links all the parts into a single whole and maintains contact between the center and the extremities. It is the channel through which life circulates through the great phalansterian body, the artery that carries blood from the heart to all the vessels."[90]

The phalanstery was to be a functional building, but it was more than just a residential machine: "Water, fire, light, granite, and metals must be harmonized. All the elements to be wedded must be molded by art's ample hands. It will be a creation!" Such an ideal, Considérant exclaimed at the end of his work, was "too beautiful not to be possible." He continued: "Although you may be housed, not everyone is. Did you know that some people are too cold in the winter and too hot in the summer? There are some whose straw mattress becomes soaked when it rains and whose floor turns to mud. Man is not made to live in caves. He is not a burrowing animal, but a man, who needs to be housed."

Of course protests were raised against what some considered to be the absurd idea of making architecture harmonious with the human organism. A graduate of the Ecole Polytechnique and a military officer, Considérant was well aware of the billions spent every year in Europe to build, maintain, and demolish fortifications of every variety. What if a fraction of that money were devoted to more productive investments, to projects easier than building a ship: "Is it easier to house 1,800 in the middle of the ocean, 1,800 leagues from the nearest shore, than to house 1,800 peasants in a harmonious building in the middle of Champagne or Beauce?"

As a deputy in the Constituent Assembly under the Second Republic, Considérant filed a bill on April 14, 1849, that would authorize the government to finance an experimental commune of five hundred people to be established near Paris. The state would bear the cost of building houses and farm structures, and ownership was to revert to the government at the expiration of the commune's lease. The Assembly would

PALAIS DE FAMILLES.

Calland-Lenoir, *Family Palaces,*
1858. The Catholic Fourierist
Victor Galland, a graduate of
the Ecole des Beaux-Arts of
Paris, hoped to realize the
master's dreams with this
palais, to be owned jointly by
people of all social classes.
Godin signed a contract with
Galland, but he was not put in
charge of building the
Familistère, for what reason we
do not know. (Paris,
Bibliothèque Nationale.)

not even debate the bill. But Fourier's followers never gave
up on this central component of Fourierist ideology. Following Considérant's lead, they recast his proposal in a variety of
forms.

Foremost among these housing activists was the novelist
Eugène Sue, who enjoyed a substantial readership among
workers. He was the writer who did most to spread Fourier's
ideas. François Hardy, the industrialist hero of Sue's *Le Juif
errant* (The Wandering Jew, 1844), was an unwitting Fourierist.
He built a "common house" on the outskirts of Paris for the
benefit of his workers. This building, which incorporated
Fourierist precepts, contained one-room apartments with bath
for unmarried workers and three-room apartments for
families.

Calland and the "Family Palace"

No phalanstery had yet appeared on the social landscape
when, in the 1850s, the architect Victor Calland revived Fourier's idea, which he renamed the "family palace." He took his
inspiration directly from the master: "The family palace is a
plan for social unity based on individual liberty applied to the

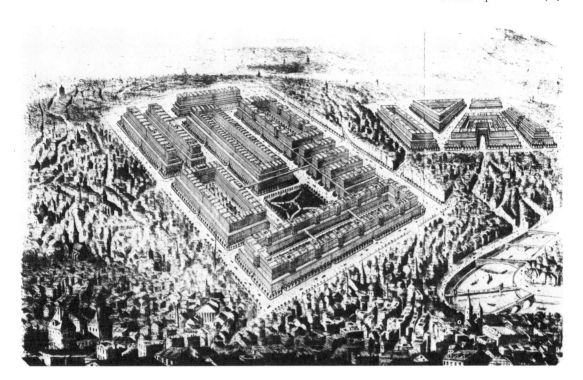

needs of domestic life and embodied in a new form of architecture suitable for any location. The basic purpose of this design is to gather at least a hundred families in one place, in a vast, harmoniously conceived monument in such a way that each individual may take full advantage of his or her freedom. It is also to encourage them to pool their strength, their expenditures, and even their social pleasures in intelligent ways, thereby multiplying their power at least fivefold. And finally, it is to help them go from a state of isolation and antagonism to one of closeness, solidarity, and association."[91]

This plan for a housing complex was included in a 45-page brochure prepared in 1865 by the engineer Jean Borie, who was very much influenced by the thinking of Fourier. Note the unified character of the whole complex and the care to separate pedestrian walkways from vehicle access. (Paris, Bibliothèque Forney.)

Although Calland, a Catholic Fourierist, enjoyed the support of Melun for a plan to build a complex of 84 apartments, 60 for workers and 24 for relatively well-to-do families, he failed to attract the interest of capitalist investors. Nevertheless, his family palace soon gained a place in the history of workers' housing, thanks to the efforts of the one disciple of Fourier whose achievements stood the test of time, the industrialist Jean-Baptiste André Godin.

There is no dearth of studies about the founder of the Familistère and his attempts to establish a working partnership between capital and labor.[92] I shall confine myself to a discussion of the Familistère of Guise, which was inspired by Fourier's idea of the phalanstery and represents a genuine attempt to put that idea into practice.

Fourier's Dream as Realized by Godin

According to Marie Moret, Godin was won over to the Fourierist ideal in 1842 after reading an article published in *Le Guetteur de Saint-Quentin,* a local newspaper. The following year he made contact with phalansterians in Paris and soon became a committed Fourierist. He read up on the subject, paid dues when necessary, wrote the editors of *Démocratie pacifique,* a Fourierist paper, and became a zealous propagandist for the sect in all the towns he visited while attempting to sell his products. He moved to Guise (in Aisne) in 1846, and his business, manufacturing stoves and ovens, prospered. He made a fortune, but for him wealth was only a means to serve mankind.

Early in the Second Empire, Godin begins to speak in his letters of constructing housing for his workers. On March 16, 1853, for example, he wrote the following lines to the phalansterian Cantagrel: "I have already asked myself many times whether my position would not allow me to build, alongside my factory, a workers' housing complex in which my employees could live, so far as their present state allows, in genuine comfort."

The November 1857 issue of the *Bulletin du mouvement sociétaire en Europe et en Amérique* drew Godin's attention to a brochure entitled "Elimination of Rents through Elevation of Tenants to the Rights of Ownership," from which extensive excerpts were cited. The author of the brochure was Calland, and Godin, after reading it, wrote him. He mentioned his plan to build workers' housing and said how sorry he was that no one had yet shown any interest in Fourier's communal architecture. Architects were interested only in isolating families. He asked Calland to state under what conditions he would accept a commission to draw up plans for workers' housing.

Godin and the first directors of the factory and of the Familistère, including his wife, who is not there just for effect. (Archives Rabaux.)

Lenoir, an architect and friend of Calland's, went to Guise and showed Godin some plans, but for the moment things went no further. In 1858 the industrialist purchased a parcel of 18 hectares and drew up his own plans for a building. The foundation was laid in April 1859. A full description of the Familistère, complete with plans and engravings, may be found in Godin's chief work, *Solutions sociales.*[93]

For the first time since Fourier had proposed the idea, a

modern residential building was made available to workers
and their families. Convinced that Considérant's ideas concerning the regulation of air, water, and light in the phalanstery
were valid, Godin worked to put those ideas into practice.
Each apartment contained a system of ventilation. Chimneys
were built into the walls with orifices to attach stoves and
furnaces. Glassed courtyards were generously ventilated. For
water, there were fountains on every floor. For laundry, there
was a special building equipped with wringers and a drying
room. There were also bathhouses and a covered swimming
pool (more than 500 square feet), with a special removable
bottom to convert it into a wading pool for children. Every
apartment had windows on both the facade and the inner
courtyard. At night all public areas were illuminated by gas.
In addition, every floor had a personal invention of Godin's,
unique for the time: a rubbish chute big enough to allow
disposal of fireplace ash.

    Eager to establish "communal institutions" to perform
the services for which the wealthy relied on their servants,
Godin set up a cleaning service in the Familistère. Courtyards,
stairways, walkways, fountains, toilets, and the like were
maintained by hired cleaners.[94]

    Like Hardy in *Le Juif errant,* Godin established a medical
service based on a mutual insurance plan. In return for payment of 1 to 2.5 francs per month, each resident was entitled
to the services of two physicians and a midwife, who visited
the premises daily. Medications were provided free of charge,

Jean-Baptiste André Godin,
Solutions sociales, 1872. This
bird's-eye view of the
Familistère follows the plan
given by Fourier in volume 2
of *Traité de l'association
domestique-agricole* (1822). (Paris,
Bibliothèque Nationale.)

The inner courtyard of every Familistère was covered with a movable glass roof. This device, combined with the series of balconies on each story of the building, made it possible to hold a variety of ceremonies and celebrations, which Godin spent a great deal of time attending. (Archives Rabaux.)

and disabled workers received a daily allowance. Those who were sick could isolate themselves from their families if they wished to avail themselves of rooms provided for that purpose.

In addition to these amenities, the Familistère offered a "culinary workshop" that prepared food and a consumer's cooperative that made many food items and manufactured goods available at reduced cost.[95] Once again Godin had a clear grasp of the problem: "Merchants buy wholesale items that the public needs and then resell those items at a profit, and the difference is paid by the consumer. Hence consumers can buy less food and other consumables because they have to give a part of their resources to unproductive middlemen. When people are scattered and do not recognize their common interests, they see the large number of middlemen as a convenience, a way of making sure that necessary items are available in every neighborhood, when in fact it imposes a very heavy burden on the consumer."[96]

Godin thus realized the Fourierist utopia: "Since we could not turn the working family's cottage or garret into a palace, we chose to put the worker's home inside a palace. The Familistère is just that—the social palace of the future." The poor man was finally granted "the equivalent of wealth." Godin's recipe was as follows: "Put the poor family in a comfortable apartment. Equip that apartment with all the resources and advantages with which the dwellings of the wealthy are equipped. See to it that the apartment is quiet, pleasant, and restful. Create communal institutions to perform the services for which the rich rely on their servants."

From the moment the central building was first occupied in 1865, Godin's social palace achieved the fame that Fourier had predicted for his phalanstery. Journalists from several countries visited it, and André Oyon wrote a book presenting it in a most favorable light.

Traditional liberals could not remain indifferent in the face of such an experiment, and soon they were attacking it with a barrage of standard arguments. In 1866 Jules Moureau expressed outrage at the way the residents of the Familistère were "made wards" of the establishment. They were given housing and clothing without having to haggle over the terms of their purchases. Communal child care was a pernicious institution that deprived the worker's wife of the most cherished responsibilities of motherhood. "One more step," Mou-

Godin was not the first industrialist to include discount stores in his workers' housing, but his stood out by being as well stocked as any store in Guise. (Archives Rabaux.)

The schools of the Familistère conformed to Fourier's precepts. They were later integrated into the French national educational system. (Archives Rabaux.)

reau fulminated, "and all will feel the leaden weight of communism pressing on their skulls." This sort of thing must not be allowed to spread. "It is a curiosity, which offers no solution to the problem at hand."[97]

Nearly fifty years later Fernand Duval presented much the same criticism in his doctoral thesis in law. The Familistère, he argued, was a barracks: "It deprives the individual of much of his freedom; it entangles him in a web of regulations that hamper his initiative."[98]

Zola Dislikes the Glass House

Zola, whose reading of popular Fourierist works had aroused his enthusiasm, also visited the Familistère.[99] His reactions are plainly evident in the notes he made in preparation for writing *Travail* (1901), a novel in which a commune is transformed into a Fourierist association. Zola did not find Godin's palace inspiring, and he rejected Fourierist principles of housing: "Glass house. Distrust of neighbor. No solitude. No freedom . . . Order, regulation, comfort, but what about thirst for adventure, risk, a free and adventurous life? Not all lives to be cast in same mold."

What could "a free and adventurous life" have meant to a nineteenth-century worker certain of finding identical slums no matter where he went? Zola's concerns would be more apt as a description of pioneers in the American West. The novelist shared all the ruling-class illusions of the day concerning the magical power of individual initiative. In Godin, the creator of a new form of communal life (a life that was not without constraint, since each "familisterian" was required to carry a small, red-covered book containing the hundred-odd regulations governing life within the Familistère), property-owners saw a traitor, a man who had broken the rules of the prevailing liberal morality.

Employers' Projects

"Respectable" industrialists who understood the benefits of a stable work force and a paternalistic system were a different story. Consider the Chagots, who founded a coal-mining concern known as the Société des Houillères de Blanzy in Montceau-les-Mines.[100] They left no doubt about their aims: "Comfortable, inexpensive housing is one of several institutions [for dealing with workers. These institutions] take charge of the individual while still very young, educate and assist him in various ways, stand by him throughout his work life, and after thirty years' service assure him of a pension of 300 francs with room and heating provided. In other words, they protect him from need and preserve the dignity of his profession and just remuneration for his labors to the end of his days." The mines were among the first industrial firms to provide single-family housing for workers.

In Briare another forward-looking industrialist, a self-taught inventor by the name of Jean-Félix Bapterosses, found his niche in ceramics. He outstripped the English in the mass-production of porcelain buttons and artificial pearls, which French explorers distributed in black Africa. By 1865 his company, purchased from a competitor twenty years before, employed a thousand workers—men, women, and children. Bapterosses took charge of everything, from child care to old age: "He knows and loves his workers; they are his children. He knows their passions, their flaws, and their perils. He handles them delicately and disciplines them firmly, as he must, but with such kindness! In order to provide them with healthy housing at below market prices he has built large apartment complexes, and it is his wish that they receive the formal blessings of religion."[101] Bapterosses preferred row houses to single-family dwellings. There were six in his complex, each more than a hundred yards long and housing 35 to 50 families. The houses stood, symbolically, between the factory and the old folks' home.

At around the same time the Schneiders, who had given up on barracks-style workers' housing well before the Second Empire, adopted the single-family house, which was better suited to the paternalistic moral rhetoric of which they were among the most enthusiastic advocates. The Schneiders won the support of the workers of Le Creusot, but a similar effort in Carmaux in 1865 ended in failure. By 1892 the Compagnie des Mines provided housing for only 201 workers, 6.9 percent of its work force.[102]

Noisiel

The most successful company town, a beacon to all champions of individual initiative, was that created by Emile Justin Menier to house his 1,700 workers. Whereas Godin had made his fortune by selling stoves and furnaces to the masses, Menier made his by bringing them chocolate. Thanks to his efforts, French chocolate consumption (including chocolate imported from South America) went from 350 tons in 1849 to 15,000 tons in 1889.

Like Godin, Menier took an active interest in social issues and published numerous books and pamphlets in praise of free trade at a time when nearly all French industrialists were protectionists. He also proposed a tax reform. Elected deputy from Meaux in 1876, he sat on the left and voted in favor of amnesty for deported communards.

After building a factory that was one of the first metal-framed buildings in the world, Menier pursued his penchant for innovation by creating, in 1874, Noisiel, a town of brick, two-family houses covering more than 20 hectares. The ground floor of each house, built above a cellar, contained one room with two windows and a kitchen with oven and sink. On the second floor there was a bedroom for the parents, another for the children, and, above, an attic. Each room was equipped with a fireplace, a closet, and shutters. In the yard was a covered shed and a portable outhouse; the privy pots, coated with cocoa leaf, furnished an excellent fertilizer that was used by all the families. Water was available from large numbers of fountains. The houses cost no more than 10,000 francs to build, or 5,000 francs per half, and they rented for 150 francs per year (12.5 francs per month). Rent bonuses

35. NOISIEL — Rue du Milieu

meant that some workers did not have to pay even this modest rent.

Like Godin, Menier established many communal institutions. A store provided low-cost food, drink, cloth, clothing, shoes, and fuel. Dining rooms served meals to workers who resided in nearby villages. Two hotel-restaurants housed and fed unmarried workers. There was a school with six grades as well as a day-care facility for children. Drugs were free, and sick workers received 2 francs per day sick pay if they were males, 1 franc per day if they were females.[103]

Just as Fourier's phalanstery was popularized by Eugène Sue, so too was this new Eden celebrated by one of the most popular late nineteenth-century writers, Hector Malot. A friend of Jules Vallès (and one of the few to help him after the Commune), Malot was a somewhat timid supporter of utopian socialism. In his novel *En famille* (1893), Paindavoine, a textile mill owner, succumbs to the influence of his granddaughter Perrine and builds a hospital and a day-care facility (called a *pouponnat,* in an explicit reference to Fourier) for his workers and their families. Unmarried men and women are housed in two hotels with restaurants that serve a substantial

In Noisiel, Menier chose to build two-family houses. Arrayed along streets, they can still be seen today.

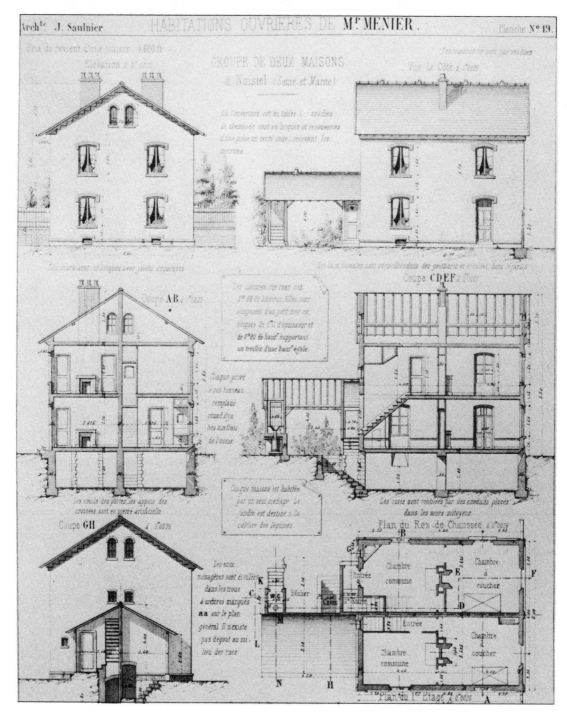

The celebrated collection of Muller and Cacheux is the most complete compilation we have of what 19th-century working-class housing was really like. This drawing shows that the houses in Noisiel were of excellent quality even though they lacked running water and sewers. (Paris, Bibliothèque Nationale.)

dinner of soup, stew or roast, bread, and cider for just 70 centimes. Each family has its own house with yard, for which the rent is just 100 francs annually. The model for the new town is explicitly stated to be Noisiel, to which Perrine sends an assistant to make a careful study of the way things work. Menier's houses were evidently to Malot's liking. Malot himself owned a single-family house, and the idea appealed to his deep-seated individualism.

As the public health movement sought to prevent tuberculosis, whose ravages were particularly devastating among workers, company towns became gardens in which every home was surrounded by greenery. At Dourges in Pas-de-Calais the Société des Mines replaced its old miners' quarters with a "regular little sanatorium" composed of more than five hundred picturesque little homes, each with a porch, a vestibule, and four rooms.[104] With the worker's cottage liberalism had finally hit on its ideal form of working-class housing.

CONFINEMENT IN THE SINGLE-FAMILY HOME

Those who believed that social and moral salvation lay in property set to work in earnest during the Second Empire. Their first undertaking, in Alsace, attracted a great deal of

Gaston Le Fol, *Petites constructions à loyer économique,* 1913. By 1909 the Société des mines de Dourges had built 500 homes of this type for its personnel. This was the golden age of the Norman-style half-timbered house, which soon vied with the Basque house throughout France. (Paris, Bibliothèque Nationale.)

attention. The Société Industrielle of Mulhouse, a company founded at the beginning of the nineteenth century, became a nonprofit foundation in 1832. On September 24, 1851, one of its members, the manufacturer Jean Zuber fils, presented a paper on workers' housing to his colleagues.[105] He submitted the plan of a model house that had been constructed in Great Britain and asked the Society to place the issue on its agenda.

His appeal was heard. During the meeting of June 30, 1852, Dr. Achille Penot reported on the results of an investigation of owners of workers' housing in the département of the Upper Rhine. There were, he said, two types of worker's residence: the barracks and the individual home. Barracks were to be rejected on moral grounds: "Bringing many strange families together under one roof rarely leads to tranquil domestic harmony and may give rise to serious disorders."

Of all the housing plans submitted, those of the Zuber Paper Mill on the Ile Napoléon appeared the most suitable. They included a cellar, two rooms and a kitchen on the first floor, and two bedrooms and a storage area on the second floor; outhouses were in the yard. For the first time a "social authority" implicitly recognized that workers might enjoy the same comforts as their employers. In conclusion, Dr. Penot expressed the wish that generous citizens might join together to build model homes patterned after those owned by the Zuber Mill. "Serious speculators" might then follow their lead.

One manufacturer, Jean Dollfus, immediately declared that he was ready to try the experiment. He commissioned the architect Emile Muller to design four houses. On November 30, 1853, Dr. Penot announced that the Société Mulhousienne des Cités Ouvrières (Mulhouse Workers' Housing Corporation) had been officially constituted on June 10 with a capital of 300,000 francs, increased to 600,000 following a contribution by Napoleon III; the original capital was divided into 600 shares of 5,000 francs each.[106] Dollfus himself held 35 shares, and the rest were divided among eleven manufacturers. Article one of the corporate bylaws is quite explicit: "The purpose of the corporation is to build homes for workers in Mulhouse and the surrounding area. Each house shall be built for a single family, without connection" to any other house. Since the purpose of the corporation was essentially philanthropic, no share would be allowed to yield a dividend of more than 4 percent.

On June 27 Dollfus submitted a comprehensive plan to

the shareholders, and on July 20 ground was broken. The corporation owned a plot of 8 hectares, on which houses were to be grouped in three ways: back to back, in blocks of four surrounded by a garden; and between a courtyard and garden.

The houses consisted of two stories with cellar. The ground floor contained a kitchen and one large room; on the second floor there were three bedrooms, a storage room, and a privy. All were to be sold for between 1,850 and 2,800 francs with special restrictions. Buyers were to make a down payment of 300 to 500 francs, depending on the type of house selected. Thereafter they were to make monthly payments of 20 to 30 francs in such a way that all registration fees, annual interest, and half the principal would be paid off within five years, sooner if possible. As for the other half of the principal, the buyer would be required to pay interest at 5 percent to the Crédit Foncier until repayment had been completed, which was to be done within roughly a thirty-year period.

Less than ten years later, in 1862, the development contained 560 homes, 488 of which had been sold as of March 31.[107] This new quarter of the old merchant republic offered nearly all the benefits of a Fourierist phalanstery: furnished apartments in seventeen-room buildings for unmarried workers, child care, medical service on the grounds, a washhouse with a centrifugal dryer, a bathhouse and swimming pool, a bakery that supplied bread at below the regulated market price, a restaurant serving inexpensive dishes, and a store that sold necessary items at reasonable prices.

The Mulhouse experiment (which continued to expand until, in 1867, the development housed some 6,000 people in 800 homes) was imitated in other cities in Upper Rhine. The industrialist Bourcart began building homes for workers in Guebwiller in 1854, and in 1860 a corporation was formed to continue what he had begun. In Beaucourt ground was broken on the Japy Estates in 1864. A similar development was begun in Colmar in 1866.[108] In all three cases the corporations formed were modeled exactly on the one in Mulhouse: a joint-stock company was administered by a committee of four or five members dominated by a majority shareholder, Dollfus in Mulhouse, Japy in Beaucourt.

These efforts were governed by a spirit of conservatism and social paternalism. Dr. Penot described them as "a work of philanthropy, whose purpose is to accustom workers to saving by offering them the attractive stimulus of ownership." In Mulhouse a prominent local personality trusted by the city's manufacturers oversaw the development of the project. Married workers were strongly discouraged from using the restaurant, an independent operation that was owned by Jean Dollfus. In Dr. Penot's sententious formulation, "the pot-au-feu is one of the cornerstones of the family, and it would be irritating to see workers turn their backs on it in order to enjoy the pointless distractions of a common table." Families were supposed to live self-contained lives and devote the bulk of their efforts to home improvements. Every year judges awarded monetary prizes to those deemed to have distinguished themselves in "order, cleanliness, and general good conduct."[109]

The Mulhouse development was completed in 1895, at which time it contained 1,240 homes housing 10,000 people, more than 10 percent of the city's population. (These homes are still occupied today.) An investigation in 1874 proves that the development did not become a working-class ghetto; more than 80 professions were represented among the population. Nevertheless, Stephan Jonas has shown that men employed as industrial workers did not earn enough to cover the monthly payments; their wives and children also had to work, and they were willing to do so because by working they could afford to own a home. In other words, the trap worked just as it was intended to.

In the Paris suburb of Clichy, the Cité Jouffroy-Renault at 14, rue des Cailloux, was modeled on the Mulhouse experiment. The development's forty homes came in five different models, containing from two to four rooms together with cellar, attic, and small yard. The maximum annual payment was 380 francs. After fifteen years of payments, or 5,700 francs (nearly double the price in Mulhouse), the occupant became a homeowner.

In the same spirit, the Dollfus' architect offered "honest, hard-working, sober workers" in the capital a chance to lease-purchase homes with garden in the faubourg Saint-Antoine during the final years of the Second Empire.[110] These spacious dwellings, large enough for ten people according to the promoter, were equipped with shop and kitchen in the basement, two rooms on the first floor, three on the second floor, wall closets, and a privy. Rent was 1 franc per day; in order to become an owner, the occupant had to pay an additional 49 centimes per day for fifteen years. The total cost of the house came to more than 8,000 francs. We do not know whether this project ever was developed, but in any case it seems to have far exceeded the financial wherewithal of workers in this period.

Early in the Third Republic the legislature initiated an unfortunately little known investigation into the situation of the French working class. One of the commission members was Armand de Melun.[111] Housing had always been among the chief concerns of the man who had inspired the law of 1850, whose effects he judged on the whole to have been greatly beneficial. As for efforts to improve working-class housing during the Second Empire, he felt that the construction of workers' barracks had not yielded good results, because such housing was at odds with the independent French character. Furthermore, there were grave drawbacks to barracks from the moral and even the political standpoint; therefore these residences should be closely watched. Developments of single-family houses did not create such problems. Melun praised industrialists who had made it easy for their workers to purchase family homes: "Property bestows one precious quality: it makes its owner more sober and hard-working. It takes him away from harmful distractions and keeps him close to home, in the bosom of his family, where he can put his leisure time to good use."

Speaking from an official podium, Melun gave renewed impetus to the concept of the worker-owner, which came to dominate the fin-de-siècle. Melun's idea was that ownership ought to be a personal vocation; proletarians would achieve it on their own, not, as some already advocated, with state assistance. In his words: "Trusting their fates to the state, which is all too widely held to be all-powerful, they dispense themselves from the need for individual effort, which is always difficult, and call, in response to their sovereign will, for a new organization of society and new policies from which they expect benefits that can only come from persevering effort and fulfillment of all their obligations."

Frédéric Le Play, who in 1856 founded the Société d'Economie Sociale, shared this view.[112] As an analyst of disorder in liberal society, Le Play stands out as one of the theorists who did most to inculcate the notion that property confers moral benefits on its owner: "The indissoluble union of the family with its home has the most salutary influence on the morality and well-being of the worker's family."[113] This idea is developed in his most important work, *La Réforme sociale*.[114]

The Correct Solution to the Problem of Social Unrest

In the first volume of that work Le Play argues that one of Europe's most fertile traditions was family home-ownership. In France, however, this tradition survived in rural areas only; in cities and manufacturing centers most housing was rented. This fact had disturbing consequences for social life: "Strict application of the principle of supply and demand has disrupted social relations in the area of rentals as well as in that of wages."[115]

The manufacturing system had uprooted people from their native soil and concentrated them in places that lacked the institutions necessary to prevent vice and profligacy. Families could not afford the individual homes that are "one of the fundamental amenities of any civilization." They had to settle for a room in a barracks, with predictably adverse consequences: "Rental dwellings lacking the most basic necessities of comfort and health suggest that the family has lost all sense of human dignity. The father is almost always away from home, either at work or in search of crude and selfish pleasures. The mother, reduced to the status of worker, also deserts the home either to engage in prostitution or to subject herself more decently to the burdens of hard labor. Young boys and girls, also subjected to hard labor at an early age, gradually become inured to profligacy and vice. Prematurely weakened by deprivation and debauch, the aging parents die in destitution well before completing the normal life span."[116]

The only cure for this terrible waste was for the ruling class to act voluntarily. Industrial leaders should make it their business to encourage workers to save in order to buy themselves homes and urge their wives not to work. The city had undermined the family's dignity and morality, and it was in the country that stable households would be restored and allowed to flourish. The rental system that occasioned "suprise and reproach" in foreigners would then die out. Once people settled down for good in houses at a comfortable distance from their neighbors, they would no longer "scatter the shreds of [their] personalities to the winds."

To Each His Home

This bizarre idea became the obsession of all bourgeois reformers in this period. The "artificial" practice of group living was condemned repeatedly at the International Hygiene congresses that began in 1876. In Brussels one speaker declared: "The material and moral well-being of workers, the health of the public, and the security of society depend on

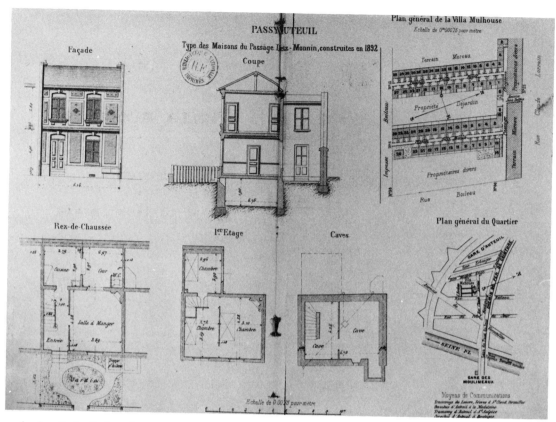

each family's living in a separate, healthy, and convenient home, which it may purchase."[117]

At the second International Hygiene Congress, held two years later in Paris, Emile Trélat, author of a report entitled "Workers' Projects, Workers' Homes," had this to say: "Efforts to improve workers' housing by lodging them in barracks are doomed to failure. It is a sign of the worker's true human dignity that he refused the economic benefits that were made available if he accepted a regimented situation in a project."[118] With a bold flourish Trélat concluded: "It is now incontrovertibly established that the barracks project is totally unsuited to serve as workers' housing."

Advocates of small family homes were quick to attempt a novel pilot project. They placed workers in an arrondissement of Paris that the bourgeoisie was in the process of appropriating for its own exclusive use. In 1880 Senator Dietz-Monin, an associate of the Japys, Paul Leroy-Beaulieu, and several other prominent conservatives, founded the Société

E. Cacheux, *L'Economie pratique.* The Société Anonyme des Habitations Ouvrières of Passy-Auteuil was a bold enterprise of "social reconciliation." The project contained a hundred homes with fenced-in front yards, still standing today. (Paris, Bibliothèque Nationale.)

Anonyme des Habitations Ouvrières (Workers' Housing Corporation) of Passy-Autueil, with a capital of 200,000 francs (2,000 shares at 100 francs).[119] Plans were made to build four-room homes with running water, gas, and sewers on land provided by Emile Cacheux, an engineer who specialized in the construction of small buildings. Purchase required a down payment of 500 francs and annual payments of about 600 francs payable over a period of twenty years. By 1893 sixty-seven houses had been built; these were occupied by some three hundred people.

The annual payments were high enough to be out of reach of all but the most "hard-working and sober" workers, meaning foremen and above all white-collar employees, members of the new stratum of low-level bureaucrats whose support the industrialists badly needed. What an honor, to be admitted onto the masters' own turf! To be sure, it was in the depths of the 16th arrondissement, along the rue Boileau, where the average rent in the early nineteenth century ran around 600 francs, that is, at the low end of the rental scale in what had become Paris's most expensive arrondissement. By comparison, rents in the Chaillot district averaged 2,000 francs; in the Porte Dauphine district, 1,900 francs; and in the Muette district, 1,100 francs.

Earnest as the applicants may have been, it was wise to be wary of the class from which they sprang, and the Société took appropriate precautions. If a "provisional" owner behaved in a notoriously "immoral" manner, his contract could be canceled and he could be thrown out of his house. In a similar spirit, subletting was prohibited. The Passy-Auteuil project enjoyed brief celebrity as a liberal showpiece; after being inaugurated by the president of the Republic, it was frequently visited by foreign dignitaries.

Its promoters anticipated the most edifying results, as is evident from a report of the first meeting of the board of directors. The report was drafted by Emile Cheysson, an engineer prominent among conservative social reformers, and published in Paul Leroy-Beaulieu's weekly magazine, *L'Economiste français:* "Home ownership effects a complete transformation [in the worker] . . . A small home and a yard turns the worker into someone who can truly be called the head of a family, a moral and prudent leader with a sense of his roots and wielding authority over his wife and children. . . . Before long his house 'owns' him. It teaches him morality, settles him down, and transforms him."[120]

No more revealing statement exists of the true motives of ruling-class thinkers. Like Le Play, whose friend and disciple he was, Cheysson was an engineer and graduate of the Ecole Polytechnique who believed that the worker, once confined in a home of his own, would lose interest in collective struggle and trade unionism. Architects, following the recommendations of social theorists, used all their ingenuity to make relations with neighbors difficult in the housing developments they designed. It was feared that communication among the residents would lead straight to that major bugbear of the nineteenth-century bourgeoisie, sexual immorality, and to political agitation fomented by irresponsible troublemakers.

Steps were taken here and there in the provinces to facilitate access to ownership of small single-family homes. Eugène Rostand, father of the poet and grandfather of the naturalist, did his utmost in Marseilles, where the Caisse d'Epargne made some extraordinary decisions. The Caisses d'Epargne were already popular savings institutions throughout France, but generally their interest in construction was limited to using the funds of the poor to build themselves splendid neoclassical headquarters resembling the private *hôtels* of the wealthy. In 1889, however, the Marseilles Caisse initiated a program to build single homes, three-room apartments, and rooming houses for unmarried workers.[121]

In Le Havre in 1889 the Société Havraise des Cités Ouvrières built forty detached and semidetached houses.[122] In

Little is known about the foundation that built these houses, which represent the most modest form of home ownership.

A "comfortable" working-class home, with two buffets, a ceiling lamp, and double curtains on the windows. (Sirot-Angel Collection.)

Beauvais in 1891 the industrialist Rupp built twenty-nine homes.[123] In Lyons the architect Roucheton designed houses on behalf of Le Cottage, a "Lyonnais corporation formed to encourage the construction of healthful, inexpensive housing and to facilitate access to ownership through work and saving." The ulterior purpose could still be openly avowed.

In 1903 building industry trade journals were filled with news of the impending international exposition of housing, construction, and public works to be held at the Grand Palais in Paris between July 30 and November 15. At the end of an article in *La Construction lyonnaise,* one journalist expressed naive satisfaction: "What this means, perhaps, is that philosophers, idealists, artists, industrialists, merchants, and workers—that is, all the hard-working sons of the great family of France—will discover that some if not all of their dreams have come true."[124] Disciples of Hennebique, the prophet of reinforced concrete, used the occasion to exalt their material, "which should be of interest to builders of low-cost housing because of its advantages in safety, hygiene, and durability, all at a cost that seldom exceeds that of local materials."[125]

The exposition, in keeping with the views of the social

authorities, promoted individual housing primarily. Several model homes were displayed, with appropriate contemporary furniture in each room; the price tags were left on. A breakdown of new construction in France in 1904 confirms the growing importance of single-family housing developments: in Dunkirk, the Cité G. Rosendaël; in Roubaix, 96 homes in La Ruche roubaisienne; in Alençon, 45 homes built by the Caisse d'Epargne; in Bordeaux, 74 homes; in Montpellier, 14 built for the Foyer par l'Epargne; in Béziers, 18 for the local Caisse d'Epargne; and in Marseilles, 24 homes already under construction at the behest of the local Caisse. The suburbs of Paris became a focus of real-estate development, which often decked itself out with social ambitions. Le Cottage d'Athis and Le Toit Familial in Argenteuil soon attracted imitators.[126]

With Zola's Approval

At that very moment the single-family home won the support of a powerful literary figure. Zola had chosen this type of home for the utopian city of Beauclair in *Travail,* one of his last works, which was published in 1901. Here there were no Familistère-type barracks surrounded by vast parks subsuming all that was left of the old peasant village, only single-family houses, "dispersed naturally to promote peace and quiet and better health." (By "dispersed naturally," Zola meant that houses were not required to be aligned along streets.) Zola's imagination soared high above the heavenly jumble of Beauclair, and it would have put lead in his wings to consider such down-to-earth problems as sewers and roads, even though Beauclair's residents were already traveling about in two-seat electric cars. He talks a great deal about the electricity that is to light every home, and one wonders if perhaps he has forgotten that wires are needed to bring electricity into the home.

Zola's naturalism is saved by a contradiction. After imagining the "tide of white houses" engulfing the old village of Beauclair, he describes other houses whose style is a good deal less pure, for they are constructed of stone decorated with the ceramic gingerbread that, after garnering applause at the 1889 exposition, was much in vogue among architects: "They were decorated with colorful pieces of sandstone and pottery, enameled tiles, gables, window frames, panels, friezes, and cornices." Zola might be moved to find these same features still intact and in some cases restored in certain suburbs of Paris today.

Competitions for the design of low-cost furniture were numerous in the early 20th century, with most of the entries designed by Art Nouveau decorators. The new designs did not achieve the popularity hoped for by the promoters, because the department stores already had a solid grip on the furniture market. The Henri II dining-room set was a best-selling item. Competition of 1905. (Paris, Bibliothèque des Arts Décoratifs.)

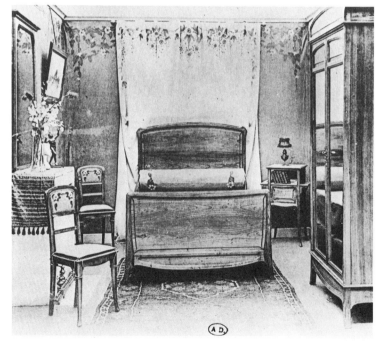

Zola's utopia reveals his true colors as a petty-bourgeois property owner, the role he played at Médan. While the French bourgeoisie attempted to resist socialist pressure by enlisting the support of a working-class elite isolated in single-family homes purchased on credit, the writer whom the bourgeoisie detested most lent it the support of his talent. Zola made a powerful contribution to the myth of the single-family home, which was just beginning to fascinate the entire French middle class.

None but the middle class could truly afford to own homes built of sandstone and granite, vulgarized versions of the bourgeois villa that soon sprang up, in ever more pictur-esque forms, throughout the Paris region. In the second decade of the twentieth century, a five-room house with garden in the Paris suburbs cost an average of 12,000 francs. Among the working class, the average annual family income in the capital was approximately 1,700 francs, and that of low-level white-collar employees was 2,200 francs. The daily wage of a con-struction worker in the Paris region in 1911 did not exceed 5.5 francs, and for France as a whole the average daily wage was 4.86 francs.

Aspiring homeowners from the lower classes therefore had no choice but to settle for the substandard models that certain architects, sensing a market, hastened to design. Petit-pas, the shrewd publisher of *Ma petite maison* (My Little House, a magazine founded in 1905), managed to build a two-room house with kitchen and indoor toilet (but no dressing room) for as little as 1,200 francs.[127] His colleague Bourniquel was later described by the publisher Garnier in terms that show how fully the lessons of Le Play and his followers had been assimilated: "Anyone who does not own his own home lives in a state of constant insecurity . . . The father who gathers his family around a true hearth spares them the need to mingle indiscriminately with people of all kinds. As a result, the dignity, moral values, and even the education of each member of the family profit."[128]

Bourniquel followed up this introduction by setting forth a full range of offerings from the worker's *maisonette* to the merchant's pied-à-terre to the industrialist's small home to the elegant bourgeois villa. In the latter a steep roof capped by weather vanes and spikes was coupled with a staircase tower, adding a tasteful medieval note to the landscape. Even the most modest homes were equipped with a porch and stairs, which became a standard feature of this type of construction.

Thus, France gradually became a straitlaced country of self-satisfied homeowners, who endlessly repeated the same platitudes: "It's all I need," "Anything good takes work," and "We're happy here." Each family shut itself up in its home, safe from "fat cats" and "foreigners." The dream lasted until the First World War, after which the miserable housing developments that were thrown up in the interwar years tarnished it somewhat. But what difference did it make, since by this time ownership had come to be considered essential? One magazine, published for more than fifteen years, was entitled simply *Not' cabane* (Our Little House)—another sign of the French fondness for anything that can be thought of as small.

But why should a "sweet" little home necessarily bring happiness? At least one writer attacked the myth. Eugène Dabit, one of France's very few proletarian writers, inexplicably neglected today, in 1932 wrote *Villa Oasis ou les Faux Bourgeois* (Villa Oasis, or The Phoney Bourgeois), which tells the story of two former hoteliers who buy a villa in a suburb of Paris. Its three stories are a mark of social success; a walled garden makes it possible to avoid contact with the neighbors; there is a decorative pool and a garage for the automobile. In short, the house has everything required for happiness, according to an ideal model that was reproduced in millions of copies. Life, however, is sometimes unkind: eventually the house kills its owners.

New Public Housing

The subversive winds of socialism and social art touched the Ecole des Beaux-Arts at the end of the nineteenth century.[129] Some young architects evidently were tormented by concerns far removed from those of their elders, priests devoted to the worship of incorruptible Beauty, and a few of them published works that might have been written by engineers or doctors.[130]

Private Initiative Takes Over

In fact a new market was about to open up, and the augurs of the profession were soon aware of it. An article published in *La Semaine des constructeurs* in 1890 stated: "The construction of low-cost housing, once a work of philanthropy, will soon achieve the status of an investment coupled with a work of enlightened socialism. It is up to our colleagues to examine the technical aspects of the question."

Gaston Le Fol, *Grandes constructions à loyer économique.* One would hardly suspect this facade, in which particular care has been taken with the lintels, of belonging to a low-cost apartment building. But in fact the building was designed for working-class families, and there were workshops in the basement. (Paris, Bibliothèque Historique.)

Gaston Le Fol, *Grandes constructions à loyer économique*. In 1908 A. Labussière built a large apartment complex at 124, avenue Daumesnil (12th arrondissement) for the Fondation du Groupe des Maisons Ouvrières. In half of the apartments, the fully equipped kitchen was separated from the dining room by a divider. The directors of the foundation considered this solution more appropriate than the traditional arrangement for the household of an ordinary employee. (Paris, Bibliothèque Historique.)

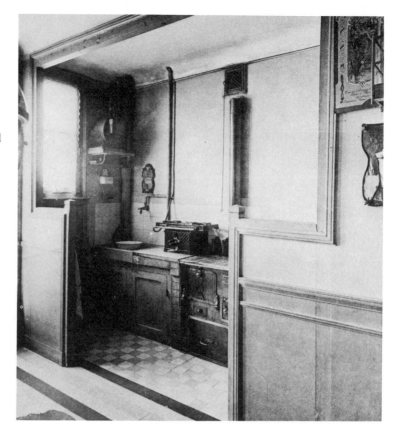

In Paris several major projects grew out of the law of 1894. The Société Philanthropique continued its efforts: 54 apartments were constructed in a building located at 19, rue d'Hautpoul (19th arrondissement) in 1897, and 38 additional apartments in a building at 77, rue de Clignancourt (18th arrondissement) in 1898. To Georges Picot's dismay, the average number of children per family in the latter building was less than one. Had neo-Malthusian propaganda done its damage here, too? But the tenants, like those in other buildings owned by the Société, paid their rent regularly. By the turn of the twentieth century the Société Philanthropique had thus rescued 190 working-class families, some 622 individuals, from the hell of the Paris slums.

In 1902 Charles Guyon was commissioned by the Groupe des Maisons Ouvrières, which was actually a foundation set up by the Lebaudy sugar concern, to build three buildings at 5, rue Jeanne-d'Arc (13th arrondissement).[131] These three buildings were to contain 71 apartments, along with amenities such a library, a storage area for bicycles and children's wagons, a laundry room, a drying room, baths and showers, and a playground. In 1905 the same group commissioned Labussière to build a complex of 175 apartments at 5–7, rue Ernest-Lefèvre (20th arrondissement).

In Saint-Denis, a suburb just outside of Paris, the Société Anonyme des Habitations Economiques was particularly active. Among its accomplishments was the construction in 1902 of a complex of 342 apartments in eleven buildings, together with twenty-one single-family homes, all designed by Charles Guyon.

Some people, including Picot, even concerned themselves with housing for single women. Writing in Le Play's journal *Réforme sociale* in 1900, he observed that "a boardinghouse is no place for a female worker who wants to work in Paris." A high police official told him: "I have come to the conclusion that 95 out of 100 girls who take up prostitution do so as a result of their living situation."[132] Various charitable organizations maintained dormitories for female workers with some one thousand beds in all. But according to the 1891 census, there were 339,344 female workers living in Paris, 165,774 of them between twenty and thirty-nine years of age.

The Société Philanthropique was not unaware of this problem, with its serious moral implications. Thanks to a gift

Plans for workers' apartments often included a library, but these were seldom actually constructed. This shows the library in a building constructed by the Fondation du Groupe des Maisons Ouvrières at 5–7, rue Ernest-Lefèvre, 1907.

Hôtel Populaire Hommes, 94, rue de Charonne, XIe arrondissement, PARIS

The tireless Labussière, here in conjunction with his colleague Longerey, designed this 743-room apartment house for single men in 1911. For the first time unmarried male workers in Paris were offered access to decent rooms with all the amenities and services of a good hotel. (Archives Bernard Marrey.)

of 500,000 francs from Baroness Hirsch, in 1902 the Société opened a boardinghouse for ladies and young women at 37, rue des Grandes-Carrières (18th arrondissement). There were twenty rooms at 1 franc per night and thirty-six studios at 60 centimes. The rooms had no facilities for washing, but baths were available for 20 centimes and showers for 10 centimes. The guard locked the establishment doors at 10 P.M. No visitors were allowed in the rooms. Residents could receive guests only in the reception room between 5 and 6:30 P.M., and male callers could be seen only in the director's office.

Soon thereafter a major government agency went to even greater lengths in behalf of its female employees. In 1906 Bliaut constructed a building at 41, rue de Lille (7th arrondissement), in the heart of a bourgeois neighborhood, directly behind the Caisse des Dépôts. The building was the Maison des Dames Employées des Postes, Télégraphes et Téléphones (dormitory for female workers employed by the PTT), a magnificent structure, influenced by Art Nouveau, which still stands. It contained 111 rooms and offered a variety of amenities to its residents.

Let us not avert our eyes, however, from the resistance and consternation of the French Friends of the Parthenon,

Hôtel Populaire Hommes, 94, rue de Charonne, XI᷊ᵉ arrondissement, PARIS

installed in their impressive headquarters opposite the Louvre and alongside the Institut in a temple that, when Napoleon III had attempted to reform the Ecole des Beaux-Arts in 1863, Ingres had declared to be devoted exclusively to the arts of Greece and Rome. Anyone who reads *L'Architecte* (published from 1906 to 1935 as the official organ of the Société des Architectes Diplômés par le Gouvernement [SADG], founded in 1877) can attest to the fact. The SADG was a power, whose membership included nearly all degree-holding architects and most of the winners of the Prix de Rome. Between 1906 and 1914, a period that saw the passage of a great deal of legislation extending the law of 1894 and intended to promote low-cost housing, *L'Architecte* published only eight articles on the subject and included plans of only one completed project, an apartment building, in 1913.

In that same year, 1913, however, another major journal, *L'Architecture,* official publication of the Société Central des Architectes, began to take notice. Its editors were not unfamiliar with the issue of workers' housing, on which they had published many articles, but they were determined to maintain

Affordable Housing Garners No Prizes

their distance. In a report on plans submitted to the juries judging various architectural prizes Henri Saladin wrote: "I then looked at workers' homes, affordable houses *(habitations à bon marché)*, low-rent apartments, and still more affordable houses. I do not wish to be regarded as a critic who is hard to please, but is the affordable house really so important from an artistic standpoint that we should receive so many submissions? These plans do not deserve to be included in the show unless they are of exceptional merit. They represent excellent architectural work, but they are not works of art."[133] The point, clearly, is that workers' housing will never be a sufficiently lofty category to qualify as a subject for Prix de Rome candidates, who would rather see their names linked to an ambassadorial residence or a pilgrimage church. Fortunately, a few independent spirits, some without degrees, broke the shackles of formalism, cast aside traditional models, and came up with solutions to the problems of working-class families.

Henri Sauvage

In June 1904 the minister of commerce, Georges Trouillot, a dyed-in-the-wool anticlerical radical, inaugurated the first building constructed by the Société des Logements Hygiéniques à Bon Marché at 7, rue de Trétaigne, in Paris's 18th arrondissement. The president of the Société was Frantz Jourdain, a pioneer in iron construction and an avowed enemy of the neoclassic.

This exemplary building—six stories, with a concrete frame, brick fill, and a perfectly legible plan reflected in the facade—was the work of a young architect, Henri Sauvage, who, though only thirty years old, was hardly unknown. Once a student at the Ecole des Beaux-Arts' Atelier Pascal, he left, as did Auguste Perret, without a degree. Yet Sauvage had attained the front rank of Art Nouveau architects, not far behind his friend Hector Guimard, by designing a villa in Nancy in 1898 for the furniture manufacturer Louis Majorelle.[134]

His design for the rue de Trétaigne incorporated all the amenities that utopians and hygienists insisted workers' housing must have: baths and showers, a cooperative store (known as La Prolétarienne), a "hygienic" restaurant, adult education classrooms, and even a hanging garden (no longer extant) for the sun cures then regarded as the best treatment for tuberculosis. For this project Sauvage abandoned the decorative neo-Gothic and vegetal touches of his Art Nouveau style,

Gaston Le Fol, *Grandes constructions à loyer économique*. This building at 165, boulevard de l'Hôpital (13th arrondissement), designed by Sauvage and Sarazin in 1909, was ahead of its time in shunning excessive ornamentation. Built of reinforced concrete, the building featured a rooftop patio for sunbathing; ornamentation was limited to a tiled facade. (Paris, Bibliothèque Historique.)

traces of which survive only in minor details. The building is an impressive masterpiece of austere understatement. Perret had chosen to renounce austerity in the building he designed on the rue Franklin, a building covered with ceramic ornament—but the two structures were also distinguished by all that divides the 16th from the 18th arrondissement.

Sauvage continued to design working-class housing in the same spirit. It culminated in the construction of the cathedral of affordable housing, a 1922 apartment building located on the rue des Amiraux in the 18th arrondissement. No one could speak any longer of "cut-rate architecture," least of all the "Messieurs Frères" of the Ecole, so sensitive to Beauty in all its manifestations.

The Haute Banque *Enters the Scene*

In January 1905 the Rothschild Foundation announced a "competition for the construction of a group of buildings offering small, healthy, and economical housing" on a triangular plot of land, measuring approximately 61,000 square feet, in the 12th arrondissement.[135] The site, not far from the Gare de Lyon, was bounded by the rue de Prague, the rue Charles-Baudelaire, and the rue Théophile-Roussel. The commission was deliberately imprecise: the buildings were to comprise several stories, to offer common amenities, and to return 3–4 percent on the investment. No promise was made that the winning plans would actually be used, but construction was to take place in two phases. On March 31, 1905, 127 anonymous contestants submitted their designs to the Hôtel de Ville, where they were to be shown in one of the reception halls. The jury included six architects and six members of the Foundation, including Cheysson, Picot, and Siegfried.

The entries were winnowed down first to twenty-five and then to seven. The grand prize, 10,000 francs, went to an outsider, Adolphe-Augustin Rey, for his design entitled "Tout pour le peuple." Second prize, 9,000 francs, went to Henry Provensal for "Utile dulci." Both were graduates of the Ecole des Beaux-Arts and government-licensed. Provensal, moreover, was a close friend of Sauvage. Anatole de Baudot, the architect of Saint-Jean in Montmartre, had been eliminated in the first round. Tony Garnier, well known for the plans of a Cité Industrielle submitted all the way from Rome, made it to the second round with a design that was the fulfillment of the hygienists' dreams. It resembled a sanatorium: there were no courtyards or air shafts; the buildings followed a zigzag pattern in order to maximize natural lighting; all the apartments were vast and equipped with bathrooms, a luxury still not found in many bourgeois apartments.

All the contestants in the second round honored the principle of the open courtyard. Rey distinguished himself by the thoroughness of his design. The ventilation system was laid out like a vertical street map. Kitchens were extraordinarily sophisticated; each was equipped with a rubbish chute, a linen closet, cabinets, a shower stall, and a pantry that admitted outside air through a filtered vent. There were joint amenities such as showers and baths, a washroom, a drying room, a bicycle shed, a hygienic restaurant, a meeting hall, rooms for single men and women, and a terrace for taking the sun. More than Sauvage had done on the rue de Trétaigne but in a similar spirit, Rey chose concrete, at that time disdained by "serious" architects, as his primary building material, but he added various fanciful decorations in the taste of the time, including projecting roofs and canopies.

None of the projects avoided issues about which hygienists had been debating for nearly thirty years: apartments large enough to accommodate families, separate rooms, rationalization of needs. The competitors were clearly less comfortable about dealing with collective amenities. Should they offer workers all desirable services at the risk of undermining their sacrosanct individual initiative? People asked, for instance, if nurseries would encourage mothers to abandon their children. Right-wing social reformers had been arguing about such questions since the beginning of the nineteenth century.

The Rothschild competition aroused the interest of the entire architectural profession, and favorable articles appeared in the press. One point stirred up considerable hostility, however. The Foundation had announced its intention to set up an agency of salaried architects, a move that leaders of various professional organizations saw as an attack on the status of architecture as an independent profession. But the Foundation took no notice of the complaints. The agency in fact functioned as a team. A marble plaque bearing the names of all employees involved in the construction, including the building inspector, was placed at the entrance of each of the Foundation's buildings.

The first groundbreaking was at 1, rue de Marché-Popincourt (11th arrondissement), where a building of 76 apartments was inaugurated in 1907. In 1908 a building of 102 apartments was constructed at 117, rue de Belleville (19th

Gaston Le Fol, *Grandes constructions à loyer économique*. This building at 10, rue de Prague, was designed in 1909 by H. Provensal and associates. Nothing sets it apart from bourgeois buildings of the same period. It is constructed of quality materials and features a monumental entry, a stone balcony, and—the one unusual note—sculptured motifs in praise of labor. (Paris, Bibliothèque Historique.)

arrondissement). In 1909, a building of 321 apartments went up at 10, rue de Prague (12th arrondissement). In 1912 a building of 206 apartments opened at 11, rue Bargue (15th arrondissement). And in 1913–1919 a building of 420 apartments went up at 256, rue Marcadet (18th arrondissement).

Of this impressive array of prize-winning testimonials to individual initiative, the building on the rue de Prague (the lot for which the contest entries had been designed) quickly became famous. It came to be known as the "Louvre of Affordable Housing" because its collective amenities (some of which can also be found in the Familistère at Guise) reflected the desires of even the most advanced utopians: a washroom with improved machines, including a hot-air dryer; showers and baths; a dispensary equipped for preventive medicine; a nursery for children from ages three to six; day care for children after school and all day Thursday; classes in home economics; and a kitchen that offered two hot meals daily and that was intended to promote a healthy, rational diet.

In this case an initiative taken by individuals thoroughly familiar with the problem and blessed with considerable financial backing proved quite influential. The two prizewinners

Gaston Le Fol, *Grandes constructions à loyer économique.* The rue de Prague building featured a model day-care center designed to conform with contemporary health norms, with such amenities as large windows and white tile, just like the Metro. The bentwood chairs came from the celebrated Austrian factory of the Thonet brothers. (Paris, Bibliothèque Historique.)

discovered themselves through the competition. Rey, winner of the grand prize, became a missionary on behalf of affordable housing. He attended countless conferences and published books and brochures in which he went so far as to advocate municipal purchase of land for low-cost housing. In 1907 he replaced Trélat on the Conseil Supérieur des Habitations à Bon Marché, where he was joined in 1912 by Schneider, secretary-general of the Rothschild Foundation, and Hatton, representing the Lebaudy Foundation—the elite of private initiative in the area of housing.

The City of Paris Competition

　　In August 1912 the city of Paris organized its first prize competition for the design of affordable housing. The contest, directly inspired by that of 1904, proved just as successful with press and public.[136] Plans were submitted for 111 projects, 58 for a plot of land on avenue Emile-Zola (15th arrondissement) and 53 for a plot on rue Henri-Becque (13th arrondissement). For the former location the commission called for a multistory apartment building that would include five types of apartments, ranging from a four-room apartment with kitchen-dining room (minimum 592 square feet) to a studio with kitchenette for bachelors (minimum 193 square feet).

　　The commission for the rue Henri-Becque aimed at something considerably below this level, an indication of the contempt in which the poor were held. The people for whom this building was intended were not considered to have any intrinsic right to space or amenities, although the organizers were careful to warn candidates that their buildings must not suggest "the idea of a barracks, a company project, or an old folks' home." At a minimum, each apartment was to include one common room and another room with a low, moveable partition; the living area was to measure at least 322 square feet. It would be interesting to know what "authority" indicated to the architects that they were under no obligation to incorporate a privy or cold-water tap in each apartment.

　　Maurice Payret-Dortail won the first prize, 15,000 francs, for a building of 143 apartments designed for the lot on the avenue Emile-Zola and similar to the Rothschild building on the rue de Belleville. At either end of the structure two service courtyards offered access to vehicles, and in the center was a square. Georges Albenque and Eugéne Gonnot were awarded prizes for their designs for the lot on rue Henri-Becque. Were they rewarded because of the concern they showed for saving money on construction costs? Going against the admonitions of all the hygienists, they provided only one privy for every two apartments—and in a few cases one privy served three apartments. The prizes launched all three architects on careers in low-cost housing. After World War I they joined Henri Sellier in the Office Public d'HBM (Public Office of Affordable Housing) of Paris and the Seine. Sellier, who headed the Office, was also the promoter of the "pink belt" of boulevards des Maréchaux, which replaced the old fortifications erected by Thiers.

Some months after this meritorious effort by the city of Paris, Henri Chéron, minister of labor and social insurance, attended ceremonies marking the completion of a housing project of great interest to the Radical government and the new society it was seeking to create. The Family Housing Corporation had just put up forty cottages arranged around a central garden at 4, rue Daviel (13th arrondissement). Intended for large families (with six or more children), each cottage contained three bedrooms of 215 square feet; such spacious accommodations had never before been offered to proletarians, and these cottages were available for rent.

The thirty-year-old architect responsible for this project hailed from Montbéliard, a remote region where conditions were harsh. The son of a Protestant industrialist born in Alsace, Jean Walter, later known the world over as Walter de Zellidja, had already established a solid reputation in eastern France. He had managed to build houses at prices that his colleagues considered impossible: a three-room house with kitchen, cellar, and attic for 2,400 francs in Montbéliard, for example. Nor did his colleagues understand his ideas about mass-producing certain house components or rationalizing the construction site.

Walter's ideas pointed toward the only possible solution of the problem of how to build single-family homes cheaply enough to rent to those whose low wages excluded them from ownership. In this period many courageous investigators set out to find low-cost mass-construction technologies. A 1913 issue of *L'Immeuble et la Construction dans l'Est* (Real Estate and Construction in the East) put it this way: "Housing for large families should be turned out by new industrial methods for

Toward the "Residential Machine"

the production of house components: frames of wood, iron, composites, or reinforced concrete, fitted panels, and so on; joists, studs, and stringers in standard dimensions; standard doors and window sashes; and standard hardware, plumbing, and equipment. The use of standard, easy-to-install materials and objects should result in noticeable savings, while allowing some diversity in external appearance, a diversity that should be easy for our architects to achieve."[137] Such practical observations quite obviously had no chance of coming to the attention of the high priests of the beautiful and thus of finding their way into the curriculum of the Ecole des Beaux-Arts, where all eyes remained focused on the lines of the imperial forums.

The government, however, took an active interest in such trivial problems. That very same year, 1913, it was announced in trade journals that the ministry of labor would issue medals in 1915 to those architects and builders who developed the best methods, materials, and techniques suitable for use in low-income housing.

If the edifying award ceremony had taken place as planned, the top prize surely would have gone to a veteran architect. Born in 1853, Georges Christie, vice-president of the Société Nationale des Architectes de France just before the war and an editor of several architectural journals, deserves a place in the history of the "residential machine" concept. He coined the notion of *villa domino* before Le Corbusier, who never gave him credit for it. The so-called domino house was a one-story, single-family dwelling with four rooms, built in groups of four according to a strictly defined plan. Christie wrote: "The problem of affordable housing can be solved only through discovery of economical methods of construction using standardized, catalogued materials in what I call industrialized methods of home building."[138]

This statement deserves a place alongside those found in the anthologies of the modern movement, along with photographs of the complex of sixty four-room apartments built for the Groupe des Maisons Ouvrières on the rue de la Säida (15th arrondissement), where Labussière successfully employed Hennebique's reinforced concrete. Built just before the war, this relatively plain building, which was a harbinger of things to come, was in a sense the swan song of the private foundations.

A law passed in 1912 finally began to produce results. In

May 1914 the Office Public d'HBM de Paris et de la Seine was set up to investigate the problem of low-income housing and to administer buildings that were to be constructed with funds raised through a 200-million-franc bond issue. The public sector did not turn its back on the skills developed in the private sector. Schneider of the Rothschild Foundation and Labussière of the Lebaudy Foundation became directors of the Office, which was set up as a collegial agency like the architectural office of the Rothschild Foundation. Provensal and Besnard, winners of the 1905 competition also served, as did Maistrasse, the future architect of the garden apartments at Suresnes.

Make no mistake, however. A glance at "Public Architectural Competitions" might suggest an outpouring of socially beneficial projects, but professionals knew full well the realities of the market. All observers agree that the construction industry in the twentieth century turned primarily toward luxury building.[139]

In the years just before World War I the cost of living increased, and rents were not exempt from the general rise in

This apartment complex on the rue de la Säida was reserved for families earning no more than 6 francs per day. Adjoining it was a public bathhouse, open daily, and a wing reserved for the elderly, married or widowed.

The banner on this building reads: "Respectful of the law, which the police have violated on behalf of the landlord, I will not leave unless compelled by force." (Sirot-Angel Collection.)

prices. Higher rents triggered reactions in the working class, reactions that various parties attempted to orchestrate. On January 6, 1910, the Union Syndicale des Locataires Ouvriers (Union of Worker Tenants) was founded at the Clichy Labor Exchange, thanks to the efforts of a man named Constant, a member of the local labor relations board and a worker in the carriage trade.[140] Anarchist violence was a thing of the past, Bonnot and his group having degenerated from political action to petty crime. Soon the tenants' union had sections in nearly all the arrondissements of Paris, and more than twenty suburban communes published a program that the left-wing political parties would ultimately be obliged to support. It called for a prohibition against the seizure of workers' furniture; elimination of annual gifts to the concierge as well as of the so-called *denier de Dieu* (God's penny), a sort of "key fee" paid to the concierge when a new tenant moved in; fixed rental payment periods; rent control; and cleanup of unhealthy buildings at the landlord's expense.

Georges Cochon and "The Tenants' Polka"

Early in 1911 Georges Cochon, a Paris worker and a colorful political activist, became secretary general of the tenants' union. Cochon was a man with a unique sense of humor and an aptitude for publicity unrivaled in the French workers' movement of his day. In 1913, after he had been expelled from the original Union Syndicale and founded a National and International Tenants' Federation, he staged a series of spectacular demonstrations in Paris and the provinces.[141]

The good old days of the Anti-Landlords League, celebrated in the 1890s for its "midnight mover" tactics to avoid payment of back rent, seemed to have returned. A spate of popular songs exalted Cochon as the Robin Hood of Paris; *La Cochonette* (The Piglet, a pun on Cochon's last name, which was obviously a boon to songwriters) and *The Tenants' Polka* were hummed in all working-class neighborhoods. Witnesses to Cochon's operations would take up the refrain:

> There goes the Pig, moving out,
> Moving out, moving out,
> There goes the Pig moving out
> By the light of the moon.

Or

> Mr. Poincaré
> Is president of the Republic
> And Mr. Pig
> Is president of the Flat-Pockets.

Or

> It's Pig, it's Pig,
> For landlords he cares not a fig.
> Pig helps a comrade move,
> Pig is the proletarian's friend,
> Pig thumbs his nose at the government.

In July 1913 Cochon pulled off one of his most stunning exploits. Antoine de La Rochefoucauld, who was moving out of a *hôtel particulier* at 17, boulevard Lannes, with eighteen months still to run on the lease, turned the premises over to Cochon, who immediately installed eight families with a total of thirty-five children on the premises. To a wall of this fortress Chabrol attached the sign, designed by Steinlen, of Cochon's Tenants' Federation.

Housing issues also attracted the attention of better behaved and less demanding personalities whom the authorities could not ignore: the champions of the French family. In 1896

Toy of wood and cardboard, 1900. With Georges Cochon the always humorous saga of anarchist antilandlord agitation came to an end. It was followed by more "serious" forms of political action, whose effectiveness still remains to be demonstrated. (Laduz, Musée Rural des Arts Populaires.)

Dr. Jacques Bertillon founded the National Alliance for the Increase of the French Population, a most respectable group whose members included Cheysson.[142] This group modestly limited its demands to a call for reform of the personal property tax. Large families—of the middle classes—were forced to live in larger apartments and were taxed more heavily than smaller families. Payment of a high personal property tax was not evidence of wealth. No frontal assault on property was to be expected from Bertillon and his friends of course, but the Ligue Populaire des Pères et Mères de Familles Nombreuses, founded in 1908 by Captain Maire, the father of ten children, was more vociferous; some of its members even took part in left-wing demonstrations against landlords.[143]

The mass media devoted considerable attention, much of it favorable, to Cochon's exploits, for the journalists themselves had been outraged by the scandal of the homeless. In 1912 *Le Matin,* with a circulation of 600,000 one of France's four largest daily papers—a paper that backed Briand and specialized in nationalist causes—organized a committee for affordable housing, whose members included two illustrious winners of the Prix de Rome: Nénot, architectural adviser to the Rothschild Foundation and Bernier, architect of the Opéra-Comique. No project ever got off the ground, however. The construction industry did not mobilize to build housing for the masses. Yet on August 2, 1914, those masses marched anyway under the banner of the Union Sacrée, proudly brandished by those who had been antimilitarists the day before, even though they had little to defend.[144]

Etienne Azambre, *Summertime*. (Salon of 1902.)

4

Backstage

Alain Corbin

Brévannes, *The Renaissance Portico*. (R. Debuisson Collection.)

Introduction

by Michelle Perrot

THE Declaration of the Rights of Man, Louis Dumont tells us, marked the triumph of the individual.[1] Yet the category "individual" remained vague and abstract in the nineteenth century. It was a long time before citizens attained their full powers. When finally established in 1848, universal suffrage meant universal male suffrage. Secret balloting was not guaranteed until 1913, when the law finally prescribed the use of the voting booth and of envelopes for ballots.

Individuals lacked legal guarantees. The Constituent Assembly would have liked to have gone further toward the establishment of individual rights, but it succumbed to "circumstances," or, at a more profound level, to a deep-seated Jacobinism, which resisted the introduction of a true principle of habeas corpus, a principle that is still lacking in French law. Yet concern for individual rights did exist. In 1792 the home was declared inviolable, and nocturnal searches were prohibited in 1795. Home and the hours of darkness: these defined the spatial and temporal limits of privacy around the individual, whose dignity and liberty were recognized. (One sign of the increased dignity of the individual was the abolition of most degrading forms of punishment.) Homosexuality, for instance, ceased to be a crime unless it manifested itself in the form of a public offense against decency.

Nineteenth-century jurists were not sure just how far to go in asserting individual rights against the rights of the family and the authorities. The right of privacy in correspondence was not recognized until quite late; it was not until the Third Republic that the authorities ceased opening mail sent through the public post. Men, however, retained the right to examine letters written by their wives, and boarding school and prison authorities had no compunctions about opening letters written by pupils and inmates.

The development of the modern media raised new problems. Armand Carrel fought a duel with Emile de Girardin when the latter "threatened to publish a biography" of Carrel in his newspaper, *La*

Presse. Carrel was killed, thus paying with his life for his right to privacy. The press was avid for miscellany concerning private scandals. In the face of such attacks, people felt a need to hide, to use pseudonyms and deception. The nineteenth century was like a masked ball. Stendhal wrote: "The disadvantage of the reign of opinion, which in one sense procures liberty, is that opinion sticks its nose where it has no business, into private life."[2]

The "will to know"—a constant concern in this century of curiosity, which always kept an eye or ear pressed to the keyhole—gave rise to countless investigations of all sorts of individuals and groups. Protection for the individual therefore became a pressing need. At the beginning of the century a significant controversy took place at Charenton. The hospital's chief physician, Royer-Collard, wanted to establish a complete medical and social history for each patient, but the director objected to what he regarded as a modern version of the religious inquisition.[3] In this controversy we see the ambiguity of a modernity in which the power of science moved forward at the same pace as concern for the self.

In both ideas and mores the individual advanced nearly everywhere, though to a degree that varied with milieu and locale. The law lagged behind the reality. More and more people rebelled against communal and family discipline and declared that they needed more time and space of their own. Individuals wanted to sleep alone, to be allowed to read books and newspapers in peace and quiet, to dress as they pleased, to come and go as they wished, to eat or drink whatever they liked, and to see and love whomever they chose. In other words, they believed in their right to pursue happiness as they saw fit. Democracy bestowed legitimacy on that right, the market stimulated it, and migration encouraged it. That new frontier, the city, weakened family and community constraints, spurred ambitions, and attenuated beliefs. Creator of liberty and dispenser of new pleasures, the city, though often a cruel stepmother, fascinated people despite the diatribes of the moralists. Paradoxically, cities engendered both crowds and loneliness. They generated activity and change.

The dandy, the artist, the intellectual, the vagabond, and the eccentric rebelled against the conformism of the masses. Yet beyond this minority of symbolic rebels, other, larger groups insistently laid claim to the right to exist: adolescents, women, proletarians. Adolescents challenged the patriarchal system first and foremost; let us hope that their cries and murmurs are present on every page of this book. Proletarians criticized chiefly the bourgeois order. Nevertheless, the strength of class consciousness, which was particularly powerful in this period, did not preclude an explosion of working-class desires or limit the variety of working-class projects. In 1890 female workers in Vienne told their employers: "We are flesh and blood, just like you." Libertarian unions adopted neo-Malthusian views regarding birth control: "Large families engender misery and slavery. Have few children." And CGT handbills exhorted women to "learn to be mothers only when you choose to be." Individualist anarchism achieved the apogee of its influence at the turn of the twentieth century.[4] Physical freedom, a taste for nature and sports, and free love all figured in the creation of so-called *milieux libres,* free milieus, whose bold innovations came into conflict with more conventional attitudes.

Although the legal rights of individuals may have been weak, the self gained new depth and complexity. The Enlightenment had conceived the idea of man in general, that tranquil creature of reason. Romanticism countered with distinctive individual features, the mystery of dream-filled nights, and the fluidity of intimate communication; it rehabilitated intuition as a mode of knowledge.[5] Inner space became an object for the self to contemplate: "For myself I am the fixed expanse within which my sun and my stars revolve," wrote Amiel. It also became the center of the world, the medium through which the world revealed its meaning: "It is within oneself that one must look at what lies outside," wrote Victor Hugo. Consciousness was relegated to a secondary role compared with that of the unconscious that governs men and reveals the key to their behavior. Even societies succumb to the power of images.

Late-nineteenth-century discoveries in neurobiology established the scientific basis of what Marcel Gauchet has called the "pure individual." Neopositivist and materialist, French medicine hesitated to embrace German somaticism; the French clung to the crumbling boundary between body and soul. Was this tenacity the source of later resistance to psychoanalysis? Or did that resistance stem from reluctance to see the sexual dynamics of the family as the cause of hysteria, neurosis, and, more generally, the structure of the personality?[6] Or did resistance to psychoanalysis develop because family structures in France were more diverse than in Freud's Vienna and the father figure was relatively weak?[7] In any event, France seems to constitute a special case in the history of Western individualism.

At a time when mass movements were gaining in importance, the individual took hold as a political, scientific, and above all, existential value. Alain Corbin invites us to examine this extraordinary discovery of the self and the way in which it changed the relation between self and others. The real drama took place in the wings of history, and we now turn our attention to that behind-the-scenes action.

Disdéri, *Grouped Visiting Cards*. Disdéri's imperious visiting cards seemed to demand a place in the family album. The techniques of posing, here quite sophisticated, became part of the strategy of self-presentation. (Paris, Bibliothèque Nationale.)

ᚼ The Secret
of the Individual

THE sense of individual identity became more distinct and spread more widely throughout the nineteenth century. One sign of this change is the history of the system by which individuals were named. Already in the eighteenth century the variety of first names had increased. This trend continued in the nineteenth century, contravening the efforts of the Catholic Church, which had sought to limit the range of given names in order to emphasize the exemplary qualities of the greatest saints. The Revolution marked no major discontinuity; at most it served to speed up a process that was already under way.

A Name of One's Own

As the decades passed, new first names were introduced at an accelerating rate that reflected an increased need for individuation, a wish to differentiate between generations, and a desire to conform to new norms set by the dominant class. Indeed, the vogue for certain first names spread vertically, from the aristocracy down to the people and from the city to the countryside. This vulgarization was hastened by the increasingly clear, if complex, structure of the social hierarchy.

At the same time, the rules governing transmission of names within families ceased to be obeyed. Children had traditionally been named after one of their godparents, which in practice usually meant after a grandparent, great-uncle, or great-aunt; an eldest son usually received the first name of his father or deceased grandfather. We must be careful not to exaggerate the decline of obedience to these rules, which had always been greater in rural areas than in the cities; nevertheless, emerging fashions did diminish the influence of the old rules. The decline of rules for naming children reflects a loss of faith in the power of a name to confer hereditary virtues and thus to determine an individual's fate. That loss of faith in turn tended to favor the development of individualism.

Where complex family structures persisted and a shortage of available names created the possibility of confusion, the naming system sometimes remained quite archaic. This occurred in certain parts of central and southern France, particularly in Gévaudan, where an individual's given name was soon forgotten and replaced in common parlance by a nickname. The patronymic was associated with the *oustal* or *maysou,* and a man who moved in with his wife's parents shed his own last name and took up hers. Nevertheless, it became more and more common, even in rural areas, for people to use their baptismal names and the family names recorded on their birth certificates. The use of nicknames was increasingly limited to marginal groups such as artists, bohemians, prostitutes, and criminals—all groups which, like *compagnons,* or journeymen (who joined organizations known as *compagnonnages*), deliberately defined themselves in terms of archaic values and types of behavior.

The desire for individuation was not the only explanation for the ongoing process of diversification of course. Urbanization increased the risk of mistaking one person for another with the same name. Advances in literacy and education created a new bond between an individual and his or her given and family names. The student's briefcase, drinking cup, and notebook, the adolescent girl's stamp and trousseau of embroidered linen, the initials sewn into the boarding school pupil's clothing—these and other practices accentuated the importance of first and last names. This new awareness of names can be measured by the increase in the number of brides and grooms able to sign their marriage certificates. During the Restoration people began leaving their initials on rocks and trees in the forest of Fontainebleau. These marks were made by humble people. Aware that, unlike the great of this earth, they would leave no trace, they counted on the ability of initials engraved in bark or stone to survive after they had gone.

During the second half of the century the mail contributed to the proliferation of symbols of the self and signs of individual possession. By 1900 some eight million postcards were being sent annually. Similar signs of change can be seen in the common use of visiting cards and personal calendars. Even

In Front of the Mirror, 1890. This fin-de-siècle artist, like his audience fascinated and disturbed by thoughts of woman's intimate sentiments, revels in the notion of lips offered twice over. (Paris, Bibliothèque des Arts Décoratifs.)

house pets gradually acquired names. As early as the July Monarchy, Eugénie de Guérin chose elegant names for her beloved dogs.

The Mirror and Physical Identity

Little by little contemplation of one's own image ceased to be a privilege. Unfortunately no comprehensive study exists of the spread and various uses of the mirror. But many signs point to the fundamental historical importance of self-regard. In nineteenth-century villages the barber was the only person who possessed a full-length mirror, whose use was limited to men. Hawkers sold small mirrors that women and girls could use to examine their faces, but full-length mirrors were all but unknown in the countryside, where peasants still discovered their physical identities through the eyes of others and relied on intuition to control their facial expressions. Véronique Nahoum wonders how people could "live in bodies they had not seen" in intimate detail.[1] That question should be put to historians of rural society. It is not hard to understand the taboos on the use of mirrors that existed in rural communities, where people believed that a child's growth could be stunted if it saw its face in a mirror and that leaving a mirror uncovered on the day after a death was an invitation to misfortune.

Among the well-to-do it was long considered improper for young women to look at themselves naked, even in the reflecting surface of the bathtub. Special powders clouded the bath water and precluded inappropriate glimpses. Such taboos increased the power of the human body to stir erotic feelings. Images of the body became an obsession; in deluxe bordellos mirrors were everywhere, and later they turned up on the doors of armoires intended for the bedrooms of the elite.

The Democratization of the Portrait

The most important factor in the development of individual self-awareness was the spread of the portrait, which, Gisèle Freund notes, was a "direct consequence of the efforts of individuals to assert their individuality and gain insight into their personalities."[2] Acquiring and displaying a portrait of oneself was a way of warding off anxieties about death, because the portrait ensured that some trace of one's existence would survive. The carefully composed portrait provided evidence of worldly success; it made a person's social position palpably manifest. For the bourgeois who saw himself, like the aristocrat of another era, in the heroic role of founder of a dynasty, the problem was not how to establish his place in an unbroken chain of generations but rather how to translate personal success into family prestige. An age of commemoration, the nineteenth century witnessed the founding of many a proud commercial lineage. The desire to imitate aristocratic behavior, to equal the great men of the past, naturally influenced fashions in portrait art. Finally, we must bear in mind the stimulus of technology, which heightened the desire for images of the self that had become both a commodity and an instrument of power.

The portrait, once the exclusive possession of the aristocracy and the wealthy bourgeoisie, by the late eighteenth century had spread to other segments of society; at the same time it took on a more intimate character. The miniature triumphed; lockets, medallions, and powder boxes all were adorned with images of the beloved. Barbey d'Aurevilly points out the enthusiasm of the Restoration elite for the

The postcard and the photographic portrait made it possible to distribute images of oneself without offending modesty. The aristocratic medallion of the early 19th century ended its long social descent in this ersatz form.

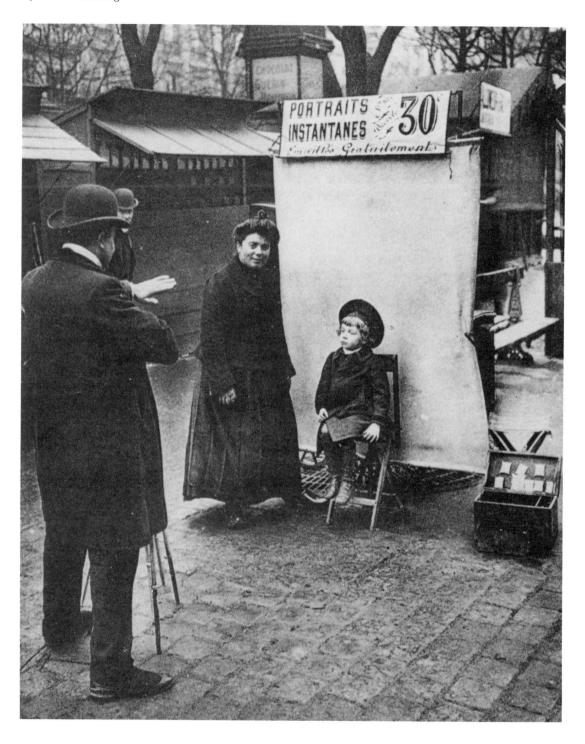

bejeweled portrait. Fashionable ladies from the boulevard Saint-Germain turned their bodies into ancestral portrait galleries in a symbolic denial of Revolution.

From 1786 to 1830 Gilles-Louis Chrétien's *physionotrace* helped to popularize portrait art, at least in Paris. Using this device an artist could in one minute trace the contours of a model's face. This profile could then be transferred to a metal plate to yield a series of accurate engraved images at relatively low cost. If desired, the portrait could be executed on wood or ivory, or English-style silhouettes could be produced by adding a hairpiece and clothing to the outline. Unfortunately, the resulting profiles, though often remarkably good likenesses, remained lifeless and expressionless. The daguerreotype, which overcame this drawback, thus met an ever more urgent social need. In 1839 L. J. M. Daguerre filed for a patent on a process that allowed him, after an exposure of fifteen minutes, to fix on a metal plate a portrait which he then sold for 50 to 100 francs. Although the daguerreotype produced clear, precise images, it did not allow for easy reproduction.

Democratization of the portrait did not really become possible until the invention of photography. Now for the first time the common man could own and distribute multiple images of himself. The photographic process, first patented in 1841, benefited from a number of technological improvements over the next ten years. Exposure times gradually decreased, until in 1851 the instantaneous snapshot was perfected. In 1854 Disdéri developed the visiting card format (6 cm x 9 cm). Photography greatly broadened the market opened up by daguerreotype. By 1862 Disdéri alone was selling 2,400 postcards daily. Now that it took only a few seconds to make a snapshot, a group of twelve portraits could be purchased for just 20 francs. Photographers set up shop in even the smallest towns. Itinerant photographers working in curbside stalls sold snapshots at 1 franc apiece.

The ability to portray the self and the possession of self-images enhanced the individual's sense of his own importance and democratized the need to stake out a social position. Well aware of this need, photographers turned their studios into theaters equipped with accessories such as columns, curtains, and pedestals and began to take full-length photographs of individuals in bombastic, grandiloquent poses. After 1861 (and the inauguration of the Second Empire of Napoleon III) some photographers even encouraged equestrian portraits. This theatrical treatment of attitudes, gestures, and facial expressions—

Photographs recorded the intensification of family feeling within the nuclear family. Beginning in the 1860s, the young child became the center of attention and the hero of a prolix normative literature. (Sirot-Angel Collection.)

Toward the end of the 19th century Europe was suddenly inundated by millions of postcards. They tightened bonds among relatives and friends and made it easy to expand one's circle of correspondents. They were also collected in souvenir albums. The cards' stereotypical formulas made writing painless and enabled even those who had difficulty expressing themselves in writing to make their feelings known.

Disdéri and his disciples knew how to exalt the maternal role. Here the photographer has arranged the children in the form of a pyramid, which emphasizes the volume of the mother's crinoline. (Sirot-Angel Collection.)

in a word, the pose—gradually became a part of daily life, a change of historical importance, as Jean-Paul Sartre noted. The millions of photographic portraits shot and religiously preserved in albums established new norms that completely transformed the private scene. They taught people to look at the body, and in particular the hands, in a new way. The photographic portrait helped to establish the physical disciplines taught in the schools, while at the same time it gave rise to a new perceptual code. From now on grandfathers learned how to behave from photographs, and thinkers learned the poses that connoted reflective activity in the same way.

The photoportrait was governed by the same rules as official painting: the idealization of appearances and the repudiation of ugliness. Crowds at the 1855 Exposition were fascinated to discover the technique of retouching, which became commonplace after 1860. Facial features were softened. Embarrassing freckles, wrinkles, and pimples disappeared from faces left smooth and wreathed in a vaguely artistic aura. Even in the countryside a new ideal of beauty challenged traditional norms.

Family photo albums illustrated the kinship structure and strengthened group ties threatened by economic development. The portrait's intrusion into new segments of society modified the way in which people conceived of life's stages as well as their sense of time. A photograph, Susan Sontag observes, is a *memento mori*.[3] Photos made it easier for people to imagine their own deaths, and anticipation of impending old age led them to reconsider the treatment of the elderly.

An aid to memory, photographs changed the nature of nostalgia. For the first time a majority of people were able to look at images of dead ancestors and unknown relatives. It became possible to see the youth of people with whom one rubbed elbows daily. The hallmarks of family memory also changed. Symbolic possession of images of loved ones channeled the emotions. Visual contact became more important than physical contact. The psychological consequences of absence changed. Photographs of the dead attenuated the anguish of loss and alleviated remorse.

Finally, the new technology multiplied images of nudity, now easier to behold than ever before. The nature of erotic stimuli changed—witness the vogue for the "1900 nude." Lawmakers were quick to notice these changes. As early as

A photograph in the family album was a way of cementing family relations. Long after brothers and sisters had gone their separate ways, the yellowing photo would reawaken warm feelings. (Sirot-Angel Collection.)

1850 a law was passed prohibiting the sale of obscene photos on public streets. After 1880 amateur photographers were able to cut out the professional middleman. Thereafter poses became less elaborate, and all of private life was laid open to the lens, whose appetite for intimate scenes was unlimited.

The Perennial Souvenir

The same wish to perpetuate oneself, to record some trace of one's existence, also manifested itself in the cemetery. Philippe Ariès has traced the triumph of individual burial and the emergence of a new cult of the dead in the early nineteenth century.[4] Here I am interested exclusively in the individual epitaph, something totally new for the vast majority of the population. The way in which this new funerary rhetoric spread is just now becoming clear. During the limited-suffrage monarchy it became increasingly common to find epitaphs praising the merits of deceased males as husbands, fathers, and citizens. The burgeoning importance of privacy was recorded on the very tombstone. Later as cemeteries grew and tombstones began to be mass-produced, standard formulas replaced individualized epitaphs, but in compensation small locket-sized photographs were embedded into the stone.

The pace of these changes varied from place to place, and there was occasional resistance. In the cemetery of Asnières, an obscure village in Ain, the first epitaph did not appear until 1847. In 1856 the widow of a minor notable who had been held in rather low esteem by his fellow citizens had a balustrade erected around her late husband's tomb. Her action aroused considerable hostility. The curé himself was incensed that the memory of this less-than-perfect Christian would be preserved by marble, when he had no idea of the precise spot where the remains of his pious churchwarden lay buried. In small rural parishes tombstones and epitaphs were long perceived as offenses against equality. In 1840 Eugénie de Guérin was obliged to mount a guard around the white column at the center of the Andillac Cemetery which celebrated the memory of her brother Maurice. In small parishes funerary rhetoric also allowed a postmortem rise in status. After death a shopkeeper could strike any pose he pleased. Yet the new durability of reputation encouraged and even magnified disparaging rumors.

A central thread links all these ways of strengthening the sense of self: the temptation of self-glorification, the hypertro-

phy of reassuring vanity. Many other signs of this temptation, which may have been associated with the rise of meritocracy, can be found in this period: the importance attached to the honor roll and school prizes, the custom of hanging diplomas on the wall of the salon or common room, and, even more, the prestige of decorations and the hagiographic tone of obituaries. For many humble people it was quite a new sensation to read their own name in the newspaper. Anyone could now strike the pose of the hero, if only at home within the family circle, which these new ambitions changed in many ways. Even criminal acts could reflect heroic aspirations. Inspired by the neo-Plutarchian memoirs of any number of latter-day dynasts, the young parricide of Aunay-sur-Odon proudly began his own startling memoirs with the words: "I, Pierre Rivière, having slit the throats of my mother, my sister, and my brother . . ."

Stereotyped epitaphs replaced earlier, individualized ones, but photographs on tombstones ensured that a person's appearance would be remembered. This practice is one of the most significant indications of a new desire to perpetuate a trace of one's existence.

The Limits of Social Control

For the authorities, the ability to identify individuals took on new importance as anonymity took the place of personal acquaintance. An increasingly dense and silent crowd filled streets now shorn of their former theatricality. The crowd moved as an aggregate of individuals, each absorbed in private thoughts and obsessed with private interests. Sophisticated identification procedures became an important instrument of social control.

Before the triumph of the Third Republic in 1876–1879, identification techniques were quite rudimentary. Technical deficiencies limited the alleged panoptic ambitions of those in power, ambitions that have probably been exaggerated. Essentially the system was based on records of vital statistics (once kept by the Church, but secularized in 1792 and codified on 28 Pluviôse, Year III); census lists drawn up every five years; and electoral lists (based on a limited suffrage until extended to the whole male population in March 1848 and again in December 1851). Certain classes of people were subject to special procedures. Workers, for example, theoretically had been required since the Consulate to submit a *livret*, or work record, to their employers; a law of 22 June 1854, passed over the strenuous objection of employers, permitted individual workers to retain possession of their records. Soldiers were subject to special requirements. Servants were required to present certificates issued by previous employers. Prostitutes were required to register with the Prefecture of Police or the municipal administration. Foundlings were assigned a birth certificate and an identification necklace. And travelers, particularly itinerants and nomads, were required to obtain passports before setting out.

Study of migrant workers in Limousin and of travelers in the Indre département shows that in this realm, as in many others, minute regulations coexisted in practice with lax enforcement, not to say total anarchy. Personal knowledge and visual memory continued to determine relations between migrants and the authorities. Nevertheless, progress in literacy, coupled with ever-increasing administrative requirements, encouraged people to obtain, decipher, and make use of "papers." This kind of knowledge was new and, coupled with the growing prevalence of contracts in rural society, made it increasingly rare, and before long improbable, that one would ever encounter a person who did not know his age—like the peasant who misstated his age by seven years, causing Eugénie de Guérin to say, "Happy man, ignorant of his life." Henceforth every person knew how to reckon his or her years. Consequently, the future became, if not predictable, at least calculable. As people became aware of personal time scales, they also began to elaborate personal histories, a prerequisite of self-identification and self-presentation.

When it became necessary to gather detailed information about another person, the most common procedure was still the investigation of morality or at least the request for a certificate of *bonne vie et moeurs* (honesty and decency). The mayor and curé were called in whenever it was necessary to judge a suitor, a candidate for employment, or a prospective servant. These officials were required to give information and opinions concerning citizens of their towns or parishioners of their parishes. Oddly enough, this practice, which in effect institutionalized rumor and led to revelations about private lives, seems to have been fairly well tolerated. The correspondence of Marthe's parents, though of fairly late date, enables us to see how these procedures worked. When it became necessary to choose, or rather to procure, a spouse for this errant young lady, a whole squadron of informers was called into action: confessors and curés acted as marriage brokers; provincial relations acted as intelligence operatives; lawyers and notaries were employed to question their colleagues; bureaucrats were questioned about the virtues of their subordinates, and servants were sent out to gather rumors. Only doctors appear to have been left out, perhaps because discretion was already required of members of the medical profession. A subtle mix of information, advice, pressure, and even blackmail worked its way into the fabric of this cornered family's private life, and its defensive squirming is revealed to us with fascinating immodesty.

In the search for identification procedures or, to put it another way, for the distinguishing characteristics of individuals, police departments served as laboratories, developing techniques that were later put to use in many other fields. The police faced the same two problems as the ordinary citizen: how to prove one's own identity, and how to ascertain that of another person (or corpse).

Until about 1880 a clever person could change identities at will. He could obtain a new birth certificate simply by knowing the date and place of birth of the person whose

The Policeman's Gaze

"The Police Photography Unit." Photography, though obviously a useful tool, did not solve the problem of identifying criminals and repeat offenders. A system of classification to allow unambiguous identification was not yet available. (*L'Illustration*, 1889.)

identity he wished to usurp. Only an unlikely encounter with a witness who knew the person in question could thwart this subterfuge, and recognition based solely on visual memory could easily be contested. Under such conditions it is not difficult to understand why the monster or avenger who assumed a false identity struck terror in people's hearts. The metamorphoses of Jacques Colin, the fate of Jean Valjean, and the strategy of Edmond Dantès probably did not strike contemporary readers as improbable. Even children's identities could not be taken for granted, and identifying signs such as bracelets, necklaces, beauty marks, and Cinderella's slipper took on tremendous importance. Recidivism posed a thorny problem for the authorities. And more than anything else, it was the difficulty of identifying prostitutes that led to the failure of the system of licensed brothels instituted under the Consulate.

Until the beginning of the Third Republic the authorities continued to rely on obvious identifying characteristics. Policemen recorded the color of hair and eyes, estimated waist measurements, and noted any physical defects. A glance at the records of parole boards, vice squads, and prisons is enough to show the ineffectiveness of these methods, which were based on unbiased but imprecise observation. To penetrate criminal disguises the police relied on the perspicacity of individual officers, especially after the law of 31 August 1832 abolished the practice of branding prisoners with a hot iron. Criminal records compiled under the 1808 law on criminal prosecution relied on these faulty methods. Until 1850 those records were kept by local police prefectures; after that date they were transferred to the courts.

At the end of the century the problem of identification was solved. New technologies made it possible to associate with each individual a fixed and easily demonstrable mark of identity. It became impossible for one person to take the place of another, even a twin. Birth certificates could no longer be falsified. In short, metamorphosis became impossible. Even bigamy became a major feat, just as divorce was reinstated. No one need any longer suffer the torment of being unable to prove his identity.

In 1876 the police began to use photographs for identifi-

Skeletal Measurements and the Search for Clues

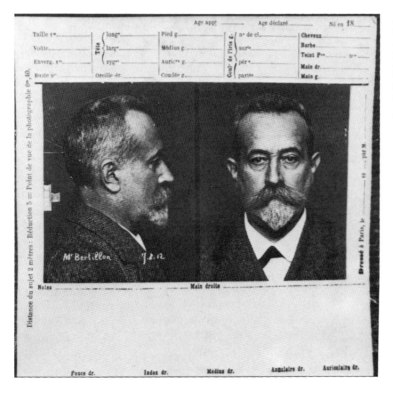

Adolphe Bertillon, considered the least gifted member of a prestigious family of physicians, won vindication and fame through his work for the police. The criminal world was his laboratory. (Paris, Musée de la Police.)

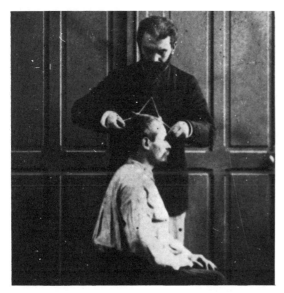
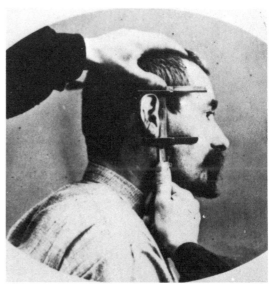

Before fingerprinting was invented, Bertillon relied on physical measurements to identify criminals. The discovery had implications beyond the world of criminality, and soon it became impossible for people to change identities.

cation purposes. By the end of the decade the Prefecture had some 60,000 slides in its possession. Shot from all angles and stored haphazardly, these mug shots were admittedly of little use. In particular, they could not help the police uncover the true identity of an impostor. But the situation changed dramatically in 1882 with the introduction of anthropometric methods developed by Alphonse Bertillon. The law of 27 May 1885 concerning recidivism soon increased the need for positive criminal identification, and Bertillon was able to show that six or seven carefully chosen skeletal measurements were enough to identify any individual.

His system, known as *bertillonage* (or, in English, the Bertillon system), culminated a lengthy series of efforts that included, most notably, Barruel's work on distinguishing characteristics of individual blood and odors and the research of Ambroise Tardieu, Quételet, and the members of the Société d'Anthropologie. But the Bertillon system reigned unchallenged until the turn of the twentieth century. In the meantime Bertillon himself introduced several improvements, such as adding other distinguishing marks to the anthropometric statistics and attaching a photograph to the record.

In truth the Bertillon system was only a phase in a long evolutionary process. Fingerprinting replaced it early in the twentieth century. An ancient Chinese invention, fingerprints had been used by the British in Bengal. Francis Galton, a friend of Bertillon, convinced him to add fingerprints to his records.

On the eve of the First World War these identification techniques were applied for the first time to people other than criminals. The law of 16 July 1912 required "nomads and itinerants," that is, hawkers, itinerant craftsmen, and the like, to carry "anthropometric identity cards." The cards, which noted first and last names, date and place of birth, parents, and identifying characteristics, also included fingerprints and a photograph—a forerunner of the identity card that every French citizen must carry today.

Such procedures posed worrisome new threats to privacy. At the height of the Dreyfus Affair, anthropometry aroused the ire of Dreyfusards and provoked spirited debate. Meanwhile, in another sign of the same anxiety, a deluge of complaints forced the prefect Lépine to suspend a police order requiring mistresses of *maisons de rendez-vous* to provide photographs of the women who frequented their establishments. Other signs of a new sensitivity to privacy no doubt exist. Philippe Boutry found, for example, that as early as 1860 in certain parishes in Ain, people began to display a previously unknown intolerance for any revelation of personal conduct by preachers.[5] Pastors who saw themselves as "eloquent denouncers of individuals' misdeeds" ultimately were forced to recognize that a new realm of private morality had come into being.

In all the areas discussed so far, change began around 1860 and was complete by around 1880. In short, the triumph of the Republic marked a moment of upheaval. Individualism, the century's guiding spirit, attained its high-water mark in this period. Meanwhile, neo-Kantian philosophy inspired France's new leaders, and Pasteur discovered the microbe. If the organism was analogous to society, then the disease-causing microbe was analogous to the individual. When the biological model was applied to the social sphere, control of the individual came to be seen as the key to group survival.

At the same time, fears of violation of the self and its secrets produced a tremendous desire to unmask others and penetrate their secrets. Incognito visits to the haunts of the poor became fashionable among the elite. Anonymous letters were sent by people who wished to pierce the walls of private life. Voyeurism came into vogue at the end of the century. And the detective with a sharp eye for hidden clues became a popular figure of fiction. Even more than Arthur Conan

"Photographs of Persons Subject to Special Surveillance at the Borders." In September 1894 France was terrorized by anarchists. Suspects were sought not merely with the aid of descriptive bulletins but with photographs, which were sent to all border posts. (Paris, Musée de la Police.)

Doyle, Gaston Leroux (creator of the detective Rouletabille) symbolized the new sensibility, because for Leroux the crux of police work was not identification but the identity—and concealment—of the guilty party.

THREATS TO THE BODY

It is pointless to try to understand the nineteenth century's notion of intimacy without first trying to grasp how the enduring dichotomy between body and soul governed attitudes. Clearly the nature of the soul-body dichotomy varied with social class, cultural level, and religious fervor. Each individual in his heart of hearts harbored layer upon layer of incompatible beliefs. Furthermore, the behavior of each segment of the population influenced that of other segments. These facts complicate the analysis, and we must not lose sight of the interrelations among systems of representation.

Anthropologists such as Françoise Loux have shown that traditional folk wisdom concerning the body formed a coherent system that exerted a powerful influence on people's minds. Oddly enough, this traditional wisdom seems to have ignored the soul-body dichotomy. Proverbs collected by folklorists at the end of the nineteenth century reflect a secularized view of existence in which organic life was paramount. These proverbs point to a morality of moderation. They suggest that by avoiding excess and steering a middle course one can achieve health and well-being, which in this value system were prized more than pleasure. Such an ethic stemmed from a hard-working peasantry, concerned about the cost of effort and suspicious of the poor, who sowed violence and disorder. The peasant mentality was a mixture of pessimism and resignation. It encouraged close attention to the messages of the body in the belief that those messages symbolically mirrored the order of the cosmos and of the plant and animal kingdoms. People paid attention to the phases of the moon, celestial arbiter of the female cycle; when death loomed, they listened anxiously to what the poulterer said; they measured the growth of the tree planted on the day a child was born; and they observed a variety of taboos concerning placentas, pared nails, and lost teeth. Though clearly archaic, these beliefs obsessed the popular mind. The common standard of hygiene held that nothing should impede natural bodily functions;

The Soul-Body Dichotomy

accordingly, people were quite tolerant of belching, farting, sneezing, sweating, and physical manifestations of desire. They did not avert their eyes from the ravages of old age.

These beliefs and attitudes encouraged resistance to the spread of scientific principles of hygiene. With the complicity of wet nurses and servants, perfidious counterattacks against those principles were mounted even in bourgeois households. Not surprisingly, the elite to some extent internalized norms that stemmed from the lower orders. At times these internalized beliefs accorded well with the routine hygienic practices recommended by simple physicians, who were also believers in the principle of "nothing to excess."

At the opposite extreme stood another set of ancient beliefs, based on the Christian opposition of body and soul, an opposition that not only persisted but in some quarters was even magnified. The mystery of the Incarnation, the sacrament of the Eucharist, and faith in resurrection set dogmatic limits to Christian contempt for the flesh. Despite those limits, however, a more pessimistic tradition can be traced back to the Church Fathers, especially Tertullian. This tradition, transmitted by Bossuet and the Jansenists, saw the body as nothing more than a temporary prison, soon to be reduced to fodder for worms. The body, to which the curé of Ars always referred as "the cadaver," was the source of instincts that compromised the soul and prevented it from ascending toward its heavenly home. Perpetual war was therefore to be waged against every physical impulse and organic drive. If the soul failed to contain the body, the body would rise up like a dragon and subjugate the soul. Compromise was impossible.

This almost schizophrenic splitting formed the intellectual basis of certain age-old ascetic practices, practices commonly found in the nineteenth century in religious orders and schools and among the growing numbers of tertiary orders. A crude asceticism, which went hand in hand with strict discipline, persisted until the dawn of the Second Empire. Frequently these practices were violent, in keeping with the romantic image of Christ at Golgotha, whom pious engravers liked to depict with blood spurting from his wounds. After midcentury mortification of the flesh lost favor as more and more women joined the ranks of ascetics. The Church, which counted on women to lead its revival, heeded the medical profession's oft-repeated warning that the daughters of Mary were a fragile lot. In place of blood and pain the Church recommended a variety of minor mortifications considered

"Doctor Lortet in 1869, observing the effects of mountain climbing on the temperature of the human body." If 19th-century men and especially women paid close attention to what their internal organs were telling them, it was because physiologists encouraged their anxiety. Scientists measured—and tended to overestimate—the effects of water, sunshine, altitude, and temperature on the human body. (*L'Illustration,* 1878.)

better suited to women's needs. As self-denial was routinized and internalized, the pious began totting up their small sacrifices.

Scientists were more innovative. The writings of Georg Stahl, which became widely known in France at the end of the eighteenth century, exerted a decisive influence on French medical thinking. Whether proponents of the vitalism of the medical school at Montpellier, of animism, or of organicism, most French physicians, especially those who, like Pierre Roussel, had had something to say about the specificity of the female sex, subscribed to the dogma of the soul's supremacy over the body.[6] The supervisory soul, privy to the secret of the body's vocation, guides the body toward fulfillment of that vocation. Hence it is not anatomy or physiology that determines woman's character and justifies her maternal vocation; rather, it is the soul that simultaneously shapes woman's body and mind. Maternity is above all a metaphysical vocation for the woman whose mission is to collaborate in the work of nature.

Coenesthesis

Nineteenth-century physicians retained many elements of a system of thought whose metaphysical underpinnings they deliberately ignored, yet they rejected the doctrine of the primacy of the soul. The Ideologues, most notably Cabanis, abandoned the ideas of the supervisory soul and the vital principle. They tried, in Jean Starobinski's words, "to unify the fields of medicine and physiology."[7] Consequently they paid greater attention than before to the relation between the physical and the moral, to the connections among organic life, social life, and mental activity. For them, therefore, femininity was a question not of ontology but of physiology and sociology. This orientation explains why they adopted an old concept that derived from Aristotle, if not from Aristippus of Cyrene, and that had been transmitted by Descartes and Stahl himself. This concept, originally referred to as "inner tact" or "touch," at the end of the eighteenth century was termed "coenesthesis." The term referred to a certain internal perception of the body, or, better perhaps, to the whole range of organic sensations, which, when translated into behavior, Cabanis argued, constituted the instincts.

Throughout the century specialists remained convinced of the fundamental importance of an "unconscious," by which they meant, again in Starobinski's words, "the obscure murmur of the visceral functions out of which acts of consciousness intermittently emerged." From the unconscious the personality leapt fully armed. Freud's genius was not to discover that large areas of subjectivity escaped consciousness yet played a part in determining mental activity, but rather to deny organic life a monopoly over the unconscious, which Freud situated within the psychic apparatus itself.

The importance ascribed at the time to coenesthesis validated a particular way of listening to the body's messages, one we no longer share. Vulgarized Hippocratic notions, still current at that time, stressed the effects of air, water, and temperature and made people sensitive to the influence of the weather and the seasons on the ease and rhythm of breathing, on the intensity of their rheumatism, and on the stability of their humors, giving rise to a sort of internal meteorology of the soul. Many also paid close attention to the organic functions and their repercussions on mental activity. These constant observations were explained primarily in terms of digestive physiology and the menstrual cycle, which could be upset by common dysentery and gynecological disease. Some people also believed in the doctrine of temperaments (bilious, lymphatic, sanguine, and nervous), to whose persistence and adaptations, despite the discredit of the theory of humors, Theodore Zeldin has called attention.[8]

A rudimentary system of images of physical and psychic health thus grew out of everyday observations, and people used it to guide their behavior and to develop strategies for dealing with others. Private documents reveal that these preoccupations constituted the very texture of private life. One need only read the journals of Maine de Biran and Eugénie de Guérin, the recently published papers of Charles-Ferdinand Gambon, the correspondence of the Boileaus of Vigné, and the letters of Marthe's family—to cite representative examples chosen arbitrarily at intervals of twenty-five years. Improbable as it may seem, comparisons of coenesthetic experiences occur in conversation as regularly as discussions of the weather. Bodily concerns determined people's attitudes toward water and sunshine, from which they sought to protect themselves, and especially toward drafts, which were the object of a genuine phobia.

We use similar observations to justify our own physical needs. We talk of compensating for the rigors of urban life, working conditions, and pollution and of procuring physical pleasures to satisfy our heightened narcissistic needs. Earlier, however, a revolution took place, about which I shall have more to say later on. The substance of that revolution was the gradual identification of the subject (in the philosophical sense) with the body. One implication of that identification was to check man's contempt for his organic, animal nature. People came to see the appetites as stemming from the self rather than as threatening (but also fascinating) demands emanating from outside. The historian who fails to note this change in the nature of desire runs the risk of psychological anachronism.

Toward the end of the ancien régime living space had begun to grow less crowded, a trend that continued into the nineteenth century. Single beds, long the rule in convents and monasteries, were adopted as a sanitary precaution, especially in hospitals. Private rooms for patients were a long time coming, however, as Olivier Faure has shown in the case of Lyons.[9] This was because privacy interfered with the rites of popular sociability, which spontaneously recreated themselves

A Room and a Bed of One's Own

Albert Morand, *La Salpêtrière*. Even in that living hell for women, the Salpêtrière, privacy and the single bed triumphed. (Paris, Musée de l'Assistance Publique.)

in the hospitals. Here I am concerned primarily with the transfer of the desire for individual accommodations from public places to private ones. This process was accelerated by the cholera epidemic of 1832, which called attention to the harmful effects of overcrowding and indiscriminate mingling in working-class housing.

Stimulated by Lavoisier's discoveries and by the new understanding of the mechanism of respiration, and persuaded of the benefits of an ample supply of oxygen, doctors waged war throughout the century against the communal bed and promiscuity. Little by little they began to be heard. It would be difficult to overstate the importance of their hard-won victory. The new solitude of the single bed strengthened the sense of individuality and independence and made room for inner monologue. The modalities of prayer, the forms of reverie, the conditions of sleep and wakefulness, and the experience of dreams and nightmares all were dramatically altered. As the warmth of fraternal closeness diminished, children began to ask for dolls or a reassuring maternal hand.

Among the petty bourgeoisie, at least, people began to have their own bedrooms. The individual bedroom was a subject of great concern to hygienists, who prescribed the size of the room and recommended keeping servants and dirty linen out. A girl's bedroom, now the temple of her private life, was appropriately bedecked with symbols. Identified with its occupant, the private bedroom gave proof of individual independence. The corner chapel, the birdcage, the vase of flowers, the printed wallpaper, the secretary that contained an album and personal correspondence, and perhaps a set of bookshelves—such items established an image of Césarine Birotteau or Henriette Gérard and even more of Eugénie de Guérin, whose diary was an endless hymn to the pleasure of inhabiting her *chambrette*. Caroline Brame experienced a similar pleasure.

The seamstress' idyllic mansard, whose decorous ambiance was a sign of virtue, was the popular version of the same model. Even in the licensed brothels on which the vice squad kept a close watch, one room per person was the rule. In farmhouses husband and wife little by little secured privacy by surrounding their bed with curtains and canopies, and in some cases by erecting rudimentary partitions. When the head of the household decided to pass the property on to his heir, it became customary for him to stipulate in the contract de-

In a bedroom filled with objects symbolizing her various pleasures, this bourgeoise enjoys her solitude despite the chill in the air. (Paris, Bibliothèque des Arts Décoratifs.)

fining the terms of his gift that one bedroom would be reserved for his own use. He thus assured himself that he would be able to end his days in privacy.

Increasingly private toilet facilities encouraged communion with the self. When a new resident of a working-class apartment building received the key to the common toilet on the landing, he began that process of familiarization with excrement that contributed substantially to the new sense of privacy. Around 1900, when lavatories and bathrooms first began to be equipped with locks, it became possible for people to experience their naked bodies without fear of intrusion. Desensualized as much as possible, the bathroom was transformed into a temple of cleanliness and decency, a place for contemplation and taking stock.

| Grooming | Improvements in cleanliness revolutionized private life and relations. Around the turn of the century numerous factors conspired to revive an interest in cleanliness that can be traced back to the convents and monasteries of the Middle Ages. With the discovery of the mechanism of perspiration and the great success of the infectionist theory of disease, people became aware of the danger of allowing pores to become clogged with disease-carrying dirt. Later, belief in the fashionable concept of purification *(dépuration)* made careful cleansing of the body's "emunctories" imperative. The recognized influence of the physical on the moral bestowed value on cleanliness and neatness. New precepts transformed manners; a greater tactfulness was required of the elite, and people shunned organic wastes, which reminded them of animality, sin, and death. In short, purification hastened progress. In addition, the elite was impelled by a desire to distinguish itself from the foul-smelling populace. All these changes helped to alter the status of sexual desire and repulsion, which in turn gave rise to new hygienic practices. |

A variety of contrary beliefs made people cautious about the new cleanliness. The use of water, whose moral as well as physical benefits were overestimated, called for precautions. Strict rules, based on sex, age, temperament, and profession, governed the frequency of bathing. Concern to avoid weakness, complacency, self-obsession, and even masturbation slowed acceptance of the practice. A firm belief in a connection between water and sterility limited the development of feminine hygiene.

Benjamin-Eugène Fichel, *Woman Bathing,* 1891. The bath is here a pretext for exaltation of the female body, hairless by convention. (Paris, Bibliothèque Nationale.)

Nevertheless, progress slowly spread from the upper classes to the petty bourgeoisie. Servants even introduced a small segment of the lower classes to the new grooming practices, though these still concerned particular parts of the body. Hands were washed frequently; the face and teeth (at least the front teeth) were cleaned daily; feet were washed once or twice a month; but the head never. A woman's bathing schedule was governed by her menstrual cycle. In this regard most female orders in the nineteenth century still followed the rule laid down by Saint Augustine. The introduction of the English-style bathtub at the end of the century, followed by the rather slow adoption of the shower, affected the amount of time spent in grooming. Showers were viewed favorably, because their vigorous action alleviated worries that washing induced weakness. Therapeutic benefits were still emphasized, however. The regulations, drafted in 1881, of the Ecole Normale of Sèvres restricted the use of the shower to students who were ill, and then only if accompanied by a nurse. By now it should be clear why sexual hygiene failed to progress. In the Nivernais the respectable bourgeoisie did not adopt the bidet or sanitary napkin before the turn of the twentieth century.[10]

Rural areas, where children were used to bathing in rivers when the weather was hot, remained unaffected by changes in grooming practices until World War I. Municipalities did of course try to secure supplies of fresh water. Fountains, storage vats, and washhouses appeared in lower Normandy during the Restoration, in the Nivernais during the July Monarchy, and at Minot in the Châtillonnais at the beginning of the Third Republic. The hospital, the prison, and later the school and barracks contributed to the task of educating the rural populace about hygiene, a campaign waged tirelessly by countless rural physicians typified by Balzac's Dr. Benassis. However, as was mentioned earlier, the hygienic precepts of science often contradicted popular beliefs: frequent washing of linen destroys the cloth; careful housekeeping is a waste of time; a crust of dirt fosters a good complexion underneath. The doctors' rules were annoying; in many cases the hygienic precepts were seen as unwanted interference by city folk in rural life.

In truth, when it came to the common people, what the elites meant by hygiene concerned primarily the appearance. Being decent meant removing grease and stains from one's clothing (in Lyons cleaners were referred to as "degreasers").

In 1886 it was fashionable to bathe in fountainlike tubs, which preceded regular bathtubs and bathrooms. (Paris, Bibliothèque Nationale.)

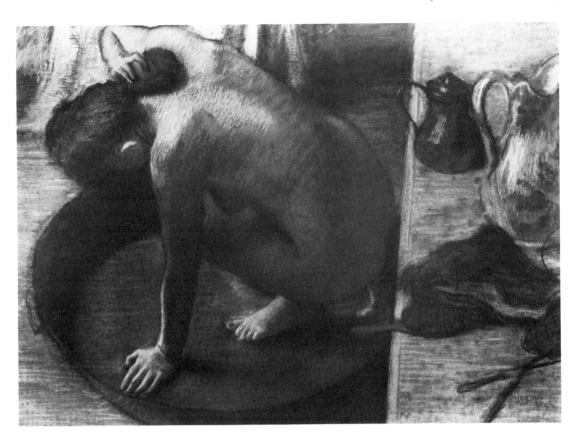

It meant polishing crude manners, combing one's hair, occasionally washing one's hands (and beard), and, later, sprinkling oneself with eau de Cologne. For Jules Renard's Ragotte, hygiene meant knowing the proper way to eat soup. Meanwhile, at the home of Fifille Migneboeuf, Ragotte's neighbor, the child was ordered to wipe up menstrual blood from the floor of the main room. Despite all the praise that has been heaped on the republican schools for their efforts to improve hygiene and their cleanliness inspection rituals, the educational authorities were actually not very ambitious. To convince ourselves of this we need only read *Le Tour de la France par deux enfants.* Crucial battles concerned the use of the comb and instruction in the discipline of defecation. Boys had to stop combing their hair with their fingers, and girls had to keep their underwear clean.

The turning point came around the beginning of the twentieth century. Limited progress in equipping apartments

Edgar Degas, *The Tub,* 1886. By displaying the intimate gestures of women, previously symbols of prostitution, Degas, an artist fascinated by the world of the bordello, conferred new respectability on the nude bather, a figure that he not only recorded in detail but also magnified. (Paris, Musée d'Orsay/Jeu de Paume.)

Alfred Stevens, *The Bathtub.*
Portable tin tubs were used
prior to the installation of
modern bathrooms, in which
the location of the tub was
fixed by plumbing. Gradually a
new private space was created,
in which a woman could relax,
read, and daydream in total
privacy, safe from intrusion.
The light gown worn by the
woman here, as well as the
boredom evident in her
posture, evokes the old pretext
of the therapeutic bath rather
than sensuality. The only note
of eroticism is the neck of
Leda's swan sculpted into the
faucetwork. (Musée de
Compiègne.)

and homes with new sanitary equipment, the use of showers
in sporting clubs, the efforts of the new public health authorities, and increased use of deluxe hotels and brothels all helped
to popularize use of the basin and pitcher. But the enameled
cast-iron sink did not catch on until the 1920s and 1930s, and
showers and bathrooms did not become common until the
1950s. Only then did a thoroughgoing revolution in hygiene
take place.

The Menace of Desire

The individual prepared in private to confront the gaze
of others. His self-presentation was based on socially defined
images of the body. Here too a revolution occurred. The
resulting strictures governed private behavior exclusively.
(Based on a heightening of the contrast between home and
the rest of the world, these rules have since lost some of their
force.) Sleepwear could no longer be worn outside the bedroom. It came to symbolize an erotic intimacy to which even
the slightest allusion, even implicit, was considered indecent,
particularly when married women began wearing nightgowns
that bore little resemblance to the simple nightshirts of little
girls. A whole range of déshabille now became possible, but
no decent woman would wish to be seen in her negligee except
by her lover. Increasingly sophisticated dressing gowns and
visible undergarments imposed new requirements of modesty.
Still, Feydeau's title *Mais n'te promène donc pas toute nue*

(Don't Go About Stark Naked) should not be taken literally. Women were seen at home with their hair down, although only maids and prostitutes appeared that way in public. These rules were only part of a more comprehensive system of prohibitions that limited women's access to the public sphere yet made sure that when they did appear, it was a solemn occasion. The distinction between home and abroad also affected the male population. No Parisian male could be seen in the street dressed as he was at home.

The extraordinary success of lingerie also influenced behavior. Unseen items of clothing took on a new sophistication, which heightened the value of nudity and deepened its mystery. Never was the female body as hidden as it was between 1830 and 1914, as Philippe Perrot has shown.[11] The success of the nightgown was followed by that of knickers, which reigned unchallenged until crinoline triumphed early in the Second Empire. By 1880 the crinoline had become de rigueur, at least among the bourgeoisie. Meanwhile, the corset withstood vehement attacks by the medical profession. Corsets that could be laced "*à la paresseuse,*" that is, without assistance, allowed women to dress themselves, which permitted greater freedom in amorous affairs.

Eugène Vincent Vidal, *Young Woman with Pink Corset.* The corset, designed to emphasize the female form, accentuated the curves of bosom and hips in slender young women and discreetly enhanced the "aesthetic dowry." Here the new "lazy lacing" system allows the young woman to lace up her own corset with a graceful gesture captured by the painter. (Paris, Musée de Luxembourg.)

Late in the century lingerie began to be made with more sumptuous embroidery and lacework than ever before. The perverse effects of modesty had never been so obvious. As undressing became a matter of degree, impatient male fingers were obliged to contend with an ever-wider variety of knots, hooks, and buttons. The erotic accumulation of undergarments, which could never be represented pictorially except in caricature, transformed the mythology of lewdness. The new fashions in undergarments spread rapidly—more rapidly than hygienic practices—to all classes of society. Before long even the peasant swain would be obliged to surmount unprecedented obstacles.

It is worth considering what this embrace of exquisite complexity meant, especially in view of the extraordinary hypertrophy of the erotic imagination evident in the bourgeoisie's obsession with drapery, slipcovers, casings, and upholstery. The desire to preserve, the concern to leave a trace of one's existence, the fear of castration, and the omnipresent reminder of the menace of desire joined in a neurotic encounter.

The prevalence of fetishism, described and documented by Binet and Kraft-Ebbing at the end of the century but previously analyzed in minute detail by Zola, Huysmans, and Maupassant, should come as no surprise. The mystique of the waistline and the small of the back, the fixation of desire on the soft curves of the bosom, the erotic value attached to the foot and to leather boots, and the desire to snip a lock of a woman's hair in order to savor its fragrance at leisure—all these fetishes became significant historical facts. So did the fetish of the apron, symbol of intimacy, which apparently made men feel entitled to all sorts of familiarities with their maids. Intimate articles of clothing that bore evidence of sexual activity, disease, or even crime were compromising in their eloquence. Servants and laundresses spread rumors based on such intimate signs. Privy to the secrets hidden in the finest linen, the château's washerwoman was an abundant source of information and enjoyed a special prestige in the village.

Strategies of Appearance

People groomed in private to appear in public. Long confined to the elite, this unproductive activity spread rapidly to the rest of society between 1880 and 1910. Men and women groomed themselves in very different ways, heightening the differentiation of sex roles. Perfume, makeup, coloring, silk, and lace were the exclusive province of women. Women also subjected themselves to a rigorous "body sculpture," presenting their figures in such a way as to counter any suspicion that they belonged to that class of people obliged to earn its daily bread. For men, condemned to a life of toil, women functioned as advertisements. Because men worked they were forced to dress in shapeless black or gray—a drabness that caused Baudelaire to exclaim that the male sex looked as if it were always in mourning. Men's undergarments also lacked refinement. The nineteenth-century male was not proud of his body, except perhaps for his hair. For women, the modern style was to wear thick curls, and the marcel, made popular by that recent innovation, the hairdresser, was all the rage. Barbers offered men a choice of no fewer than fifteen to twenty different types of mustaches, beards, and sideburns.

The historical importance of these fashions is not to be laughed at. They inaugurated a new style of private life. Again the crucial change seems to have occurred between 1860 and 1880. Until then country folk seem to have been suspicious of all that came from the cities. On fair and market days peasants still proudly wore traditional costumes in city streets. The period between 1840 and 1860, a time of rural prosperity,

As leisure time increased, more and more attention was devoted to appearances. Aided by her maid, a petty bourgeoise prepares to go out in public. Because so many different outfits were worn in the course of the day, wardrobes had to be carefully arranged in order to avoid turning the bedroom into a theatrical dressing room. (Sirot-Angel Collection.)

was a golden age for traditional regional dress. Afterward a period of mimicry began. Peasant traditions were lost, and regional costumes, no longer worn, were piously collected by folklorists. While bonnets and overalls gradually disappeared, fashion prints began to appear in even the most remote rural areas. Mail-order purchases, provincial branches of the Printemps department store, the establishment of millinery shops in small towns, and especially the increase in the number of dressmakers at the end of the century—all these hastened the change. The lives of adolescent girls, now forced to keep up with the latest fashions, were transformed, as Yvonne Verdier has demonstrated in her work on Minot.[12] She fails to note, however, that the phenomenon was confined to a very brief period.

Urban workers were not exempt from these changes. In the past the way a man dressed revealed his occupation. Until the middle of the Second Empire it was easy to distinguish the worker's blouse from the magistrate's black robes from the clerk's collar. After 1860, however, the temptation to "dress up" on Sundays became hard to resist. A worker might don the suit of a bourgeois and mingle happily with the urban

Henri Evenpoel, *Sunday Stroll,* 1899. When the workers' movement joined the clergy in insisting that Sunday ought to be a day of rest, the ritual of the Sunday stroll, long confined to the bourgeoisie, suddenly became popular. Greater leisure time and a desire to show off one's best clothes also contributed to the phenomenon, which tended to blur social status distinctions and encourage dreams of fleeting encounters. (Liège, Musée des Beaux-Arts.)

crowd. Sunday dinner took on new meaning. Dressing up demonstrated familiarity with the new standards of cleanliness. Young female workers adopted the latest in seductive fashions: the ankle boot, the perfumed handkerchief, the molded bosom, even a new posture. Shopping became an obsession, as women adopted new standards for deciding when clothing was no longer fit to wear. Many Maupassant stories and songs from around 1900 reflect these changes, symbolized by the emergence of the *trottin,* or dressmaker's assistant, a latter-day version of the *grisette.*

In the nineteenth century modesty and shame were important determinants of behavior. Behind these terms lurked two fears: fear of allowing the Other—the body—to express itself, and fear that an indiscretion might give away one's most intimate secrets. The first fear led to self-discipline, as people sought to prevent any organic manifestation of the body's existence. Richard Sennett has described the "green disease," a form of constipation from which women suffered as a result of fear of breaking wind in public.[13] Physicians described the clinical symptoms of "ereuthophobia," modesty of the second degree: a morbid fear of being unable to refrain from blushing. The second fear was responsible, among other things, for the reluctance of physicians to employ the speculum, use of which was for a long time regarded as "medical rape." Opponents of legalized prostitution in the late nineteenth century continued to raise this argument in their campaigns. The same type of anxiety was at the root of the "white ailment" in women, that is, the refusal to go out of the house for fear of being seen by strangers.

    From these two fears stemmed an insistence on "modest" comportment, which formed a prominent part of the teaching of nuns. One purpose of that teaching was to curb the spontaneity of children. Natural impulses were disciplined, but, beyond that, the very sources of youthful energy were sapped and sensuality's contribution to that energy was strictly checked. Since the senses were the devil's portals, young people had to be taught prudence. They had to learn to keep their hands busy, to avoid staring, to speak in a low voice or, better still, to steep themselves in the virtues of silence.

    The precepts taught in convents became stricter around the middle of the century, following a period of relative freedom, not to say genuine spontaneity.[14] The denial of corporeal

Modesty and Shame

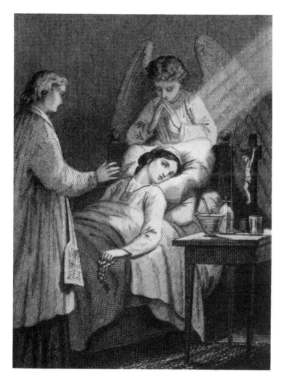

Pious images, omnipresent in the lives of young women, insisted on their need to protect themselves from harm. Here, the heroine, conscious of her ardent desire, knows that without divine assistance she will be unable to resist the temptations of the ball. Images exalted the guardian angel, who in the minds of the pious was often confused with the religious daughter eager to ascend to heaven. (Paris, Bibliothèque Nationale.)

existence was intensified when angels were held up as models with which many young girls actually identified. This illusion, which has been attributed in part to the influence of neo-Platonism, quickly gained ground.[15] Quite noticeable in the postures assumed in prayer, angelism was accompanied by exaltation of virginity and by a new lyricism of chastity. A revealing sign of these attitudes was the rapid spread of the cult of Saint Philomena after 1834. Although Philomena never existed, numerous biographies of her were written, and prayers, emblems, and even chastity belts were made available to girls who wished to keep their virginity intact. It is worth remembering that in a century in which the words of men reigned supreme, women's preaching was couched in the rhetoric of the body, the elevation of the gaze, and the fervor of gesture.

A question remains, however: how did the new patterns of behavior spread? Suzanne Voilquin, a woman of modest background, has left a record of the veritable novitiate she was forced to undergo at the cloister school of Saint-Merry between 1805 and 1809 and of her later apprenticeship, begun at age nine, with lugubrious Norman spinsters.[16] Still, the angelic anthropology that was reactivated in the romantic period did not become widespread until after a Catholic counteroffensive was launched in 1850. Techniques of self-discipline developed in the convents spread to laymen and laywomen. By patiently exploring folk memories Marie-José Garniche-Merritt has been able to paint an extraordinary portrait of the way in which the behavior of young girls was minutely scrutinized by the nuns of Bué-en-Sancerrois between 1900 and 1914.[17] Young people's congregations were set up in rural parishes. There were countless associations of Children of Mary and Servants of Mary and of *rosières,* girls to whom a wreath of roses was given in reward for virtuous behavior. Martine Segalen has put the number of such organizations at around a thousand; they reinforced the moral teachings and behavioral discipline dispensed by the republican schools, which themselves drew heavily on Lasalle's manual of civility, the primer widely used in schools during the July Monarchy.[18] In Touraine the mayor and curé jointly chose and honored the village *rosière,* who was required, on the morning of the prize ceremony, to appear before the physician to give proof of her virginity. In Nanterre de-Christianization proved no obstacle to the preservation of this model of domestic and private virtue.

Within ordinary homes the new concern with distinction went hand in hand with a new physical discipline. Louis-Ferdinand Céline, in his semi-autobiographical novel *Death on the Installment Plan,* recounts the tortures the young hero is forced to endure at the hands of his father, a clerk, and his mother, who works in a shop in a central Paris mall. This is not the place to list the various regimens by means of which once-public acts were transformed into private ones. Among the practices now considered "shameful" were undressing in the open before slipping into bed with one's brother, grooming oneself in front of other people, and making love in the family bedroom.

The case of the nubile adolescent girl, who attracted so much of the moralists' solicitude, is worth exploring in somewhat greater detail. Thick books of physiology and hygiene were devoted to pubescent girls. This learned literature conjured up the quite fantastic image of a child frightened or surprised by the radical metamorphosis taking place within her own body, a metamorphosis marked by the onset of menstruation. She was a strange creature with incomprehensible tastes, all the more dangerous because she had not yet learned the nature of the female condition and because she remained too close to the natural forces just then making their presence felt within her. Her strangeness, which manifested itself in the form of languor, sighs, and involuntary tears, called for the solicitude of those around her. Her existence was to be hedged about with taboos, many of which admittedly were ignored. Doctors recommended that her curiosity about sexual matters not be aroused. The number of "innocents" soared, partly as a result of urbanization, which deprived young people of the chance to witness copulation between animals, partly because sexual relations between husband and wife were now relegated to the privacy of their own bedroom. The myth that babies were brought by storks gained credence. Unfortunately we have no idea about how much of this innocence was faked, about how much distance there was between external attitudes and inner thoughts—and sadly we probably never will know. When Colette's heroine Claudine and her school friends compare breasts to see whose are largest, we glimpse a very different image of what young ladies were like.

Solitary Pleasure

The horror aroused by solitary sexual activities provides a useful index of the depths of hypocrisy. Historians from Jean-Louis Flandrin to Jean-Paul Aron have called attention to the incredible alarm of physicians at a scourge long since denounced by the clergy. The publication, in 1760, of Dr. Tissot's celebrated treatise *Onania,* which was repeatedly reprinted as late as 1905, marks a crucial date. There was controversy among specialists as to whether masturbation was on the rise, but quantitative history is powerless to enlighten us on this question. The later age of marriage, the creation of veritable bachelors' ghettos in the cities, the vanishing of traditional forms of premarital sex in rural areas, the growing numbers of boys' boarding schools, the switch to single beds and private rooms, and heightened fears of venereal disease all suggest an increase in masturbation, unless we assume that sublimation somehow kept pace with all these changes. Everything that exalted the individual and encouraged inner dialogue with himself surely must have tended in the same direction. Other contributing factors include fascination with transgression, the pleasures of subterfuge and sin, and, for unsatisfied wives, a desire for compensation or revenge coupled with a fear of the difficulties that might result from taking a lover. There is every reason to believe that the moralists' campaign against masturbation would never have achieved such a fever pitch of intensity if the practice itself had not been rampant.

Let us return to the terrifying rhetoric of the physicians, whose dissuasive effects should not be underestimated. The doctors' interminable diatribe, a part of a broader strategy of sexualization of childhood noted by Michel Foucault, was based in the first instance on the fantasy of loss, on the need to regulate every expenditure of precious bodily fluid in order to achieve a sound spermatic economy.[19] Men were repeatedly warned that masturbation would rapidly deplete their reserves. Consumption, premature senility, and death marked the stages of decline visible in the haggard, pale, doddering males who seem to have crowded the doctors' offices. The dramatization of the clinical account reflects fears that the expenditure of energy in masturbation might sap a man's force and render him incapable of work. Above all, the account hides a refusal to learn about pleasure, a denial of the hedonic functions of sexuality.

Female orgasm without male participation seems to have been particularly intolerable. In "manualization" lay the very essence of vice. For men it represented the absolute secret, infinitely more mysterious than the transports of sexual intercourse. With women the risks of depletion could not be an issue, since woman's "venereal capacity" appeared to be infinite. But other, equally terrible punishments lay in store for the woman who violated this taboo. Not a single clinical or biographical account of a nymphomaniac, hysteric, or prostitute failed to begin with the portrait of a little girl given to vice. Here we encounter the well-known hostility of nineteenth-century physicians to the clitoris, which was denounced as a mere instrument of pleasure with no procreative function.

When surveillance by parents and teachers failed, only a special orthopedic device could quell the adolescent's irrepressible need for solitary release and save him from premature senility or even death from loss of precious bodily fluid. (Paris, Bibliothèque de l'Ancienne Faculté de Médecine.)

The battle against the scourge of masturbation was waged by parents, priests, and above all physicians. Weighty tomes exhorted parents to keep their children under surveillance at home. For clerical educators, sleep was supposed to be the equivalent of death; the bed symbolized the tomb, and waking symbolized resurrection. In girls' boarding schools a nun was present at bedtime and wakeup time to ensure that modesty was preserved. During the day it was considered unwise to leave a child alone for long periods. In schools run by the Ursulines, the rules stipulated that each female pupil must remain at all times in sight of several classmates. Physicians

The Surveillance of the Onanist

recommended against warm and damp beds; they prescribed down comforters and several blankets and specified the proper sleeping position. Women who rode horseback aroused their suspicion, as did the sewing machine, which was denounced by the Académie de Médecine in 1866.

Manufacturers and orthopedists took part in the effort of prevention. In 1878 specialists recommended the use of toilet stalls equipped with doors provided with cutouts at top and bottom to allow checking on the position of the occupant. Certain doctors recommended that boys wear long shirts with tails. For those who persisted in masturbating, special bandages were available until 1914, and "self-disciplinary belts" were available for girls. In mental hospitals nymphomaniacs were handcuffed or strapped, and sometimes special devices were placed between their thighs to prevent them from being rubbed together. If the affliction persisted, surgery might be attempted. Cauterization of the urethra seems to have been fairly widespread. Theodore Zeldin cites the martyrdom of one department-store clerk, aged eighteen, who was cauterized seven times, ostensibly to treat involuntary seminal emissions.[20] Even more revealing were the tortures of Amiel, recounted in detail by the victim himself. This unfortunate young man, who regularly "succumbed" to "seminal losses," was told by a specialist that "every pollution is a dagger in your eyes." Frightened, Amiel thereafter recorded each nocturnal emission. He promised to repent and made repeated resolutions. At night he took cold baths, ate ground glass, and washed his abdomen with vinegar. Nothing worked. On June 12, 1841, he decided that he would henceforth sleep no more than four to five hours a night, and seated in an armchair.

Cauterizations of the clitoris and vulva were infrequent, and clitoridectomies even rarer, although the operation was performed by Dr. Robert as early as 1837 and by Dr. Demetrius Zambaco at the end of the century. Although such frightful mutilations were undoubtedly significant, their frequency should not be overestimated.

Clearly that the body had become an obsession. Awareness of the obscure signs of coenesthesis, vigilance against temptation, sensitivity to the omnipresent threats to modesty, and fascination with the ubiquitous possibility of transgression tended to focus attention on the body's presence. People now shunned the sight of copulating animals. Simple allusions formed the basis of dirty jokes that seem remarkably unfunny today. Singing clubs and social circles formed solely to hear and talk about sex. Deeply hidden, nakedness stirred fantasies in men. The guests of Countess Sabine, one of the heroines of Zola's *Nana,* speculate endlessly about the shape of her thighs. By comparison, today's much-touted indulgence of sensuality seems mild, even nonchalant.

UNDERSTANDING AND SELF-CONTROL

As inwardness flourished in literature, people began to feel more of a need to understand themselves. Introspection became commonplace, aided by the spread of spiritual exercises developed by Catholics in connection with post-Tridentine efforts to restore religious discipline. Examination of the conscience was more widely practiced than ever, even as the number of practicing Catholics decreased. A new understanding of the requirements of moral theology made a once elitist mental discipline accessible to the masses of lay Catholics. Retreats and missions, both opportunities for extended self-scrutiny ending in confession, were a common feature of the Restoration. Claude Langlois has shown that ordinary lay people in the diocese of Vannes took part in these religious retreats. According to Gérard Cholvy, six thousand men, all carrying candles, participated on March 24, 1821, in the ceremony of public penitence that marked the culmination of the great Montpellier mission.[21] Nearly half a century later, the rude peasants who occupied the *oustaux* of Chasseradès, a humble commune in the inaccessible Gévaudan region, looked deep within themselves and suddenly found their tongues untied after the preachers came to their village in 1866. For several decades in the nineteenth century confessors deferred absolution until time had passed and they had heard a second confession, and general confessions with intervening periods for self-examination became a common practice, as recommended by the curé of Ars, who, during the July Monarchy, became a settled missionary. By such means people were encouraged to scour their consciences for the least memory of sin.

Along with the closer examination of conscience went growing numbers of rules and ever more detailed resolutions. Preachers and religious teachers exhorted the pious to master these new skills, and thus they exerted control over private behavior. On advice of the nuns, parents imposed strict rules on daughters who returned home from boarding school in order to protect them from the temptations of a life that seemed destined for idleness. Léopoldine Hugo's moving *Cahier de résolutions* (Notebook of Resolutions) gives an idea of what these rules were like. Some good souls even urged girls of quite tender age to keep diaries as an aid in fulfilling the penitential sacrament. In Marseilles, Isabelle Fraissinet, age twelve, was required to write a certain number of lines each day. Adults too recorded their spiritual progress on paper and by so doing alleviated the remorse they felt for minor, everyday sins. After 1850 women kept conversion diaries modeled on that of Mme Swetchine, which was published by Falloux. These diaries reflected a similar desire to adapt the growing need to write about oneself to some edifying purpose.

The crucial point, however, is that techniques of self-comprehension developed for the confessional were being secularized. In the nineteenth century people became obsessed with accounting for their time. It was not only their obsession with sin that was responsible. Their need stemmed from the same fantasies of loss that impelled them to keep detailed household accounts and that engendered certain fears, such as the fear of squandering sperm or of watching life grow shorter with each passing day. A determination to stem these losses led to the keeping of private diaries.

The Diarist's Search

This link is clearly evident in the extraordinary *Essay on the Use of Time, or Method for Regulating the Use of Time, the Primary Means of Achieving Happiness,* which was written in 1810 by one Jullien, a retired military officer. The author, who claimed to have taken his inspiration from Locke and Franklin and whose work was hailed by Fourcroy, recommended dividing the day into three periods of eight hours each. The first of these periods was to be devoted to sleep, the second to study and to the "duties of one's employment," and the third to meals, relaxation, and physical exercise. Most important of all, he recommended keeping three diaries, or "open accounts," which were to be filled with observations on one's health, moral development, and intellectual activities. Every three to six months an "analytical memoir" and three-part situation table were to be prepared, and these summaries were to be submitted to a friendly volunteer, who would judge the individual's progress. Here the desire for inner illumination coupled with the obsession with loss gave rise to a practice not justified by any kind of dialogue with the Creator. The result was a permanent, obsessive self-scrutiny shaped by a person's view of himself and others. This ongoing inner monologue enabled each individual to control how he looked to others, and thus to make himself more indecipherable. The very need for personal privacy contributed to the need for introspection.

The great diarists of the first half of the nineteenth century pursued their goal of illumination without the least shadow of literary ambition. Their works, which often recorded their labors, expenditures, leisure activities, and loves indiscriminately, served as meters, registering every loss. The purpose of the private diary was to exorcise the very same anxiety about death that keeping such a diary engendered. By detecting the ways in which one's substance was wasted, the diary became an element in a strategy of thrift. "By keeping the history of what I feel," Delacroix wrote on April 7, 1824, "I live doubly; the past will come back to me. The future is always there." A memoir, at once an antidote to amnesia and an instrument of commemoration, thus took shape.

Keeping a journal was also a form of inner discipline. Discreet confessions were recorded on paper. Writing things down made it possible to analyze one's inner guilt, to record the failures of sexual desire and the stifling awareness of an inability to act. Private resolutions were preserved for reexamination.

Many other factors contributed to the rise of this fascinating practice. For Maine de Biran, keeping a diary was a way of founding the science of man on observation and, to that end, of understanding the relation between the physical and the moral. The quest for the self was spurred by all the historical factors that deepened the individual's sense of identity. Of these, the most important was the insecurity that stemmed from social mobility. Diarists questioned their own position and speculated about the judgments of others. Society's mute presence haunted the private and solitary life of the journal author. The new mode of interpersonal relations dictated by urbanization multiplied man's narcissistic wounds, engendering frustration which in turn caused individuals to turn inward in search of refuge. In 1816 Maine de Biran predicted the need for psychological revenge. He anticipated a time when "men, tired of feeling, will find it easier to retreat into themselves, there to seek repose and that sort of calm, those kinds of consolation, that one finds only in the intimacy of conscience."[22]

The growing attachment to property was not unrelated

Philippe Jolyet, *The Letter.* Literacy, nearly universal by the time the republican school system was established, enabled young people for the first time to express themselves in various forms of writing. (Salon of 1908.)

Vicomtesse de Cistello, *The Reply.* An aristocratic or bourgeois lady devoted several hours a day to correspondence. Letters, which helped to cement group ties, also played an increasingly important role in love. In the heyday of adultery men usually discovered their wife's guilty secret when they happened upon a letter or diary. (Salon of 1909.)

to the quest for individuality, as Maine de Biran again sensed. He was pleased that his friend the abbé Morellet, in his memoir on property, had founded property rights on what "each man possesses for himself, his faculties and his ego."

Writing about Oneself

What kind of people wrote about themselves? The question is easily answered if we concern ourselves exclusively with those recognized by history as great diarists. Many women, prohibited from publishing by the proprieties of the day, kept diaries in order to satisfy their urge, not to say their mania, to write. Eugénie de Guérin confessed that writing assuaged an irrepressible desire, and there is every reason to think that the same was true of Mme de Lamartine, the poet's mother.

Diarists often were people obliged to live in societies to which they were not well suited, people who suffered from their inability to communicate with others. Often too they were people who found it difficult to make decisions. In May 1848 Amiel, then twenty-seven, endlessly mulled over the question of marriage. And Maine de Biran, overwhelmed by what he called his "preoccupation" and what we would call his anxiety, which he attributed to "mistrust of himself," confessed: "I create phantoms and difficulties for myself out of nothing."

The great diarist could easily be seen as a neurotic, or at the very least as a timid, ineffectual man, overwhelmed by homosexual tendencies that he was incapable of satisfying. The provincial bourgeois family was the ideal breeding ground for personal diaries. The nuclear family structure encouraged the child's attachment to the mother and to childhood. Béatrice Didier argues that diarists suffered from regression, from a desire to return to the womb, and it is undeniable that the daily chore of writing was like a perpetual classroom task or homework assignment.[23]

A diary, in a first and perhaps most important sense, is an activity. It requires tiresome labor: think of the 17,000 pages written by Amiel. For those who savored interior monologue, keeping a diary was also a source of sophisticated pleasure. "When I am alone," Maine de Biran declared, "I have plenty to do in following the movement of my ideas and impressions, in exploring myself, in examining my dispositions and my various ways of being, in drawing the best out of myself, in registering the ideas that come to me by chance or that are suggested to me by my reading." In this respect the diary was privacy's crowning joy: "I aspire to become myself upon returning to private, family life," the same writer confessed. "Until then I shall be beneath myself; I shall be nothing." Yet, not surprisingly, the diary was the enemy of matrimonial bliss. Wives especially were obliged to write in secret. Eugénie de Guérin hid, even from her adored father, the notebook that she filled at night in her tiny room while contemplating the stars. Keeping a diary did indeed have the masturbatory character that Béatrice Didier has noted.

Historians have yet to measure accurately the social distribution of the diary, which in many ways remains the exclusive province of literary critics. The fact that many diaries have not survived has led to underestimating their number. Several indications suggest that diaries formed a counterpoint to countless lives. Even among the petite bourgeoisie diaries were not unknown, as evidenced by that of P. H. Azaïs, a Parisian autodidact of modest background. At this level the diary may be seen as the heir of the old *livre de raison* and the companion of the account book. There is reason to suspect, moreover, that the number of young girls who poured their feelings into diaries is legion. Caroline Brame, whose papers were found at a flea market, and Marie Bashkirtseff were certainly not isolated examples, nor was Isabelle Fraissinet.

The great vogue of the scrapbook should also be mentioned. Pierre Georgel notes that during the July Monarchy every daughter of good family kept one and showed it to family friends.[24] Lamartine perused that of Léopoldine Hugo, in which little Didine recorded her games, her childish dreams, and her readings until the age of thirteen. Later she recalled the sighs over and confessions about the first admirers who began to attract her attention. She started to be concerned with her appearance and with remarks on the dances and plays she saw, and she also recorded notes on her travels. The scrapbook was a catch-all: report cards were glued to some of its pages, and picturesque engravings stuck between others. After Léopoldine married, her scrapbook joined other notebooks in the new museum of family archives.

Symbolic equivalents of the scrapbook and perhaps the diary existed at lower levels of society. Was not the trousseau that an adolescent girl embroidered a kind of record of her private feelings and dreams of the future? Its function was certainly more than to ensure an adequate supply of linen after marriage. Agnès Fine has written of the care with which marriageable girls in the Pyrenees sewed, embroidered, and monogrammed with red thread a treasure that would subsequently prove of little use.[25] Even young heiresses engaged in this ritual activity, which in their case could be of no practical use. Women were extremely attached to this symbolic hoard, and Cabet was accused of having proposed in *Icarie* to confiscate these prized trousseaus. By attaching extreme value to the chest of linen that Gilliat inherits from her mother, the author of *Travailleurs de la mer* did indeed mean to single out a major component of the popular sensibility.

Wise Ambitions

The diarist's retrospective search for self stimulated regret and spurred nostalgia; it simultaneously conferred value on aspiration and encouraged individuals to dream of what they might become. What we need is a history of ambition, a history that unfortunately remains beyond reach. But one thing is clear: people's images of the future were quite modest.

Such prudence contradicts the superficial idea that the nineteenth century was one of boundless appetites. We must not forget the allure of the status quo and the powerful mechanisms that maintained it. For a long time widespread reliance on patronage, recommendations, connections, and intertwined family strategies impeded the rise of meritocracy, which even after the triumph of the Republic continued to be tempered by other factors. Fears of overexertion and excess, backed by medical wisdom, helped restrain ambition. Classical humanism also played a part, despite a condescending contempt which today seeks to minimize its influence. How many mature men, readers of Horace, did not strive above all else for *otium* and adhere to the precept *carpe diem*? Among them were the poet-prefects described by Vincent Wright, and the président de Neuville, the magistrate who figures in Duranty's play *Le Malheur d'Henriette Gérard*. The thirst for public esteem evident in the obsession with decorations often exceeded the desire for riches, and the difficulties faced by the parvenu show that social mobility was not merely a matter of wealth.

With these facts in mind it becomes easier to understand some of the results of quantitative history, such as the continuing attraction of the professions and the civil service. A survey, commissioned by Duruy in 1864, of students studying the classics at provincial lycées showed that most planned to attend law school, medical school, or the military academy at Saint-Cyr. The bourgeoisie preferred state service to business. Christophe Charle has been able to gauge the durability of the mechanisms of social reproduction and the persistent attractiveness of the high civil service.[26] The Ecole Polytechnique and other *grandes écoles* fascinated bourgeois youth, even though the practice of moving back and forth between the civil service and the private sector had yet to develop, so that entering the civil service was not a sure means of amassing great wealth.

Workers, proud of their skills and expertise, were less anxious to escape their social background. There was, consequently, a high rate of intermarriage among the sons and daughters of men in a given trade and a low degree of upward mobility. The frequency of occupational changes from generation to generation should not be allowed to conceal the overall stability of social status.

Between 1830 and 1850, however, a minority of workers suffered profoundly from a new frustration.[27] These were individuals who felt destined to a calling other than that of being

Heroism, virility, literary and artistic creation, and oratorical talent all figured in dreams of self-fulfillment. The 19th-century elite reproduced itself by means of schools of law and medicine—and especially by the so-called *grandes écoles,* whose uniforms, shown here, continued to attract ambitious young scholars.

exploited workers, and who were pained by the hours squandered on their jobs. They suffered in a sense from a superfluity of sensibility and sought to assuage their pain by throwing themselves body and soul into "bedroom fantasies." The nights of these proletarians, filled with dreams of the future, were haunted by the paradise of identity. Living like workers but striving to talk and write like bourgeois, this minority of the working class experienced its own peculiar form of stress. The ambitions of these men cost them an immense effort of reading difficult works, copying out sections, and learning whole passages by heart. Another sign of the spread of proletarian ambition is the much larger number of Parisian workers who attended night courses during the July Monarchy. The history of these singular individuals casts a new light on the mute quantitative data and tells us something about the origins of desire.

In the countryside too, people little by little began to dream of individual futures. Evidence of these tentative first steps must be sought in deeds more than in words. Thus, Pierre Rivière's horrible crime may be interpreted as an individual response to a collective malaise. The formulation of individual ambitions caused family structures to disintegrate slowly, at a pace that varied from region to region and according to the nature of the structure concerned. Strategies of inheritance were disrupted, yet the problem of how to deal with younger children in the stem-family system was neatly resolved just in the nick of time. According to Gregor Dallas, who has studied the peasantry in the Orléanais, developing individualization weakened the bond between mother and children, heightened feelings of insecurity, and destroyed a "peasant economy" that might otherwise have resisted ongoing economic upheavals.[28] Families did not turn inward and make the child king; rather, they fell apart as the emotional bonds that had held them together withered away. Innumerable signs of growing disregard for family members and of the evaporation of family feeling could be mentioned. To give just one example, during the Restoration migrant workers from Creuse began to refuse to hand over their savings to their fathers, and before long they stopped coming home to hug their mothers and sisters.

Young men in the countryside were torn between three types of ambition, which were subject to the influence of subtle intrafamilial hierarchies, particularly that determined by the relative age of the brothers. First, there was the traditional ambition to own land. This was easier to achieve now than in the past; it was reflected in the rising price of land, in the fragmentation of farms, and in the resumption of large-scale land-clearing. Second, there was a wish to rise socially by taking a rare post in one of the ancillary rural occupations such as miller or, above all, taverner. Such positions were indispensable springboards to social success in rural Pas-de-Calais.[29] The third ambition was to move permanently to the city, where the risks of exile were reduced by networks of migrants that offered solidarity, assistance in finding lodging and work, and mutual defense. Usually regionally based, such networks had grown up in the cities over decades; the contacts developed in one generation made it possible for subsequent generations to rise socially.

Religious Vocations

At the summit of the scale of ambitions were religious vocations. Irrepressible urges to embrace the religious life frequently disrupted, and in some cases exalted, nineteenth-century family life. The upsurge in vocations is evident from the increase in the number of ecclesiastics up to the beginning of the Third Republic. The social background of those entering the Church varied so much from diocese to diocese that it is pointless to attempt even a brief summary. Overall, however, the clergy had a markedly more rural coloration than in the past. The original call often came on the eve of a young person's First Communion, during that mystical crisis that George Sand recounted so well after the fact and that the unfortunate Caroline Brame experienced with such intensity. After 1850 angelic symbolism, Marian devotion, the dogma of the Immaculate Conception, the revival of hitherto neglected saints, and the waning of antimystical attitudes all encouraged a juvenile sentimentality whose impulses were contained by a simultaneous denial of the body. Apparitions of the Virgin from La Salette (1846) to Pontmain (1871) attested to her divine presence and stimulated additional vocations.

A secular equivalent of the religious vocation also merits attention. Certain bourgeois politicians led lives that suggest they thought of themselves as apostles of the people. Charles-Ferdinand Gambon, a fabulously wealthy participant in the revolution of 1848, spent fifteen years of his life in prison, withstood the pleading of his family and fiancée, and endured the subtle tortures of his jailers rather than seek the emperor's

pardon. When finally freed, he devoted the rest of his life to the republican cause. Countless working-class militants who lived an almost apostolic life on the road, feminists who chose to remain virgins, or at least not to marry, and ascetic teachers more or less consciously modeled their behavior on the ancient model of the religious vocation. And Françoise Mayeur has shown how life at the Ecole Normale of Sèvres resembled that of a convent.[30] It would no doubt be fruitful to reexamine in this light the brief biographical notices in the *Dictionnaire du mouvement ouvrier* (Dictionary of the Worker's Movement), published by the indefatigable Jean Maitron, to see what they reveal concerning the consecration of individual lives and the dissolution of the one in the dreams of the many.

In the meantime, and by way of conclusion to this brief history of ambition, one thing is certain: disappointment was a common and profound experience. In 1864 students of the

Jules James Rougeron, *A Carmelite Takes the Habit.* Between the signing of the Concordat (1801) and the end of the Second Empire, the number of female vocations increased sharply. The Church in France counted on women to conquer souls in society as well as in the family. (Musée de Dijon.)

classics dreamed of becoming generals, captains of industry, great lawyers; many found themselves employed as school-teachers, accountants, and law clerks. And girls who dreamed of marrying Prince Charming or a handsome artisan were perfectly well aware that the family's marriage strategy, whose requirements they knew by heart, would force them into the arms of some graying bachelor or hapless oaf.

THE SOUL'S WANDERINGS

A revolution in travel occurred during the first half of the nineteenth century. A new experience would occupy a prominent place in people's dreams. The old model of a calm, peaceful journey, punctuated by stops in major cities during which the tourist satisfied his appetite for works of art and visited monuments, gradually gave way to a new type of travel first developed in the eighteenth century and based on such models as Saussure's excursions in the Alps, Ramond de Carbonnières's hikes in the Pyrenees, and Cambry's hikes in Finistère. The chief aims of travel became self-affirmation and self-enrichment.

The New Experience of Space

Travelers set out to acquire a new experience of space and of other people outside the normal context. They thirsted for grandiose scenery and wild landscapes, camped out on mountainsides and contemplated the sunny peaks above and calm valleys below. They read books that invited them to compare themselves to the noble savages who inhabited the places they visited. Images of the highlander from the *Waverley* novels and of Indians from Chateaubriand gave rise to a crude ethnology, composed largely of fantasies. The learned members of the Celtic Academy and the archaeologists of other learned societies pointed out traces of the past embedded in the soil and suggested mysterious correspondences between the mineral, the vegetable, and the human.

Tourists staying in crowded spas ventured out in groups to assault the foothills of nearby mountains. In 1816 Maine de Biran, Ramond in hand, hazarded the slopes of the Pyrenees. Tourist guides published during the July Monarchy indicated outlooks and scenic views. Along with the picture magazines, soon aided by the invention of the snapshot, these guides educated the public's vision. Fashionable itineraries came and went: after the Alps and Auvergne came the turn of Nor-

mandy and later Brittany, despite the inadequacy of tourist lodging. During the July Monarchy and Second Empire the new tourism caught on with people of all classes. Social differences in the timing of various travel fads are easily explained. While good bourgeois from Rouen were setting out for Switzerland, Perrichon was braving death on the *mer de Glace,* a glacier in the vicinity of Mont Blanc.

Even the ordinary act of strolling was transformed. The desire to find a refuge where one could commune with oneself and enjoy the consoling spectacle of nature—in a word, to share Rousseau's experience on the Ile Saint-Pierre—retained its prestige even as its content was modernized. The ideal places for contemplation now became the grotto, the windswept countryside, the wave-wracked coast, the promontory with lighthouse. Readers of *René* and *Dominique* were quick to adopt the new fashions. Jean-Pierre Chaline has found that the bourgeois of Rouen preferred, despite the proximity of the coast and beaches, to take long walks and enjoy lonely reveries in woods and fields.[31]

During the July Monarchy people turned toward a new type of experience, exemplified by Flaubert and Du Camp's hike through Brittany. They ceased to look for revelation from the earth, to search for metaphysical and anthropological meaning, to divine mysterious correspondences. On the other

Family expeditions to the mountains became popular during the Belle Epoque. The new interest in sports revived an old interest in excursions to the Alps and Pyrenees.

Heroic memories of excursions helped to bind family and friends. Although workers no longer embarked on temporary travels, tourism opened up a new range of experiences to a broad segment of the population. The discovery of new vistas was no longer the exclusive province of the Paris elite and wealthy foreigners. (Paris, Bibliothèque Nationale.)

hand, they were more open to sensation, to the messages of their own bodies. In this new form of hiking the body was more deeply implicated than in the past. This first step in the undressing of the body is evident in the country picnics of Courbet's sleeping nudes and Maupassant's boaters, in the vogue for beaches, where people went in search not of sun—not yet—but of cool, fresh air, and in the rigors of bathing in fifty-five-degree ocean water that Didine Hugo mentions in her scrapbook.

Equally important for cultivated young men was the initiatory function of the great "oriental" journey—the trip to Spain, Greece, Egypt, and the Bosporus. The increasingly common honeymoon trip, now open to people from all levels of society, was an opportunity for initiation in two senses. Young couples were drawn to Venice and Tunis on the one hand, to the coasts of Brittany and the Norwegian fjords, on the other.

Travel was still a diversion from the ordinary course of life. People came away from their journeys with a collection of souvenirs whose importance it is difficult even to imagine today. Scrapbooks filled with fragmentary impressions and impressions modeled after those in the fashionable *Voyage pittoresque* were indispensable mementos, and the many notebooks and travel stories published by the greatest writers,

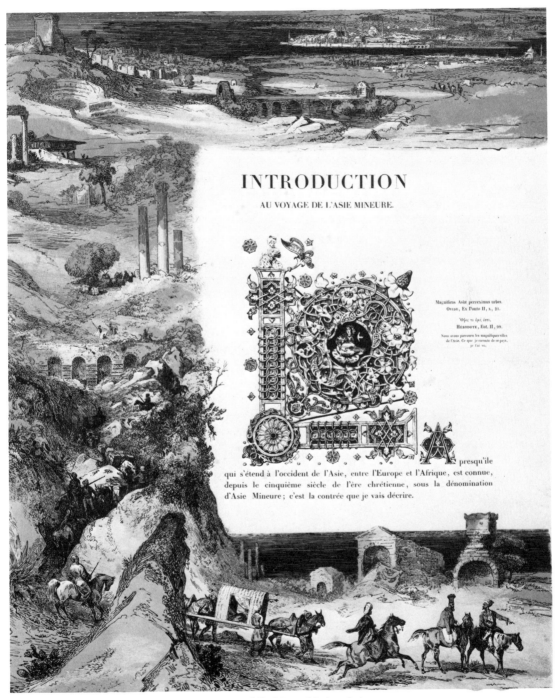

Laborde, *Journey to the Orient*, 1837. (Paris, Bibliothèque Nationale.)

from Stendhal to Flaubert, from Gautier to Nerval, attest to the intensity of the experience. It was only much later, however, with the introduction of pleasure trains and especially the organization of mass pilgrimages in the wake of the Assumptionists' offensive (1871–1879), that the rural masses began to experience the same transports of emotion that had enriched the lives of the elite for more than a century.

In the cities the emergence of the *flâneur,* or idle stroller, noted by Hugo and acutely analyzed by Baudelaire, reflected both the transformation of public space and the new importance of privacy. In his strolls through the city's stony vistas the flâneur invented strategies for appropriating public space; he should therefore be regarded as a transitional figure. In his urban explorations he searched for places where it might be possible to reconstitute the conditions of private life. In his eyes the street itself resembled an apartment. The arcades constructed by the urban planners of the July Monarchy and the cafés tucked away in them were ideal settings for the new forms of public comportment. To the flâneur they were like sham interiors. Later, in the age of Haussmanization, the railway stations and huge department stores—those new mazes of merchandise—would become the flâneur's last refuge. Now viewed as a quaintly odd figure, he gradually relinquished the sidewalk to people in a hurry. Pressed pedestrians, worried about their safety and absorbed in preoccupations of their own, lacked the leisure to attend to the spectacle of the street, which ceased to be seen as an extension of the home.

The Paths of Reverie

The audacity with which the romantics transformed the imagination, blazed new paths for reverie, enriched the forms of interior monologue, and invited their readers to engage in meditation, contemplation, and even mystical ecstasy is well known. Here I can do no more than give a brief resumé of this prodigious change. Rousseau and later Lamartine developed the sensuous reverie in which the mind contemplated its own inner life. This new genre dominated the literature of the Restoration, in which private meditations were set against the themes of death, the flight of time (recalled by relics of the past), the ocean, the starry night, the song of the nightingale. After 1830 wider avenues opened up to the imagination. Exotic myths, which allowed exploration of faraway lands and the remote past, supplanted private reverie.

To what extent did literature influence people's behavior?

New walls around private life, stricter hygiene, more strenuous exercise, the new concern with modesty, and closer management of time must have encouraged some to seek escape through the imagination. Young girls, whose lives were most closely regulated of all, dreamed ethereal dreams of love, as evidenced by works of fiction from Balzac to Edmond de Goncourt and Marcel Prévost. Boys, sent away to boarding schools and isolated from girls their own age, dreamed of diaphanous sylphs; some experimented with degrading sexual practices. A slender silhouette glimpsed in church or an oval face framed in a window was all it took to kindle a fantasy.

Innumerable traces of this penchant for fantasy can be found in the archives of youth. Eugénie de Guérin's walks in the cemetery seem to have been inspired, down to the very poses she struck, by the iconography of death and the maiden. The "style book" that Léopoldine Hugo kept when she was sixteen or seventeen shows that she excelled at "pensive dissertations" and reveals an astonishingly mature mastery of the techniques of meditation. One of her texts, entitled "The Night," is a lengthy analysis of reverie. George Sand recounts how, as an adolescent, she imagined a park at Versailles, which she had never seen. Later, young Aurore developed the habit of plunging herself wholeheartedly into the illusions of the moment, abandoning herself to the most insane ideas. Exotic reveries became a mania. Her writings attest to aspects of virginal behavior that were widely discussed in the medical literature. The Flaubertian temptation, of a life dreamed rather than lived, also has its place here, though we cannot measure how widely it was diffused through society.

Dream Imagery

Jean Bousquet believes that people in the nineteenth century needed to dream more than people in earlier times; this may account for their lively interest in the subject. Dreams were supposed to reveal the true core of the personality, hidden during the day beneath numerous shrouds. Freud's influence has tended to obscure certain of the nineteenth century's beliefs about dreams. During the first few decades of the century philosophers pondered the nocturnal status of the soul. Maine de Biran believed that just as the body slept, so too did the soul. Jouffroy, however, held that the soul remained awake, and Lélut maintained that it rested. For the romantics, dreaming was nothing less than a resurrection of the soul, and dreams revealed the very depths of being.

For a long time scientific accounts of the mechanism of dreaming were influenced by the Idéologues' interest in co-enesthesis and by the belief that the physical affects the moral. Messages from the body's organs, especially the brain, determined the content of dreams; the previous day's concerns and residues of daily sensations were crucial. Maine de Biran and, later, Moreau de Tours, Alfred Maury, and Macario, distinguished between sensory, affective, and intellectual dreams.

Between 1845 and 1860 a galaxy of French thinkers revolutionized dream theory. Dreams, they argued, were simply one of several mechanisms whereby higher psychic forms suffered regression and dissolution. The dream was thus relegated to the realm of pathology, along with delirium and madness. Researchers devoted a great deal of attention to the phenomenon of somnambulism as well as to the hypnagogic process, that is, to the imprecise sensations that one experiences on the threshold of dreaming, when thought ceases to be coherent. The "psychiatrization" of dreaming is evident in Moreau de Tours's *De l'identité de l'état de rêve et de la folie* (On the Identity of the Dream State and Madness, 1855) as well as in the fascination with Nerval's *Aurélia*. The dream science developed in this period reigned unchallenged, in France at any rate, until the introduction of psychoanalysis.

A more difficult historical problem concerns the phenomenology of dreams and the social distribution of oneiric practices. Bousquet opened the debate with a peremptory dictum: "Only since roughly 1780 have men dreamed the strange scenes and bizarre, meaningless puzzles" that constitute the substance of modern dreams. In his view, the form, content, and function of dreaming all changed dramatically at the end of the eighteenth century.[32]

Be that as it may, specialists agree that premonitory dreams disappeared in this period. Dreams ceased to be focused on the future. According to George Steiner, the spread of Newtonian cosmology and, later, of Darwin's theory of evolution made it impossible to look for signs of the future in the obscurity of the individual night.[33] Nevertheless, "Dream Keys" distributed by hawkers continued to be best-sellers among the lower classes—proof that theory outpaced practice and that archaic beliefs survived in the populace. Dreams now frequently related to the personal history of the dreamer. The romantics led the way with their insistence that dreams represented a return to the very roots of being, preserved in memories of early childhood. Recall that the whole place of childhood in the family was being reevaluated at the same time.

We cannot say with equal assurance what changes took place in erotic dreams. If we confine our attention to erotic dreams in literature, quite common in the eighteenth century, it is clear that their frequency diminishes up to around 1840 or 1850, to be replaced by images of platonic love. Dreams thus evolved in much the same manner as waking reverie. After 1850, however, eroticism made a remarkable comeback. Salacious dreams of brothels, such as those reported by Flaubert, begin to appear for the first time. According to Chantal Briend, this change occurred between 1850 and 1870. Even the hours of sleep were haunted by the allure of purchased sex and the licentiousness of imperial revelry. In this return of eroticism Alfred Maury sees a need for what he calls "de-repression," whose purpose was supposedly to counteract the contemporary religious campaign against the pleasures of the flesh. In fact, the upsurge of sexual dreams coincided precisely with the spread of angelic imagery. Most likely to succumb to the temptations of the sexual dream were hysterical women and virginal young men (many of whom suffered from nocturnal emissions), as well as "individuals engaged in intellectual work and meditation" (according to Macario). Some of the dreams reported by Edmond de Goncourt and, even more, the incest dreams that Jules Renard recounts in his diary attest to an acute awareness of the relation that was developing between dreams and sexual desire at precisely the moment when the seeds of psychoanalysis were being sown.

The frequency of dreams about travel, stagecoaches, trains, and landscapes is also worth noting, for it tends to confirm the psychological importance of the new experience of time. Maury himself dreamed of majestic sites and of paintings he had contemplated as a tourist. No fewer than six cities occur in the dreams he relates. And concerning a particular form of hypnagogic sensation he confesses that "it is chiefly while traveling that I am subject to these picturesque hallucinations."[34]

It would be interesting to catalogue the political themes that cropped up in nineteenth-century dreams. Revolutionary acts are a leitmotif in dream literature. This frequency may be an unconscious sign of the depths of anxiety about revolution. Maury's guillotine dream became famous after Bergson chose to analyze it, as did his dream of the forceps, inspired by an episode that occurred during the June Days. But perhaps these

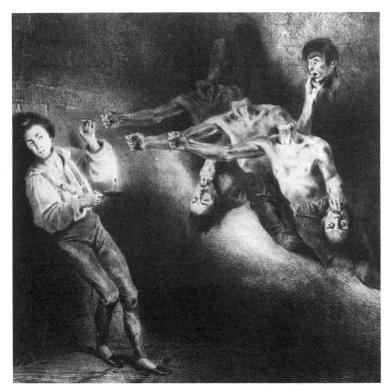

The creatures of nightmare have their own history. Between the invention of the guillotine and the neuroses of the fin de siècle, the elimination of certain forms of torture and the development of new varieties of anxiety and suffering changed the ways in which people dreamed. Page 516: Gustave Doré, *La Rue de la Vieille-Lanterne,* 1855. (Paris, Bibliothèque Nationale.) Left: Louis Boulanger, lithograph illustrating "the lidless eye," taken from *Contes bruns.* (Paris, Bibliothèque Nationale.)

should be interpreted as instances of the sadistic dreams that became common, according to Chantal Briend, at the end of the nineteenth century.

These remarks may seem rather unmethodical compared with the majestic structure erected by Jean Bousquet on the basis of his analysis of hundreds of literary dreams. According to him, the variety of dream images, previously limited to symbols of heaven and hell, gradually expanded after the fall of the ancien régime. Among the offshoots of dreams of Eden we must count dreams of gardens and natural landscapes; among the derivatives of dreams of hell were dreams of caves and cities, as well as anxiety dreams stemming from well-known forms of delirium. These new infernal visions transformed the nightmare. Dreams also conveyed images of inhibition, involuntary actions, and split personalities. After 1850 the two types of dreams gradually converged as dreaming became increasingly secularized. Thereafter, the contemporary type of dream, absurd or bizarre, was free to develop.

Bousquet's fascinating survey, together with my earlier remarks, lends credence to the anti-Freudian hypothesis that dreams have a history. We cannot fail to be struck by the many correlations between the history of the imagination and the evolution of dream content.

MEDIATORS OF MONOLOGUE

At the height of the Second Empire, more old works of pious literature were reprinted than new works were published.[35] This continuity with the past probably would seem even more striking were we to focus exclusively on the literature hawked to the lower classes. The facts suggest that religious sentiment and the forms of individual prayer evolved quite slowly. Spiritual practices still conformed closely to the teachings of earlier masters. For a long time the *Imitation,* of which Lamennais provided a new translation, remained the most widely used guide of zealous Christians. The "good curé" of Ars was a model of atemporal spiritual eclecticism; the pious Eugénie de Guérin still read with veneration the works of Saint Augustine, Saint François de Sales, Bossuet, and Fénelon. Restoration missionaries drew inspiration for their endless accounts of the tortures of hell from the dramatic tone of earlier preachers. Fascinated by death, the Romantics trembled at the terrifying words of Tertullian and Saint Bernard. Meditation on the Last Things quite naturally found its way into new dramatizations of melancholia.

Solitary Prayer and Meditation

Even after all due allowance for continuity has been made, however, it is impossible to deny the nineteenth century's originality in matters of piety, a topic that has been unduly neglected by religious sociologists bent on measuring the extent of de-Christianization. When the intentions of prayer and expressions of gratitude are analyzed, it becomes clear that people prayed for more specific purposes and were more concerned with family matters than ever before. Prayers for the conversion or salvation of a husband or brother and for prosperity and success in business joined the traditional stock of prayers for individual recovery from disease, for a safe ocean voyage, or for the safe return of a soldier.

Ex-votos were never so widespread as in the nineteenth century. In Provence their numbers did not begin to decline until the 1870s. This material sign of gratitude bears the hallmark of petty bourgeois preoccupations; indeed, for the petty bourgeoisie the ex-voto became one of the primary forms of expression. The growing attention devoted to the person of the beneficiary reconfirms the rise of individualism, which we have encountered at every step.

The increasingly family-oriented nature of prayer is also evident in the growing popularity of prayers for souls in purgatory. In order to relieve the suffering of deceased family members a pious son, presumably having heard their appeals for prayer, paid for masses to be celebrated, received communion, said prayers, and did his best to obtain indulgences. In 1884 a country curate, the abbé Burguet, who called himself the "traveling salesman for souls in purgatory," founded an organization known as the Oeuvre Expiatoire in La Chapelle-Montligeon. Its success was astonishing: by 1892 it boasted more than three million associates. This rapid growth attests to a need for the presence of the dead in the midst of life, a feeling reflected in the vogue for spiritualism that swept cultivated circles at the beginning of the Second Empire. Codification of family rituals for the veneration of the dead only increased the desire to make contact with departed souls. The emphasis understandably shifted from the flames of purgatory and its transitory tortures to a more reassuring image of communication with souls now conceived of as waiting in what Philippe Ariès has called a kind of "parlor."

EX V. F. G. LA SIG: ANGELA MARIA MANGIAPAN. SUCESSO LI 19 LUGLIO 1834.

This ex-voto illustrates the structural changes that took place. The space allotted to heavenly intercessors shrank, while more space was devoted to episodes of private life that elicited gratitude. (Notre-Dame-de-Laghet.)

The nature of spiritual life changed, and the soul was obliged to undergo new rites of passage. Meanwhile, agnosticism and freethinking were on the rise. Growing numbers of people lost their faith. Gender differences became more noticeable. Young men almost invariably grappled with doubt as they embarked on adult social life between the ages of sixteen and twenty-five. Lurking in many minds was the tragic image of the renegade priest who mocked the priesthood during the Revolution, an image that inspired the most dazzling of Barbey d'Aurevilley's novels. By contrast, the convert acquired new stature. Zealous missionaries who sought to bring new souls into the Church delighted in recounting conversion experiences. From Mme Swetchine (1815) to Eve Lavallière (1917), from Huysmans to Claudel kneeling at one of the pillars of Notre-Dame, a host of celebrated converts, galvanized by faith, would help quell the doubts and alleviate the tortures of those who had fallen away from religion.

The Exaltation of Suffering

The nineteenth century can be divided into two distinct periods. The first was marked by a baroque sensibility that reached its apogee during the Restoration, a sensibility in which the dominant element, as attested by iconography and pious literature, was the exaltation of pain. Christ's suffering was described with a realism bordering on sadism. The publication of Grou's *L'Intérieur de Jésus et Marie* and the translation, in 1835, of Anne Catherine Emmerich's *Visions of the Life of Jesus and His Doleful Passion* mark the beginning and end of this period. Frightful pages were written about the agony in the Garden of Gethsemane. In this literature, which inspired the neo-Lamartinian school, blood flowed, spurted, and drenched the body of Christ. It became customary to portray Jesus wearing the crown of thorns as a belt around his body. Images of Christ pointing a finger at the gaping hole in his chest became commonplace. The Romantics turned even the Infant Jesus into a figure of suffering. It was in this period that the iconography of the Child of the Sacred Heart surrounded by the bloody crown was developed. Our Lady of the Seven Sorrows and the image of the *Stabat Mater* became focal points of Marian piety. As late as 1846 the Virgin of La Salette bore the symbols of the Passion.

Religious practice reflected this tragic sensibility, which was reinforced by the belief that the blood of Christ circulates throughout human history. Countless women and even young

Top: Emile Charlet, *The End of the Procession*. (Salon of 1913.) Bottom: Jules Breton, *Placing a Calvary*. (Musée de Lille.) Most of the calvaries that dot the French countryside date from the 19th century and attest to the tragic aspect of that era's religious sensibility. The girls' white gowns, on the other hand, illustrate the seraphic aspect of mid-century piety, deeply influenced by Marial devotion.

girls—some of them members of tertiary orders, others not—emulated celebrated ecclesiastics by wearing sackcloth, hair shirts, and even horrible metal belts. The curé of Ars flagellated his "cadaver," while Lacordaire arranged for people to walk on his body and spit in his face. It was no longer enough merely to imitate Christ; the new prayers exalted the ideal of progress toward the perfect refuge. They harped on the notion of inhabiting the Heart of Christ, to be achieved by contemplation of his wounds. The practice of visiting the stations of the cross, which stemmed from the same sensibility, became widespread in the second half of the century, to judge from research in the dioceses of Arras and Orléans. More calvaries were erected in the nineteenth century than in any other period.[35]

Toward a Seraphic Piety

Piety became less intense after the fraternal revolution of February 1848. Ten years before the Trappist physician Pierre Debreyne had criticized the violence of the ascetic life on the grounds that it bred hysteria and tuberculosis. A more sentimental religion challenged the reign of fear and antimystical attitudes. Iconography evolved toward more placid themes. New apparitions of Mary and evolution in Church dogma favored a seraphic piety. The radiant white lady of Lourdes was a long way from the *Mater Dolorosa* of La Salette. The gentle image of the Immaculate Conception of Sées went well with the reassuring figure of the guardian angel that would soon be widely reproduced in color prints. No longer was there anything tragic about even the Virgin of the Sacred Heart of Issoudun.

Mother and child praying together symbolized the new relaxed piety. Religious manuals praised this "touching tableau." Mothers were urged to place the child on the lap, join its tiny hands together in a gesture of prayer, and encourage it to stammer its first words. Young hearts would thus learn to associate the Virgin and the Infant Jesus with mother. This gentle catechism transformed domestic religion, about which we still know very little. Ultimately, in 1910, it resulted in the papal decree *Quam Singulari,* which authorized private communion.

Veneration of the Most Holy Sacrament and increasingly frequent communion further contributed to the relaxation of piety. Perpetual Adoration, instituted in 1852 in the diocese of Orléans and revived the following year in the diocese of

Domestic worship was greatly influenced by the new figures of private life. Prayer and religious instruction tightened the bonds between mothers and children. The feelings evoked by the Christ Child intensified emotional life in general.

Arras, gave rise to a new source of individual emotion. Even the simplest Christians were impressed by the new egalitarianism that enabled them to stand alone, face to face with their God, and watch over him individually. In the entourage of the *"bon curé"* stories were often told about the uneducated peasant who spent hours in the tiny church staring at the statue of Jesus. When questioned about the nature of his meditation, he replied: "I look at him and he looks at me." This sublime "degree zero" of prayer reminds us not to overlook the importance of saying the rosary and meditating on its mysteries. Aided by the revival of old confraternities and the creation of new ones, between 1850 and 1880 these practices spread to growing numbers of people and lower strata of society.

After 1850 private worship proliferated. The decentralization of prayer and adoption of new interlocutors, evident from the new popularity of religious statuary, proved to be a shrewd maneuver, for it enabled the Church to wage war against the widespread veneration of miracle-working saints and magical fountains, which historians have shown persisted

Pious imagery pulled out all the stops in exalting Christ's pain and suffering. These widely distributed prayer cards of the Sacred Heart focused the attention of sensitive souls on death.

Early in the Third Republic
dolls still resembled little girls
and therefore encouraged
identification and confidences.
By the end of the century they
had become chiefly devices for
teaching maternal
responsibilities.

Henri Laurent–Desrousseaux,
Dolly Bath. Salon of 1904.
(Paris, Bibliothèque des Arts
Décoratifs.)

in Charente, Limousin, the Loir-et-Cher, and Morbihan. The same strategy may account in part for the revival or foundation of pilgrimages in many dioceses and cantons. Somewhat later, after France's defeat in the Franco-Prussian War and the episode of the Commune, the Assumptionists orchestrated great religious events on a nationwide scale.

In the early 1860s the image of religion changed. It became serious, moralistic, and above all calculating, showing little concern for impulsiveness or spontaneity. The discourse of piety drew on the language of capitalism.[36] The new utilitarian conception of prayer, confirmed by the vogue for votive objects, transformed the nature of asceticism. The bourgeois prie-dieu became more comfortable, while at the same time the physical violence of earlier asceticism was supplanted by a totting up of merits and demerits. The daily discipline of impulses, the offering up of labor, and the observance of moderate abstinences encouraged constant calculation of the soul's condition and thus led to the integration of prayer into everyday private life.

Inner monologue requires silent interlocutors to perpetuate the soul's exalted state. Three such interlocutors played an important role in the nineteenth century; one of them was the doll.

The Doll and Inner Monologue

During the first half of the nineteenth century, "the French doll resembled not a small, but a scaled-down, woman, whose careful attire closely followed trends in fashion."[37] Nipped-in waist and broad hips reflected contemporary canons of female beauty. There were rag dolls and sheepskin dolls stuffed with sawdust. The head and neck were made of papier-mâché, the teeth of straw or metal. Little girls went walking with their dolls. Because the range of models, the sumptuousness of their trousseaus, and the size of their dollhouses reflected the social hierarchy, dolls helped children become aware of their social identities. It was therefore quite easy for the doll to assume the role of confidant. Stories in which dolls came to life and talked contributed to the doll's ability to perform this psychological function. So did technological progress. Talking dolls were manufactured as early as 1824; the first walking dolls appeared in 1826.

Around the middle of the century, in 1855, a revolution took place. Dolls, now increasingly made of gutta-percha, more often than not represented young girls and were improperly referred to as "babies." As the years went by, the new model gained in popularity, for it was easier for children to identify with these child dolls. Dolls encouraged daughters to think about their relation to their own mothers and to imagine becoming mothers in turn. During the Second Empire the coexistence of adult and "baby" dolls encouraged an exceptionally rich ambiguity. Embroidering the doll's trousseau, organizing a ball in her honor, and imagining her impending marriage encouraged young girls to learn their future roles as women and to familiarize themselves with the society's customs.

As dolls began to represent younger children, the psychological content of this activity was diminished. When the first "nursing doll" appeared in 1879, its attire reduced to diapers and swaddling, and the dollhouse shrank to the dimensions of a cradle, identification became impossible and dolls ceased to serve as girls' confidants. The new toys were useless for learning any role other than that of mother. This transformation is evident in the new language of childhood and, later, in the curriculum of home economics courses.

By 1909 the transformation was complete. That year a new type of doll appeared: a newborn baby boy. Its success was immediate, and it was followed in 1920 by the introduction of a celluloid doll that could be bathed. Meanwhile stuffed animals had appeared on the scene. These reproduced—and stimulated—a type of relationship that has continued to develop throughout the twentieth century.

The Animal, Object of Affection

The history of pets emphasizes the importance of the transformation that occurred in the middle of the Second Empire. Until then elitist practices that had survived from the ancien régime continued to dominate. The court of Louis XVI had already rejected the Christian tradition of indifference toward, not to say suspicion of, soulless animals; it had also rejected the Cartesian notion of the animal-machine. People no longer behaved like Malebranche, who kicked his pregnant cat in the stomach and then blamed its cries on "animal spirits." The salons took to heart the lesson of Rousseau's affection for his dog. People stopped looking at animals as living dolls and began to see them as individuals, worthy of sentiment.

By the turn of the nineteenth century affection toward animals was not simply permissible but firmly established.[38] But that affection took two primary forms. The first was the bond between a woman and her dog. Fond smiles, affectionate

Valerie Rottenbourg, *Beg!* Woman with dog: an increasingly common duo. Tenderness toward pets accorded well with ideas about the feminine sensibility. (Salon of 1912.)

Man's best friend recorded for posterity in a daguerrotype. (Paris, Bibliothèque Nationale.)

looks, "innocent caresses," and "wild games" attested to woman's inclination toward tenderness and pity, an inclination widely acknowledged in medical literature. These womanly acts of compassion were messages addressed to men. Animals were thus assigned a new domestic function; they taught children about the emotions.

Emotional bonds also developed between the elderly and their companions in decline. A number of important texts mark the progressive exaltation of the dog's loyalty: Lacordaire's sermon on the old man's last friend, the curé's white dog in *Jocelyn,* and finally, in Victor Hugo's *L'Homme qui rit,* the silhouette of Homo, the tireless wolf.

If the wealthy now treated animals with affection in their homes, the poor displayed violence toward animals in public. The slaughter of animals was a familiar spectacle, but one that came to be thought of as detrimental to society. During the July Monarchy the government began to require that slaughtering, at least in Paris, be done out of sight. In 1850 the Legislative Assembly passed the Grammont Law, which made it illegal to beat domestic animals in public. This measure had little effect, other than to emphasize the solidity of the walls that had been erected around private life.

Many instances of affectionate treatment of pets can be found in the romantic era. Eugénie de Guérin loved her little dogs; she petted them, groomed them, and prayed for them. When one died, she cried and insisted on a dignified burial. This aspect of her emotional life occupies a great deal of space in her diary. Her love also embraced birds, particularly the nightingale. Her concern even extended to the tiny gnats that scurried across the pages of her book. Already animals were being transformed into a balm for the tortures of solitude. When Stendhal found himself alone in Civitavecchia in 1841, with no one to love, he petted his two dogs. In old age Mérimée lived alone with a cat and a tortoise. Victor Hugo was quite attached to the loyal dog that followed him into exile. Gambon's notebooks are particularly revealing when it comes to feelings about pets. The Forty-Eighter was capable of being moved by the eyes of a steer, the friskiness of a horse, or the vulnerability of a sheep. Like Silvio Pellico, he fed a spider in his prison cell and kept company with a snail. At Doullens, Mazas, and Belle-Ile he raised warblers, which became his closest friends. From one of his companions in misfortune, a poor Limousin peasant, he learned the song of the goldfinch and attempted to transcribe it into musical notation.

All of this gives us a clear indication of the common man's regard for animals. We must not be blinded by all the rhetoric regarding the carter's brutality to his horse or the bloody-mindedness of the men who organized cock- and dog-fights. In the 1820s the peasants of Aunay-sur-Odon were astonished by Pierre Rivière's cruelty toward frogs and birds and outraged by the way he tortured horses. From Odoard de Mercurol's correspondence we learn that the peasants of Drôme did not slaughter animals that had served them well. And the passion of workers in the Nord for pigeons is well known. In 1839 J. B. Rochas Séon published his *Histoire d'un cheval de troupe* (The Story of a Cavalry Horse), an edifying tale in which a young peasant is unafraid to enlist in order to follow his horse, which has been bought by the army. When he dies of tuberculosis, the animal refuses to go on living.

Affection for animals developed even more after 1860, when a veritable collective neurosis set in. In 1845 the Society

Charles Trevor Garland, *Little Girl Defending Her Cat*. At the end of the century, relations of dependency in private space were reversed. (Paris, Bibliothèque des Arts Décoratifs.)

for the Protection of Animals had been established in Paris. Its existence was in one sense a reflection of Anglomania, but it also reflected the efforts of French animal-lovers, led by Dr. Pariset. During the second Empire the keeping of pets, especially poodles, in apartments became an accepted fact. Dog shows came into vogue. As people became obsessed with pedigrees and grooming, photographs of the family pet began to appear in albums alongside the children. It became customary to bury pets in the yard. Pet cemeteries inaugurated a new form of veneration of the dead. Dogs even posed a problem to railroad companies, which put on special cars for pets. Meanwhile, young women, from bourgeois matrons in their private rooms to seamstresses in their garrets, kept birds in cages as a mark of their sensitivity and a token of their virtue. In 1856 Michelet wrote a book on birds that strengthened this attachment.

During the final quarter of the century the status of animals changed somewhat. The growing influence of freethinkers gave rise to a new fraternity between man and beast. Guarantees for the rights of animals and concern for their well-being were ways of alleviating the new solitude of the human race. The problem was posed not in ecological terms but in terms of encouraging humanitarian sentiments and maximizing social utility. Primary schools aided the effort by focusing attention on animals. The spread of evolutionary theories, the extension of veterinary medicine, and the success of animal husbandry all encouraged the new fraternity. Anthropomorphism reached a peak, and books such as Alphonse Toussenel's *Zoologie passionnelle* all too plainly betrayed man's newfound desire to communicate with animals.

Yet here too Pasteur's discoveries changed behavior. To be sure, the fear of germs, which persuaded some people that animals could be petted safely only by wearing gloves, apparently did not survive the initial vogue for the new theories. That fear even worked in favor of the house cat, which smelled less than its rival and was reputed to take better care of itself. Cats, until then confined to high society and artistic circles, now became pets of the common people. The imperial family kept Siamese cats, and Gautier and Baudelaire chose cats for companions; concierges showed a new appreciation of the virtues of the cat apart from its function in controlling the population of rats and mice. By the turn of the twentieth century animals no longer depended on men; men depended on animals, at least in an emotional sense, and animals were on the verge of becoming sovereign masters of domestic space.

Edmond de Goncourt was scarcely exaggerating when he baptized the piano the "lady's hashish." Danièle Pistone has found two thousand scenes in nineteenth-century novels in which a piano appears. Half of them involved young, single women; one-quarter involved married women. The great vogue for the instrument began in 1815. Prudery helped, because the harp, the cello, and the violin all came to be seen as indecent. During the July Monarchy the piano spread to the petite bourgeoisie, and after that it was fully democratized. By 1870 it was considered somewhat vulgar, and its popularity began to decline.

The most obvious conclusion to be drawn from Pistone's work is that the social function of the instrument was of primary importance. The ability to play the piano well established a child's reputation and gave public proof of a good education. Virtuosity figured, along with the rest of the "aesthetic dowry," in marriage strategies. Pianos were rarely the site of an amorous exchange or dialogue, however. That role

The Lady's Hashish

Dejonghe, *Young Woman at the Piano,* 1880. The ability to play the piano enhanced a woman's chances on the matrimonial market. Agile fingers created a sonorous environment that comforted children as they played and inspired daydreams in loved ones. When a woman married, her silent piano reminded her parents how much they missed her.

Auguste Renoir, *Woman at the Piano,* 1875. (Chicago Art Institute. Martin A. Ryerson Collection.)

belonged to the song, especially the ballad. Still, in four stock scenes from nineteenth-century literature, the piano, played by a solitary woman, usually in the evening, can be seen to fill the roles of friend, confidant, soul mate, and aid to self-expression. These conventions gradually disappeared as the piano was transformed from soul mate into inert furniture.

Even the innocent fingers of an inexperienced young girl could express through the keyboard feelings that could never be stated in language. For that reason Balzac advised his sister, Laure Surville, to buy a piano. The instrument was seen as an outlet for the timid. Accordingly, it was a literary convention to portray a young girl at the piano who, believing that she is alone, reveals unsuspected feelings to an indiscreet listener. The piano, which lifted the girl's soul toward the lofty realm of the ideal, even helped her to conceal those feelings from herself.

Less frequently the piano expressed nostalgia for thwarted love or served as a messenger to an absent lover. It could also convey the pain of the soul wounded by the end of love. According to Edmond About, it was customary for a man to send a piano to a woman he had jilted.[39] This custom can be seen in the literary stereotype of the good but not very pretty woman who, sensitive and understanding, improvises wrenching tunes though her heart is broken—the woman of whom Jules Laforgue wrote that she "performs her own autopsy with a few bars of Chopin."

A third literary convention was the most common of all. In it the piano serves as outlet for irrepressible passions. It is a piano that calms the tumultuous feelings of the duchesse de Langeais. In this role the instrument replaced the horseback ride and the walk through a storm. (Note the proximity of the three semantic fields.) Well before psychoanalysis, Edmond de Goncourt saw a connection betwen playing the piano and masturbation.

Finally, the piano helped women idle away the hours while awaiting the arrival of a man. According to Hippolyte Taine, playing the piano helped women resign themselves to the "nullity of the feminine condition." Note, however, that all these conventional scenes, which attest to the importance of the piano in private life, tell us primarily about the way men thought of women at the piano. Hair down, face illuminated by candles, eyes vacant, the female pianist was depicted as a prey to male desire.

Lonely Leisure and Secret Treasures

Books were expensive during the first half of the nineteenth century. Under the Restoration a new novel would have claimed one-third of a farm worker's monthly wages. Until well into the Second Empire, therefore, booksellers were few and far between. Rental libraries were the rule. These *cabinets de lecture* played an important role in Restoration Paris.[40] Libraries lent either by single volume or by subscription. A reader about to leave for his or her country home could borrow twenty to one hundred books at a time. Forty thousand Parisians availed themselves of these libraries. Most apparently were members of the new bourgeoisie, particularly the petite bourgeoisie, which was well satisfied with the rental system. In the lending libraries one met not only rentiers and students but many people who lived in contact with the upper classes: chambermaids, building superintendents, and shop girls. Servants were sent out to borrow books to read to their masters on the boulevard Saint-Germain. In the Temple district the bulk of the libraries' clientele consisted of seamstresses, *grisettes,* and artisans; workers seldom visited. Lending libraries existed in the provinces, but they were slower to develop there than in the capital. In cantonal seats in the Limousin during the July Monarchy and the Second

Mary Shepard Greene, *A Short Story*. Clearly this young woman is reading not a pious work but a novel, a decent one, no doubt, but still instructive enough to teach the young innocent things she might otherwise never know. (Salon of 1902.)

Empire, haberdashers' wives, often widows, occasionally borrowed novels from the less expensive collections.

People who lived in remote rural areas were obliged to order books by mail. A book was a precious commodity. The surprise gift of a book could be an occasion for rejoicing. When the residents of poor Cayla near Albi received works by Walter Scott or Victor Hugo, they were overcome with joy. Hawkers, usually Pyreneans, traveled through such areas selling the books of major publishers. This method of book selling reached its apogee during the Second Empire. These publishers' men supplanted the humble traveling salesmen who had distributed countless copies of *Télémaque, Simon de Nantua, Geneviève de Brabant,* and *Robinson Crusoe* in earlier decades.

In the 1860s a more efficient system of distribution was established. The public libraries continued to slumber. Their collections of classic and scientific works, partly inherited from ancient monasteries and convents, interested few people other than specialists, who were hindered by limited hours of access. The silence that reigned in these austere establishments and the attire required of readers went too much against the grain of working-class habits to allow public libraries to play much of a role. But city dwellers now had access to a fairly decent range of bookstores, and these were complemented by railway station libraries. Meanwhile, the advent of inexpensive, mass-circulation newspapers rendered the broadsheets of the early nineteenth century obsolete. Peasants, however, continued to find useful reading in their almanacs.

Louis Tesson, *Meditation.* Historians of 19th-century literature have long noted the importance of the window in representations of the female sensibility. For young women at home awaiting the arrival of their man, the window offered a view of the world. It let in light for reading, but it also allowed women to look out on the wider scene, whose tumult was muffled by the glass.

Changes in Reading Habits

Three different library systems came into being: parish libraries, popular libraries, and school libraries. The parish libraries, which began to appear in even the smallest towns during the July Monarchy, specialized in works of piety. The popular libraries, established in 1865, were frequented mainly by young people who had developed a taste for reading in school. The school libraries played the same role as the collection of prize books that some peasants kept on a shelf. For rural people starved for reading, these meager resources were hardly enough to fill the gap that developed after the book hawkers vanished but before the development of a mass-circulation regional press.

As the system of distribution changed, so did the nature of reading. Reading aloud in the home declined, as did the

The almanac's contents may have changed, but it remained the peasant's primary reading matter up to the First World War. Easily carried from place to place, it entertained the whole community during evening gatherings. In a paradoxical way it also helped peasants to understand the larger society. (Paris, Bibliothèque Nationale.)

practice of writing from dictation. During the July Monarchy the bourgeois of Rouen continued to read in the salon by the fireplace in the evenings. Later, however, singing, playing music, and painting supplanted an activity that had come to be seen as old-fashioned, suitable only for the sick and elderly. Reading aloud thus became the exclusive province of the devoted daughter or companion who attended to the needs of an elderly person. The reading of pious works to illiterate servants, an exercise performed several times daily by Mademoiselle d'Ars, the curé's châtelaine, also fell out of fashion.

By contrast, until the First World War reading aloud remained a traditional activity among peasants gathered together for the evening. The texts to be read were necessarily short. Their purpose was to stimulate conversation, to provide a subject for comment by all present. Such an activity was naturally very different from the monotone reading style of the bourgeois salon, always a potential soporific. At the end of the century porcelain workers at Limoges read aloud to one another in their workshops, a late instance of a practice whose origins can be traced back to convent refectories and which is still practiced in religious boarding schools. But for the most part reading aloud gave way to silent reading.

Silent reading did not necessarily mean solitary reading. People read in libraries, clubs, cafés, and reading rooms. But reading to oneself did imply self-absorption and abstraction from the environment—in short, a whole range of attitudes from which the lower classes long felt excluded. By contrast, for some people reading in solitude was a way of consciously joining a group of other readers, a way of engaging in conversation with imaginary partners. During the July Monarchy the man who read his newspaper in his salon was taking part in public life, and his activity was perceived accordingly. To subscribe to *La Quotidienne* in Nancy during the time of Lucien Leuwen was to join the small circle of legitimists. The bourgeoisie of Rouen read a great deal, Flaubert's opinion to the contrary notwithstanding. Conversations in high society were filled with comments on the novelties of the day, knowledge of which required reading in private before venturing out into society. Such reading was done in the salon or bedroom, on the garden bench, or in the great outdoors.

Once an elitist pastime, reading spread throughout society as literacy improved. Parent-Duchâtelet discovered to his astonishment that some prostitutes spent hours reading love novels. Nocturnal reading exerted, as we saw earlier, a pow-

erful attraction on a small working-class elite after the revolution of 1830. Even as early as 1826 or 1827 Agricol Perdiguier nourished himself on disparate and haphazard reading during his tour of France. Besides devouring the kinds of books sold by hawkers and indulging his love for the songs of journeymen, he also developed a passion for some of the most insipid authors of the eighteenth century, whose works had just been published in definitive editions.

Reading habits varied widely with age and sex. More than ever people tried to limit children's reading to once-popular fairy tales and legends. Innumerable new editions of Perrault and Mme d'Aulnoy were now joined by a host of works whose authors, from the comtesse de Ségur to Jean Macé, attempted to capture the peculiarities of the child's imagination. A new development was a literature aimed at the children of the bourgeoisie and intended to justify social supremacy on the grounds of moral superiority. Led by Mme Necker de Saussure and Mme Guizot, a stellar array of well-intentioned ladies drew their inspiration from a model developed by Mme de Genlis. All these women agreed with the

Emile Adan, *The Reader.* Reading aloud, once practiced in the salon, was rarely done in the late 19th century, except, as here, when a companion read to an elderly woman.

Jules Trayer, *The Picture Book*. Looking at picture books drew siblings together. The book offered a calm, meditative alternative to the bustle of the yard and helped to shape the image of the well-behaved child.

physicians that the reading of young ladies must be closely monitored. All denounced the nefarious influence of the novel, which became the focus of the tension between desire and taboo.

A reader's social background obviously affected the way in which he or she consumed books. Before there were school libraries, the young peasant starved for reading matter had no choice but to read whatever came his way. Sometimes he overestimated the importance of what he read; the influence of haphazard reading could be tremendous. Pierre Rivière responded to what he read in 1820 in much the same way as the seventeenth-century Friulian miller studied by Carlo Ginzburg. Both were unfortunate victims of undisciplined habits of mind. For a long time to come, autodidacts would continue to suffer the consequences of their boundless appetite for the printed word, so cruelly mocked by Sartre in *Nausea*. A half-century after Agricol Perdiguier, the Valenciennes miner Jules Mousseron devoured whatever books he could get his hands on the moment he emerged from underground. Female workers during the Belle Epoque were less bold; when reading they felt that they were stealing time normally devoted to work. They did not boast of their reading and were careful not to express personal tastes. Nevertheless, they avidly devoured popular novels whose style was suited to being read piecemeal and commented on at the workplace or while riding the bus to and from home.

What did people read once they had reached an age when they were free to choose for themselves? Literary history can be misleading; the most significant genres were not necessarily the most prestigious. Works of piety were widely read in 1861, and estate inventories reveal the importance of professional books. The magistrates of Poitiers filled their libraries with law books, and country doctors equipped theirs with books of medicine. The works of classical authors continued to accumulate on the shelves; the Parisian bourgeois disdained contemporary literature.[41] Eugène Boileau, who in 1872 retired to his château at Vigné, passed his time annotating Seneca and Benjamin Franklin, the two authors from whom he had derived his personal code of conduct. Poetry was widely read in the nineteenth century. Familiarity with the lectern, the need to listen to long liturgical texts, the taste for Latin poets among the largely bilingual cultivated public, the vogue for postpran-

The Contents of Books

Forbidden Fruit, based on a painting by Auguste Toulmouche, Salon of 1865. Toulmouche is suggesting
that despite the wide distribution of pious literature demonstrated by Claude Savart, young women
during the Second Empire still knew how to amuse themselves with books from the upper shelves.
(Paris, Bibliothèque des Arts Décoratifs.)

dial amateur poems that were later dutifully copied out into family scrapbooks, the proliferation of poetry societies, and, perhaps most significant of all, the vogue for singing and the growing numbers of working-class poets—all these things ensured that poetry was an important presence at all levels of society. To mention just two indications of this ubiquity: in Valenciennes, during the Belle Epoque, nearly all the miners' daughters kept notebooks of songs; the same custom existed among hatmakers in the Aude Valley.[42]

Contemporaries noted the steady inroads made by the novel at the expense of the classical authors and works of history. From the time of the July Monarchy serialized fiction enjoyed extraordinary success. Lower prices made possible larger editions, as the publisher Charpentier successfully demonstrated, and novels were read even by the lower classes. The teaching of science and patriotic values in the schools contributed to the success of contemporary authors. By the end of the century people in small hamlets in the Creuse had begun to collect modest libraries in which the works of Victor and Paul Margueritte stood alongside those of Verne and Erckmann-Chatrian.

The Home Museum

The progress of silent reading was matched by a growing interest in the solitary pleasures of the study. In the nineteenth century collecting was still primarily a masculine pastime. It was men who invented and defined the project of accumulation. Women were capable only of trivial creations. In 1892 and 1895 shows of women's collections attracted ironic comment from the critics, who refused to see any value in these contemptible products of idleness. At best a woman might be moved by affection or piety to accumulate particularly moving family souvenirs in the drawers of her writing desk.

The nature of collecting changed in the first half of the nineteenth century. Objects that once had embellished aristocratic studies had been scattered by the Revolution and reduced to cast-offs. Many turned up in curiosity shops, of which Victor Hugo paints a remarkable portrait in *Quatre-Vingt-Treize*. At a time when great public collections were being assembled, the revision of old hierarchies disrupted the traditional signs of social supremacy.

A new breed of collector appeared on the scene. From 1815 to 1840 it was a buyer's market. Like Balzac's Cousin Pons, antique dealers, many of them people of modest means and no social position, quickly amassed astonishing collections. Between 1840 and 1845 collecting suddenly became fashionable. The bourgeoisie crowded antique shops. New rules were codified. People studied antiques and visited shops to engage in patient research. The July Monarchy was the golden age of the "archaeological" study, the home museum, and of collecting without regard to the marketplace. Collectors favored antiques; their ambition was to "preserve history," not to make a killing. When a collector died, his treasures were dispersed. Collectors existed even in the provinces; a dozen or so were active in Toulouse.

By 1850 the antique business was fully organized and antiques had acquired real value. The fact that Pons's treasures end up in the hands of the uncultivated Popinot foreshadows the coming influence of profit. The behavior of collectors changed. A galaxy of extremely wealthy collectors set the tone. All the great businessmen felt a need to accumulate valuable collections; with some this passion seems to have outstripped all others. Banking magnates such as the Pereire brothers, who owned a hôtel in the faubourg Saint-Honoré, and the Rothschilds, who had one in Ferrières, were smitten by the collector's lust. So were many industrialists: Eugène Schneider collected Dutch painting and drawing. He kept his treasures locked in a room where no one could see them and carried the key with him at all times. The heads of the great department stores, most of whom were parvenus, were also gripped by the new frenzy. Boucicaut collected jewels; Ernest Cognacq and Louise Jay, founders of La Samaritaine, collected eighteenth-century objets d'art.

All these collectors were also patrons of the arts who exerted a great deal of influence on fashions. Impressionism and Art Nouveau both owed a great deal to these ambitious bourgeois. After 1870 great collectors were no longer willing to allow their highly eclectic collections to be broken up when they died. In the hope of achieving posthumous celebrity and ensuring the survival of their name, they donated their collections to state museums, and in return rooms were named after them.

The Solitary Pleasures of the Study

Collectors' appetites seem to have had two sources. For those who aspired to found a dynasty, accumulation of symbolic objects was a way of legitimating a recently acquired social position. Collecting brought social prestige; when con-

These photographs, which date from the early Third Republic, of the Rothschild estate at Ferrières are food for thought for all who would analyze the need for legitimation of new dynasties, the desire to commemorate individual lives, and the bourgeois need for cultivated leisure. (Paris, Bibliothèque Nationale.)

Arthur Henry Roberts, *M. Sauvageot's Study*. A prisoner among apparently unrelated objects that fill all available space, this collector seems to be checking the lock on the cabinet. (Paris, Louvre.)

nected with patronage, it enabled a person to influence artistic taste and production. As a result, aristocracy and bourgeoisie became so thoroughly confused that even a historian like Arno Mayer could be misled, in the case of France at any rate, into confounding bourgeois eclecticism with the ancien régime.[43]

The desire to collect revealed a hidden psychology with deep roots in private life. Many different desires led people to create private museums in their homes. Some collections were little more than accumulations of personal souvenirs. The chest in which Nerval kept Jenny Colon's locks of hair and letters, like the collection of perfumed dainties that reminded Flaubert in Croisset of his rapturous nights with Louise Colet, was a source of individual pleasure, at once nostalgic and anxious. One possible reason for such behavior was a need, common in men over the age of forty, to control or check the libido.

Pure possession without functional justification, collecting satisfied the individual passion for private property. In some cases, however, it was also a passionate form of escape, a way of seeking refuge among objects that were nothing less than narcissistic equivalents of the self. Snobbery and aesthetic pleasure were sometimes mere alibis; we sense that for some people collecting was actually a way of compensating for real or imagined failures. When the imperial administration destroyed the career of Henri Odoard, a minor magistrate, he retired to Chantemerle, where he piously catalogued his family's archives and collected shells and medals. This retreat into domesticity confirmed a failure to connect with others, a failure that is also evident in the chiaroscuro bourgeois interior of the 1880s, with its upholstered furniture and heavy wall hangings. Can we interpret this retreat as a sign of unconscious fear of the masses, or of remorse for the spoliation attested by the accumulation of precious objects? The neurosis of Des Esseintes (in Huysmans's *A Rebours*) suggests that the answer might be yes.

Private collecting was probably a manifestation of the same regressive processes responsible for the keeping of diaries. Intended to conjure away the specter of death, both pastimes offered solitary pleasures yet were at the same time forms of self-destruction. Whatever its meaning, the ubiquity of collecting is one of the most telling facts of nineteenth-century upper-class history. To ignore it is to misunderstand completely the motives of the day's most important economic leaders.

James Collinson, *The Empty Purse*. This young lady has spent all her money on pictures, trinkets, flowers, and bibelots, typical items of women's "collections." (London, Tate Gallery.)

Collecting Spreads to Other Segments of Society

Collecting, long an elitist activity, ultimately spread to other segments of society. Stamp collecting was already popular when people began, between 1890 and 1914, to explore new types of collections, such as postcards, shells, medals, and dolls. The petite bourgeoisie, especially in the provinces, soon succumbed to the desire to amass family archives and collections of souvenirs. These practices spread down to the lowest levels of society.[44] Shortly after Henri Odoard reverently catalogued his family correspondence, people at every level of society began collecting photographs, inlays, wedding dresses, bouquets, and bridal wreaths. These handmade treasures were stored away with legal documents and military records to create a treasury of pious souvenirs that became valueless after death. Was this a democratization of the impulse to collect, a desire on the part of people at the bottom of the social ladder to emulate the rich? Of course. But it also represents a diffusion throughout society of a sense that the values of the past were threatened and of a refusal to accept the severing of continuity between generations. The inability to ensure transmission of this legacy engendered at this level of society a new guilt, which impelled people to gather together items capable at least of recording a trace of the past. The same desire that led to increasingly personalized epitaphs was at work here. "Joseph Brunet is a man. Believe me when I tell you," one obscure landowner wrote on the flyleaf of a book in his collection.

Other phenomena partook of the process of imitation. In the 1880s, as bourgeois interiors grew more lavish, people of more modest background became avid buyers of reproductions. A brisk trade developed in false antiques. People even began to collect fakes. The "Louis XV" bedroom set and "Henri II" dining room set changed the way people related to their furniture and their homes. The whole ritual of private life was affected.

Charles Cres, *Lovers' Banter.* (Salon of 1906.)

✒ Intimate Relations

T HE feelings of vulnerability that accompanied the progress of individuation; the failure to connect, which forced members of the dominant classes to retreat into solitary pleasures; the internalization of ever more strict rules of sexual morality, which intensified feelings of guilt—all these things enhanced the prestige of genuine encounter with another individual in whom one could confide. New trails of confidence were blazed, and both the pleasures and miseries of confession reached new heights of sophistication.

The Century of Confession

The nineteenth century is regarded as the golden age of the confessional. The lord's tribunal formed the heart of what Philippe Boutry calls "introspective religion."[1] Confessors "conducted investigations and assigned guilt." Introspection was in fact the hallmark of nineteenth-century Catholicism, whose two primary prerequisites of salvation were examination and confession. The confessional was an important element in the Church's moral strategy. Confessors rescued youths from the brink of the abyss, prevented adultery, and hindered divorce. They also helped to preserve the social order by forming what the obscure abbé Debeney in 1853 called a "barrier to socialism" that would ensure "the salvation of France."

On occasion priests heard confession in private homes. Such visits were extremely rare, however, and generally reserved for the sick or for the few who could afford private chapels or employed family chaplains. Confessions usually were heard in the church or sacristy. Confessionals, at first quite simple but later increasingly elaborate, came into widespread use around the turn of the nineteenth century. When

In the darkness of one of the 40,000 "oak closets" that Michelet would soon denounce, a Restoration priest listens to a woman's confession and measures the degree of her repentance. (Paris, Bibliothèque des Arts Décoratifs.)

the curé of Ars heard confession, he sat in a simple armchair flanked by two boards, but more ornate confessionals of polished oak enveloped priest and confessor in a shadowy intimacy that drew the scorn of Michelet.

A superficial comparison between the confessional and the psychoanalyst's couch is sometimes made. There are similarities, to be sure: the priest, like the doctor, must be sober, attentive, discerning, and discreet. Hidden behind his grille, he must not reveal his face or his eyes. The secrecy of the confessional was respected throughout the century; the honor of the priesthood depended on it. Yet the behavior of the penitent has little in common with that of a psychoanalytic patient. In attitude, gesture, and attire the penitent expressed humility. Kneeling, hatless, hands joined, veil lowered in the case of a woman, the penitent submitted in advance to the priest's judgment. He or she quietly recited a list of sins in the language of the confessional, a language that did not come easily to rural people used to expressing themselves in the strongest of terms.

Confession was supposed to be accompanied by contrition. Only then would the priest grant the absolution that wiped away sin and guaranteed salvation. When, around the middle of the eighteenth century, priests began to refuse absolution, it was a matter of immense significance. Refusal to absolve was a drastic step, for it meant public exclusion from Easter communion. The effect was to confront the sinner with the possibility of damnation. "My friend, you are lost," Jean-Marie Vianney did not shrink from telling one of his penitents. "My boy, you are damned," he warned another.

It is misleading to draw any hard and fast distinction between confession and spiritual supervision. Most ecclesiastics, some young girls, and a few zealous women, chiefly aristocrats or bourgeoises along with a few spinsters who happened to live close to the church, enjoyed the benefit of continuing, personalized spiritual supervision. But these privileged few remained a distinct minority. Nevertheless, a confession was also a judgment and always implied submission to the authority of the spiritual magistrate. The few words uttered before penance was imposed, the exhortation to the sinner to amend his ways, constituted a form—admittedly a rather crude form—of spiritual guidance.

In theory a Catholic was supposed to confess to the curé of his parish. Until around 1830 the rural clergy jealously guarded this prerogative. After that date a certain freedom of

Prior to the vogue for Marial devotion that developed around midcentury, the pious sought out not a woman but a man, and a living one at that. The "good curé," a missionary who stayed in one place and let the crowds come to him, was primarily a confessor. Day and night he answered the questions of the faithful, consoled grieving souls, blasted unrepentant sinners, and mingled his own tears with those of his penitents.

choice was tolerated. In pious circles the choice of a confessor was a veritable rite of passage. For a young girl home from boarding school and about to make her debut in society, the decision was one of great importance. The correspondence of young Fanny Odoard reveals the decisive influence of her confessor, the abbé Sibour, future archbishop of Paris. Devout ladies often discussed the relative merits of various confessors. In urban parishes some priests specialized in hearing particular types of confession: some preferred children and adolescents; others liked to deal with servants. Certain pastors enjoyed considerable renown. When a difficult case of conscience arose, their judgment might be solicited. The curé of Ars remains the foremost of these apostles of the confessional. For nearly thirty years he remained, for seventeen hours a day, the prisoner of the lines of the faithful that formed outside his confessional under the watchful eyes of squads of ushers. The fact that the reputation of the "good curé" drew pilgrims from throughout the region is clear evidence of the importance of the sacrament. But Jean-Marie Vianney was not the only celebrated confessor. Father P. A. Mercier, who retired to Fourvière at the age of sixty-six, heard twenty thousand penitents in less than four years.

A Catholic unsatisfied with a routine confession might undertake to make a general confession of his sins. Converts often chose this course. One professor, fascinated by the curé of Ars, chose to make a general confession after forty-four years without having visited a priest. A general confession sometimes marked the culmination of a retreat, a mission, or a pilgrimage. It was compulsory for the dying person who remained in possession of his or her faculties.

The Practice of Confession

In the diocese of Vannes in the period from 1800 to 1830, the frequency of confession varied widely from individual to individual.[2] By this time monthly confession was obligatory in secondary schools. Certain pious souls, generally whole families, had already formed the habit of frequent confession and communion. The number of these zealous Catholics was so large that the bishop expressed his concern about the additional workload for his clergy. The intensity of this new popular demand should not be overestimated, however. Throughout the century the rural population of the diocese of Belley remained hostile to frequent confession. In the diocese of Arras a persistent strictness made pastors wary of the practice. In upper Brittany frequent confession did not become common until the twentieth century; prior to that time most Catholics were content to visit the confessional three or four times a year.

The sexual dichotomy typical of nineteenth-century religious practice in general also affected the sacrament of penitence. Statistics, compiled at the behest of Msgr. Dupanloup, concerning the diocese of Orléans, a quantitative analysis of the penitents who visited the curé of Ars, and the complaints made by pastors on pastoral visits—in a word, all the sources—stress the feminization of the sacrament. This tendency was further accentuated by what Boutry has called "confession in dependency": the priest was assigned the mission of monitoring the purity of young girls, the fidelity of wives, and the honesty of servants.

During the first half of the nineteenth century the French clergy showed little interest in the confessions of children. In Brittany children rarely confessed before their First Communion, that is, at the age of twelve.[3] In 1855 this delay drew criticism from Rome, and the French clergy began to reform its practice to bring it into line with the new rules. In 1861 the synod of Breton bishops asked priests to lend more than just a polite ear to the confessions of the young. Before long children were going to confession more and more frequently. By the end of the nineteenth century their practice more or

Jules Alexis Muenier, *Catechism*, 1891. Under the July Monarchy the good curé of Ars was already playing on the emotions of his listeners in catechism class. By the end of the century the French clergy had learned to pay greater attention to the young.

less mimicked that of their elders. In 1910, following issuance of the papal decree *Quam Singulari,* private communion was instituted in the dioceses. Yet in the diocese of Saint-Brieuc, to take just one example, people still had misgivings about the new practice.

The vast majority of young men ceased to frequent the confessional after their First Communion. This lack of male confession varied from region to region, however. In the Lys Valley at the end of the nineteenth century, 60 percent of the men received communion at Eastertime, yet the comparable figure for nearby southern Artois was only 20 percent. Some young workers found the experience of confession disappointing. Norbert Truquin humorously recounts how he flabbergasted the good priest who immediately asked if his penitent "saw women."[4] In its efforts to lure men back to the confessional, which most of them had abandoned, the clergy was tireless but largely ineffectual. When necessary it knew how to bend the rules. In 1877 the synodal statutes of Montpellier advised confessors not to keep men waiting, to avoid spending too much time on the subject of lust, and to show lenience.

The Evolution of Theology

Moral theology and with it the attitudes of confessors evolved over the course of the century. From the time of the Concordat until about 1830 the French Church favored rigorism, which had always been an important element in Gallican, and even more in Jansenist, tradition. Thoughts of damnation and fears of sacrilegious confession obsessed its pastors. One result of this rigorist attitude was the frequency of sermons concerned with the Last Things. Refusals to grant absolution and postponements of absolution were commonplace, although they usually were inflicted on notorious and habitual sinners, not on those whom the theologians characterized as "occasional" or "recidivist." It is not surprising that the asylums were filled with women suffering from religious delusions, women who tortured themselves with endless self-inflicted punishments or who succumbed to anorexia so that God would not punish the rest of humanity for their sins.

The rigorism of the confessional was aimed in particular at festive revelry over which the clergy had no control. Balls, "assemblies," Breton *pardons* (folk festivals), taverns, peasant *veillées* (evening gatherings), wedding banquets, youthful revels, and even mere flirtation, that symbol of the body's pride, all stirred the fury of somber curés. The old theme of indecent décolletage was given new life by lurid descriptions of the guillotine, which wreaked its terrible vengeance on the vices of the ancien régime. Jean-Marie Vianney denounced youths and their parents, while the curé of Véretz prevented his peasants from dancing. Even as late as the Second Empire, the curé of Massac in the Tarn walked through his church before mass in order to inspect the women's attire; when he found one whose coiffure he deemed unseemly, he did not hesitate to trim her locks.

After 1830, however, this strictness eased up somewhat. Over the next twenty years the doctrines of Alfonso da Liguori, translated by Thomas Gousset and spread through seminaries and clerical meetings, gradually gained influence with help from determined pastors such as Msgr. Devie, bishop of Belley. The new moral theology taught that confessors should be prudent and tolerant and should avoid plunging sinners into despair. Calming souls was deemed more beneficial to salvation than frightening them. The Jesuits, Lamennais, and later the growing influence of ultramontane piety all contributed to the humanization of penitence. Once the vast majority of the faithful began to assimilate these simplified rules of moral theology, preaching could become less lugubrious. Even the once terrifying curé of Ars, now mellowed, no longer refrained from mingling his tears with those of his penitents.

Rigorism made something of a comeback during the Second Empire. Sexuality in marriage now became the focus of clerical wrath. While Dr. Bergeret tracked "conjugal deception" from his office, the clergy decided to attack "marital onanism." From 1815 to 1850, Jean-Louis Flandrin remarks, the Church was notably passive in this area.[5] This was a period in which contraceptive practices enjoyed a "discreet diffusion." Birth control spread through the parish of Ars and, as the bishop Msgr. Bouvier noted, through the diocese of Le Mans. Nevertheless, Roman theologians continued to hold that a woman could engage in sexual relations even though she knew from experience that her husband practiced coitus interruptus. The Church regarded such laxity as a way to prevent wife-beating and fornication.

After 1851, however, Rome's attitude hardened. The developing rivalry between man and God for control of the sources of life was a cause of anxiety. The theologians of the Holy See now firmly condemned any form of cooperation, even passive, by women whose husbands practiced onanism.

Luis Jimeñez Aranda, *Penitent,* 1902. During the Second Empire confessors began to focus attention on sins of the flesh, which also became the central issue in the debate with anticlericals. It is hard to imagine that the artist intended to suggest anything else with this drawing of a beautiful penitent on her knees.

The Church of France appears to have adopted the new attitude more quickly than Flandrin once believed. As early as the beginning of the Second Empire, Msgr. Parisis exhorted the clergy of the diocese of Arras to show more firmness. The new bishop of Belley took a similar position in 1860. The defeat of the Commune accentuated the new rigorism. Confessors who had previously been quite discreet about matters of the flesh now probed more deeply. They no longer waited for their penitents to raise the issue.

The Insidious Power of the Confessor

At the same time that confessors began asking more searching questions, an anticlerical offensive was getting under way. In 1845 Michelet's *Du Prêtre, de la femme, de la famille* (On the Priest, Woman, and the Family) provoked a storm of controversy. Novelists soon took up the theme: Zola *(La Conquête de Plassans)*, Edmond de Goncourt *(Madame Gervaisais)*, George Sand *(Mademoiselle de la Quintinie)*, and Pèladan *(Le Vice suprême)* all treated confession as one of the major problems of the day. Pamphleteers broadened the campaign. In 1885 Léo Taxil and Karl Milo published *Les Débauches d'un confesseur,* and militantly anticlerical newspapers filled their pages with reports of clerical immorality. Many joined the attack. As early as 1839 the peasants of Dompierre-en-Dombes petitioned against their curé, whose questions were allegedly "teaching too much," that is, putting immoral ideas into young people's heads. Even in the shadows of the confessional the priest was vulnerable to rumor. Among workers his spying had long been considered a persistent annoyance.

The anticlerical offensive revolved around four central themes. Confessors, it was alleged, wielded insidious power and hindered the free development of the individual. Clerical judgment conflicted with individual autonomy, which for neo-Kantians was the cornerstone of morality. Priests were allegedly indiscreet and curious about the most intimate aspects of a person's life. They questioned family members and neighbors in their quest for total control, which threatened to produce what Michelet called "transhumanization," a loss of individual autonomy.

Clerical sexuality was challenged in various, at times contradictory, ways. Well versed in the sins of the flesh, the confessor asked too many questions and allegedly stimulated an interest in vice in otherwise innocent souls. Frightened and disgusted by the words of her confessor, fourteen-year-old Suzanne Voilquin decided to stop going to confession.

It was further charged that priests were obsessed with women, whom they resembled in dress and sensibility. Sexually frustrated by his vow of chastity, the priest was alleged to be vulnerable to the frankness of women's confessions, which could easily shock or even arouse him. Anticlerical literature was filled with images of the priest as seducer. Graver still was the charge that the confessor, through his questions, insisted on knowing everything that went on between husband and wife, even in bed. After ferreting out their most intimate secrets, he sought to control relations between them. The pleasures of marriage were subject to his approval. Marriage plans could be wrecked by his obsessive concern with the purity of virgins. Even a freethinker's daughter might be persuaded to enter a convent by her confessor.

To the husband jealous of his authority, the priest became a rival. Anticlericals, themselves sticklers for womanly virtue, were no champions of freedom for women. The priest's meddling shocked their sense of propriety. They were jealous of an intruder who, they claimed, sought to control people's private lives, who took advantage of his access to people's homes, and who always kept an eye out for the moment when the wife's delicate soul might be vulnerable to his blandishments. Jean Faury has called this jealousy of the priest "anticlerical machismo."[6]

The last major theme of the anticlerical movement concerned the influence of confessors over people's wills. This allegedly posed a threat to family fortunes. To guard against it, article 909 of the Civil Code stipulated that no confessor could inherit from his penitents. To anticlericals, any bequest to the Church was a form of clerical spoliation.

The heat of these controversies gives some idea of the importance of the stakes. In the eyes of its enemies confession threatened the privacy of the home, the new individualist ethic, and the development of the fraternal couple of which Michelet dreamed. A historian who possessed all the sources of this dialogue of transgression and guilt could go straight to the heart of private life.

The discovery of a rich cache of letters has lifted the veil from one drama of the confessional. Eugène Boileau was a wealthy young anticlerical who collected press clippings about the scandalous behavior of priests. In a moving series of letters written in 1872 and 1873 to his fiancée, he explained his conception of their impending marriage. Upon learning that his future wife was terrified of a confessor who, it seemed, was out both to take her fortune and to seduce her, the outraged Boileau ordered her to end all relations with the scoundrel. The couple's children were not baptized.

Sexual Confession and Medical Secrecy

How difficult was it to confess a moral defect or sexual disease? The fear of uttering certain words is one indication that the difficulty was enormous. In good society people did not refer to sexual parts or acts by name. When novelists dealt with impotence, they merely hinted at the problem. Syphilis required a circumlocution; the victim was said to "frequent Saint Veronica." After 1902 he was described as having "gone rotten." This rather mild expression, taken from Brieux's plays, finally allowed the subject to be broached, timidly, in drawing-room conversation. In the 11,000 letters in the Boileau family collection, sexual transgressions and venereal disease are never once mentioned. Nor is there any allusion to diseases of the chest, which were subject to a similar taboo.

Medical literature confirms the difficulty of confession. Professor Alfred Fournier, author of *La Syphilis des innocents*, cited the case of a young virgin who had been infected by a kiss and who, though her body was covered with lesions, kept her terrible secret to herself. After leaving his doctor's office one officer shot himself so that he would not to have to write to his chaste fiancée that he was suffering from syphilis. A young man could not tell his mother that he was contaminated; it was difficult even to inform his father. "Do not be afraid to tell me," Marie-Laurent Odoard wrote her son Henri, a student in Paris.

In this realm the primary, and often the only, confidant was the doctor. But even in the privacy of a doctor's office, confession was difficult. Doctors often complained about the difficulty of getting young masturbators to admit their vice. It took all of Bergeret's patience to persuade his clients to own up to their marital infidelities. Women were reluctant to submit to the speculum. In the 1880s people became obsessed with congenital disease. The reigning dogma of hereditary syphilis encouraged the search for an impossible cure. Sufferers from the disease were convinced that they could never have children and would die an early death. Eugenics seemed a tempting prospect. Medical secrecy was threatened.

Lucien-Hector Jonas, *Physicians.* Physicians' private clients were drawn from the bourgeoisie. Even with several consultants involved, as in this case, secrets were easier to keep than in a hospital ward. The practitioners' grave air, a far cry from the imperious pose of the lecturer, was a guarantee of discretion. (Salon of 1911.)

Actually few people enjoyed complete medical secrecy. A man's medical history was subject to public review when he entered the army. Tuberculosis victims were displayed to medical students in the hospitals. Charcot exhibited the hysterics of the Salpêtrière to the cream of Paris society. The victims of venereal disease crowded into Lourcine and Saint-Lazare in Paris and the syphilitics confined to special wards and units in provincial hospitals and prisons had no hope of hiding their condition. Clever pimps recruited prostitutes right out of hospital beds. Men knew which neighborhood prostitutes were healthy and which were not. In rural areas everyone in the village knew whose blood was "rotten." Not until the very end of the century did the dermatology clinic at the Saint-Louis Hospital begin to used coded names and offer common people the new privilege of comparative secrecy.

With the upper class, from which the specialists drew their private patients, matters were quite different. A congenital defect posed a potential threat to a family's marital strategy. Not even a cure could repair the damaged prospects of a young person known to suffer from a pulmonary disease; the danger of relapse remained, and there was also the fear that the disease might be transmitted to children. Hence secrecy was important. Marthe's family was afraid that the alleged hysteria of this young Norman woman might compromise the marriage prospects of her cousins in Burgundy. Fortunately, article 378 of the penal code obliged the physician to hold his tongue.

Between 1862 and 1902 some leading physicians, influenced by the prevailing belief in hereditary disease, challenged the doctrine of secrecy. To them the most important thing was to prevent the birth of degenerates. Professors Brouardel, Lacassagne, and Gilbert-Ballet proposed resorting to subterfuge. They might, for example, advise the parents of a prospective bride to ask her fiancé to apply for a life insurance policy. He would then be forced to submit to a stringent medical examination. Brouardel also recommended arranging for the two family physicians to meet. Each could then give a recommendation to his clients without betraying medical secrets. Duclaux proposed asking the fiancé to give his word of honor. A small minority of physicians, led by Louis-Adolphe Bertillon, recommended that every individual be issued a personal medical record card, which would indicate the medical history of that person and his or her ancestors. Some of Galton's disciples held that single men should be examined and issued a certificate attesting to their qualification for marriage, but this suggestion was not taken up until after the First World War. In 1903 an investigation conducted by *La Chronique médicale* showed that medical practitioners were hostile to the matrimonial law. By this time the "hereditarianist" terror had waned somewhat. Pasteur's disciples were less fearful than Benedict Morel's and Prosper Lucas's had been. Clearly, however, the upper classes were extremely vigilant when it came to protecting the secrets of their private life.

The sons and daughters of the bourgeoisie were carefully isolated from the social life of the lower classes. Governed by a strict code, their social activities tended to encourage exclusive and passionate friendships. The difficulty of confession kindled a desire to recount one's experiences to a chosen companion. These childhood confidences respected the division between the sexes; they played a crucial role in the development of the personality.

Childhood Confidences

Choosing an intimate friend was an important moment in the life of an adolescent. Mothers encouraged long-term and totally candid relationships between serious girls. The hope was that a firm friendship of this sort, the opposite of the frivolous acquaintances that one struck up in society, would help the girls find their way in life. When the social rituals of childhood ceased to function effectively, a similar concern to encourage children to enter into special friendships developed in the countryside. For Catholic girls this best friend was usually a classmate in the child's First Communion class. When elderly women in Bué-en-Sancerrois were questioned in 1976, they all agreed on the importance of this particular friendship.

When a young girl was suddenly plucked from the warmth of the family and immersed in the hostile boarding school environment, she felt an urgent need for a best friend. Ever since the time of Mme de Maintenon, the rules of these institutions had encouraged older children to take younger new arrivals under their wing. George Sand has left a detailed account of the pleasures of these special friendships. In the hermetic world of the schools, segregation of the sexes fostered an ambiguous kind of closeness. Girls exchanged pictures and oaths. Often these friendships proved durable. "Grown girls" who had left boarding school to await marriage exchanged long letters and visits. Examples of fast friendships

Suzanne Hurel. Historians have paid too little attention to friendship and to the pleasures of confidential conversation. (Salon of 1911.)

abound. Eugénie de Guérin was astonished to discover that she had put together a whole network of sober, gentle girls who had matured early owing to a death in the family.

Cousins often occupied a special position. In the Boileau family, cousins conversed together in English to spite their curious parents. Fanny and Sabine Odoard exchanged letters filled with hundreds of petty secrets between their homes in Nîmes and Mercurol. Their correspondence was remarkably serious; the two girls discussed not Prince Charming but questions of conscience and rules of conduct. When cholera broke out, young Fanny took the necessary precautions, placed her private papers in a safe place, and prepared herself for the hereafter. Accustomed to serving as nurses within the family and as angelic benefactors to the local poor, girls of this class were on familiar terms with suffering. Correspondence such as this tends to cast doubt on the largely masculine notion that the young girl's chief curiosity was for news of her best friend's wedding night. Yet that notion occurred widely in literature from *Mémoires de deux jeunes mariées* (1842) to *Chérie* (1889) by Edmond de Goncourt.

Different from, but just as intense as, these female friendships were the male friendships that developed in boarding schools, preparatory schools, and university lecture halls. Most young men had had sexual experience, but quite often it was of an indecent sort that could not be discussed with family members, and few of these youths went to confession. Nor were their sexual partners likely to welcome confidences, and in any case those partners were the Other, the prey, to whom men did not reveal themselves. Even though these bourgeois youths knew in their hearts that they would end up as lawyers or notaries, many harbored boundless ambitions. They abhorred the commonplace and believed themselves called to do great things. Their culture filled them with pride. Friendship was an important aspect of a man's sentimental and sexual education, because it provided an opportunity to comment on experience. Derision, laughter, and joking took on tremendous importance, as can be seen from Flaubert's experience with with what Sartre called the "bachelor freemasonry" of the *collège* of Rouen, in which humor played a key role.

That kind of friendship was a group experience, however; close personal friendships were different. Friends opened their hearts in fireside chats during evening or nighttime visits. Flaubert cherished memories of his evenings at Croisset, which he spent smoking in the company of one of his friends— Alfred Le Poittevin, Ernest Chevalier, or Maxime du Camp. Friendships were sealed by long walks in the country or, even more, by joint visits to brothels. Sartre observes: "Whores were common property. Men shared them and told each other crude stories about their frolics." In doing so they betrayed their "wish to sacrifice the other sex to virile camaraderie— virile and just a tinge homosexual, like all flaunting of virility." Abundant correspondence, filled largely with sexual confidences, maintained these friendships in later life. Keeping score of conquests in brothels, crude jibes at the expense of the bourgeoisie, and retelling old jokes were ways of salving wounds inflicted by adult life.

When conscription was introduced in 1872, the "army buddy" became an important figure in the popular mind. In the meantime, young urban workers were kept on the move in search of employment and housing, so that it was more difficult for these young men to form fast friendships than it was for peasants, who tended to stay in one place, or for upper-class males, who enjoyed the benefits of privacy. The few working-class memoirs that have survived are filled with fond memories of chance encounters with a coworker or fellow boarder, resulting in friendships that lasted only a few weeks or months. Migrant workers' friendships were similar, but too little is known about migrants' lives to permit any confident conclusion.

Brothers and Sisters

To return to the bourgeoisie, there was one breach in the barrier between the sexes. Brother and sister enjoyed a special relationship whose importance has too often been neglected. The bond that developed between mother and daughter, a bond that was strengthened by strict sex-role differentiation, no doubt overshadowed the brother–sister connection in early childhood. A brother was the only male with whom a young girl was allowed to behave familiarly. Similarly, a sister was the only decent girl of whom a boy possessed intimate knowledge. The stern moral climate and strict rules governing visits between boys and girls both magnified the importance of the sibling relationship and limited its emotional range. Mutual fantasies sustained a confidential relationship in a minor key, one free from the burden of desire and the fear of succumbing. When Flaubert wrote his younger sister Caroline, to whom he was deeply attached, he restrained his style and avoided crude stories.

Sisters, usually oppressed by the culture and by their experience of the male world, felt not only admiration but a solicitous, almost maternal affection for their brothers. They worried about the dangers of disease, loss of faith, and failure. Parents counted on their daughters to instill morality in their sons. Eugénie de Guérin's devotion to her brother Maurice was no doubt an extreme case, but similar if less intense feelings bound Sabine Odoard to her brother Henri, a student in Paris, to whom she seems to have been closer than she was to the lackluster husband her family had chosen for her. In both cases the sister's feelings were more intense than the brother's; the sisters complained constantly about lack of mail from their brothers and about a shortage of confidential information.

Sisters were soft, malleable wax, and their brothers liked to play Pygmalion, quietly fashioning a double of themselves. Imagining the woman of their dreams helped prepare them for marriage, which, owing to the exigencies of their social position, had to be deferred. Beginning with the troubled relationship of René and Lucile, one could cite any number of such sibling couples: Balzac and Laure, Stendhal and Pauline, Marie de Flavigny and Maurice, and of course the Guérins. Such couples—the brother and sister made for one another, a version of the myth of the androgyne—enjoyed a particular honor as long as romanticism continued to hold sway. By the end of the century relations between brother and sister were no longer so close: Jules Renard's older sister, though sweet and good, nevertheless irritated him.

Family Secrets

Family correspondence in this period was exceptionally abundant. Though scattered, members of the extended family stayed in touch with one another. Chance has determined which collections of letters survived and which vanished, but wherever we look—at the Odoards of Mercurol or the Dalzons of Chandolas or the Boileaus of Vigné—we find the same density of correspondence.

Letter-writing was an obligatory ritual prior to family visits. Letters accompanied gifts and acknowledged favors that relatives were able to do for one another by virtue of their geographical location or professional and social contacts. The mail carried information about people, personal recommendations, tips on the stock market, and other advice. The pattern of exchange reveals the family hierarchy, determined in part by birth, in part by individual success. Aimé Dalzon, an engineer from Saint-Etienne, enjoyed a brilliant career. An admirable brother, he felt a powerful affection for his sister Arsène, who continued to live where the two children had grown up. He helped his family from afar by taking care of numerous bureaucratic matters. He described the new methods of silkworm breeding to his brother and kept him informed of likely changes in the price of silk. He also put his brother in touch with people whom he knew through his father-in-law. In addition, he selected the boarding schools for his nephews and nieces.

Few confidences or personal confessions are found in letters written by mature adults. Sex was not discussed. Adult correspondence was more reserved, less filled with illusions, than were the letters of more youthful writers. No doubt settled adults had fewer indiscretions to recount. Nevertheless, their letters contain plenty of family secrets. (The Boileau letters, which were read aloud to small gatherings of relatives and friends and accordingly contain very few confidences, were an exception to this rule.) Those responsible for the family's well-being were obsessed with the skeletons in the closet. The Odoards' principal concerns were the mental illness of the eldest son, Auguste, and the misdeeds of an ecclesiastical uncle who was obliged, for reasons that will always remain a mystery, to take refuge in a Trappist monastery. Marthe's family goes to extraordinary lengths to conceal its secrets. The daughter's sin—sleeping with the coachman—is forthrightly stated in the very earliest letters, written in 1892. But it is a long time before a word is breathed about her late father's syphilis. Veiled allusions to the mother's "misfortune" and the daughter's hysteria arouse the reader's suspicions well before the son-in-law blurts out the dreaded word. We understand why marriage between cousins aroused such fears, and we learn too of the sad fate of Marthe's sister Eléonore, who never married. Only after her death do we discover that she was mildly hydrocephalic. Compared with this tragic fate, the figure of Aunt Dide in Zola's saga of the Rougon-Macquart family seems rather muted.

When it came to hiding skeletons in the closet, the family closed ranks. Secrecy was total. To compensate for the absolute ban on leaks to outsiders, the family endlessly ruminated upon its own misfortunes; this interminable private discussion reduced the temptation of public avowal. Oddly enough, some of this upper-class behavior is reminiscent of practices that anthropologists have found in rural societies. The peasants of Gévaudan considered secrecy of fundamental importance, a matter of family honor, just as it was among the northern bourgeoisie. In both milieus it was also essential to know other families' secrets. The peasants of Lozère sent their children to the cafés to pick up rumors that might be of use in planning the family's marriage strategy. Bourgeois families investigating the background of a marriage prospect similarly drew on a wide range of intelligence sources.

Sentimental Education

The nature of love and the behavior associated with it can tell us a great deal about a society's erotic aspirations and tensions. Here too ideas and practices changed dramatically, yet for the most part historians have ignored this aspect of nineteenth-century culture. Enamored of statistics, the profession has preferred quantitative studies of premarital pregnancies to qualitative studies of private correspondence.

In matters of love the grip of the past was particularly firm. Ancient codes continued to govern the way people felt. Whether they knew it or not, nineteenth-century lovers were influenced by a variety of traditional models: courtly love and its procedures of deliberation; Renaissance neo-Platonism and its angelic anthropology; classical rhetoric, with its tropes about the hurricane of the passions; the condemnation of "love's folly" by the clergy of the Counter-Reformation. Even more influential, obviously, were the theories inherited from the Enlightenment. The metaphysicians' reflections on the essence of the soul; physicians' and psychiatrists' views on the nature of passion, the existence of two sexual natures, and the dangers of physiological excess; theological controversy over the relative gravity of sexual sins—these too helped shape amorous behavior.

The crucial phenomenon, however, was first the elaboration, then the decline, of the notion of romantic love. Underlying the new view of love were multiple and various theories of the relation between body and soul, a subject that I shall not explore here because there is more to be gained by examining a rather different idea. The nineteenth century believed that woman possessed a dual nature, that she partook of both good and evil. This belief is, I think, a key to understanding attitudes toward love in this period. Marked by her ancient pact with the serpent, the daughter of Eve lived in constant danger of succumbing to sin; the need for exorcism was part of her very being. Close to nature, women possessed intimate knowledge of life and death. Females were presumed to be vulnerable to telluric forces, whose effects were evident in nymphomania and hysteria. In short, woman was a smoldering volcano, and when she erupted the furies of her sex were unleashed; she became insatiable in her loves and fanatical in her beliefs, and her gestures resembled the gesticulations of madmen. Inspired by the new system of representation that had come into being a century earlier, late-nineteenth-century artists called attention to the enigma of femininity. They portrayed women as both bestial and pure: the female sphinx with serpent wrapped around her waist and eyes gleaming with a savage light. Modernism's hieratic code required just such a symbol, as Claude Quiguer has shown in a brilliant analysis.[7] Novelists, Zola in particular, drew on this model of the devouring female even for their portraits of the working class. Obsessed by fear of women, men felt an urgent need to ap-

Paul Albert Steck, *Melody*. Late
19th-century symbolism had a
tremendous influence on the
image of woman. Emphasizing
the dichotomy between the
ethereal and the venomous in
female imagery was
symbolism's way of expressing
the fear that women aroused in
the men of this period. (Paris,
Musée de Luxembourg.)

pease the sexuality of their companions and subject them to the discipline of the masculine order.

Religious symbolism also influenced the representation of women. The offspring of Eve was also the spiritual daughter of Mary, and the Virgin represented the positive aspect of femininity. Methodism had exalted the redemptress in an earlier period. The nineteenth century looked to woman as man's guardian angel. Capable of being moved by pity, and by nature born for charity, women were messengers from on high. Since angels were known to exist, other intermediaries between man and God must also exist, for otherwise the chain of being would be discontinuous. Woman's vocation was to ennoble herself, that she might fill this role of mediator. She might also inspire men by appearing to them in the guise of an angel from above.

Even before the dogma of the Immaculate Conception became official Church doctrine in 1854 and a wave of Marian apparitions swept Europe (1846–1871), pious literature and mystical painting depicted the flight from the flesh and its burdens, the aspiration to emulate the angels. Influenced by Lyonnaise illuminism, the painting of Louis Janmot reflected that aspiration. In his fine *Virginitas* the young woman raises

Louis Janmot, *Virginitas*. No one was better than Janmot at capturing the ambiguous understanding of diaphanous, ethereal romantic lovers. (Lyons, Musée des Beaux-Arts.)

her eyes to heaven, thereby putting her companion into contact with the invisible world. In this perspective love was like a second heaven, an affinity associated with a shared spiritual adventure.

A close relation developed between the procedures of confession and the dialectics of love. Lucienne Frappier-Mazur remarks that it was as if the return of the repressed followed the same associative pathways as repression itself.[8] Romantic love borrowed from the sacrament of confession the religious language of avowal, the redemption of suffering, and the anticipation of reward. In love, spiritual authority belonged to the woman; it was she who judged right and wrong.

Romantic love was more complex than this description suggests. It grew out of a combination of religious language with the new status of passion. Love as a chaos of the emotions, a cataclysm of being, a form of derangement—a code elaborated in the seventeenth century at the latest and much in vogue in the period from 1720 to 1760—was now downgraded. Between 1820 and 1860 the sentiment of love was reinvented in France. Passion was reduced to a mere form of energy, the source of the electric shock that preceded love. Passionate energy created a bond between two individuals and lifted them into a magical sphere, effecting a transition from the natural to the poetic order. Love implied a spiritual affinity close enough to convince both partners that the harmony that existed between them would endure for all eternity. "Love," wrote Paul Hoffmann, "in the fullness of its being escapes from reality and subsists on the frontiers of life, where presence and absence are confounded, where the face of the beloved becomes confused with images from memory and dreams."[9]

Woman's mission was to awaken man, to stir "turbulence in [his] soul," to encourage an inextinguishable nostalgia for the ideal. This image of perfect plenitude was bequeathed to the romantics by Rousseau, who reworked the myth of the spiritual androgyne. It is highly reductionist to see Sophie as nothing more than a male chauvinist model of a submissive companion. Rousseau's refurbishing of the ancient myth according to which male and female were originally parts of a single being encouraged a certain sexual ambiguity, as is quite evident in Janmot's painting. This blurring of distinctions permitted men and women to engage together in a fraternal quest for the ideal.

Surprisingly, however, the same blurring of distinctions

brings us back to the negative aspect of femininity. So thoroughly does the ethereal, diaphanous virgin deny the sexuality of her companion that she herself becomes a disturbing, insidiously castrating figure. Man falls victim to the woman whom he has raised up to the level of the angels the better to exorcise his own animality.

Popular literature illustrated the new system of love with edifying models and stories. Certain clichés emerged: the first encounter, the woman as "apparition," the glimpse of a fleeting silhouette. The garden path and nature trail supplanted the bower as the preferred settings for lovemaking. The language of love was mediated; messages from a distance were more important than direct communication. The glance, the sound of a far-off voice, the sweet, natural fragrance that filtered its way through the lightest of attire—these were forms of communication that protected female modesty even as they forged indestructible chains.

Romantic love affected the role of confession, heightened the sense of shame, and introduced new forms of judgment. A more refined eroticism made it possible to overcome the incompatibility between male desire and the representation of women as angels. In situations where words would have been scandalous, glances, smiles, even light caresses took their place. Possible responses included discomfiture, blushing, or sustained silence.

All these things constituted the curriculum, as it were, of sentimental education, a constant theme of romantic literature. Sentimental education was a part of the difficult process of maturation. A woman made up for a man's loss of his mother's love. The comfort she offered, the total confidence she inspired, made possible a miraculous second birth, a return to paradise in compensation for initiatory suffering. Mme de Warens, Mme de Rênal, Mme de Couaën, Mme de Mortsauf, and many other women acted as second mothers who sat in judgment of a man's desire for amorous initiation. Yet the mother remained inaccessible. Behind the maternal image in romantic literature lurked a terrifying, castrating female who exacted a heavy tribute for the outpouring of romantic sexuality.

After 1850 romantic love ceased to exist as a coherent model, although dictionaries like that of Larousse continued to reflect the idealist image. The semantic content of the word

Love at First Sight

Edouard Gelhay, *Plans for the Future*. A striking evocation of the social degradation of the romantic code of sentiment. The lovers seated at their table in this sylvan tavern are more reminiscent of Frédéric and Rosanette in Flaubert's *L'Education sentimentale* than they are of the heroes of *Volupté* or *Le Lys dans la Vallée*. (Salon of 1897.)

"love" remained unchanged, but the various meanings of the word no longer constituted a system. The failure of the generation of 1848 culminated in the irony of Flaubert, which marked the end of the representation of women as angels. Barricades blocked the avenues of sentimental education. Loss of faith in the romantic model of love went hand in hand with its diffusion—one might even say its democratization. It became a consumer item, almost a commodity. The reveries of Emma and her lover Rodolphe toward the end of *Madame Bovary* are filled with the now incoherent elements of amorous feeling, which float through consciousness like the scattered leaves that drift on the nearby stream. This incoherence would endure for the next fifty years. As the sphinx supplanted the angel, a vague, shifting complex of sensations, reveries, souvenirs, and fears supplanted the irresistible impulse toward the ideal.

Real Behavior

Historians in recent years have learned a great deal about the imagery of love. We now need to study how people actually behaved. A few pioneering works have shown that, while the romantic models were influential, there was a growing gap between their more sophisticated elaborations and actual behavior.

Nicole Castan notes that by the end of the eighteenth century the rhetoric of passionate love had penetrated to the lowest strata of society and that a new rhetoric had already begun to make its influence felt.[10] Even illiterates spoke of "tender oaths" and "abundant tears," echoing the sentiments of Rousseau's *La Nouvelle Héloïse*. Through study of private correspondence from the early nineteenth century, Jean-Marie Gautier has discovered the violence of passionate language in the years after the Revolution. Love became frenzy; jealousy took the form of madness. The emotion was so overwhelming that it made even death tempting.[11] In short, the privatization of tears coincided with an intensification of love's traditional power to derange. Simultaneously women began to be portrayed as angels. Religious metaphors became commonplace: lovers were "heavenly" creatures to be honored by veneration.

A half-century later (1850–1853), the petite bourgeoisie took up these same metaphors. Young Jules Odoard found himself madly in love with a rural schoolmistress, the daughter of peasants. Copious letters he wrote tell of the ravages wrought by his stormy passion. He sent his beloved "long, ardent kisses" by mail. He likened his bleeding heart to the heart of Christ as portrayed in romantic iconography: "My God . . . may your will be done," he wrote when deprived of the "divine balm" of his mistress' body.

This is not the place to attempt a full inventory of amorous behavior, although systematic analysis is not beyond reach. Strolls in the garden, glances, confessions, and squeezes of the hand marked the early stages of Victor Hugo's love for Adèle; Stendhal's passion for Métilde went no further. The stern Protestant François Guizot's sentimental education was typical of the time, as Guizot himself recognized. Hippolyte Pouthas has retraced Guizot's passion for a friend of his mother's. The future minister came close to committing suicide out of frustration.

Lovemaking in the Village

In matters of love traditional society sometimes seems totally different from modern society. Nineteenth-century peasants did not speak of their emotions. The few letters that Limousin migrants sent their wives do not speak the language of the heart but are concerned almost exclusively with running the farm.

That said, we must proceed with caution. Our information comes from people who judged rural folk with an ethnologist's eye, blinkered by prejudice. Influenced by Enlightenment anthropology, they saw the peasant as a savage whose need to adapt to the "climate" slowed progress toward civilization. Vague disciples of Condillac and the Idéologues, these observers were also persuaded that man's faculties were at war with one another: the brute strength and even violence required by manual labor, as well as the unhygienic conditions in which peasants lived, had prevented their senses, hence their sentiments, from developing refined powers of discrimination. Their souls, made of less sensitive fiber than the souls of other men, lacked refinement. Hence the peasant was capable of experiencing passion only in a monstrous form. He was totally insensible to romantic love, which required a certain delicacy of communication. Vitalists pointed to the peasant's gnarled exterior as proof of the poverty of his soul. Either brute instinct or superstitious abstention—these two extremes defined the peasant's experience of love.

Anthropologists and historians have long since deciphered this code. Love, they have learned, was indeed recognized in rural society. "People talked about love, and they made love,"

Martine Segalen remarks.[12] But because their code of love differed from that of contemporary observers, surviving accounts are misleading. There were, moreover, significant regional variations in the manifestations of love.

Love was usually expressed not by words but by deeds. During a festival or at the fairgrounds, during an evening vigil or after mass, a man and a woman might exchange approving glances. Men were generally miserly with words. A man's only way of acknowledging his preference was to deny it, and he did so through mockery and crude jokes. Gestures marked the progress of a love affair. Lovers shook hands so tightly that the bones cracked; they twisted each other's wrists; they rubbed cheeks and thighs. A slap on the shoulder, a pat on the back, or a shower of stones might signify that affection was reciprocated. Everyone knew the meaning of such behavior and the gradation of responses.

With approval from their families, young people could begin to "make love," that is, to court. From that point on their visits were a matter of strict ritual, subject to the oversight of the group. Courting often took place in silence. Various means of coping with sexual needs before marriage were employed. Fondling and petting were codified and monitored by the group, in this case not the whole community but the peer group consisting of other youths. Premarital sexual activity stopped short of mutual masturbation, but girls were willing to bare their bosoms and allow their breasts to be fondled.

Difficulties of Interpretation

Much is known about the various kinds of behavior, but many problems remain. Engaging in foreplay with others of one's own age was not the same as engaging in foreplay with one particular partner. Singling out a partner reflected a personal preference, and relationships of this kind were subject to rules of their own. Public declarations of love often followed a highly ritualized pattern, which anthropologists have been quick to note, but such declarations may have been preceded by more discreet seductions that escaped the notice of outside observers. Young men and women had plenty of occasions to meet while tending the cows, traveling to market, or walking to church. No doubt real emotions were expressed in these moments of temporary freedom from the apparatus of social control.

According to Edward Shorter, a first sexual revolution

took place in the eighteenth century.[13] Little by little young people felt a growing desire to emancipate themselves from all the rituals and all the surveillance by peers and family members. A new, more individualistic model of amorous behavior developed, encouraged by the rural exodus, the breakdown of village systems, and the growing spontaneity, tenderness, and empathy of relations between the sexes. This account of the diffusion of the romantic love model so clearly resembles the picture I painted above that it would be churlish of me to criticize Shorter's version. Nevertheless, it is a mistake to believe that acceptance of the traditional social code proves that individual feelings were missing. Family strategies were not always incompatible with personal sympathy. As Pierre Bourdieu has noted in the case of Béarn, those strategies left some room for maneuver and for the assertion of individuality.[14] Recommendations based on prior experience should not be mistaken for injunctions. In any case, family norms were internalized from early childhood, and they therefore affected the individual's very susceptibility to romantic feelings.

Matrimonial strategies, far from disappearing in the nineteenth century, were actually encouraged by prosperity. A successful marriage became an even greater imperative than in the past, especially for children designated as heirs. The gap between siblings actually widened; younger sons were freer than before, but the behavior of elder sons was rigorously determined. Similarly, the daughter of a day laborer enjoyed greater freedom than did a daughter chosen to inherit the family farm. Ronald Hubscher notes that in rural Pas-de-Calais some girls of very modest background were able to win the hearts of men of markedly higher station.[15]

The importance of stricter segregation of the sexes, the result of a clerical offensive that reached its peak between 1870 and 1880, should not be minimized. In that decade rural youth in some areas were subject to extremely strict controls. Clearly emancipation was not without its setbacks. In Bué-en-Sancerrois supervision of girls was never stricter than on the eve of World War I.

Amorous behavior always conforms to certain models. Socioeconomic factors are an important determinant. Young people may have yearned to be free, but what that notorious desire meant in practice was usually that they mimicked the behavior of an admired model. Shorter is certainly right that among peasants romantic love was more individualistic than traditional forms of love. Still, the spontaneity of romantic love should not be overestimated. Nor should the freedom of the peasant who moved to the city be exaggerated. The whole image of liberation derives from an old stereotype, first created by bourgeois worried about the expansion of the allegedly dangerous, vice-ridden lower class. That stereotype was accepted uncritically by historians studying the way in which new arrivals were integrated into the city. In urban neighborhoods colonized by migrant workers from a particular region, the mechanisms of social control were identical to those that governed village society; freedom was limited by rumor in exactly the same way.

A key problem is to determine how romantic love spread to the lower levels of the social pyramid. The Church of course popularized the angelic image of women. New images of love were also promulgated by romantic fiction and by the poetry of wit, which, according to one observer, was extremely popular in rural Limousin during the July Monarchy, as well as by the success of tear-jerking melodramas, by reading rooms, and by serialized fiction. Café-concerts and music halls helped shape the sensibility of the upper Aude Valley after 1870.[16] After 1890 lovers in search of a model could look to postcards for ready-made attitudes, dramatized sentiments, and emblems of Saint Valentine. The postcard democratized the declaration of love.

Alfred-Philippe Roll, *Woman in Love*. (Salon of 1895.)

Adult sexuality was often socially asymmetrical; a student might keep a seamstress as his mistress. Yet these dissonant unions also hastened the spread of romantic images of love and lust. The young bourgeois taught, at times unwittingly, new gestures and attitudes to his *grisette,* thus rejuvenating the theater of love. The nonchalant gesture, the seduction on the sofa, the evening passed in the private room of a restaurant, the picnic in the country—all were lessons in the new romantic code.

Carnal Love in the Romantic Era

The subject of sex is a dark continent. Because of the persistent prejudice that sex has no place in history, it is also a continent enveloped in a heavy shroud of silence. It will therefore be useful to attempt, even at the risk of being somewhat schematic, a rough periodization. Once again, a turning point can be located in the 1860s. Let us begin, therefore, by considering the period of more than half a century—from the

Consulate to the heyday of imperial revelry—which led up to that crucial moment of change.

Forms of Pleasure

The language of sexuality shaped dreams and governed behavior. To ignore the importance of language is to run the risk of anachronism. According to Bronislaw Baczko, the word "sexuality" was first used in 1859 (or perhaps, at the earliest, in 1845).[17] At first it denoted the distinctively sexual features of living things. Prior to the elaboration of the *scientia sexualis* people spoke of "love" and "amorous passions," of "desires" and "genetic instincts," of "carnal" or "venereal" acts. Physicians used the terms "copulation" and "coitus." Describing acts of physical love was virtually a monopoly of males, yet even men had to talk around the subject. Only doctors could discuss sex openly, and they invoked the concept of the "genetic instinct" to distinguish sexuality from passion. Sexuality was thus characterized as a force necessary for the reproduction of the species and thereby relegated to an inferior status. Doctors merely shrugged their shoulders at the various degrading forms that sexual relations were known to take. They codified all sexual activity and catalogued the varieties of orgasm. Already some doctors were fulminating against what they saw as "aberrations" of the genetic instinct in the form of "deviant" behavior. The onanist was the first target of the budding field of sexual pathology.

Physical love was a constant obsession of fiction and poetry. Obscenity, omnipresent yet hidden in the depths of the text, forced readers to decode the message as they read, thus heightening the pleasures of transgression. Ellipsis, litotes, periphrasis, and metaphor called the imagination into play. Descriptions of sexual climax are a case in point. In this literature men "took" women, while women "gave" themselves. "Pleasure"—meaning sometimes coitus, sometimes orgasm—consisted of "indescribable ecstasies," "extraordinary delights," "frenzied, almost convulsive transports." Novels explored, or at any rate touched on, the secrets of sexual life, once the province of libertine literature. They alluded to frigidity and impotence and delighted in homosexual scandals.

Laughter was another device. "Frank, healthy" gaiety served as a pretext for broad and raunchy humor. Racy songs, which often dated back to the swashbuckling age of aristocratic gallantry, were popular among the petite bourgeoisie and lower classes. Licentious ditties supposedly lifted people's

spirits. Sometimes a story's meaning was veiled by a rebus. Spoonerisms gave license to make obscene allusions for the reader to decode. The standard tropes of obscene songs and literature flattered the narcissism of the male sex. Marie-Véronique Gautier observes that "the songwriters dreamed of always avid women, their eyes riveted on the instrument of their pleasure." Sexual metaphors often coupled Eros with Mars: women were constantly "laying down their arms" and men "hitting the bullseye."[18]

The positive–negative duality of the female influenced the imagery of sexual pleasure. There was, as Jean Borie has noted, a continual alternation between idealization and degradation, an inexorable fall from the heights of angelic yearning to the pit of the brothel.[19] According to the code of romantic love, women were supposed to behave so chastely in bed that today one can only smile at the descriptions. Feminine desire was so taboo that women had to pretend to

Hubert-Denis Etcheverry, *The Swoon*. In this scene of seduction amidst luxury and finery, the woman's posture foretells and mimics abandonment. The sofa with its piles of cushions allowed a woman to give herself as if by surprise. Unlike the bed, it permitted her to pretend that she had swooned or been overcome, thus salving her conscience. (Salon of 1903.)

Achille Devéria, *Morning and Night*. Devéria, a rather timid painter of erotic scenes in the early July Monarchy, here portrays a reserve that seems more apt to describe marital relations, even the wedding night, than the excesses of debauchery. Vanquished yet yielding, the woman clumsily abandons herself and allows the man to lift her into the bed. The next morning, the contentment evident in her expression belies her feigned modesty and attests to the satisfaction of her desires. Her bare breasts are the only sign of the night's ardor. (Paris, Bibliothèque Nationale.)

be prey, who "gave themselves" only when assaulted vigorously enough to justify "defeat." A body that spoke too eloquently of its pleasures was obliged, after experiencing "ecstasy," to assume the redemptive postures of purity. Louise Colet was no prude; it was she who hurled herself upon the young Flaubert as they rode together in a cab. Yet after their first lovemaking, in a dubious hotel, she remained stretched out on the bed, "her hair spread over the pillow, her eyes lifted up to heaven, her hands joined, offering up her crazy words." In commenting on the scene, Sartre noted: "In 1846 a woman of bourgeois society who had just behaved like an animal was required to play the angel."

Men suffered from a growing sense of sexual inferiority. When a character in Musset speaks of his sexual pleasures, his boasting is a long way from the triumphal chortle of a Restif de La Bretonne. Nineteenth-century literature emphasized the paroxystic aspects of sexual pleasure. Not only novelists but also physicians called attention to the individual's total abandonment, to the annihilation of self in ecstasy—even, or perhaps especially, in degradation. Namouna is devastated by her orgasm, as evidenced by "a slight trembling, an extreme pallor, / a convulsion of the throat, a blasphemy, / [and] some meaningless words muttered in a very low voice."

This romantic image of sensual pleasure, very different from the Sadian pleasure from which it derived, was accompanied by an obsession with the arithmetic of intercourse, a concern that grew out of fear of exhaustion and depletion. The bourgeois male in this period required reassurance of his prowess or, at the very least, mathematical proof of constant regularity. The fact that Vigny and Hugo counted their orgasms, that Flaubert totaled up his exploits, and that Michelet kept annual accounts of his genital activity leads us to think that such sexual bookkeeping must have been common in their milieu.

The drama of sensual desire, in which ecstasy mingled with degradation, unfolded on the fringes of society. The shape of pleasure was defined in the brothels, in encounters on the streets, in the sumptuous apartments of courtesans, and in the midst of adultery.

Premarital Sex

The period between puberty and marriage was very long in the nineteenth century. In the case of women it was lengthened even more by the decline of almost two years in the average age of menarche. The increase in the average life expectancy forced people to wait longer for the inheritance that would at last permit them to marry. Hence celibacy increased, and that, together with the growth of urban ghettos, resulted in a strong demand for premarital intercourse. Migrant workers living in rented rooms in the center of Paris; soldiers stationed in the capital; students; office and shop workers without sufficient income to set up the modest household of their dreams—a whole army of males kept female virtue under constant siege. Under the July Monarchy, moreover, the cities filled with countless permanent migrants, whose presence created a marked imbalance in the numbers of males and females in certain neighborhoods.[20] In rural areas where the stem-family system predominated, younger sons were more likely to survive than in the past, and many knew that they were unlikely to find wives. In Berry members of the growing servant class suffered the pangs of sexual deprivation.

Physicians recognized the violence of the "genetic in-

Edmond de Goncourt, *La Fille Elisa*, 1877. This bordello scene, based on what the artist saw in soldiers' brothels adjacent to the Ecole Militaire, depicts the lassitude of prostitutes in a variety of bizarre postures; it contrasts sharply with the modest transports of the woman in Devéria's painting. (Paris, Bibliothèque Nationale.)

stinct" and attempted to measure its frequency. Belief in its existence justified the conviction that there ought to be a double standard of sexual morality. The moral realism of the Church Fathers, particularly Saint Augustine, led to minimizing the gravity of the most bestial acts and to tolerating a complex system of masculine sexual gratification. Efforts were made to circumscribe the resulting sexual hell. To counteract its baneful influence, an amorous heaven was also created— the heaven to which Louis Janmot's angelic lovers so plainly aspired. Degraded sexuality flourished, compensated by an idealization of love.

The First Circles of Hell

Masturbation, the first circle of this sexual hell, need not detain us. But the demographic evidence shows that premarital sex also took other forms. Between 1750 and 1860 the number of illegitimate births and premarital conceptions increased. These facts are of considerable importance, but, unfortunately, quantitative methods alone are inadequate for interpreting them. According to some historians, these statistics prove that more and more people were free to make sexual choices, that individualism was on the rise in matters of love, and consequently that traditional mechanisms for choosing marriage partners were breaking down. A weakening of the rules that governed permissible behavior during engagement—rules elaborated in the seventeenth and early eighteenth century and based largely on self-control—may also be indicated. The Church, it should be noted, never wavered in its opposition to young men and women spending time together, a custom in which it saw the seeds of vice. But now that young women were no longer subject to surveillance by their peers, they became vulnerable to seduction.

Others argue that the rise in the number of premarital conceptions indicates that young men were obliged more often than in the past to marry the women they seduced. But the parallel increase in the number of illegitimate births weighs against this hypothesis. It may well be that the rise in illegitimacy reflects not a weakening but an accentuation of family matrimonial strategies. Lovers without hope of legal satisfaction had no recourse but the hayloft or the meadow.

In some rural areas elaborate forms of premarital sexuality evolved in the nineteenth century. Sometimes the rules of fraternization permitted young men and women to spend the night together; but they did not necessarily engage in sexual intercourse. In Corsica young people practiced premarital concubinage. In the Basque country they engaged in trial marriages. Women who intended to earn money as wet nurses in the Morvan were required, prior to marriage, to demonstrate the fertility on which their earnings would depend. Forty percent of all brides in the diocese of Arras were pregnant. According to Yves-Marie Hilaire, women there were obliged to prove their childbearing abilities.[21] People were quite tolerant. Between 1838 and 1880 youngsters aged fifteen to seventeen went off in pairs to private rooms, lofts, and "secret places." This institution ultimately succumbed to the protests of the clergy, however.

Less ritualized forms of union also existed. Young men in the *oustaux* of Gévaudan slept in the stable with servants, who taught them the facts of life. A worldly serving girl might forsake the arms of the hired man in order to instruct her employer's eager son in the rudiments of love. Life was brutal in this part of Lozère. If a younger son with no chance of marrying raped a shepherdess, he was likely to go unpunished. If he went about it a little more brutally than usual and trouble ensued, no one in the village would talk, so it was impossible for the police to uncover the guilty party. The sexuality of the celibate here resulted in the tacit subjugation of the female proletariat. The *oustaux* kept close watch on their "heiresses" to ensure their virginity. In this devout milieu a pregnant girl attracted a great deal of attention. To stem the rumors for a time, girls would lace themselves tightly into their clothing, not spend too much time in confession, go ostentatiously to communion, and work especially hard in the hope of deflecting attention from their condition.

Forms of Concubinage

Louis Chevalier and, more recently, Edward Shorter have suggested that concubinage as practiced by urban workers in the early nineteenth century became a new model for illegitimate sexuality.[22] Tired of being manipulated, young migrant workers who only recently had escaped the confines of the village and now felt beyond the reach of the community entered into informal relationships that allowed them to express their feelings. Thus, the working class allegedly created its own form of extramarital relationship at a time when the nuclear family structure was being reinforced by the middle class.

The facts, however, do not entirely support this account of illegitimate sexuality among the working class. Michel Frey has examined a sample of 8,588 unmarried couples in Paris during the July Monarchy. Only two-thirds of the men involved were workers, compared with nine-tenths of the concubines. Furthermore, the men referred to as workers were for the most part artisans and shopkeepers, along with a few servants, laborers, and street vendors. Only 10.4 percent were factory workers. Nearly all the concubines were servants or factory hands, however. This asymmetry suggests that concubinage was a complex phenomenon. Frey has shown, moreover, that in Paris in 1847 there was no correlation between the density of the working-class population and the prevalence of concubinage. Moreover, the working class even at this early date seems to have exhibited a remarkable propensity toward marriage.[23]

This research, though limited, suggests the need for caution. The term "concubinage" actually concealed a variety of practices. The point is not to deny that illegitimate sexuality was common among the poorer classes of society. Many couples behaved as though they were married but delayed the formal ceremony because of the heavy cost of marriage. In

Lille, for example, the cost of wedding attire, a trousseau, fees for the mass and the publishing of banns, and the cost of the wedding banquet made many couples think twice about the wisdom of tying the knot.[24] It was difficult to gather the papers required by the government. For individuals uprooted from their native soil, obtaining the necessary documents meant engaging in unaccustomed correspondence and filing costly applications. Prior to 1850 indigents did not enjoy the benefit of free filing. Twenty percent of the Lyonnais silk workers who married in 1844 were already living in concubinage, and the vast majority (80 percent) already had children upon whom marriage bestowed legitimacy. "It is clear," writes Laura Strumingher, "that, according to the cultural norms of artisans, sexual relations and the birth of children were not sufficient reasons to wed."[25]

Urban populations were more tolerant than rural communities. Also, family controls were less powerful in the cities. A daughter could be allowed to "enjoy her youth" in an environment where concubinage and marriage meant virtually the same thing and where no inheritance was at stake. In any case, young women who earned wages had the wherewithal to press their own demands. Social investigators remarked repeatedly on how difficult it was for a woman to live without a man in a large city. Hence the concubine's position was one of inferiority to her companion, which made it hard for her to insist on legitimizing their union. Young urban males were also less vulnerable to censorious rumor than were their peasant counterparts.

The nature of concubinage varied with the length of cohabitation. In Paris in 1847, 43 percent of unmarried couples had been together for less than three years. These unions may thus be regarded as trial marriages. But 34 percent had been together for more than six years. Such longevity reveals an undeniable contempt for the normal standards.

In addition to what Frey has called "working-class illegitimacy," which as we have seen turns out to have been a phenomenon that left women at a disadvantage, there was also concubinage under conditions of dependency, that is, relations between a member of the grande or petite bourgeoisie and a seamstress, laundress, or shopgirl. In some cases, such as relationships between students and their *grisettes,* the men were satisfying their sexual needs prior to marriage. Novels have made us familiar with the guileless and none too virtuous young lady who loves to dance and who brings to her bourgeois companion some of the energy, directness, and sincerity of the *faubourgs*. The function of this ubiquitous simplicity and frivolity was no doubt to make the inevitable breakup at the conclusion of the student's studies seem less cynical. According to Jean Estèbe, who has analyzed the youthful activities of men who became ministers under the Third Republic, students at all the major schools depended on the fierce devotion of these young women, who were such a permanent fixture of the student scene that they were referred to as *étudiantes*.[26] Every student of the Ecole Polytechnique had his *grisette,* who accompanied him to class gatherings. Over the years a young man might adopt a more settled attitude toward his mistress. Or, if he could afford it, he might abandon his girlfriend for a more elegant companion or, to simplify matters, pay a prostitute to be his mistress. Although the venality of prostitutes caused concern, ultimately prostitution would compensate for the decline of the *grisette*.

For army officers marriage was difficult owing to draconian regulations, frequent transfers, and the difficulty of supporting a wife. Many waited to marry until they retired. In order to avoid becoming regular customers of the brothels,

Eugène Edmond Thierry, *In an Attic*. The young student or clerk enjoys a pleasant interlude with his *grisette*. Such pictures reminded the 19th-century bourgeois of the freer moments of his sentimental education.

officers were permitted to take concubines, provided that the relationship remained discreet and the woman displayed a certain distinction. Many officers of the Second Empire re-signed themselves to this temporary solution.[27] The love affair between an artist and his model was a cliché of fiction, but in the absence of research we cannot gauge its validity.

Some of these dependent relationships proved durable. The sober bachelor felt an urgent need to establish a "house-hold." In those days it was difficult—and would have seemed ridiculous—for a man to do household chores, which took a great deal of time and required a constant presence at home. Tending the fire, fetching fresh water, disposing of waste, cooking, and taking care of the linen were tasks before which more than one unmarried clerk, tired of taking his suppers in cheap restaurants, recoiled. In the countryside tongues wagged if a man allowed himself to perform "woman's work." It was therefore tempting for a lonely man to set up housekeeping with a good, placid, reassuring woman, and who is to say whether her devotion was more that of a wife or a servant? In rural Gévaudan the master who took his servant for his concubine avoided the problem of the dowry. While waiting for his financial situation to improve, he embarked upon the only kind of union open to him.

Such cozy domestic arrangements were a world apart from the escapades of the married man with a yen for young flesh. In the countryside older men continued, as they had always done, to prey on younger women. From court records in any number of child-murder cases we learn of "masters" who, abetted by wives or even mothers-in-law, had no com-punctions about dismissing serving girls whom they had made pregnant. By the end of the eighteenth century, however, there is evidence from Nantes that this type of dependency, tinged with venality, was gradually giving way to a more respectable and even sentimental relationship. Men now preferred to keep young girlfriends in apartments of their own. Caution is in order, however: evidence that men in this period were more likely than before to become involved in multiple extramarital affairs has been uncovered.[28] The provisions of the Code Civil may have had something to do with this.

The kept woman soon became a familiar urban figure under the July Monarchy. Balzac's novel *Une Double famille* dissects the pleasures and torments of the carefully divided life. The vogue for privacy even affected a man's behavior with his mistress, in whose apartment the bourgeois male

Pierre Jules Tranchant, *Breakup*. When a man was about to marry, he usually told his mistress that it was all over and hoped to avoid any "embarrassment." In the Belle Epoque it was riskier for a man to keep a mistress than to seduce a married woman. (Salon of 1808.)

expected to find all the comforts of home with the zest of the erotic as a bonus. The image of the honorable mistress who never betrayed her lover had its counterpart in the reassuring and tactful wife: both women lived in impatient expectation of their man's return.

Prostitutes and courtesans were a very different matter. The authorities of the Empire and July Monarchy were the first to dream of regulating brothels. They developed the so-called French system, which became a model for all Europe. In its time the licensed bordello served three functions. First, it initiated minors, especially young students, although this function was officially forbidden by the rules. Second, it satisfied the "genetic instincts" of unmarried males living in sexual ghettos; most clients in this category came from the working classes. And third, it serviced, discreetly, the needs of frustrated husbands. Many things drove such men to the brothels: unyielding wives, often retiring women forced into unsuitable marriages; the chilling influence of the confessor; castrating mother images; the frequent interruption of sexual relations owing to menstruation, pregnancy, and breast-feeding; cessation of sexual relations after menopause; the prevalence of gynecological diseases; and the need for contraception. Then too the bordello was a jovial place where an otherwise upstanding citizen could relax and forget his starchy pose. Fascination with the "animality" and salty language of the lower classes also contributed to the desire some men felt to spend time with naked women who reeked of cheap perfume.

Ever since the first steps toward regulation under Pasquier, champions of the licensed brothel had dreamed of providing a safe, discreet outlet for an urge that could not be eliminated. Sophisticated eroticism and emotional effusions had no place in these sexual service stations, which were intended to deal quickly and efficiently with a purely physical need. The antithesis of the illegal whorehouse, licensed brothels were conceived as temples of utilitarian sexuality. Registered prostitutes were examined by police physicians; their bodies were constantly scrutinized, and all activities were closely monitored by the house madame. The prostitute's mission was to return her client, satisfied but intact, to his family and society.

Actually the system, which reached its peak of perfection in 1830 when Mangin, then prefect of Paris, managed for a

Paid Pleasures

Théophile Alexandre Steinlen, *The Roundup*. Regulated prostitution could succeed only if the authorities could prevent licensed prostitutes from going underground and unlicensed ones from soliciting customers. The police therefore made periodic sweeps. These arbitary methods aroused the furor of abolitionists, who seized on the arrest of certain nonprostitutes to denounce the illegality of police behavior. (Paris, Bibliothèque Nationale.)

few weeks to confine all the city's prostitutes to licensed houses, never worked perfectly. It was easy for women to slip through the net, and the police were never able to stamp out illegal prostitution. Even Parent-Duchâtelet's subtle realism proved helpless. Unlicensed houses continued to operate. Wretched *pierreuses* sold themselves for a few sous at construction sites and in the ditches adjacent to the city walls. Though obsessed with fear of the authorities, camp followers congregated in the areas around army barracks. There was a constant traffic between the the licensed houses with their bright lights and the unlicensed ones that flourished in dubious darkness.

In the meantime a series of sexual images of the working-class woman became rooted in people's minds. These images, involving stench, filth, disease, and death, still influence historians' views. We also need to consider the dionysiac functions of the various vulgar pleasures that the authorities hoped to relegate to the lower depths.

Through skillful use of their charms some women of humble background had remarkable careers as kept mistresses. Obscure shopkeepers turned procuresses and arranged encounters for their protégées. In the dark recesses of the July Monarchy the stage was being set for the triumph of the famous *cocottes* and *horizontales* of the next generation. We still know very little, however, about this prehistory of the imperial feast.

The Marriage Bed

Let us turn now to sexuality in marriage, the culmination, in this century of virginity, of the dreams and apprehensions of young women and the final stage in the initiation of young men. Perhaps because nineteenth-century writers were struck dumb on the threshold of that sanctuary, or perhaps because what went on there was not spicy enough to hold their attention, they had little to say on the subject of the marriage bed. Historical demography has traced the cycles of fertility, but the results tell us little about what people did for pleasure. We are left with the clergy's extremely vague diatribes and the rather more eloquent prescriptions of the physicians. Close reading of all the sources leads to several important conclusions. First, the initiation of the bride on her wedding night remained a matter of great importance throughout the century. All physicians allude to the modesty, fear, and ignorance of newly married women, and in fact the wedding night was a ritual dramatization of those feminine qualities. The vogue for honeymoon travel stemmed in part from a desire to remove the scene of defloration from embarrassing proximity to the family. Initiation was often brutal, countless witnesses testified, because many husbands concealed their true nature until the wedding night. In 1905 Dr. Forel pointed out that prospective bridegrooms among his patients were prevented by good manners from discussing their sexual needs.

After the first night it was the husband's responsibility to control his wife's sexual needs. Like all women, she could easily—and even unwittingly—become an unrestrained sensualist. Only by tempering her sexual appetites could a husband spare his wife the torments of nymphomania or the more common problem of "enervation." Fortunately a woman's desire needed to be stimulated—or so people believed. Thus the medical profession placed a heavy burden of responsibility on the shoulders of the husband. Given these beliefs, we can more readily understand the anxiety of the young man who discovered that his wife was only too well versed in sexual matters. The record of certain first-night dramas has been preserved. For young Mme Lafarge, who married in 1839, the act, unconsummated, took place in a nondescript provincial hotel and ended in violence. Fifty years later, Zélie Guérin, the mother of Saint Theresa, went into shock during her initiation.

Physicians repeatedly warned men of the dangers of depletion. In keeping with prevalent upper-class attitudes, they advocated careful management of spermatic reserves. Overindulgence in intercourse, even between husband and wife, could easily ruin a man's health. The doctors therefore proposed guidelines setting forth the recommended frequency of intercourse for men of various ages, based on such old works as Lignac's and Nicolas Venette's. It is impossible of course to know to what extent these guidelines were followed. The medical profession opposed intercourse after a certain age. Sexual relations for postmenopausal and sterile women were superfluous, and doctors warned men against their insatiable desires, which could not be quenched by pregnancy. Many doctors considered fifty to be the upper limit for male sexual activity; after this age indulging in intercourse only hastened death.

Vigorous intercourse was believed to increase the likelihood of successful conception. Medical literature associated skill in lovemaking not with quality or delicacy of touch but with virile energy and speed. The problem of premature ejac-

Frédéric Louis Levé, *A Cloud.* This painting, of what is probably the beginning of a marital dispute, reflects the growing interest in psychological analysis of emotional life. It harmonizes well with the discreetly erotic novel made fashionable by Paul Bourget and avidly read by women in the know. (Salon of 1907.)

ulation, so frustrating for women, was ignored, although frequent mention of involuntary loss of semen suggests that it was widespread. Brevity of intercourse was clearly the rule throughout the century, hence it seems likely that simultaneous orgasm was rare. In 1905 Forel explicitly mentions the rarity of simultaneous orgasm among his bourgeois clients.

It is anachronistic to put the issue in these terms. People simply did not pay much attention to their partner's pleasure. The discovery of the mechanism of ovulation at the end of the July Monarchy proved that women were not mere "vessels," as Aristotle had believed. Rather, as Galen had suspected, they played an active part in conception. Contrary to Galen's view, however, participation did not require that the woman experience pleasure. Ovulation was a mechanical affair, and the satisfaction of the female could safely be ignored. Science justified masculine egoism, inaugurating a period in which the female orgasm was viewed with misgiving and the useless clitoris treated with hostility. Yet the same discovery may have liberated some women, who, unwilling to become pregnant, had deliberately avoided orgasm in the belief that it played an essential part in conception. Even at the end of the century some women refused to believe that they were pregnant because they had never experienced orgasm—proof, if proof were needed, of the gap between scientific knowledge and everyday behavior.

In view of the cult of virginity, the angelic imagery of the romantics, and the exaltation of modesty, the religious bourgeois could not help thinking of the bedroom as a sanctuary and of the marriage bed as the altar on which the sacred act of procreation was performed. Young Auguste Vacquerie placed a prie-dieu in the bedroom of his wife, Léopoldine. The presence of bed, crucifix, and instrument of prayer heightened the room's religious atmosphere. Modesty dictated that lovemaking take place in darkness and out of sight of any mirror. Although physicians recommended that couples use only the "missionary position," like eighteenth-century physicians and theologians, they approved of practices such as rear entry that were believed to aid conception.

To what extent did the sexual apprenticeship of males outside the marriage bed influence what they did with their wives? How bold could men be, and how much pleasure could women admit, without offending modesty or arousing their partner's contempt or disgust? How far would husbands inflamed by desire permit themselves to go despite their fears of disease and damnation? On all these points the sources are silent. When a couple went to court to obtain a legal separation, sexual incompatibility was never mentioned except when camouflaged as "cruelty" or "injuries." Not until the end of the century did women dare to say publicly that they refused to perform fellatio.

The Danger of Anachronism

Sexuality, a central part of every modern marriage, in the nineteenth century was merely a backdrop to married life. What usually held bourgeois households together was the need to protect inherited wealth. Legal documents such as wills and donations *inter vivos* frequently stipulated that anything left over after all children were settled should go to the surviving spouse—a sign of genuine affection. In this segment of society, a childless husband would rarely favor his own family over his wife. The very language of wills is further evidence of the affection between husbands and wives; the extreme rarity of separations is additional proof.

Little is known about the sexual relations of peasant couples. Let us be wary, however, of accepting uncritically allegations of lack of privacy and of promiscuity in rural households. In the countryside lovemaking was not confined to the bedroom. The barn, the hayloft, and the woods were always available for discreet satisfaction of desires. Country people did not yet wear underclothing or complicated corsets, and they knew nothing of intimate hygiene. They coupled in sublime ignorance of sophisticated bourgeois impediments and distastes. Still, as Martine Segalen reminds us, we must not underestimate the affection that existed between husband and wife. Working together at the difficult tasks of running a farm and raising children created close and lasting marital bonds. In Marlhes, a small village in the Loire Valley, James Lehning found a sharp increase in the number of marriage contracts specifying joint ownership of property acquired by the couple after marriage, as well as evidence of property transfers between husbands and wives.[29]

THE ADVENT OF SEXUALITY

The contemporary history of sexuality began around 1860. Dull rumblings shook the traditional culture; the imagery of the erotic was transformed. Locked in the private sphere, the bourgeoisie began to suffer from its morality. The myth of a bestial and liberated lower-class sexuality made escape from the confines of bourgeois morality an enticing prospect. The dark allure of prostitution increased. When the industrialist Hennebeau watches his young employees making love, his poignant response reveals the depths of this doleful longing: "He would gladly have died of hunger, as some day they would die, if only he could have started life over again with a woman ready to lie down on gravel and give herself to him with all her heart and all her loins."

The Mutation of the Erotic Imagination

The romantic code was on the wane. With it went women's anxieties about sexual transgression. Seduction became commonplace. The degraded modern Don Juan seemed a strangely passive figure. Bel-Ami no longer had to feign emotion. Passion succumbed to fear of "complications." Meanwhile, men's dread of women increased. After France's defeat in the Franco-Prussian War and in the wake of the Commune, notables, afraid that all the carefully erected barriers against female sexuality were about to fall, attempted to establish a

Félicien Rops, *The Massage,*
1870–1880. (Paris, Ordre
National des Pharmaciens,
Bouvet Collection.)

"moral order," but to no avail. The terrifying thought that
the bestiality of the lower orders might penetrate and contam-
inate the bourgeoisie stirred sexual anxieties. Literature took
up the theme of prostitution. Maxime Du Camp denounced
the new traffic in vice, and Zola tried to illustrate it in *Nana.*
A new and ultimately worrisome portrait was painted of seduction. Gone were the burning eyes and elevated gaze, the
diaphanous gowns, the tears, the sighs, the timid avowals of
passionate feelings that had typified another age. Now women
deliberately aroused desire. They scented themselves with
musk. The demimonde fascinated many people. Before long
the temptress began to wrap herself in vines and exotic plants
and tried to pass herself off as an alabaster princess, a priestess
of sexuality.

　　At the same time researchers from Moll to Hirschfeld,
from Féré to Binet, from Krafft-Ebing to Forel, elaborated a
new *scientia sexualis,* which transformed the tactics of sexual
discipline. This first generation of sexologists analyzed the
subspecies of the erotic, classified perversions, and applied the

label "pathological" to conduct that had previously been condemned only as immoral. The ground was thus prepared for the coming reign of sex. Eroticism also invaded the home, and it was there that the epicenter of the impending earthquake would be located.

Flirtation

Toward the end of the century the young men and women of the bourgeoisie began to relate to one another in new ways. No study exists of this transformation of behavior, which would shape young love in the West for a century to come. Rather than invoke Marcel Prévost's "semivirginal" Maud de Rouvre as an example from literature, let me leave the task of describing the change to a specialist in the subject, Auguste Forel. Like the amorous code of the romantics, the new rules of flirtation required that male and female initially keep their distance. Forel stressed the importance of the glance prior to the actual encounter. The eyes met and caressed: this was the first step along a well-blazed trail. Other preliminaries included the "merest touch" of the other person's clothing, then the skin, then squeezes of the hand. Knees and legs drew near, then touched at the table or in the coupe or railway car. Foreplay followed: kisses, caresses, touches. According to Forel, this careful orchestration of desire often led to "orgasm without intercourse." Many young people "avoided giving themselves away with words." Flirtation involved a surprisingly "mute conversation regarding the sexual appetite."

The new style of lovemaking very quickly came to be associated with certain locales: spas, coastal resorts, casinos, luxury hotels, sanatoriums. Flirtation preserved virginity and modesty while accommodating the imperatives of desire. Even married women became infatuated with the ritual. The woman who only hinted at her sexuality did not compromise herself completely. Furthermore, the new eroticism required tact. It introduced refinement and complexity into the game of making love and allowed artistic and intellectual qualities to be brought into play. The engagement ritual was soon subject to the new rules. Even this sophisticated form of lovemaking had its "deviants," however: men and women who, according to Forel, preferred flirtation to love and copulation. Today the flirt seems to have been a transitional figure, midway between the old innocent and the modern liberated woman. She could satisfy a desire, and she could experience a pleasure that was still difficult to avow openly.

Félicien Rops, *Homage to Pan,* and *Fig Leaf* (opposite page). All of Rops's work attests to the new importance of sexuality. The threatening nudity and tragic immodesty of women evoked the fantasies of men obsessed with the danger of unrestrained female sexuality. (Musée Royal de Mariemont, and Namur, Musée Félicien-Rops.)

There has been a great deal of debate about the relation of flirtation to other forms of premarital sexuality. Edward Shorter, who believes that flirtation was a new development, has challenged Jean-Louis Flandrin's well-known hypothesis that the Vendean practice known as *maraîchinage,* mutual masturbation by a young couple hidden in a ditch beneath a large umbrella, was simply an old-fashioned relic of earlier juvenile sexual rituals.[30] No doubt Flandrin is correct, but it is worth noting that although *maraîchinage* was described as traditional by Dr. Baudoin in 1900 and by a Vendean priest as early as 1880, it still may have been influenced by upper-class practices. Flandrin is rather hasty in his assertion that nothing similar existed at the time among the bourgeoisie. The importance of reciprocal borrowing and of the circulation of cultural models should not be underestimated. In 1905 Forel observed that flirtation hit the lower classes like a tidal wave. In his view, this vulgar flirtation was merely an inept, clumsy imitation of the delicacy of the elite. Hence there is no reason why *maraîchinage* might not have been revitalized and imbued with a new subtlety inspired by the upper-class model.

The Eroticization of Marriage

Flirtation put marital sexuality in a new light. Clearly the modern "semivirgin" did not come to the marriage bed with the same attitudes as the complete innocent of an earlier era. Women were no longer so inhibited about admitting their pleasure. During the final quarter of the century husbands and wives began to feel a need for greater closeness and unity. No longer were husband and wife separated by disparities in sexual knowledge or by the injunctions of the confessor. Republican prophets painted the portrait of a new type of couple: the republican couple. These apologists for the new regime were the very same people who worked with Camille Sée to open the doors of secondary schools to female students. Husbands and wives began to refer to each other as "dear," and young woman no longer shied away from the veiled eroticism of the day's best-selling novels.

With women more aware of the facts of life and men more concerned about their partners' pleasure, a new understanding became possible. Shared pleasure replaced selfish assault. Some moralists and educators encouraged the change. In 1903 the threat of venereal disease moved Dr. Burlureaux to write a primer in sexual education for young women. Urged on by female educators and mothers, the Society for

Sanitary and Moral Prophylaxis took up the cause. Pressure was brought to bear on Louis Liard, the rector of Paris, but he did not dare to make sex education an official part of the girls' curriculum for fear of providing ammunition to his adversaries.

As early as 1878 Dr. Dartigues had published *De l'amour expérimental ou des causes de l'adultère chez la femme au XIXe siècle* (On Experimental Love, or the Causes of Adultery in Women in the Nineteenth Century). The book contained a plea in favor of female orgasm, which Dartigues saw as the best defense against the spread of adultery. Meanwhile, Dr. Montalban and several of his colleagues, also concerned about the pleasure of the female partner, recommended that husbands be gentler and more patient in their caresses. Such voices were no doubt in the minority. But there was simultaneous progress in contraception, which suggests a shift toward a more erotic, sensual conception of sexuality and away from exclusive emphasis on procreation.

Edouard Gelhay, *The Homecoming*. This artist openly celebrated the eroticization of married life. In this painting there is no sofa, no voluptuous luxury, nothing at all to accentuate the ardor of the kiss. The scene, a prelude to making love, takes place in the couple's own quite proper salon. (Salon of 1906.)

Physicians first mounted an assault on "conjugal onanism" in the late 1850s. In 1857 Dr. Bergeret compiled a list of the techniques used by his patients in Arbois. Of these, coitus

Pleasure without Risk

Birth-control industries were concentrated in a limited area of the capital. Manufacturers of pessaries and other contraceptive devices were all located on one of Paris's busiest streets. At the turn of the century the galleries of the Palais-Royal were filled with condom merchants. (Paris, Musée d'Histoire de la Médecine.)

interruptus was the most common. It required a self-control which accorded well with the neo-Kantian concept of moral autonomy praised by the founders of the republican system of public education. Bergeret was also highly critical of mutual masturbation (which he characterized as "ignoble service"), fellatio ("buccal coitus," he called it), and anal intercourse (more common than the "buccal" variety if Dr. Fiaux's judgment is to be trusted). The wealthy used condoms, while workers continued to believe that making love while standing up prevented pregnancy.

The end of the century saw the spread of neo-Malthusian propaganda in favor of birth control. Led by Paul Robin and Eugène Humbert, the League for Human Regeneration (1896) and the group that published *Génération consciente* (1908) advocated "*la grève des ventres,*" a strike of the wombs. The neo-Malthusians targeted a part of their effort at the working class, and their propaganda reached workers in the Nord. It was also prevalent in Paris's 20th arrondissement.[31] Several prefects noted that workers were inundated with information about contraceptive techniques. Tracts and brochures advocated methods less onerous and more reliable than coitus interruptus, methods with which Dr. Forel's clients were thoroughly familiar. Some women used injections of warm water tinged with vinegar. Others used sponges soaked in disinfectant and inserted into the vagina or more elaborate "occlusive pessaries," membranes of rubber encircled by rings of bone. Marthe, on advice of her doctor, chose the pessary. Thin rubber condoms were just coming into widespread use. They were less expensive than condoms made of animal intestines, which required careful handling. In short, contraception progressed simultaneously with sexual hygiene. The "English rubber" kept company with the bidet.

The introduction of antiseptic techniques in 1882 permitted an increase in the number of ovariectomies. Professor Péan performed 777 of these operations at the Saint-Louis Hospital between January 1888 and July 1891. In 1897 a scandalized Dr. Etienne Cam estimated that in Paris alone between 30,000 and 40,000 women had been surgically "neutered." Zola denounced this "conjugal fraud" (which deceived the husbands of women thus rendered sterile) in *Fécondité*. An even more dreadful operation was also performed, although it is impossible to say how often: some women submitted to the so-called Baldwin Mari procedure, which resulted in the creation of an artificial vagina.

At the end of the nineteenth century, however, to practice contraception and engage in what Guy de Téramond in 1902 called "perpetual adoration" meant ignoring the injunctions of confessors and of most of the medical profession. Most doctors remained convinced that "conjugal fraud" resulted in a variety of female pathologies: "frightful hemorrhages" (Bergeret), gastralgias, consumption, "enervation," and mental illness awaited the woman whose thirst was not slaked by regular drafts of seminal liquor and above all by repeated pregnancy.

Many patients shared their doctors' convictions. Marthe's family worried that her husband was exhausting her by indulging her hunger for pleasure. When her mother noticed that no pregnancy had come to assuage her daughter's feminine temperament, she expressed fears for her daughter's sanity and longevity. The husband's relatives, for their part, felt that Marthe was depleting his energies.

The way in which contraceptive techniques were propagated remains obscure. Neo-Malthusian propaganda did not reach all segments of society, yet "conjugal fraud" rose sharply according to an investigation conducted by Dr. Jacques Bertillon in 1911. Frequent recourse to prostitutes, traditional users of injections, probably familiarized many men with the technique and its erotic possibilities.

Although smallholding peasants traditionally practiced withdrawal during intercourse, workers continued to take virile pride in their wives' fertility. That pride, coupled with the cavalier attitude of many men, hindered the spread of contraception. Nevertheless, what Angus MacLaren has called "domestic feminism" developed among working-class women in the 1880s; at the same time the dangers of infection decreased.[32] Solidarity among women made it possible to limit the size of families. Workers' wives, less skilled than their bourgeois counterparts when it came to using contraceptive devices and less able to insist that their husbands withdraw prior to ejaculation, began to seek abortions in large numbers. When violent exercise, herbal potions, and injections failed to do the job, women turned to one of the many *faiseuses d'anges* (angel-makers, as abortionists were known) to be found in the cities. Many women even performed abortions on themselves, only to be rushed to the hospital afterward.

Attitudes grew increasingly permissive. Just before World War I the number of abortions rose sharply. Experts have estimated that anywhere from 100,000 to 400,000 pregnancies

A Shady Profession, April 13, 1907. In the early 20th century abortion ceased to be limited to prostitutes and deviants. Respectable bourgeoises and working-class mothers were no longer afraid to seek out unlicensed physicians and "angel makers." (Paris, Bibliothèque Marguerite-Durand.)

were terminated by abortion every year. At the beginning of the nineteenth century it had been mainly young single women and widows threatened with dishonor who resorted to abortion; now married women constituted the bulk of the abortionists' clientele. What had been a desperate emergency measure became a common practice as women assumed control of their bodies.

Outside Temptations

Even as bourgeois households felt themselves drawn toward a still timid hedonism, the threat of adultery once again loomed on the horizon. Having a maid became a criterion of social distinction; every middle-class housewife wanted one. A new type of promiscuity flourished in apartments that were often quite small. The presence of a young peasant girl introduced a permanent temptation into the hitherto tranquil household. Once Haussmannization and the subsequent transformation of urban architecture had relegated servants to upper-story garrets, it became easy for the men of the house to hasten up the service stairway for a brief fling. Offering the

The Treacherous Mirror, lithograph after Duboulez, 1863. The presence of maids, readily accessible and accustomed to furtive and imperious caresses, tended to eroticize the atmosphere of the bourgeois home. Such affairs were the bane of the bourgeoise, whose reserve and sophistication contrasted with the free ways of her lowly and sometimes vengeful rival.

master consolation and listening to him pour out his woes onto her bosom allowed a maid to take sweet revenge on a domineering mistress.

The bourgeois of the younger generation, raised by live-in nannies, were used to having their physical needs attended to by women of the servant class. When the age of initiation and puberty arrived, a young man of this sort might easily turn to a familiar housemaid. Hers was just one more of the many bodies sacrificed to the needs of the bourgeois libido. Psychoanalysts could probably tell us a great deal about the fetish of the apron, which symbolized both the familiarity of the home and the availability of the female body. Sometimes the mistress of the house willingly lent herself to a ménage à trois. By doing so the sick, frigid, or abandoned wife could confine her husband's (or her son's) sport within her own walls. An affair with the maid posed no risk of squandering the family fortune or compromising the man's health. It was a way of avoiding "complications."

The fiction of the time was filled with these adulterous frolics. Zola, Maupassant, and Mirbeau rehearsed them endlessly. Yet the extent of the practice cannot be measured. Because the prolific imaginations of these writers all too obviously reflect the fantasies of men fascinated by the accessible and domesticated bodies of the lower classes, caution is in order.

Under the head of sexual relations with dependents the harassment of young female workers by employers and especially by foremen should also be mentioned. Militant workers, anarcho-syndicalists in particular, frequently expressed their indignation over this new *droit de cuissage* (an allusion to the medieval *jus primae noctis,* the right of the lord to deflower women who married his dependents). According to these militants, the exploitation of working women's bodies undermined the morality of the working class, a view we know not to have been fanciful. In Limoges in 1905 a demonstration against one abusive employer led to the man's being pursued through the streets, followed by cries of "Satyr!" Out of this incident grew the serious riots that saw blood flow that year in the streets of the city of porcelain.

Infidelity and the Courts

The eroticization of married women led to fear of adultery. In the eyes of the law the positions of husband and wife were very different. A man could not be prosecuted for adul-

Emile Tabary, *Adultery*. Adultery appeared not just on stage but also in the salons of the bourgeoisie. In this case the painter accentuates the possibility of a tragic outcome. The more married life was eroticized, the more fascinated men became with the flesh possessed by other men. (Salon of 1909.)

tery in criminal court unless he kept a concubine under the same roof as his wife. Such conduct, which came close to bigamy, was considered a danger to the family. In this one instance, therefore, the wife was allowed to bring charges against her husband, who then faced a stiff fine. A woman could also file for separation from her husband, particularly if his adultery was accompanied by grievous insult or cruelty. From 1884 on she could also file for divorce. By contrast, adultery by the wife, no matter where it took place, was always a crime. An unfaithful wife risked up to two years in prison. After bringing charges and obtaining a conviction, a husband could ask for a stay of execution of the sentence and permit the guilty woman to return home; he then held a sword over his wife's head. The adulterous woman's accomplice also risked jail. Clearly the lawmakers did not wish solely and exclusively to favor men over women; above all they aimed to protect the family. Be that as it may, the laws amounted to what Naquet called a "quasi-encouragement to male adultery." In the same vein, after obtaining a separation, a woman was still obliged to remain faithful to her husband, while he could

Oswaldo Tofani, drawing, 1896. Adultery could lead to separation or crime, but it could also end in forgiveness. Rich or poor, 19th-century women were accustomed to asking for pity. The exaltation of pity served as a counterweight to the excesses of masculine power.

Verification of Adultery, 1885. This painting was shown one year after the reinstitution of divorce. It dealt with a topical subject, with which Maupassant also dealt in his *Bel-Ami*. Here again, the tragedy serves as a pretext for the representation of female nudity. The guilty woman, her hair down, shows off her body with considerable abandon to the disapproving man in black, whose duty is to violate the couple's illicit privacy. (Paris, Bibliothèque Nationale.)

do just as he pleased since the family household no longer existed.

Jurists justified this unequal treatment in two ways. Because women were inferior to men, they had no right to scrutinize the behavior of their husbands, who must be presumed to be faithful. Furthermore, a wife's adultery raised the threat that patrimonial property would fall into the hands of another man's children; a husband's adultery posed no such danger.

In fact, this inequality between men and women was greatly alleviated in case law. Women were permitted to prosecute husbands in cases where the adultery was notorious or involved injurious behavior (1828) and where the husband abandoned his family (1843) or refused to cohabit (1848) or even refused to have sexual relations with his wife (1869). Female adultery was no more harshly punished than male adultery between 1890 and 1914.[33] In this sense woman's legal inferiority had become entirely theoretical. Furthermore, judges ascribed little importance to what they now regarded as a minor offense.

Between 1816 and 1844, moreover, cheating was only a

secondary factor in separations. The procedure was used primarily by women who sought protection against beatings by their husbands, behavior that had for some years been less and less tolerated. After 1884 mistreatment and lack of money were cited far more often than adultery as grounds for divorce.

Numerous factors contributed to the rise of adultery, particularly among the petty bourgeoisie. The relaxation of surveillance of grown daughters, which came rather late; a moderate improvement in sexual hygiene; bathing, tennis, and later, bicycling; and the habit of allowing oneself to be caressed—all these gradually liberated men and women from the taboos that had attached to contemplation and exhibition of the body and to the acquisition of erotic experience. The new sensuality of marriage, the spread of contraceptive practices, and, as Madeleine Pelletier has shown, women's insistence on their right to feel pleasure all undermined the model of the virtuous wife. Growing familiarity with the techniques of seduction, the indulgence of judges, the fear of venereal disease, and the need for greater discretion at the time of the inevitable breakup induced men to shift the focus of their desires to married women, who were less ignorant and more accessible than in the past.

The Married Woman's Desire

Haussmann's urban renewal made it possible for proper ladies to venture out into the streets of the capital. By the 1880s they could show themselves in outdoor cafés flooded with light from gas, and later electric, lamps. Innumerable new pretexts for meetings and possible locations for rendezvous came into being. Large department stores served as excuses for discreet disappearances. Even philanthropy had useful service to perform. In 1897 a number of men who believed that their wives had died in the fire at the Bazar de la Charité were astonished and delighted when the women returned from the dead—or so rumor had it, and the gossip is significant whether or not the story is true. Cabs, private rooms, and *maisons de rendez-vous* offered opportunities for brief encounters. There were many new and relatively lengthy interruptions to the normal course of married life: rail travel, separate vacations, group pilgrimages, sojourns at watering holes and in coastal resorts, and even single-day excursions by train—all of which offered opportunities for adventure.

Adultery was a frequent topic of afternoon conversation. In high political circles, Jean Estèbe tells us, it was normal to

Léon Laurent Galand, *Party*. Reveling with the *grandes horizontales* of the Third Republic did not require abandoning respectable bourgeois surroundings. This painting deliberately maintains the ambiguity of the situation. Are these women wives or courtesans? The viewer is not sure. Without being shocking, the painting portrays the comfortable private debauchery of mature men. (Salon of 1909.)

have a mistress: "An affair with a lady of high society might even attract appreciative notice."[34] Novels and plays encouraged infidelity. Alexandre Dumas fils, Feydeau, Becque, and Bataille harped endlessly on the theme of adulterous love in plays in which the ménage à trois functioned with all the efficiency of a bourgeois marriage. An illicit affair calmed the nerves and piqued the senses, with secrecy as an added spice. The philandering male could avoid any danger to his health or reputation. But adulterous farce did more than hint at the pleasures of extramarital love. The theater also alleviated vague anxieties brought about by the blurring of distinctions between licit and illicit. The man who took his wife to laugh at a Feydeau comedy simultaneously quelled any fear that his comfortable vice might somehow undermine his family.

Criticism of matrimony was heard from the emancipated few. A few militants advocated free love. In 1907 Léon Blum expressed approval of premarital sexual experience. Fifteen years later in several large tomes Georges Anquetil persua-

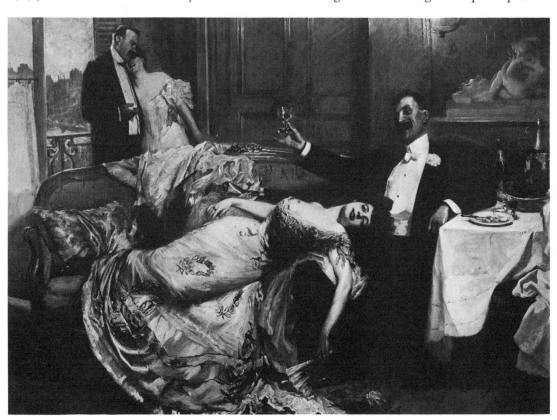

sively depicted man and his mistress as legitimate members of society.

We must not overestimate the frequency of adultery, however. Large segments of the population shunned these latest modifications to the marriage code. In the thinking of most members of the bourgeoisie, woman retained her virtuous image. The German threat brought renewed emphasis on motherhood as a civic duty, an emphasis that can of course be interpreted as yet another sign of anxiety but which reinforced the traditional morality. In her careful investigation of the wives of northern French industrialists Bonnie Smith calls attention to the virtues of these respectable women, who devoted so much of their energy to good works.[35] Between 1890 and 1914 leagues of morality sponsored by Senator Béranger and various Protestant leaders spearheaded ferocious assaults on obscenity, licentious public behavior, and the demoralization of the military. In the years just prior to World War I, when the tide of nationalism crested, these leagues appear to have made some headway. Neglect of marital obligations was not tolerated in certain quarters. A frivolous wife was a handicap to the career of a magistrate or subprefect. Rumor and anonymous libel also posed a threat to the careers of civil servants, who were expected to display a certain reserve.

The Two-Faced Mistress

In the Belle Epoque a durable affair was a very different thing from the illegitimate amours of the emancipated single woman. The emancipated woman's relationships were usually asymmetrical; in more than half the cases studied by Anne-Marie Sohn, the lover was a bourgeois, usually a bachelor or widower, while his mistress was a descendant of the *grisette* of an earlier period. The mistress of the subprefect de Forcalquier was a young seamstress. By contrast, the adulterous woman deceived her husband with a man of her own class, usually bestowing her favors on a gentleman of her own age. Court records suggest that women who discreetly deceived their husbands with a single lover felt little remorse. They looked upon their affairs as foreseeable consequences of unhappy marriages. In some cases they saw them as revenge for the husband's infidelity or syphilis. In other words, these women seem to have been formulating an implicit critique of the institution of matrimony. The debate over the evils of the *régime dotal* was another sign of doubts about the wisdom of mercenary marriage. Fiction suggests, however, that it was mothers, not wives, who usually repented when a marriage was contracted for financial gain.

If a woman's adultery was uncovered, the consequences varied with her social position. Among the bourgeoisie indiscreet correspondence usually gave the game away. At this level of society few offended husbands took the law into their own hands; some even went to court. To salve his vanity and account for his wife's behavior, the aggrieved husband might blame her misconduct on mental illness. Lower down on the social scale, men stung by ridicule often resorted to violence, particularly in the south of France. Most of the crimes and murders committed by deceived husbands occurred in this segment of society. In Belleville a great many criminal cases originated with allusions or insults that impugned a wife's morals. Workingmen got drunk at night and insults flew. Violent words were hurled back and forth across narrow streets from one apartment to another. Shouts of "whore" or "lesbian" often led to fisticuffs. Whole neighborhoods became involved.

For married women, regardless of social class, the discovery of a husband's infidelity was an emotional drama, as was the divorce that sometimes ensued. Wives recovered from divorce, however, more easily than did their husbands, who found it difficult to accept that a woman who had once been theirs might regain her sexual freedom. Brutality sometimes resulted. When an illicit relationship was broken off, emancipated single women sometimes reacted violently. A woman who had lived for a long time as the concubine of a widower or bachelor found it difficult to face a breakup that would leave her alone to face hostile public opinion; passion had been her alibi for flouting the prevailing morality, and the end of an affair also eliminated the justification. Men always faced the possibility of a violent reaction. Some jilted women caused public scandals; others avenged themselves by writing slanderous letters; a few even doused their former lovers with acid.

Some men attempted to get rid of troublesome mistresses by offering a parting gift. The stern Jules Ferry sent his brother Charles to work things out with a pretty blonde *cousette* from rue Saint-Georges. An exasperated lover might denounce his former mistress to the authorities. A few came to feel that murder was the only way out. They had the public on their side, for people took a dim view of women who would not let go. Not surprisingly, men who had had affairs with emancipated women in their youth preferred moderate adultery after marriage.

Prostitution changed in response to the still hesitant revolution in marital sexuality. Support for licensing prostitutes evaporated as men rejected the brothel in favor of more refined entertainment. The naked flesh and docility of the prostitutes humiliated and disgusted many clients. The neighborhood bordello fell on hard times, except in certain outlying provinces, where tradition impeded change. Licensed prostitution came under violent attack by a new movement, supported by the radical left, in favor of abolishing prostitution. In order to survive, licensed houses had to meet new demands from clients. In 1872 the older residents of Château-Gontier expressed indignation that newer girls were willing to perform fellatio, which had previously been prohibited in licensed brothels.

The great Paris bordellos of the late nineteenth century reflected these developments. Through clever use of incense, sumptuous decoration, mirrors, carpeting, and a riot of electric lights the brothel was transformed. Nymphs awaited their clients in Calypso's grotto, while well-rehearsed "nuns" re-

The Myth of Venal Adultery

There were more sumptuous bordellos than the houses of the rue de Londres. But note the profusion of rugs, curtains, and wall hangings, intended to make the premises as respectable as a bourgeois salon. Nothing, not even the bibelots on the mantelpiece, alludes in any way to unbridled sensuality. (Paris, Musée Carnavalet.)

ceived theirs in Sadian convents. Voyeurs delighted in tableaux vivants and discreet booths with peepholes. Some houses offered special services. For each of the "perversions" catalogued by the new sexology clients knew just where to go.

New forms of prostitution developed in response to the clients' new desires. As early as the July Monarchy dancers at the Opera had regularly granted their favors to respectable gentlemen willing to pay their expenses. The far more provocative *cocottes* of the imperial years had made womanizing respectable again. The new fashion spread to lower strata of society. Petty bourgeois males dreamed of debauching themselves like aristocrats. Café-concerts, dance halls, and taverns sustained the illusion. These new establishments employed poor artists who were obliged to sell themselves to drunken gentlemen in cozy private rooms. In the Latin Quarter bar girls compensated for the decline of the *grisette* by offering students the illusion of love.

The best solution to the problems created by the changing nature of desire, however, was the clandestine or at any rate discreet, *maison de rendez-vous*. The "houses" were so useful that Lépine, the prefect of Paris, decided to tolerate them, the better to keep an eye on what went on. Generally a lady of respectable appearance ran the house, which usually occupied the main floor of a fairly decent apartment building. It served clients only during daylight hours. Introductions took place in a comfortably furnished salon. The woman arrived wearing a hat and dressed like a respectable lady of the upper class. Without a trace of vulgarity she consented to go to the handsomely furnished bedroom, where the couple made love for an extended period. The gentleman of course then left a gift. Men who frequented these places were willing to pay for the illusion of fashionable adultery. They were men who coveted their friends' wives but who lacked the charm to seduce them. The madame of the house always insisted, usually falsely, that the women who came to her salon were respectable wives, socialites fallen on hard times, or women whose sensual appetites were frustrated. Many provincial rentiers who came to the big city found a visit to one of these houses an irresistible temptation. In any case, after the transgression came the inevitable moment of escape, which so obsessed Huysmans and Maupassant, and it was less humiliating to slink away from a respectable *maison* than from a garish bordello.

This need to maintain at least the illusion of feeling, to preserve the possibility of communication with one's sexual partner, affected the social hierarchy from top to bottom. The relaxation of laws governing the serving of alcoholic beverages in the 1880s cleared the way for prostitution in the taverns, a prostitution that was less humiliating for both client and prostitute than was the naked display of the brothels. So-called clandestine prostitution also experienced a sharp upturn in the 1880s. Streetwalkers mingled with the crowds on the boulevards. Some even pretended to be decent women and cleverly allowed themselves to be "seduced" by out-of-town rubes.

The importance of the half-century that runs from the heyday of the Second Empire to the First World War should by now stand out quite clearly. A slow but profound change was under way, one that altered the nature of the couple and set the stage for a revolution in sexual mores. We must not allow ourselves to be blinded by any rigid, monolithic concept of Victorian morality. In my view, this half-century was more innovative than the sixty years between the Consulate and the Second Empire.

The blows that transformed the structure of private life after 1860 derived much of their force from imitation. Models of behavior developed first by the aristocracy and later by the bourgeoisie proved more influential than models stemming from the lower classes. People were admittedly fascinated by the sexuality of the lower classes, and it is true that a certain erotic freedom did develop in the working class during the July Monarchy, before workers embraced the family model. But these lower-class models were not the ones that most people adopted. In France the present liberalization of sexual behavior was shaped by the upper classes. Playwrights, left-wing politicians, bourgeois feminists, neo-Malthusian propagandists, advocates of free love, and above all the scientists who created the discipline of sexology did more to shape modern sensibilities than did immigrants to Louis-Philippe's Paris with all their confused and erratic relationships.

Jean François Raffaëlli, *Old Convalescents,* 1892. The solitary suffering of old age has attracted little notice from 19th-century historians, blinded by the social dominance of youth. (Paris, Louvre.)

❧ Cries and Whispers

Symptoms of Individual Suffering

Progress toward individuation gave rise to new subjective forms of suffering. People were obliged to fashion images of themselves, and those images caused dissatisfaction. Little by little birth ceased to provide a clear definition of someone's place in the world; thereafter each individual had to define that place for him- or herself. The increase in social mobility, the vagueness and vulnerability of social hierarchies, and the growing complexity of signs of social rank not only complicated the question of ambition but also resulted in indecisiveness, confusion, and anxiety. Susceptibility to the judgment of others made people displeased or even disgusted with their own behavior. Diarists were frequently merciless on themselves. Competition, less disciplined than it had been under the ancien régime, raised fear of failure, leading to overwork and magnifying occupational anxieties. Accustomed to constant examination from childhood on, people were afraid of failing. The need to adapt to ever-changing circumstances, coupled with fears of abandonment, caused some to draw back from the world; they suffered from paralysis of the will, which Alfred de Musset called the affliction of the age.

The decline of certitude was complicated by a new sense of obligatory happiness, which altered the relation between desire and suffering. Emptiness of heart and soul was now experienced as a misfortune. This new culpability vis-à-vis the self was reflected in the ennui experienced by the day's most refined spirits—Baudelaire's "spleen."

Private diaries and letters make it clear that people felt a new uneasiness. The rise of the psychiatric clinic only magnified the effects of the mutually reinforcing factors just mentioned. The proliferating nosology and long-winded descriptions of mental illness heightened anxieties. Such new disease categories as *manie raisonnante* and *folie lucide* permitted specialists to ferret out mental illness hidden in the calm and privacy of seemingly tranquil lives. More generally, the triumph of clinical medicine tended to modify the way individuals looked at their bodies. How many previously normal recruits were terrified to learn of the pathological conditions from which they suffered when they appeared before the army's medical examiners?

The Evolution of Monstrosity

Two images of savagery struck panic into the heart of the upper class. The urban working class, which expanded rapidly in the first half of the nineteenth century, aroused revulsion, terror, and fascination. Countless novels evoked this new menace; social investigators analyzed it; philanthropy attempted to exorcise it. The initial optimism of the Restoration turned to pessimism under the July Monarchy. Members of the elite set out in search of the hidden France and discovered savages: ignorant herdsmen in the mountains, uncouth fishermen on the Léon coast, cottagers in the marshes of Poitou, a dark race inhabiting the swamps of Dombe and Brenne. These people seemed mired in the past and bound to some primitive condition of the soil, at one with the plants and rocks; they were scarcely more than animals.

Vague anxieties stemming from the proximity of these primitive tribes were compounded by the discovery of veritable monsters living within the bosom of society. A number of sensational crimes called attention to man's proximity to the beasts. Among the most notorious criminals were the parricide Pierre Rivière; the ogress of Sélestat, who in 1817 murdered her child, cooked one of its thighs in a cabbage stew, and served a piece to her husband; and the vintner Antoine Léger, who in 1823 eviscerated a little girl and sucked the blood from her heart. Scandal sheets were filled with stories of cruelty, which cast the torments of private life in a tragic light. When the king was put to death on January 21, 1793, the monster was let loose. Ogres, Jean-Pierre Peter tells us, were no longer confined to tranquil fairy tales.[1] In 1831 Quasimodo made his appearance, confirming the association between the monstrous and *le peuple*.

Proletarian violence declined after the trauma of the Commune, yet savagery persisted. Now, however, it lurked within the breast of each individual, manifesting itself in the form of

Under the July Monarchy people exhibited a powerful curiosity regarding moral monstrosity. Although the courts no longer tortured prisoners, memories of the Terror and the execution of the king gave rise to obscure anxieties, which partly explain the fascination with fratricide, parricide, and infanticide. (Paris, Bibliothèque Nationale and Musée des Arts et Traditions Populaires.)

wild fantasies. One paramount fear was that an ancestor would return from the dead; such ghosts were always seen as harmful.

The Pathological Family

The idea of the pathological family was characteristic of the time. The concept influenced scientists, ideologues, and artists. Heredity, a very old idea, had been held in high esteem by eighteenth-century thinkers. Physicians in those days believed that the offspring of elderly parents were likely to be sickly; that love children were likely to be beautiful; and that a drunken parent was likely to give birth to a monster. In order to neutralize the most extreme idiosyncrasies, neo-Hippocratic medicine recommended that different temperaments be mixed. Later, studies of industrial and urban pathologies, fear of "insurrectional hysteria," and the prevalence of neuropathy among artists suggested a link between civilization and degeneration and led many doctors to take a pessimistic view of the future.

The Book of Genesis provided the myth that the human race, perfect at the Creation, would slowly degenerate in punishment for the original sin. In 1857 Benedict Morel, inspired by Buchez, breathed new life into this old belief. Man, he said, had strayed from his initial nature; he had become degenerate. As a result, he was less and less governed by moral law and more and more subservient to his physical desires. In other words, man was moving closer and closer to the level of the animals. For more than thirty years (1857–1890) educated people believed in the theory of morbid heredity in its secularized form. Ignorant of Mendel's laws, they believed in the inheritance of acquired characters. A progressive degeneration of the species was therefore a distinct possibility. Scientific study of the causes of monstrous births quickly led to the elaboration of a social teratology, which amassed a fabulous array of monsters, freaks, and degenerates. Heredity was reduced to a morbid process. The "stamp" or "seal" that marked a person's face or physique obscured the individual and called attention to the flaws of his ancestors. Moreau de Tours's notion of an "unfortunate hereditary disposition" combined with the belief in an incredible range of latent defects to render all hope of redemption idle. "Every family," Jean Borie tells us, "lived in a feudal tower with a horde of frightened folk cowering in the depths of the oubliettes."[2]

After 1870 the influence of Darwin's theory in medical circles forced what Jacques Léonard considers an evolutionist reinterpretation of ideas about heredity.[3] Scientists stressed the defects from which various morbid processes derived. The finger of blame was quickly pointed at the poor. Misery, unhealthy conditions, lack of hygiene, immorality, and drunkenness triggered, revealed, or accelerated the hereditary process. The genetic patrimony of the elite was menaced by unseen influences emanating from the streets, the factories, and the garrets. The fear of being infected by teeming urban masses metamorphosed into a fear of degeneration. Owing to the dominance of neurology, that fear focused primarily on nervous pathology.

Félicien Rops, *Rape and Prostitution Rule the World.* (Paris, Bibliothèque Nationale.)

The naturalization of sin, indeed of mere negligence, placed new responsibilities on the shoulders of every individual. The myth of hereditary syphilis transformed desire into what Jean Borie has called an "infernal machine." The pox became a pervasive symbol in novels and iconography. Huysmans' heroes and Félicien Rops's hideous portraits reflected collective anxieties reinforced by the tragic fates of well-known syphilitics. The risks of debauchery now became more serious; the impossibility of biological redemption supplanted or reinforced existing fears of sin and hellfire. The belief in morbid heredity made it imperative for man to rise above animality.

These new fears should not be exaggerated, however. There was resistance to the new ideas. Scientists loyal to Catholic tradition, optimistic republican ideologues, older physicians inspired by a combination of neo-Hippocratism and vitalism, and above all the Pasteurian contagionists, who were hostile to Darwinism—all held that there was nothing inevitable about morbid heredity. While Weismann undermined belief in the inheritance of acquired characters, Léonard notes that "the rise of microbial etiologies shot holes in hereditarian accounts."[4] Many scientists advocated transforming the environment through social reforms and sanitary measures. They believed that joint action could yield tremendous benefits. Some even favored scientific guidance for procreation. Eugenic concerns led to criticism of institutions such as the dowry and arranged marriage. They also led to calls for sex education and sexual self-control and gave further impetus to the newly emerging image of the married couple—better informed, more united, and more harmonious.

Policlinique du Mardi, 15 Novembre 1887.

Objet de la Leçon:

1: Syphilis, ataxie locomotrice progressive, paralysie faciale;
2: Monoplégie brachiale hystérique, forme douloureuse;
3: Épilepsie partielle.

M. Charcot _ Contrairement à mes habitudes, j'ai fait venir ici des malades que je connais un peu.

Vous savez que d'ordinaire, dans la leçon d'aujourd'hui, je n'examine ici que des malades du dehors venus pour la consultation; vous savez aussi quel est le but de cet enseignement, c'est de vous exposer la véritable méthode du traitement des malades atteints d'affections du système nerveux.

Ce que nous appelons des leçons ex cathedra est chose un peu artificielle. Si vous n'aviez pour vous que cet enseignement, quand vous vous trouveriez en face des malades, vous pourriez être singulièrement embarrassés et aboutir facilement à de redoutables erreurs. C'est pour ne pas vous tromper que je me jette à l'eau et que je procède un peu devant vous comme je le fais dans ma clinique particulière. Je fais venir ordinairement des malades que je ne connais pas moi-même, mais aujourd'hui le cas est différent. Je connais le malade que je vous présente, il est très intéressant et je vais l'interroger comme si je ne le connaissais pas.

Il s'agit d'un cas complexe qui me permettra de discuter devant vous plusieurs points controversés. Le diagnostic n'est pas bien difficile à établir. Ce qui est plus difficile, c'est d'arriver à la connaissance des différents éléments qui établissent l'état pathologique du malade. Je vais l'interroger.

(au malade) Vous avez été atteint de la Syphilis? A quelle époque?

Le malade: En 1880.

M. Charcot: La chose n'est pas douteuse. Il a été soigné par M. le Docteur Fournier. En 1880, il a eu une éruption sur tout le corps.

Le malade: M. Fournier m'a dit quand je suis allé le trouver: votre maladie remonte

---

Dr. Charcot's Tuesday lectures were a major social event. Few celebrities of the day failed to attend once or twice to listen to the celebrated doctor whose successes, and claims of success, helped make neurology fashionable. This lecture reminds us that the "venereal peril" was a major worry of the day. (Paris, Bibliothèque Charcot.)

Individual feelings of malaise assumed considerable historical importance in this period. People constantly scrutinized themselves for signs of disease; the vagueness of the boundary between the normal and the pathological was troubling. Biological and social anxieties, disappointments, and failures manifested themselves in the form of depression and in the very heart of private life, the home. Men and women were afflicted to different degrees because their roles were different and because the adversities of the workplace affected them differently.

Men defined the nature of suffering and imposed their definition on women. The nineteenth century was a time of self-restraint, however, and men's suffering remained discreet—at least in public. According to Moreau de Tours, every hereditary defect was a mute object lesson, an edifying spectacle from which others could learn. People may have tried to conceal their afflictions, and men may have left it to women to exhibit the suffering that they tried to hide.

Among the many symptoms of male malaise, fear of women, which reflected man's problematic relation to his own desires, was paramount. The image of Eve as temptress, the permanent fear of the dark side of femininity and of all-devouring female sexuality, terror of the enigmatic sphinx —all these things prevented couples from experiencing shared pleasure. Medical treatises, which emphasized the risks of masturbation and debauch, aroused feelings of guilt that led to impotence.

In nineteenth-century male images of sexuality, fear of failure always lurked in the background. Stendhal's intermittent failures with the prostitute Alexandrine and Flaubert's with Louise Colet are famous. Fear that the virile member would not rise at the appropriate moment was for Edmond de Goncourt the constant anxiety of the debonair seducer. Dr. Roubaud devoted a lengthy treatise to this affliction, in which he noted the existence of an idiopathic impotence resulting from shame. Stendhal, in a chapter on fiasco, recounts a conversation he had with five handsome young men between the ages of twenty-five and thirty: "It turned out that except for one conceited fool, who probably was not telling the truth, we had all failed the first time with our most celebrated mistresses." Anxieties about impotence were especially acute because the mechanism of erection was not well understood. Many quacks got rich offering a variety of treatments. Fin-de-siècle newspapers were filled, especially in springtime, with ads for manual flagellations, douches, massages, electrical treatments, penile urtication, acupuncture, and magnetic therapies.

Increased life expectancy and the problems of old age gave rise to a variety of personality disorders. When alienists focused their clinical gaze on these afflictions, psychiatry began to make great strides. Nevertheless, until around 1860 doctors continued to believe in the moral etiology of mental illness. Earlier in the century the frequency of hypochondria had increased sharply. This malady afflicted mainly men, particularly professional men. Toward the end of the century neurasthenia and psychasthenia were common diagnoses. The competitive life and its "vexations" made headaches a common problem.

First-person accounts of mental illness began to appear in literature for the first time. In 1887, forty years after Théophile Gautier's opium dreams and Nerval's *Aurélia,* Maupassant in *Le Horla* painted a terrifying portrait of a split personality. A new anxiety was thus born, one that continues to haunt the twentieth century. The monstrous now revealed itself in forms other than bestial desire. No longer the Other, the monster now dwelt within, and its presence could result in dissolution of the personality itself.

Anemic Young Women

The symptoms of the nineteenth century female differed notably from those of the male. Doctors found female physiology fascinating. They were struck by the fragility of the weaker sex and believed that woman's sexual organs were the cause of all her troubles, which were conveniently classed under the head "female diseases." This polymorphous morbidity was an everyday problem for families, and it consumed much of the time of physicians who ministered to the bourgeoisie. The disease that claimed the youngest victims was chlorosis, or green sickness, which became increasingly prevalent. Novels and medical anthologies were filled with images of young girls with greenish-white complexions. Among the elite the representation of women as angels, the exaltation of virginity, the fear of the sun, and, later, the symbolists' veneration of snow-white skin combined to create the image of the pallid female. Indeed, her very pallor attested to both delicacy and weakness.

The sheer volume of treatises and variety of scientific theories of the disease give an idea of the anxieties it aroused. Until around 1860 a number of related explanations held sway.

Physicians who clung to ancient Hippocratic notions held that chlorosis was the result of a dysfunction in the menstrual cycle and an involuntary manifestation of awakening sexual desire. Preventive therapy was therefore appropriate. Young women suffering from the malady were to be deprived of anything that might arouse their passions until it became possible to administer the one true remedy, namely, marriage. More prudish practitioners held that chlorosis was caused by a malfunction of the stomach, a symbolic equivalent for the womb. Still others maintained that it was caused by inadequate vitality. Hence it was a consequence not of plethora or retention but of what Jean Starobinski reports was seen as a "failure to become a woman," a failure generally believed to be hereditary.[5] This theory attached particular importance to female puberty, a subject that fascinated both novelists and doctors; the difficulties that Zola's heroines faced in overcoming this hurdle are a good example. Associated with menarche, chlorosis was believed to attack the nerves in a manner similar to hysteria. It was related to "pubescent madness."

James Tissot, *A Convalescent,* circa 1875–1876. Young bourgeois women were a source of anxiety. Between puberty and marriage this fragile creature was subject to a strange, often painful metamorphosis, which called for close surveillance by those around her and for urgent medical intervention. (Sheffield, City Art Galleries.)

In the final third of the century, however, a new view became prevalent. It was widely believed that chlorosis was the result of some kind of deficiency. A new understanding of anemia, coupled with the new technology of counting red blood cells, served to justify an ancient treatment of the disease, namely, the administration of iron supplements.

Thus the progress of science encouraged adults to scrutinize young girls for the moment of sexual awakening and to attempt to delay that moment by means of moral hygiene. As the age of menarche lowered, beliefs about the sexual etiology of female diseases served to justify early marriage. Fantasies inspired by the blood of women actually contributed to shaping the female condition.

The Womb and the Brain of the Hysteric

Another image, that of the hysteric, was even more influential. It affected domestic life, sexual relations, and daily routines. The hysteric began to intrude upon private life after the grimacing figure of the witch vanished from the public arena. Throughout most of the nineteenth century hysteria, as the name implies, was seen almost exclusively as a disease of women. When some physicians protested that men also suffered from the malady, they were ignored. Not until the final decades of the century did the image of the male hysteric begin to gain ground. The first photograph in the archives of the Salpêtrière of a male victim of this curious affliction dates

Obvious but inexplicable pain: a phase of hysteria as described by Charcot. (Paris, Bibliothèque Charcot.)

from 1888. Hysteria, a disease that developed without physical signs, had posed a conundrum to physicians since Hippocrates. The doctors of antiquity attributed it to the uterus, which they believed was an autonomous animal that led a life of its own inside the body of its female host. In this way physicians were able to explain the autonomy of desire and its power to subdue the will. The body, they believed, was distinct from the self. In a hysterical crisis a woman succumbed to dark forces; because those forces overcame her resistance, they also relieved her of guilt.

In the late eighteenth century hysteria once again became an object of intense scrutiny. Medical science developed a theory which in circular fashion explained the disease as a consequence of woman's nature. Nineteenth-century physicians for a long time adhered to treatments that reflected these beliefs, which emphasized the role of the womb and of sexual desire. Hysterics were sent to gynecologists for therapy. Laymen, influenced by this kind of thinking long before Michelet confessed his interest in the mechanism of ovulation, often were willing to overlook peculiarities in their wives' behavior as the menstrual period approached. Some husbands carefully monitored their wives' menstrual cycles to make sure that all was well.

Among physicians, however, there was a long-standing controversy regarding the relative importance of the genital and nervous systems in the etiology of the disease. In the mid-nineteenth century opinion shifted in favor of the brain. Briquet in 1859 described hysteria as a neurosis of the encephalum. The change was important, because for the first time hysteria was linked to the positive qualities of women: only those with the most refined sensibilities succumbed to the disease, to which they were vulnerable precisely because they were capable of experiencing noble emotions and sentiments. It was their female nature that made women susceptible to hysteria; they paid a heavy tribute for the very virtues that made them good wives and good mothers. Suddenly hysteria ceased to be pathological.[6] Briquet's book appeared, incidentally, five years after the dogma of the Immaculate Conception became official Church doctrine and shortly after the apparitions of the Virgin at Lourdes, at a time when the curriculum of girls' boarding schools reflected the Church's angelic anthropology.

From 1863 to 1893 Charcot continued to believe in the overwhelming importance of neurosis, which he attributed to

These slides, from the archives of the Salpêtrière, are eloquent evidence of the suffering caused by nervous diseases. Patients acted out for the camera, often in bizarre ways, and it is hard to know how much of this tragic theater was play-acting and how much was real. The behavior of hysterics influenced the behavior of other women both at home and on the stage. (Paris, Bibliothèque Charcot.)

a morbid heredity whose consequences were triggered by a "nervous shock." The reason why the disease left no organic traces was that it affected only the cerebral cortex.

Whether hysteria was seen as a disease of the womb or a disease of the brain, it was a disturbance produced by the body, hence external to the self. Gladys Swain notes that it was always "experienced by the person it inhabited as something other than herself."[7] It was an anonymous force to which women had to submit, just as they had to submit to the violence of men's desires. A woman known to be a chaste—not to say a frigid and indifferent—wife might succumb, like the possessed women of another age, to natural forces capable of transforming her into a nymphomaniac.

Because of these beliefs it was advocated that woman's desires and needs for affection be satisfied to a "reasonable" degree. Fear of hysteria convinced many of the wisdom of a moderate sexual regime and peaceful home life, which allowed women to express the virtues that made them devoted wives and loving mothers without risk to their health. Husband were responsible for exercising their wives' sensibility without indulging their sensuality and thus provoking hysteria.

Another long-running controversy complicated the issue, however. Eighteenth-century animists saw hysteria as the result not of a tension or misfit between the self and its physical shell but rather of a disorder of the soul. Stahl, for example, held that hysteria indicated an eruption of passion, the conflict of a divided soul. Such a soul, Paul Hoffmann wrote, "cannot openly satisfy a desire which it is nevertheless incapable of not at least expressing."[8]

Clearly this view was the forerunner of that subjectivization of the body that occurred, Swain notes, between 1880 and 1914, a subjectivization that gave us first Janet's psychological analysis and later Freud's psychoanalysis. For these thinkers hysteria was the manifestation of a divided consciousness, of a dissociated self. It represented an inner division in the subject. For the first time in history the convulsive attitudes that reflected the old belief in the exteriority of the body began to disappear, and simultaneously hysteria ceased to symbolize, in its theatrical way, the fate of woman.

For the student of private life, however, the ubiquity of hysteria on the domestic front remains crucial. In this period the woman who was not forced to resort to raving and madness in order to make herself heard used a variety of discomforts and ailments to draw the attention of those around her

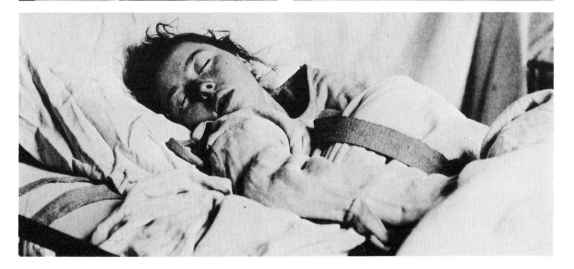

to her private suffering. Historians are just beginning to pay attention to this substitute for direct expression.

The Quest for Feminine Identity

Hysteria sometimes manifested itself in spectacular forms. Collective hysterias occurred in both private and public settings. Some cases were blamed, as of old, on demonic possession. Others were said to result from convulsive rituals. From 1783 to 1792 young women in the tiny commune of Fareins, two miles from Ars, remained under the spell of two ecclesiastics, the brothers Bonjour. The women refused to obey their fathers, submitted to flagellation by their priests, and perpetrated a variety of outrages. One of them allowed herself to be crucified in the small village church. The most fanatical of the lot became the mistress of François Bonjour and gave birth to a new messiah. From this beginning stemmed a strange rural heresy that still flourished as late as the Third Republic. The *aboyeuses* (barking women) of Josselin (1855) and the *possédées* (possessed women) of Plédran (1881) attest to the persistence of these collective manias.

The hysterics of Morzine, an isolated Alpine village, are better known. Because of the large number of unmarried women living in the town, a specifically female social life had developed there. The clergy, which exercised tight control over all activities, prohibited any kind of festival or carnival. This constraint, coupled with fears of modern life, gave rise to hysterical manifestations among the women of the town, manifestations that lasted from 1857 to 1873 and that tell us a great deal about the discomforts of women in the nineteenth century.

The first signs of trouble appeared in the spring of 1857 in two girls preparing for their First Communion. They screamed, writhed, blasphemed, and insulted adults who tried to comfort them. Soon they were imitated by other adolescent girls, and then by older women, the guardians of community values in a town that had not managed to adapt to changes in the world around it and that wished to go on living in isolation.

The hysteria also—perhaps primarily—reflected the uneasiness of adolescents in search of their identity, young women who were not allowed to dance, who lived in fear of not finding a husband, and who somehow derived pleasure from imitating one another in a collective frenzy. The young turned their backs on their parents, and mothers in turn shunned their children. Daughters insulted their fathers and refused to obey them. Wives rose up and beat their husbands. Religion was mocked by women, who inverted Church ritual. On April 30, 1864, hysterical women ran amok and cast an evil spell on a bishop who had refused to allow them to be exorcised. Even more revealing was the women's refusal to work. Instead, they sat down and played cards, drank liquor reserved for the men, turned up their noses at potatoes, and insisted on eating only white bread.

The local priest ignored the recommendations of his superiors and privately resorted to exorcism, without success. The French authorities, who became involved in 1860, launched nothing less than a civilizing crusade in an effort to calm the town's women. Roads were built, a garrison was installed in the town, and dances were organized. Most important of all, the alienist Constans was granted broad powers in the hope that he would be able, by isolating the afflicted and conducting individual treatment, to confine manifestations of the disease to the private sphere. On the eve of the Third Republic he finally succeeded.

Other neglected traces of women's suffering and rebellion can be found. I shall mention only a few. In 1848 an epidemic of hysteria broke out in a Paris factory that employed four hundred female workers. In 1860 young women studying at the *école normale* in Strasbourg were afflicted. In 1861 female communicants in Montmartre parish were afflicted. In 1880 students at a girls' boarding school in Bordeaux succumbed to the disease. In 1883 there was an outbreak of hysteria in a factory in Ardèche, where young females both lived and worked in the silk trade.

Between 1863 and 1893 hysteria was featured in a fascinating theatrical display at the Salpêtrière. Here the anguish of nineteenth-century woman was heard in its pure form. The cries of these hysterics tell us more than any other source about people's private suffering.

The Theater of the Salpêtrière

Jean Martin Charcot, the neurologist who described and analyzed the phases of the hysterical attack, put obedient hysterics on display at the Salpêtrière, a psychiatric hospital in Paris. The women who performed at Dr. Charcot's behest were eager to capture the attention of the great man and his entourage. Though apparently thrilled by the dramatization of their narcissistic pain, they never allowed their desires to

Pierre André Brouillet, *Dr. Charcot Lecturing at the Salpêtrière,* 1886. (Paris, Fondation Nationale d'Art Contemporain; presently at the Hôpital Neurologique of Lyons.)

interfere with the master's orders. Charcot exhibited his patients to an audience of artists, writers, journalists, and politicians. Some of his Tuesday lectures were attended by men such as Lavigerie, Maupassant, and Lépine. The orchestration of hysteria—recorded on film by the photographers Régnard and Londe—accentuated the signs of the disease, called attention to the appearance of the victim, encouraged imitation, and revealed the erotic side of the patients' behavior. The interest of the public was thus focused on nervous diseases. Hysterical gestures found their way onto the Paris stage. Sarah Bernhardt mimicked the great doctor's patients, or perhaps one should say the great director's actresses. The great divas of opera strove to outdo the now universally famous stars of the Salpêtrière, from the Wagnerian Kundry's display of remorse in 1882 to the long vindictive cry in Richard Strauss's *Elektra* (1905).

A subtle relation developed between literature and psychiatry. Edmond de Goncourt painted portraits of man-hating hysteria *(La Fille Elisa)*, religious hysteria *(Madame Gervaisais)*, and neurosis in young girls *(Chérie)*. The troubles of Marthe Mouret as described by Zola in *La Conquête de Plassans* (1874) and those of Hyacinthe Chantelouve in J.-K. Huysmans's *Là-bas* helped to establish the image of madness codified at the Salpêtrière. Meanwhile, writers dazzled by Charcot or swept away by fashion posed as hysterics themselves or confessed to suffering bouts of hysteria.

Everyday scenes were staged in such a way that the woman, simulating her symptoms, believed that she was performing a role. The hysteric's equivocal wink and smile offered a pathological image of female seduction. Men found it tempting to confuse the manifestations of the illness with those of orgasm and with the provocative behavior of streetwalkers. Any woman who propositioned a man was mimicking, whether she knew it or not, Augustine, the pretty young leading lady of the Salpêtrière. Charcot and his disciples never tired of her glances, her "passionate poses," her "ecstasies." They had her reenact her rape countless times until one day she took it into her head to escape.

What was the reason for this theater? Why did doctors take such endless delight in the dubious transferences they inspired? What accounts for the extraordinary influence of this great teacher, whom his students took—and who at times seems to have taken himself—to be either Napoleon or Jesus? Undeniably there was a therapeutic intent, but that in itself is not a sufficient explanation. Nor was the need to perfect the clinical technique of young doctors enough to account for Charcot's eagerness to elicit expressions of erotic pleasure mixed with pain, to witness the simulation of rapture. The theater of hysteria may have been a mere tactic in a subtle economy of male desire. It was above all a symptom, and perhaps an unwitting therapy, for an affliction of men. The complex game of exhibitionism and voyeurism that was enacted on the stage of the Salpêtrière dramatized a sick relation to desire on the part of both participants and onlookers.

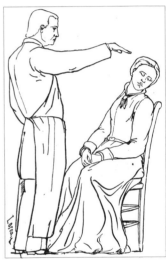

Doctors deliberately directed the actors in their theater of hysterics. Hypnosis was fashionable for years, primarily in Nancy but also in Paris. (Paris, Bibliothèque Charcot.)

Charcot had an enormous number of private patients, many of them foreigners. The master saw some five thousand outpatients annually. Under these conditions it is hardly surprising that his hospital was filled with so many hysterics, or that Marthe, a young woman with ardent desires, was considered by her family to be incurably ill.

All this bustling activity gave rise to some cruel—and useless—therapies. The worst was not the theater itself, which bestowed on its performers a privileged status within the bedlam of the Salpêtrière. It was the proliferation, over Charcot's objections, of hysterectomies; it was cervical cauterization, a

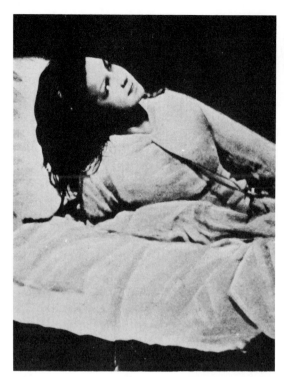

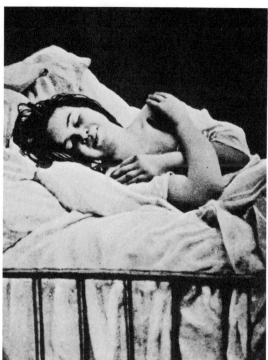

Augustine, a girl of sixteen, seems to have been the favorite patient of the Salpêtrière's staff. The photographers obviously liked to capture this pretty girl's "passionate poses" as she reenacted the rape of which she was a victim and which continued to obsess her. (Paris, Bibliothèque Charcot.)

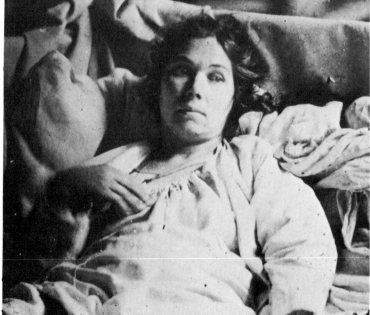

procedure performed by Charcot himself; it was experimentation with inducing hysteria through hypnosis; and it was the damage done to these tortured women, many of whom wound up addicted to alcohol, ether, or morphine.

Getting drunk can be a pleasure. More often, however, it is a sign of difficulty with life. The nineteenth century witnessed the birth of alcoholism and the emergence of the solitary drinker. The new scourge was attacked on two fronts. The upper classes, backed by the medical profession, saw a connection between alcoholism and the supposed immorality of the working class. Hence the best way to overcome this plague—which disrupted families, depleted savings, lowered the birth rate, hastened degeneration of the race, stirred social discord, and tarnished the nation's grandeur—was to preach morality to the proletariat. In 1873 a campaign against alcoholism was organized. Schools, barracks, cooperative apartments, and supervisors of recreational activities for workers were expected to play a part, but above all the campaign relied on the influence of women. In a quieter way the organizers also hoped to do something about alcohol consumption among the upper classes. Absinthe was particularly worrisome because it was believed to damage the brain cells and cause epilepsy. Like its cousin syphilis, this menace posed a threat to the genetic patrimony of the ruling class. Furthermore, the respectable male who openly drank himself into a stupor in a café was an obscene spectacle that had best be limited to isolated individuals.

In the 1890s the workers' movement took up where the notables' antialcohol campaign left off. Although the movement's analysis of the problem was quite different, blaming alcoholism on the poverty of the working class did not diminish the activists' ardor. Organizers accused alcohol, the new opium of the people, of impeding the organization of workers. Just as religion was losing its grip, alcohol arrived on the scene to cloud the minds of working men and women and to prevent the class struggle from coming to a head. Once again, women were assigned the role of preachers. The worker's wife was supposed to convert her husband to temperance, just as the bourgeois redemptress of an earlier day had been assigned the role of bringing her unbelieving husband back into the orthodox fold.

Although the different origins of these two campaigns

The Desire for Alcohol

Félicien Rops, *Absinthe Drinker.* Rops did not miss a single opportunity to portray worrisome femininity: here, an alcoholic seductress. (Paris, Bibliothèque Nationale.)

Jules Adler, *Mother*, 1899. On the eve of the First World War, alcohol was denounced by spokesmen for both the bourgeoisie and the workers' movement. It destroyed families and led to poverty and degeneracy.

against alcohol may mislead historians, all witnesses agree that a change took place in the image of the drinker. "In place of the jovial, red-faced, talkative, expansive, happy drinker," Chantal Plonévez notes, "we find the pallid, depressed, sometimes violent, aggressive, and occasionally criminal alcoholic." This change coincided with a change in drinking customs, which is best explored by considering the example of Normandy and Brittany. During the first half of the nineteenth century, Thierry Fillaut tells us, "undisciplined inebriation" and "loud, disorderly drunkenness" were still the rule in this region. At every break in the ordinary rhythm of life the peasant got drunk. *Pardons* and other festivals, fairs, and family occasions provided opportunities to drink to excess in a festive atmosphere. The resulting public intoxication was not well understood by bourgeois observers. Parisians who visited Brittany on these occasions and who were astonished to find so many people passed out along the roads were quick to overstate the evidence of debauch, which only confirmed their prejudice that the peasants of western France were barely more civilized than animals.

Beginning in the 1870s these offensive public manifestations of drunkenness were replaced by a more restrained but chronic brand of alcoholism. Identified and denounced in 1849 by the Swede Magnus Huss, the disease quickly came to be seen as one of the primary causes of degeneracy. A transitional period lasted from 1850 to 1870, during which time, according to Fillaut, "[periodic] inebriation went hand in hand with everyday consumption."[9] Drinking thus shifted from the public to the private sphere. The distinction was recognized by the authorities. An 1873 law made public drunkenness a crime but said nothing about concealed alcoholism. Unevenly enforced and largely ineffective, the law affected mainly people on the fringes of society, often homeless drunkards unable to hide their consumption of alcohol behind walls.

Alcohol and Physical Waste

All signs indicated that the changes in the west of France also occurred in other parts of the country, with differences according to social class. Apparently alcohol consumption in private originated among the bourgeoisie, although no case studies have yet been done. Drinking apéritifs, having cognac with coffee, and the use of absinthe long retained marks of their elitist origins and never became truly democratized. Absinthe—*la fée verte*—was customarily drunk in a long, slow

Edgar Degas, *Absinthe,* 1876–1877. Henri de Toulouse-Lautrec, *The Drinking Woman, or Hangover,* 1889. Degas and Toulouse-Lautrec highlighted the features of alcoholism as described by Magnus Huss. Both artists portrayed not drunkenness but lonely, morose absorption with the liquor itself, which the drinker hoped would cure her ills. And both observed the novel presence of women in Paris cafés in the early Third Republic. (Albi, Musée Toulouse-Lautrec.)

ritual, which suggests refinement of manners and acceptance of the self-destructive consequences.

Alcoholism quite early began to wreak havoc on the urban working class. Migrant masons from Limousin consumed greater quantities of alcohol than did peasants who remained home—and did so as early as the 1830s and 1840s. Some may object that this type of alcoholism is not our concern here, since it was public and involved the sociability of the tavern. But the working-class tavern and wine shop were places where the boundary between public and private broke down. The tavernkeeper was a friend, one who took part in private conversations. He served as a confidant and lent money or invested it as needed. In this context alcohol did not simply meet a physical need but also served as a pretext for private relations. It is not an exaggeration to describe such drinking as a substitute for confession.

It also cemented the social relations of the workplace. The worker who did not drink risked being shut out. He might easily be accused of being an *aristo* (aristocrat), one who "thought himself better than other people."[10] The consumption of alcohol, an accepted sign of virility, helped to create an individual's image. Denis Poulot's *Sublime* gives some idea of the discredit that attached to sobriety. A round of drinks accompanied every happy event: a birthday, a meeting with a

friend, the arrival of a telegram, a new job, and of course receipt of a pay check.

The influence of the thermodynamic model led to comparison of the body with a furnace or motor that required a constant supply of fuel. This view reinforced beliefs in the virtues of alcohol. The illusion that alcohol provided a needed "kick" governed the consumption of drinks at regular intervals by masons in Paris, dockers in Rouen, and metalworkers in Valenciennes. The pick-me-up, quaffed in a single gulp at five in the morning, helped the worker, for a little while at least, to forget about his fatigue, the dangers of the job, and the wretchedness of his condition. Alcohol played an important part in the economy of weariness and fatigue, a fact that explains in part why the consumption of alcoholic beverages by men was so much greater than consumption by women. Female workers relied on other techniques, out of the question for men, to ward off premature decline.

Historians have proposed many other explanations for the rise in solitary drinking, but it is not easy to substantiate their claims. The decline of the festival tradition, the loss of skills that had been the source of so much worker pride, the growing monotony of work, the increase in wages and expansion of leisure time (which heightened the need for escape yet made it more difficult to kill time) may have compounded psychological ills and led workers to try to drown their sorrows in drink. Indeed, the workers most likely to be tempted by the taverns were those who had achieved a certain prosperity without having had a chance to learn how to make use of their newfound leisure.

The growth in urban alcohol consumption was encouraged by lower liquor prices owing to the introduction of industrial production methods, as well as by relaxation of regulations governing the sale of alcoholic beverages under the law of 1880. Research on workers in Paris has shed light on their tastes. They liked wine, bitters, quinine, and absinthe, although they tried to conceal their fondness for the latter; they also preferred spirits to rum. Cider and beer were apparently of little interest. Women who drank showed a preference for apéritifs, liqueurs, and macerated fruits.

The Opium of the Countryside	Alcohol played a ubiquitous part in the private life of Belleville workers.[11] Drunkenness led to domestic disputes, heightened jealousy, magnified suspicions to the point of violence, and often ended in wife-beating. Drunken brawls were commonplace, as were delirium tremens, tragic evidence of the physical perils of drinking.

Alcohol's invasion of the countryside came after its conquest of the cities. For many years peasants were content to drink water, milk, cheap wine, or mildly fermented juices (called simply *la boisson,* the beverage, in west central France). As late as the Second Empire the vast majority of Limousin peasants drank only wine with meals. The chronology of the alcohol invasion varies according to the region. In western France it began in the 1870s and coincided with a major agricultural crisis and with the advent of the public schools, despite efforts by those schools to warn against the dangers of alcoholism. In some parts of lower Normandy the ravages of drink were noticeable as early as the middle of the century. Outlying areas such as Vendée and Finistère, where older drinking manners more effectively resisted change, did not show signs of the scourge until much later. Incidentally, it is a mistake to believe that alcoholism rates were substantially lower in winemaking regions. Shrewd propaganda by the wine industry has created a false image of the vintner as a person of exceptional sobriety.

In addition to the falling price of liquor and the rising standard of living, other factors that stimulated rural alcohol

consumption included improvement in communications, a growing urban influence in the countryside, and the introduction of conscription in 1872. In addition, Hervé Le Bras and Emmanuel Todd single out the collapse of older rural social structures and religious beliefs.[12] The mass exodus from rural areas exacerbated the isolation of individuals and nuclear families. Even where the stem-family persisted, the decline of the "house" often left children who were unable to marry in a desperate situation. In rural Creuse, for example, only the elderly remained on the land, and the condition of older farmhouses deteriorated. The bicycle facilitated the desertion of the young, who were drawn to the towns and their taverns.

Research might help explain why men and women were almost equally apt to become secret alcoholics. In lower Normandy women in the privacy of their own homes readily succumbed to the temptation of the "drop." The preaching of the temperance movement was not heard in the depths of the countryside. Couples often found solace in drinking together. Drink did not lead, as in the cities, to private violence, but it did affect the whole atmosphere of domestic life. In Normandy daily indulgence in cider, brandy, and above all coffee spiked with calvados gradually undermined the health of the

Peasants began to drink in private. Meanwhile, regulations governing alcoholic beverages in the towns were loosened.

peasantry. The peasants of the Mortanais, known for drinking half a liter of spirits a day, were no longer exceptions to the rule. A majority of households consumed from fifty to seventy-five liters of alcohol annually. As the decades passed, the range of beverages consumed by rural drinkers broadened. In the Porzay region vermouth was introduced in 1879, rum in 1880, kirsch and curaçao in 1889, and absinthe in 1901. Yet brandy remained the drink of choice.

The Emergence of a New Species

Homosexuality in the late eighteenth century was relatively uncomplicated. It was generally a matter of chance encounters, and most homosexuals also engaged in heterosexual activities. Under the scrutiny of the clinician, however, in the nineteenth century the homosexual was transformed into a new species. Out of the multifarious realm of debauchery a new type of human being, the curious product of a form of biological determinism, was singled out, initiating what Michel Foucault has called the "dispersion of sexualities."[13]

The "pederast," it was alleged, loved jewelry, cosmetics, and perfumes; he swished his hips and curled his hair. Hence, owing to the belief in a close relation between the physical and the moral, the new species took on a female image. The homosexual shared the characteristic vices of women: gossip, indiscretion, vanity, inconstancy, duplicity. Seeking to unmask him, forensic medicine painted a fantastic portrait, which incorporated every one of the era's marks of infamy. In 1857 Dr. Ambroise Tardieu showed how the pederast violated the rules of hygiene and cleanliness, how he shunned purifying ablutions. He could be recognized by certain morphological signs, most notably the condition of the buttocks. A relaxed sphincter, an anus shaped like a funnel or adapted to accommodate an object the shape and size of a penis—these were unmistakable signs of belonging to the recently identified species. Similarly, a "twisted mouth" along with "very short teeth and thick, curled, deformed lips" indicated familiarity with the practice of fellatio. In short, the pederast was a new kind of monster, an animal whose sexual activities resembled those of a dog. By nature he was linked with excrement; he was drawn to the stench of the public toilet.

To the police the homosexual was a person who disdained social barriers. His "unnatural" activities were no longer the exclusive province of the aristocracy. The grande bourgeoisie and artistic circles had allowed themselves to become contaminated. Police records indicate that people of this class often associated with proletarians. Pederasts were even more susceptible to fascination with the lower orders than were men who frequented prostitutes. Homosexuals felt no compunctions about crossing boundaries of class and race. For all these reasons, homosexual behavior seemed abominable to members of the bourgeoisie, who worried about preserving their bodies from contamination and who were as devoted to the purity of sex as aristocrats were to the nobility of blood.

During the final third of the century the composite image of the "invert" reflected the heightening of biological anxieties. The nascent discipline of sexology classified his various perversions and thus magnified the threat. The invert became one of a broad spectrum of sexual deviants ranging from the exhibitionist to the zoophile. All suffered from some kind of pathology, from "moral insanity" to "genital neurosis" to hopeless degeneracy. Among the victims of morbid heredity

In 1872, with the imperial fête at an end and Ordre Moral soon to take over the government, the police were not about to relax their surveillance of "pederasts." This young transvestite, arrested six times, was well aware of their efforts. (Paris, Police Archives.)

Magnan and Charcot reserved a special place for the invert.

The homosexual (the word was first used in 1809) thus became more than just a profile, a set of morphological features, a type of temperament. He took on an individual history and was associated with a particular way of acting and feeling. The history of his childhood, even of his life in the womb, played a part in determining his fate. He was afforded the pleasure of becoming grist for the interpretive mill. Having ceased to be a sinner, the homosexual became a patient, a congenital victim. He cried out for treatment. Accordingly, therapies were developed; these included hypnosis, gymnastics, outdoor activities, enforced chastity, or, at the opposite extreme, enforced relations with prostitutes.

Social Stigmatization

There has been a great deal of controversy concerning the degree of repression of "sodomites" in the eighteenth century. This crime, which was very difficult to detect, appears to have been tolerated among the nobility but prosecuted in the rest of the population. Generally it was punished only when it accompanied another crime. Historians are not sure just how far liberalization went during the revolutionary period. After the Revolution, however, repression was reinstated and intensified.

Justification of surveillance of homosexuals was based on medical as well as legal arguments. Tardieu, a physician, lent credibility to Carlier, a police official. The Penal Code of 1810 did not mention pederasty as a specific crime. The law of April 28, 1832, defined the crime of "pedophilia" as a homosexual act with a child under the age of eleven. It was also a crime to attempt to seduce or to fondle a child. On March 13, 1863, the minority age was increased to thirteen. In practice, the courts and the police were tougher than the rather mild letter of the law. In 1834 the police began making sweeps of public places in search of homosexuals. One such sweep, carried out on July 20, 1845, in the Tuileries Garden, is infamous because it resulted in the alleged pederasts' being beaten by a mob. From 1850 to 1880 the repression of homosexuals was patterned after the repression of prostitutes, although at times the former was more severe than the latter. In 1852 judges decided to exile from the Seine département all professional pederasts with no fixed abode or occupation. In 1872, in a precedent-setting case, a homosexual prostitute named Alfred, known as La Saqui, was sentenced to two years in prison for flagrant solicitation of clients.

The repression of homosexuality gives some idea of what the private life of homosexuals must have been like. They were obliged to hide their behavior. In large cities they developed unique social patterns; for want of an alternative, some homosexuals came to resemble the portrait that had been painted of them. During the Second Empire anthropologists joined doctors and criminologists in studying the homosexual. Homosexuals somehow had to signal their desire, and repression forced them to find very subtle ways of doing so in quiet, out-of-the-way meeting places. Fear of police spies gave rise to an exclusive argot and to a complex set of recognition signals.

Philippe Ariès observed that stigmatization by society sometimes induced suffering victims to make pathetic confession of their supposed sins.[14] Others, crushed by exposure, never recovered from the reproaches of their friends. Villemain, minister of public instruction under Louis-Philippe was unable to come to terms with his desire for men and died insane. We should not paint too bleak a picture, however. In the first half of the nineteenth century at least, homosexuals such as Cambacérès and Junot enjoyed brilliant careers. Homosexual lovers were tolerated as long as any overt display of affection between men was kept strictly private. Parisian high society acquiesced in Destutt de Tracy's decision to share his life with a fellow Idéologue. The marquis de Custine and his English lover Saint-Barbe were also accepted. Joseph Fiévée lived with Théodore Leclercq, a writer of didactic plays; the lovers were laid to rest in the same tomb at Père-Lachaise.

When all is said and done, the pederasts of the nineteenth century were the first to develop the model of a strictly hedonistic sexuality, which was destined to enjoy a brilliant future. When homosexuals finally emerged from hiding to proclaim their normality, it was, as Philippe Ariès remarked, as the bearers of a triumphant new model of virility.

At present the sources for a history of female homosexuality are nonexistent. Apart from high-society lesbianism, whose history runs from the *anandrines* of the late eighteenth century to the wealthy American sapphics who settled in the Paris of the Belle Epoque, we know little beyond the inter-

The Lesbian, Symptom of Male Fantasies

Jean-Alexandre Coraboeuf, *Abandon*. Throughout the century female homosexuality enjoyed the complicity of males, whose fantasies it gratified. Painters found a pretext for portraying the sensuality of the female body. Despite its title, this painting did not shock the organizers of the Salon of 1909. A painting of male homosexuality would no doubt have been greeted with less indulgence. (Salon of 1909.)

minable diatribes of physicians and magistrates against the proliferation of Amazons in the brothels and prisons. We do, however, know a great deal about the fascination that the lesbian exerted on the male imagination, a fascination that can be read as yet another symptom of the morbid character of male desire in the nineteenth century. The discussion of sapphism was very different from the discussion of pederasty. If male fantasies medicalized the latter, they poeticized the former. The nineteenth century invented the "lesbian," that paragon of gentleness, delicacy, and cleanliness; the very word, notes Jean-Pierre Jacques, caressed the tongue.[15]

Of course the doctors worried about women who experienced pleasure without any male to control their ecstasy. The medical fraternity categorically asserted that one of the two lesbian partners invariably assumed the male role, a belief that gave rise to the most incredible statements about enormous clitorises and deformed vulvas. The police issued an order that any woman who wished to dress as a man must apply for authorization, an order with which the painter Rosa Bonheur complied. The male view of lesbianism did not persuade everyone, however. Early in the century Parent-Duchâtelet demonstrated that no clinical sign distinguished the lesbian from the heterosexual woman.

The image of Sappho elaborated by men in this period was an ambiguous one. Men were fascinated by women's enormous capacity for pleasure; at the same time they feared any pleasure that women experienced in their absence. Sapphism was a favorite topic of conversation among men, whose fantasies were greatly influenced by images of the harem. Convinced of their sexual inferiority, men dreamed of the insatiability of women left to govern their own desires. In pursuit of satisfaction, they imagined, frantic lesbians pulled out all the stops. It was this fantasy, quite evident in *La Fille aux yeux d'or,* that drove Fourier as well as the voyeurs who frequented brothels later in the century to delight in tableaux vivants in which all the roles were filled by women. As in the theatrical display of hysteria at the Salpêtrière, men found this exhibition of female bodies somehow therapeutic.

Paradoxically, men found the insatiability of the sapphic reassuring, because it proved that in their absence women experienced a dissatisfaction, a lack. Maupassant to the contrary notwithstanding, men do not seem to have felt truly deceived when their lovers slept with other women. According to the Goncourt brothers, the duc de Morny, a wizened sensualist if ever there was one, held that sapphism introduced adolescent females to an eroticism of which men ultimately reaped the benefits. This opinion probably explains why nine-teenth-century males, like the husband of Colette's *Claudine,* were so tolerant of a practice whose actual prevalence we shall probably never know.

What we know of such couples as Renée Vivien and Nathalie Clifford-Barney confirms the notion that relations between women were affectionate and tender. The depth of their feeling for each other is reminiscent of the early stages of a love affair. In Nathalie's salon, which according to Marie-Jo Bonnet became a "crucible of passion and freedom," lesbians were lured out of the closet. Liberated women emancipated themselves from the male gaze.

The Rise of Suicide

When suffering became too great, suicide was a possible option. A private act, taking one's own life was also a cry for help, a desperate protest against the failure of communication. Suicide was on the rise everywhere in nineteenth-century Europe. France, where the suicide rate did not begin to decline until 1894, was no exception. All or part of this increase may be the result, however, of improvements in record-keeping that were instituted in 1826.

Suicide has long been a fascinating subject. Leading psychiatrists and sociologists such as Guerry, Quételet, Falret, Brierre de Boismont, and of course Durkheim have attempted to analyze the phenomenon. Visits to the morgue to gaze at recovered bodies cooling on marble slabs became a regular Sunday ritual for some Parisian families.

A growing sense of insecurity weakened the will to live. Durkheim in 1897 distinguished between egoistic suicide and anomic suicide. The former was a product of disillusionment, the latter of unrestrained desire and competition. Statistics suggest that loneliness and the various social factors that encouraged it were important determinants of suicide. Also striking is the very high rate of suicide among unmarried, widowed, and divorced men and women in the nineteenth century. Marriage, or at any rate the presence of children, seems to have protected people against the self-destructive urge. Still, the relative importance of social factors as opposed to individual factors of a psychiatric or genetic nature has been a matter of debate for more than a century and a half.

The causes adduced by victims and witnesses are not very convincing. Families and the authorities sometimes attempted to conceal the facts, manipulate witnesses, and destroy evidence. One vague indication is that among the causes blamed for suicides in the period from 1860 to 1865, mental illness came first, followed by "love, jealousy, and immorality," followed by poverty and family troubles.

Thanks to detailed official investigations, we know exactly what people killed themselves in nineteenth-century France. Among men the suicide rate was relatively high, three to four times greater than the rate for women, depending on the decade. Quételet was quick to note that the likelihood of suicide increased with age. There is more controversy, however, concerning the relative probability of suicide in various occupational groups. Broadly speaking, the suicide rate was extremely high at opposite ends of the social spectrum. Rentiers, intellectuals, professionals, and military officers, particularly those serving in the colonies, attempted suicide more often than the average. These figures may be read as suggesting that the death instinct increases with level of education and degree of individual self-awareness.

Equally clear, however, is the very high rate of suicide among domestic servants, especially toward the end of the nineteenth century, when many servants first became aware of the misery of their condition. Similarly, the probability of suicide was extremely high among the unemployed and rootless, as well as among inmates of the state prisons.

In Paris during the July Monarchy *les misérables* committed suicide in large numbers, as if they were incapable of adapting to the inescapable conditions of life in a large city. In contrast to the situation that exists today, however, the suicide rate among peasants in the nineteenth century was very low.

More than half of all male suicides chose to hang themselves, a quarter chose drowning, and 15 to 20 percent opted for a bullet in the head or the heart, the latter being the "noble" choice preferred by the elite. Half of all successful female suicides chose drowning, while from 20 to 30 percent, depending on the period, chose hanging; asphyxia and poison became increasingly common as time went by.

Most nineteenth-century suicides were committed in the morning or afternoon, occasionally in the evening; nighttime was seldom chosen. Between Friday and Sunday suicides were less common than during the week; the rate rose from January to June, then declined from July to December. Long days,

sunshine, the spectacle of people outdoors, and the beauty of nature seem to have provoked more suicides than did the solitude of evening, the tortures of the night, or the chill of winter.

TREATMENT TRANSFORMED

From the beginning of the century onward, the presence of the medical profession was increasingly noticeable at the bedsides of aristocratic and bourgeois clients, for whom the family doctor was someone with a background similar to their own, even a close friend. The patient and the patient's family listened to the physician's diagnosis and heeded his advice. They knew how to comply with his orders and could afford to take the hygienic measures he prescribed. "Their will to live," Jacques Léonard writes, "enabled them to see eye-to-eye with medical rationality."[16] Close relations between doctor and patients led to frequent visits, and it is sometimes hard to tell whether those visits were made out of friendship, politeness, or professional obligation. Doctors often took tea with patients and spent evenings in their homes. Medical duties brought them into close contact with local magistrates. Because the doctor knew how to ride a horse, he cut a fine figure at the hunts staged by the local aristocracy. Jules Sandeau's "good Doctor Herbeau," Stendhal's Dr. Sansfin, and the cynical Torty of Barbey d'Aurevilly's *Bonheur dans le crime* give some idea of the close relations that existed between doctors and patients.

At the end of the century rural physicians felt no compunctions about openly entering into friendships with schoolteachers and public officials. Growing numbers of the newly rich and lesser local luminaries—lumber dealers, livestock merchants, tavernkeepers, millers, gelders—were apt to seek out the town doctor as an educated companion, and they in turn served as mediators who carried word of scientific advances to the rural masses.

These prosperous clients could afford to pay the doctor for his services, often by subscription, as evidenced by countless household account books. In this segment of society, moreover, people felt considerable gratitude toward the competent, respectable physician, whose devotion was priceless.

For the peasant or worker, hanging was considered the manly way to end one's own life. Drowning and poison were preferred by women. Octave Tassaert, *Suicide,* 1852. (Montpellier, Musée Fabre.) Honoré Daumier, *Suicide.* (Paris, Musée Carnavalet.)

Family medicine had a rhythm all its own. The general practitioner was free to use his time as he saw fit. If need be

Women and Medicine

Albert Guillaume, *Vaccination,*
1908. The doctor's auscultation
was long an embarrassment to
the modest woman. In 1908,
however, the young beauty's
attempt to cover her breasts
must have seemed rather
prudish and old-fashioned.
(Paris, Bibliothèque Nationale.)

he could remain in a patient's home for hours, compensating
for his therapeutic shortcomings by being a patient listener
and a polite, refined guest. The physician knew the family and
its secrets. When necessary he acted as its ally, concealing a
hereditary defect or helping a family get rid of a troublesome
member. He could aid in finding a mate for a child. Women
were his natural allies. Every doctor had to please the ladies,
who made and unmade reputations and who had charge of
domestic health matters. The growing importance of "wom-
en's diseases" justified this special attention to women. Treating highly emotional patients whose modesty was easily
offended took skill and tact. When a doctor, in the course of
treatment, became privy to a person's sexual needs and desires,
he needed to understand what was only half-spoken and had
to be able to offer guidance without frightening or offending
his patient. Doctors, whose image was modeled on that of the
father and husband, were able to increase their authority over
the years. Gradually they learned to use women as their mes-

sengers. "Together," writes Jean-Pierre Peter, "they set out to discipline, to save lives, to make marriages, to restore health."[17]

It has often been deplored that the doctor's newfound authority came at the expense of the traditional therapeutic role of women. The habit of following doctors' orders, we are told, interfered with the transmission of traditional remedies from mothers to daughters. There are in fact many indications of the medical profession's growing influence over child-rearing. Doctors increasingly insisted that families hire a live-in nanny. They waged successful war against swaddling and favored slowly introducing the infant to solid food rather than abrupt weaning. Mothers relied on doctors to familiarize their daughters with the signs of puberty. Still, the rapidity of this medicalization of childhood should not be overestimated; change was actually quite slow.

Doctors and the Poor

The physician's relation to poor families was quite different from his relation to the well-to-do, even though the same physician often treated both. The cultural gap between practitioners and their clients led to misunderstandings. When treating the poor, physicians never ventured into the psychological terrain they sometimes explored with wealthier patients. Medical treatment was sporadic and limited to a specific purpose, usually an emergency such as an epidemic or an illness so serious as to require obedience to medical authority. Medicine was associated with charity, and often doctors were sent to the homes of the poor by charitable agencies. In such cases they charged practically nothing. In other circumstances, doctors were obliged to extend credit, which encouraged them to adopt a paternalistic pose.

Some sense of the attitudes of rural clients can be gained through study of proverbs. The beliefs of country people were a long way from the rationality and optimism of the Enlightenment. To them disease seemed inevitable and quite often incurable. The peasant had little interest in physiological explanations. He believed in the medicine of signs, based on supposed analogies between the plant and animal kingdoms and the cosmic order. The patient was largely responsible for his own condition. Disease came from the outside as the result of some act of negligence, sin, or predisposition. To overcome the malady the patient first had to describe the symptoms; then he (or she) had to battle the disease with stoic discretion.

Hence it seemed pointless to bring in a learned doctor to treat a child who was incapable of describing his ailment. A suffering individual deserved compassion, but that compassion was hardly therapeutic. For peasants, the doctor was only one of several possible avenues of recourse. He was expected to take a determined, energetic approach—to set fractures and boldly probe even the deepest wounds. Yet he worked in a hostile, or at any rate suspicious, environment. Youth, flirtatiousness, and greed were easily held against him. Tardiness was inexcusable. Mocking the physician was one way for peasants to take revenge on the dominant classes.

Less is known about workers' attitudes toward disease prior to the triumph of Pasteur's theories. The working class did employ some rather primitive preventive techniques. Ways of warding off physical decline were developed spontaneously in response to the accelerating pace of work. In response to the threat of tuberculosis, workers tried to save their strength, to find moments for rest in their rather flexible schedules.

Folk Medicine

Medical anthropologists have found a flourishing tradition of folk medicine in the nineteenth century. This durable tradition, a compound of magical formulas and ancient practices, survived by borrowing from modern medical practice in ways that did not challenge the fundamental integrity of folk beliefs. Throughout the century people continued to turn for help to witches and herbalists; they made pilgrimages to the graves of "good saints" and to magical fountains. Bonesetters, sorcerers, and healers of every variety served a vast clientele, often with cruel or tragic consequences.

The healers' techniques were not always very different from those of the learned doctors. Folk medicine often borrowed from the medical science of an earlier period, even though the borrowed practice belonged to a different system of ideas about health and disease. There was constant interchange between one cultural level and another. Physicians themselves were not above borrowing from other disciplines when necessary. Some encouraged their patients to go on pilgrimages. Throughout the century quacks with diplomas prospered.

Among the upper classes, in addition to official medicine, a range of alternative therapies was available. The priest and his maid and nuns who taught in religious schools distributed medication and advice. Aristocrats kept rather rudimentary

Folk medicine played an important role in the economy of health under the Second Empire. (*L'Illustration,* 1856.)

private pharmacies in their châteaux; the lady of the manor used the medicines it contained to treat the poor of the hamlet. In the upper classes mothers did not hesitate to use grandma's old-fashioned remedies to treat minor ailments. The Boileaus of Vigné-en-Saumurois rarely called on the services of their physician, relying instead on familiar remedies.

At the same time, hawkers and barkers sold medicines from the official pharmacopoeia as well as prosthetic devices. In fact, they borrowed so heavily from official medicine that they may be regarded as pioneers of medicalization. Their sales pitches helped peasants to overcome their fatalistic outlook. Other healers, whose practice was increasingly limited by laws against the unlicensed practice of medicine, were vaguely influenced by progress in surgical and orthopedic practice.

The influence of medical authority on private life varied with the nature of the doctor-patient relationship and with the period. Until 1880 or so doctors enjoyed greater prestige

Family Hygiene and Contagious Disease

among the bourgeoisie than the efficacy of their treatment warranted. For the most part therapy was limited to enemas, leeching, cupping, and other quite simple techniques, regardless of the physician's theoretical allegiances. Medicine's shortcomings allowed considerable room for improvements in hygiene, the importance of which cannot be overemphasized. The nature of the hygiene varied with sex, age, position, profession, temperament, and climate and affected all aspects of family life. Individuals were encouraged to practice bodily cleanliness. Changes were made in the family diet. More generally, behavior was regulated in a variety of ways. The hygienist—and in those days every doctor was to some extent a hygienist—insisted on the need to regulate exercise, horseback riding, dancing, novel reading, and sexual relations. Medical science issued injunctions pertaining to the discourse of the passions, the vagaries of the soul, and, in quite a minute way, the use of the senses. Even the content of dreams was a matter of medical interest. In general, doctors encouraged moderation, avoidance of extremes, and restraint.

The same period witnessed the development of a kind of

"Family hygiene" occupied 19th-century doctors as much as did clinical practice. The doctor's orders cemented the relationship between the physician and the woman of the house, who carried medicine's message into the home. (Paris, Bibliothèque Nationale.)

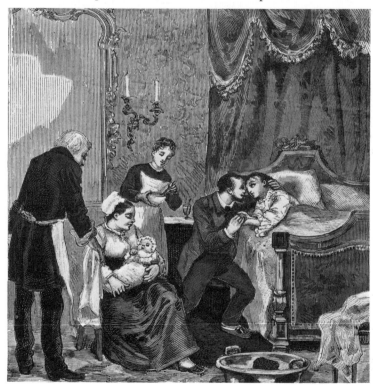

Edward Loevy, *Treatment of Tuberculosis at the Hôpital Saint-Louis.* After the discovery of Koch's bacillus, proof that tuberculosis was contagious, and given the inefficacy of treatment, the fate of the victim became even more tragic than before. Families often wished to get rid of sufferers who were now seen as dangerous. Brief periods of remission no longer raised false hopes, and the disease had lost the aura it had in the romantic era. (Paris, Bibliothèque Nationale.)

natural medicine associated with a still ill-defined ecological project. New urban pathologies coupled with the anarchic growth of industry led people to ask whether the conditions necessary for good health had not been radically compromised. The question plagued the upper class. Doctors recommended fresh-air "cures" as well as mineral baths, thus contributing to the resurgence of the spas and, during the July Monarchy, to the growth of coastal resorts. What might be called a bourgeois style of relaxation developed in response to the fear of tuberculosis. The ill were isolated, not so much to avoid contagion, in which few people believed, as to hide the victim of tuberculosis or mental illness who posed a threat to the family's genetic capital.

The triumph of contagionism and of Pasteur's theories in the 1880s transformed images of disease, altered people's attitudes, and disrupted their habits. Doctor-patient relations also changed. Doctors now wished to demonstrate the efficacy of their treatment. Their mission no longer was to keep up the patient's morale or to protect him from excess but to heal. The course of therapy was well marked, simplifying the doctor's task. As for hygiene, the war against the microbe now became the primary focus. Water, soap, and antiseptics made yesterday's complex prescriptions seem old-fashioned. When a doctor, before coming to his patient's bedside, carefully washed his hands, he was setting an example for others to follow. The doctor's constant presence was no longer as pressing a concern as in the past, hence physicians were more likely to do their work quickly and move on. By the same token, people were less willing to forgive medical errors and failures.

The new theories emphasized the dangerous sources of contagion that lurked in the home. Leading physicians were slow to recognize that tuberculosis was a contagious disease. Although Villemin in 1865 gave proof that it was, the fact still had not been accepted by the Academy of Medicine in 1867. Pidoux declared that even if the danger were real, it would be better to say nothing lest families be tempted to spurn diseased members. After Koch isolated the bacillus in 1882, however, the truth could no longer be hidden.

Hunting the Microbe

Before that date, doctors who treated the urban poor did all they could to diminish the danger of infection and epidemic that resulted from crowded housing. Rural physicians acted as mentors, helping peasants to clean up their homes and the areas around them. That was about as far as prevention went. After 1880 medical practice became more methodical. New therapies reached rural areas at about the same time as knowledge of antiseptic practices. Modern medication reached the Nivernais between 1870 and 1890, for example.

To be sure, Pasteur's followers continued to analyze the morbid menace in environmental rather than social terms. Nevertheless, the new theories were fraught with consequences. They prompted sanitary and social reforms that led to closer surveillance of individual families. Luc Boltanski has investigated the halting progress of new child-care methods among the working class.[18] The need to prevent epidemics and track the course of a disease led to interventions by the authorities that tended to blur the boundary between public and private; so did the obligation to remove contagious patients from the family and to oversee the application of prophylactic measures. The situation was complicated by the fact that microbes could not be seen with the naked eye, so that preventive measures had to be broader and more systematic than those used in an earlier period to detect and remove so-called sources of infection.

The nurse and the social worker appeared on the scene for the first time. The traditional charitable visits to the poor by ladies of the aristocracy gave way to more systematic methods. Daughters of well-to-do families, eager to escape from the house and in some cases from marrriage as well, took on new responsibilities, particularly in the war against tuberculosis. Dr. Calmette was the first to propose sending "health monitors" into workers' homes in Lille. Soon the monitors were superseded by "social health inspectors." Schools were set up to train the new health personnel. The most celebrated of these, located on rue Amyot in Paris, opened its doors in 1903.

The development of these new roles confirms the relation between the rise of medical power and the triumph of Pasteur's theory of contagion. It was that triumph that permitted the *coup d'état sanitaire* whose history Jacques Léonard has so ably reconstructed.

We must not think that interest in psychic phenomena grew inordinately between 1800 and 1914. What changed was the nature of the response to those phenomena. For at least the first two-thirds of the nineteenth century the medicine of the soul was characterized by inefficacy, a syncretic methodology, long-windedness in describing such afflictions as chlorosis, hysteria, hypochondria, and the dangers of the passions, and belief in a close relation between the physical and the moral.

Psychiatry and Private Life

With bourgeois clients, sober, well-meaning physicians employed crude, empirical psychotherapeutic techniques. Even rural practitioners, though much less sophisticated than the great alienists of the day, were careful not to neglect such symptoms as dizziness, nightmares, phobias, and outbursts of passion.

With victims of more severe mental illness relatives and doctors faced a much more difficult problem. The presence of insanity in a home or community could arouse anxiety in a great many people. Madness was a terrible secret, which could compromise a family's honor or wreck a carefully laid matrimonial strategy. When the victim of mental illness was a child, it seemed natural to keep the patient in the home. Overwhelmed by his responsibilities as an eldest son, Auguste Odoard showed signs of derangement. He was confined first in his bedroom, then in a study near his father's office, and finally in a small cell in the manor's dovecote. His younger

The Second Empire established the modern hospital. Therapy began to take precedence over charity. The new hospitals were not like the old Hôtel-Dieu to which the poor came in search of a comfortable death in a bed with sheets. People now came to the hospital in the hope of being cured. (Hôpital Fernand Widal. Paris, Musée Carnavalet.)

sisters, Sabine and Julienne, brought him food and cut his hair. The family doctor called in an alienist as a consultant. We still know very little about the practice of psychiatry in these early days. In 1866, 58,687 mentally ill individuals were cared for by their families, compared with 323,972 in asylums.

If the insane person was an adult, however, remaining at home was impossible. The rest of the family usually decided to send the victim away, especially if the patient was an unmarried woman, who contributed less than a man to the family's well-being. Before the law of 1838 defined the legal status of the mentally ill, anarchy reigned. A family could have a person committed simply by applying to the mayor, the priest, or some local ecclesiastic or official. In other cases confinement followed a decision by the courts. In Maine-et-Loire after 1835 commitment papers had to be issued by a physician. The law of 1838, which tried to bring order to commitment procedures, insisted that the medical authorities be involved. Once a family had rid itself of an insane member, relatives quickly forgot about the person. According to Yanick

Ripa, 29 percent of female inmates held in Paris asylums between 1844 and 1858 eventually were released.[19] During the same period, however, only 3 percent of Parisian women held in provincial asylums were ever released.

Special wards in public asylums were reserved for paying customers, who were divided into several classes at such places as Charenton, Limoges, Mareville (near Nancy), and Yon (in Seine-Inférieure). Patients from well-to-do families enjoyed special treatment. Their rooms were more spacious than those of other inmates. They could choose what they ate. Some were even attended by servants, an indication that they led relatively private lives. When the time came for "ergotherapy," they were able to circumvent the work requirement. Of 40,804 inmates held in special asylums in 1874, 5,067 were exempt from the usual rules.

A network of so-called *maisons de santé* also developed, forerunners of private mental hospitals. These were reserved for the wealthy. In 1874, 1,632 patients were distributed among twenty-five such institutions, the most famous of which were Esquirol, located at one time near the Jardin des Plantes in Paris and later in Ivry; the Château Saint-James in Neuilly, where Casimir Pinel did his work; and the Passy clinic. In 1853 Gérard de Nerval, who had been hospitalized

Cells of inmates of the Salpêtrière led to attacks on the confinement of mental patients.

Hydrotherapy was the primary treatment of mental illness throughout most of the 19th century. Few drugs were available. (*L'Illustration*, 1868.)

twice in a municipal asylum known as the Maison Dubois, entered Dr. Blanche's clinic. He brought with him his furniture and collections. Released for a time, he returned the following year to a clinic that would later receive Guy de Maupassant. Less well-known clinics operated in the provinces, like the one that Dr. Guérin opened at Grand-Launay (Maine-et-Loire) in 1829, where wealthy patients had private rooms.

A substantial number of private institutions treated wealthy patients suffering from relatively mild neurotic conditions. In all these institutions patients enjoyed close relations with their doctors, relations that did not exist in the more anonymous environment of the large mental hospital.[20] These private institutions were the breeding ground of the class-based practice that psychoanalysis would later adopt.

The Demand for New Psychological Therapies

During the final quarter of the nineteenth century a new demand developed for psychological services unrelated to mental illness, a demand that not only influenced private life but also revealed something about its nature. People called upon the services of psychiatrists, as evidenced by the size of

Charcot's private practice. We have already examined many of the causes of malaise. Anxiety over morbid heredity, the considerable prestige of neurology, and growing belief in the efficacy of psychological intervention contributed to the new demand. General practitioners influenced by Pasteur's theories had begun to make inroads in the war against contagious disease and were no longer as willing as in the past to listen patiently to endless accounts of their patients' troubles. Listening became a specialty.

The change coincided with substantial progress in science. The prestige of Hippolyte Taine inspired the development of a new discipline, experimental psychology, devoted particularly to the study of intelligence. The new field was soon dominated by the personality of Pierre Janet. The work of Alfred Binet and Théodule Ribot attracted a great deal of attention, as did Bergson's introspective techniques. The development of psychology proceeded in two main directions. Psychological analysis, first defined by Janet in 1889, was a major innovation. Free association was used to explore the mind of the individual, particularly the subconscious, which was believed to be related in some way to conscious thought. The other main area of investigation was intelligence testing, based on the belief that every intelligence, from the idiot to the genius, could be assigned a precise point on a continuum. The intelligence quotient and the test to measure it, developed by Binet and Simon between 1903 and 1905, became part of the new credo of French psychology.

The implications of these discoveries were numerous. Psychological analysis established a new therapeutic ideal; it led to abandonment of authoritarian methods and to repudiation of hypnosis. Janet's method substituted hearing for seeing. The theatricality of the mental hospital gave way to the hushed silence of the psychiatrist's office. Psychiatry thus entered a new realm even before the advent of psychoanalysis.

Indeed, for the time being those who advocated the French view of the unconscious rejected Freud's pansexual theories; until the First World War they effectively prevented their promulgation in France. Théodore Flournoy's efforts in 1903 to introduce Freud's ideas and, on a broader scale, those of Moricheau–Beauchant, an obscure professor from Poitiers, met with little success. Nevertheless, the groundwork for the widespread influence of psychological thinking today was effectively laid by psychological analysis and other triumphs of experimental psychology, such as Binet's theory of fetishism and Charles Féré's work on the pathology of the emotions.

Intelligence testing, made important by the still recent innovation of compulsory education, affected the lives of countless children. Thanks to Binet's discovery, the schools, which in the words of Robert Castel and Jean-François Le Cerf, functioned as a "sort of grand democratic tribunal,"[21] were able to detect abnormalities that once would have gone unnoticed. Idiots, imbeciles, and other children with mental disabilities could now be identified. From the once undifferentiated mass of childhood one now singled out the backward, unstable, and retarded. The law of 1909, which established special classes for the handicapped, bestowed official recognition on this new system of classification, but until the 1950s nothing was done to implement the law.

Training the Body

Social and economic needs determined certain bodily images and attitudes, which in turn influenced the teaching of gestures and postures in the schools. This physical discipline also provoked a liberation movement, which accompanied what historians of psychology have described as "the subjectivization of the body." The nineteenth century witnessed the development of a variety of physical disciplines, not all of which have yet been classified. In this as in many other areas, historians are still at the stage of studying what was said, not what was actually done. The sign language of good manners, influenced by Lasalle's manuals of civility, has yet to be studied. The teaching of postures and attitudes to schoolchildren, soldiers, and prisoners; the gestures of the laborer and the ways in which he rested or relaxed; the desire to move more freely that manifested itself during the Belle Epoque—all belong to a vast and largely unexplored field of study.

This physical training and the reaction to it influenced people's behavior in private, but once again certain elementary distinctions can be seen. Change was particularly slow in the countryside. To us the postures and gestures of Millet's peasants seem to hark back to a distant past, but this perception may be a product of our ignorance. Guy Thuillier, to date the only historian who has examined the question, has looked at the gestures of peasants in the Nivernais and concluded that until the middle of the nineteenth century there is little evidence of any change.[22] Anthropologists associated with the Musée des Arts et Traditions Populaires have also investigated this difficult area. Their tentative hypothesis is that the ges-

This new treatment for ataxia accorded well with 19th-century ideas about orthopedics, which often relied on cruel devices to put the body back into shape. (*L'Illustration*, 1889.)

tures associated with the use of kitchen utensils show no signs of evolution from the fourteenth century until 1850. From 1850 until 1920 technological and material improvements slowly influenced traditional practices. After 1920 a profound upheaval took place, resulting in a total transformation of the everyday acts that define the texture of private life. This chronology urgently needs to be fleshed out. Philippe Joutard is right to point out that gestures are not unrelated to one another but form a coherent system. The way in which a peasant grabs a bale of hay gives clues to the way in which he makes love.

Country folk who believed that the body was malleable clung to certain corrective techniques. Nineteenth-century midwives were in the habit of modeling the heads of newborns. The use of swaddling, in a modified form that allowed the baby's arms to move freely, persisted in certain rural areas until the early years of the Third Republic. Various devices were used to correct faulty posture. Bourgeois mothers forced daughters with slightly curved spines to wear dreadful iron braces in the hope of augmenting the "aesthetic dowry" of their marriageable offspring.

Correcting Posture and Proscribing Laziness

Thanks to the work of Georges Vigarello, we now know a great deal about the history of physical training. Images of the body were greatly influenced in the first half of the nineteenth century by mechanics and, after 1851, by thermodynamics. Initially the body was seen as a set of forces, then as a kind of motor. The aim was no longer to mold it but to train it. The meaning of exercise ceased to be primarily military. A new kind of physical training emerged, whose purpose was to maximize the body's strength.

Great stress was placed on proper posture. Men were exhorted to tighten their belts, stick out their chests, and tuck in their bellies. Corsets reshaped the female body, so that nearly all women in the latter third of the nineteenth century suffered from mild curvature of the spine. Children were constantly reminded to stand up straight and tuck in their bellies. Fear of tuberculosis persuaded people of the wisdom of doing breathing exercises designed to increase lung capacity. Orthopedic medicine was transformed. Older devices designed to reshape the body were replaced by machines that aided exercise and facilitated training. A remedial gymnastics based on a careful analysis of physical movements was developed.

Top: Jules Scalbert, *Come On In!* Ocean swimming, fashionable in France since the Restoration, ceased to be regarded as a therapeutic activity in the Belle Epoque. Rather than a salutary ordeal, it had become a pleasure to be enjoyed by the young, male and female alike. (Paris, Bibliothèque Nationale.) Bottom: Another manifestation of the new concern for the body. (*L'Illustration,* 1892.)

By the end of the century, a respectable woman could ride a bicycle, especially if accompanied by her husband. (Sirot-Angel Collection.)

These various physical disciplines influenced teaching both in the schools and at home. Teachers and parents worked to stamp out laziness and the slack posture that suggested idleness. The time of vigorous physical activity had arrived. In schools and factories new physical disciplines standardized postures and eliminated idle time. Emphasis was placed on the beneficial consequences of what Georges Vigarello calls "muscle-strengthening chores."[23] After 1860 fears of degeneracy and advances in microbiology reinforced belief in the new disciplines.

At the end of the century, as Eugen Weber and Marcel Spivak have shown, physical training came to be seen as an instrument of national revenge. Gymnastics became a civic duty. For a time students trained as soldiers and people steeled themselves by taking long hikes. Gymnastics then merged with the less strenuous physical activities of the aristocracy to produce that new phenomenon whose name was borrowed from the English: sport. Horseback riding, hunting, and various games played with balls spread from the top of the social hierarchy downward. Darwinian theories and the German menace contributed to the new emphasis on sport, which supposedly fostered self-reliance.

The New Physical Freedom

A third element contributed to the late-nineteenth-century emphasis on physical development. Homeopathic medicine advocated walks in the country, excursions to the mountains, ocean bathing, and bicycle riding. Over the years these activities broke free of the medical realm. It was no longer discipline, exercise, or health that motivated participants, but the desire to enjoy the unfettered experience of their own bodies. Isadora Duncan, who danced in Paris, may have evoked the ancients with her movements, but what her dancing really symbolized was the freedom to experience the body as something no longer external to the self. Significantly, this new freedom coincided with the new demand for psychological services as well as with the eroticization of marriage. No longer was the sense of the body dominated by its disorders. People began to notice health and its pleasures. Soon even the austere Paul Valéry would be analyzing the pleasures of nude ocean bathing.

Marcel Proust, who found watching pretty cyclists on the beach all the more fascinating because he was unable to share their delight, noticed this revolution as it was happening. Revolution: the word is not too strong, for the changes under way in the late nineteenth and early twentieth centuries totally transformed what we think of as private life.

The petty bourgeois male who dreamed of seducing a singer or dancer was drawn to the café-concert, where for a price he could find a woman to satisfy his illusions. Most of these singers and dancers were also prostitutes. In the 1860s a form of lascivious behavior once limited to the aristocracy thus began to spread to lower levels of society, to the ever more complex middle class.

ᴈ Conclusion

Michelle Perrot

ESTABLISHING an equilibrium between public and private was a delicate matter, and political theory was constantly tinkering with the balance. Rousseau dreamed of absolute transparency: "If I had had to choose my place of birth, I would have chosen a state in which everyone knew everyone else, so that neither the obscure tactics of vice nor the modesty of virtue could have escaped public scrutiny and judgment." In contrast, Tocqueville stressed the advantages of individualism, which, writing in 1850, he called a "recently coined term." Essentially he took it to mean private social relations: "Individualism is a feeling of comfort, which allows each citizen to withdraw from the mass of his fellow men in order to keep company with his family and friends, in such a way that, having created a small society that suits him, he willingly leaves the larger society to its own devices." At the beginning of the twentieth century Léon Bourgeois saw "solidarism" as the means of reconciling the rights of the triumphant individual with his obligations—his "debt"—to the preexisting larger society of which he was an organic member. "Social justice," a consequence of the organic nature of society, precluded not only laissez-faire liberal but also totalitarian solutions to social problems; it justified increasing state intervention.

The nineteenth century made a desperate effort to stabilize the boundary between public and private by mooring it to the family, with the father as sovereign. But just when things seemed firmly in place, they began to slip and slide. In some ways the twentieth century ushered in yet another form of modernity. Expansion of the market, growth of production, and the explosion of technology led to increased consumption and trade. Advertising stirred new desires. Improved communications set people on the move. Trains, bicycles, and automobiles encouraged the circulation of human beings and goods. The allure of fashion diversified appearances. Photographs greatly increased people's access to images of themselves. At times, however, these spectacular signs of change serve only to conceal an unchanging backdrop.

Now that individuals were relatively free of the constraints of time and space, they began to feel deceptively free in their choice of ambitions. Concern for the self, for a body that was better groomed and whose complexity was better understood, for the depths of the psyche that were only now coming into clear focus, for sexuality liberated from procreation and marriage—all these things were at the heart of twentieth-century aesthetics and philosophy.

The rise of individualism affected all strata of society to one degree or another, especially in the cities. As discipline in the factories was tightened, for example, workers began to place greater stress on leisure time and to insist on space for themselves. The affirmation of working-class consciousness was by no means incompatible with a desire on the part of workers to move up to a higher class. Even rural people who had long lived as their ancestors had done before them succumbed to the influence of migrant workers, who served as cultural mediators. They no longer embraced as inevitable the old ways of living, loving, and dying.

Three groups of people were especially successful in breaking free of old habits: the young, women, and members of the intellectual and artistic avant-garde. "To will, to achieve, to live": those were the three aspirations that the twenty-seven-year-old Roger Martin du Gard attributed to his double in *Devenir* (1908). As women entered new occupations and acquired new freedom, they began to insist on the right to work, to travel, and to love whomever they pleased. Feminism, the collective expression of a much broader range of aspirations, had been a relatively sporadic movement in the nineteenth century, a movement that reared its head whenever a chink appeared in the armor of the powers-that-be. In the twentieth century it developed into a more persistent force. Through newspapers such as *La Fronde,* groups, and conventions, women demanded equality of civic and political rights. They justified their demands on two grounds: the social and maternal role of women and the logic of natural rights. If women are individuals, why treat them as minors? The "new woman," hailed in sometimes ambiguous terms by men eager to change the nature of male-female relations, became an important figure throughout Europe.

These changes, which had only just begun and were far from complete, encountered formidable resistance on religious, moral, and political grounds. The resistance was bolstered by surviving elements of the ancien régime, which, as Arno Mayer has pointed out, continued to flourish long after the Revolution. Organizations such as the Boy Scouts attempted to regiment newly emancipated youth. A virulent strain of antifeminist sentiment grew out of the crisis in male identity brought about by the subversion of sex roles that had endured for centuries. Women were accused of responsibility for a decline of morals that was in turn blamed for the decline of nations. A variety of moralistic movements set out to clean up the streets and bookstores, to ban public displays of affection and erotic reading matter. One symptom of the evolving climate was the change in attitude of the writer Maurice Barrès. At one time he had celebrated the cult of the self; now he extolled a life rooted in the soil and steeped in ancestral memories.

Stronger than ever at the turn of the twentieth century, European states sought to enhance their power by influencing the psychology of the masses. Governments mobilized public opinion in favor of national defense and national values. In 1909 the Futurist manifesto proclaimed: "We want to demolish museums and libraries and combat moralism and feminism . . . We want to glorify warfare—the world's one true hygiene."

The declaration of war in 1914 abruptly reminded everyone of the primacy of the public and the limits of private life. Recess was over. With the support of powerful governments and efficient new technologies, the war mobilized the energies of youth suddenly recalled to duty. Men and women were put back in their places; each citizen was restored to his proper rank. Of course nothing can really interrupt private life for long, and in some ways the war actually created new opportunities. But people had to dissimulate and hide these new private activities, especially if they did not contribute directly to the war effort. Subsequent developments would reveal what the war impeded, halted, diverted, and produced.

Class 16 departs Paris's Gare Montparnasse on April 12, 1915. (Paris, Bibliothèque Nationale.)

Even before the First World War, however, a new system of relations had begun to take shape. What thoughts were on the minds of the young men who marched off, apparently happy, to a war that everyone said would surely be short? What were those boys thinking of as they prepared to play in this new game of whose cruelty they as yet had no inkling? What thoughts were on the minds of the young and not-so-young women who waved their handkerchiefs in an outpouring of patriotic emotion whose meaning surpassed them? What friendships and loves were ended? What old hopes were shattered, and what new hopes replaced them? So many ordinary lives, all similar yet each different from the others, were for a moment welded into a single substance and swept away by the tide of history. In that moment the fate of the modern age was fittingly symbolized by two things: a railway station and a train.

Notes

Bibliography

Credits

Index

Notes

1. The Curtain Rises

THE UNSTABLE BOUNDARIES OF THE FRENCH REVOLUTION (LYNN HUNT)

1. Ferdinand Brunot, *Histoire de la langue française, des origines à nos jours,* 13 vols. (Paris: Armand Colin, 1967), vol. 9, *La Révolution et l'Empire,* p. 823.

2. *L'Ami du peuple,* 16 October 1790, p. 8.

3. John Moore, *A View of the Causes and Progress of the French Revolution,* 2 vols. (London: G. G. and J. Robinson, 1795), I, 150.

4. Fabre d'Eglantine, *Réimpression de l'Ancien Moniteur,* 18: 290 (session of 8 Brumaire, year II [29 October 1793]).

5. Quote from Darline Gay Levy, Harriet Branson Applewhite, and Mary Durham Johnson, *Women in Revolutionary Paris, 1789–1795* (Urbana: University of Illinois Press, 1979), p. 219.

6. See Brunot, *Histoire de la langue française,* vol. 10, *La Langue classique dans la tourmente,* p. 191.

7. Archives Nationales F7 3699(2). This document was provided to me by Professor Suzanne Desan from her own work on the religious revival.

8. Quoted in Dominique Dessertine, *Divorcer à Lyon sous la Révolution et l'Empire* (Lyons: Presses Universitaires de Lyon, 1981), p. 276.

9. Quotes from "Mémoires particuliers," in *Mémoires de Madame Roland,* ed. Paul de Roux (Paris: Mercure de France, 1986), pp. 201, 330; and *Lettres en partie inédits de Madame Roland,* ed. C. A. Dauban, 2 vols. (Paris, 1867), II, 576.

10. Roland Barthes, *Sade, Fourier, Loyola* (Paris: Seuil, 1971), p. 22.

THE SWEET DELIGHTS OF HOME (CATHERINE HALL)

1. John Bull, "Ode to George IV and Caroline his wife," British Library collection of pamphlets and poems on Queen Caroline.

2. Rev. George S. Bull, "Home and How to Make It Happy," lecture in the Town Hall, Birmingham, 1854.

3. This quotation from John Milton's *Paradise Lost* serves as an epigraph to Hannah More's *Coelebs in Search of a Wife, comprehending of domestic habits and manners, religion and morals,* 9th ed. (London: T. Caddell and W. Davies, 1809).

4. The Marsh Children, *Memorials of a Beloved Mother by her Children* (Birmingham: John Knott, 1837), p. 26.

5. Hannah More, *Strictures on the Modern System of Female Education. The Works of Hannah More,* 11 vols. (London: T. Caddell, 1830), VIII, 27.

6. The Epistle of Paul the Apostle to the Ephesians, 5:22.

7. These popular lines from William Cowper were often quoted in diaries, letters, and commonplace books. See, for example, Charlotte Sturge, *Family Records* (London: Privately published by Abraham Kingdon, 1882), p. 107.

8. Rev. Edward Bickersteth, quoted in Owen Chadwick, *The Victorian Church,* 2 vols. (London: Adam and Charles Black, 1966), I, 443.

9. The Epistle of Paul the Apostle to the Galatians, 3:28.

10. Richard Tapper Cadbury to Elizabeth Cadbury, February 10, 1815. Cadbury Family Letters, 1806–1855. Birmingham Reference Library, 466/300/1–21.

11. Elizabeth Cadbury to Maria Cadbury and Sarah Barrow, June 3, 1828. Ibid.

12. Maria Cadbury, "The Happy Days of Our Childhood," Birmingham Reference Library, 466/344.

13. General Report, *Census of Great Britain, 1851* (1852), I, xxxvi.

14. *Aris's Birmingham Gazette,* January 13, 1834.

15. For the relation between middle- and working-class cultures, see, for example, Robert Q. Gray, *The Labour Aristocracy in Victorian Edinburgh* (Oxford: Clarendon, 1976); David Vincent, *Bread, Knowledge and Freedom. A Study of Nineteenth Century Working Class Autobiography* (London: Methuen, 1981); Angela John, *By the Sweat of their Brow. Women Workers at Victorian Coal Mines* (London: Routledge and Kegan Paul, 1984); Thomas W. Laqueur, *Religion and*

Respectability. Sunday Schools and English Working Class Culture, 1780–1850 (New Haven: Yale University Press, 1976).

16. Birmingham Temperance, *A Selection of Tracts and Handbills published in aid of the Temperance Reformation* (Birmingham: R. Davies, 1839).

17. John Smith, Speech at the Birmingham Temperance Meeting, December 14, 1835 (Birmingham: Wrightson and Webb, 1835).

18. Francis Place, *The Autobiography of Francis Place, 1771–1854,* ed. Mary Thrale (Cambridge: Cambridge University Press, 1972), pp. 116, 138.

19. Edward P. Thompson, *The Making of the English Working Class* (London: Victor Gollancz, 1963), p. 746.

20. William Cobbett, *Cottage Economy* (London: C. Clement, 1822), p. 199.

21. William Cobbett, *Advice to Young Men, and incidentally to Young Women in the Middle and Higher Ranks of Life* (Oxford: Oxford University Press, 1980), p. 317.

22. Hugh S. Tremenheere, quoted in Angela John, "Colliery Legislation and its Consequences: 1842 and the Women Miners of Lancashire," *Bulletin of John Rylands* (University Library of Manchester) 61 (1978): 90.

23. Lawrence Stone, *The Family, Sex and Marriage in England, 1500–1800* (London: Weidenfeld and Nicholson, 1977); Rudolph Trumbach, *The Rise of the Egalitarian Family. Aristocratic Kinship and Domestic Relations in Eighteenth Century England* (New York: Academic Press, 1978).

24. Leonore Davidoff, *The Best Circles. Society Etiquette and the Season* (London: Croom Helm; Totawa, N.J.: Rowman and Littlefield, 1973), p. 36.

25. Mark Girouard, *Life in the English Country House* (Harmondsworth: Penguin, 1980), p. 270.

26. James Luckcock, "My House and Garden: Lime Grove, Edgbaston," Birmingham Reference Library, 375/948.

27. James Luckcock, *Sequel to Memoirs in Humble Life* (Birmingham: T. Belcher, 1825).

2. The Actors

THE FAMILY TRIUMPHANT (MICHELLE PERROT)

1. Benjamin Constant, *Journaux intimes (1803–1816); quoted in André Jardin, *Histoire du libéralisme politique. De la crise de l'absolutisme à la Constitution de 1875* (Paris: Hachette, 1985), p. 233.

2. G. W. F. Hegel, *Principles of the Philosophy of Right,* 1821, pt. 3.

3. Kant, quoted by Bernard Edelman, *La Maison de Kant* (Paris: Payot, 1984), pp. 27, 31.

4. Germaine de Staël, quoted in Jardin, *Histoire du libéralisme politique,* p. 204.

5. Constant, quoted in Jardin, ibid.

6. Pierre Rosanvallon, *Le Moment Guizot* (Paris: Gallimard, 1985), p. 71.

7. Pierre-Paul Royer-Collard, quoted in Jardin, *Histoire du libéralisme politique,* p. 255.

8. Alexis de Tocqueville, *Democracy in America,* book 2, chap. 8.

9. See Raymond Deniel, *Une Image de la famille et de la société sous la Restauration (1815–1830)* (Paris: Ouvrières, 1965); Mona Ozouf, *La Fête révolutionnaire (1789–1799)* (Paris: Gallimard, 1976), trans. by Alan Sheridan as *Festivals and the French Revolution* (Cambridge, Mass.: Harvard University Press, 1988); and Robert Paxton, *Vichy France: Old Guard and New Order, 1940–1944* (New York: Knopf, 1972).

10. See Françoise Arnoult, "Histoire de Frédéric Le Play. De la métallurgie à la science sociale," unpub. diss., University of Nantes, 1986.

11. See Louis Devance, "La pensée socialiste et la famille de Fourier à Proudhon," unpub. diss., University of Dijon, 1976.

12. Fourier's *Le Nouveau Monde amoureux* was finally published in 1967 by Simone Debout.

13. See Jacques Capdevielle, *Fétichisme du patrimoine. Essai sur un fondement de la classe moyenne* (Paris: Fondation nationale des sciences politiques, 1986).

14. See Hervé Le Bras and Emmanuel Todd, *L'Invention de la France* (Paris: Pluriel, 1981).

15. Compare Jules Simon, *Le devoir,* 1878.

16. Paul Ourliac has shown this in countless case studies.

17. Jean-Pierre Chaline, *Le Bourgeois de Rouen. Une élite urbaine du XIXe siècle* (Paris: Fondation nationale des sciences politiques, 1982).

18. See Elisabeth Claverie and Pierre Lamaison, *L'Impossible mariage. Violence et parenté en Gévaudan. XVIIe, XVIIIe et XIXe siècle* (Paris: Hachette, 1982).

19. See Adeline Daumard and François Codaccioni, *Les fortunes françaises du XIXe siècle* (Paris: Mouton, 1973).

20. Capdevielle, *Fétichisme du patrimoine.*

21. One of the most interesting developments in recent research has been the growth of a new discipline, economic anthropology, whose pioneers were Chayanov and Jacques Gody. See Yves Lequin, *Histoire des Français, XIX et XX siècles.* Vol. 1, *Un peuple et son pays.* Vol. 2, *La Société.* Vol. 3, *Les Citoyens et la démocratie* (Paris: Armand Colin, 1983–1985).

22. For evidence of this nostalgia, see Serge Grafteaux, *Méme Santerre. Une vie* (Paris: Marabout, 1975).

23. See Maurizio Gribaudi, "Procès de mobilité et d'intégration. Le monde ouvrier turinois dans le premier demi-siècle," unpub. diss., Ecole des Hautes Etudes en Sciences Sociales, 1985.

24. See Françoise Raison-Jourde, *La Colonie auvergnate de Paris au XIX siècle* (Paris: Bibliothèque Historique de la Ville de Paris, 1976).

25. Jacques Rancière, "Savoirs hérétiques et émancipation du pauvre," in Jacques Borreil, ed., *Les Sauvages dans la Cité. Auto-émancipation du peuple et instruction du prolétaire au XIX siècle* (Seyssel: Champ Vallon, 1985), p. 44.

26. Louis Bergeron, "Permanences et renouvellement du Patronat," in Lequin, ed., *Histoire des Français, XIX et XX siècles.* Vol. 2, *La Société,* pp. 153–293.

27. Ibid.

28. Pierre Bourdieu and Monique de Saint Martin have reported similar findings. See Bourdieu, "La Capital Social," and Saint Martin, "Une grande famille,"*Actes de la Recherche en Sciences Sociales,* 31 (January 1980): 2–4, 4–22.

29. Jean-Paul Sartre, *L'Idiot de la famille: Gustave Flaubert de 1821 à 1857,* 3 vols. (Paris: Gallimard, 1971–72), II, 1117.

30. Michel Foucault, *Le Souci de soi* (Paris: Gallimard, 1984), trans. by Robert Hurley as *The Care of the Self* (New York: Pantheon, 1987).

31. Le Bras and Todd, *L'Invention de la France.*

32. Eugen Weber, *Peasants Into Frenchmen: The Modernization of Rural France, 1870–1914* (Stanford, Calif.: Stanford University Press, 1976).

33. Caroline Chotard-Lioret, "La Socialité familiale en province: une correspondance privée entre 1868 et 1920," unpub. diss., University of Paris V, 1983.

34. Mireille Bossis, "La Correspondance comme figure du compromis," in *Ecrire, Publier, Lire. Les Correspondances (problématique et économie) d'un "genre littéraire."* Papers of the Colloquium "Les Correspondances," Nantes, October 1982 (Nantes, 1982).

35. Anne Martin-Fugier has studied such gatherings as well as the ritual. See "Bourgeois Rituals" in this volume.

36. Hélène Sarrazin was able to follow the family's evolution by comparing photographs taken at this annual occasion. See *Elisée Reclus ou la passion du monde* (Paris: La Découverte, 1985).

37. Hans Naeff, *Die Bildniszeichnungen von J. A. D. Ingres,* 5 vols. (Berne: Benteli, 1978).

38. See Philippe Lejeune, *L'Autobiographie en France* (Paris: Armand Colin, 1971).

39. See, for the Camisards, Philippe Joutard, *Le Légende des Camisards* (Paris: Gallimard, 1977).

40. Norbert Elias, *Über den Prozess der Zivilisation* (Basel, 1939); *The Civilizing Process,* trans. Edmund Jephcott (New York: Pantheon, 1982).

41. François Tricaud, *L'Accusation. Recherches sur les figures de l'aggression éthique* (Paris: Dalloz, 1977).

42. Henri Leyret, *En plein faubourg* (Paris, 1895), p. 51.

43. Tricaud, *L'Accusation,* p. 136.

44. Lejeune, *L'Autobiographie en France.*

45. Joëlle Guillais-Maury, *La Chair de l'autre. Le crime passionnel au XIXe siècle* (Paris: Olivier Orban, 1986).

46. Anne-Marie Sohn, "Les Rôles féminins dans la vie privée: approche méthodologique et bilan de recherches," *Revue d'histoire moderne et contemporaine,* October–December 1981.

47. Louis Chevalier, *Classes laborieuses et classes dangereuses à Paris pendant la première moitié du XIXe siècle* (Paris: Plon, 1958).

48. Claverie and Lamaison, *L'Impossible mariage.*

49. Yves Castan, *Honnêteté et relations sociales en Languedoc, 1750–1780* (Paris: Plon, 1974); Nicole Castan, *Justice et répression en Languedoc à l'epoque des Lumières* (Paris: Flammarion, 1980) and *Les Criminels de Languedoc. Les Exigences d'ordre et les voies du ressentiment dans une société prérévolutionnaire (1759–1790)* (Toulouse, 1980).

50. Arlette Farge and Michel Foucault, *Le Désordre des familles. Lettres de cachet des Archives de la Bastille* (Paris: Gallimard/Julliard, 1972). See also Arlette Farge, "The Honor and Secrecy of Families," in Roger Chartier, ed., *A History of Private Life.* Vol. 3, *Passions of the Renaissance* (Cambridge, Mass.: Harvard University Press, 1989), pp. 588–600.

51. See Bernard Schnapper, "La Correction paternelle et le mouvement des idées au XIXe siècle," *Revue historique,* April–June 1980.

52. The importance of this innovation was stressed by Robert Castel. See *L'Ordre Psychiatrique.* Vol. 1, *L'Age d'or de l'aliénisme* (Paris: Minuit, 1976).

53. This subject has been studied by Yanick Ripa, *La Ronde des folles* (Paris: Aubier, 1986).

54. Ulysse Trélat, *La Folie lucide* (Paris, 1861).

55. Schnapper, "La Correction paternelle."

ROLES AND CHARACTERS (MICHELLE PERROT)

1. Françoise Mayeur, "Jules Ferry et l'enseignement des filles," in François Furet, ed., *Actes du colloque Jules Ferry* (Paris, 1985).

2. Jules Simon, *La Liberté,* 1869; quoted by Bernard Schnapper, "La Correction paternelle et le mouvement des idées au XIX siècle," *Revue Historique,* April–June 1980, p. 345.

3. Yanick Ripa, *La Ronde des folles. Femme, folie et enfermement au XIXe siècle* (Paris: Aubier, 1986).

4. Henri Guillemin, *L'Engloutie, Adèle, fille de Victor Hugo (1830–1915)* (Paris: Seuil, 1985), p. 105.

5. Bonnie Smith, *Ladies of the Leisure Class. The Bourgeoises of Northern France in the Nineteenth Century* (Princeton: Princeton University Press, 1981).

6. See Lafont de Sentenac, *Des droits du mari sur la correspondence de sa femme,* Court of Appeals of Toulouse, lecture at annual opening session, October 16, 1897 (Toulouse, 1897).

7. See Hélène Sarrazin, *Elisée Reclus ou la passion du monde* (Paris: La Découverte, 1985).

8. Fresnette Pisani-Ferry, "Jules Ferry, L'homme intime," in Furet, ed., *Colloque Jules Ferry.*

9. Jean-Paul Sartre, *L'Idiot de la famille: Gustave Flaubert de 1821 à 1857,* 3 vols. (Paris: Gallimard, 1971–72), II, 1882.

10. Michel Foucault, *La Volonté de savoir* (Paris: Gallimard, 1976), p. 143.

11. Hervé Le Bras and Emmanuel Todd, *L'Invention de la France* (Paris: Pluriel, 1981), p. 29.

12. Martine Segalen, *Nuptialité et alliance. Le Choix du conjoint dans une commune de l'Eure* (Paris: Maisonneuve et Larose, 1972), p. 90.

13. Gérard Jacquement, *Belleville au XIXe siècle* (Paris: EHESS, 1984).

14. See Yves Lequin, *Les Ouvriers de la région lyonnaise (1848–1914).* Vol. I, *La Formation de la classe ouvrière régionale* (Lyons: Presses Universitaires, 1977); Elinor A. Accampo, "Industrialization and the Working-Class Family: Saint-Chamond, 1815–1880" (Ann Arbor, Mich.: University Microfilms International, 1984).

15. See Elisabeth Claverie and Pierre Lamaison, *L'Impossible mariage. Violence et parenté en Gévaudan. XVIIe, XVIIIe et XIXe siècle* (Paris: Hachette, 1982), p. 139.

16. Caroline Chotard-Lioret, "La Socialité familiale en province: une correspondance privée entre 1868 et 1920," unpub. diss., University of Paris V, 1983.

17. Martine Segalen, *Mari et femme dans la société paysanne* (Paris: Flammarion, 1980).

18. Yvonne Verdier, *Façons de dire, façons de faire. La laveuse, la couturière, la cuisinière* (Paris: Gallimard, 1979), p. 79.

19. Agnès Fine, "A propos du trousseau: une culture féminine?," in Michelle Perrot, ed., *Une Histoire des Femmes est-elle possible?* (Marseilles: Rivages, 1984), pp. 156–180.

20. Claverie and Lamaison, *L'Impossible mariage,* p. 218.

21. Camphor was indeed used extensively by the wife of a Paris carpenter studied in an 1856 monograph by Le Play and Focillon.

22. See François Ewald, *L'Etat-providence* (Paris: Grasset, 1986).

23. Le Bras and Todd, *L'Invention de la France.*

24. See Edward Shorter, *A History of Women's Bodies* (New York: Basic Books, 1982).

25. J.-P. Goubert, *La Conquête de l'eau. L'Avènement de la santé à l'âge industriel* (Paris: Laffont, 1986).

26. Angus MacLaren, *Sexuality and Social Order: The Debate over the Fertility of Women and Workers in France, 1770–1920* (New York: Holmes and Meier, 1983).

27. Le Bras and Todd, *L'Invention de la France,* p. 168.

28. Jules Simon, *L'Ouvrier de huit ans.*

29. See M.-F. Lévy, *De mères en filles. L'Education des Françaises, 1850–1880* (Paris: Callman-Lévy, 1984).

30. Fine, "A propos du trousseau."

31. George Sand, *Histoire de ma vie,* ed. Georges Lubin, 2 vols. (Paris: Gallimard, 1970–71), II, 179.

32. Michel Bouillé, "Les Pédagogies du corps. Lieux et corps pédagogiques du XVIIIe au XIXe siècle," unpub. diss., University of Paris VIII, 1984.

33. Georges Navel, *Travaux* (Paris, 1945).

34. Foucault, *La Volonté de savoir.*

35. Sand, *Histoire de ma vie,* I, 76.

36. Elisée Reclus and his siblings are a good example of this. See Sarrazin, *Elisée Reclus ou la passion du monde.*

37. For a case in point, see Michel Braudeau's novel *Naissance d'une passion* (Paris: Seuil, 1985).

38. Marie Lafarge, *Mémoires de Marie Cappelle veuve Lafarge écrits par elle-même,* 4 vols. (Paris: René et Cie, 1841–1844), II, 103.

39. Pierre Sansot, *La France sensible* (Seyssel: Champ Vallon, 1985), p. 85.

40. Michel de Certeau, *L'Invention du quotidien.* Vol. 1, *Arts de faire* (Paris: UGE, 1980).

41. Louis Chevalier, *Classes laborieuses et classes dangereuses à Paris pendant la première moitié du XIX siècle* (Paris: Plon, 1958).

42. Nancy Green, in *Les Travailleurs immigrés juifs à la Belle Epoque. Le "Pletzl" de Paris* (Paris: Fayard, 1985), has studied the differences that existed between the rue des Francs-Bourgeois, where the upper crust of the Jewish quarter lived, and the dirtier, more densely populated rue des Rosiers.

43. George Vigarello, *Le Propre et le sale. L'Hygiène du corps depuis le Moyen Age* (Paris: Seuil, 1985).

44. Anne Martin-Fugier, *La Place des bonnes. La Domesticité féminine à Paris en 1900* (Paris: Grasset, 1979).

45. For insane asylums, see Marcel Gauchet and Gladys Swain, *La Pratique de l'esprit humain. L'Institution asilaire et la révolution démocratique* (Paris: Gallimard, 1981). For sanatoria, see Pierre Guillaume, *Du Désespoir au salut: les tuberculeux aux XIXe et XXe siècles* (Paris: Aubier, 1986).

46. See Odile Arnold, *Le Corps et l'âme. La Vie des religieuses au XIXe siècle* (Paris: Seuil, 1984).

47. Patricia O'Brien, *The Promise of Punishment: Prisons in Nineteenth-Century France* (Princeton: Princeton University Press, 1981).

48. Erving Goffman, *Asylums: Essays on the Social Situation of Mental Patients and Other Inmates* (New York: Aldine, 1961).

49. See Jean Borie, *Le Célibataire français* (Paris: Sagittaire, 1976).

50. See Jean-Claude Caron, "Maintenir l'ordre au Pays latin: la Jeunesse des Ecoles sous surveillance (1815–1848)," in Philippe Vigier, ed., *Maintien de l'ordre et polices en France et en Europe au XIXe siècle* (Paris: Créaphis, 1987), pp. 329–347.

51. Jerrold Seigel, *Bohemian Paris: Culture, Politics, and the Boundaries of Bourgeois Life, 1830–1930* (New York: Viking, 1986).

52. For studies of the novel features of dandyism, see Roger Kempf, *Dandies. Baudelaire et Cie* (Paris: Seuil, 1984), and Marylène Delbourg-Delphis, *Masculin singulier. Le dandysme et son histoire* (Paris: Hachette, 1985).

53. J.-P. Burdy has studied the "forewomen" of Saint-Etienne's Soleil district, women who were admired and criticized at the same time. See "Le Soleil noir. Formation sociale et mémoire ouvrière dans un quartier de Saint-Etienne (1840–1940)," unpub. diss., University of Lyons II, 1986.

54. See Cécile Dauphin, "Histoire d'un stéréotype: la Vieille Fille," and Pierrette Pézerat and Danièle Poublan, "Femmes sans maris: les employées des postes," in Arlette Farge and Christiane Klapisch-Zuber, *Madame ou Mademoiselle? Itinéraires de la solitude féminine au XIX siècle* (Paris: Montalba, 1984), pp. 207–231, 117–162.

55. Louis-René Villermé, *Tableau de l'etat physique et moral des ouvriers qui travaillent dans les manufactures de coton, de laine et de soie,* 2 vols. (Paris: Renouard, 1840); ed. Yves Tyl (Paris: UGE, 1971).

56. See J.-C. Beaune, *Le Vagabond et la machine. Essai sur l'automatisme ambulatoire. Médecine, technique et société, 1880–1910* (Seyssel: Champ Vallon, 1983).

Bourgeois Rituals (Anne Martin-Fugier)

1. Caroline Chotard-Lioret, "La Sociabilité familiale en province: une correspondance privée entre 1868 et 1920," unpub. diss., University of Paris, 1983.

2. Renée Berruel, "Journal," 1905–1916. Manuscript. Private Collection.

3. George Sand, *Histoire de ma vie,* ed. Georges Lubin, 2 vols. (Paris: Gallimard, 1970), I, 661–662. Maurice Genevoix, *Trente mille jours* (Paris: France-loisirs, 1981), p. 36.

4. Jean-Pierre Chaline, *Les Bourgeois de Rouen. Une Elite urbaine du XIX siècle* (Paris: Fondation nationale des sciences politiques, 1982), p. 203.

5. Alida de Savignac, *La Jeune maîtresse de maison, moeurs parisiennes* (Paris, 1836).

6. Sand, *Histoire de ma vie,* I, 844.

7. Ibid., I, 532–533.

8. Elisabeth Leseur, *Journal d'enfant* (Paris, 1934). Subsequent Arrighi quotations are from this source. See also R. P. M. A. Leseur, *Vie de Elisabeth Leseur* (Paris, 1931).

9. Pierre Laffitte, quoted by Philippe Ariès, *L'Homme devant la mort* (Paris: Seuil, 1983), p. 536.

10. Robert Mauzi has studied the development of the taste for nature in the eighteenth century. See *L'idée du bonheur au XVIIIe siècle* (Paris: Armand Colin, 1966). Henri Boiraud, *Contribution à l'étude historique des congés et des vacances scolaires en France du Moyen Age à 1914* (Paris: Vrin, 1971).

11. Louis Weiss, *Mémoires d'une Européenne.* Vol. 1, 1893–1919 (Paris, 1968).

12. Adrienne Cambry, *Fiançailles et fiancés* (Paris, 1913).

13. See Adeline Daumard, *La Bourgeoisie parisienne de 1815 à 1848* (Paris: SEVPEN, 1963), and other works; and Chaline, *Les Bourgeois de Rouen.*

14. Georges Vigarello. *Le Propre et le sale. L'hygiène du corps depuis le Moyen Age* (Paris: Seuil, 1985).

15. Marcel Prévost, *Lettres à Françoise* (Paris, 1902), letter XXIX.

16. G. d'Avenel, quoted by Maurice Crubellier, *Histoire culturelle de la France, XIXe–XXe siècle* (Paris: Armand Colin, 1974), p. 205.

17. François René de Chateaubriand, *Mémoires d'outre-tombe* (Paris, 1848–1850).

18. Marcel Reinhard, André Armengaud, and Jacques Dupâquier, *Histoire générale de la population mondiale* (Paris, 1968), p. 352.

19. Henri Hatzfeld, *Du paupérisme à la sécurité sociale (1850–1940)* (Paris: Armand Colin, 1971).

20. Victor Hugo, "Recueil Victor Hugo," manuscript annotated by Claire P. de Chateaufort, 1893–1919. Private Collection.

3. Scenes and Places

At Home (Michelle Perrot)

1. Maurice Agulhon, *Le Cercle dans la France bourgeoise (1810–1848). Etude d'une mutation de sociabilité* (Paris: Armand Colin, 1977). On the notion of semiprivate spaces, see Isaac Joseph's remarks in *Urbi*, no. 3 (1980).

2. Gustave Flaubert, *Correspondance,* ed. Jean Bruneau, 2 vols. (Paris: Gallimard, 1973, 1980), II, 518; letter to Louise Colet, 29 January 1854; on the hackney carriage as Temple of Priapus, see his letter to Louise Colet of 29 November 1853 and the scene in *Madame Bovary* involving Léon and Emma in a hackney in Rouen.

3. Bernard Edelman, *La Maison de Kant* (Paris: Payot, 1984), pp. 25–26.

4. M. Richard, "Conseils pratiques aux instituteurs," *Revue pédagogique* 4 (April 1881), cited by Francine Muel, "Enseignement primaire et éducation spécialisée," unpub. diss., Ecole des Hautes Etudes en Sciences Sociales, 1982, pp. 51–52.

5. Gustave de Beaumont, *Correspondance Beaumont-Tocqueville,* in Tocqueville, *Oeuvres complètes,* 3 vols. (Paris: André Jardin, 1967), letter no. 106, 31 July 1839.

6. Marc Regaldo, "Un Milieu intellectuel: 'La Décade philosophique' (1794–1807)" (Lille: Université de Lille III, Service de reproduction des thèses, 1976), 5 vols. (offset), p. 876.

7. Jacques Capdevielle, *Fétichisme du patrimoine. Essai sur un fondement de la classe moyenne* (Paris: Fondation nationale des sciences politiques, 1986).

8. See Denis Bertholet, "Conscience et inconscience bourgeoise. La mentalité des classes moyennes françaises, décrite à travers deux magazines illustrés de la Belle Epoque," 2 vols., unpub. diss., University of Geneva, 1985. On the appropriation of the world through books, more generally, see *Les Français peints par eux-mêmes,* the *Physiologies*—the reflection of Walter Benjamin. Cf. Richard Sieburth,

"Une idéologie du lisible: le phénomène des Physiologies," *Romantisme* (1987): 39–61.

9. Anne-Lise Maugue stresses this theme in "La Littérature antiféministe en France de 1871 à 1914," unpub. diss., University of Paris III, 1983.

10. Elias Canetti, *The Tongue Set Free: Remembrance of a European Childhood,* trans. Joachim Neugroschel (New York: Farrar, Straus & Giroux, 1983).

11. Elisabeth Claverie and Pierre Lamaison, *L'Impossible mariage. Violence et parenté en Gévaudan aux XVIIe, XVIIIe et XIXe siècles* (Paris: Hachette, 1982), p. 80; Ronald Hubscher, "L'Identité de l'homme et de la terre," in Yves Lequin, ed., *Histoire des Français, XIXe-XXe siècle.* Vol. 1, *La Société* (Paris: Armand Colin, 1983), pp. 11–57.

12. Jean-Paul Flamand, ed., *La Question du logement et le mouvement ouvrier français* (Paris: Villette, 1981).

13. On this subject, see Michelle Perrot, "Les Ouvriers, l'habitat et la ville au XIXe siècle," in Flamand, ed., *La Question du logement,* pp. 19–39; Yves Lequin, "Les Espaces de la société citadine," *Histoire des Français,* I, 341–383; and Yves Lequin's contribution to "Workers in the City," the special issue of *Mouvement social* I, no. 118 (1982).

14. Maurizio Gribaudi, *Itinéraires ouvriers. Espaces et groupes sociaux à Turin au début du XX siècle* (Paris: Ecole des Hautes Etudes en Sciences Sociales, 1987).

15. Patrick Gervaise, "Les Passages de Levallois-Perret (1860–1930), unpub. diss., University of Paris VII, 1985. On life in the alleyways of Lille, see Lise Vanderwielen, *Lise du Plat-Pays* (Lille: Presses Universitaires de Lille, 1983), with an afterword by Françoise Cribier.

16. Michelle Perrot, "Les Ménagères dans l'espace parisien au XIXe siècle," *Annales de la recherche urbaine* 9 (Autumn 1980).

17. Armand Audiganne, *Les Populations ouvrières et les industries de la France* (Paris, 1860), II, 3315–316.

18. Louis Reybaud, *Le Coton, son régime, ses problèmes, son influence en Europe* (Paris: Calmann-Lévy, 1863), noted the weavers' attachment to their homes: "They would accept a large discount rather than move their place of work, to which they were attached because they toiled under their own roof, close to their friends and to some extent as they pleased" (p. 222).

19. Texts quoted by Jacques Rancière, *La Nuit des prolétaires. Archives du rêve ouvrier* (Paris: Fayard, 1981).

20. Perrot, "Les Ouvriers," p. 28.

21. François Bédarida, "La Vie de quartier en Angleterre. Enquêtes empiriques et approches théoriques," *Le Mouvement social* 1 (1982): 14.

22. Michel Verret, *L'Ouvrier français. L'Espace ouvrier* (Paris: Armand Colin, 1979), esp. p. 153.

23. Daniel Robert and André Encrevé, "Mémoires de l'évangéliste David Gétaz," *Bulletin de la société d'histoire du protestantisme français* 130 (October–December 1984): 480–555.

24. Michelle Perrot and Georges Ribeill, eds., *Le Journal intime de Caroline B.* (Paris: Montalba, 1985), p. 211: "No one will ever see me so affectionate in public."

25. Quoted by Véronique Leroux-Hugon, "Infirmières des hôpitaux parisiens (1871–1914). Ebauches d'une profession," unpub. diss., University of Paris VII, 1981, p. 160.

26. Norbert Truquin, *Mémoires et aventures d'un prolétaire à travers les révolutions* (Paris, 1888), pp. 203–204.

27. Guillaumin, "Hospices," *Dictionnaire d'économie politique*, p. 868.

28. Flaubert, *Correspondance*, p. 701, letter to Maurice Schlésinger, early April 1857; p. 666, letter to Elisa Schlésinger, 14 January 1857.

29. Martin du Gard's largely autobiographical posthumous novel abounds in descriptions of interiors modeled on the long description of Princess Mathilde's salon by the Goncourt brothers.

30. Lytton Strachey, "Lancaster Gate," *Urbi* 9 (1984): iii–xi.

Private Spaces (Roger-Henri Guerrand)

1. Leo Taxil, *Topographie physique et médicale de Brest et de sa banlieue*, 1834.

2. Adeline Daumard, *La Bourgeoisie parisienne de 1815 à 1848* (Paris, SEVPEN, 1963).

3. F.-P. Codaccioni, *De l'inégalité sociale dans une grande ville industrielle: le drame de Lille de 1850 à 1914* (Lille, 1976).

4. Louis Roux, "Le Cabinet de lecture," December 1838; lithography by John Quartley in *Le Magasin pittoresque*, December 1847.

5. Honoré de Balzac, *La Cousine Bette*, 1848.

6. Order issued 15 July 1848.

7. 22 July 1882.

8. Decree of 23 July 1884.

9. Decree of 13 August 1902.

10. On this question in general, see Louis Hautecoeur, *Histoire de l'architecture classique en France*, vols. 6, 7 (Paris: Picard, 1955, 1957).

11. Louis Reybaud, *Jérôme Paturot à la recherche d'une position sociale*, 1864.

12. Balzac, *Ferragus*, 1833.

13. Eugène Sue, *Les Mystères de Paris*, 1844–45.

14. Jean-Louis Deaucourt. "Le Concierge, mythe et réalité," unpub. diss., University of Paris VIII, December 1981.

15. Paul de Kock, *Un Concierge de la rue du Bac*, 1868.

16. Emile Zola, *Pot-Bouille*, 1882.

17. Balzac, *La Cousine Bette*.

18. Jean-Paul Aron, *Le Mangeur du XIXe siècle* (Paris: Laffont, 1973).

19. Emile Cardon, *L'Art au foyer domestique*, 1884.

20. Maxime Du Camp, *Souvenirs littéraires*, 1882; Henri Rochefort, *Les Aventures de ma vie*, 1896–1898; Henry Bataille, *L'Enfance éternelle*, 1922.

21. Daumard, *La Bourgeoisie parisienne de 1815 à 1848*.

22. The celebrated hygienist who felt more at home in the sewers of Paris than in the salons and said so was the exception that confirms the rule. The case is mentioned by Alain Corbin in his introduction to Dr. Alexandre Parent-Duchâtelet, *La Prostitution à Paris au XIXe siècle* (Paris, 1981).

23. Cardon's book, which is devoted exclusively to the grand rooms, says nothing about kitchens.

24. Pierre-Jean Mariette, *L'Architecture française, recueil de plans, élévations, des maisons particulières, châteaux, maisons de campagne, bâtis nouvellement par les plus habiles architectes*, 1727.

25. Stevens Hellyer, *The Plumber and Sanitary Houses* (London, 1884); translated as *La Plomberie au point de vue de la salubrité des maisons*, published with the approval of the Chambre Syndicale des Entrepreneurs de Plomberie de la Ville de Paris, 1886.

26. Wazon, *Principes techniques d'assainissement des villes et habitations suivis en Angleterre, France, Allemagne, Etats-Unis et présentés sous forme d'études sur l'assainissement de Paris*, 1884.

27. Roger-Henri Guerrand, "La Bataille du tout-à-l'égout," *L'Histoire* 53 (February 1983): 66–74.

28. Anne Martin-Fugier, *La Place des bonnes: la domesticité féminine à Paris en 1900* (Paris: Grasset, 1979).

29. Louis Hautecoeur, *Histoire de l'architecture classique en France; Le Parisien chez lui au XIXe siècle, 1814–1914* (Archives nationales, 1976).

30. *Le Siècle de l'éclectisme, Lille, 1830–1930*, vol. 1 (Brussels, 1979).

31. Jean-Yves Veillard, *Rennes au XIXe siècle, architectes, urbanisme et architecture* (Rennes: Thabor, 1978).

32. Jean-Pierre Chaline, *Le Bourgeois de Rouen. Une élite urbaine au XIXe siècle* (Paris: Fondation nationale des sciences politiques, 1982).

33. Théodore Bourgeois, *La Villa moderne* (Paris: Librairie Centrale de Beaux-Arts, 1899).

34. Emile Zola, *La Curée*, 1871.

35. Bernard Marrey and J.-P. Monnet, *La Grande histoire des serres et des jardins d'hiver, 1780–1900* (Paris: Graphite, 1984).

36. Christian Derouet, *Grandes demeures angevines au XIXe siècle. L'oeuvre de René Hodé entre 1840 et 1870* (Paris: Caisse nationale des monuments historiques, 1976).

37. Paul Bois, *Paysans de l'Ouest. Des Structures économiques et sociales aux options politiques depuis l'époque révolutionnaire dans la Sarthe* (Paris: Flammarion, 1971).

38. Maurice Bedon, *Le Château au XIXe siècle en Vendée* (Fontenay-le-Comte: Lussaud, 1971).

39. *Viollet-le-Duc*, catalogue of the Galeries Nationales du Grand Palais (Paris, 1980).

40. Too far from the site to supervise the construction personally, Viollet-le-Duc entrusted it to his student Edmond Duthoit.

41. Guy de Rothschild, *Contre bonne fortune* (Paris: Balland, 1983).

42. Paul Chabot, *Jean et Yvonne, domestiques en 1900* (Paris: Tema-Editions, 1977).

43. Louis Burnet, *Villégiature et tourisme sur les côtes de France* (Paris: Hachette, 1963).

44. *La Ville d'hiver d'Arcachon* (Paris, 1983).

45. Gabriel Désert, *La Vie quotidienne sur les plages normandes du Second Empire aux années folles* (Paris: Hachette, 1983).

46. See Jean-Hervé Donnard, *Les Réalités économiques et sociales dans la Comédie humaine* (Paris, 1961), pp. 173–194.

47. Balzac's *Le Médecin de campagne, Le Curé de village,* and *Les Paysans*; George Sand's *François le Champi, La Petite Fadette,* and *La Mare au diable.*

48. François Cointeraux, *Cahiers de l'architecture rurale,* 1790–91.

49. Lasteyrie du Saillant, *Traité des constructions rurales,* 1802.

50. Léon Perthuis de Laillevault, *Traité d'architecture rurale,* 1810; Urbain Vitry, *Le Propriétaire architecte,* 1827; A. Roux, *Recueil de constructions rurales et commerciales,* 1843.

51. Louis Bouchard-Huzard, *Traité des constructions rurales et de leur disposition,* 2 vols., 1858–1860.

52. Charles Fourier, *Destinée sociale,* 1834.

53. *Recueil des principaux travaux des conseils de salubrité du département de l'Aube,* 1835.

54. Henri Bon, *Recherches hygiéniques sur les habitants de la campagne de la commune de Lacaune,* 1837.

55. Villermé, "Rapport d'un voyage fait dans les cinq départements de la Bretagne pendant les années 1840 et 1841," *Mémoires de l'Institut (Académie des sciences morales et politiques)* 4 (1844): 635–794.

56. Jacques Cambry, *Voyage dans le Finistère ou Etat de ce département en 1794 et 1795,* 3 vols., 1800.

57. A. de Bourgoing, *Mémoire en faveur des travailleurs et des indigents de la classe agricole des communes rurales de France,* 1844.

58. *Séance du conseil général du 30 août 1850, rapport sur la question des logements insalubres,* Archives nationales, F8 210.

59. Dr. Charles-Alexandre Bertrand, *Mémoire sur la topographie médicale du département du Puy-de-Dôme,* 1849; J.-S. Edouard Noël, *Quelques Considérations générales sur l'hygiène dans les campagnes des Vosges,* 1851.

60. "Tableau des populations rurales de la France en 1850," *Journal des économistes,* January 1851, pp. 9–27.

61. J. F. Eugène Deflandre, *Essai sur l'hygiène des campagnes de la Picardie,* unpub. diss., University of Paris, 1853; N. P. Abel-Poullain, *Essai sur l'hygiène des habitants dans le canton d'Arc-en-Barrois (Haute-Marne),* unpub. Ph.D. diss., University of Montpellier, 1855; J. B. M. Henri Demathieu, *Essai sur l'hygiène du paysan du haut Limousin,* unpub. Ph.D. diss., University of Paris, 1863; Paul Castenau, *Quelques considérations sur l'hygiène d'une partie de la population de la Haute-Garonne,* unpub. diss., University of Montpellier, 1864.

62. Louis Caradec, *Topographie médico-hygiénique du département du Finistère ou Guide sanitaire de l'habitant,* 1860.

63. Henri Baudrillart, *Les Populations agricoles de la France,* 3 vols., 1885–1893.

64. Alexandre Layet, *Hygiène et maladies des paysans, étude sur la vie matérielle des campagnards en Europe,* 1882, part 1, chap. 3, "Les Habitations rurales: principales causes de leur insalubrité," pp. 36–76.

65. Docteur A. le Chevallier, *Essai sur l'habitation rurale en Bretagne,* 1898.

66. Arthur Young, *Travels during the years 1787, 1788 and 1789* (Bury St. Edmund's: printed by J. Rackham, 1792); repr. *Voyages en France,* 3 vols., 1931, see preface to vol. 1.

67. Louis Girard, *Nouvelle Histoire de Paris, La Deuxième République et le Second Empire, 1848–1870* (Paris, 1981).

68. Louis Chevalier, *Classes laborieuses et classes dangereuses à Paris pendant la première moitié du XIXe siècle, 1809–1880,* rev. ed. (Paris: Plon, 1965); Roger-Henri Guerrand, *Les Origines du logement social en France* (Paris: Ouvrières, 1966).

69. *Rapport sur la marche et les effets du choléra-morbus dans Paris et les communes rurales du département de la Seine,* 1854; Ange-Pierre Leca, *Et le choléra s'abattit sur Paris* (Paris, 1982).

70. Jeanne Gaillard, *Paris, la ville, 1852–1870* (Paris: Champion, 1976).

71. Dr. Octave du Mesnil, *L'Habitation du pauvre* (1890); comte d'Haussonville, *Misère et Remèdes* (1886).

72. Madeleine Fernandez, "La Ceinture noire de Paris," unpub. diss., University of Paris VII, 1983.

73. Jules Bucquoy, *Rapport général sur les épidémies pendant l'année 1882,* 1884.

74. *L'Epidémie cholérique de 1892 dans le département de la Seine,* Conseil d'hygiène et de salubrité du département de la Seine, 1893.

75. Jacques Bertillon, *Essai de statistique comparée du surpeuplement des habitations à Paris et dans les grandes capitales européennes,* 1894.

76. Du Mesnil, *L'Habitation du pauvre.*

77. Louis-René Villermé, *Tableau de l'état physique et moral des ouvriers employés dans les manufactures de coton, de laine et de soie,* 2 vols., 1840. Adolphe Blanqui, *Des classes ouvrières en France pendant l'année 1848,* 1849.

78. Jules Simon, *L'Ouvrière,* 1861, chap. 4, "Logements d'ouvriers," pp. 146–176.

79. Jean-Pierre Babelon, "Les Cités ouvrières de Paris," *Monuments historiques,* no. 3, 1977, pp. 50–54.

80. Jean-Baptiste Duroselle, *Les Débuts du catholicisme social en France (1822–1870)* (Paris, 1951).

81. Adeline Daumard, *Maisons de Paris et propriétaires parisiens au XIXe siècle* (Paris: Cujas, 1965), p. 167.

82. *La Construction moderne,* February 1, 1890, pp. 200–202; September 20, 1890, pp. 598–600; *Bulletins de la Société française des habitations à bon marché* 2 (1890): 119–152.

83. *L'Architecture et la Construction dans l'Ouest,* September 1907, pp. 102–107.

84. In 1891 Félix Mangini published a work entitled *Les Petits logements dans les grandes villes et plus particulièrement à Lyon,* in which he accused architects of being incapable of constructing buildings economically. On Mangini, see Edouard Aynard, *La Vie et les oeuvres de F. Mangini,* 1903.

85. *Bulletin de la Société française des habitations à bon marché* 3 (1890): 204–224, and 3 (1891): 316–346. See also Bernard Marrey, *Rhône-Alpes* (Paris, 1982).

86. The number of companies whose stock was traded on the Paris Bourse was 938 in 1894, according to the *Annuaire statistique de la France;* compare this with 402 in 1869.

87. Charles Fourier, *La Fausse industrie,* 2 vols., 1835–1836.

88. Brochure issued by the *Nouveau monde industriel et sociétaire,* 1830. Summary of *Traité de l'association domestique-agricole,* 1822.

89. Victor Considérant, *Destinée sociale,* 2 vols., 1834.

90. The street-gallery apparently was of great interest to Fourier's contemporaries. As early as 1830 Amédée de Tissot, in a work entitled *Paris et Londres comparés,* envisioned an almost identical arrangement that was clearly based on the phalanstery, from which he also borrowed the central heating system. Another new amenity was the use of elevators: "For traveling up and down between floors one could use machines moved by steam or other mechanical means."

91. On Calland, see Roger-Henri Guerrand, *Les Origines du logement social* (Paris: Ouvrières, 1966), pp. 153-160.

92. The essential work was written by Godin's wife: Marie Moret, *Documents pour une biographie complète de J.-B. A. Godin,* 3 vols. (Familistère de Guise, 1901, 1906, 1910). More recent studies include Henri Desroche, *La Société festive: du fouriérisme écrit aux fouriérismes pratiqués* (Paris: Seuil, 1975); Annick Brauman, *Le Familistère de Guise ou les Equivalents de la richesse* (Brussels, 1976); *Le Familistère Godin à Guise. Habiter l'Utopie* (Paris: Villette, 1982); Guy Delabre and J.-M. Gautier, *Godin et le Familistère de Guise* (Laon, 1983).

93. J.-B. A. Godin, *Solutions sociales,* 1871, pt 4, chap. 20, "Le Palais social," pp. 435–625. This book was reprinted with notes and an introduction by J.-F. Rey and J.-L. Pinol (Quimperlé: La Digitale, 1979).

94. According to André Oyon, who wrote the first account of the Familistère in 1865, these were cleaned three times a day.

95. Godin discontinued this experiment, because the tenants of the palace preferred to cook their own meals.

96. Godin, *Solutions sociales,* pt 4, chap. 20, p. 461.

97. Jules Moureau, *Des Associations coopératives,* 1866.

98. Fernand Duval, *J.-B. André Godin et le Familistère de Guise,* 1905.

99. Alfred Dominic Roberts, "Zola and Fourier," unpub. diss., University of Pennsylvania, 1959.

100. J. Figueroa, "La Politique du logement de la Société des Houillières de Blanzy de 1833 à 1900," *Milieux* 2 (June 1980): 34–39.

101. M. Bougaud, *Communication à la Société d'encouragement à l'industrie nationale, le 26 mars 1886.* Bapterosses had died the previous year.

102. Christian Devillers and Bernard Huet, *Le Creusot, naissance et développement d'une ville industrielle, 1872–1914* (Seyssel: Champ-Vallon, 1981). Rolande Trempé, *Les Mineurs de Carmaux, 1848–1914*, 2 vols. (Paris, 1971), I, 258–286.

103. Exposition de 1889, *Menier, type des maisons de Noisiel; Bulletin de la Société française des habitations à bon marché* 4 (1892): 450–455; Bernard Marrey, *Un Capitalisme idéal (Menier à Noisiel)* (Paris: Clancier-Guénaud, 1984).

104. Société des mines de Dourges, *Habitations ouvrières*, 1909.

105. *Bulletin de la Société industrielle de Mulhouse* 117 (August 1852): 127–129.

106. "Rapport du Comité d'économie sociale sur la construction d'une cité ouvrière à Mulhouse," ibid. 124 (April 1854): 299–316.

107. "Rapport sur les forces matérielles et morales de l'industrie du Haut-Rhin pendant les dix dernières années (1851–1861)," ibid. 157 (October 1862): 469–473.

108. "Les Institutions privées du Haut-Rhin, notes remises au comité départemental de l'Exposition universelle de 1867," ibid. 175 (October 1862): 469–473.

109. On the history of the project, see Stephan Jonas, *La Cité de Mulhouse (1853–1870): un modèle d'habitat économique et social du XIXe siècle*, 2 vols. (Paris: Ministère de l'Urbanisme et du Logement, secrétariat de la Recherche architecturale, 1981). The contemporary views of members of the Société industrielle is discussed by J.-P. Hohly in 1975 in a note celebrating the hundred and fiftieth anniversary of its founding, no. 3, 1976, pp. 111–115.

110. Emile Muller, *Cité ouvrière à Paris, faubourg Saint-Antoine. Maisons isolées avec jardins*, n.d.

111. *Journal officiel* of August 14, 1875, no. 222, app. 3,283, session of July 27, pp. 6788–6792.

112. On Le Play, see Duroselle, *Les Débuts*, pt 3, chap. 4, sec. 2, pp. 672–684.

113. Frédéric Le Play, *L'Ecole de la paix sociale, son histoire, sa méthode et sa doctrine*, 1881, plan of government, article 2: "Make it easier for a family to accumulate wealth and own its own home."

114. Frédéric Le Play, *La Réforme sociale*, 2 vols., 1864.

115. Ibid., "La Famille," I, 170–181.

116. Ibid., "Les Rapports privés," II, 14–21.

117. *Congrès international d'hygiène, de sauvetage et d'économie sociale tenu à Bruxelles du 27 septembre au 4 octobre 1876*, 2 vols, II, 487–550.

118. Emile Trélat, "Des logements des classes nécessiteuses," 4th question, *Congrès international d'hygiène tenu à Paris du 1er au 10 août 1878*, 1878, pp. 1–8.

119. The statutes and aims of this society were reproduced in *Bulletin de la Société française des habitations à bon marché* 3 (1893): 250–279.

120. *L'Economiste français*, August 27, 1881.

121. Eugène Rostand, "L'Action sociale par l'initiative privée, 1892. L'Habitation du peuple," pp. 147–348; Guy Dumont, "La Question du logement social à Marseille de 1875 à 1939," both unpub. diss., University of Aix-Marseilles, 1973.

122. *Bulletin de la Société française des habitations à bon marché* 1 (1890): 35–75.

123. *La Construction moderne*, July 29, 1898, pp. 210–212.

124. *La Construction lyonnaise*, February 1 and March 1, 1903.

125. *Le Béton armé*, newsletter published by owners of franchises and sales representatives of the Hennebique system, September 1903, pp. 49–51.

126. Most of the projects discussed here were treated in articles, sometimes with illustrations, in such journals as *La Construction moderne* and *Bulletin de la Société française des habitations à bon marché*.

127. *Maisons de campagne, Villas et Cottages*, 1913.

128. Hippolyte Garnier, ed., *Pour construire sa maison*, 1919, 281 plates.

129. See Roger-Henri Guerrand, *L'Art nouveau en Europe* (Paris: Plon, 1965).

130. Charles Lucas, *Etude sur les habitations à bon marché en France et à l'étranger*, 1899; Henry Provensal, *L'Habitation salubre et à bon marché*, 1908; Eduard Schatzmann, *Conditions hygiéniques nécessaires dans l'habitation des enfants*, 1911; Emile Guillot, *La Maison salubre*, 1914.

131. Eugène Hatton, *Fondation "Groupe des maisons ouvrières," ses immeubles en 1907, leur exploitation, services généraux*, 1907.

132. *Les Garnis d'ouvriers à Paris*, June 1, 1900, pp. 823–851, and *L'Habitation de la jeune fille dans les grandes villes*, July 16, 1901, pp. 145–153.

133. Henri Saladin, *L'Architecture aux salons de 1913*, June 14, 1913.

134. On Sauvage, see the catalogue of the show organized at the headquarters of the Société des ar-

chitectes diplômés par le gouvernement in Paris in 1976, published in Brussels.

135. Thus far there has been only one work on the Rothschild Foundation: Marie-Jeanne Dumont, "La Fondation Rothschild et les premières habitations à bon marché de Paris, 1900–1914," unpub. diss., Unité pédagogique d'architecture no. 1, 1980.

136. City of Paris, *Premier Concours pour la construction d'HBM, rapport du jury*, n.d.

137. *L'Immeuble et la Construction dans L'Est*, October 12, 1913, pp. 461–463.

138. Georges Christie, *Moniteur des beaux-arts et de la construction*, August–September 1913, pp. 1854–1855; January 1914, pp. 1909–1914.

139. André Gaillardin, in *La Construction moderne*, February 2, 1913.

140. For pioneering work on the tenants' movement in Paris, see Susanna Magri, *Le Mouvement des locataires à Paris et dans la banlieue parisienne, 1919–1925* (Paris: Centre de sociologie urbaine, 1982).

141. Cochon's actions were featured in a column published in the newspaper *Humanité* from November 17, 1935, to January 17, 1936, entitled "The Memoirs of Cochon, or the Bust-up of Saint Polycarp." The author, who signed himself Casimir Lecomte, was actually André Wurmser.

142. On Bertillon as "repopulator" of France, see Roger-Henri Guerrand, *La Libre Maternité, 1896–1969* (Paris, 1971).

143. On the family movement, see Robert Talmy, *Histoire du mouvement familial en France, 1896–1939*, 2 vols. (Paris: L'Union des Caisses de l'Allocation Familiales, n.d.).

144. With the exception of some anarchists and neo-Malthusians, such as Eugène Humbert, who went to Spain; Cochon served until 1917, when he deserted.

4. Backstage

INTRODUCTION (MICHELLE PERROT)

1. See Louis Dumont, *Essai sur l'individualisme. Une perspective anthropologique sur l'ideologie moderne* (Paris: Seuil, 1983), *Essays on Individualism: Modern Ideology in Anthropological Perspective* (Chicago: University of Chicago Press, 1986).

2. Stendhal, *La Rouge et le Noir* (Paris: Gallimard, 1830), p. 697.

3. See Jan Goldstein, "Foucault among the Sociologists: The 'Disciplines' and the History of the Professions," *History and Theory* 184: 170–192.

4. See M. J. Dhavernas, "Les Anarchistes individualistes devant la société de la Belle Epoque (1895–1914)," unpub. diss., Paris X-Nanterre, 1982.

5. See Georges Gusdorf, *L'Homme romantique* (Paris: Payot, 1984).

6. See Elisabeth Roudinesco, *La Bataille de cent ans. Histoire de la psychoanalyse en France*, 2 vols. (Paris: Seuil, 1986).

7. See Hervé Le Bras and Emmanuel Todd, *La Invention de la France* (Paris: Pluriel, 1981).

THE SECRET OF THE INDIVIDUAL (ALAIN CORBIN)

1. Veronique Nahoum, "La Belle Femme ou le stade du miroir en histoire," *Communications*, no. 31, 1979.

2. Gisèle Freund, *Photographie et société* (Paris: Seuil, 1974), p. 11.

3. Susan Sontag, *On Photography* (New York: Farrar, Straus, and Giroux, 1977).

4. Philippe Ariès, *L'Homme devant la mort* (Paris: Seuil, 1977).

5. Philippe Boutry, "Les Vénérés pasteurs du diocèse du Belley, Cheminement des mentalités et des opinions religieuses dans les paroisses du diocèse de l'Ain de 1815 à 1880," unpub. diss., University of Paris I, 1983.

6. See Pierre Roussel, *Système physique et moral de la femme . . .* (Paris, 1775).

7. Jean Starobinski, "Breve histoire de la conscience du corps," *Revue française de psychanalyse* 2 (1981): 272.

8. See Theodore Zeldin, *Ambition, Love and Politics* (Oxford: Oxford University Press, 1973).

9. Olivier Faure, *Genèse de l'hôpital moderne: Les Hospices civils de Lyon de 1802 à 1845* (London and Paris: C.N.R.S. and Presses universitaires de Lyon, 1982).

10. See Guy Thuillier, *Pour une histoire du quotidien en Nivernais au XIXe siècle* (Paris: Mouton, 1977).

11. Philippe Perrot, *Le Travail des apparences ou les transformations du corps féminin (XVIIIe–XIXe siècle)* (Paris: Seuil, 1984).

12. Yvonne Verdier, *Façons de dire, façons de faire. La laveuse, la couturier, la cuisinière* (Paris: Gallimard, 1979).

13. Richard Sennett, *The Fall of Public Man* (New York: Knopf, 1974).

14. See Odile Arnold, *Le Corps et l'âme. La vie des religieuses au XIXe siècle.* (Paris: Seuil, 1984).

15. See Jean Delumeau, *La Péché et la peur* (Paris: Fayard, 1983).

16. Suzanne Voilquin, *Souvenirs d'une fille du peuple* (Paris: Maspero, 1978).

17. Marie-José Garniche-Merritt, "Vivre à Bué-en-Sancerrois," unpub. diss., University of Paris VII, 1982.

18. Martine Segalen and Josselyne Chamarat, "La Rosièze et la *Miss:* Les Reines des fêtes populaires," *L'Histoire* 53 (February 1983): 44–56.

19. Michel Foucault, *The History of Sexuality,* trans. Robert Hurley, Vol. 1, *Introduction* (New York: Pantheon, 1978).

20. Theodore Zeldin, *Intellect, Taste and Anxiety* (Oxford: Oxford University Press, 1977).

21. Claude Langlois, *Le Diocèses de Vanne au XIXe siècle (1800–1830)* (Paris: Klincksieck, 1974); Gérard Cholvy, "Religion et société. Le diocèse de Montpellier au XIXe siècle," unpub. diss., University of Paris IV, 1972.

22. Maine de Biran, *Journal,* 3 vols. (Paris: Vrin, 1955).

23. Béatrice Didier, *Le Journal intime* (Paris: PUF, 1976).

24. Pierre Georgel, *Léopoldine Hugo, une jeune fille romantique* (Paris: Catalogue du musée Victor-Hugo, 1967).

25. Agnès Fine, "A propos du trousseau: Une culture féminine," in Michelle Perrot, ed., *Une Histoire des femmes est-elle possible?* (Marseilles: Rivages, 1984).

26. Christophe Charle, *Les Hauts fonctionnaires en France au XIXe siècle* (Paris: Gallimard/Julliard, 1980).

27. See Jacques Rancière, *La Nuit des prolétaires. Archives du rêve ouvrier* (Paris: Fayard, 1981).

28. Gregor Dallas, *The Imperfect Peasant Economy. The Loire Country. 1800–1914* (Cambridge: Cambridge University Press, 1982).

29. See Ronald Hubscher, *L'Agriculture et la société rurale dans le Pas-de-Calais du milieu de XIXe siècle à 1914,* 2 vols. (Arras, 1979).

30. Françoise Mayeur, *L'Enseignement secondaire des jeunes filles sous la Troisième République* (Paris: Fondation nationale des sciences politiques, 1977).

31. Jean-Pierre Chaline, *Les Bourgeois de Rouen. Une élite urbaine du XIXe siècle* (Paris: Fondation nationale des sciences politiques, 1982).

32. Jean Bousquet, *Les Thèmes du rêve dans la littérature romantique* (Paris: Didier, 1964), p. 52.

33. George Steiner, "Les Rêves participent-ils de l'histoire? Deux questions adressées à Freud," *Le Débat,* no. 25, May 1983.

34. Alfred Maury, *Le Sommeil et les rêves* (Paris, 1861), p. 62.

35. See Yves-Marie Hilaire, *Une Chrétienté au XIXe siècle. La vie religieuse des populations du diocèse d'Arras, 1840–1914* (Lille: Presses universitaires, 1977).

36. See Claude Savart, "Le Livre catholique témoin de la conscience religieuse en France au XIXe siècle," unpub. diss., University of Paris-Sorbonne, 1981. This quantitative survey of the distribution of pious literature is a reminder to historians of the need to proceed with caution.

37. Robert Capia, "L'Age d'or de la poupée au XIXe siècle," *Histoire de la poupée,* Catalog of the Courbevoie Exhibition, 1973.

38. See Valentin Pelosse, "Imaginaire social et protection de l'animal. Des amis des bêtes de l'an X législateur de 1850," *L'Homme,* nos. 21–22, October–December 1981 and January–March 1987.

39. Cited in Danièle Pistone, *Le Piano dans la littérature française des origines jusque vers 1900* (Paris: Champion, 1975).

40. See Françoise Parent-Lardeur, *Lire à Paris au temps de Balzac. Les cabinets de lecture à Paris, 1815–1830* (Paris: EHESS, 1981).

41. See Adeline Daumard, *Le Bourgeoisie parisienne de 1815 à 1848* (Paris: SEVPEN, 1963).

42. See Marie-Dominique Amaouche-Antoine, "Espéranza, 1870–1940: une ville ouvrière chante," *Ethnologie française,* 1986.

43. Arno J. Mayer, *The Persistence of the Old Regime: Europe to the Great War* (New York: Pantheon, 1982).

44. See Chantal Martinet, "Objets de famille, objets de musée, ethnologie ou muséologie," *Ethnologie française* 1 (1980).

INTIMATE RELATIONS (ALAIN CORBIN)

1. Philippe Boutry, "L'Anticlérical, la femme et le confessional," *L'Histoire* 16 (October 1979): 94.

2. See Claude Langlois, *Le Diocèses de Vannes au XIXe siècle (1800–1830)* (Paris: Klincksieck, 1974).

3. See Michel Lagrée, "Confession et pénitence dans les visites pastorales et les statuts synodaux bretons, XIXe–XXe siècle," *Pratiques de la confession des Pères du désert à Vatican II* (Paris: Cerf, 1983).

4. Norbert Truquin, *Mémoires et aventures d'un prolétaire à travers la Révolution (1888)* (Paris: Maspero, 1977).

5. Jean-Louis Flandrin, *L'Eglise et le contrôle des naissances* (Paris: Flammarion, 1970).

6. Jean Faury, *Cléricalisme et anticléricalisme dans le Tarn* (Université de Toulouse–Le Mirail, 1930).

7. Claude Quiguer, *Femmes et machines 1900. Lectures d'une obsession modern style* (Paris: Klincksieck, 1979).

8. Lucienne Frappier-Mazur, "Le Régime de l'aveu dans *Le Lys dans la vallée*," in Paul Viallaneix and Jean Ehrard, eds., *Aimer en France 1760–1860*, International Colloquium of Clermont-Ferrand, Proceedings, 2 vols. (Clermont-Ferrand, 1980).

9. Paul Hoffmann, "L'Héritage des Lumières: mythes et modèles de la féminité au XVIIIe siècle," *Mythes et représentations de la femme*, special number of *Romantisme* (Paris: Champion, 1976), p. 17.

10. Nicole Castan, "Inégalités sociales et différences de conditions dans les liaisons amoureuses et les tentatives conjugales," in Viallaneix and Ehrard, *Aimer en France*.

11. Jean-Maurice Gautier, "Amours romantiques, Amours frénétiques," in *Aimer en France*, ibid.

12. Martine Segalen, *Love and Power in the Peasant Family* (London: Blackwell, 1983), p. 75.

13. Edward Shorter, *The Making of the Modern Family* (New York: Basic Books, 1975).

14. Pierre Bourdieu, "Les Stratégies matrimoniales dans le système de reproduction," *Annales. Economies. Sociétés. Civilisations*, July–August 1972.

15. Ronald Hubscher, *L'Agriculture et la société rural dans le Pas-de-Calais du milieu du XIXe siècle à 1914*, 2 vols. (Arras, 1979).

16. See Marie-Dominique Amaouche-Antoine, "Espéranza, 1870–1940: une ville ouvrière chante," *Ethnologie française*, 1986.

17. Bronislaw Baczko, "Le Calendrier républicain. Décréter l'éternité," in Pierre Nora, ed., *Les Lieux de mémoire*, vol. 1: *La République* (Paris: Gallimard, 1984).

18. Marie-Véronique Gautier, "Les Sociétés chantantes au XIXe siècle," unpub. diss., University of Paris I, 1989.

19. Jean Borie, *Le Célibataire français* (Paris: Sagittaire, 1976).

20. See Jeanne Gaillard, *Paris, la ville, 1852–1870* (Paris: Champion, 1976).

21. Yves-Marie Hilaire, *Une chrétienté au XIXe siècle. La vie religieuse des populations du diocèse d'Arras, 1840–1914* (Lille: Presses universitaires, 1977).

22. Louis Chevalier, *Classes laborieuses et classes dangereuses à Paris pendant la première moitié du XIXe siècle* (Paris: Plon, 1958); Shorter, *Making of the Modern Family*.

23. Michel Frey, "Du mariage et du concubinage dans les classes populaires à Paris en 1846–1847," *Annales ESC*, July–August 1978.

24. See Pierre Pierrard, *La Vie ouvrière à Lille sous le Second Empire* (Paris: Bloud et Gay, 1965).

25. Laura Strumingher, "The Artisan Family: Tradition and Transition in Nineteenth Century Lyon," *Journal of Family History* (Fall 1977): 218.

26. Jean Estèbe, *Les Ministres de la République, 1871–1914* (Paris: Fondation nationale des sciences politiques, 1982).

27. See William Serman, *Les Officiers français dans la nation, 1848–1914* (Paris: Aubier, 1982).

28. See Marie-Claude Phan, "Typologies d'aventures amoureuses . . . Carcassonne de 1676 à 1786," in Viallaneix and Ehrard, *Aimer en France*.

29. James R. Lehning, *Peasants of Marlhes: Economic Development and Family Organization in Nineteenth-Century France* (Chapel Hill: University of North Carolina Press, 1980).

30. Shorter, *Making of the Modern Family*; Flandrin, *Les Amours paysannes. Amour et sexualité dans les campagnes de l'ancienne France, XVIe–XIXe siècle* (Paris: Gallimard/Julliard, 1975).

31. See Gérard Jacquemet, "Médecins et maladies populaires dans le Paris de la fin du XIXe siècle," *Recherches*, no. 29, December 1977.

32. Angus MacLaren, *Sexuality and Social Order: The Debate over the Fertility of Women and Workers in France, 1770–1920* (New York: Holmes and Meier, 1983).

33. See Anne-Marie Sohn, "Les Rôles féminins dans la vie privée: approche méthodologique et bilan de recherches," *Revue d'histoire moderne et contemporaine*, October–December 1981.

34. Estèbe, *Ministres de la République*, p. 85.

35. Bonnie Smith, *Ladies of the Leisure Class: The Bourgeois of Northern France in the Nineteenth Century* (Princeton: Princeton University Press, 1981).

CRIES AND WHISPERS (ALAIN CORBIN)

1. Jean-Pierre Peter, "Ogres d'archives," *Nouvelle Revue de psychoanalyse*, no. 3, 1972.

2. See M. Jeanneret, "La Folie est un rêve. Nerval et le Dr. Moreau de Tours," *Romantisme*, no. 27, 1980; Jean Borie, *Mythologies de l'hérédité au XIXe siècle* (Paris: Galilée, 1981), pp. 144, 124.

3. See Jacques Léonard, "Eugénisme et darwinisme. Espoirs et perplexités chez les médecins du XIXe siècle et du début de XXe siècle," *De Darwin au darwinisme* (Paris: Vrin, 1983).

4. Ibid.

5. Jean Starobinski, "Sur la chlorose," *Romantisme*, no. 31, 1981.

6. See Gérard Wajeman, *Le Maître et l'hystérique* (Paris, 1982).

7. Gladys Swain, "L'Ame, la femme, le sexe et le corps. Les métamorphoses de l'hystérie à la fin du XIXe siècle," *Le Débat*, March 1983.

8. Paul Hoffmann, "Le Discours médical sur les passions de l'amour. De Boissier de Sauvages à Pinel," in Paul Viallaneix and Jean Ehrard, eds., *Aimer en France (1760–1860),* International Colloquium of Clermont-Ferrand, Proceedings, 2 vols. (Clermont-Ferrand, 1980), II, 346.

9. Thierry Fillaut, "Manières de boize et alcoolisme dans l'ouest de la France au XIXe siècle, *Ethnologie française* 14 (October–December 1984): 382, 385.

10. Chantal Plonévez, "L'Alcoolisme dans les milieus ouvriers à Paris, 1880–1914," unpub. diss., University of Paris, 1975.

11. See Gérard Jacquemet, *Belleville au XIXe siècle* (Paris: EHESS, 1984).

12. Hervé Le Bras and Emmanuel Todd, *L'Invention de la France* (Paris: Pluriel, 1981).

13. Michel Foucault, *The History of Sexuality.* Vol. 1, *Introduction* (New York: Pantheon, 1978).

14. Philippe Ariès, "Reflexions sur l'histoire de la sexualité," *Sexualités occidentales,* special number of *Communications,* no. 35, p. 589.

15. See Jean-Pierre Jacques, *Les Malheurs de Sapho* (Paris: Grasset, 1981).

16. Léonard, *La Vie quotidienne du médecin de province au XIXe siècle* (Paris: Hachette, 1977), p. 190.

17. Jean-Pierre Peter, "Les Médecins et les femmes," *Misérable et glorieuse: la femme du XIXe siècle* (Paris: Fayard, 1981).

18. Luc Boltanski, *Prime éducation et morale de classe* (Paris and The Hague: Mouton, 1977).

19. Yanick Ripa, *Le Ronde des folles. Femme, folie et enfermement au XIXe siècle* (Paris: Aubier, 1986).

20. See Robert Castel, *L'Ordre psychiatrique,* vol. 1: *L'Age d'or de l'aliénisme* (Paris: Minuit, 1976).

21. Robert Castel and Jean-François Le Cerf, "Le Phénomène *psy.* et la société française," *Le Débat,* May 1980.

22. Guy Thuillier, *Pour une histoire du quotidien en Nivernais au XIXe siècle* (Paris: Mouton, 1977).

23. Georges Vigarello, *Le Corps redressé. Histoire d'un pouvoir pédagogique* (Paris: Delarge, 1978), p. 111.

Bibliography

Accampo, Elinor A. "Industrialization and the Working Class Family: Saint-Chamond, 1815–1880." Ann Arbor, Mich.: University Microfilms International, 1984.

Actes de la recherche en sciences sociales, nos. 21–22, 1978: Special issue on "Le Patronat."

Adler, Laure. *L'Amour à l'arsenic. Histoire de Marie Lafarge.* Paris: Denoël, 1985.

——— *Secrets d'alcôve. Histoire du couple de 1830 à 1930.* Paris: Hachette, 1983.

Agulhon, Maurice. "Le Sang des bêtes. Le problème de la protection des animaux en France au XIXe siècle," *Romantisme,* no. 31, 1981.

Allaire, L. "Une famille de bourgeoisie rurale en Ardèche au XIXe siècle." Thesis, University of Paris I, 1980.

Amaouche-Antoine, Marie-Dominique. "Espéranza, 1870–1940: une ville ouvrière chante," *Ethnologie française,* 1986.

Amiel, Henri Frédéric. *Journal intime.* Lausanne: L'Age de l'homme, 1976–1979.

Annales de démographie historique, 1973. See the special issue on "Enfance et société" for an important bibliography.

Archives d'architecture moderne. *Jean-Baptiste Godin et le Familistère de Guise.* Brussels, 1976.

Aimer en France (1760–1860). See Viallaneix and Ehrard, eds.

Archives d'architecture moderne. *Le Siècle de l'eclectisme, Lille 1830–1930,* vol. 1. Brussels, 1979.

Archives Nationales. *Le Parisien chez lui au XIXe siècle, 1814–1914.* Exhibition catalogue, November 1976–February 1977.

Ariès, Philippe. *L'Enfant et la vie familiale sous l'Ancien Régime.* Paris: Plon, 1960; Seuil, 1975. Trans. by Robert Baldick as *Centuries of Childhood: A Social History of Family Life.* New York: Knopf, 1962.

——— *Histoires des populations françaises et de leurs attitudes devant la vie depuis le XVIIIe siècle.* Paris: Self, 1948.

——— *L'Homme devant la mort.* Paris: Seuil, 1977.

——— *Images de l'homme devant la mort.* Paris: Seuil, 1983. Trans. by Janet Lloyd as *Images of Man and Death.* Cambridge, Mass.: Harvard University Press, 1985.

Armengaud, André. *Les Français et Malthus.* Paris: PUF, 1975.

Armogathe, Daniel, and Maïte Albistur. *Histoire du féminisme français. Du Moyen Age à nos jours.* Paris: Ed. des Femmes, 1977.

Arnaud-Duc, Nicole. *Droit, mentalités et changement social en Provence occidentale. Une étude sur les stratégies et la pratique notariale en matière de régime matrimonial, de 1785 à 1855.* Aix-en-Provence: Edisud, 1985.

Arnold, Odile. *Le Corps et l'âme. La Vie des religieuses au XIXe siècle.* Paris: Seuil, 1984.

Arnoult, Françoise. "Histoire de Frédéric Le Play. De la métallurgie à la science sociale." Thesis, University of Nantes, 1986.

Aron, Jean-Paul. *Le Mangeur du XIXe siècle.* Paris: Laffont, 1973.

——— ed. *Misérable et glorieuse: la femme du XIXe siècle.* Paris: Fayard, 1981.

———, and Roger Kempf. *Le Pénis et la démoralisation de l'occident.* Paris: Grasset, 1978.

Baczko, Bronislaw. "Le Calendrier républicain. Décréter l'éternité," in Pierre Nora, ed., *Les Lieux de mémoire.* Vol. 1, *La République.* Paris: Gallimard, 1984.

Baechler, Jean. *Les Suicides.* Paris: Calmann-Lévy, 1975.

Bailbe, Joseph-Marc. *Le Roman et la musique en France sous la monarchie de Juillet.* Paris: Minard, 1969.

Barthes, Roland. *Sade, Fourier, Loyola.* Paris, 1971. Trans. by Richard Miller as *Sade, Fourier, Loyola.* New York: Hill & Wang, 1976.

Basch, Françoise. *Les Femmes victoriennes. Roman et société, 1837–1867.* Paris: Payot, 1979.

Bashkirtseff, Marie. *Journal.* Paris: Mazarine, 1985.

Baude, Maurice. "P. H. Azaïs, témoin de son temps, d'après son journal inédit (1811–1844)." Thesis, University of Lille III, 1980.

Baudrillard, Jean. *Le Système des objets.* Paris: PUF, 1968.

Baudrillart, Henri. *Les Populations agricoles de la France.* 3 vols. 1885–1893.

Baumfelder-Bloch, Eliane. "Médecine et société face à l'enfance anormale de 1800 à 1940." Thesis, Ecole des Hautes Etudes en Sciences Sociales, 1983.

Beaune, J.-C. *Le Vagabond et la machine. Essai sur l'automatisme ambulatoire. Médecine, technique et société, 1880–1910.* Seyssel: Champ Vallon, 1983.

Bedon, Maurice. *Le Château au XIXe siècle en Vendée.* Fontenay-le-Comte: Lussard, 1971.

Beguin, Albert. *L'Ame romantique et le rêve.* Paris: José Corti, 1937.

Benjamin, Walter. *Charles Baudelaire. Un poète lyrique à l'apogée du capitalisme.* Paris: Payot, 1982.

—— and Paris, International Colloquium on *Passagen-Werk,* 1983, introduction by Henry Wismann. Paris: Cerf, 1986.

Bercherie, Pierre. "Les Fondements de la clinique," *Ornicar,* 1980.

Berlanstein, L. R. "Growing Up as Workers in Nineteenth-Century Paris: The Case of the Orphans of the Prince Imperial," *French Historical Studies* 11, no. 4 (1980).

Bernard, Daniel. "Itinérants et ambulants dans l'Indre au XIXe siècle." Thesis, Ecole des Hautes Etudes en Sciences Sociales, 1982.

Bernos, Marcel. "De l'influence salutaire ou pernicieuse de la femme dans la famille et la société," *Revue d'histoire moderne et contemporaine,* July–September 1982.

Berruel, Renée. "Journal," 1905–1916. Manuscript.

Bertillon, Dr. Jacques. *Essai de statistique comparée du surpeuplement des habitations à Paris et dans les grandes capitales européennes.* 1894.

Besançon, Alain. *Histoire et expérience du moi.* Paris: Flammarion, 1971.

Biasi, Jean-Marc de. "Système et déviance de la collection de l'époque romantique," *Romantisme,* no. 27, 1980.

Blanchot, Maurice. *Lautréamont et Sade.* Paris, 1949.

Blunden, Katerine. *Le Travail et la Vertu. Femmes au foyer: une mystification de la révolution industrielle.* Paris: Payot, 1982.

Boime, Albert. "Les Hommes d'affaires et les arts en France au XIXe siècle," *Actes de la recherche en sciences sociales* 28 (June 1979).

Boiraud, Henri. *Contribution à l'étude historique des congés et des vacances scolaires en France du Moyen Age à 1914.* Paris: Vrin, 1971.

Boltanski, Luc. "Pouvoir et impuissance: projet intellectuel et impuissance dans le *Journal* d'Amiel," *Actes de la recherche en sciences sociales* 5–6 (November 1975).

—— *Prime éducation et morale de classe.* Paris and The Hague: Mouton, 1969.

Bonello, Charles. "Le Discours médical sur l'homosexualité au XIXe siècle." Thesis, University of Paris VII, 1984.

Bonnet, Marie-Jo. *Un Choix sans équivoque. Recherches historiques sur les relations amoureuses entre les femmes, XVIe-XXe siècle.* Paris: Denoël-Gonthier, 1981.

Bonnet, Serge, and André Cottin. *La Communion solenelle.* Paris, 1969.

Bordeaux, Michèle. "Droit et femmes seules. Les pièges de la discrimination," in Arlette Farge and Christiane Klapische, *Madame ou Mademoiselle?*

Borie, Jean. *Le Célibataire français.* Paris: Sagittaire, 1976.

—— *Mythologies de l'hérédité au XIXe siècle.* Paris: Galilée, 1981.

—— *Le Tyran timide: le naturalisme de la femme au XIXe siècle.* Paris: Klincksieck, 1973.

Borreil, Jacques, ed. *Les Sauvages dans la cité. Auto-émancipation du peuple et instruction du prolétaire au XIXe siècle.* Seyssel: Champ Vallon, 1985.

Bouchard-Huzard, Louis. *Traité des constructions rurales et de leurs dispositions.* 2 vols. 1858–1860.

Bouillé, Michel. "Les Pédagogies du corps. Lieux et corps pédagogiques du XVIIIe au XIXe siècle." Thesis, University of Paris VIII, 1984.

Bourniquel, M. *Pour construire sa maison.* 1919.

Bousquet, Jean. *Les Thèmes du rêve dans la littérature romantique.* Paris: Didier, 1964.

Boutry, Philippe. "L'Anticlérical, la femme et le confessional," *L'Histoire* 16 (October 1979): 94.

—— "Réflexions sur la confession au XIXe siècle," *Pratiques de la confession des Pères du désert à Vatican II.* Paris, 1983.

—— "Les Vénérés pasteurs du diocèse de Belley, Cheminement des mentalités et des opinions religieuses dans les paroisses du diocèse de l'Ain de 1815 à 1880." Thesis, University of Paris I, 1983.

Bouvier, Jeanne. *Mes Mémoires ou Cinquante-Neuf Années d'activité industrielle, sociale et intellectuelle d'une ouvrière (1876–1935).* New edition edited by Daniel Armogathe and Maïte Albistur. Paris: Maspero, 1983.

Brame, Caroline. *Journal intime. Enquête de M. Perrot et G. Ribeill.* Paris: Montalba, 1985.

Bréton, Geneviève. *Journal.* Paris: Ramsay, 1985.

Burdy, J.-P. "Le Soleil noir. Formation sociale et mémoire ouvrière dans un quartier de Saint-Etienne (1840–1940)." Thesis, University of Lyons II, 1986.

Burnand, Robert. *La Vie quotidienne en 1830.* Paris: Hachette, 1957.

———— *La Vie quotidienne en France, 1870–1900.* Paris: Hachette, 1947.

Burnet, Louis. *Villégiature et tourisme sur les côtes de France.* Paris: Hachette, 1963.

Cabanis, José. *Michelet, le prêtre et la femme.* Paris: Gallimard, 1978.

Canetti, Elias. *The Tongue Set Free: Remembrance of a European Childhood,* trans. by Joachim Neugroschel. New York, 1979.

Capdevielle, Jacques. *Fétichisme du patrimoine. Essai sur un fondement de la classe moyenne.* Paris: Fondation nationale des sciences politiques, 1986.

Capia, Robert. "L'Age d'or de la poupée au XIXe siècle," *Histoire de la poupée.* Courbevoie Exhibition, 1973.

———— *Les Poupées françaises.* Paris, 1979.

Cardon, Emile. *L'Art au foyer domestique.* 1884.

Carroy-Thirard, Jacqueline. "Figures de femmes hystériques dans la psychiatrie française au XIXe siècle," *Psychanalyse à l'université,* March 1979.

———— "Hystérie et littérature au XIXe siècle." *Psychanalyse à l'université,* March 1982.

———— "Possession, extase, hystérie au XIXe siècle," *Psychanalyse à l'université,* June 1980.

Castel, Robert. *L'Ordre psychiatrique.* Vol. 1, *L'Age d'or de l'aliénisme.* Paris: Minuit, 1976.

Centre National de la Photographie. *Identités,* exhibition catalogue, Palais de Tokyo. Paris, 1986.

Cerisy Colloquium, *Individualisme et Autobiographie en Occident,* 1979. Brussels: Ed. universitaires, 1983.

Certeau, Michel de. *L'Invention du quotidien.* Vol. 1, *Arts de faire.* Paris: UGE, 1980.

Chabot, Paul. *Jean et Yvonne, domestiques en 1900.* Paris: Tema-Editions, 1977.

Chaline, Jean-Pierre. *Les Bourgeois de Rouen. Une élite urbaine du XIXe siècle.* Paris: Fondation nationale des sciences politiques, 1982.

Charle, Christophe. *Les Hauts fonctionnaires en France au XIXe siècle.* Paris: Gallimard/Julliard, 1980.

Charuty, Giordana. *Le Couvent des fous. L'internement et ses usages en Languedoc aux XIXe et XXe siècles.* Paris: Flammarion, 1985.

Chateaubriand, François René de. *Mémoires d'outre tombe.* Paris, 1848–1850.

———— *René.* Paris, 1802.

Chesnais, Jean-Claude. *Histoire de la violence.* Paris: Hachette, 1982.

———— *Les Morts violentes en France depuis 1826.* Paris: PUF, 1976.

Chevalier, Louis. *Classes laborieuses et classes dangereuses à Paris pendant la première moitié du XIXe siècle.* Paris: Plon, 1958.

Cholvy, Gérard. "Religion et société. Le diocèse de Montpellier au XIXe siècle." Thesis, University of Paris, 1972.

Chotard-Lioret, Caroline. "La Sociabilité familiale en province: une correspondance privée entre 1868 et 1920." Thesis, University of Paris V, 1983.

Claverie, Elisabeth, and Pierre Lamaison. *L'Impossible mariage. Violence et parenté en Gévaudan. XVIIe, XVIIIe et XIXe siècle.* Paris: Hachette, 1982.

Cobb, Richard. *Death in Paris.* Oxford: Oxford University Press, 1978.

Communications, no. 35. Special issue on "Sexualités occidentales." See articles by Philippe Ariès, A. Bejin, Michel Pollak, and others.

Compère, M.-M. *Du collège au lycée (1500–1850). Généalogie de l'enseignement secondaire français.* Paris: Gallimard/Julliard, 1985.

Constant, Benjamin. *Journaux intimes (1803–1816).* Paris: Gallimard, 1957.

Corbin, Alain. *Les Filles de noce. Misère sexuelle et prostitution aux XIXe-XXe siècles.* Paris: Aubier, 1978.

———— *Le Miasme et la jonquille. L'odorat et l'imaginaire social, XVIIIe-XXe siècle.* Paris: Aubier-Montaigne, 1982. *The Foul and the Fragrant: Odor and the French Social Imagination.* Cambridge, Mass.: Harvard University Press, 1986.

Cottereau, Alain. "Travail, école, famille. Aspects de la vie des enfants ouvriers à Paris au XIXe siècle," *Autrement,* no. 9, 1977.

———— "La Tuberculose: maladie urbaine ou maladie de l'usure du travail? Critique d'une épidémiologie officielle: le cas de Paris," *Sociologie du travail,* no. 78.

———— ed. "L'Usure au travail," special issue of *Le Mouvement Social,* no. 124 (July–September 1983).

Cousin, Bernard. "Le Miracle et le quotidien. Les ex-voto provençaux, images d'une société." Thesis, University of Aix, 1983.

Crubellier, Maurice. *L'Enfance et la jeunesse dans la société française (1800–1950).* Paris: Armand Colin, 1970.

Dallas, Gregor. *The Imperfect Peasant Economy: The Loire Country, 1800–1914.* Cambridge: Cambridge University Press, 1982.

Danet, Jean. *Discours juridique et perversions sexuelles (XIXe et XXe siècle).* Nantes: Centre de recherche politique de l'université de Nantes, 1977.

Darmon, Pierre. *Le Tribunal de l'impuissance. Virilité et défaillances conjugales dans l'ancienne France*. Paris: Seuil, 1979.

Daudet, Mme Alphonse. *L'Enfance d'une Parisienne. Enfants et mères*. Paris, 1892.

Daumard, Adeline. *La Bourgeoisie parisienne de 1815 à 1848*. Paris: SEVPEN, 1963.

——— ed. *Les Fortunes françaises au XIXe siècle*. Paris: Mouton, 1973.

——— *Maisons de Paris et propriétaires parisiens au XIXe siècle, 1809–1880*. Paris: Cujas, 1965.

——— ed. *Oisiveté et loisirs dans les sociétés occidentales au XIXe siècle*. Interdisciplinary colloquium. Amiens, November 1982. Abbeville: Paillart, 1983.

Davidoff, Leonore. *The Best Circles. Society, Etiquette, and the Season*. London: Croom Helm; Totawa, N.J.: Rowman and Littlefield, 1973.

Delacroix, Eugène. *Journal, 1822–1863*. Paris: Plon, 1980.

Delbourg-Delphis, Marylène. *Masculin singulier. Le dandysme et son histoire*. Paris: Hachette, 1985.

Delumeau, Jean. *Le Péché et la peur*. Paris: Fayard, 1983.

Deniel, Raymond. *Une Image de la famille et de la société sous la Restauration (1815–1830), étude de la presse catholique*. Paris: Ouvrières, 1965.

Derouet, Christian. *Grandes demeures angevines au XIXe siècle. L'oeuvre de René Hodé entre 1840 et 1870*. Paris: Caisse nationale des monuments historiques, 1976.

Desaive, Jean-Paul. "Le Nu hurluberlu," *Ethnologie française*, nos. 3–4, 1976.

Désert, Gabriel. *La Vie quotidienne sur les plages normandes du Second Empire aux années folles*. Paris: Hachette, 1983.

Dessertine, Dominique. *Divorcer à Lyon sous la Révolution française et la famille*. Paris: Presses Universitaires de Lyon, 1978.

Devance, Louis. "La Pensée socialiste et la famille de Fourier à Proudhon." Thesis, University of Dijon, 1976.

Devillers, Charles, and Bernard Huet. *Le Creusot, naissance et développement d'une ville industrielle, 1872–1914*. Seyssel: Champ Vallon, 1981.

Dhavernas, Odile. *Droit des femmes, pouvoir des hommes*. Paris: Seuil, 1978.

Didi-Huberman, Georges. *Invention de l'hystérie. Charcot et l'iconographie de la Salpêtrière*. Paris: Macula, 1982.

Didier, Béatrice. *Le Journal intime*. Paris: PUF, 1976.

Donzelot, Jacques. *La Police des familles*. Paris: Minuit, 1977.

Dumay, J.-B. *Mémoires d'un militant ouvrier du Creusot (1841–1926)*. Edited by Pierre Ponsot. Paris: Maspero, 1976.

Dumont, Louis. *Essai sur l'individualisme. Une perspective anthropologique sur l'idéologie moderne*. Paris: Seuil, 1983.

Durkheim, Emile. *Le Suicide*. Paris: PUF, 1930.

Edelman, Bernard. *La Maison de Kant*. Paris: Payot, 1984.

Eleb-Vidal, Monique, and Anne Debarre-Blanchard. *Architecture domestique et mentalités. Les traités et les pratiques, XVIe-XIXe siècle*, nos. 2 (1984) and 5 (1984–1985).

——— *La Maison. Espaces et intimités*. Paris and Villemin: Ecole d'Architecture, 1986.

Elias, Norbert. *Über den Prozess der Zivilisation. Soziogenetische und Psychogenetische Untersuchungen*. Basel, 1939. Trans. by Edmund Jephcott as *The Civilizing Process: The History of Manners*. New York: Pantheon, 1982.

Elshtain, J. B. *Public Man, Private Woman. Women in Social and Political Thought*. Princeton: Princeton University Press, 1981.

Estèbe, Jean. *Les Ministres de la République, 1871-1914*. Paris: Fondation nationale des sciences politiques, 1982.

Ethnologie française, April–June 1980: special issue on "Provinciaux et province à Paris."

Ewald, François. *L'Etat-providence*. Paris: Grasset, 1986.

Fabre, Daniel. "Le Livre et sa magie. Les liseurs dans les sociétés pyrénéennes aux XIXe et XXe siècles," in Roger Chartier, ed., *Pratiques de la lecture*. Marseilles: Rivages, 1985.

Farge, Arlette, and Christiane Klapisch. *Madame ou Mademoiselle? Itinéraires de la solitude féminine au XIXe siècle*. Paris: Montalba, 1984.

Fay-Sallois, Fanny. *Les Nourrices à Paris au XIXe siècle*. Paris: Payot, 1980.

Fernandez, Madeleine. "La Ceinture noire de Paris, histoire de la Zone." Thesis, University of Paris VII, 1983.

Feuillet, Mme O. *Quelques années de ma vie*. Paris, 1894.

Fillaut, Thierry. *L'Alcoolisme dans l'ouest de la France pendant la seconde moitié du XIXe siècle*. Paris: La Documentation française, 1982.

Flamand, Jean-Paul, ed. *La Question du logement et le mouvement ouvrier français*. Paris: Villette, 1981.

Flandrin, Jean-Louis. *Les Amours paysannes. Amour et sexualité dans les campagnes de l'ancienne France (XVIe-XIXe siècle)*. Paris: Gallimard/Julliard, 1975.

———— *L'Eglise et le contrôle des naissances.* Paris: Flammarion, 1970.

———— *Le Sexe et l'Occident. Evolution des attitudes et des comportements.* Paris: Seuil, 1981.

Foucault, Michel. *Histoire de la folie à l'âge classique.* Paris: Gallimard, 1972.

———— *Histoire de la sexualité.* Vol. 1, *La Volonté de savoir.* Vol. 2, *L'Usage des plaisirs.* Vol. 3, *Le Souci de soi.* Paris: Gallimard, 1976–1984. Trans. by Robert Hurley as *The History of Sexuality:* Vol. 1, *Introduction;* Vol. 2, *The Uses of Pleasure;* Vol. 3, *The Care of the Self.* New York: Pantheon, 1978, 1985, 1987.

———— *Naissance de la clinique. Une archéologie du regard médical.* Paris: PUF, 1963. Trans. by A. M. Sheridan-Smith as *The Birth of the Clinic.* New York, 1973.

———— ed. *Herculine Barbin dite Alexina B.* Paris: Gallimard, 1978.

———— et al. *Moi, Pierre Rivière, ayant égorgé ma mère, ma soeur et mon frère . . .* Paris: Gallimard, 1973.

Foville, Armand de. *Les Maisons types.* 1894.

Fraisse, Geneviève. *Femmes toutes mains. Essai sur le service domestique.* Paris: Seuil, 1979.

Fraser, Derek and Antony Sutcliffe, eds. *The Pursuit of Urban History.* London: Edward Arnold, 1983.

Fréminville, Bernard de, ed. *Lettres de Emilie (1802–1872).* Paris, 1985.

———— *Lettres de Marthe (1892–1902).* Paris, 1982.

Frère, Claude, and Aline Ripert. *La Carte postale. Son histoire, sa fonction sociale.* Paris: CNRS, 1983.

Freund, Gisèle. *Photographie et société.* Paris: Seuil, 1974.

Frey, Michel. "Du mariage et du concubinage dans les classes populaires à Paris en 1846–1847," *Annales ESC,* July–August 1978.

Furet, François, ed. *Colloque Jules Ferry.* Paris, 1985.

Gaillard, Jeanne. *Paris, la ville, 1852–1870.* Paris: Champion, 1976.

Gambon, Charles-Ferdinand. *Dans les bagnes de Napoléon III. Mémoires.* Introduction by J.-Y. Mollier. Paris: PUF, 1983.

Garaud, Marcel, and R. Szramkiewicz. *La Révolution française et la Famille.* Paris: PUF, 1978.

Garniche-Merritt, Marie-José. "Vivre à Bué-en-Sancerrois." Thesis, University of Paris VII, 1982.

Gauchet, Marcel, and Gladys Swain. *La Pratique de l'esprit humain. L'Institution asilaire et la révolution démocratique.* Paris: Gallimard, 1981.

Gauny, Gabriel. *Le Philosophe plébéien.* Edited by Jacques Rancière. Paris: Maspero, 1983.

Gay, Peter. *The Bourgeois Experience. Victoria to Freud.* I, *Education of the Senses.* II, *The Tender Passion.* New York: Oxford University Press, 1984, 1986.

Gélis, Jacques, M. Laget, and M.-F. Morel. *Entrer dans la vie. Naissances et enfances dans la France traditionnelle.* Paris: Gallimard/Julliard, 1981.

Georgel, Pierre. *Léopoldine Hugo, une jeune fille romantique.* Paris: Catalogue du Musée Victor-Hugo, 1967.

Georges, Rambert. *Chronique intime d'une famille de notables au XIXe siècle. Les Odoard de Mercurol.* Lyons: PUL, 1981.

Gerbod, Paul. "Les Métiers de la coiffure dans la première moitié du XXe siècle," *Ethnologie française,* January–March 1983.

———— *La Condition universitaire en France au XIXe siècle.* Paris, 1965.

Gilbert, A. D. *Religion and Society in Industrial England: Church, Chapel and Social Change.* London: Longman, 1976.

Gillet, Marcel. *L'Homme, la vie et la mort dans le Nord au XIXe siècle.* Lille: Presses universitaires, 1972.

Gillis, John R. *For Better, For Worse. British Marriages, 1600 to the Present.* Oxford: Oxford University Press, 1985.

———— *Youth and History. Tradition and Change in European Age Relations, 1770 to the Present.* New York and London: Academic Press, 1974.

Ginzburg, Carlo. "Signes, traces, pistes. Racines d'un paradigme de l'indice," *Le Débat,* November 1980.

Girard, Alain. *Le Journal intime.* Paris: PUF, 1963.

Girouard, Mark. *Life in the English Country House.* Harmondsworth: Penguin, 1980.

Godin, J.-B. *Solutions sociales.* Quimperlé: La Digitale, 1979.

Goffman, Erving. *Asylums: Essays on the Social Situation of Mental Patients and Other Inmates.* New York: Aldine, 1961.

———— *The Presentation of Self in Everyday Life.* New York: Doubleday, 1959.

Goody, Jack. *The Development of the Family and Marriage in Europe.* Cambridge: Cambridge University Press, 1983.

Goubert, Jean-Pierre. *La Conquête de l'eau. L'Avènement de la santé à l'âge industriel.* Paris: Laffont, 1986.

Grafteaux, Serge. *Mémé Santerre. Une vie.* Paris: Marabout, 1975.

Gray, Robert Q. *The Labour Aristocracy in Victorian Edinburgh.* Oxford: Clarendon, 1976.

Green, Nancy. *Les Travailleurs immigrés juifs à la Belle Epoque. Le "Pletzl" de Paris.* Paris: Fayard, 1985.

Gribaudi, Maurizio. *Itinéraires ouvriers. Espaces et*

groupes sociaux à Turin au début du XX siècle. Paris: Ecole des Hautes Etudes en Sciences Sociales, 1987.

Guérin, Eugénie de. *Journal et fragments.* Paris: V. Lecoffre, 1884.

Guermont, Marie-Françoise. "La 'Grande fille.' L'Hygiène de la jeune fille d'après les ouvrages médicaux (fin XIXe–début XXe siècle)." Thesis, University of Tours, 1981.

Guerrand, Roger-Henri. *La Libre Maternité, 1896–1969.* Paris, 1971.

—— *Les Lieux, histoire des commodités.* Paris: La Découverte, 1985.

—— *Les Origines du logement social en France.* Paris: Ouvrières, 1966.

Guillais-Maury, Joëlle. *La Chair de l'autre. Le crime passionnel au XIXe siècle.* Paris: Olivier Orban, 1986.

Guillaume, Pierre. *Du Désespoir au salut: les tuberculeux aux XIXe et XXe siècles.* Paris: Aubier, 1986.

—— *Individus, Familles, Nations. Essai d'histoire démographique, XIXe–XXe siècle.* Paris: SEDES, 1985.

—— *La Population de Bordeaux au XIXe siècle.* Paris, 1972.

Guillemin, Henri. *L'Engloutie, Adèle, fille de Victor Hugo (1830–1915).* Paris: Seuil, 1985.

Guillot, Emile. *La Maison salubre.* 1914.

Gusdorf, Georges. *L'Homme romantique.* Paris: Payot, 1984.

Haan, Pierre. *Nos ancêtres les pervers.* Paris: Olivier Orban, 1979.

Halévy, Daniel. *Visites aux paysans du Centre (1907–1934).* Paris, 1978.

Hall, Catherine. "The Early Formation of Victorian Domestic Ideology," in Sandra Burman, ed., *Fit Work for Women.* London: Croom Helm, 1979.

—— "Private Persons Versus Public Someones: Class, Gender and Politics in England, 1780–1850," in Carolyn S. Steedman, Cathy U. Urwin, and Valerie W. Walkerdine, *Language, Gender and Childhood.* London: Routledge and Kegan Paul, 1985.

—— "The Tale of Samuel and Jemima: Gender and Working Class Culture in Early Nineteenth Century England," in Tony Bennett, Colin Mercer, and Janet Woollacott, *Popular Culture and Social Relations.* London: Open University Educational Enterprises, Milton Keynes, 1986.

—— with Leonore Davidoff, *Family Fortunes: Men and Women of the English Middle Class, 1780–1850.* Chicago: University of Chicago Press; London: Hutchinson, 1987.

Hau, C. *Le Messie de l'an XIII.* Paris: Denoël, 1955.

Heller, Geneviève. *Propre en ordre, habitation et vie domestique, 1850–1930: l'exemple vaudois.* Lausanne: Ed. d'En bas, 1979.

Hervier, Denis. "Cafés et cabarets en Berry de 1851 à 1914." Thesis, University of Tours, 1979.

Hilaire, Yves-Marie. *Une chrétienté au XIXe siècle. La vie religieuse des populations du diocèse d'Arras, 1840–1914.* Lille: Presses universitaires, 1977.

Hirschman, Albert O. *Shifting Involvements: Private Interest and Public Action.* Princeton: Princeton University Press, 1981.

Hobsbawm, Eric J., and T. Ranger, eds. *The Invention of Tradition.* Cambridge: Cambridge University Press, 1983.

Hoffman, Paul. *La Femme dans la pensée des Lumières.* Paris, 1977.

Hubscher, Ronald. *L'Agriculture et la société rurale dans le Pas-de-Calais du milieu du XIXe siècle à 1914.* 2 vols. Arras, 1979.

Hugo, Victor. "Recueil Victor Hugo." Annotated by Claire P. de Chateaufort. 1893–1919. Manuscript.

Institut Français d'Architecture. *La Ville d'hiver d'Arcachon.* Paris, 1983.

Isambert-Jamati, Viviane, and R. Sirota. "La Barrière, oui, mais le niveau?" *Cahiers internationaux de sociologie* 70 (1981): 5–33.

Jacquemet, Gérard. *Belleville au XIXe siècle.* Paris: EHESS, 1984.

—— "Médecins et maladies populaires dans le Paris de la fin du XIXe siècle." *Recherches,* no. 29, December 1977.

Jacques, Jean-Pierre. *Les Malheurs de Sapho.* Paris: Grasset, 1981.

Jeanneret, Michel. "La Folie est un rêve: Nerval et le Dr. Moreau de Tours," *Romantisme,* no. 27, 1980.

John, Angela. *By the Sweat of Their Brow. Women Workers at Victorian Coal Mines.* London: Routledge and Kegan Paul, 1984.

Jonas, Stephan. *La Cité de Mulhouse (1853–1870): un modèle d'habitation économique et social du XIXe siècle.* 2 vols. Paris: Ministère de l'Urbanisme et du Logement, secrétariat de la Recherche architecturale, 1981.

Joutard, Philippe. "L'Homme et son corps," *L'Histoire,* no. 22.

Kaluszynski, Martine. "Alphonse Bertillon, savant et policier. L'Anthropométrie ou le début du fichage." Thesis, University of Paris VII, 1981.

Kaplow, Jeffry. "Concubinage and the Working Class in Early Nineteenth Century Paris," *Von Ancien Regime zur französischen Revolution.* Göttingen, 1978.

Kempf, Roger. *Dandies. Baudelaire et Cie.* Paris: Seuil, 1984.

Knibiehler, Yvonne. *Nous, les assistances sociales.* Paris: Aubier, 1980.

——— et al. *De la pucelle à la minette. Les jeunes filles de l'âge classique à nos jours.* Paris: Temps actuels, 1983.

Kniebiehler, Yvonne, and Catherine Fouquet. *La Femme et les médecins.* Paris: Hachette, 1983.

——— *Histoire des mères du Moyen Age à nos jours.* Paris: Montalba, 1977.

L'Histoire, January 1984. Special issue on "Amour et sexualité."

L'Homme, no. 4, 1980: special issue on naming. See the articles by André Burguière, Martine Segalen, F. Zonabend, and others.

La Révellière-Lépeaux, Louis-Marie. *Mémoires.* Paris, 1895.

Lafarge, Marie. *Mémoires de Marie Cappelle veuve Lafarge écrits par elle-même.* 4 vols. Paris: René & Cie, 1841–1844.

Lagree, Michel. "Confession et pénitence dans les visites pastorales et les statuts synodaux bretons, XIXe–XXe siècle," *Pratiques de la confession des Pères du désert à Vatican II.* Paris: Cerf, 1983.

Laguin, Gabrielle. "Journal," 1890–1891. Manuscript.

Lalouette, Jacqueline. "Le Discours bourgeois sur les débits de boisson aux alentours de 1900," *Recherches,* no. 29, December 1977.

Lamarre, Anne. "L'Enfer de la IIIe République. Entrepreneurs moraux et pornographes." Thesis, University of Paris VII, 1986.

Lamartine, Alphonse de. *Le Manuscrit de ma mère.* Paris: Hachette, 1924.

Langlois, Claude. *Le Diocèse de Vannes au XIXe siècle (1800–1830).* Paris.

Laplaige. Danièle. "Paris et ses sans-famille au XIXe siècle." Thesis, University of Paris VII, 1981.

Layet, Alexandre. *Hygiène et maladies des paysans. Etude sur la vie matérielle des campagnards en Europe.* 1882.

Le Bras, Hervé, and Emmanuel Todd. *L'Invention de la France.* Paris: Pluriel, 1981.

Lehning, James R. *Peasants of Marlhes, Economic Development and Family Organization in Nineteenth Century France.* Chapel Hill: University of North Carolina Press, 1980.

Lejeune, Philippe. *L'Autobiographie en France.* Paris: Armand Colin, 1971.

——— *Je est un autre.* Paris: Seuil, 1980.

——— *Moi aussi.* Paris: Seuil, 1986.

——— *Le Pacte autobiographique.* Paris: Seuil, 1975.

Lejeune, X. E. *Calicot. Enquête de Michel et Philippe Lejeune.* Paris: Montalba, 1984.

Leleu, Michèle. *Les Journaux intimes.* Paris: PUP, 1952.

Lemoine, Albert. *Du Sommeil au point de vue physiologique et psychologique.* Paris, 1855.

Lenoir, Rémi. "Note pour une histoire sociale du piano," *Actes de la recherche en sciences sociales,* no. 28, June 1979.

Leonard, Jacques. *De Darwin au darwinisme.* Paris: Vrin, 1983.

——— *La France médicale. Médecins et malades au XIXe siècle.* Paris: Gallimard, 1978.

——— *La Médecine entre les pouvoirs et les savoirs.* Paris: Aubier, 1979.

——— *La Vie quotidienne du médecin de province au XIXe siècle.* Paris: Hachette, 1977.

Leplaige, Danièle. "Paris et ses san-famille." Thesis, University of Paris VII, 1983.

Lequin, Yves. *Histoire des Français, XIXe–XXe siècle.* Vol. 1, *Un Peuple et son pays.* Vol. 2, *La Société.* Vol. 3, *Les Citoyens et la démocratie.* Paris: Armand Colin, 1983–1985.

——— *Les Ouvriers de la région lyonnaise (1848–1914).* 2 vols. Lyons: PUL, 1977.

Lévy, F.-P. *L'Amour nomade. La mère et l'enfant hors mariage (XVIe–XXe siècle).* Paris: Seuil, 1981.

Lévy, Marie-Françoise. *De mères en filles. L'Education des Françaises, 1850–1880.* Paris: Calmann-Lévy, 1984.

Liederkerke, Anatole de. *La Belle Epoque de l'opium.* Paris: La Différence-Le Sphinx, 1984.

Loux, Françoise. *Le Jeune enfant et son corps dans la médecine traditionnelle.* Paris: Flammarion, 1978.

——— and Philippe Richard. *Sagesses du corps: la santé et la maladie dans les proverbes français.* Paris: Maisonneuve et Larose, 1978.

Lucas, Charles. *Etude sur les habitations à bon marché en France et à l'étranger.* 1899.

Lynch, L. W. *The Marquis de Sade.* Boston: Twayne, 1984.

McBride, Theresa. *The Domestic Revolution. The Modernization of Household in England and France (1820–1920).* London: Croom Helm, 1976.

MacLaren, Angus. *Sexuality and Social Order: The Debate over the Fertility of Women and Workers in France, 1770–1920.* New York: Holmes and Meier, 1983.

McMillan, James F. *Housewife or Harlot: The Women Question in France Under the Third Republic.* New York: St. Martin's, 1981.

Maine de Biran. *Journal.* 3 vols. Paris: Vrin, 1955.

Maire, Catherine-Laurence. *Les Possédées de Morzine, 1857–1873.* Lyons: PUL, 1981.

Manson, Michel. "La Poupée au XIXe siècle," *Histoire de l'éducation,* no. 18, April 1983.

Marcilhacy, Christian. *Le Diocèse d'Orléans sous l'épiscopat de Mgr. Dupanloup.* Paris: Plon, 1962.

Marrey, Bernard. *Un Capitalisme idéal (Menier à Noisiel).* Paris: Clancier-Guénaud, 1984.

———— and J.-P. Monnet. *La Grande histoire des serres et des jardins d'hiver, 1780–1900.* Paris: Graphite, 1984.

Marrus, Michael R. "L'Alcoolisme social à la Belle Epoque," *Recherches,* no. 29, December 1977.

Marthe. Paris: Le Seuil, 1982.

Martin du Gard, Roger. *Souvenirs autobiographiques et littéraires.* Paris: Gallimard, 1955.

Martin, Henri-Jean, and Roger Chartier, eds. *Histoire de l'édition française.* Vol. 3, *Le Temps des éditeurs: Du romantisme à la Belle Epoque.* Paris: Promodis, 1985.

Martin-Fugier, Anne. *La Bourgeoise. Femme au temps de Paul Bourget.* Paris: Grasset, 1983.

———— "La Douceur du nid. Les Arts de la femme à la Belle Epoque," *Urbi,* no. 5.

———— *La Place des bonnes. La Domesticité féminine à Paris en 1900.* Paris: Grasset, 1979.

Martinet, Chantal. "Objets de famille, objets de musée, ethnologie ou muséologie," *Ethnologie française,* no. 1, 1980.

Marx (the daughters of Karl Marx), *Lettres inédites,* with an introduction by Michelle Perrot. Paris: Albin Michel, 1979.

Mayer, Arno J. *The Persistence of the Old Regime: Europe to the Great War.* New York: Pantheon, 1982.

Mayeur, Françoise. *L'Enseignement secondaire des jeunes filles sous la Troisième République.* Paris: Fondation nationale des sciences politiques, 1977.

———— *Histoire générale de l'enseignement et de l'éducation en France.* Vol. III, *De la Révolution à l'école républicaine.* Paris: Nouvelle librairie de France, 1981.

———— and Jacques Gadille, eds. *Education et images de la femme chrétienne en France au début du XXe siècle.* Lyons: L'Hermès, 1980.

Mesnil, Dr. Octave du. *L'Habitation du pauvre.* 1890.

Métral, Marie-Odile. *Mariage: Les Hésitations de l'Occident.* Paris: Aubier, 1977.

Meyer, Philippe. *L'Enfant et la raison d'état.* Paris: Seuil, 1977.

Michaud, Stéphane. *Muse et Madone. Visages de la femme de la Révolution française aux apparitions de Lourdes.* Paris: Seuil, 1985.

Miller, M. B. *The Bon Marché: Bourgeois Culture and the Department Store, 1869–1920.* Princeton: Princeton University Press, 1981.

Mitchell, Judith, and Ann Oakley, eds. *The Rights and Wrongs of Women.* Harmondsworth, 1976.

Moore, Barrington. *Privacy.* Princeton: Princeton University Press, 1984.

Moreau, Thérèse. *Le Sang de l'histoire. Michelet, l'histoire et l'idée de la femme au XIXe siècle.* Paris: Flammarion, 1982.

Murard, Lion, and Patrick Zylbermann. *Sanitas sanitatum et omnia sanitas.* CERFI, 1980.

Nadaud, Martin. *Mémoires de Léonard, ancien garçon maçon* (1895). Introduction by Maurice Agulhon. Paris: Hachette, 1976.

Nahoum, Véronique. "La Belle femme ou le stade du miroir en histoire," *Communications,* no. 31, 1979.

Navaille, J.-P. *La Famille ouvrière dans l'Angleterre victorienne. Des regards aux mentalités.* Seyssel: Champ Vallon, 1983.

Noiriel, Gérard. *Les Ouvriers dans la société française, XIXe–XXe siècle.* Paris: Seuil, 1986.

Noiriel, G. *Longwy. Immigrés et prolétaires (1880–1980).* Paris: PUF, 1984.

Noonan, John T. *Contraception: A History of Its Treatment by the Catholic Theologians and Canonists.* Cambridge, Mass.: Harvard University Press, 1986.

O'Brien, Patricia. *The Promise of Punishment: Prisons in Nineteenth-Century France.* Princeton: Princeton University Press, 1981.

Ourliac, Paul, and Léon Gazzaniga. *Histoire du droit civil français de l'an mil au Code civil.* Paris: Albin Michel, 1985.

Ourliac, Paul, and Jehan de Malafosse. *Histoire du droit privé,* vol. 3. Paris: PUF, 1971.

Ozouf, Jacques. *Nous les maîtres d'école.* Paris: Gallimard/Julliard, 1967.

———— and François Furet. *Lire et écrire. L'alphabétisation des Français de Calvin à Jules Ferry.* Paris: Minuit, 1977.

Ozouf, Jacques, and Mona Ozouf. *La Classe ininterrompue. Cahiers de la famille Sandre, enseignants, 1780–1860.* Paris: Hachette, 1979.

Ozouf, Mona. *La Fête révolutionnaire (1789–1799).* Paris: Gallimard, 1976. Trans. by Alan Sheridan as *Festivals and the French Revolution.* Cambridge, Mass.: Harvard University Press, 1988.

Pange, Comtesse de. *Comment j'ai vu 1900.* Vol. 1, *A l'ombre de la tour Eiffel.* Vol. 2, *Confidences d'une jeune fille.* Vol. 3, *Derniers bals avant l'orage.* Paris, 1962, 1965, 1968.

Parent-Lardeur, Françoise. *Lire à Paris au temps de Balzac. Les cabinets de lecture à Paris, 1815–1830.* Paris: EHESS, 1981.

Pelckmans, Paul. "Le Prêtre, la femme et la famille: notes sur l'anticléricalisme de Michelet," *Romantisme,* no. 28, 1980.

Pélicier, Yves, ed. *L'Imaginaire quotidien au XIXe siècle.* Paris: Economica, 1985.

Pelosse, Valentin. "Imaginaire social et protection de l'animal. Des amis des bêtes de l'an X au législateur de 1850," *L'Homme,* nos. 21–22, October–December 1981 and January–March 1982.

Perdiguier, Agricol. *Mémoires d'un compagnon.* Introduction by A. Faure. Paris: Maspero, 1977.

Perouas, Louis, et al. *Etude de l'évolution des prénoms depuis un millénaire.* Paris: CNRS, 1984.

Perrot, Michelle. *Enquêtes sur la condition ouvrière en France au XIXe siècle.* Paris: Microéditions Hachette, 1972.

———— *Le Mode de vie des familles bourgeoises, 1873–1953.* Paris: Armand Colin, 1961.

———— "Quand la société prend peur de sa jeunesse au XIXe siècle," in Annick Percheron and Michelle Perrot, eds., *Les Jeunes et les Autres.* 2 vols. Paris, 1986.

———— "Sur la ségrégation de l'enfance au XIXe siècle," *La Psychiatrie de l'enfant,* vol. 25, no. 1, 1982, pp. 179–207.

———— ed. *Une Histoire des femmes est-elle possible?* Marseilles: Rivages, 1984.

Perrot, Philippe. *Le Travail des apparences ou les transformations du corps féminin (XVIIIe–XIXe siècle).* Paris: Seuil, 1984.

———— *Les Dessus et les dessous de la bourgeoisie. Une histoire du vêtement au XIXe siècle.* Paris: Fayard, 1981.

Perthuis de Laillevaut. *Traité d'architecture rurale.* 1810.

Peter, Jean-Pierre. "Le Corps du délit," *Nouvelle Revue de psychanalyse,* no. 3, 1971.

———— "Les Médecins et les femmes," in Jean-Paul Aron, *Misérable et glorieuse: la femme du XIXe siècle.*

———— "Ogres d'archives," *Nouvelle Revue de psychanalyse,* no. 3, 1972.

Petit, Jacques. "Folie, langage, pouvoirs en Maine-et-Loire (1800–1841)," *Revue d'histoire moderne et contemporaine.* October–December 1980.

Petitpas, M. *Maisons de campagne, villas, et cottages.* 1913.

Pich, Edgard. "Pour une définition de la poésie comme phénomène social au XIXe siècle," *Romantisme,* no. 39, 1983.

Picq, Françoise. "Sur la théorie du droit maternel. Discours anthropologiques et discours socialistes." Thesis, University of Paris IX, 1979.

Pierrard, Pierre. *L'Eglise et les ouvriers en France (1840-1940).* Paris: Hachette, 1984.

———— *La Vie ouvrière à Lille sous le Second Empire.* Paris: Bloud et Gay, 1965.

Pierre, Eric. "Histoire de la protection des animaux en France au XIXe siècle." Thesis, University of Paris, VII, 1982.

Pinchbeck, Irvy. *Women Workers and the Industrial Revolution, 1750–1850.* Second edition. London: Frank Cass, 1969.

Pinell, Patrice, and Markos Zafiropoulous. "La Medicalisation de l'échec scolaire. De la pédopsychiatrie à la psychanalyse infantile," *Actes de la recherche en sciences sociales,* no. 24, November 1978.

Pistone, Danièle. *Le Piano dans la littérature française des origines jusque vers 1900.* Paris: Champion, 1975.

Plonévez, Chantal. "L'Alcoolisme dans les milieux ouvriers à Paris, 1880–1914." Thesis, University of Paris VII, 1975.

Pomian, Kristof. "Entre l'invisible et le visible: la collection," *Libre,* nos. 2–3, 1978.

Postel, J., and Claude Quetel, eds. *Nouvelle Histoire de la psychiatrie.* Toulouse: Privately printed, 1983.

Pouthas, Hippolyte. *La Jeunesse de Guizot.* Paris: Alcan, 1936.

Prigent, Robert, ed. *Renouveau des idées sur la famille.* Cahier de l'INED, vol. 18, 1954.

Proceedings of the International Colloquium on Correspondence, Nantes, October 1982. *Ecrire, Publier, Lire. Les correspondances (problématique et économie) d'un "genre littéraire."* Offset, The University of Nantes, 1982.

Proudhon, P. J. *Mémoires de ma vie.* Edited by Bernard Voyenne. Paris: Maspero, 1983.

Quiguer, Claude. *Femmes et machines 1900. Lectures d'une obsession modern style.* Paris: Klincksieck, 1979.

Quinlan, Maurice. *Victorian Prelude. A History of English Manners, 1700–1830.* London: Cass, 1965.

Raison-Jourde, Françoise. *La Colonie auvergnate de Paris au XIXe siècle.* Paris: Bibliothèque historique de la Ville de Paris, 1976.

Rancière, Jacques. "En allant à l'expo: l'ouvrier, sa femme et les machines," *Les Révoltes logiques,* no. 1, 1975.

———— *La Nuit des prolétaires. Archives du rêve ouvrier.* Paris: Fayard, 1981.

Raymond, Marcel. *Romantisme et rêverie*. Paris: José Corti, 1978.

Reddy, William. "Family and Factory: French Linen Weavers in the Belle Epoque," *Journal of Social History*, 1975, pp. 102-112.

———— *The Rise of Market Culture. The Textile Trade and French Society, 1750–1900*. Cambridge: Cambridge University Press, and Paris: Maison des sciences de l'homme, 1984.

Renard, Jules. *Journal, 1887–1910*. Paris: Gallimard, 1960.

Reytier, Daniel. "L'Adultère sous le Second Empire." Thesis, University of Paris VII, 1981.

Ripa, Yanick. *La Ronde des folles. Femme, folie et enfermement au XIXe siècle*. Paris: Aubier, 1986.

Roderick, Philip. *Family Breakdown in Late Eighteenth-Century France: Divorce in Rouen, 1792–1803*. Oxford: Clarendon, 1980.

Roland, Mme de. *Mémoires*. 2 vols. Paris: Badouin Frères, 1820; *Memoires de Madame Roland*, ed. Paul de Roux. Paris: Mercure de France, 1986.

Romantisme, no. 4, 1976. Special issue on "Mythe et représentation de la femme au XIXe siècle."

Ronsin, Francis. *La Grève des ventres*. Paris: Aubier, 1979.

Rosanvallon, Pierre. *Le Moment Guizot*. Paris: Gallimard, 1985.

Roudinesco, Elisabeth. *La Bataille de cent ans. Histoire de la psychanalyse en France*. 2 vols. Paris: Seuil, 1986.

Rouillé, André. *L'Empire de la photographie, 1839–1980*. Paris, 1982.

Roux, A. *Recueil de constructions rurales et communales*. 1843.

Rouy, Hersilie. *Mémoires d'une aliénée*. Paris: P. Ollendorff, 1883.

Royer, Jean-Pierre, R. Martinage, and P. Lecoq. *Juges et notables au XIXe siècle*. Paris: PUF, 1982.

Sand, George. *Histoire de ma vie*. Edited by Georges Lubin. 2 vols. Paris: Gallimard, 1970–1971.

Sarrazin, Hélène. *Elisée Reclus ou la passion du monde*. Paris: La Découverte, 1985.

Sartre, Jean-Paul. *L'Idiot de la famille: Gustave Flaubert de 1821 à 1857*. 3 vols. Paris: Gallimard, 1971–1972.

———— *Les Mots*. Paris: Gallimard, 1964.

Savart, Claude. "Le Livre catholique témoin de la conscience religieuse en France au XIXe siècle." Thesis, University of Paris-Sorbonne, 1981.

Schnapper, Bernard. "La Correction paternelle et le mouvement des idées au XIXe siècle," *Revue historique*, April–June 1980.

———— "La Séparation de corps de 1837 à 1914. Essai de sociologie juridique," *Revue historique*, April–June 1978.

Segalen, Martine. *Mari et femme dans la société paysanne*. Paris: Flammarion, 1980. *Love and Power in the Peasant Family*. London: Blackwell, 1983.

———— *Nuptialité et alliance. Le choix du conjoint dans une commune de l'Eure*. Paris: Maisoneuve et Larose, 1972.

———— *Sociologie de la famille*. Paris: A. Colin, 1981.

Seigel, Jerrold. *Bohemian Paris: Culture, Politics, and the Boundaries of Bourgeois Life, 1830–1930*. New York: Viking, 1986.

Sennett, Richard. *The Fall of Public Man*. New York: Knopf, 1974.

———— *Families against the City: Middle Class Homes of Industrial Chicago, 1872–1890*. Cambridge, Mass.: Harvard University Press, 1970.

———— *Classic Essays on the Culture of Cities*. Englewood Cliffs, N.J.: Appleton, 1969.

Serman, William. *Les Officiers français dans la nation, 1848-1914*. Paris: Aubier, 1982.

Shorter, Edward. *A History of Women's Bodies*. New York: Basic Books, 1982.

———— *The Making of the Modern Family*. New York: Basic Books, 1975.

Simonin, Albert. *Confessions d'un enfant de La Chapelle. Le faubourg*. Paris: Gallimard, 1977.

Smith, Bonnie. *Ladies of the Leisure Class. The Bourgeoises of Northern France in the Nineteenth Century*. Princeton: Princeton University Press, 1981.

Sohn, Anne-Marie. "Les Rôles féminins dans la vie privée: approche méthodologique et bilan de recherches," *Revue d'histoire moderne et contemporaine*, October–December 1981.

Sontag, Susan. *On Photography*. New York: Farrar, Straus, and Giroux, 1977.

Spivak, Marcel. "L'Education physique et le sport français, 1852-1914," *Revue d'histoire moderne et contemporaine*. January–March 1977.

Starobinski, Jean. "Brève histoire de la conscience du corps," *Revue française de psychanalyse*, no. 2, 1981.

———— "Sur la chlorose," *Romantisme*, no. 31, 1981.

Staum, M. S. *Cabanis: Enlightenment and Medical Philosophy in the French Revolution*. Princeton: Princeton University Press, 1980.

Steedman, Caroline S., Cathy U. Urwin, and Valerie W. Walkerdine, eds. *Language, Gender and Childhood*. London: Routledge and Kegan Paul, 1985.

Steiner, George. "Les Rêves participent-ils de l'histoire? Deux questions adressées à Freud," *Le Débat,* no. 25, May 1983.

Stendhal, *Journal, 1801–1823.* Paris: Gallimard, 1955.

———— *Oeuvres intimes.* Edited by Henri Martineau. Paris: Gallimard, 1955.

Stone, Lawrence. *The Family, Sex and Marriage in England, 1500–1800.* London: Weidenfeld and Nicholson, 1977.

Swain, Gladys. "L'Ame, la femme, le sexe et le corps. Les métamorphoses de l'hystérie à la fin du XIXe siècle," *Le Débat,* March 1983.

Swetchine, Mme. *Lettres de Mme Swetchine. Journal.* Edited by Comte Falloux. Paris: Didier, 1862.

Taricat, J., and M. Villars. *Le Logement à bon marché. Chronique, Paris, 1850–1930.* Paris: Apogée, 1982.

Taylor, Barbara. *Eve and the New Jerusalem. Socialism and Feminism in the Nineteenth Century.* London, 1983.

Termeau, Jacques. *Maisons closes de province (Maine-et-Loire, Sarthe, Mayenne).* Le Mans: Cenomane, 1986.

Thiesse, A.-M. *Le Roman du quotidien. Lecteurs et lectures populaires à la Belle Epoque.* Paris: Chemin vert, 1984.

Thornton, Peter. *Authentic Decor. The Domestic Interior, 1620–1920.* London: Weidenfeld, 1984.

Thuillier, Guy. *Pour une histoire du quotidien en Nivernais au XIXe siècle.* Paris: Mouton, 1977.

Tilly, Louise A., and Joan W. Scott. *Women, Work and Family.* New York: Holt, Rinehart and Winston, 1978.

Trempé, Rolande. *Les Mineurs de Carmaux, 1848–1914.* 2 vols. Paris, 1971.

Tricaud, François. *L'Accusation. Recherches sur les figures de l'agression éthique.* Paris: Dalloz, 1977.

Truquin, Norbert. *Mémoires et aventures d'un prolétaire à travers la Révolution (1888).* Paris: Maspero, 1977.

Tulard, Jean. *La Vie quotidienne des Français sous Napoléon.* Paris: Hachette, 1978.

Vallès, Jules. *L'Enfant* (1881), *Le Bachelier* (1881), *L'Insurgé* (1882), in *Oeuvres complètes,* edited by L. Scheler and M.-C. Bancquart. 4 vols. Paris: Livre-Club Diderot, 1969–1970.

Vanderwielen, Lise. *Lise du Plat-Pays.* Lille: Presses universitaires, 1983.

Veillard, Jean-Yves. *Rennes au XIXe siècle, architectes, urbanisme et architecture.* Rennes: Thabor, 1978.

Verdier, Yvonne. *Façons de dire, façons de faire. La Laveuse, la couturière, la cuisinière.* Paris: Gallimard, 1979.

Viallaneix, Paul, and Jean Ehrard, eds. *Aimer en France (1760-1860).* International Colloquium of Clermont-Ferrand. Proceedings. 2 vols. Clermont-Ferrand, 1980.

Vicinus, Martha. *Independent Women. Work and Community for Single Women, 1850–1920.* London: Virago, 1985.

Vigarello, Georges. *Le Corps redressé. Histoire d'un pouvoir pédagogique.* Paris: Delarge, 1978.

———— *Le Propre et le sale. L'hygiène du corps depuis le Moyen Age.* Paris: Seuil, 1985.

Vincent, Anne. *Histoire des larmes, XVIIIe–XIXe siècle.* Marseilles: Rivages, 1986.

Vincent, David. *Bread, Knowledge and Freedom. A Study of Nineteenth Century Working Class Autobiography.* London and New York: Methuen, 1981.

Vitry, U. *Le Propriétaire architecte.* 1827.

Voilquin, Suzanne. *Souvenirs d'une fille du peuple.* Paris: Maspero, 1978.

Wajeman, Gérard. *Le Maître et l'hystérique.* Paris, 1982.

Weber, Eugen. *France: Fin de Siècle.* Cambridge, Mass.: Harvard University Press, 1986.

———— "Gymnastic and Sports in Fin de Siècle France: Opium of the Classes," *American Historical Review,* 76 (1971): 70–98.

———— *Peasants into Frenchmen. The Modernization of Rural France, 1870–1914.* Stanford, Calif.: Stanford University Press, 1976.

Weiss, Louise. *Mémoires d'une Européenne.* Vol. 1, *1893–1919.* Paris, 1968.

Zeldin, Theodore. *Ambition, Love and Politics.* Oxford: Oxford University Press, 1973.

———— *Intellect, Taste and Anxiety.* Oxford: Oxford University Press, 1977.

Credits

The objects illustrated in this book (on the pages noted) are found in various locations, as follows: Archives Bernard Marrey, 434, 435; Archives Départementales du Nord, Lille, 372, 377a; Archives of Haut-Rhin, Colmar, 233; Archives of Indre, Châteauroux, 306; Archives Raboux, 408, 410, 411, 412; Bibliothèque de l'Ancienne Faculté de Médecine, Paris, 495; Bibliothèque des Arts Décoratifs, Paris, 103, 138, 151, 163, 172, 287, 294, 297ab, 371ab, 428ab, 459, 481, 524b, 529, 540, 550; Bibliothèque Charcot, Paris, 620, 624, 626, 627abc, 631ab, 632abcd; Bibliothèque Forney, Paris, 407; Bibliothèque Historique, Paris, 235, 282, 338, 350, 376, 396b, 431, 432, 437, 440, 441; Bibliothèque Marguerite-Durand, Paris, 121, 161a, 164, 165, 182, 601; Bibliothèque Nationale, Paris, 15, 16, 17ab, 18, 19, 23, 24, 25, 26, 27, 28, 29a, 32b, 42, 48, 86ab, 90, 92, 105, 106, 118, 119, 135, 144, 148, 158, 174a, 178, 195ab, 206, 210, 212, 234, 244, 247, 250, 252ab, 259b, 263, 288, 289, 300, 305, 311, 312, 313, 324, 325, 326, 333, 340, 348, 349, 361, 362, 363, 364, 367, 370, 373, 377b, 378, 385ab, 389, 396a, 398, 406, 409, 416, 417, 423, 456, 483, 484, 492ab, 510, 511, 516, 517, 528, 536, 543ab, 580, 582, 589, 606, 617a, 619, 633, 650, 654, 655, 665a, 671; Birmingham Reference Library, 65, 69, 70; Borgé Collection, 391; Capodimonte Museum, Naples, 238; Chicago Art Institute, 532 (Martin A. Ryerson Collections); Collection of H.M. Elizabeth II, 46; Debuisson Collection, 452; Dorville Collection, Paris, 279a; Fondation Nationale d'Art Contemporain, Paris, 630; Galerie de l'Imagerie, Paris, 279b; Harris Museum, Preston, 51; INRP, Historical Collection, Paris, 296; Jean Migrenne Collection, 353; L'Illustration, 125, 145, 168, 232, 243, 249, 284, 470, 477, 653, 660, 663, 665b; Le Lillois, 372; Louvre, Paris, 98, 246, 269, 544, 614; Manchester City Art Gallery, 285; Michigan Institute of Arts, Detroit, 264; Musée des Arts Décoratifs, Paris, 366, 368, 369, 379; Musée des Arts et Traditions Populaires, Paris, 155, 617b; Musée de l'Assistance Publique, Paris, 480; Musée des Beaux-Arts, Angers, 381; Musée des Beaux-Arts, Liège, 490; Musée des Beaux-Arts, Lyons, 569; Musée des Beaux-Arts, Nancy, 298 (photo Gilbert Mangin); Musée des Beaux-Arts, Nantes, 202; Musée des Beaux-Arts, Rouen, 114, 177, 189, 203, 240, 327; Musée Carnavalet, Paris, 20, 32a, 39, 272, 280, 283, 291, 611, 649, 658; Musée de Compiègne, 486; Musée de Dijon, 507; Musée Fabre, Montpellier, 648; Musée Félicien-Rops, Namur, 597 (photo Speltdoorn); Musée d'Histoire de la Médecine, Paris, 600; Musée de Lille, 521b; Musée de Luxembourg, Paris, 487, 568; Musée Nationale de l'Education, Rouen, 216; Musée d'Orsay, Paris, 166; Musée d'Orsay/Jeu de Paume, Paris, 260, 323 (Kaganovitch Collection), 485; Musée de la Police, Paris, 474; Musée Royal de Mariemont, 596; Musée Rural des Arts Populaires, Laduz, 448; Musée Toulouse-Lautrec, 636, 637; Musée Victor Hugo, Paris, 161b, 337; Museum of Fine Arts, Boston, 275 (Mary Hopkins Foundation); Museum of Fine Arts, Lille, 12; Museum of the French Revolution, Vizille, 6, 22, 29b, 31; Museum of History, Versailles, 14; National Galleries of Scotland, Edinburgh, 53; National Gallery of Art, Washington, D.C., 197 (Chester Dale Fund), 345; Notre-Dame-de-Laghet, 519; Ordre National des Pharmaciens, Paris (Bouvet Collection), 595; Petit Palais, Paris, 101, 110; Police Archives, Paris, 641; Prado, Madrid, 152; Private Collections, 96, 128 (Paris), 150, 193 (Stanford, Calif.), 219b, 303, 314, 315, 320; Réunion des Musées Nationaux, Paris, 14, 155, 246, 486, 544, 617b; St. John's College, Cambridge, 54b; St. Louis University Gallery of Art, 142; Sheffield City Art Galleries, 623; Sirot-Angel Collection, 94, 116, 117, 122, 127, 169, 180, 199, 219a, 220, 224ab, 226, 230, 259a, 271, 276ab, 302, 328ab, 358, 387, 426, 446, 462, 463ab, 464b, 465, 489ab, 666; Städelsches Kunstinstitut, Frankfurt, 188; Tate Gallery, London, 8, 546; University of Manchester, 75; Victoria and Albert Museum, London, 80, 357.

Photographs were supplied by the following agencies and individuals: A. C. Cooper Ltd., London, 46; André Martin, 461ab, 466, 467; Archives photographiques, Paris, 637; Bernard Marrey, 365ab, 415, 433, 434, 435; Bridgeman-Giraudon, 197; Bulloz, 39, 101, 128, 214, 219b, 280, 291; CAP Roger-Viollet, 504b; Christie's Collection, Toronto, 197; Édimédia, 519; Founders Society Purchase, Robert H. Tannahill Foundation, 264; François Rophé, 445; G. Dagli Orti, 152, 238, 279b, 283, 371a, 481, 648; Giraudon, 98, 193, 269, 279, 630, 634, 636; Harlingue-Viollet, 464a; J.-L. Charmet, 103, 138, 148, 150, 151, 158, 163, 172, 216, 218, 234, 287a, 294,

296, 297ab, 303, 320, 371b, 459, 471, 474, 480, 495, 523b, 524a, 529, 536, 540, 551, 553, 595, 600, 611, 624, 633, 641ab, 649, 658; Lauros-Giraudon, 12, 20, 32a, 110, 114, 142, 166, 177, 189, 203, 240, 260, 272, 323, 327, 345, 485, 490, 614, 655; Mansell Collection, London, 68, 72, 76a, 88; Mary Evans Picture Library, London, 54a, 60, 61, 73, 76b; NBA Roger-Viollet, 524b; Patrick Jean, 202; Radio Times Hulton Picture Library, London, 78, 79ab, 82; Roger-Viollet, 130, 174b, 194, 205, 209, 215, 217, 221, 236, 237, 242, 248, 254, 255, 256, 257, 287b, 331, 334, 395, 425, 472ab, 504a, 509, 517, 523a, 531, 538, 551, 564, 568, 602, 605, 639, 659; Seuil Archives, 108, 125, 145, 168, 229, 232, 243, 249, 284, 470, 477, 525, 653, 660, 663, 664b; Seuil/Bibliothèque des Arts Décoratifs, 428ab; Seuil/Bibliothèque Charcot, 620, 626, 627abc, 631ab, 632abcd; Seuil/Bibliothèque Forney, 407; Seuil/Bibliothèque Historique, 235, 282, 338, 350, 376, 396b, 431, 432, 437, 440, 441; Seuil/Bibliothèque Marguerite-Durand, 121, 161a, 164, 165, 182, 601; Seuil/Bibliothèque Nationale, 86ab, 90, 92, 340, 348, 349, 363, 364, 373, 378, 389, 406, 409, 416, 417, 423; Seuil/Jean Migrenne Collection, 353; Seuil/Rabaux Collection, 408, 410, 411, 412; Visual Arts Library, London, 188.

Credits for color plates in order of appearance are: Wolverhampton Art Library, Bridgeman-Giraudon; Bridgeman-Giraudon; Harrogate Art Gallery; Museum of the French Revolution, Vizille; Museum of the French Revolution, Vizille; Magyar Nemzeti Gallery, Budapest, G. Dagli Orti; Musée des Beaux-Arts, Rennes, G. Dagli Orti; Musée Historique Lorrain, Nancy, G. Dagli Orti; State Russian Museum, Leningrad, G. Dagli Orti; Bibliothèque Historique de la Ville de Paris; Bibliothèque Historique de la Ville de Paris; J.-L. Charmet; G. Dagli Orti; Bibliothèque des Arts Décoratifs, G. Dagli Orti; Musée des Beaux-Arts, Dijon, Bulloz; University Library, West Berlin, G. Dagli Orti.

Index